DICTIONARY OF ART AND ARCHAEOLOGY

APSE OF THE BASILICA OF ST. PAUL-WITHOUT-THE-WALLS, ROME.

[*See* BASILICA, *p.* 37.

DICTIONARY OF
ART AND
ARCHAEOLOGY

J. W. MOLLETT

BRACKEN BOOKS
LONDON

Dictionary of Art and Archaeology

First published in 1883 by Sampson Low, Marston, Searle and
Rivington, London

This edition published in 1994 by Bracken Books, an imprint of
Studio Editions Ltd, Princess House, 50 Eastcastle Street, London
W1N 7AP, England

ISBN 1 85891 140 0

Printed at Thomson Press (India) Ltd.

PREFACE.

THIS Dictionary was commenced as an amended edition of that written by M. Ernest Bosc, architect of Paris, and contains the 450 engravings published in the French work, to which about 250 more have been added. Little or nothing, however, of the text of M. Bosc's work has been left standing; his definitions having, in the process of revision under reference to original works, almost entirely disappeared. The whole work, as it now stands, has been drawn from, or carefully corrected by, the best authorities in each of its special branches. Considerable prominence has been given to ARCHITECTURE, from the French original corrected from English writers; to CHRISTIAN ANTIQUITIES from *Martigny*, and the Dictionary of *Dr. Smith and Professor Cheetham*, and other authorities; to MEDIÆVAL ARMOUR, and terms of CHIVALRY, chiefly from *Meyrick's Ancient Armour;* to COSTUME from *Planché* and *Fairholt;* to HERALDRY from *Boutell's* and *Mrs. Bury Palliser's* works; to POTTERY, the substance of the articles on this subject being derived from *M. Jacquemart's* work; to NEEDLEWORK, IVORIES, MUSICAL INSTRUMENTS, GOLDSMITHS' WORK, PAINTERS' MATERIALS AND PROCESSES ANCIENT AND MODERN, COLOUR, &c., with references to the several authorities referred to.

The GREEK AND ROMAN ANTIQUITIES, which are the principal part of M. Bosc's work, have been in this volume reduced to the smallest possible compass: the Dictionaries of Dr. Smith and Rich must be referred to by those who require fuller definitions upon this subject, which would of itself fill ten such books as the present.

A few INDIAN, CHINESE, and JAPANESE TERMS, which have come into ordinary use in art, have been sought out and inserted : in the first-mentioned

Dr. Birdwood's Handbooks have been a most useful guide. Finally, it is necessary to state, that many words essential to the completeness of the work would have been in danger of omission, if I had not had before me *Mr. Fairholt's* admirable *Dictionary of Art Terms*, which, occupying a more restricted ground than this, is so thorough and accurate in dealing with all that it professes to include, that the only *raison d'être* of this work is the very much wider and different ground that it covers, and the greater condensation of its definitions. Obviously the substance of every statement in the work is borrowed from some previous writer on the subject, and it is evident that a Dictionary of Reference is not a convenient vehicle for theory or invention.

The appended list of CLASSIFIED CATALOGUES which have been prepared by direction of the authorities of the South Kensington Museum, will have the additional use of referring the reader to the fountain-head at which he can verify and amplify the condensed information that this work supplies.

J. W. MOLLETT.

October, 1882.

ILLUSTRATED DICTIONARY OF WORDS

USED IN

ART AND ARCHÆOLOGY.

ABBREVIATIONS—Arch. *Architectural;* Chr. *Christian;* Egyp. *Egyptian;* Fr. *French;* Gr. *Greek;* Her. *Heraldic;* It. *Italian;* Lat. *Latin;* Med. *Meaiæval;* O. E. *Old English;* Orient. *Oriental;* R. *Roman.*

Aar or **Aarou**, Egyp. A plain in a supra-terrestrial region, which corresponded, with the Egyptians, to the Elysian Fields of the Greeks and the Asgard of Scandinavian mythology.

Fig. 1. Abaculi used as pavement.

Abaculus, Gr. and R. (a diminutive of *abacus,* q.v.). A small square or cube of glass, or some vitreous composition made to imitate stone or glass of various colours. *Abaculi* were employed for the inlaid-work of pavements, or the incrustations of mosaic.

Abacus, Gr. and R. (ἄβαξ, a slab or board). 1. In general a rectangular slab of stone, marble, or terra-cotta. 2. A board or tray used in arithmetical calculations, and constructed for reckoning by tens. 3. A play-board divided into compartments, a kind of back-gammon in use in antiquity. The same term was also applied to a board used for another game of skill, the *ludus latrunculorum,* which was more like our chess. 4. A side-board on which were displayed, in the *triclinium,* or dining-room, silver plate and other table utensils. 5. A slab of marble, used for a coating in the decoration of a room or apartment of any kind. 6. A square slab of terra-cotta or wood, placed by the earliest builders at the top of wooden columns, in order to give them a broader head, and so afford a better support to the beams which rested on them. It was this motive that gave rise to the formation of the *abacus of the capital of a column.*

Abaton or **Abatos,** Gr. (α, βᾰτὸs, inaccessible). A term used generally to denote any inaccessible place, such as the *cella* of a temple, an adytum from which the profane were excluded. The term *Abaton* denoted more particularly a building in the city of Rhodes, which contained, together with two statues in bronze, a trophy commemorating a victory gained over the Rhodians. This memorial had been placed in the building by queen Artemisia, who had consecrated it to a divinity. To destroy it would have been a sacrilege, and as no one could be allowed to penetrate into the interior of the *Abaton,* without the defeat of the Rhodians becoming known, all access to it was forbidden.

Abezzo, Olio di, It. Strasburg Turpentine (q.v.).

Ablutions, Chr. There were various ablutions: that of the head (*capitilavium*), as a preparation for unction in baptism; that of the hands (*aquamanile*), during Mass, &c.; that of the feet (*pedilavium*), including the ceremony of washing the feet of the poor, performed on Maundy Thursday, by the Pope. (Fig. 2.)

Abococke, Med. Cap of estate, worn by kings on their helmets: "a huge cappe of estate. called

B

Abococke, garnished with two rich crownes ;"
15th century.

Abolla, Gr. and R. (ἀναβολὴ, a throwing back
and around). A cloak made of a piece of cloth
folded double and fastened round the throat by a
brooch. *Abolla maior* was the name given to

Fig. 2. Ewer for ablutions (Persian).

the ample blanket in which the Greek philosophers were accustomed to wrap themselves.
This cloak was adopted by the philosophers as
an instance of their humility, because it was
mostly worn by the poorer classes at Rome. Fig. 3
is a representation of one of the lictors, with
his fasces on his shoulder, and wearing the *abolla.*

Abraxas, Gr. (a mystical or cabalistic word
formed of the Greek letters α, β, ρ, α, ξ, α, s).
Cut stones or gems of very various shapes, upon
which are engraved the words Abraxas, Abrasax.
They are also known as *Basilidian* stones or
gems, because they constituted the symbols of
the gnostic sect of the Basilidians. Certain
peoples looked upon them as magic amulets
against particular maladies and demoniacal
influences. The impressions on these stones are
very varied ; cabalistic figures, the signs A and Ω,
and the word IAΩ, which designates the Supreme
Being. Numerous explanations have been
sought for this term *abraxas ;* some philologists
assert that it comes from the Persian [or Pehlvi],
and that it signifies *Mithra ;* others derive it from
the Hebrew, or the Coptic, while others again
recognize in it only a numerical sign, the letters
of which, added together, would give the number

365, or the number of days that make up the
year, and in this case *abraxas* would symbolize
the annual revolution of the sun. A figure
often found upon Abraxas stones is that of a
serpent with a radiated lion's head (Chnouphis),
which rears itself amid seven stars. The reverse
of these stones often bears the inscription TΩ
XNOYΦI, "To Chnouphis."

Fig. 3. A Lictor with the fasces, wearing the *abolla.*

Absidiole. Diminutive of *apse,* and thus used
to denote a small apse terminating a lateral nave,
while the apse closes the central or chief nave.
(See Absis.)

Absis or **Apse,** R. (ἀψὶς, a bow or vault). Any
enclosure of semicircular form terminating a
room, hall, &c. There was an *absis* in the

Basilica (q.v.), or court of justice, and it was in the semicircular recess thus formed that the judges' seats were placed. Many temples also had an *absis* attached to them, and there is one in particular of this description well known to all archæologists. This is the *absis* of the temple of Venus at Rome, which was built by the emperor architect Hadrian. (See APSE.)

Abutment, Arch. called also **Impost**. The solid part of a pier from which an arch immediately springs.

Abydos, Tablets of, Egyp. Under this term are designated two hieroglyphic inscriptions containing the names of Egyptian kings. These tablets were graven upon the walls of a *cella* in a small temple at Abydos, in Upper Egypt; hence their name. The first tablet, the beginning of which was destroyed at the time of its discovery, contains the names of the kings of the twelfth and eighteenth dynasties; this inscription was discovered in 1817 or 1818 by J. W. Bankes, and drawn by Caillund in 1832; it had been taken down from the wall of the temple by Mimaut, the French consul at Alexandria. It is now at the British Museum. The second tablet, which begins with Menes, who is generally supposed to have been one of the first kings of Egypt, contains a complete list of the two first dynasties, as well as a great number of names belonging to kings of the third, fourth, fifth, sixth, ninth, tenth, and eleventh dynasties. This tablet was discovered in 1864 by M. Mariette. It is reproduced in De Rougé's treatise on the six first dynasties.

Abyssus, Egyp. A Coptic word, read by some archæologists as NOUN (q.v.), and which signifies the *abyss*, the immensity of the celestial waters upon which sails the solar bark.

Acacia, R. A term employed by some antiquaries to denote an object held in the hand of the statue of an emperor of the Lower Empire. It usually consists of a piece of cloth, which the emperor unfurled as a signal for the games to commence.

Academies of Italy. Literary societies established during the middle ages. The principal were the Accesi, Affidati, Amorevole of Verona, Animosi of Milan, Arcadi of Rome, Ardenti of Pisa, Ardenti of Naples, Ardenti of Viterbo, Catenati of Macerata, Chiave of Pavia, Crusca of Florence, Elevati of Ferrara, Eterea of Padua, Florimontana of Annecy, Granelleschi of Venice, Infiammati of Padua, Infocati, Insensati of Perugia, Intronati of Siena, Lincei of Rome, Occulti, Offuscati, Ostinati, Rinovati, Sonnachiosi of Bologna, Trasformati of Milan, Travagliati, Unanimi. Their devices are described under the respective headings.

Acæna, Gr. (ἀκαίνη), a measuring-rod; ten Greek feet in length.

Acanthus, Gr. and R. (ἀκή, a point, and

ἄνθος, a flower). A plant, the ornamental foliage of which has been largely employed as an architectural decoration by different peoples. The acanthus has been applied to the ornamentation of friezes, cornices, modillions, and

Fig. 4. Architectural acanthus.

various other members of architecture, but in especial to the decoration of modillions (projecting brackets) (Fig. 4) and of Corinthian and composite capitals. There are several varieties of the acanthus; those most in use are the cultivated acanthus, or Brankursine (*Acanthus mollis*), and the spring acanthus (*Acanthus spinosa*), the foliage of which is much less beautiful, and furnished with small

Fig. 5. Bracket decorated with acanthus.

spikes which make the plant resemble a thistle. This last has also often been applied to decoration, in the Romano-Byzantine and lanceolated styles of architecture. An English name for this ornament is the "bear's claw."

Acapna, Gr. (α, priv., and καπνός, i.e. without smoke). Wood for fuel, which had undergone several operations to hinder it from smoking when put on the fire. One of the methods employed consisted in stripping the bough of the bark, immersing it in water for some days, and then leaving it to dry. In a second method, the surface was rubbed with oil or oil-lees, or else the piece of wood was plunged into the oil for a few moments. A third method consisted in slightly charring the surface of the wood by passing it through the flame. The wood prepared by this last process was also called *cocta* and *coctilia*.

Acatium, Gr. and R. (ἀκάτιον, dimin. of ἄκατος, a light boat). A description of vessel belonging to the class called *actuariæ*, i.e. were propelled either by sails or oars. The *acatium* was a fast-sailer much employed by the Greek pirates. The stern was of a rounded concave form (*inflexa*), and the prow was adorned with a beak (*rostrum*). (See also ACTUARIÆ.) The name *acatium* was also given to a drinking-vessel which was in the form of a boat. The Roman *scapha* was a similar vessel.

Acca. A word used in the 14th century for a cloth of gold shot with coloured silk, figured with animals: from Acre in Syria.

Accesi, It. (*inflamed*). One of the Italian Literary Academies. Their device was a fir-cone placed over a fire, with the motto "hinc odor et fructus."

Accetta, Med. Lat. A battle-axe, or hache-d'armes.

Accidental or **complementary colour,** the prismatic complement of a ray of light : such are *orange* to *blue*, *green* to *red*, and *purple* to *yellow*.

Accidental light. An effect of light in a picture independent of the principal light, such as that on the Holy Child in the *Notte* of Correggio, or that of a candle, &c.

Acclamations, Chr. Formulas employed by the first Christians to express their grief on the occurrence of some misfortune, or on the other hand, to testify their joy at some piece of good fortune These acclamations were imitated from the nations of antiquity [e. g. at *marriages*, " Io Hymen, Hymenæe, Talassio :" at *triumphs*, " Io, triumphe," &c.].

Accollée, Her. (1) placed side by side : (2) entwined about the neck.

Accosted, Her. Side by side.

Accrued, Her. Grown to maturity.

Accubitum, R. (*ad* and *tubitum*, an elbow). A bed or rather couch of a peculiar kind, upon which the Romans reclined at meals, and which replaced the *lectus triclinarius*. It was a kind of sofa holding only a single person, while the *lectus triclinarius* held two or three. The act of reclining on this sofa was called *accubitio* or *accubitus*, a term derived from *accubo*, to recline at table.

Acerra or **Acerna,** R. (prob. from *acer*, maple). A small square box with a hinged lid ; a coffer used to hold the incense for sacrifices ; whence its Latin names *arca turalis*, *arcula turalis*, *acerra turis custos*. The *acerra* appears on certain bas-reliefs among the sacred utensils. It is to be seen represented on the altar of the small temple of Quirinus, at Pompeii, underneath a garland, and above an augur's wand. It is generally met with, as being carried by the officiating priests, at religious ceremonies. The attendant carried the *acerra* in the left hand and employed the right hand to sprinkle the incense on the flame of the altar; whence the expression *libare acerra*. The term *acerra* was also used to denote a small portable altar placed before the dead, on which incense was burnt during the time the corpse was exposed to view (*collocatio*). The altar was also named, from this circumstance, *ara turicrema*.

Acetabula, R. A kind of bronze cymbals,

attached to the hands and feet, as also to the knees. The same name was also given to silver cymbals which were played by striking them with a stick of hard wood.

Acetabulum, R. (from *acetum*, vinegar). A cup for vinegar used by the Romans at meals.

The *acetabulum* was also a goblet used by jugglers among the Greeks and Romans to make nutmegs disappear. By the latter these jugglers were called *præstigiatores*, by the former ψηφο-κλέπται or ψηφοπαίκται. Lastly, we find in Pliny the Elder that *acetabulum* was the name given to a dry measure of capacity, equal to the quarter of a *hemina* or the half of the *quartarius*, and equivalent to .1238 of a pint. [The Greek *Oxybaphon.*]

Acha, Achia, Hachia, Lat. A battle-axe.

Achelor, Achlere or **Ashlar.** (Arch.) Hewn stone.

Achromatic, Gr. (α priv. χρόμος, colour). The effect of an arrangement of lenses by which a coloured ray of light is rendered colourless.

Acicula, Gr. (dimin. of *acus*, a needle or pin). In particular a bodkin used by the Roman ladies to keep the hair in its place when curled or plaited, and to keep on false hair. The words *acicula* and *acus* are however all but synonymous. The former does not denote a bodkin of smaller size than the *acus*, but an object made of an inferior material ; the *acus* being of silver, ivory or gold, while the *acicula* was simply of bone or some hard wood such as box, myrtle, olive, &c.

Fig. 6. Acinaces.

Acinaces, Orient. (ἀκινάκης; orig. a Persian word). A straight poniard resembling a very short Roman sword, used by the Eastern nations of antiquity, especially, the Medes, Persians and Scythians. It was worn by soldiers suspended from a belt round the waist, but the weapon hung either at the right or the left side, according to the nationality and accoutrements of the soldier. When, however, he wore a sword, this was always placed at the left, and the *acinaces* at the right side of the body. The handles of these weapons are generally extremely rich.

Acisculus, R. (Diminutive of *ascia*, an adze = a small adze). A small pick employed by stone-cutters and masons in early times. Representations of it may be seen pretty frequently on medals, in especial those of the Valerian family. [See ASCIA.]

Acketon, Fr. A quilted leathern jacket, worn under the armour, introduced from the East by the Crusaders.

Aclis or **Aclyx,** R. A sort of harpoon, consisting of a thick short stock set with spikes. This massive weapon was chiefly employed by foreign nations, but not by the Romans. It was launched against the enemy, and drawn back by means of a cord to which it was attached, to be launched a second time. This weapon bears some resemblance to a particular kind of *angon* (or trident). (See ANGONES.)

Acoustic Vases, R. (Gr. ἀκουστικὸς, pertaining to the sense of hearing). Vases of earthenware or more often of bronze, which, in the theatres of antiquity, served the purpose of strengthening the voices of the actors. Vases of this kind would also seem to have been employed for the same purpose during the middle ages, for the architect Oberlin, when repairing the vault of the choir, in the ancient church of the Dominicans at Strasburg, discovered some acoustic vases there.

Fig. 7. Acratophorum, Roman.

Acratophorum, Gr. and R. (ἀκρατο-φόρος, holding unmixed wine). A table vessel for holding pure wine, while the crater (κρατὴρ), on the other hand, contained wine mixed with water. These vessels were often dedicated to Bacchus. They were made in earthenware and metal, but those that were dedicated to the gods were of gold and silver, and had their place among the treasures of the temples. Fig. 7 represents a silver acratophorum found at Hildesheim.

Acrolith, Gr. (ἄκρον, end, and λίθος stone). A statue covered with garments which in many cases were gilded. The extremities of these statues were of marble or stone— whence their name—more rarely of gold and ivory. The Minerva of Areia, at Platæa in Bœotia, described by Pausanius, was an *acrolith.* This was by Pheidias. The *acrolith* period is the infancy of the Greek plastic art.

Acropodium, Gr. (ἄκρον, end or point ; and πόδιον, a foot). A low square plinth serving for basement to a statue and often forming part of it.

Acropolis, Gr. (ἀκρό-πολις, upper or higher city). From its primary meaning the term came to signify a fortified city. They were very numerous, in ancient times, in Italy, Greece

and the colonies of Asia Minor. Most ancient Greek cities were built upon hills, and the citadel on the summit of the hill was called the *acropolis.*

Acrostic, Chr. (ἄκρον, end, and στίχος, a row or line). A combination of letters formed out of some word, which is thus made to express a thought differing from its own meaning. For instance, the Greek word ΙΧΘΥΣ (ICHTHUS, fish), symbolizes, in the primitive church, the name of Christ. The following is the acrostic of this word : Ιησους, Χριστος, Θεου, Υίος, Σωτηρ I, CH, TH, U, S.

Fig. 8. Roman acrostolium.

Acrostolium, Gr. and R. (ἀκροστόλιον, extremity of beak of a ship). An ornament employed by the ancients to decorate the upper extremity of the prows of ships. This ornament often figured among trophies, since it was the custom for the victor in a naval combat to take the *acrostolia* from the captured ships. It is frequently to be met with on the bas-reliefs of triumphal monuments. Fig. 8 shows an *acrostolium* taken from a bas-relief in the Museum of the Capitol. The object seen projecting from the acrostolium is a sounding lead.

Acroterium, Gr. and R. (ἀκρωτήριον, the extremity of anything). In a signification more restricted than the primary one, yet generally admitted, the term *acroteria* is applied to the plain socles and pedestals placed at the summit of buildings to support statues, groups, or other crownings. ACROTERIUM was the common name for the *acrostolium,* and the taking of it away as a trophy was called *acroteriazein.*

Actia, Gr., festivals held every fourth year, at Actium, in Epirus, in honour of Apollo.

Actinic (rays of light:) chemically active.

Actuariæ, R. (see Naves). Open boats, built to attain a high degree of speed, propelled by sails and sweeps, and never fitted with less than eighteen oars. Pirates used this class of vessel exclusively.

Actuarii, R. The shorthand writers who took

down speeches in the senate. Also certain officials who answered to our commissariat officers.

Acuminated, Arch. Finishing in a point, like a lofty Gothic roof.

Acus, R. (Gr. ἀκὴ, a point). A bodkin, needle, or pin. The *acus* denoted both a needle for sewing and a pin for fastening anything. When used for the hair it was called *acus crinalis* or *comatoria*. In Christian archæology the word applies to the jewelled pins used as fastenings to papal or archiepiscopal vestments. The Roman *acus* is worn in the hair by the Italian peasant woman of the present day.

Addorsed, Her. (1) Back to back ; (2) pointing backwards.

Adespotoi, Gr. (ἀ-δέσποτοι, i.e. without masters). A name given to a certain class of freedmen at Sparta.

Adobare, Med. To entrust with arms (to "dub" a knight). Meyrick.

Adobes. Bricks manufactured by the ancient Peruvians.

Adramire, Med. To challenge to a duel or tournament. (Meyrick.)

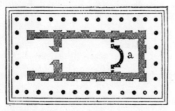

Fig. 9. Plan of a Roman temple, showing the adytum.

Adytum or **Adyton**, Gr. and R. (ἄδυτον, from α, priv., and δύω, to enter). An obscure and secret sanctuary in certain temples from which the public was excluded, and into which the priests alone might enter. The little temple of Pompeii possessed an *adytum*, and it was here that was discovered the Portici Diana now in the Naples Museum. There was also an *adytum* in the temple of Delphi, which was burnt down in the first year of the 58th Olym., and rebuilt by the Corinthian Spintharus. The temple of Paphos contained in its *adytum* a representation of the goddess under the form of a column pointed at the top and surrounded by candelabra. The engraving shows the position of the adytum of a small Doric temple, now destroyed, which once stood near the theatre of Marcellus at Rome. The *adytum* was the name given to the *cella* of a temple, in which oracles were given, or the worship was connected with mysteries. See ABATON and CELLA.

Ædicula, R. (dimin. of *Ædes*, q.v.). A small house, temple, chapel, tabernacle, or even shrine. Thus the name was given to a small wooden shrine, constructed to imitate the front of a temple, and in which were preserved the ancestors of the family (*imagines majorum*), together with the Lares and tutelar divinities.

Ægicranes, Gr. (αἴγειος, of a goat ; κρανίον, the skull). A goat's [or ram's] head employed as a decoration by ancient sculptors. It was used chiefly to adorn altars which were dedicated to rural divinities.

Æginetan marbles. Two remarkable groups of very early (archaic) Greek sculpture, in the Glyptothek at Munich—discovered in the temple of Pallas-Athene at Ægina, and arranged by Thorwaldsen. They illustrate "the infancy of art, which lingers round symbolic representation, and has not yet grasped the full meaning and truth of nature." (*Butler's Imitative Art.*) The anatomy of the bodies and limbs at this period is greatly superior to the expression of the heads.

Ægis, Gr. In its primary meaning, a *goatskin*. The primitive inhabitants of Greece used the skins of goats and other animals for clothing, and defence. At a later period the *Ægis* became a protective mantle ; the shield of Minerva, beneath which the goddess sheltered those whom she wished to protect from the enemy's missiles. Later still the *Ægis* denoted the breastplate of a divinity, in especial that of Jupiter or Minerva, as opposed to the *lorica*, which was the breastplate of a mere mortal. The ægis bore in its centre the Gorgon's head, of which the serpents were arranged round the border. Minerva is generally represented wearing it, either as a cuirass or a scarf passed over the right shoulder.

Aëneator (Lat. *aëneus*, brazen). The name given to any musician who played on an instrument of brass (*aëneum*) ; such as the *buccinatores, cornicines, liticines, tubicines*, &c. They formed a college.

Fig. 10. Eolipyle.

Æolipilæ or **Æolipylæ**, Gr. (αἴολος, the wind ; and πύλη, an orifice). A metal vase with a narrow orifice, which was filled with water and placed upon the fire, either to make the chimney draw better, or, according to Vitruvius, to show which way the wind blew.

Æolian Harp, Gr. A musical instrument that is played on by the wind passing over its strings.

Ærarium, R. (*æs*, money). The public treasury as distinguished from the private treasury of the Emperors (*fiscus*). Under the Republic the temple of Saturn served as the public treasury, and here were preserved the produce of the revenue, the public accounts and other public records. The army had a separate treasury of its own called *ærarium militare*, entirely distinct from the *ærarium publicum*. It was established by Augustus to provide for the special expenditure of the army.

Aerial perspective. The realization of the effect of intervening atmosphere in the distances of a landscape.

Æro, R. A basket made of rushes or broom, but still more commonly of osier, and used for conveying sand. It was employed by the Roman soldiery when at work on intrenchments, excavations, or fortifications, as may be seen from bas-reliefs ; more particularly some of those which adorn the column of Trajan.

Æruca, R. (*æs*, bronze). A very brilliant green colour artificially made to imitate *verdigris*.

Ærugo, R. *Verdigris*, the same colour as *æruca* (q. v.), but obtained from oxide of bronze. It is difficult to establish a real distinction between the two terms, as Pliny gives the name of *ærugo* (the rust of bronze) to what Vitruvius calls *æruca*. It is probable, however, that *æruca* was a kind of verdigris obtained by artificial means, while *ærugo* was the natural verdigris. This has given rise to the two terms, which by many archæologists are confused together. *Æruca*, the artificial copper rust, formed by the action of wine refuse upon copper, is an acetate of copper (verdigris): while the genuine copper rust, *Ærugo*, is a carbonate of copper.

Ærumna, R. A kind of fork by which travellers carried their baggage over the shoulder. 2. An instrument of punishment for slaves. (See FURCA.)

Æs. A term used in antiquity to denote brass, copper, bronze, or any alloy of these metals. It also serves, in various connexions, to denote a number of different objects. Such as *æs candidum*, a brass mixed with silver ; *æs Corinthum*, a brass mixed with gold ; *æs Cyprium*, the ancient name for copper. (See also BRONZE.)

Æs grave, R. A general term current in Rome to denote any bronze money at the period when the *as* was equal to about a pound in value.

Æs rude, R. The name given to the bronze ingots employed at Rome as ready money in exchanges and other commercial transactions.

Æs thermarum, Gr. and R. A bronze gong or metal bell hung up in the public baths, the sound of which, when struck, gave notice to the public that the baths were sufficiently warm to be ready for use.

Æs ustum. Peroxide of copper, or calcined copper.

Æsthetics, Gr. (αἰσθάνομαι, to comprehend). The science of the instinctive apprehension of the harmonies.

Aetos, Gr. (Ἀετός). A Greek word signifying *eagle*, and by analogy, a gable, pediment, or higher part of a building generally, so-called from the resemblance which these parts bear to an eagle with outstretched wings. In the same way the Greeks gave the name of πτερὰ (wings), to the outer rows of columns flanking each side of a temple.

Affidati, It. One of the Italian literary academies. Their device was a nautilus, with the motto "tutus per suprema per ima."

Affrontée, Her. Showing the full front.

Agalma, Agalmata, Gr. (ἄγαλμα, from ἀγάλλω, to glorify). Any work of art dedicated to a god, whether it were placed in his temple ór not ; such as tripods; [braziers for incense], or other accessories of a temple. The low pillar placed over a tomb, or the statue of a god might be *agalmata*.

Agate. A variety of quartz often employed by the engravers of antiquity. The term is a corruption of the word *Achates*, a river of Sicily, on the banks of which numerous varieties of the stone abound. Among these may be mentioned the *cerachates*, or white wax-like agate ; *dendrachates*, or arborescent agate ; *hemachates*, or blood-agate, so-called from its blood-like spots ; and *leucachates*, or white agate. Agates were often carved into scarabæi by the Egyptians, and Babylonian cylinders have been found, made of the same material. The oriental agate is semi-transparent, the occidental is opaque, of various tints, often *veined* with quartz and jasper; hence its fitness for cutting cameos.

Agathodæmon, Cup of, Gr. (Ἀγαθο-δαίμων). A name given by the Greeks to a cup consecrated to Bacchus, and meaning literally, the "Cup of the Good Genius." It was sent round after a feast, in order that each guest might partake of the wine.

Agea, R. A narrow passage or gangway in a boat, by means of which the boatswain (*hortator*) communicated with the rowers.

Agger, R. A general term to denote a mound of any materials, such as that formed by a dyke, quay, roadway, or earthwork ; and particularly a rampart composed of trunks of trees and employed in offensive or defensive warfare. A celebrated *agger* was that of Servius Tullius at Rome. The art of constructing *aggeres* and other fortifications, had been learnt by the Romans from the Greeks, who in their turn had derived it from the East. It was after having penetrated into the heart of Asia under Alexander the Great, that the Greeks learned the use of siege works employed in the attack or defence of strong places, and became acquainted with various kinds of warlike engines such as the ACROBATICON, &c.

Agnus Bell, Chr. A sacring bell.

Agnus Dei, Chr. The LAMB OF GOD, or lamb bearing the banner of the cross. The term is also used to denote certain ornaments or medallions of wax impressed with a figure of the lamb. They represented the ancient custom of distributing to worshippers, on the first Sunday after Easter, particles of wax from the consecrated paschal taper.

Agolum, R. A long sharp-pointed shepherd's stick used by the Roman herdsmen for driving their cattle. The *agolum* was made out of a straight shoot of the prickly pear ; it is still in use among the herdsmen of the Roman campagna at the present day.

Agonalia or **Agonia**, R. A Roman festival, which derived its name from the word *agone* (shall I proceed?) the question asked of the *rex sacrificulus* by the attendant, before he sacrificed the victim. The Quirinal was called *Mons agonus*, from a festival being held there on the 17th or 18th of March, in honour of Mars. The day itself was called *Agonium martiale* or day of the Liberalia. Another explanation of the etymology of the name is that the sacrifice was offered on the Quirinal hill, which was originally called *Agonus*. (Consult Ovid. Fasti, i. 319—332, he suggests several explanations.)

Agonistic, (ἀγωνιστική, from ἀγών, a contest). With the ancients, that part of gymnastics in which athletes contended with arms.

Agora, Gr. (ἀγορὰ, from ἀγείρω, to assemble). A place of assembly or public market. The *agora* was to the Greeks what the *forum* was

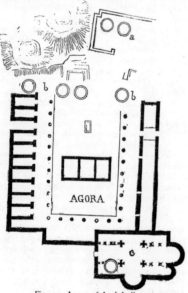

Fig. 11. Agora of Antiphellus.

to the Romans. There were numerous agoræ in Greece and Asia Minor. Fig. 11, represents the plan of the *agora* of Antiphellus ; in which *a* and *b* indicate the sites of the corn-pits ; *c*, that of a basilica. *Agora* is also used to denote the general assembly of freemen in contradistinction to the *Boulè* (q.v.).

Agraulia. An Athenian festival.

Agrenon, Gr. and R. A net, or garment of netted wool, worn over their other dress by the priests of Bacchus and by soothsayers.

Aguinia, Med. A corruption of *ingenia*, engines of war. (Meyrick.)

Aguzo, It. A spear-head ; a spear.

Ahenum or **Aenum**. A bronze vessel furnished with a handle for suspending it over the fire, and so-named from the material out of which it was made. (2) The coppers used in the public baths for heating the water in.

Fig. 12. Aiglets.

Aiglet, Fr. (*aiguillette*). A metal tag or point to a lace ; sometimes used to signify the lace itself, as in the military costume of the present day. They were formerly used to fasten the slashed dresses of the middle ages ; and sometimes to fasten armour, when they were made of leather with metal points. In civilian costume they were of silk. The term Aiguillette is also applied to the shoulder-knot worn by soldiers and livery servants.

Ailettes (little wings). Armour worn on the shoulders to protect the back of the neck ; found in monumental brasses of the 13th century.

Aisle (*ala*, a wing). The wing of a building ; the side passages of a Roman house. In buildings of vast size, such as a basilica or temple, comprising a central and two lateral naves, the latter are called aisles.

Alabarda, Med. A halberd.

Alabaster or **Alabastrum**, (ἀλάβαστρον). A small vase for holding precious perfumes ; so-called from the alabaster of which it was generally made. It was of various shapes, but chiefly assumed an elongated form resembling a long pear, a pearl-drop, &c. [Many of these perfume vessels are made of stalactite.] (2) A calcareous substance of white colour, translucent or semi-transparent, and presenting, according to the variety, undulating and continuous veins. The various kinds of ancient alabaster are very numerous ; the following may be named ; flowered alabaster (*alabastro fiorito*) ; golden (*dorato*) ; quince coloured (*cotognino*) ; eyed (*occhii*) ; tortoiseshell (*tartaruga*) ; foam-white (*pecorella*) ; Busca de Palombara (*palombara*) ;

onyx (*onice*), &c. The Egyptians used alabaster for making statues, phials, panegyric vases, canopea, small figures, and even sarcophagi ; of which last that of Seti I., now in the British Museum, is an example. Alabaster was at one time frequently used for tombs and carved figures, and is now used for pulpits and other ecclesiastical purposes. False alabaster is the name given to a gypseous variety of this substance, of which there are rich quarries at Volterra, in Tuscany. It is called " Gesso Volterrano," and is much used in Italy for the *grounds* of pictures.

Alabastrotheca, R. (θήκη, a chest). A box or casket containing alabaster flasks or vases.

Aland, Alant, Her. A mastiff with short ears.

Alapa. The blow on the shoulder in dubbing a knight.

Alba creta. Latin for white chalk, a term used by writers on art for gypsum.

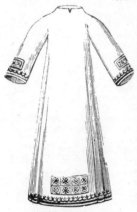

Fig. 13. Albe.

Albani stone. A pepper-coloured stone used in ancient buildings at Rome before the introduction of marble.

Albarium (opus), R. (*albus*, white). A white coating or kind of stucco with which brick walls were covered after a previous application of ordinary cement. This stucco, which was also called simply *albarium*, was made by a mixture of chalk, plaster, and white marble.

Albalista, Arbalest. A cross-bow.

Albe, (*albus*, white). An ancient ecclesiastical vestment, common in old brasses. It was a long white linen gown, reaching to the feet, and secured by a girdle. The surplice is an *albe* with wider sleeves. (Fig. 13.)

Alberk, for **Hauberk.** A cuirass.

Album, Gr. and R. (*albus*, white). A space on the surface of a wall covered with white plaster, upon which were written advertisements or public announcements. By analogy the term was used to denote any kind of white tablets bearing an inscription, such as edicts, decrees, &c. These tablets were very numerous ; there were the *album pontificis, prætoris, centuriæ, decurionum, judicum, senatorum,* &c.

Alcato, Arab. In armour, a gorget.

Alcora pottery (See DENIA.)

Alcove. A niche or recess in a room.

Aldobrandini, Marriage, R. A celebrated fresco from the gardens of Mecænas, discovered at Rome near the church of Santa Maria Maggiore, whence it was conveyed to the villa Aldobrandini, and afterwards sold to the Borghese family. This painting which indisputably dates from the reign of Augustus, consists of a group of ten figures, representing, according to some, the marriage of Peleus and Thetis ; and cording to others, that of Manlius and Julia.

Fig. 14. Point d'Alençon.

Alençon, Point d'. Lace formerly known as Point de France. It is the only French lace not made on the pillow, but worked entirely by hand with a fine needle, on a parchment pattern; it is called " Vilain" in the French provinces, and in England is known as needle-point. (Fig. 14.)

Alerion, Her. An eagle, in early Her., represented without feet or beak. (See EAGLE.)

Ale-stake. In the middle ages the roadside ale-house was distinguished by a stake projecting from the house, on which some object was hung for a sign.

Alexandrinum (opus), R. A kind of mosaic employed especially for the pavement of rooms. The distinctive feature of these mosaics is that the lines or figures composing the designs are in two colours only, the prevailing ones being red and black upon a white ground. A large number of mosaics of this description exist at Pompeii, which are also called *sectilia.*

Alexikakos (Apollo). Another name of the celebrated statue generally called the Belvedere Apollo ; from Nero's villa at Antium.

Algaroth powder. An ingredient in the manufacture of an Antimony white pigment.

Alhambraic. Ornamentation in the Moorish style of the Alhambra, the characteristic of which is a faithful imitation of natural combinations of form and colour, with a rigid avoidance of the representation of natural objects. (Fig. 15.)

Alicula, R. A kind of large mantle, furnished sometimes with a hood. The term is derived

Fig. 15. Alhambraic ornament.

from the Greek ἄλλιξ, the name given to the Thessalian chlamys. (See CHLAMYS.)

Alizarin, the colouring principle of the madder.

Allecret or **Hallecret**. A light armour for cavalry and infantry, consisting of a breastplate and tassets (or gussets), 16th century.

Allegory in art, is allegorically represented as a female figure veiled.

All Halowes or **All Hallowes**. O. E. for All Saints.

Alloys of Gold. Gold is found alloyed with various metals, never without silver, often with copper, iron, or other substances in small quantities, and sometimes with mercury, when it is called an *amalgam*. Gold alloyed with silver is called *native gold*. See ELECTRUM.

Allouyère Fr. (Lat. *alloverium*). A purse or pouch often carried at the girdle, for holding papers, jewels, and money.

Almayne Rivets (German Rivets). Rivets used in plates of armour made to slide and thus give play to the arms and legs, invented in the 17th century, in Germany ; hence their name.

Almery, Aumery, or **Ambry**, Arch. Chr. A niche or cupboard by the side of an altar, to contain the utensils belonging thereto.

Almond, Chr. An aureole of elliptic form, which is frequently met with encircling representations of saints, or of God the Father, God the Son, or the Virgin. A more common name, however, for this aureole is VESICA PISCIS (q.v.). The term of *mystical almond* was applied to the symbol expressive of the virginity of the Virgin Mary. The mystical meaning attached to this symbol is explained by reference to the rod of Aaron, which consisted of the bough of an almond-tree that had flowered in a single night and produced an almond on the morrow.

Almonry, Almonarium, Arch. Chr. A room where alms were distributed.

Almuce, Aumuce, Amess, Chr. (*almutium*). A furred hood worn by the clergy for the sake of warmth, from the 13th to 16th centuries. Common in brasses of the 15th century. (Fig. 16.)

Aloa, or **Haloa**. An Attic festival, in honour of Demeter and Dionysus.

Alostel, O. E. A cry of heralds at the close of a tournament, ordering the combatants to quit the lists and retire to their lodgings.

Alpha and **Omega**, Chr. (ἄλφα and ὠμέγα). These two letters, respectively the first and the last of the Greek alphabet, symbolize our earthly life, since this has a beginning and an end. They are also a symbol of God as being the beginning and end of everything.

Altar. A kind of platform or table upon which sacrifices were offered to the gods. Hence, in Christian art, the table upon which the Eucharistic sacrifice is offered. (See ANTEPENDIUM, CIBORIUM, REREDOS, &c. See ALTARE and ARA.)

Altar cards, Chr. Portions of the service of the mass printed separately on cards, and placed against the reredos of an altar.

Altar cloth, Chr. The linen coverings, and embroidered hangings of an altar.

Altare, R. (*alta ara*, high altar). A raised altar as contradistinguished from the *ara* which was of no great height. (Fig. 17.)

Altar front, Chr. An antependium (q.v.).

Altar screen, Chr. The partition behind the high altar, separating it from the Lady Chapel.

Alto-rilievo (Ital.) High Relief. See RILIEVO.

Alum is used in many processes—in the preparation of paper for water-colour painting,

Fig. 16. Almuce.

and of *lakes*, and *carmine*, from cochineal. *Roche alum*, or roach alum, *Roman alum*, and *Turkey alum*, are varieties of the common alum, described by mediæval writers as *alumens*.

Alumen (Lat.), Greek, (*stypteria*). Mediæval writers confused this word with the alums.

Fig. 17. Circular Roman altar.

The name was applied by the classics to several salts of the nature of vitriols, and among them to the natural sulphate of iron (*copperas* or *green vitriol* of commerce).

Alur, Aloring, or **Alurde,** &c., O.E. Parapet wall.

Alvéole; see NIMBUS.

Alveus, R. (*alvus*, the belly). (1) A bath constructed in the floor of a room, the upper part of it projected above the floor, the lower part being sunk into the floor itself. (2) A playing-board, which was divided in the same manner as the ABACUS (q. v.). (3) A canoe hollowed out of the trunk of a tree, the Greek μονόξυλον. (4) The hull of a ship. (5) A wooden trough or tray.

Ama or **Amula,** Chr. A long phial for holding the wine presented at the altar at the moment of offering.

Amassette, Fr. An instrument of horn used for spreading colours on the stone in the process of grinding.

Amatito, Ital. Lapis Amatita. Amatito is the *soft* red hæmatite, and is called also *matita rossa*. Lapis amatita is the *compact* red hæmatite, and is also called in Italy *mineral cinnabar*, and in Spain *albin*. When this word is used by early writers on art, it probably indicates *red ochre*, the red hæmatite of mineralogists. (Fairholt.)

Amber. There are two varieties of this substance, viz., the grey and the yellow amber, of which the latter only need here be more particularly noticed. Its use may be traced back to a very early antiquity, the purposes to which it was applied being the setting of jewels and furniture. It was employed by the Jews for making amulets. Amber was also used by the Egyptians in the fabrication of necklaces composed of pearls or other delicate materials. By the Romans it was sculptured into vases or statuettes. The name of *vasa electrina* was given to amber vases set with silver, and that of *electrina patera* to pateræ made of amber alone. Amber was largely used by early painters as a *varnish*, and also as a *vehicle*. It is harder than copal, and is said to be the most durable of all varnishes. It requires a long time to fit it for *polishing*. Amber is supposed to be a vegetable fossil; it is washed up by the sea, especially on the shores of the Baltic.

Amber Yellow, is an *ochre* of a rich amber colour in its raw state; when burned it yields a fine *brown-red*.

Ambitus, Gr. R. and Chr. (*ambio*, to go round about). A small niche in underground Greek or Roman tombs forming a receptacle for a cinerary urn. In the Middle Ages these niches were so far enlarged as to admit coffins; the name under which they then went being ENFEUS (q.v.). During the same period the term *ambitus* was also applied to the consecrated ground by which a church was surrounded. It served as a place of asylum as well as for burial. The term is also applied to the process of canvassing for votes.

Ambivium, R. (*ambi* and *via*, a way round). Any road or street leading *round* a place.

Ambo, Chr. (perhaps from ἀναβαίνειν, to ascend). A tribune of stone or marble in the

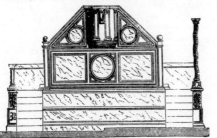

Fig. 18. The ambo of St. Lawrence at Rome.

ancient Latin basilicas, a pulpit. Fig. 18 gives a representation of the ambo in the church of St. Lawrence without the walls at Rome.

Ambrices, R. The cross laths (*regulæ*) inserted between the rafters and the tiles of a roof.

Ambry; see ALMERY.

Ambulant, Her. In the act of walking.

Ambulatory, Chr. (*ambulo*, to walk). Part of a cloister, forming a kind of gallery for taking exercise in.

Amenti or **Amenthi**, Egyp. One of the names given to the nether world of the Egyptians. It means the *unseen region*. We learn from Plutarch's treatise on Osiris that, "the subterranean regions whither souls betake themselves after death is called *Amenthes.*" Osiris is the lord and god of Amenti, which was also called by the Egyptians the *country of truth*.

Amentum, R. A thong attached to the shaft of a lance at the centre of gravity. The soldier placed the fingers of his right hand between the two ends of the thong, gave the weapon a rapid turn, and then hurled it. *Amentum* was also used to denote the leather strap by which certain kinds of boots, such as the *crepidæ, solæ*, &c., were fastened above the instep.

Amess. (See ALMUCE.)

Amethyst, (ἀμέθυστος, without intoxication.) A precious stone of a more or less deep violet colour. The engravers of antiquity carved figures upon it, in especial those of Bacchus, since the stone was also used, in preference to any other, for making drinking-cups, from a belief that it possessed the virtue of dispelling intoxication. This was the origin of the Greek term. Among the ancient Jews the amethyst was one of the twelve stones compos-

ing the breastplate of the high priest; it occupied the eighth or ninth row. In Christian symbolism the amethyst (or the colour violet) signifies humility and modesty.

Amiantus, (ἀμίαντος [? undefiled]. A fibrous uninflammable mineral substance. It was used by the ancients for making fire-proof clothing. It was known by the name of *asbestus* (ἄσβεστος, uninflammable).

Amice. A piece of fine linen in the form of an oblong square, suspended over the shoulders of the clergy. *Pugin* says it is "a white linen napkin or veil worn by all the clergy above the four minor orders." *Durand* says it is a proper covering for the head, typical of the helmet of salvation alluded to by the apostle; or of the cloth with which the Jews covered the Saviour's face, when they asked him to prophecy who struck him. Milton, in *Paradise Regained*, alludes to it,—

> "Morning fair
> Came forth with pilgrim steps, in *amice* grey."

Amma, Egyp. (1) A measure of length in use among the ancient Egyptians. It was about sixty feet. (2) A kind of line used in land surveying.

Ammah, Egyp. The door which formed the exit from the abode of the dead. Chapters lxxiii. and cxv. of the *Book of the Dead* are entitled,— *On passing Ammah*; i.e. *directing one's course to heaven by stepping over the Ammah*.

Amorevole of Verona. One of the Italian literary academies. Their device was a hedgehog with its spines laden with grapes (for its young). Motto, "non solum nobis."

Amorini, Ital. Cupids.

Ampelitis, Gr. (ἄμπελος, a vine). A black pigment prepared by the ancients from the burnt branches of the vine.

Amphibalus, Chr. A vestment, used on Sundays and high festivals; peculiar to the Gallican Church.

Amphidromia. Family festival held by the Athenians upon the occasion of the birth of a child. The carrying of the child round the hearth gave the name to the festival.

Amphimallum, Gr. and R. (ἀμφί-μαλλον, woolly on both sides). A description of woollen cloth more or less rough, and having a nap on both sides.

Amphiprostylos, Gr. and R. (ἀμφι-πρόστυλος). A temple or other building having two open porticoes (*porticum* and *posticum*), both in front and rear. They are so constructed as to project beyond the *cella*, or main body of the building.

Amphitapus, Gr. and R. (ἀμφί-ταπος, hairy on both sides). A particular kind of cloth, made of some material resembling Vicuna wool, and having, like the *amphimallum*, a nap on both sides. It was probably of Eastern origin.

Amphitheatre, R. (ἀμφι-θέατρον). A building which was at first constructed for the purpose of exhibiting gladiatorial shows to the Roman populace ; but later on any kind of spectacle, even to a *naumachia*, or sea-fight, was exhibited there. In the engraving, A shows the

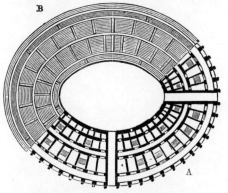

Fig. 19. Ground-plan of an amphitheatre.

ground-plan of an amphitheatre, and B the plan of the seats.

Amphora, Gr. and R. (ἀμφὶ-φορέω). A large earthenware vessel, having a handle on each side of its neck (whence the name), and terminating in a point. Amphoræ were used for holding various kinds of produce, especially wine ; they were placed side by side in an upright position in the cellar, the floor of which was covered with a deep bed of sand. The engravings represent amphoræ from Cnidus, Chio, and Samos. Amphoræ were also made of glass ; and a specimen is

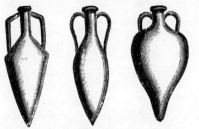

Fig. 20. Greek Amphoræ.

mentioned by Nepos of one made of onyx. Homer mentions them of gold and stone ; and the Egyptians had them of brass.

Amphotis, Gr. and R. 1. A brass cap lined with cloth inside. 2. A simple woollen cap worn by athletes to protect their temples and ears from the blows of the *cestus*, in a boxing match. 3. A wooden vessel in use among the ancient Greek peasants, as a milking-pail. It derived its name from having two handles or ears.

Ampulla, Gr. and R. A phial or flask with short and narrow neck and spherical body, which was used to hold the oil requisite for bathers (*ampulla oleria*) ; it could also be used to hold vinegar, wine, and other beverages, and was then called *ampulla potaria*. The ampulla generally took the form of a globe or bladder, but not invariably ; a lentil-shaped variety with rounded sides was very common. *Ampulla rubida* was the name given to the leather-covered flasks which were made use of by travellers or sportsmen to carry wine, vinegar, or oil. The vessel or cruet used in Christian churches for the consecrated oil or wine was hence called the AMPUL.

Ampyx, Gr. and R. (ἄμπυξ, from ἀμπέχω, to surround). Latin *frontale*. A general term to denote any net composed of strings, bands, or ribbons, which forms a head-band. It thus denotes at once a woman's head-dress, or the ornamental strips of leather which serve as head-band for a horse. The *ampyx* worn by women was in some cases very costly, being made of gold or silver, and adorned with precious stones. The term was also applied, by analogy, to the cover of a vase. Another word for it is *ampicter*.

Amulets. Objects of a very heterogeneous description, to which is superstitiously attributed the power of healing certain diseases, or averting them from men and animals. This is the meaning which attaches, in its widest sense, to the term amulet (*amuletum*). Amulets are unquestionably of Eastern origin; by the Egyptians they were looked upon as preservatives against dangers, unlucky days, enemies, &c. The varieties of them were very numerous ; among others, were scarabæi, small columns, cartouches, symbolic eyes, interlacing fingers, heads of uræus, &c. A large number of stones were also employed as amulets ; those of commonest occurrence are hematite, jasper, lapis lazuli, amethysts, diamonds, heliotropes, &c. Each of these amulets had its special virtue ; for instance, the clear crystal worn during prayer rendered the god propitious, and compelled him to give ear to the suppliant. Coral kept every evil influence away from a house ; and in Italy it is looked upon, even at the present day, as a preservative against the evil eye. In Christian archæology, the name of amulets, or in some instances, ENCOLPIA (q.v.), was given to relics, or objects of devotion, such as crosses, medals, wood from the true cross, the bones of saints, &c. Amulets were also called *periapta* (περί-απτα), i.e. suspended, because they were hung round the neck, and also *pyctacium*, because some amulets were folded in two. The Arabic word amulet means the same as *periapta*, that which is suspended.

Amussis, R. The exact sense of this term is not clearly defined by ancient authors, beyond the fact that it denotes generally any kind of instrument employed by builders—especially masons—for testing the accuracy, regularity, and evenness of their work. The term is used to denote sometimes the plumb-line, rule, or square; sometimes the level, measuring-line, &c.

Anabathra, Gr. and R. (ἀνά-βαθρα, steps up). Steps or stairs ; a raised step ; a mounting block. These last were often placed along the high roads.

Anabologium, Chr. Another name for the Humerale or AMICE (q.v.).

Anaceia or **Anakeia**, Gr. (from ἄναξ, a king). A festival held at Athens in honour of Castor and Pollux, who were also called *Anaktes* and *Anakestes*. (See ANACEIUM). Similar festivals were held at Sparta, Argos, and other cities of Greece.

Anaceium, Gr. A temple of ancient Athens, dedicated to Castor and Pollux. Slaves used to be sold there.

Anaclinterium, Gr. (ἀνακλιντήριον). The head-board of a sofa or bed, which served as a support for the bolster and the pillow on which the sleeper's head rested.

Anadem, Gr. (ἀνάδημα). In general a fillet or head-band ; but in a more restricted acceptation, an ornamental band, such as was worn by women and youths among the Greeks. It was thus distinguished from the *diadema* and the *vitta*, which were also head-bands, but worn solely as the insignia of honorary, regal, or religious distinctions.

Anaglyph, (ἀνὰ and γλύφειν, to carve). A general term to denote any work of art that is sculptured, chased, carved, or embossed, such as cameos, bas-reliefs, or other raised work, whether in metal, marble, or ivory. When such sculptures or chasings are incised or sunk, they are called INTAGLIOS or DIAGLYPHS (q.v.). According to St. Clement of Alexandria, ana-glyphs were employed by the Egyptians when they wished to hand down a panegyric of any king under the form of a religious myth. Although the words of St. Clement are very obscure, and have furnished materials for count-less discussions, it is now admitted that the anaglyphs in question belong to the group of hieroglyphics which may be deciphered on the cartouches of the Pharaohs, and in which we have, in fact, panegyrics of the Egyptian kings veiled in religious myths. The Egyptians also gave the name of anaglyphs to a kind of secret writing, understood only by the initiated ; even at the present day it remains undecipherable, owing to our imperfect knowledge of Egyptian mythology. (See CÆLATURA.)

Anagogia. A festival at Eryx, in Sicily, in honour of Aphrodite.

Analemma, Gr. and R. (ἀνάλημμα). Any raised construction which serves for a support

or rest, and more particularly a pier, wall, or buttress. (2) The pedestal of a sun-dial, and so the sun-dial itself.

Anancœum, R. A drinking cup of great capacity, the form of which is unknown. If we may credit Varro it was sometimes richly chased.

Anankaion, Gr. (ἀναγκαῖον, from ἀνάγκη, restraint). A kind of prison the purpose of which is not exactly known. According to some archæologists it was a private prison for slaves, or for freedmen, who, from some fault, were reduced to servitude again ; others assert that it was a public prison.

Anapiesma, Gr. and R. (ἀνα-πίεσμα, that which is pressed back). An appliance used in ancient theatres. It was a kind of trap-door by means of which deities were raised from beneath the stage so as to make them visible to the spectators. The *proscenium* contained a certain number of these trap-doors ; one of them, lead-ing from the orchestra to the front of the stage, enabled the Furies to appear; by another, marine deities made their appearance ; while that through which passed the shades who as-cended Charon's staircase was called *Charon's anapiesma*.

Anastatic. An ingenious modern process of reproducing copies of printed matter, engravings, ink drawings, &c., by transferring them to a sheet of polished zinc.

Anathēma, Chr. (ἀνάθημα, an offering). Anything offered up in churches by the faithful ; as, for instance, vases and other utensils for sacrifice, altar ornaments, &c.

Anathĕma, Chr. The greater excommunica-tion, answering to the Hebrew *cherem*.

Anchor. In Christian Art, the emblem of Hope. The attribute of S. Clement, the Pope, who was bound to an anchor, and thrown into the sea. (See ANCORA.)

Ancile, R. A shield of the shape of a violin case. It was the sacred shield which, according to tradition, had fallen from heaven into the palace of Numa. It occurs frequently on medals, especially those of Augustus. The two incava-tions of the shield were more or less deep, and usually semicircular. But Ovid describes it as of an entirely different shape, being cut evenly all round ; *Idque ancile vocat, quod ab omni parte recisum est* (Ovid, Fast. iii. 377). The SALII, or twelve priests of Mars Gradivus, had twelve such shields. The form was oval, with the two sides curving evenly inwards, so as to make it broader at the ends than in the middle. They used to beat their shields and dance.

Anclabris, Gr. and R. A small table used instead of an altar at sacrifices ; it was slightly concave, so as to adapt it to hold the entrails of the victim for the inspection of the diviners. (See ALTAR.)

Ancon, Gr. and R. (αγκων). A term admitting

various meanings. (1) A small console on each side of a door supporting an ornamental cornice. (2) The arm of a chair or arm-chair. (3) A cramp of wood or metal serving to connect together courses of masonry or blocks of stone. (4) The prongs or forks at the end of the props employed by hunters to hang their nets upon. (5) An earthenware vessel used in Roman taverns for holding wine. According to the etymology of the word which in Greek signifies hollow or elbow, this bottle must have been shaped like a retort. (6) The arms or branches of the square used by carpenters and stone masons, which form an angle similar to that formed by the bent arm.

Ancora, Gr. and R. (ἀγκύρα, from ἄγκος, a bend). An anchor or piece of iron used to stop a ship. Like those now in use, the ancient anchors were generally furnished with two flukes or arms, but sometimes they had only one. In the latter case they were called *terostomos*,

a term corresponding to our modern blind anchor. A bas-relief on the column of Trajan represents an anchor placed at the bow of the vessel. In Christian archæology the anchor is a symbol of hope; an anchor is frequently met with, among Christian symbols, associated with a fish; the emblem of the Saviour (See ACROSTIC).

Fig. 21. Roman anchor, rom a bas-relief.

Ancorale, Gr. and R. Literally the cable of an anchor, and then the buoy-rope, or even the buoy itself. The ancient anchors had a ring at the end of the shank to which the buoy-rope was attached. The latter served not only to indicate the place where the anchor lay, but also to drag the flukes out of the ground when the anchor was raised.

Andiron. Iron standards with bars for supporting logs of wood fires, frequently richly ornamented, and sometimes made partly of silver.

Andriantes, Gr. (ἀνδριάντες, images of men). Statues set up by the Greeks in honour of the victors in the public games. This custom dated from 50 Olym., or 584 B.C.

Androgeonia. An Athenian annual festival, in honour of Androgeus, the son of Minos.

Andron, Andronitis, Gr. and Gr.-R. (ἀνδρὼν, from ἀνὴρ, a man). That part of the Greek or Græco-Roman house exclusively set apart for men. Fig. 22 represents the ground-plan of a

Greek house; the *andron* occupies all that part of the building which surrounds the open court, and consists of the apartments numbered 1 to 9.

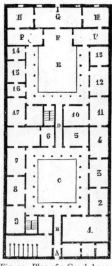

The Romans applied the term simply to a passage separating a house or part of a house from another.

Anelace, O. E. A knife or dagger worn at the girdle; broad, two-edged and sharp.

"An *anelace* and a gip-
ciere all of silk,
Hung at his girdle, white
as morwe milk."
(CHAUCER, *Canterbury Tales.*)

Fig. 22. Plan of a Greek house, showing the andron.

Angel. A gold coin current in England and France in the 15th and 16th centuries. It derived its name from the figure of an angel stamped upon it. A similar coin, either of gold or silver, was current in France at various periods. From the time of Louis IX. to that of Louis XI., the gold angel was equal in value to a crown of fine gold, or a little more than fourteen francs. It was stamped with a figure of St. Michael, holding in his right hand a sword, and in his left a shield with three fleur-de-lys. Henry VI., king of England, when he was in possession of Paris, had a gold angel struck which was not above seven francs in value. It was stamped with the figure of an angel holding in his hand the shields of France and England. The same king also had a silver angel struck which was only worth about five and a half francs.

Fig. 23. Angel of the reign of Elizabeth.

Angels, (Gr. ἄγγελος, a messenger) in Christian Art are represented in nine degrees, which are divided into three categories. The first consists of Seraphim, Cherubim, and Thrones; the

Fig. 24. Arms of France with Angels as supporters. XIV. century.

second of Dominations, Virtues, Powers ; and the third of Princedoms, Archangels, and Angels. They are represented as young, to show their continued strength; winged as messengers of speed ; barefooted and girt to show their readiness ; in robes of white indicative of purity, or in cloth of gold for their glory ; the cloth of gold diapered with bands of precious stones ; the emerald, emblem of *unfading youth*; the crystal, of *purity*; the sapphire, of *celestial contemplation*; and the ruby, of *divine love*. During the renaissance, Pugin complains, "the edifying and traditional representations of angelic spirits were abandoned, and, in lieu of the albe of purity and golden vests of glory, the artists indulged in pretty cupids sporting in clouds, &c." The proper attributes of the angels are trumpets, for the *voice of God*; flaming swords, for the *wrath of God*; sceptres, for the *power of God*; thuribles or censers for the *prayers of saints*, and musical instruments to emblem their *felicity*.

Angiportus or **Angiportum**, R. A narrow road passing between two houses or rows of houses, or an alley leading to a single house.

Angleterre, Point d'. Lace made by Flemish makers who were invited to settle in England in the reign of Charles II., the English Parliament having passed an act prohibiting the importation of all foreign lace. England, however, could not produce the necessary flax, and the lace was of inferior quality. The merchants of the time remedied this by smuggling large quantities of lace from the Brussels market, selling it as English Point or Point d'Angleterre, by which latter name it is still known, effacing the old name "Point de Bruxelles." (Fig. 25.)

Anglicanum Opus. (See EMBROIDERY.)

Angones. French weapons of the Middle Ages furnished with three blades, one of which was straight, broad and keen, the remaining two curving outwards. Some angons have a lozenge-shaped head-blade. They were used as a kind of pike, and sometimes hurled like javelins. The latter kind somewhat resembled the *aclis*.

Anguilla, R. A whip made use of by Roman schoolmasters for punishing their scholars. It was so called because made from the skin of an eel (*anguis*).

Anguis, R. A serpent which among the Romans symbolized the local spirit (*genius loci*).

Serpents were painted upon a wall to deter the public from defiling the spot thus indicated. At

Fig. 25. Point d'Angleterre.

Pompeii these representations of serpents are found in the bakehouses, kitchens, and similar places where cleanliness is peculiarly desirable. The same term was applied to a military ensign in the shape of a serpent.

Anime. Gum anime is a resin, which is mixed with copal in making varnish, causing it to dry quickly and firmly.

Animosi of Milan. One of the Italian literary academies. Their device was "stags passing a river, resting on the heads of each other." Motto, "Dant animos vices." (Mutual help gives strength.)

Anklets, Gr. (See PERISCELIS.)

Annealing. The process of tempering brittle glass and metals by heat.

Annulet, Her. A plain ring, or false roundle.

Annulets, Arch. The rings or mouldings about the lower part of the echinos or ovolo of Doric capitals.

Annulus or **Anulus,** Gr. and R. (dimin. of *anus,* a ring). A finger-ring. They were originally made of iron, and used as a signet for sealing. Later on they were made of gold. Among the Greeks and Romans they were worn on the fourth finger of the left hand, whence the expression *sedere ad anulos alicui,* to be seated at any one's left hand. The *anulus bigemmis* was a ring set with two precious stones ; *anulus velaris* was a curtain ring. A plait of hair arranged in circles round the back of the head was also called *anulus.* In architecture the term was formerly employed instead of *anulet.* The stone most

frequently used for rings was the onyx, upon which devices were carved with wonderful skill. The *bezel,* or part of the ring which contained the gem, was called PALA. (See RINGS.)

Ansa, Gr. and R. A term signifying both haft and handle, and even eyelet or hole. Any vessel or vase which has large ears or circular handles on the neck or body, is said to be furnished with *ansæ. Ansa ostii* was the term applied to the handle by which a door is pulled or shut to. The bronze or iron eyelet on the top of a steelyard were also called *ansæ stateræ.* The holes or eyelets made in the side leathers of a Greek or Roman shoe were called *ansæ crepidæ;* the handle of the rudder, *ansa gubernaculi;* lastly an iron cramp was called *ansa ferrea.*

Fig. 26. Templum in antis.

Antæ, R. Square or rectangular pilasters supporting the walls of a temple, which was thence called *templum in antis.* (Fig. 26.) The *antæ* thus formed the end of the walls of the *cella.* The capitals of *antæ* and the friezes abutting on them were sometimes richly ornamented, as may be seen by referring to Fig. 27, which repre-

Fig. 27. Capital and frieze of one of the Antæ in the temple of Augustus.

C

sents, in their restored state, the frieze and one of the antæ in the temple of Augustus, at Ancyra, in Galatia.

Antarius, Antarii funes, R. Ropes employed for raising into the proper position any object of considerable weight, such as a column, mast, &c.

Antefixa. Ornaments of terra cotta which were placed above the cornice, at the end of each row of tiles on a roof (Fig. 29). They were also used in ancient times for decorating the ridge of a roof. We possess specimens of antefixa remarkable for delicacy of design and execution ; such were the antefixa of the temple of Diana Propylæa at Eleusis, and the various Etruscan specimens to be found in our museums. They were decorated with masks, leaves, and especially palms painted to imitate nature or in different colours. The Etruscans employed coloured antefixa only ; many specimens of these last may be

Fig. 29. Archaic Antefixa in terra cotta.

seen at the Louvre, and in the museums of Perugia, Florence, and Naples. The Antefixa of the Parthenon were of marble. (Fig. 30.)

Antemural. A term referring either to the outworks protecting the approach to a castle, or to the wall surrounding the castle.

Antenna, R. The yard-arm of a ship.

Antepagmentum, R. The jamb of a door. *Antepagmentum superius,* the lintel.

Antependium. Richly ornamented hangings of precious metal, wood, or textile fabrics, in front of a Christian altar.

Anteportico. A synonym of PORCH (q.v.) ; but little used.

Anterides, Gr. and R. (? ἀντερείδω, to stand firm). A structure employed to strengthen a weaker one. It consisted of a kind of buttress

placed against an outer wall, chiefly in subterranean constructions, such as a sewer or aque-

Fig. 30. Antefixa in marble from the Parthenon.

duct. Fig. 31 represents the *anterides* of the Cloaca Maxima at Rome.

Fig. 31. Anterides of the Cloaca Maxima at Rome.

Anthony, Cross of St., in the form of the letter T. It is the idealized representation of a crutch. (See CROSSES.)

Anthropomorphic. Man-shaped ; said for example of the character of the Greek Religion, whose gods and demi-gods were only ideal men, from which circumstance the representation of the human form became the first object of their plastic art.

Antia. The iron handle of a shield.

Antiæ, R. The ringlets of hair worn by men and women which hung about the ears and the temples.

Antick. Strange, irregular, or fantastic in composition.

Antilena, R. An appliance attached to the pack-saddle of a beast of burden. It was a broad strap passing in front of the animal's breast so as to prevent the saddle from slipping backwards. It was employed especially in mountainous districts.

Antimensium, Chr. A consecrated altar-cloth.

Antimony. The oxide of this metal is employed in the preparation of yellow pigments for enamel or porcelain painting. Glass is coloured yellow by antimony. (See NAPLES, GUIMET'S YELLOWS.)

Antipendium, Chr. (See ANTEPENDIUM.)

Antiphoner, Chr. An antiphonarium ; a book of responses set to music.

Antique. Pertaining to ancient Greek or Roman art : more freely used in recent times to describe the quality of ancient art in general, but properly applicable only to classical art.

Fig. 32. Opus Antiquum.

Antiquum Opus, Arch. An ancient kind of stone-work or masonry composed of irregular stones. Another name for it was *opus incertum.*

Antiseptic varnish. A glazing composed to protect vegetable or animal pigments.

Antitype. The realization of the *type.*

Antonine Column. One of the most valuable architectural monuments in Rome. It is a lofty pillar ornamented with a series of bas-reliefs extending spirally from the base to the summit, representing the victories of the Emperor Marcus Aurelius Antoninus.

Anulus. (See ANNULUS.)

Anvil. In Christian art the attribute of St. Adrian, and of St. Eloy, the patron saint of the smiths.

Apalare, R. A kitchen utensil ; a sort of large metal spoon or ladle.

Ape. In Christian art the emblem of malice and of lust. Common in illuminations of the penitential psalms, in allusion to David's fall.

Apex, R. (*apex,* the top). A piece of olive wood pointed at the end, and set in a flock of wool. It formed the head-dress of the *Flamines*

and *Salii.* By analogy, the term was furtherused to denote a cap, and also the ridge on the top of ahelmet towhich the horsehair crest wasattached.

Aphractus, Gr. and R. (ἄφρακτον, lit. un-guarded). A vessel without a deck, or only partly decked fore and aft.

Aphrodisia, Gr. (Ἀφροδίσια). A general term under which were comprised all the festivals held in honour of Venus (*Aphroditè*).

Fig. 33. Aplustre and anchor of a Roman ship.—From bas-relief.

Aplustre, Gr. and R. (ἄφλαστον). An orna-ment placed at a ship's stern. It was constructed of flexible wooden planks, in imitation of the feather of a bird's wing.

Apobates, Gr. (Lat. Desultor). One who

Fig. 34. Apostle Mug.

dismounts. (1) Soldiers in chariots who leaped in and out in the fight. (2) The circus riders who leaped from one horse to another.

Apodyterium, R. and Gr.-R. (from ἀπὸ δύω, to put off). In a general sense, an undressing-room, and more particularly the apartment in the baths where the bathers undressed. As little light penetrated from without, there was generally a lamp burning in a niche. An *apodyterium* such as that just described may still be seen at Pompeii.

Apollino, It. The name usually given to the beautiful " Apollo of Florence," attributed to Praxiteles.

Apophyge or **Apophysis**, Arch. The small fascia or band at the top and base of the shaft of columns.

Apostle Mug. The mug or tankard shown in the engraving is of Nanconian or Nurem-berg stone-ware, with figures of the twelve apostles enamelled in colours upon it. (Fig. 34.) APOSTLE SPOONS are well known to have received their names from the figures of the Apostles forming the handles.

Apostyls Coats, O. E. Probably garments used for mystery plays.

Apotheca, Gr. and R. (ἀποθήκη, a granary). A store-room or magazine for containing any kind of stock. The Romans also applied the term specially to a wine store-room situated in the upper part of the house ; this was sometimes called the *fumarium*. Here the wine was placed in amphoræ to ripen it more quickly, whereas when stored in the *cella vinaria*, it was placed in CUPÆ and DOLIA (q.v.).

Apotheosis, Gr. (ἀπὸ, θεὸς god, to deify). A deification ; the ceremony by which a mortal was introduced among the number of the gods. The proper term in Latin is *consecratio* (q.v.). The funeral pile, in such cases, was built several stories in height, and an eagle was let loose from the top storey, to carry the soul of the emperor from earth to heaven. This is commemorated upon the medals struck on the occasion, which represent an altar with a fire on it, from which an eagle ascends.

Apparel, Chr. Embroidered additions to the vestments of the clergy.

Appaumée, Her. Said of a *hand*, open, erect, and showing the palm.

Appianum, Lat. Appian green, a pigment used by the ancients, prepared from green earth, now known as *Cyprus* or *Verona green*, because the best is found at those places.

Apple. The emblem in classical art of victory, and in Christian art of the fall of man.

Appliqué, Fr. Applied ornament, as of metal or porcelain upon wood. In embroidery, Appliqué work is used, when a pattern cut out of one colour or stuff is applied, or laid on, to another.

Apse, Apsis, or **Chevet** (ἀψὶς, bow or vault). The termination of a church. It is generally of semicircular form, and surmounted by a demi-

cupola, but there are instances of rectangular apses. Fig. 35 represents the apse of St. William in the Desert. (See ABSIS.)

Apsis gradata, Chr. The chair occupied by bishops in the early Christian basilicas.

Apteral, Arch. Without wings. A temple thout columns on the sides.

Aqua fortis (nitric acid). Used by engravers

Fig. 35. Apse of St. William in the Desert, a monastery in the South of France.—Built about A.D. 820.

and etchers for biting in on copper and steel.

Aqua marina. A transparent green stone, frequently used by the gem engravers of antiquity.

Aquæmanalis. (See AQUIMINARIUM.)

Aquamanile, Chr. The basin used for washing the hands of the celebrant in the liturgy. A. of great splendour are frequently mentioned in the ancient records. The corresponding ewer was called URCEUS.

Aqua-tint. A method of engraving with the help of mastic. (*Consult* Fielding's " Art of Engraving.")

Aqueduct, Gen. (*aqua*, water, and *duco*, to lead). An artificial canal for conveying water from one point to another, and often to a considerable distance from the source. Many ancient nations have executed works of this description, but the Roman aqueducts are especially celebrated. The most perfect is that which still exists, in a ruined state, over the river Gard, near Nismes in the South of France, called *Pont-du-Gard.* (Fig. 36.) Aqueducts were often discharged into reservoirs.

Aquilæ, R. The eagles, or ensigns, of the

Fig. 63. Pont-du-Gard, a Roman aqueduct near Nismes.
(*Restored*)

Roman legion under the Empire. They were of silver or bronze, and had the wings outstretched. As an architectural term *aquila* denotes the triangular face formed by the tympanum of a pediment, because the latter was often ornamented with an eagle. (See ENSIGN.)

Aquiminarium, R. An ewer for pouring water over the hands of the guests after a banquet. Other terms for this ewer were *aquæmanalis* and *aquimanale.*

Ara, R. The Latin term for ALTAR. (See this word and ALTARE.)

Arab Pottery. (See GARGOULETTE.)

Arabesque, Gen. An ornament of a pattern more or less intricate, composed of stems, foliage, leaves, fruits, scrolls, or leafage, as well as of curious and fantastic animals. It is an error to suppose that arabesque, as its name might seem to indicate, was an Arab invention; it was known to the Greeks and Romans, and was largely employed in Græco-Roman architecture.

Aræostylē, Arch. An order of temples, in which the space between the columns is four diameters in width.

Arbalest. (See CROSSBOW.)

Arca, R. (*arceo,* to enclose, preserve). (1) A kind of box or strong chest used by the ancients as a receptacle for money, clothes, or any valu-

able effects. (2) A strong box or money chest; (3) a rough chest used for a coffin ; (4) a cage for criminals, made of oak ; (5) a wooden caisson, answering the purpose of a modern coffer-dam.

Arcade. A series of arches.

Arcadi. A Literary Academy established at Rome in 1690. The members adopted pastoral names. Their device was a Pandæan pipe, surrounded by a wreath of olive and pine.

Arcatures, Arch. A series of blind arcades represented on a wall, in relief or painting. Carved arcatures are those forming a kind of screen ; they are detached from the wall, and have an inner and outer face.

Arcera, R. A cart boarded all over so as to resemble a huge chest (*arca*). The inmate reclined on cushions and pillows covered with drapery ; and the exterior was covered with hangings, the richness of which varied with the rank and fortune of the owner.

Arch (*arcus,* a bow). A structure the form of which is based on the segment of a circle. The kinds of arches are named according to the curve which they make. *Round-headed arches :* semicircular, segmental or stilted, introduced by the Romans. *Triangular arches,* of very early date. *Horse-shoe arches ;* the Moorish, the common horse-shoe and the pointed (which is also a Moorish form). Then the *trefoil arch* of the Early English style : with its variations, including the square-headed trefoil of the 13th century. The *lancet* or acute-pointed ; the *equilateral ;* the *pointed trefoil ;* the *ogee,* of the 14th and 15th century ; the *Tudor* arch, of the reigns of Henry VII. and VIII.; and the decorative forms, not used in construction; the *flamboyant,* the *cinquefoil* and the *multifoil* are all described under the headings printed above in *Italics.*

Archaic (art). The first period of Art is distinguished by stiffness and conventionality of treatment, directed much more to the symbolic representation of an idea than to beauty or true imitation. It is properly called also the *hieratic* type, from its intimate relation to religious symbolism. See SELINUNTIAN ; ÆGINETAN MARBLES.

Archangels. The seven angels of the Christian hierarchy who stand in the presence of God. *St. Michael,* sometimes in complete armour, bears a sword and scales, as the Angel of Judgment, also a rod with a cross ; *St. Raphael* bears a fish, and a pilgrim's staff and gourd ; *St. Gabriel* bears a lily ; *Uriel* carries a parchment roll and a book, as the interpreter of prophecies ; *Chamuel* bears a cup and a staff; *Zophiel* a flaming sword ; and *Zadchiel* the sacrificial knife which he took from Abraham. The Archangels are generally represented with the nimbus, and clothed as princes and warriors ; their ensign is a banner and cross, and they are armed with a sword and a dart in one hand.

Arched or **Archy,** Her. Bent or bowed.

Arched-buttress or **Flying Buttress**, Arch. An incomplete arch supporting the spandrels of a roof. It springs from a BUTTRESS (q.v.).

Archeria, Med. Lat. A vertical loophole from which arrows could be discharged.

Archibault. (See ARCHIVOLT.)

Architrave, Gr. and R. (ἀρχὸς, chief; and Ital. *trave*, a beam). That part of a structure which rests immediately on the capital of a column or pilaster. Architraves are surmounted by a frieze and a cornice.

Archivium, Gr. and R. A building in which archives (charters and records) of a city or state were deposited. It was also called ARCHEION or TABULARIUM (q.v.).

Archivolt or **Archibault**, (*arcus*, and *volutus*, rolled round). The whole of the mouldings decorating an arch or arcade, and following the contour of the same.

Archlute, old Eng. A kind of *theorbo*, or double-necked lute. 16th century.

Archy. (See ARCHED.)

Arcosolium, Chr. (*arcus*, and *solium*, a coffin). An arched or vaulted sepulchral chamber in the catacombs, sanctified by the interment of martyrs and holy persons; and in later generations often richly decorated, as with marble incrustations, paintings, and mosaics. The *arcosolia* in which Christians of small means were buried are constructed in the walls of the passages in the catacombs. The wealthier Christians, however, had *arcosolia* specially excavated for their family and friends; the following inscription is frequently found on them: *Nobis et nostris et amicis.*

Arcuatio, R. A structure formed by means of arches or arcades, and employed to support a construction of any kind, such as a bridge, aqueducts, &c.

Arcubalista, R. (βάλλω, to throw). A machine for hurling arrows, somewhat similar to a cross-bow.

Arcubus. (See ARQUEBUS.)

Arcula, R. Diminutive of ARCA (q.v.). (1) A small chest. (2) A colour-box used by encaustic painters. (3) A small sepulchre, or stone coffin.

Arculum, R. A garland which the *Dialis* (Priest of Jupiter) wore on his head while sacrificing; it consisted of one or two pomegranate boughs bent into a circle and fastened with fillets of white or red wool.

Arcuma, R. A small carriage constructed to hold only one person. (See PLAUSTRUM, CHIRAMAXIUM, VEHICULUM.)

Arcus, R. (1) A bow for discharging arrows. There were many kinds in use among the ancients. Those of the Greeks and Romans presented on the whole much analogy with each other, while the Scythian bow differed entirely from both. (2) An arch of masonry; the *arcus triumphalis* was a trimphal arch. The Romans never used any other form of arch than the semi-circle.

Ardenti. Literary Academies of this name existed at Pisa, at Naples, and at Viterbò.

Area, R. (1) Any broad, open and level space, and so a square or parade. *Areæ* were adorned with fountains and statues set up in honour of some divinity, who frequently gave his name to the spot. Thus at Rome there were the *area Apollinis, area Mercurii,* &c. (2) A threshing-floor in a field.

Arena, R. (1) Sand; a material employed in building. (2) The level space forming the area of an amphitheatre.

Arenaria, R. A Roman game of ball for two persons; it derived its name from the fact that the ball was made to rebound from the ground (*arena*).

Areste. A cloth of gold, elaborately figured, used for vestments. 13th century. It is not to be confounded with *arras*.

Arezzo Vase. Many fine examples of old Etruscan pottery have been found in or near the town of Arezzo in Tuscany. They are of red lustred ware ornamented in relief, and show evident traces of Greek origin. (Fig. 37.)

Fig. 37. Arezzo vase.

Argei, R. (1) Certain sites at Rome, having a small temple attached to them. (2) Images or lay-figures made of bulrushes, which were cast into the Tiber, on the Ides of May, from the Sublician bridge. This custom is still kept up in the south of France, where, in certain

Fig. 38. Point d'Argentan.

towns, on Ash-Wednesday, they drown an image called *Caramentran* who represents the god of the carnival.

Argent, Her. The metal silver, represented in engravings by a plain white.

Argentan, Point d'. Lace made much in the same way as Point d'Alençon, but having the flowers bolder and larger in pattern and in higher relief; the foundation, called the bride-ground, is also coarser. It takes its name from the little town of Argentan in Normandy, where it was made. (Fig. 38.)

Fig. 39. Argentella lace.

Argentella. A name given to a lace made in Genoa, but worked much like Point d'Alençon.

Argive. A school of sculpture, contemporary with the ATTIC SCHOOL of Pheidias; of which Polycletus was the head. He was the author of the *Canon*, or law of proportion in sculpture, exemplified in his *Doryphorus* (spear-bearer); he worked principally in bronze, and was famous for his chryselephantine statues. A specimen of the Argive school of sculpture is the *Discobolus* of Myron (a contemporary of Polycletus) in the British Museum. It is an ancient copy in marble from the original bronze statue. Closeness to Nature is a distinguishing characteristic of the Argive School.

Aries or **Ram**. A battering-ram. It consisted of a stout beam, furnished at one end with an iron head, shaped like that of a ram,

and was used to batter the walls of a city till a breach was effected. The battering-ram was at first worked by men, who simply carried it in their arms, but in course of time it was suspended from a wooden tower (Fig. 40), or a

Fig. 40. Battering-ram.

vertical beam, and worked with the aid of ropes. When the battering-ram was enclosed in a kind of wooden shed bearing some resemblance to the shell of a tortoise, it was called by the name of that animal (*testudo*) (Fig. 41).

Ark, Chr. A symbol of the church.

Armanahuasi, Peruv. The baths of the ancient Peruvians. They were remarkable for the elegance and luxury displayed in their ornamentation. They were furnished with magnificent fountains, some of which threw their jets upwards (*huraea*), others in a horizontal direction (*paccha*).

Armarium, R. A cabinet, cupboard, or bookcase. Originally a place for keeping arms. Some were ornamented with plates of brass set in links of gold; others were made of gold inlaid with precious stones of various shapes. (See also ALMERY.)

Fig. 41. Battering-ram in *testudo*.

Armatura, R. (1) In a general sense, armour of every kind. Thus *armatura levis* denoted the light infantry; and soldiers armed only with a *hasta*, and the dart, *gæsa* (of Gallic invention) were called *leves milites*. (2) The art of fencing. (3) The pieces of iron or bronze which connect stones or the parts of a structure. (4) The iron framework in a window or casement.

Armed, Her. Having natural weapons of offence, &c. A lion is *armed* of his claws and teeth, a bull of his horns, &c.

Armenian Green. (See CHRYSOCOLLA.)

Armet, Old Eng. A kind of helmet of the 16th century, worn with or without the *beaver*.

Armilausa, Lat. A classical garment adopted in England and elsewhere, worn by knights over their armour. Strutt describes it as "a round curtal weed, which they called a cloak, and in Latin *armilausa*, as only covering the shoulders."

Fig. 42. Armilla. Celtic Bracelet.

Fig. 43. Armilla. Gaulish Bracelet.

Armilla. In general, any circlet of gold or silver which forms a bracelet for men or women, whether worn on the wrist, arm, or ankle. Bracelets worn by men often consisted of three or four massive bands of bronze, silver, or gold, and thus covered a considerable portion of the arm. Bracelets were worn by the Assyrians, the Babylonians, the Medes, the Persians, the Celts (Fig. 42), and the Gauls (Fig. 43). The Egyptians in some instances employed ivory and porcelain in their manufacture.

Armillum, R. A kind of *urceolus*, or small pitcher for holding a particular kind of wine. It was among the number of the sacrificial vessels, and was well known from the Latin proverb : *Anus ad armillum* (an old woman returns to her bottle).

Armilustrium. A Roman festival for the purification of arms.

Arming Points. The "points" or ties of armour.

Armins. Cloth or velvet coverings for pike-handles.

Armory, Her. (1) Heraldry. (2) A list of names and titles with the arms belonging to them.

Armour, Arms. In almost every deposit where *prehistoric* remains are buried, we find clubs, hatchets, arrows, hammers, or other arms, mostly, even in the *stone age*, carefully ornamented. The ancient *Egyptians* were armed with "the bow, spear, two species of javelin, sling, a short and straight sword, dagger, knife, falchion, axe or hatchet, battle-axe, pole-axe, mace or club, &c. Their defensive arms consisted of a helmet of plate, or quilted head-piece,

a cuirass, or coat of armour made of metal plates, or quilted with metal bands, and an ample shield" (*Wilkinson*). Among the Greeks, the heavy-armed warrior wore the greaves, cuirass, with the mitra underneath, and the zone or cingulum above ; his sword, ensis or gladius, hung on his left side, and the large round shield,

Fig. 44. Primitive Roman Armour.

sacus, aspis, clipeus or scutum, hung from his shoulder ; his helmet, corys, cunea, cassis or galea ; his spear, enkus, doru or hasta, or two spears. The defensive armour, the shield and thorax, were called hopla, and the man hoplites. The light-armed, psiloi, anoploi, gymnai, gymnetai, had a slighter covering of skins, or cloth, and fought with darts, stones, bows and arrows or slings. There were also the peltastæ, so called from their small shield pelte. All the above-mentioned parts of classical armour, and their modifications in that of mediæval times are described under their respective headings ; as well as much of mediæval armour.

Arnis, Gr. and R. An expiatory festival held in honour of Linus and his mother Psamathê, the daughter of Crotopus, king of Argos. Various legends are extant regarding the origin of this festival, which was called *Arnis* from the sheep (ἀρνειòs) that were sacrificed.

Arotoi-Hieroi, Gr. Literally : *sacred labours,* a term used to denote three agricultural festivals which took place in Attica ; the first was held in commemoration of the first sowing ; the second, on occasion of reaping the earliest crop of barley in a field near Eleusis ; the third, by way of invoking the blessings of Ceres on the field of corn specially set apart for the worship of Athena.

Arquebus. A hand-gun, larger than a musket. The man using it was called an *arquebusier.*

Arra or **Arrha,** R. A deposit, or earnest-money to a contract.

Arras. Tapestry. Textile hangings for walls ; first made at Arras in the 14th century. It was originally called Opus Saracenicum.

Arrhæ Sponsalitiæ, called also ARRABO, was the name of the betrothal money paid to the parents of a bride ; a practice of the Hebrews, continued by Christians.

Arrhephoria, Gr. ('Αρρηφόρια). A festival held at Athens in the month of June or *Sciro-phorium.* The maidens who took part in it were called ἀρρηφόροι or ἐροηφόροι. Four little girls and a priestess carried some sacred vessels to a grotto.

Arricciate, Ital. One of the coats of mortar laid on to a wall to receive fresco painting.

Arrondie, Her. Curved, round.

Arrows, in Christian art, are the emblems of pestilence, death, and destruction.

Arsenicon, Greek for *orpiment* (q. v.).

Artemisia, Gr. A general term to denote all the festivals of *Diana Artemis.* The most cele-brated were those held at Ephesus, Delphi, and Syracuse.

Articulation. The anatomical study of the uncture of the bones.

Artolaganus, R. (ἀρτο-λάγανον, i. e. bread-cake). A kind of dough-cake made with wine, milk, oil, and pepper. Cicero, in one of his letters, asserts that it was delicious.

Artophorium (bread-bearer), Chr. Another name for the ciborium or costly box prepared to contain the consecrated Host.

Artopta, Gr. and R. (from ἀρτάω, to bake). A mould in which bread and pastry were baked.

Artopticius, R. (sc. *panis*). A roll or loaf of

bread baked in an *artopta,* many examples of which may be seen in the small museum at Pompeii; owing to their having become hardened, these loaves have retained their shape perfectly when taken from the oven after eighteen centuries.

Arundel Device.

Fig. 45. Arundel device.

A chapeau *or,* and *gules,* sur-mounted by a fret *or,* and an acorn leaved *vert.* This is only one of the numerous badges of the house of Arundel, which is peculiarly rich in armorial bearings.

Arundel Marbles. A collection of ancient sculptures found in Greece and Asia Minor in the early part of the 17th century and brought to England at the expense of Thomas Howard, Earl of Arundel. In 1667 his grandson presented them to the University of Oxford.

Arundo, R. A term with various significations. (1) A reed or cane. (2) An arrow or bow made of cane. (3) A fishing-rod. (4) A cane rod tipped with bird-lime for catching birds. (5) A reed pen for writing. (6) A Pan's pipe in which the reeds were joined together by wax ; whence its name *arundo cerata.* (See CALAMUS.)

Arx, R. (*arceo,* to enclose). A citadel or for-tress. *Arx* is almost equivalent to ACROPOLIS (q. v.), since citadels were usually built on elevated sites, thus forming an upper city (ἀκρόπολις).

Fig. 46. Greek Aryballos.

Aryballos. A Greek flask or vase used for oil or wine. It was commonly of a bladder shape with a thin neck. The example engraved (Fig. 46) is painted in the Asiatic style. On some of these vases the ornament is engraved.

Arystichos, Gr. and R. (from ἀρύω, to draw water). A vessel for drawing water, especially from the AMPHORA (q.v.). It was also called *ephebos* (ἔφηβος), because, at banquets, it was the duty of youths to mix the wine with water before handing it to the guests. This term has as synonyms *aruter, arusane, arustis* and *oinerusis.*

Arzica. (1) An artificial pigment of a yellow colour, used for miniature painting. (2) A yellow lake made from the herb "reseda luteola." (3) A yellow earth for painting, of which the moulds for casting brass are formed; it yields an ochreous pigment of a pale-yellow colour, which, when burned, changes to an orange colour.

Arzicon. A contraction of *Arsenicon,* for *orpiment* (q.v.).

As, R. The unit of value in the bronze currency of the Romans. Originally the *as* weighed one pound, whence its name *as liberalis;* and as it was composed of a mixture of copper and tin (*æs*), it was also called *æs grave.* At a later period the *as* had much declined in value; under Augustus it was only worth somewhat less than a penny.

Asaminthos, Gr. (ἀσάμινθος). A large vase of the Homeric epoch, large enough to admit of a person bathing in it. It is supposed that this was the *tub* of Diogenes.

Asbestus. (See AMIANTUS.)

Ascendant, Her. Issuing upwards, as a flower.

Ascia, Gr. and R. A term applied to instruments of various shapes and employed for different purposes, but all bearing a general resemblance to a carpenter's adze. The expression *sub ascia dedicavit,* which is frequently found engraved on tombs together with the representation of an *ascia,* has given rise to numerous interpretations. It is supposed that this expression signified: This tomb [never before used] has been dedicated to the memory of the person in whose honour it was erected; or possibly the formula implied that the plot upon which the memorial stood had been granted in perpetuity. After all the discussion to which the formula has given rise, these are the two hypotheses most generally accepted. (See ACISCULUS.)

Ascopera, Gr. and R. (ἀσκὸς, leathern bag or wine-skin; πήρα, a pouch). A large bag made of undressed leather, carried as knapsack by foot-travellers, and thus distinguished from the HIPPOPERA (q.v.).

Ascolia, Ascolias, Gr. and R. (from ἀσκὸς, a wine-skin). An Athenian game which consisted in leaping upon a wine-skin, filled with wine and greased over with oil, during the festivals in honour of Dionysus.

Ashlar, Achelor, &c.; also ASTLER or ESTLAR, O. E. Hewn stone for the facings of walls. "Clene hewen Ashler."

Asilla, R. A yoke, like a milkman's, or the Malay *picol,* for carrying burdens; is a common object in Egyptian and all other ancient representations of domestic appliances.

Asinarii. A term of reproach inherited by the early Christians from the Jews, who were accused of worshipping an ass.

Askos, Gr. and R. (ἀσκός). A vessel, originally shaped like a leather bottle (*uter*) for holding water or wine. It was furnished with a handle at the top, and had sometimes two mouths, one of which served to fill, the other to empty it. Later on, the *askos* assumed the form of an earthenware pitcher.

Asor, Heb. A musical instrument of ten strings played with the plectrum.

Asp. In Egyptian art the emblem of royalty; in Christian art, under the feet of saints, of conquered malice.

Aspectant, Her. Looking at one another.

Asperges, Aspergillum, Chr. The rod for sprinkling holy water.

Aspersed, Her. Scattered over,—the same as Semée.

Aspersorium, Chr. The stoup, or holy water basin.

Asphaltum. A brown carbonaceous pigment used in painting. It is found in various parts of the world, more particularly in Egypt, China, Naples, and Trinidad. The best is the Egyptian. (See BITUMEN, MUMMY.)

Aspic. (See OIL OF SPIKE.)

Ass, Chr. An emblem of patience and sobriety; but also of idleness and obstinacy; sometimes of the Jewish nation.

Ass, Festival of the. A grotesque Christian festival of the Middle Ages, connected with the prominence of the ass in religious history.

Asser, R. (1) A beam, pole, or joist. (2) The rafters of a wooden roof. (3) *Asser falcatus* was a kind of ram which was launched, with the aid of machinery, by the garrison of a fortified town, against the enemy's siege works.

Assett, O. E. A salver.

Assommoir, Fr. A sort of gallery built over a door or passage of a fortified place, from which stones, lead, and other heavy objects could be hurled down to *overwhelm* (*assommer*) the besiegers. Hence the name.

Asterisk, Chr. Sometimes called STELLULA. A kind of crossed framework made of gold or silver, consisting of two arched bands which are sometimes surmounted, at the point of intersection, by a cross. The asterisk is placed upon the patera for the purpose of keeping up the cloth which covers the consecrated wafers of the host.

Astler. (See ASHLAR.)

Astragal (ἀστράγαλος, knuckle-bone). A

small semicircular moulding, so called from its resemblance to a row of knuckle-bones placed side by side. As it is decorated with beads, or berries of laurel or olive, separated by discs, it is now commonly known as a *chaplet*. Astragals are placed at the top of a column, beneath the capital, and divide the architrave into two or three parts. They are also used to decorate any kind of base. (See TORUS.)

Astragalus, R. The ancient game of knuckle-bones ; a common subject in classical sculpture, called also TALI.

Astreated, Arch. Star-shaped ornaments, used in Norman mouldings.

Asylum, Gr. and R. (ἄ-συλον, safe from violence). A place of refuge, to which was attached the privilege of inviolability called *asulia.* This privilege belonged to certain temples, woods, or other sacred enclosures. There were a con-

Fig. 47. One of the Atlantes of the Theatre of Bacchus at Athens.

siderable number of such retreats in Greece and the Greek colonies.

At Gaze, Her. Said of animals of the chase "standing still and looking about them."

Atach-gah, Pers. The fire-altar of the ancient Persians ; mentioned in the writings of Pausanias and Strabo.

Atellanæ (sc. *fabulæ*), R. A farce, so called from its having originated in *Atella*, a city of the Osci, in Campania. Hence the name of Oscan games (*ludi Osci*). *Atellanæ* were played by youths of good family, on the conclusion of a tragedy. They were introduced into Rome in the fourth century B.C. These farces were distinguished by their refinement, and freedom from low buffoonery.

Athenæum. A university for literary and scientific studies at Rome, on the Capitoline Hill.

Athyr, Egyp. One of the months of the ancient Egyptians. It was the third of the four months called the months of inundation.

Atlantes, Gr. and R. (from τλῆναι). Human figures so called, in allusion to the story of the Titan Atlas, which were employed instead of columns to support entablatures (Fig. 47). The Latin equivalent for the term is TELAMONES. Similar *female* figures were CARYATIDES.

Fig. 48. Atlas, a device used by Philip II. of Spain.

Atlas. One of the several devices adopted by Philip II. of Spain was a figure of Hercules bearing on his shoulders and kneeling beneath, the weight of the world ; a feat recorded to have been performed by him in order to give relief to Atlas from his customary burden. The motto "Ut quiescat Atlas," is written on a ribbon.

Atramentale, Atramentarium, Gr. and R. (*atramentum*, q.v.). An inkstand, of any shape or material whatsoever. Inkstands were made of terra cotta, bronze, and silver. There is a Pompeian painting in which a *double* inkstand is represented, one side of which contains black ink, the other an ink of some different colour.

There were also portable inkstands called *theca*. (See THECA.)

Atramentum, Gr. and R. (*ater*, black). A general term to denote any kind of black liquid; such were *atramentum scriptorum*, *atramentum librarium*, or simply *atramentum*—all terms for writing ink ; *atramentum sutorum*, the black used by shoemakers for dyeing their leather, another name for which was *chalcamentum* (q.v.) ; and *atramentum tectorium*, a kind of ink used for writing inscriptions with a brush. In ancient times, all descriptions of ink were made with soot and gum, forming a kind of Indian ink which was diluted with water. Vitruvius (Book VII.) thus describes the process by which *atramentum* was obtained: " Soot is first procured by burning rosin in a vaulted chamber, and the black (*atramentum*) thus obtained is then mixed with gum."

Atriolum, R. (dimin. of *Atrium*). (1) A small atrium. It might be either a smaller atrium adjoining the principal one in a house, or the atrium of a dwelling of inferior size. (2) A small antechamber forming the entrance of a tomb.

Atrium, R. and Mod. A term perhaps derived from *Atria*, a city of Tuscany in which structures of this description were first built. It consisted of a kind of covered court (*cavædium*), round which were grouped the different apartments of the house. In the centre of the roof was an aperture with sloping sides called the *compluvium*, and in the court beneath, a basin which collected the rain water from the roof. This was called the *impluvium*. There were besides, the *atrium displuviatum* and the *atrium testudinatum*. The atrium was unquestionably

Fig. 49. Atrium, with Ionic columns.

the most essential and the most interesting part of a Roman mansion ; it was here that numbers assembled daily to pay their respects to their patron, to consult the legislator, to attract the notice of the statesman, or to derive importance in the eyes of the public from an apparent intimacy with a man in power. — *Moule*.

Fig. 50. Atrium, with Doric columns.

During the Middle Ages the term *atrium* was used to denote the open plot of ground surrounding a church, which served for a cemetery, and the close or courtyard of certain churches.

Attegia, R. A hut or cabin made of reeds, and covered with thatch.

Attic-order, Arch. An arrangement of low pilasters, surmounting a building.

Attiourge, Arch. (Ἀττικουργὴς, wrought in Attic fashion). A doorway, the uprights of which, instead of being perpendicular, inclined slightly inwards, so that the opening was wider at the threshold than immediately under the lintel. Fig. 51 represents the doorway of an ancient monument at Agrigentum, in Sicily.

Attires, Attired, Her. The antlers of a stag or "hart" having antlers.

Attributes. Conventional symbols of the character, or the agency, or the history, of subjects of art representation.

Auditorium, R. (a place for hearing). A lecture-room, assembly-room, court of justice. or generally any place in which orators, poets, &c., were heard. The BASILICÆ contained halls so named, in which courts of justice were held.

Augmentation, Her. An honourable addition to a coat of arms.

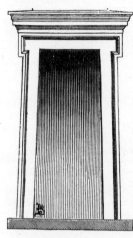

Fig. 51. Atticurge doorway at Agrigentum.

Augurale, R. (*augur*, a sooth-sayer). In a Roman camp the *augurale* was a place situated to the right of the general's tent or PRÆTORIUM (q.v.). It was so called because the augurs there took their station to observe the flight of birds. In Greece, the *oracles* were consulted; but in Rome questions were addressed to Jupiter, who answered simply "*Do*" or "*Do not*," by his messengers the birds. They gave no prophecies.

Augustine's Oak, at Aust on the Severn; the scene of the conference between St. Augustine and the British bishops, A.D. 602.

Aula, Gr. and R. (αὐλή). (1) An open court attached to a house. It was usually in front, and on either side of it were the stables and offices. When it belonged to a farm it was round this courtyard that the stabling, sheepfolds, and other outhouses were arranged. (2) *Aula regia* was the central part of the scene in a Greek or Roman theatre.

Aulæa or **Aulæum**, R. (*aula*, a hall). (1) Hangings or tapestry used to decorate the dining-room or *triclinium*, or generally, any piece of tapestry used as a curtain, whether to cover a doorway, act as a screen, or hide the stage in a theatre. (2) The covering of a sofa or dining-couch, also called, from the way in which it hung all round it, *peristroma* (περίστρωμα). Aulæa is almost synonymous with VELUM (q v.).

Aulmonière. The Norman name for the pouch, bag, or purse appended to the girdle of noble persons, and derived from the same root as "alms" and "almoner." It was more or less ornamented and hung from long laces of silk or gold; it was sometimes called Alner. (Fig. 52.) (See ALLOUYÈRE.)

> I will give thee an *alner*
> Made of silk and gold clear.
> (*Lay of Sir Launfal.*)

Aulos, Gr. The Greeks gave this name to all wind instruments of the *flute*, or *oboe*, kind; it was not blown at the side like a flute, but by a vibrating reed in the mouthpiece, like a clarionet. The single flute was called *monaulos*, and the double one *diaulos*.

Fig. 52. Aulmonière.

Aumbrie, **Aumery**, **Almery**, O. E. A cupboard or closet.

Aumery of Here, O. E. A cupboard with hair-cloth sides for ventilation. A meat-safe.

Aureola, Chr. (*aurum*, gold). A quadrangular, circular, or elliptic halo surrounding the bodies of Christ, the Virgin, or certain saints. Another name for this ornament is the *mystical almond* or VESICA PISCIS (q.v.). When it envelopes the head only it is called the NIMBUS.

Aureole. (See AUREOLA.)

Aureus, R. (sc. nummus, golden). The unit of value for gold currency under the Roman emperors, worth about a guinea.

Auripetrum. A cheap imitation of gold leaf; made of tinfoil coloured with saffron.

Auspicium, R. (*aves aspicio*). Divination from observation of the flight of birds. (*Auspicium ex avibus, signa ex avibus.*) There was also the *auspicium cœleste* or *signa ex cœlo*, of which the most important was a flash of lightning from a clear sky. Besides these there were the *auspicia pullaria*, or auspices taken from the sacred chickens; the *auspicia pedestria, caduca*, &c. (See AUGURALE.)

Authepsa, Gr. and R. (αὐθέψης). Literally a *self-boiler*; it was a sort of kettle or cauldron, which was exposed to the rays of the sun, to heat the water within it; whether, however, the ancients had attained the art of raising water to boiling heat, in this manner, it is impossible to say. The apparatus is mentioned by Cicero and Lampridius, but neither of them gives any description of it.

Avellane. A variety of the heraldic cross. (See CROSSES.)

Avena, R. (oats). A Pandæan pipe, made of the stalk of the wild oat.

Aventail, Fr. (*avant taille*). The movable front of a helmet.

Aventurine. A kind of brown glass, mixed with bright copper filings, formerly made at Venice.

Averta, R. A trunk, bag, or portmanteau, carried on the crupper by travellers who rode on horseback.

Aviarium, R. (*avis*, a bird). (1) A poultry-yard. (2) An aviary in which birds—and more particularly those of rare breeds—were kept.

Axis, R. (1) The axle-tree of a carriage. (2) *Axis versatilis* was a cylinder worked by a crank, and used for drawing water from a well by means of a cord which rolled round it as it revolved. (3) The upright pivot upon which a door turned. It worked in two sockets, placed respectively in the upper and lower lintels.

Azarcon. The Spanish name for red lead.

Azure. A blue colour known from the very earliest times. Azure stone was the name given to the lapis lazuli. The name is given also to COBALT. In heraldry it is the name for the blues in the arms of persons whose rank is below that of a baron; it is represented in heraldic engraving by regular horizontal lines.

Azyme, Chr. Unleavened bread.

B.

Baccalarii, Med. Lat. A contraction of bas-chevaliers: poor knights; distinct from knights bannerets, who were also termed rich knights.

Baccelleria, Med. Lat. The order of bachelors. Thus we read,

> " La flor de France et la bachelerie."

Bachelor or Bachelier has been derived from *bas échelle*, the lowest step of the ladder. (*Meyrick.*)

Baccha, Gr. and R. A Bacchante; a woman who celebrates the mysteries of Bacchus, in the temples of the god, or in the Bacchic orgies. In the numerous representations of Bacchantes which occur on monuments of ancient art, they carry the *thyrsus* in their right hands, and wear a wreath of ivy or vine-leaves on their heads. They appear also in the disguise of Lenæ, Thyades, Naiads, Nymphs, &c.

Bacchanalia, R. (Greek, *Dionysia*). Festivals held in honour of Dionysus or Bacchus.

Bacchos, Gr. and R. A short, richly-ornamented *thyrsus*, carried by the Mystæ, at Éleusis, on occasion of their being initiated in the

mentioned in a MS. of the 13th century. The name of *bag-gamon* is first found in 1646.

Baculum, Baculus, R. A general term to denote any kind of staff, except such as form the insignia of any rank or office, or are employed in certain professions.

Fig. 53. Planta genista, or broom.

Badges. Small heraldic shields, worn by servants and others, showing, in embroidered cloth or silver, a figure or device; common also "in the furniture of houses, on robes of state, on the caparisons of horses, on seals, and in the details of Gothic edifices." (*Lower, " Curiosities of Heraldry.*") Fig. 54 from the cornice of King Henry's chantry in Westminster Abbey shows the adaptation of heraldic badges in architectural ornament. (The description is inserted under BLAZON, q.v.) The Badges worn by the mili-

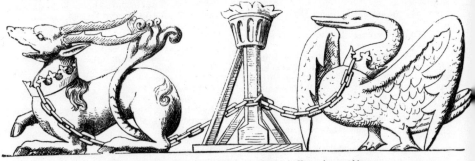

Fig. 54. Badge of King Henry V. in his chantry in Westminster Abbey.

mysteries. There was a proverb in Greece which said: " Many carry the *Bacchos*, but few are inspired by the gods."

Bacillum (dimin. of BACULUM, q.v.). A small wand, especially the lictor's wand.

Backgammon, originally called *table board*, is

tary followers of the feudal leaders answered the purpose of our modern uniforms. Among remarkable badges are the "Bear and ragged staff" of the Earls of Warwick, the red and white roses of Lancaster and York, the sprig of broom (Fig. 53) of the Plantagenets.

Badgers. Brushes of badger's hair, for blending or softening. (See BLENDING.)

Bagordare, Med. It. A burlesque tournament in which the combatants were attended by fools instead of heralds and esquires.

Bagpipe. This ancient and favourite instrument of the Celtic races is represented in an O. E. MS. of the 14th century. Several of the Hebrew instruments mentioned in the Bible and in the Talmud were kinds of bagpipes. So was a Greek instrument called "Magadis." In Russia and Poland, and in the Ukraine, it used to be made of a whole goat's skin, and was called "Kosa," a goat. It is of high antiquity in Ireland, and a pig playing the bagpipe is represented in an illuminated Irish MS. of A.D. 1300.

Baijoire. (1) A medal or coin on the obverse or reverse of which were two faces in profile, placed one over the other. (2) An ancient silver coin of Genoa, and an ancient Dutch gold coin. The term is certainly derived from an old word Baisoire [*baiser*, to kiss].

Bai-Kriem, Hindoo. Literally, roasted rice ; a stone employed in some of the monuments of the ancient Cambodia. (See BIEN-HOA.)

Bailey. (See BALLIUM.)

Bainbergs (Germ. *Bein-bergen*). Shin-guards or modern greaves.

Baisoire. (See BAIJOIRE.)

Balance or **Scales.** In Christian symbolism the balance symbolizes the Last Judgment. The Scales and Sword are also, generally, the attribute of personified Justice.

Balandrana. A large cloak, of the 12th and 13th centuries.

Balayn, O. E. Whalebone for crests of helmets.

Baldachin, It. A canopy of wood, stone, or metal over seats and other places of honour, common also over fireplaces and beds, and carried in coronation and other processions over the most honoured persons.

Baldric, Baudrier, or **Baudrick,** O. E. A girdle or sash, usually a belt of leather, and worn over the shoulder. They were sometimes hung with bells. (See BALTEUS.)

Balea, Balia, Med. Lat. (from βάλλω, to throw). (1) A sling. (2) A *ballista.* From their skill in the use of slings, the inhabitants of Majorca, Minorca, and Ivica had the appellation Baleares.

Bales, O. E. (Lat. *balascus* ; Fr. *balais*). An inferior kind of ruby.

Baleyn. (See BALAYN.)

Balista. (See BALLISTA.)

Balista a pectore, Med. Lat. A hand cross-bow.

Balistrariæ, Med. Lat., Arch. Cruciform openings in the wall of a fortress to shoot quarrels through from cross-bows.

Balletys or **Tuptai,** Gr. A ceremony consisting in a mock combat with stones, which took place at the Eleusinian festival.

Ball-flower. An ornament characteristic of the Decorated style of the 14th century. It represents the "knop" of a flower. *Ball-flowers* may be seen in the Cathedrals of Bristol, Gloucester, and Hereford.

Fig. 55. Ball-flower.

Ballista or **Balista,** Gr. and R. (βάλλω, to throw). A military engine for hurling large missiles. It was constructed of wood, and consisted of two uprights connected horizontally by a double cross-beam. Strands of twisted fibre formed the motive power of the engine, which was fitted with an iron groove. The cord was drawn back by men, with the aid of a drum or pulleys. The ancient balista was used to shoot *stones;* the catapult to project *heavy darts.* Some balistæ threw stones weighing three cwt. The mediæval balistæ threw *quarrels* or stones.

Ballistarium or **Balistarium,** Gr. and R. A shed or magazine in which *ballistæ* were kept.

Ballium, Med. Lat. (1) (from Ital. *battaglia*) The *Bailey* or courtyard of a castle. (2) The bulwark which contained such a Bailey.

Balneæ or **Balineæ.** (See BALNEUM.)

Balnearia, R. A general term for all the utensils used in a bath, such as strigils, *unguentaria, guttæ,* oils, perfumes, essences, &c.

Balneum, Balneæ, Thermæ, Gr. and R. *Balneum* meant originally a tub or other vessel to bathe in ; next, the room in which it was placed; when there were many such rooms the plural *balnea* was used. *Balneæ* were the public baths, under the Republic, when they consisted of ordinary baths of hot and cold water. *Thermæ* were the magnificent and luxurious buildings adapted for the hot air system. They contained (1) the *Apodyterium,* or dressing-room; (2) the *Frigidarium,* where the cold bath was taken ; (3) the *Tepidarium,* a bath of warm air ; (4) the *Caldarium,* with a vapour bath at one end, a warm water bath at the other, and a *Sudatorium,* or sweating bath in the middle. The pavement, called *suspensura,* was over a furnace, *hypocaustum.* The bathers were currycombed with *strigils,* which the Greeks called *stlengis* or *xystra;* and they dropped oil over their bodies from narrow-necked vessels called *guttus* or *ampullæ.* The *Thermæ* contained *exedræ,* or open-air chambers, where philosophers lectured, and libraries, and had gardens, and shady walks, and fountains, with statuary attached to them. The ruins of

Fig. 56. Balneæ. The Caldarium.

the *Thermæ* built by Titus, Caracalla, and Domitian remain visible (Fig. 56).

Balon, Balein, Balayn, O. E. Whalebone.

Balsam of Copaiba. An oleo-resin, used as a *varnish*, and as a vehicle, for oil-painting.

Balteolus. Dimin. of BALTEUS (q.v.).

Balteus or **Balteum** (a belt), R. (1) A baldric or wide belt which passed over one shoulder and beneath the other, for the purpose of suspending a sword, buckler, or any other arm. (2) The ornament on the baldric on which was marked the number of the legion to which a soldier belonged. (3) A richly ornamented band of leather placed round a horse's breast,

Fig. 57. Balustrade.

below the MONILE, or throat-band (q.v.). (4) The broad belt in the sphere, which contains the signs of the Zodiac. (5) The bands surrounding the volutes of an Ionic capital. (6) The *præcinctiones*, or small walls, or parapets, separating the different tiers in a theatre or amphitheatre. (Generally a BELT.)

Baltheus, Med. Lat. for BALTEUS.

Baluster. A small pillar, swelling in the centre or towards the base.

Balustrade, Arch. An enclosure or parapet composed of ballisters (q.v.), and by analogy, an enclosure consisting of any other ornament, such as trefoils, carved work, &c. Fig. 57 represents a balustrade of the pointed Gothic style.

Bambino, It. A babe. Image of the infant Christ.

Bambocciata, It. The style of genre painting of Teniers, Van Ostade, Wilkie, and others. It was introduced into Rome in 1626 by Peter Van Laar, who was called, from an unfortunate deformity that he had, Il Bamboccio, or the Cripple.

Banded, Her. Encircled with a band.

Banderolle. (1) A small flag, about a yard square, upon which arms were emblazoned, displayed at important funerals. (2) In architecture of the Renaissance, a flat scroll, inscribed.

Bands. Originally the name given to the collars which (in the 17th century) replaced the ruff of Elizabeth's reign. At first they were made of stitched linen or cambric edged with lace, stiffened so as to stand up round the neck. Contemporary with these were the falling bands. The engraving (by Hollar, 1640) shows a merchant's wife with collar or falling band of cambric edged with lace. The term bandbox has descended to us from those days, when similar boxes were made expressly for keeping bands and ruffs in. (Fig. 58.)

Fig. 58. Falling Band.

Bands, Arch., are either small strings round shafts, or a horizontal line of square, round, or other panels used to ornament towers, spires, and other works. (See BALTEUS.)

Bandum, Banderia, Med. Lat. A small banner. The French poets called it "*ban*," a word probably of Celtic origin, signifying "exalted." (*Meyrick*.)

Bankard, O. E. (Fr. *banquier*). A carpet or cloth covering for a table, form, or bench.

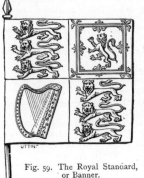

Fig. 59. The Royal Standard, or Banner.

Banner. In heraldry, a square, or narrow oblong flag, larger than the pennon (q.v.), charged with the coat of arms of the owner displayed over its entire surface, precisely as it is blazoned on a shield, as in the illustration of the Royal Standard,

which should properly be styled the Royal *Banner*. (See STANDARD.) The Union Jack is also a banner, in which the blazonry of the two nations of England and Scotland are combined, not by "quartering," but by an earlier process of "blending" the cross and the saltire in a single composition. The profusion of banners at tournaments, in feudal times, when each noble planted his own in the lists, was an element of picturesque effect. The term applies to all kinds of flags, or colours, proper to individuals, or corporations, &c., who display them. It does not appear that *military* banners were used by the ancients. The banners used in Roman Catholic countries bear the representation of patron saints, or symbols of religious mysteries.

Banner-cloth, Chr. A processional flag.

Banneret. A knight entitled to display a banner.

Baphium, Gr. and R. (βάπτω, to dye). A dyer's workshop.

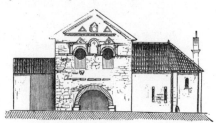

Fig. 60. Baptistery of St. Jean, Poitiers.

Baptisterium, R. (from βάπτω, to dip). A kind of cold plunging-bath, constructed in the FRIGIDARIUM (q.v.), or the room itself. In

Fig. 61. Baptistery of St. Constance, Rome.

Christian archæology, *baptistery* was the name given to a building adjoining a basilica, or situated near it, in which baptism was adminis-

D

tered. Such is the baptistery of St. John Lateran at Rome. One of the most ancient baptisteries in France is that of St. Jean, at

Fig. 62. Interior of the Baptistery of St. Constance.

Poitiers, represented in Fig. 60. It dates from the fourth century; that of St. Constance, at Rome (Figs. 61, 62), belongs to the same period.

Bar, Her. A horizontal line across a shield.

Barathron or **Orugma,** Gr. (βάραθρον). A deep cleft behind the Acropolis at Athens, into which criminals were thrown, either under sentence of death by this means, or after they had been put to death by hemlock or other poisons. It was situated near the temple of Diana Aristobulê.

Barba, Gen. The beard, whence the attributive *barbatus*, frequently employed to denote one who wears a beard. Thus *bene barbatus*, a man with a well-trimmed beard; *barbatulus*, a young man whose youthful beard had never been touched with the razor. Among many nations of antiquity the custom prevailed of curling the beard artificially, so as to obtain long curls or ringlets, *cincinni*. (See CINCINNUS.) The Assyrians, Egyptians, Jews, Persians, Greeks, and Romans may be particularly enumerated. Shaving the beard was introduced into Rome about B.C. 300, and became the regular practice. In the later times of the republic many persons began to wear it trimmed, and the terms *bene barbati* and *barbatuli* were applied to them. Under Hadrian the practice of wearing beards was revived, and the emperors until Constantine wore them. The Romans let the beard grow as a sign of mourning; the Greeks shaved. The beard is an attribute of the prophets, apostles, and evangelists (excepting St. John); and, in ancient art, of Jupiter, Serapis, Neptune, &c. Neptune has a straight beard; Jupiter a curly silky one. The early Britons shaved generally, but always had long moustachios. The Anglo-Saxon beard was neatly trimmed or parted into double locks. The Normans originally shaved

clean, but when settled in England let all their beard grow. Close shaving prevailed among the young men in England in the 14th century; older men wore a forked beard. After sundry changes, clean shaving obtained in the reign of Henry VI., and the beard was rarely cultivated from then until the middle of the 16th century. The most extravagant fashions arose in Elizabeth's reign, and were succeeded by variations too numerous to detail.

Barbatina, It. A preparation of clay mixed with the shavings of woollen cloth, used in the manufacture of pottery to attach the handles and other moulded ornaments. (*Fortnum.*)

Barbed, Her. Pointed, as an arrow.

Barbican, Mod. (1) A long narrow opening made in a wall, especially in a foundation wall, to let the water flow away. (2) The term also denotes an outwork placed in front of a fortified castle or any other

Fig. 63. Barbican.

military post. In the latter acceptation the term ANTEMURAL (q.v.) is also used. The illustration is taken from the arms of Antoine de Burgundy. In this instance the barbican is a small double tower, or out-post watch-house, and the shutter-like pent-house protection of the unglazed window openings bears a striking resemblance to a modern sun-blind.

Barbitos, Gr. and R. (βάρβιτος). A stringed instrument which dates from a very high antiquity; it was much larger than the CITHARA (q.v.). To strike the long thick strings of the *barbitos*, a PLECTRUM (q.v.) was used instead of the fingers. The invention of this instrument is attributed to Terpander; Horace, on the contrary, says it was invented by Alcæus, and Athenæus by Anacreon. It was a kind of lyre with a large body.

Barbotine, Fr. A primitive method of decorating coarse pottery with clays laid on it in relief. (*Jacquemart.*)

Barca. A boat for pleasure, or for transport. It was also a long-boat. (See BARI.)

Barde, Barred, Her. In horizontal stripes.

Barded, Her. Having horse-trappings, or—

Bardings, which were often enriched with armorial blazonry.

Bardocucullus, R. and Gaul. (*bardus* and *cucullus*, i.e. monk's-hood). A garment with sleeves and hood worn by the poorer classes among the Gauls. It bore some resemblance to the Roman PÆNULA (q.v.).

Barge-board, or **Verge-board**, is the external gable-board of a house ; which is often elaborately ornamented with carvings.

Bari or **Baris**, Gr. and Egyp. (βᾶρις). A shallow Egyptian boat, used on the Nile to transport merchandise, and in funeral processions. The Egyptian sacred barks, with which they formed processions on the Nile, were made of costly woods, and ornamented with plates of gold or silver, and carried a miniature temple (*naos*), which contained the image of a divinity. The prow and the poop were ornamented with religious symbols of the richest workmanship.

Fig. 64. Barnacles or Breys.

Barnacles or **Breys**. An instrument used in breaking horses.

Baron, in heraldic language, signifies a husband. The rank of Baron in the peerage corresponds with that of the Saxon Thane ; it is the lowest.

Baronet. An hereditary rank instituted by James I. in 1612.

Baron's Coronet, first granted by Charles II., has, on a golden circlet, six large pearls ; of which four are shown in representations.

Baroque. In bad taste, florid and incongruous ornamentation. The same as *rococo*.

Barrulet, Her. The diminutive of a BAR (q.v.).

Barry, Her. Divided into an even number of bars, which all lie in the same plane.

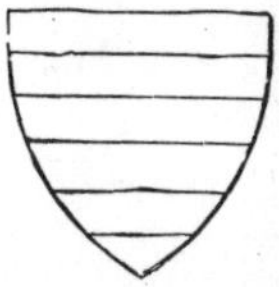

Fig. 66. Barry of six.

Barry-Bendy, Her. Having the field divided by lines drawn *bar-wise*, which are crossed by others drawn *bend-wise*.

Bartizan, Watch-turret, Arch. A small watch-tower made to project from the top of a tower or a curtain-wall, generally at the angles. City-gates were in some instances furnished with bartizans. Originally they were of wood, but from the 11th century they were made of masonry, and so formed part of the structure on which they rested ; they were, in fact, turrets. (Fig. 67.) (Compare BARBICAN.)

Bar-wise, Her. Disposed after the manner of a BAR (q.v.).

Barytes. A heavy spar, or sulphate, the *white* varieties of which are ground and made into paint (*constant* or *Hume's white*). Mixed with an equal quantity of *white lead*, it produces *Venice white*, and with half as much "*Hamburg*," or with one-third "*Dutch*" white.

Basalt is a very hard stone, much like lava in appearance, and black or green in colour, used

for statuary. The principal specimens are Egyptian and Grecian.

Fig. 67. Bartizan.

Basanos, Gr. (1) (Lat. *lapis Lydius*) The touchstone ; a dark-coloured stone on which gold leaves a peculiar mark. Hence (2) trial by torture. (3) A military engine, the form of which is not exactly known.

Bascauda, R. A basket, introduced from Britain as a table utensil, considered as an object of luxury. It was the old Welsh "basgawd," and served to hold bread or fruits.

Fig. 68. Bar-wise.

Bascinet. A light helmet, round or conical, with a pointed apex, and fitting close to the head, mentioned in the 13th century.

Bascule, O. E. (1) The counterpoise to a drawbridge. (2) A kind of trap-door. (A badge of the Herbert family.)

Base, Arch. The lower part of a pillar, wall, &c. ; the division of a column on which the shaft is placed. The Grecian Doric order has no base.

D 2

Base, Her. The lowest extremity.

Baselard, Fr. An ornamental short dagger, worn at the girdle; 15th century. With such a

Fig. 69. Ionic Base.

weapon the Lord Mayor of London "transfixit Jack Straw in gutture." The weapon is preserved by the Fishmongers' Company.

Bases. A kind of embroidered mantle, which hung down from the middle to about the knees, or lower; worn by knights on horseback. (*Nares.*)

Basileia, Gr. (βασίλεια). A festival instituted in honour of Jupiter *Basileus*. It was in commemoration of the victory which the Bœotians had won at Leuctra, and in which success had been promised them by the oracle of Trophonius.

Fig. 70. Basilica at Pompeii (restored).

Basilica (sc. aula), Gr. and R. (Βασιλικὴ, sc. στοὰ, i. e. royal hall). This term owes its original meaning to the fact that in Macedonia the kings, and in Greece the archon Basileus dispensed justice in buildings of this description. The Romans, who adopted the basilica from the above-named countries, used it as a court of justice, but besides this it became a branch of the forum, and even when it did not form a part of the latter was constructed near it, as was the case at Pompeii. Fig. 71 represents the ground-plan of this basilica, and Fig. 70 a view of the same building restored. The ground-plan of the basilica is rectangular, the width not more than half nor less than a third of the length. It was divided by two single rows of columns into three naves, or aisles, and the tribunal of the judge was at one end of the centre aisle. In the centre of the tribunal was the *curule chair* of the prætor, and seats for the judices and advocates. Over each of the side aisles there was a gallery, from which shorter columns supported the roofs; these were connected by a parapet wall or balustrade. The central nave was open to the air. Under Constantine the basilicæ were adopted for Christian churches. The early Norman churches were built upon the same plan, and the circular apsis, where the judges originally sat, used for the central altar, was the origin of the apsidal termination of the Gothic cathedrals. The first basilica was built at Rome, B.C. 182. In the Middle Ages structures resembling small churches erected over tombs were called Basilica.

Fig. 71. Ground-plan of a Basilica.

Basilidian Gems. (See ABRAXAS.)

Fig. 72. Basilisk.

Basilinda, Gr. and R. (Βασιλίνδα). Literally, the game of the king; it was often played by Greek and Roman children. The king was appointed by lot, the rest being his subjects, and bound to obey him, during the game.

Basilisk. A fabulous animal, having the body of a cock, beak and claws of brass, and a triple serpent tail. The emblem of the Spirit of Evil. In heraldry, a cockatrice having its tail ending in a dragon's head.

Basilium, Gr. (βασίλειον). A royal diadem, of a very tall form, of Egyptian origin. Isis-Fortuna is often represented wearing the *basilium* on her head.

Basinet. (See BASCINET.)

Basons for ecclesiastical ceremonies, for collecting alms or for holding the sacramental vessels, were a favourite subject for the goldsmith's art. Some beautifully enamelled basons of the 13th century represent subjects of hawking and hunting, &c.

Bas-relief, Basso-relievo, sculptured figures projecting less than half of their true proportions; **Mezzo-relievo** projecting exactly half; **Alto-relievo** more than half, from the ground upon which they are carved.

Bassara or **Bassaris**, Gr. (a fox, or fox-skin). A long tunic of Lydian origin worn by the Mænads of Lydia and Thrace, who were often called, from this circumstance, *Bassaræ* and *Bassarides*.

Basterna, R. A closed litter appropriated especially to the use of ladies, as the *Anthologia Latina* says : "The gilded basterna conceals the chaste matrons." It was carried by two mules harnessed in shafts, one in front and one behind; the LECTICA (q.v.), on the contrary, was carried by men. During the Middle Ages the same form of litter was a common means of conveyance in England.

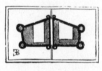

Fig. 73. Ground-plan of the Bastile.

Bastile, Arch. An outwork placed so as to defend the approach to a castle or fortified place. A famous Bastile which had been converted into a state prison was that of Paris, destroyed in 1789. Fig. 73 shows the ground-plan of it. The diminutive of this term is Bastillon, which has been changed into *Bastion*.

Bastion, Mod. A projecting polygonal buttress on a fortification. The anterior portions of a bastion are the *faces ;* the lateral portions, the *flanks ;* the space comprised between the two flanks, the *gorge ;* and the part of the fortification connecting two bastions together, the *curtain.*

Bastisonus, Med. Lat. A bastion or bulwark.

Batagion or **Batagium**. (See PATAGIUM.)

Bath, Order of the, numbers 985 members, including the Sovereign; viz. *First Class :* Knights Grand Cross—G.C.B.—50 Naval and Military and 25 Civil Knights. *Second Class :* Knights Commanders — K.C.B. — 120 Naval and Military and 50 Civil. *Third Class :*

Companions—C.B.—525 Naval and Military and 200 Civil.

Fig. 74. Naval and Military Badge of the "Bath."

Fig. 75. Civil Badge of the "Bath."

Batiaca or **Batioca**, Gr. and R. A vase of a very costly description, used as a drinking-vessel.

Batiere, Fr., Arch. (See SADDLE-ROOF.) A roof is said to be "*en batière*" when it is in the form of a pack-saddle; that is, when it has only two slopes or eaves, the two other sides being gables.

Batillum or **Vatillum**, R. (1) A hand-shovel used for burning scented herbs to fumigate. (2) Any kind of small shovel.

Baton. In heraldry, a diminutive of the BEND SINISTER couped at its extremities.

Baton. The military baton, or staff, was of Greek origin. (See SCYTALE.)

Batter, Arch. Said of walls that slope inwards from the base. Walls of wharfs and of fortifications generally *batter*.

Battle-axe is one of the most ancient of weapons. The *pole-axe* is distinguished by a spike on the back of the axe. (See BIPENNIS.)

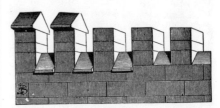

Fig. 76. Embattled

Battled, Embattled, Her. Having battlements.

Battlement, Embattailment, Bateling, O.E. (Fr. *Créneau, Merlet, Bretesse*). A parapet in fortifications, consisting of a series of rising

Fig. 77. Battlement.

parts, called MERLONS or COPS, separated by spaces called CRENELS, EMBRASURES, or LOOPS.

Batuz. Norman French for *battus*, beaten with hammered up gold; said of silken stuffs so adorned.

Baucalia or **Baucalis**, Gr. and R. (βαυκάλιον, βαύκαλις). A drinking-vessel, which varied in shape and material.

Baucens, Bauceant, Med. A black and white banner used in the 13th century. (*Meyrick.*)

Baudekyn, O.E. A fabric of silk and gold thread.

Baudekyn (Lat. *Baldakinus*). Cloth of gold, brocade: "pannus omnium ditissimus."

Baudrick or **Baldrock**, O.E., of a church bell. The strap by which the clapper is hung in the crown of the bell.

Baukides, Gr. (βαυκίδες). A kind of shoe worn by women; it was of a saffron colour. This elegantly-shaped shoe was highly esteemed by courtezans, who often placed cork soles inside their *baukides*, to make themselves appear taller.

Baxa or **Baxea**, Gr. Sandals made of textile plants, such as the palm, rush, willow, papyrus, and a kind of alfa. They were worn by comic actors on the stage.

Bay, Arch. (Fr. *Travée*). A principal compartment or division in a structure, marked off by buttresses or pilasters on the walls, or by the disposition of the vaulting, the main arches, &c. The French word *baie* means an opening made in a wall for a door or window.

Bayeux Tapestry. A roll of unbleached linen worked in coloured worsted with illustrations of the Norman Conquest (about A.D. 1068); preserved in the public library at Bayeux. A full-sized copy may be seen in the South Kensington Museum.

Bayle, Arch. The open space contained between the first and second walls of a fortified castle. These buildings often had two bayles; in this case, the second was contained between the inner wall and the donjon.

Bayonet. A weapon, so called after the town of Bayonne in France, where it was invented about A.D. 1650.—

Bay-stall, Arch. The stall or seat in the bay (of a window).

Beads, Arch. An architectural ornament of mouldings consisting of small round carved beads, called also Astragal. Another name for this ornament is Paternosters.

Beaker (Fr. *cornet*). A trumpet-shaped vase, or drinking-cup.

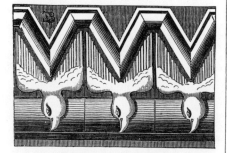

Fig. 78. Moulding with Beak-heads and Tooth-ornament.

Beak-heads (Fr. *becs d'oiseau*), Mod. An ornament peculiar to English architecture, representing heads and beaks of birds. The ancient Peruvians used the same ornament in their architecture, as shown in Fig. 79, taken from the decoration of the monolithic door of Tianuaco.

Fig. 79. Peruvian ornament (Beak-heads).

Bear. Dancing bears are represented in Anglo-Saxon MSS.

Beards. (See *barba*.)

Beaver. The movable face-guard of a helmet.

Beds. Anglo-Saxon beds usually consisted merely of a sack (*sæccing*) filled with straw, and laid on a bench or board, which was ordinarily in a recess at the side of the room, as we still see in Scotland. The word *bedstead* means only "a place for a bed." *Tester beds*, or beds with a roof, were introduced by the Normans. Early in the 13th century beds were covered much as now, with 'quilte,' counterpane, bolster, sheets, and coverlet; and stood behind curtains which hung from the ceiling. In the 15th century the beds became much more ornamental, having canopy and curtains, and these, as well as the *tester* or back, decorated with heraldic, religious, or other devices. At the sides were *costers*, or ornamental cloths. Between the curtains and the wall a space was left called the *ruelle*, or little street.

Beech Black. A blue-black vegetable pigment.

Bees, in Christian art, are an attribute of St. Ambrose.

Belfry (Fr. *Beffroi*). The campanile or bell-tower of a church. Frequently detached from the church, as at Chichester Cathedral. (See BELL-GABLE.)

Bell. An attribute of St. Anthony, referring to his power of exorcising evil spirits. In heraldry, the bell is drawn and blazoned as a church bell.

Bell-cot, Arch. A BELL-GABLE (q.v.).

Belled, Her. Having bells attached, like the cows in the device of the city of Béarn. (Fig. 80.)

Bell-gable, Arch. A tur-

Fig. 80. Belled.

ret raised over the west end of small churches and chapels that have no towers to hang a bell in. This is distinct from the smaller turret at the east end of the nave for the SANCTUS BELL (q.v.).

Bellicrepa, Med. Lat. A military dance, of Italian origin.

Bellows were called in A.S. *bælg* or *blast-bælg*. A MS. of the 14th century represents a man blowing at a three-legged caldron with a perfectly modern-looking pair of bellows. Bellows, in Christian art, are an attribute of Ste. Geneviève.

Bell-ring, Mod. The ring in the CROWN of a bell from which the clapper hangs.

Bells on the caparisons of horses were common in the Middle Ages. A passage in the romance of Richard Cœur de Lion describes a messenger "with five hundred belles rygande." Chaucer's monk has also bells on his horse's "bridel" which "gyngle as lowde as doth the chapel belle."

Belt, Chr. A girdle used to confine the alb at the waist.

Belt of Beads, Chr. A rosary was sometimes so called.

Belvidere, It. A prospect tower over a building.

Bema, Gr. (1) A stone platform or hustings, used as a pulpit in early Christian churches. (2) The term is synonymous with sanctuary. (3) It also serves to denote an ambo and a bishop's chair. (See AMBO.) The Athenian *bema* was a stone platform from which orators spoke at the assemblies (*ecclesiæ*) in the Pnyx.

Bembix, Gr. and R. (Lat. *Turbo*). (1) A child's whipping-top. (2) The whorl of a spindle.

Benches, for seats, are represented in the 14th century formed by laying a plank upon two trestles.

Fig. 81. Bend.
Arms of Le Scrope.

Bend, Her. One of the Ordinaries. It crosses the field diagonally, from the dexter chief to the sinister base, as in Fig. 81, the arms of Richard Le Scrope: *Azure, a bend or.*

Bendideia, Gr. (Βεν-δίδεια). A festival held in the Piræeus in honour of the goddess *Bendis* (the Thracian name of Artemis or Diana).

Bendlet, Her. The diminutive of Bend.

Bend-wise, or **In bend**, Her. Arranged *in the direction of a* bend.

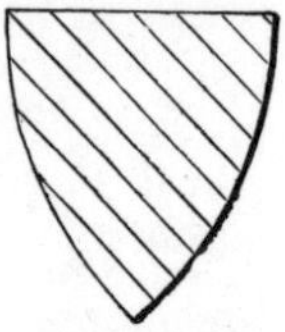

Fig. 82. Bendy.

Bendy, Her. Parted bend-wise into an even number of divisions.

Benna, Gaul. and R. This term, borrowed either from the Welsh or the Gauls, denoted among the Romans a four-wheeled cart or carriage made of wicker-work. A *benna* may be seen on the bas-reliefs of the column of Marcus Aurelius.

Bennou, Egyp. A mythical bird resembling the phœnix, which sprang from its own ashes, and was made the emblem of the resurrection. It symbolized the return of Osiris to the light, and was therefore consecrated to that god.

Benzoin. A gum-resin used as an ingredient in *spirit varnishes.*

Berlin Porcelain. The manufactory was first founded in 1750, under Frederick the Great. Fig. 83 is a specimen of Berlin hard porcelain.

Beryl. A gem of an iridescent green colour.

Bes, R. (*bi*, twice, and *as*). A fraction of value equivalent to two-thirds of an *as*.

Besa, Gr. and R. A drinking-vessel, also called *bessa* and *bession*. It was wider at the bottom than at the top, and in shape much resembled the BOMBYLOS (q.v.).

Bessa (Fr. *beysse ferrée*), Med. An instrument like a pickaxe or mattock used by the pioneers of an army ; 15th century. (*Meyrick*.)

Bession. (See BESA.)

Bestions, Arch. This term is applied by Philibert Delorme to the fantastic animals which

Fig. 83. Berlin porcelain jug.

occur in sculptures of the decorative or florid period of architecture.

Beten, O. E. Embroidered with fancy subjects.

     " A coronall on her hedd sett,
       Her clothes with beasts and birdes were *bete*."

Beveled, Arch. Having a sloped surface. (See SPLAY.)

Bever. A Norman word for "taking a drink" between breakfast and dinner; elsewhere called "a myd-diner under-mete."

Bezant, Her. A golden "roundle" or disk, flat like a coin.

Biacca, It. White carbonate of lead ; a pigment.

Fig. 84. Bezant.

Biblia, Med. Lat. A war engine for attack.

Bibliotheca, Gr. and R. (βιβλίον, book, and θήκη, case). Primarily the place where books were kept, and hence used for the collection of books or MSS. itself. The most celebrated library of antiquity was that founded by the Ptolemies at Alexandria, destroyed by the Arabs, A.D. 640.

Bibliothecula, Gr. and R. (dimin. of *bibliotheca*). A small library.

Bice. The name of certain very ancient blue and green pigments, known also as *Mountain* (or *Saunders'*) *blue*, and *Mountain green*, and by other names. (See CARBONATES OF COPPER.)

Biclinium, Gr. and R. A couch or sofa on which two persons could recline at table.

Bicos, Gr. (See BIKOS.)

Bidens, R. (*dens*, a tooth). Literally, with two teeth, forks, or blades. The term was applied to a hoe, a pair of scissors, and an anchor (*ancora bidens*). A two-forked weapon of the same name occurs in some representations of Pluto.

Bidental, R. (*bidens*). A structure consecrated by the augurs or haruspices, through the sacrifice of an animal. This was generally a sheep of two years old, whence the name *bidens* applied to the victim. The *bidental* was often an altar surrounded with a peristyle, as may be seen from the remains of one of them at Pompeii. A *bidental* was set up in any place which had been struck by lightning. A cippus or *puteal* placed on the exact spot which had been struck bore the inscription : *Fulmen* or *fulgur conditum*.

Bien-hoa or **Ben-hoa**, Hind. A kind of stone employed by the Khmers or ancient inhabitants of Camboja for their sculpture ; they also called it *baï-kriem* (roasted rice), which it exactly resembles. Its deep yellow colour recalls in a striking degree that of old white marbles which have been long exposed to the sun and air in warm countries.

Fig. 85. Bifrons.

Bifrons, R. (*frons*, a forehead). Having two fronts or faces. Libraries and picture galleries generally contained statuary of heads or busts coupled together back to back, but especially of Janus, emblematic of his knowledge both of the past and the future. The illustration represents a Greek vase, in imitation of the statuary described.

Biga, R. (*bi* and *juga*, double-yoked). A car drawn by two horses. *Bigæ* also denoted, like *bijugus* or *bijugis*, two horses harnessed together. [The Greeks called this method "Synoris."]

Bigatus, R. (sc. *nummus*). A silver denarius (one of the earliest Roman coins) which had a BIGA on the reverse. Other denarii were *quadrigati*, having a *four-horse chariot* on the reverse.

Biggon, O. E. "A kind of quoif formerly worn by men ;" hence "Béguines," the nuns at the Béguinage at Ghent, who still wear the *biggon*.

Bikos, Gr. and R. A large earthenware vase adapted to hold dry provisions, such as figs, plums, &c.

Bilanx, R. (double-dish). A balance with two scales. (See LIBRA.)

Bilbo. A light rapier invented at Bilboa.

Bilix, R. (double-thread). A texture like "twill," or "dimity," made by a double set of leashes (*licia*).

Fig. 86. Bill-head.

Bill, O. E. A weapon made of a long staff with a broad curved blade, a short pike at the back, and a pike at the top, used by infantry of the 14th and 15th centuries. (Fig. 86.)

Billet, Her. A small oblong figure.

Billet, Arch. A moulding of the Roman epoch, consisting of short rods separated from each other by a space equal to their own length. Some billets are arranged in several rows.

Bilychnis, Gr. and R. A double lamp with two beaks and two wicks, so as to give out two separate flames.

Binio, R. A gold coin current at Rome. It was worth two *aurei* or fifty silver *denarii*. (See AUREUS.)

Bipalium, R. A spade, furnished with a cross-bar, by pressing the foot on which the instrument could be pushed into the ground. Representations of this tool occur pretty frequently on tombs.

Fig. 87. Bipennis.

Bipennis or **Bipenne**, Gen. (*penna*, a wing). An axe with a double blade or edge, used as an agricultural implement, an adze, or a military weapon. The Greeks, who called it βουπλῆξ, never made use of it. It was used especially by barbarous nations, such as the Amazons, Scythians, Gauls, &c. Fig. 87 represents a Gaulish *bipennis* taken from one of the bas-reliefs on the triumphal arch at Orange.

Bird, in Egyptian hieroglyphics, signified the soul of man, and in Christian art had *originally* a similar meaning afterwards forgotten.

Bird-bolt. A short thick arrow, with a blunt head. about the breadth of a shilling.

Biremis, R. (*remus,* an oar). A pair-oared boat, or a vessel having two banks of oars.

Fig. 88. Biretta. (Portrait of a Rector of Padua.)

Biretta, It. A cap. In its restricted meaning the term is applied to that worn by priests and academical persons. The illustration shows the state costume of the Rector of the University of Padua, who wears a sacerdotal biretta.

Birotus and **Birota,** R. (*rota,* a wheel). Anything having two wheels, and so a two-wheeled carriage, car, or chariot.

Birrus and **Byrrus,** R. A russet-coloured capote with a hood. It was made of a coarse cloth (*bure*) with a long nap. Such was, at first, the meaning of the term, but in course of time *birri* of a fine quality were made.

Bisaccium (It. *bisacce*). Saddle-bags of coarse sacking.

Biscuit, Fr. A kind of porcelain, unglazed. The finest is the so-called Parian porcelain.

Bisellium, R. (*sella,* a seat). A seat of honour or state chair, reserved for persons of note, or who had done service to the state. There was room on the seat for two persons.

Bishop's Length. Technical name for a portrait-canvas of 58 inches by 94 inches.

Bismuth. The pigment, called pearl white, which is the sub-nitrate of this metal, is very susceptible to the action of sulphurous vapours, which turn it black.

Bisomus, Chr. A sarcophagus with two compartments ; that is, capable of holding two dead bodies. (See SARCOPHAGUS.)

Bistre. A warm brown water-colour-pigment, made of the soot of beech-wood, water, and gum. It is the mediæval fuligo and fuligine.

Biting-in. The action of aqua fortis upon copper or steel in engraving.

Bitumen. This pigment *should* be genuine *Asphaltum,* diluted and ground up with drying-oil or varnish. It dries quickly. There is a substance *sold as bitumen* which will not dry at all. (See ASPHALTUM.)

Bivium, R. (*via,* a way). A street or road branching out into two different directions ; at the corner there was almost always a fountain.

Bizarre, Fr. Fantastic, capricious of kind.

Black is the resultant of the combination in unequal proportions of blue, red, and yellow.

Black, in Christian art, expressed the earth ; darkness, mourning, wickedness, negation, death ; and was appropriate to the Prince of Darkness. White and black together signify purity of life, and mourning or humiliation ; hence adopted by the Dominicans and Carmelites. In blazonry, black, called sable, signifies prudence, wisdom, and constancy in adversity and love, and is represented by horizontal and perpendicular lines crossing each other.

Black Pigments are very numerous, of different degrees of transparency, and of various hues, in which either red or blue predominates, producing brown blacks or blue blacks. The most important are *beech black,* or *vegetable blue black ; bone black,* or *Paris black,* called also *ivory black ; Cassel* or *Cologne black, cork black, Frankfort black,* and *lamp black.* (See ASPHALTUM.)

Blades, Arch. The principal rafters of a roof.

Blasted, Her. Leafless, withered.

Blautai, Gr. (Lat. *soleæ*). A richly-made shoe ; a kind of sandal worn by men.

Blazon, Her. Armorial compositions. To blazon is to describe or to represent them in an heraldic manner. The representation is called Blazonry. For example, the *blazoning* of the BADGES on the cornice of King Henry's chantry in Westminster Abbey is as follows :—On the dexter, a white antelope, ducally collared, chained, and armed *or*; and on the sinister a swan gorged with a crown and chain. The beacon or cresset *or*, inflamed proper. (See Fig. 54.)

Blending. Passing over painting with a soft brush of badger's hair made for the purpose, by which the pigments are fused together and the painting softened.

Blindman's Buff. Called "hoodman-blind," *temp*. Elizabeth.

Blind-story, Arch. The TRIFORIUM in a church. Opposed to the CLEAR or CLERESTORY (q.v.).

Blocking-course, Arch. The last course in a wall, especially of a parapet. The surface is made slightly convex to allow of water flowing off more easily.

Blodbendes (O. E. for blood-bands). Narrow strips of linen to bind round the arm after bleeding.

Blodius, O. E. Sky blue.

Bloom. The clouded appearance which varnish sometimes takes upon the surface of a picture.

Blue. One of the three primary colours, the complementary to orange. Blue, in Christian art, or the sapphire, expressed heaven, the firmament, truth, constancy, fidelity. Its symbolism as the dress worn by the Virgin Mary is of *modesty*. In blazonry it signifies chastity, loyalty, fidelity, and good reputation. Engravers represent it by horizontal lines.

Blue Black, or **Charcoal Black,** is a pigment prepared by burning vine-twigs in close vessels. Mixed with *white lead* it yields very fine silvery greys. (See also BLACK PIGMENTS.)

Blue Pigments. Minerals:— see ULTRAMARINE, COBALT, BLUE VERDITER. Vegetable:—*Indigo*. Animal :—*Prussian blue*. (See CARBONATE OF COPPER, INTENSE BLUE.)

Blue Verditer. (See VERDITER.)

Boar. In mediæval art, emblem of ferocity and sensuality. In heraldry the boar is called Sanglier. The military ensigns of the Gauls were surmounted by figures of the wild boar.

Figs. 89, 90. Boars. Gallic ensigns.

Boclerus, Med. Lat. A buckler; 14th century. The word is derived from the German Bock, a goat. Compare ÆGIS.

Bodkin, Saxon. A dagger, a hair-pin, a blunt flat needle.

> " With *bodkins* was Cæsar Julius
> Murdred at Rome, of Brutus, Cassius."
> (*The Serpent of Division*, 1590.)

" He pulls her bodkin that is tied in a piece of black ribbon." (*The Parson's Wedding*, 1663.)

The Latin name for this classical head-dress was *acus*.

Body Colour. In speaking of oil colours the term applies to their solidity, or degree of opacity; water-colour painting is said to be in body colours when the pigments are laid on thickly, or mixed with white, as in oil painting.

Boedromia, Gr. and R. A festival instituted in honour of Apollo the Helper—βοηδρόμιος. It was held at Athens on the sixth day of September, a month thence called *Boedromion*.

Bohemian Glass. The manufacture of a pure crystal glass well adapted for engraving became an important industry in Germany about the year 1600, and the art of engraving was admirably developed during the century. Of Johann Schapper, especially, Jacquemart says that he produced "subjects and arabesques of such delicacy of execution that at first sight they seemed merely like a cloud on the glass."

Bohordamentum, Med. Lat. A joust with mock lances called "bouhours."

Bojæ, R. (*bos*, an ox). (1) A heavy collar of wood or iron for dangerous dogs. (2) A similar collar placed round the necks of criminals or slaves.

Boletar, R. A dish on which mushrooms (*boleti*) were served, and thence transferred to dishes of various forms.

Bolevardus, Med. Lat. A boulevard or rampart.

Bombard, O. E. A machine for projecting stones or iron balls ; the precursor of the cannon. First used in the 14th century.

Bombards, O. E. Padded breeches. In Elizabeth's reign the breeches, then called BOMBARDS, were stuffed so wide that a gallery or scaffold was erected to accommodate members of Parliament who wore them. The engraving shows James I. (painted 1614) attired for hawking. (Fig. 91.)

Bombax, O. E. The stuff now called Bombasin. "A sort of fine silk or cotton cloth well known upon the continent during the 13th century." (*Strutt*.)

Bombê, Fr. Curved furniture, introduced in the 18th century.

Bombulom or **Bunibulum,** O. E. (from the Greek βόμβος, a hollow deep sound). A musical instrument consisting of an angular frame with metal plates, which sounded when shaken like the *sistrum* of the Egyptians.

Bombylos and **Bombylê**, Gr. and R. A vase so called from the gurgling noise which the

Fig. 91. Bombards worn by King James I. of England.

liquid makes in pouring out through its narrow neck.

Bone Black. (See IVORY BLACK.)

Book. In mediæval art an attribute of the fathers of the Church ; in the hands of evangelists and apostles it represents the Gospel. St. Boniface carries a book pierced with a sword. St. Stephen, St. Catherine, St. Bonaventura, and St. Thomas Aquinas also carry books.

Bordure, Her. A border to a shield.

Boreasmos, Gr. A festival held at Athens in honour of Boreas, the god of the north wind.

Borto or **Burdo**, Med. Lat. A lance.

Boss. The centre of a shield; also an architectural ornament for ceilings, put where the ribs of a vault meet, or in other situations.

Bossage, Arch. An arrangement of plain or ornamental projections on the surface of a wall of dressed masonry. Figs. 92 and 93 represent two Greek walls

Fig. 92. Greek Bossage.

finished in this manner.

Boston, O. E. A flower so called.

Botéga, It. A manufactory or artist's workshop where pottery is made.

Fig. 93. Bossage.

Botonée, Fitchée, Her. Varieties of the heraldic cross, called also treflée. (Fig. 94.)

Fig. 94. Botonée Fitchée.

Bottcher Ware. Early Dresden pottery. (1) A very hard red stoneware, made of a red clay of Okrilla, invented at Meissen by John Frederick Bottcher. (2) Porcelain. Bottcher, finding his wig very heavy one day, examined the powder upon it, and discovered it to be the fine kaolin of Aue, from which the Dresden (or Meissen) china is made. Bottcher's first object was to obtain a paste as white and as perfect as that of the COREA ; he succeeded at his first trial, and

Fig. 95. Coffee-pot of Bottcher Ware.

produced pieces with archaic decoration so perfectly imitated, that one would hesitate to declare them European.

Bottle, Boutell, Bowtell, or **Boltell,** Arch. An old English term for a bead moulding ; also for small shafts of clustered columns resting against the pillars of a nave, in the Romano-Byzantine and Gothic periods. These shafts spring from the ground and rise to the height of the bend of the roof, the diagonal ribs of which

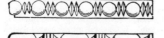

Fig. 96. Bottle-mouldings.

they receive on coupled columns. Probably from *bolt*, an arrow.

Fig. 97. Water Bouget.

Bougets or **Water Bougets**, Fr., were pouches of leather, which were used by the Crusaders for carrying water in the deserts. Fig. 97 is a heraldic representation of the coat of arms of De Ros.

Boulé, Bouleuterion, Gr. An assembly composed of the foremost men of the nation. It was a kind of senate or higher council which deliberated on the affairs of the republic. The popular assembly, on the other hand, composed of all the males of free birth, was called *agora*, and was held in a place called by the same name. (See AGORA.)

Boule. A peculiar kind of marquetry, composed of tortoise-shell and thin brass, to which are sometimes added ivory and enamelled metal. Named from its inventor, André Charles Boule, born 1642.

Boulting-mill. A mill for winnowing the flour from the bran (*crusca*); the device of the Academy of La Crusca. (See CRUSCA.)

Bourdon. A pilgrim's staff. On the walls of Hôtel Cluny, at Paris, the pilgrim's *bourdon* and cockle-shells are sculptured. Piers Plowman describes a pilgrim's

"*burdoun* y-bounde
With a broad liste, in a withwynde wise
Y-wounden about."

Fig. 98. Bourgogne Point Lace.

Bourginot. A close helmet of the 15th century, first used in Burgundy.

Bourgogne, Point de, is a beautifully fine and well-finished pillow lace resembling old Mechlin. No record remains of its manufacture. (Fig. 98.)

Bovile. (See BUBILE.)

Bow. Represented in the most ancient monuments. In classical art an attribute of Apollo, Cupid, Diana, Hercules, and the Centaurs.

Bow, Arch., O.E. A flying buttress, or archbuttress.

Bowed, Her. Having a convex contour.

Bower or **Bowre,** O. E. The Anglo-Saxon name for a bed-chamber, "*bird in bure*" = a lady in her chamber. The bed-chambers were separate buildings grouped round or near the central hall.

" Up then rose fair Annet's father,
Twa hours or it wer day,
And he is gane into the *bower*
Wherein fair Annet lay."
(*Percy Ballads.*)

Bowls of metal, generally bronze or copper, found in early Anglo-Saxon *barrows* or graves, are probably of Roman workmanship. Some beautiful *buckets* (A.S. *bucas*) were made of wood, generally of ash, whence they had another name *æscen*. They are ornamented with designs, and figures of animals, and were probably used at festivities to contain ale or mead.

Bowtell or **Boutell,** Arch. (See BOTTLE.)

Brabeum, Brabium, or **Bravium,** Gr. (βρα-βεῖον, from βραβεὺς, judge). Three terms denoting the prize assigned to the victor in the public games.

Braccæ, Bracæ, or **Bragæ** (Celtic breac). Trousers worn principally by barbarous nations,

Fig. 99. Figures with Braccæ.

such as the Amazons, Gauls, Persians, and Scythians. *Anaxyrides* was the name given to close-fitting trousers, *braccæ laxæ* to wider pantaloons, such as those worn by the Gaul in the left-hand corner of Fig. 99, from a bas-relief taken from the sarcophagus of the *vigna* Ammendola. The *braccæ virgatæ* were striped pantaloons worn especially by Asiatics ; *braccæ pictæ*, variegated or embroidered trousers. (See BREECHES.)

Braced or **Brazed**, Her. Interlaced, as in the illustration of the arms of Cosmo, the founder of the Medici family. (Fig. 100.) (See also the illustration to FRET.)

Bracelet. Bracelets were, among the ancients, a symbol of marriage. (See ARMILLA.)

Bracelets. (See PERISCELIS.)

Fig. 100. Three diamond rings interlaced.

Brachiale, R. (*brachium*, the arm). An armlet, or piece of defensive armour covering the *brachium* or forearm. It was worn by gladiators in the circus. Some beautifully ornamented specimens were found among the excavations at Pompeii.

Brackets, Arch., in mediæval architecture, are usually called Corbels. (See Fig. 5.)

Braconniere, O. E. A skirt of armour, worn hanging from the breast and back plates ; 16th century.

Bractea or **Brattea**, R. Leaves of metal, especially of gold, beaten out.

Braga, Bragæ. (See BRACCÆ.)

Bragamas, O. E. (See BRAQUEMARD.) "Un grant coustel, que l'en dit bragamas ;" 14th cent.

Braggers, O. E. An obsolete term for timber BRACKETS.

Brake, O. E. A quern or handmill.

Brand, A.S. A torch ; hence, from its shining appearance, a sword. (*Meyrick*.)

Brandrate, O. E. An iron tripod fixed over the fire, on which to set a pot or kettle.

Braquemard, O. E. A kind of sabre—"un grant coustel d'Alemaigne, nommé braquemart ;" 14th century.

Brass, Gen. An alloy made by mixing copper with tin, or else with zinc or silver. Another name for it is BRONZE (q.v.). Corinthian brass is very celebrated, but little is known of its composition even at the

Fig. 101. Brassart.

present day. Mosaic gold, pinchbeck, prince's metal, &c., are varieties of brass differing in the proportions of the ingredients. Brass beaten into very thin leaves is called Dutch Metal.

Brassart. Plate armour for the arm. (Fig. 101.)

Brasses. Engraved metal plates inlaid in the pavements or walls of churches as monuments. The material was called *cullen* (or Cologne) plate. The engravings were made black with mastic or bitumen, and the field or background was coarsely enamelled in various colours.

Brattach, Celtic. A standard ; literally, a cloth.

Braunshid, O. E. Branched.

Breadth "in painting is a term which denotes largeness, space, vastness," &c. (Consult J. B. Pyne "*On the Nomenclature of Pictorial Art*," Art Union, 1843.)

Fig. 102. Bridle-device of the Arbusani.

Breccia, It. A conglomerate used by the ancients in architecture and sculpture.

Breeches (*breac* Celtic, *braccæ* Lat.). The word breeches in its present acceptance was first used towards the end of the 16th century ; previously, breeches were called hose, upper socks, and slop. (See BOMBARDS and BRACCÆ.)

Bremen Green. (See VERDITER.)

Breys, Her. (See BARNACLES.)

Bridges, O. E. A kind of satin manufactured at Bruges.

Bridle. A favourite Scriptural emblem of self-restraint and self-denial. The illustration is the device of Benedetto Arbusani of Padua ; with the motto which, according to Epictetus, contains every essential to human happiness. (Fig. 102.) (See "*Historic Devices.*")

Fig. 103. Broad arrow.

Broach or **Broch**, O. E. A church spire, or *any sharp-pointed object*, was frequently so called.

Broad Arrow, now used as the Royal mark on all Government stores, &c., was first employed as a regal badge by Richard I. (Fig. 103.)

Brocade. A stout silken stuff of variegated pattern. Strutt says it was composed of silk interwoven with threads of gold and silver. The state or "ducal" costume of the Dogeressa of Venice, represented in the illustration, con-

Fig. 104. Gold Brocade State or "Ducal" costume of the Dogeressa of Venice.

sisted principally of an ample robe of the finest gold brocade, lined with ermine. (Figs. 88, 104.)

Broella. Coarse cloth worn by monks in the Middle Ages.

Bromias, Gr. A drinking-vessel of wood, or silver, resembling a large SCYPHUS (q.v.).

Bronze. *Antique* bronze was composed of tin

and copper; the *modern* bronze contains also zinc and lead, by which the fluidity is increased, and the brittleness diminished.

Bronzes (ancient Chinese) are rarely seen out of the province of Fokien. The lines of metal are small and delicate, and are made to represent flowers, trees, animals of various kinds, and sometimes Chinese characters. Some fine bronzes, inlaid with gold, are met with in this province. As a general rule, Chinese bronzes are more remarkable for their peculiar and certainly not very handsome form than for anything else.

Bronzing. The art of laying a coating of bronze powder on wood, gypsum, or other material. Another method is the electrotype process. (Consult Walker's *Electrotype Manipulation.*)

Brooch. (See FIBULA.) Anglo-Saxon and Irish specimens of magnificent workmanship are de-

Figs. 105 to 112. Gallic and Merovingian brooches.

scribed in the *Archæological Album.* In the Middle Ages brooches bore quaint inscriptions: Chaucer's "prioress" wore

> "*a broche* of gold ful shene.
> On which was first y-wretten a crouned A,
> And after, *Amor vincit omnia.*"

Leather brooches for hats are mentioned by

Dekker in *Satiromastix*, 1602. Figs. 205, 206, 207 represent different brooches found in

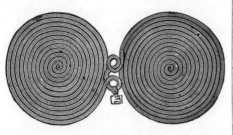

Fig. 113. Gallic brooch.

France of the Gallic and Merovingian periods. (Compare FIBULA, PHALERÆ.)

Brown, in Egyptian art, was the colour consecrated to Typhon ; in ancient times it was the sign of mourning. Regarded as a compound of red and black, BISTRE, it is the symbol of all evil deeds and treason. In a monastic costume it signifies renunciation. With the Moors it was emblematic of all evil. Christian symbolism appropriates the colour of the dead leaf for the type of "spiritual death," &c. (Consult Portal, *Essai sur les Couleurs symboliques.*)

Brown Madder. (See MADDER.)

Brown Ochre. A strong, dark, yellow, opaque pigment. (See OCHRES.)

Brown Pigments are *asphaltum, bistre, umber, sienna, Mars brown, Cassel earth, Cappagh brown, brown madder*, and burnt *terra verde ;*—chiefly calcined earths. (See also INDIGO.)

Fig. 114. Brussels Lace.

Brown Pink (Fr. *stil de grain*). A vegetable yellow pigment. (See PINKS.)

Brown Red is generally made from burnt *yellow ochre*, or *Roman ochre*, or from calcined sulphate of iron. (See MARS.)

Brunswick Green. A modification of MOUNTAIN GREEN (q.v.).

Bruny, Byrne, or **Byrnan.** Saxon for a breastplate or cuirass, called by the Normans "*broigne.*"

Brushes. (See HAIR PENCILS.)

Brussels Point à l'Aiguille differs somewhat from the lace usually known as Brussels Lace or Point d'Angleterre, but resembles Point d'Alençon in the réseau ground. (Fig. 114.) (See POINT D'ANGLETERRE.)

Buccina (Gr. βυκάνη). A kind of trumpet anciently made of a conch-shell, represented in the hands of Tritons.

Buccula, R. (*bucca*, a cheek). The chin-piece or cheek-piece of a helmet, which could be raised or lowered by the soldier at will.

Bucentaur. A monster, half man and half ox. The name of the Venetian state galley.

Buckets, Anglo-Saxon. (See BOWLS.)

Fig. 115. Heraldic buckle.

Buckle, Her. The crest of the Pelham family, now represented by the Earls of Chichester. It is a common ornament of ecclesiastical buildings, houses, and other objects in Sussex. (Fig. 115.)

Buckler. (See CLIPEUS and SCUTUM.)

Buckram. A cloth stiffened with gum, so called from Bokhara, where it was originally made.

Bucranium, R. (βουκράνιον). An ox's head from which the flesh has been stripped ; an ox-skull employed in the decoration of friezes by Greek and Roman architects. Fig. 116 represents a *bucranium* in the temple of Vespasian at Rome.

Budge, O. E. Lambskin with the wool dressed outwards. Mentioned by Chaucer.

Buffett-stoole, O. E. A stool with three legs.

Buffin, O. E. Coarse cloth of Elizabeth's time.

Bugles, O. E. Glass beads in the hair, *temp.* Elizabeth and James I.

Buldiellus, Med. Lat. A baudric.

Bulga, R. A purse or leathern bag for money which was carried on the arm. According to Festus the word is of Gallic origin.

Bulla, R. (*bullo*, to bubble). A term denoting objects of various kinds, but all more or less approximating in shape to a water-bubble. The heads of certain nails were called *bullæ*; Fig. 117 shows one of the *bullæ* decorating an ancient bronze door in the Pantheon at Rome. The *bulla aurea* was an ornament of globular shape,

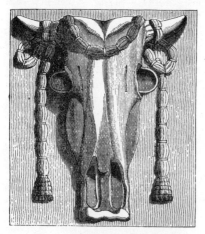

Fig. 116. Bucranium.

worn round the neck by children of patrician family. The *bulla scortea* was an ornament

Fig. 117. Bulla (on a door).

made of leather, worn by freedmen or individuals of the lower orders.

Bulting-pipe, O. E. A bolting-cloth for sifting meal.

Bullula, R. (*bulla*). Diminutive of BULLA (q. v.).

Bur. A term in etching for the rough edge of a line, commonly removed, but by Rembrandt and other great masters made effective.

Burdalisaunder, Bourde de Elisandre. Burda, a stuff for clothing (mentioned in the 4th century) from Alexandria. A silken web in different coloured stripes; 14th century.

Burgau. A univalve shell, *Turbo marmoratus*, producing a mother of pearl; and hence all works in mother of pearl, of whatever material, are called "burgau." (*Jacquemart.*)

Burin. An instrument for engraving on copper.

Burnisher. A steel instrument used by engravers to soften lines or efface them. An agate is used to burnish gold.

Burnt Sienna. (See SIENNA.)

Burnt Terra Verde. (See GREEN EARTH.)

Burnt Umber. (See UMBER.)

Burr, O. E. (1) The broad iron ring on a tilting-lance, just below the gripe, to prevent the hand slipping back. (2) Projecting defences at the front of a saddle. (*Meyrick.*) (3) The rough edge produced on the metal by an incised or etched line in an engraving.

Buskin. (See COTHURNUS.)

Bustum, R. (*buro*, to burn). An open spot upon which a pyre was raised for burning the corpse of a person of distinction. When the area adjoined the burying-ground, it was called *bustum*; when it was separate from it, it was called *ustrina*.

Fig. 118. Arch-buttress.

Buttress, Arch. An abutment employed to increase the solidity or stability of a wall; it may either immediately abut on the wall, or be connected with it by a flying or arch buttress (Fig. 118). In the Romano-Byzantine and lanceolated styles buttresses are largely employed to strengthen the walls of naves which have to support high vaulted roofs.

Buxum, R. (πύξος). Box, an evergreen, the wood of which was used for various purposes, as with us. By analogy, the term *buxum* was applied to objects made of this wood, such as combs, flutes, children's shoes, and waxed tablets for writing.

Buzo, O. E. The arrow for an arquebus, or cross-bow. French, *boujon:* "a boult, an arrow with a great or broad head." (*Cotgrave.*)

Byrrus. (See BIRRUS.)

Byssus, Gr. and R. (βύσσος). The precise meaning of this term is unknown; there is no doubt it was a texture made of some very costly

E

material, since we learn from Pliny that the byssus cloth which he calls *linum byssinum* was exceedingly dear. Everything leads us to suppose that it was a linen material of the finest quality. This opinion would seem to be confirmed by Herodotus and Æschylus. The word comes from the Hebrew *butz*.

Fig. 119. Byzantine Font.

Byzantine Period. Time, about 6th to 12th century A.D. (*Byzantium*, the Latin name of Constantinople.) Byzantine Architecture is noteworthy for a bold development of the plan of Christian places of worship. It introduced the cupola, or dome, which was often sur-rounded by semi-domes; an almost square ground-plan in place of the long aisles of the Roman church ; and piers instead of columns. The apse always formed part of Byzantine buildings, which were richly decorated, and contained marble in great profusion. St. Sophia, Constantinople (A.D. 532—537), is the finest example of Byzantine architecture. St. Mark's, Venice (A.D. 977), and the Cathedral of Aix-la-Chapelle (A.D. 796—804), are also of pure Byzantine style. Byzantine Painting was that which succeeded the decline of the early Christian Art in the catacombs and basilicas of Rome, and which preceded and foreshadowed the Renaissance of Art in Italy. In style it was based on that of the catacombs, but with a reminiscence of the excellence of ancient Greece ; it was, however, restrained and kept within narrow limits by the conventionalities which were imposed upon it by the Church, and which almost reduced it to a mechanical art. The mosaics of the 10th and 11th centuries in St. Mark's, Venice, are perhaps the best existing examples of the Byzantine period. Specimens are also to be seen in St. Sophia, Constantinople ; and at Ravenna.

Fig. 121. Roman-Byzantine Cross at Carew.

Fig. 120. Byzantine ornament on an English font.

C.

Caaba, Arabic (lit. square house). The sacred mosque at Mecca. The temple is an almost cubical edifice, whence its name. It is a favourite subject of representation upon Mussulman works of art.

Caballaria, Cavalherium, hevallerie (Gr. κλῆρος ἱππικὸς), Med. A meadow set apart for military exercises.

Caballerius, Med. Lat. A cavalier or knight.

Cabeiri were the personification of the element of fire. The precise nature attributed to them is unknown. There were two principal branches of their worship, the Pelasgian and the Phœnician. It is probable that this religion originated in Asia Minor, and penetrated to the island of

Samothrace, in remote antiquity; it was very popular throughout Greece in the Pelasgic period. The principal temples were at Samothrace, Lemnos, Imbros, Anthedon, and other places.

Cabeiria, Gr. (καβείρια). Annual festivals in honour of the Cabeiri. (See THRONISMUS.)

Cabinet Pictures. Small, highly-finished pictures, suited for a small room.

Fig. 122. Cable and tooth-mouldings.

Cabling, or **Cable-moulding.** A moulding in Roman architecture, made in imitation of a thick rope or cable.

Fig. 123. Lion's head cabossed.

Cabossed, Her. Said of the head of an animal represented full-face, so as to show the face only. (Fig. 123.)

Cabulus, Med. Latin (Old French, *chaable*). A machine for hurling stones; a large BALLISTA.

Caccabus, Gr. and R. (κάκκαβος or κακκάβη). A sort of pot or vessel for cooking any kind of food. It was made of bronze, silver, or earthenware, and assumed a variety of forms; but the one in ordinary use resembled an egg with an opening at the top which closed by a lid. The *caccabus* rested upon a trivet (*tripus*).

Cadafalsus, Cadafaudus. (See CAGASUPTUS.)

Cadas, O. E. An inferior silken stuff used for wadding; 13th century.

Cadency, Her. Figures and devices, by which different members and branches of a family are distinguished.

Cadet, Her. Junior.

Cadlys-drain, Welsh. Chevaux-de-frise.

Cadmium Yellow is the sulphide of cadmium, the finest and most permanent of all the yellow pigments in use.

Cadpen, Welsh. A chief of battle; captain.

Cadrelli, Med. Lat. Cross-bow quarrels. (See CARREAUX.)

Cādūceus or **Caduceum.** A wand of laurel or olive, given by Apollo to Mercury in exchange for the lyre invented by the latter. Mercury, it is said, seeing two snakes struggling together, separated them with his wand, whereupon the snakes immediately twined themselves round it.

This was the origin of the caduceus, as we know it; it was always an attribute of Mercury, who thence obtained his name of *Caducifer*, or caduceus-bearer. The caduceus was an emblem of peace.

Cadurcum, R. This term is applied to two distinct things: (1) the fine linen coverlets, and (2) the earthenware vases, manufactured by the Cadurci, or Gauls inhabiting the district now called Cahors.

Cadus, Gr. and R. (from χανδάνω, to contain). (1) A large earthenware jar, used for the same purposes as the amphora; especially to hold wine. An ordinary *cadus* was about three feet high, and broad enough in the mouth to allow of the contents being baled out. (2) The ballot-urn in which the Athenian juries recorded their votes with pebbles, at a trial.

Cælatura (*cælum*, a chisel). A general term for working in metal by raised work or intaglio, such as engraving, carving, chasing, riveting, soldering, smelting, &c. Greek, the *toreutic* art. Similar work on wood, ivory, marble, glass, or precious stones was called SCULPTURA.

Cæmenticius, Cæmenticia (structura). A kind of masonry formed of rough stones. There were two methods of construction to which this name applied. The first, called *cæmenticia structura incerta*, consisted in embedding stones of more or less irregular shape in mortar, so as to give them any architectural form, and then covering the whole over with cement. The second, called *cæmenticia structura antiqua*, consisted in laying rough stones one on the top of the other, without mortar, the interstices being filled by chippings or smaller stones.

Cæmentum. Unhewn stones employed in the erection of walls or buildings of any kind.

Caer, British (Lat. *castrum*; Saxon, *chester*). A camp or fortress.

Cæsaries (akin to Sanscrit *keça*, hair, or to *cæsius*, bluish-grey). This term is almost synonymous with COMA (q.v.), but there is also implied in it an idea of beauty and profusion, not attaching to *coma*, which is the expression as well for an ordinary head of hair.

Cæstus, Cestus. A boxing gauntlet. It consisted of a series of leather thongs, armed with lead or metal bosses, and was fitted to the hands and wrists.

Cætra. (See CETRA.)

Cagasuptus, Med. Lat. A CHAT-FAUX, or wooden shed, under which the soldiers carried on the operations of attack. (*Meyrick*.)

Cailloutage, Fr. Fine earthenware; pipeclay; a kind of hard paste; opaque pottery. "Fine earthenware is most frequently decorated by the 'muffle;' the oldest specimens, those made in France in the 16th century, are ornamented by incrustation." (*Jacquemart*.)

Cairelli, Med. Lat. (See CADRELLI.)

Cairn. A heap of stones raised over a grave,

to which friends as they pass add a stone. The custom still prevails in Scotland and Ireland.

Caisson, Arch. A sunken panel in a ceiling or soffit. (See COFFER.)

Calamarius (*calamus*, q.v.). A case for carrying writing-reeds (*calami*). Another name for this case was *theca calamaria*.

Calamister and **Calamistrum**. A curling-iron, so named because the interior was partly hollow like a reed (*calamus*), or perhaps because in very early times a reed heated in the ashes was employed for the purpose; hence, CALAMISTRATUS, an effeminate man, or discourse. (Compare CINIFLO.)

Calamus (κάλαμος, a reed or cane). A haulm, reed, or cane. The term was applied to a variety of objects made out of reeds, such as a Pan's pipe, a shepherd's flute (*tibia*), a fishing-rod (*piscatio*), a rod tipped with lime, for fowling, &c. (See ARUNDO.) It was specially used, however, to denote a reed cut into proper shape, and used as a pen for writing.

Calantica. (See CALAUTICA.)

Calash (Fr. *calèche*).

Fig. 124. Calash.

A hood made like that of the carriage called in France *calèche*, whence its name. It is said to have been introduced into England in 1765 by the Duchess of Bedford, and was used by ladies to protect their heads when dressed for the opera or other entertainments.

Calathiscus (καλαθίσκος). A small wicker basket.

Calathus (κάλαθος, a basket; Lat. *qualus* or *quasillus*). A basket made of rushes or osiers plaited, employed for many purposes, but above all as a woman's work-basket. The *calathus* was the emblem of the γυναικεῖον or women's apartments, and of the housewife who devoted herself to domestic duties. The same term denoted earthenware or metal vases of various shapes; among others a drinking-cup.

Calautica or **Calvatica**, R. (Gr. κρήδεμνον, from κρὰς and δέω; fastened to the head). A head-dress worn by women; the Greek MITRA (q.v.).

Calcar (*calx*, the heel). A spur. It was also called *calcis aculeus* (lit. heel-goad), a term specially applied to the spur of a cock. The latter, however, was just as often called *calcar*. In mediæval Latin *calcaria aurea* are the golden, or gilt, spurs which were a distinctive mark of knighthood; *calcaria argentea*, the silver spurs worn only by esquires. *Calcaria amputari*, to hack off the spurs, when a knight was degraded :—

"Li esperons li soit copé parmi
    Prés del talon au branc acier forbi."
                            (*Roman de Garin MS.*)

Calcatorium (*calco*, to tread under foot). A raised platform of masonry, set up in the cellar where the wine was kept (*cella vinaria*), and raised above the level of the cellar-floor, to a height of three or four steps. On either side of this platform were ranged the casks (*dolia*) or large earthenware vessels in which the wine was made. The *calcatorium* served as a receptacle for the grapes when crushed (whence its name), and as a convenient place from whence to superintend the making of the wine.

Calceamen. Synonym of CALCEUS (q.v.), a term far more frequently employed.

Calceamentum. A general term denoting any description of boot and shoe. (Each will be found separately noticed in its place.)

Calcedony or **Chalcedony** (from the town *Chalcedon*). A kind of agate, of a milky colour, diversified with yellow, bluish, or green tints. The Babylonians have left us a large number of chalcedony cylinders, covered with inscriptions. (See also AGATE, CAMEOS.)

Calceolus (dimin. of CALCEUS, q.v.). A small shoe or ankle-boot worn by women. There were three kinds : the first had a slit over the instep, which was laced up when the boot was on. A second shape had a very wide opening, and could be fastened above the ankle by a string passed through a hem round the top. In the third description there was neither cord, lace, nor slit. The shoe was always low in the heel, and was worn like a slipper.

Calceus (*calx*, the heel). A shoe or boot made sufficiently high to completely cover the foot. The Romans put off their shoes at table ; hence *calceos poscere* meant " to rise from table."

Calculus (dimin. of *calx*, a small stone or counter). A pebble, or small stone worn by friction to present the appearance of a pebble. *Calculi* were used in antiquity for recording votes (for which purpose they were thrown into the urn), for reckoning, and for mosaic paving (hence the English word "calculation").

Caldarium (*calidus*, warm). The apartment in a set of Roman baths which was used as a kind of sweating-room. This chamber, which is constructed nearly always on the same plan in the different baths which have been discovered, included a LACONICUM, a LABRUM, a SUDATORIUM, and an ALVEUS. (See these words.) Fig. 56 (on p. 32) represents a portion of the *caldarium* of Pompeii, restored.

Caldas Porcelain is from the Portuguese factory of that name, specialized for faiences in relief; the greater number are covered with a black coating ; the others with the customary enamels of the country, violet, yellow, and green.

Caldron, for domestic use of the 14th century, is depicted as a tripod with a globular body, and broad mouth and two handles.

Calibre (or **Caliper**) **Compasses.** Compasses made with arched legs.

Caliga. A military boot worn by Roman soldiers and officers of inferior rank. The *caliga* consisted of a strong sole, studded with heavy pointed nails, and bound on by a network of leather thongs, which covered the heel and the foot as high as the ankle.

Caliptra. (See CALYPTRA.)

Caliver. A harquebus of a standard "calibre," introduced during the reign of Queen Elizabeth.

Calix. A cup-shaped vase, used as a drinking-goblet. It was of circular shape, had two handles, and was mounted on a tolerably high stand. The term also denotes a water-meter, or copper tube of a specified diameter, which was attached like a kind of branch-pipe to a main one.

Calliculæ. A kind of very thin metal disk, more or less ornamented, worn by rich Christians, and especially priests, as an ornament for the dress. *Calliculæ* were also made of purple-coloured cloth. Many of the pictures in the catacombs represent persons wearing *calliculæ* on their *colobia* and other garments. (See COLOBIUM.)

Callisteia (καλλιστεῖα). A Lesbian festival of women, in which a prize was awarded to the most beautiful.

Callot. A plain coif or skull-cap (English).

Calones (κᾶλα, wood). (1) Roman slaves who carried wood for the soldiers. (2) Farm servants.

Calote, Fr. A species of sabre-proof skull-cap worn in the French cavalry.

Calotype. A process of printing by photography, called also *Talbotype*.

Calpis, Gr. A water-jar with three handles, two at the shoulders and one at the neck.

Calthrops. (See CALTRAPS.)

Caltraps (for *cheval*-traps). Spikes of metal thrown on the ground to resist a charge of cavalry. In Christian art, attributes of St. Themistocles.

Calvary, Chr. An arrangement of
Fig. 125. small chapels or shrines in which the
Caltrap. incidents of the progress to the scene of the crucifixion are represented. To each such "station" appropriate prayers and meditations are allotted.

Calvatica. (See CALAUTICA.)

Calyptra (from καλύπτω, to hide). A veil worn by young Greek and Roman women over the face. It is also called *caliptra*, but this term is less used.

Camail (for cap-mail). A tippet of mail attached to the helmet. In mediæval Latin called *camale, camallus, camelaucum, calamaucus, calamaucum.*

Camara. (See CAMERA.)

Camayeu. Monochrome painting, i. e. in shades of one colour, or in conventional colours not copied from nature.

Camber, Arch. A curve or arch.

Camboge or **Gamboge.** A gum-resin, forming a yellow water-colour. The best gamboge is from Siam, and the kingdom of Camboja (whence its name). It should be brittle, inodorous, of conchoidal fracture, orange-coloured or reddish yellow, smooth and somewhat glistening. Its powder is bright yellow. An artificial gamboge, of little value, is manufactured with turmeric and other materials.

Cambresian Faience. The "poterie blance" of Cambrai is mentioned in a MS. of the 16th century. It was an enamelled faience.

Camella. An earthenware or wooden vessel employed in certain religious ceremonies. It probably served for making libations of milk.

Cameo (Ital. *cammeo*). A precious stone engraved in relief ; it is thus opposed to the INTAGLIO (q. v.), which is cut into the stone. Cameos are generally carved from stones having several layers. They were employed in the decoration of furniture, vases, clasps, girdles, and to make bracelets, rings, &c. Cameos were largely made by the Egyptians, Greeks, and Romans ; by the two latter generally of sardonyx and onyx. (See INTAGLIO, SHELL CAMEO, &c.)

Cameo-glass. (See GLASS.)

Camera, more rarely **Camara.** The vault or vaulted ceiling of an apartment. *Camera vitrea*, a vaulted ceiling, the surface of which was lined with plates of glass. The term was also used to denote a chariot with an arched cover formed by hoops ; an underground passage ; a pirate-vessel with a decked cabin ; and, in short, any chamber having an arched roof, as for instance the interior of a tomb.

Camera Lucida. An optical instrument for reflecting the outlines of objects from a prism, so that they can be traced upon paper by a person unacquainted with the art of drawing.

Camera Obscura. A darkened room in which the coloured reflections of surrounding objects are thrown upon a white ground.

Camfuri, Camphio, Med. Lat. A decreed duel : from the German "kampf," battle ; and the Danish "vug," manslaughter. (*Meyrick.*)

Camies, O. E. A light thin material, probably of silken texture.

Caminus. Literally, a smelting furnace, and then an oven for baking bread ; also, a hearth or fireplace. Fig. 126 represents a baker's oven at Pompeii.

Camisado, O. E. A sudden attack on a small party ; a Spanish term.

"To give camisadoes on troupes that are lodged a farre off." (*Briefe Discourse of Warre.*)

Camisia (a Gallic word, whence prob. Ital.

camicia). A light linen tunic worn next the skin (*tunica intima*).

Camlet or **Chamlet,** O. E. Originally a tissue of goat's and camel's hair interwoven. In Elizabeth's reign the name was given to a cloth of mixed wool and silk, first manufactured in Montgomeryshire, on the banks of the river Camlet.

Cammaka. A cloth of which church vestments were made, *temp.* Edward III.

Camoca, O. E., 14th century. A textile probably of fine camel's hair and silk, and of Asiatic workmanship, much used for church vestments, dress, and hangings.

Fig. 126. Caminus.

Campagus or **Compagus.** A kind of sandal. It was worn especially by the Roman patricians.

Campana, It. A bell; hence, CAMPANOLOGY, the science or study of bells.

Campanile. A belfry.

Camp-ceiling. Where all the sides are equally inclined to meet the horizontal part in the centre (as in an attic).

Campestre, R. (from *campester*, i. e. pertaining to the Field of Mars). A short kilt worn by gladiators and soldiers when going through violent exercises in public. The kilt fitted close to the body, and reached two-thirds down the thigh.

Campio Regis, Engl. The king's champion, who on the day of the coronation challenges any one who disputes the title to the crown.

Campus Martius (i. e. Field of Mars). At Rome, as in the provinces, this term had the same meaning which it bears in some countries at the present day; i. e. a ground on which soldiers went through their exercises. In ancient times, however, the Field of Mars, or simply the Field, served also as a place of assembly for the *comitia*.

Canaba, Gr. and R. A Low Latin name for the slight structures common in country places, such as we should now call sheds or hovels. Those who lived in them were called *canabenses*. Fig. 127 is from a terra-cotta vase found near the lake Albano.

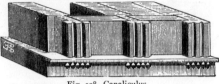

Fig. 127. Canaba.

Canaliculus (dimin. of CANALIS, q.v.). A small channel or groove; or a fluting carved on the face of a triglyph. (Fig. 128.)

Fig. 128. Canaliculus.

Canalis (akin to Sanscrit root KHAN, to dig). An artificial channel or conduit for water. The term *canalis* is also given to the fillet or flat surface lying between the abacus and echinus of an Ionic capital. It terminates in the eye of the volute, which it follows in such a way as to give it the proper contour.

Canathron (Gr. κάναθρον). A carriage, of which the upper part was made of basket-work.

Canberia, Med. Lat. (Fr. *jambières*). Armour for the legs.

Cancelli (from *cancer*, a lattice). A trellis, iron grating, or generally an ornamental barrier separating one place from another. In some amphitheatres the PODIUM (q.v.) had *cancelli* at the top. In a court of law the judges and clerks were divided from the place set apart for the public by *cancelli* (hence "*chancel*").

Candela. A torch, made of rope, coated with tallow, resin, or pitch. It was carried in funeral processions (hence "*candle*").

Candelabrum. A candlestick, candelabrum, or generally any kind of stand by which a light can be supported. There were many different kinds. The same term is also used to denote the tall pedestal of a portable lamp (Fig. 129). (See CANDLEBEAM.)

Candellieri, It. A style of grotesque ornamentation, characteristic of the Urbino majolica ware.

Candlebeam. O. E. A chandelier of the Middle Ages with

Fig. 129. Candelabrum.

"*bellys of laton*" (or brass cups) slung by a pulley from the ceiling.

Candles. The A.S. poets called the sun "rodores candel," the candle of the firmament, "woruld candel," "heofon candel," &c. Originally, no doubt, the candle was a mere mass of fat plastered round a wick (candel-weoc) and stuck upon a "candel-sticca," or upright stick ; when the candle-stick had several branches, it was called a candle-*tree*. There were iron, bone, silvergilt, and ornamented candlesticks. Through the Middle Ages candles were stuck on a spike, not in a socket, and a chandelier of the 16th century shows the same arrangement.

Fig. 130. Persain Candys.

Candys (κάνδυς). A Persian cloak of woollen cloth, generally purple in colour.

Canephoria. Greek festivals of Diana ; *or* an incident of another feast, called *pratelia*, in which virgins about to marry presented baskets (*canea*) to Minerva. The name, CANEPHORUS, or "basket-bearer," was common to the virgins who attended processions of Ceres, Minerva, and Bacchus, with the consecrated cakes, incense, and other sacrificial accessories, in the flat baskets called *canea*.

Canette. A conic-shaped German drinking-mug, resembling the modern "schoppen," of which highly ornamented examples in white stone-ware have been produced by the potters of Cologne and other parts of Germany. (Fig. 131.)

Fig. 131. Canette of white stone-ware, 1574.

Caniple, O. E. A small knife or dagger.

Canis (akin to Sanscrit çVAN, Gr. κύων). A dog. This term has numerous diminutives : *catulus, catellus, canicula*. However ancient any civilization, the dog is always met with as the companion of man, and in each nation it follows a particular type. Thus a distinct difference is perceptible in the dogs of the Etruscans, Greeks, Romans, Egyptians, Indians, and Gauls. The Egyptians had terriers and greyhounds, wolf-dogs, and others for hunting or watchdogs. All these breeds are met with on the bas-reliefs of Egyptian monuments. The Egyptian name for a dog, *wou, wouwou*, is evidently onomatopoietic or imitative. (See also DOG.)

Canistrum, Canister, or **Caneum** (κάνιστρον, from κάνη, a reed). A wide shallow basket for carrying the instruments of sacrifice and offerings for the gods. It was generally carried on the head by young girls, who were called *Canephoræ* (κανηφόραι, i. e. basket-bearers), q.v.

Canon (κανών, from κάνη, i. e. anything straight like a reed). A fixed rule or standard which is supposed to have served, in antiquity, as a basis or model in forming statues, the various members of which bore a definite proportion one to the other. The Greeks had some such *canon*. The δορυφόρος (spearman) of Polycletus was, it is said, looked upon as affording a standard for the proportions of the human body. The Egyptians are also supposed to have had a canon, in which the middle finger formed the unit of measurement.

Canopea or **Canopic Vases.** An Egyptian vase, made of clay, and so named from its being manufactured at Canopus, a town of Lower Egypt, the present Aboukir. The same name was given to funereal urns made in the shape of the god *Canopus*, who is described by Russin as *pedibus exiguis, attracto collo, ventre tumido in modum hydriæ, cum dorso æqualiter tereti* (i. e. having small feet, a short neck, a belly as round

and swelling as a water-jar, and a back to
match). Canopean vases were made of earthenware, alabaster, and limestone. They were
placed at the four corners of tombs or sarcophagi containing mummies. In them were deposited the viscera of the dead, which were
placed under the protection of the four genii,
symbolized each by the head of some animal
which served at the same time for the lid of the
canopea.

Cant, Arch. (1) To truncate. (2) To turn
anything over on its angle.

Cantabrarii, Med. Lat. Standard-bearers :
from CANTABRUM, a kind of standard used by
the Roman emperors. (Consult *Meyrick*.)

Canted Column, Arch. A column polygonal
in section.

Cantellus, Med. Lat. (Fr. *chanteau* and *cantel;*
Lat. *quantillus*). (1) A cut with a weapon, or
the portion cut away. (2) Heraldic for the fourth
part of a shield, since called a canton. (3) The
hind part of a saddle.

Canteriolus (dimin. of *canterius*, a prop).
A painter's easel. The term, which is of doubtful Latinity, corresponds to the Greek ὀκρίβας.

Canterius, R. This term has numerous
meanings ; it serves to denote a gelding, a prop,
the rafters forming part of the woodwork of a
roof, and a surgical contrivance, of which the
form is unknown, but which was used for suspending horses whose legs chanced to be broken,
in such a way as to allow the bone to set.

Fig. 132. Cantharus (Greek).

Cantharus (κάνθαρος, a kind of beetle). A
two-handled vase or drinking-cup, of Greek in-

vention. It was particularly consecrated to
Bacchus, and accordingly, in representations of
the festivals of that god, it figures constantly
in the hands of satyrs and other personages.
(Fig. 132.)

Cantherius. (See CANTERIUS.)

Canthus (κανθὸς, the felloe of a wheel). A
hoop of iron or bronze forming the *tire* of a
wheel. The Greeks called this tire ἐπίσωτρον
(i. e. that which is fastened to the felloe).

Canticum. An interlude of music in a Roman
play.

Cantilevers or **Cantalivers**, Arch. Blocks
framed into a wall under the eaves, projecting so
as to carry a moulding. (See MODILLION.)

Cant-moulding, Arch. Any moulding with a
bevelled face.

Canum. A Greek basket, more generally
called CANISTRUM (q.v.).

Canvas prepared for painting is kept stretched
upon frames of various sizes : e. g. *kit-cat*, 28 or
29 inches by 36 ; *three-quarters*, 25 by 30 ; *half-
length*, 40 by 50 ; *bishop's half-length*, 44 or 45
by 56 ; *bishop's whole-length*, 58 by 94.

Cap-a-pie (Fr.). In full armour, from *head to
foot.*

Caparison. The complete trappings of a war-
horse.

Capellina, Med. Lat. The chapeline or small
CHAPEL DE FER.

Capellum, Med. Lat. A scabbard (*not* the
hilt of a sword).

Capellus ferreus. (See CHAPEL DE FER.)

Capillamentum, R. A wig of false hair, in
which the hair was long and abundant. (See
COMA.)

Capillus (from *caput*, the head). Hair ; the
hair of the head in general. (See COMA.)

Capis, R. A kind of earthenware jug, with a
handle. Vessels of this kind were used in
sacrifices, and the *capis* is often found represented on medals. Other names for it were
capedo, capeduncula, and *capula.*

Capisterium (deriv. from σκάφη or σκάφος,
i. e. that which is scooped out). A vessel
resembling the *alveus*, or wooden trough, and
which was employed for cleansing the ears
of corn after they had been threshed and
winnowed.

Capistrum (from *capio*, i. e. that which takes
or holds). (1) A halter or head-stall. (2) A
rope employed for suspending the end of the
beam in a wine-press. (3) A muzzle made to
prevent young animals from sucking after they
have been weaned. (4) A broad leather band
or cheek-piece worn by flute-players. It had an
opening for the mouth to blow through.

Capita aut Navia (lit. *heads or ships ;* of coins
having the head of *Janus* on one side and a ship
on the reverse). A game of "heads or tails"
played by the Romans and Greeks.

Capital (*caput*, a head). A strip of cloth worn round the head, in primitive times, by Roman women, to keep in their hair. Later on it was worn only by women attached to the service of religion. (See CAPITULUM.)

Capitellum. (See CAPITULUM.)

Capitium. An article of female dress ; a kind of corset or bodice.

Capitolium (i. e. the place of the *caput;* because a human head was supposed to have been discovered, in digging the foundations). The Capitol, or enclosure containing the temple raised in honour of Jupiter. The first Capitol of Rome was built on the *Mons Capitolinus* or *Capitolium.* The chief cities of Italy possessed each its *Capitolium.*

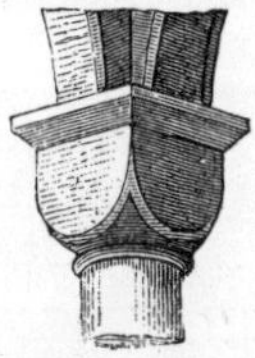

Fig. 133.

Fig. 134.

Capital. A term which denotes the member of architecture crowning the top of a column, pillar, or pilaster. Figs. 133 and 134 represent cushion capitals of the Romano-Byzantine epoch. Orders of Architecture are known by their Capitals. (See COMPOSITE, CORINTHIAN, DORIC, IONIC, and TUSCAN.)

Capo di Monte, Naples. A manufactory of faience, established by Charles III.

Cappagh Browns, Light and **Dark.** Rich brown pigments, made of a bituminous earth from Ireland. Called also *Mineral* or *Manganese Brown.*

Capreolus, R. (lit. a wild goat or roebuck). A fork for digging, with two prongs converging together like the horns of a roebuck. The term is also used for a strut or brace. The tie-beams and king-posts in the frame of a roof are often connected by *capreoli.*

Capriccio, It. Caprice in art.

Capricornus. The zodiacal sign of September employed by Augustus Cæsar in commemoration of his victory at Actium on the day when the sun enters that sign. The same device was used by Cosmo dè' Medici, and by the Emperor Rodolph II. of Germany, with the motto, "Fulget Cæsaris Astrum." (Fig. 135.)

Caprimulgus, Lat. A goat-milker, a common device on antique gems and bas-reliefs, representing a man or a faun milking a goat.

Capronæ, R. (from *caput* and *pronus,* i. e. that which hangs down the forehead). The forelock of a horse, and by analogy, a lock of curling hair falling down over the centre of the forehead, in a man or woman.

Fig. 135. Capricornus. The device of Cosmo de' Medici.

Capsa or **Scrinium,** R. A box or case of cylindrical form, used for several purposes, but more particularly for the transport of rolls or volumes (*volumina*). The *capsæ* were generally provided with straps and locks, the former serving as a handle.

Capsella and **Capsula,** R. (dimin. of CAPSA, q. v.). A case or casket for jewels, &c.

Capuchon. A hood with neck-piece and mantle. The engraving (Fig. 136) is a portrait of Cimabue.

Capula. Dimin. of CAPIS (q.v.).

Capularis, R. The straight handle or hilt of any kind of instrument or weapon, in contradistinction to *ansa,* which signifies a curved haft or handle. The term *capularis* was applied indifferently to the handle of a sword, a sceptre, &c.

Car, Chariot, or **Carriage.** (See CARRUS and CURRUS.)

Carabaga, Med. Lat. Also CALABRA. A kind of catapult or balista.

Carabine. (See CARBINE.)

Carabus (κάραβος). A small boat made of wicker-work ; a kind of shallop covered with raw hides. It was either propelled by itself or attached to the stern of a larger vessel. Similar to the coracle.

Caracalla (a Celtic word). A military garment introduced from Gaul into Rome by the Emperor Antonine, who obtained thus his surname of *Caracalla.*

Caracole, Arch. A spiral staircase.

Carbassus or **Carbassum** (κάρπασος, fine Spanish flax). This term was used indifferently to denote all textures made of the fine Spanish flax. Thus any kind of linen garment, the sails of a ship, the awning of a theatre or amphitheatre, all came under the term of *carbassus.*

Carbatinæ (καρβάτιναι). A rough kind of boot in common use, made of a single piece of leather, and worn by peasants.

Carbine, or **Carabine,** or **Caraben.** A short gun with a wheel lock and a wide bore, introduced in the 16th century.

Fig. 136. Capuchon and mantle.
From an Italian painting of the 13th century.

Carbonate of Lead, or *white lead,* is the principal white pigment. It is prepared by exposing sheets of lead to the action of acetic and carbonic acids. It is called also *Ceruse, Flake white, Krems* (or *Vienna*) *white, Nottingham white.* It is also known, under different modifications of colour, as *Venice,* or as *Hamburg,* or as *Dutch white.* It is a pigment very liable to injury from exposure to certain gases. (See OXIDE OF ZINC.)

Carbonates of Copper yield blue and green pigments, known from the earliest times, and under many names, as *Mountain* blue and green, blue and green *Ash,* or *Saunders'* (for *cendres'*) blue and green. These names are also applied to the manufactured imitations of the native carbonates of copper. Powdered *Malachite* is a form of the native green carbonate. The colours

called *Emerald Green* and *Paul Veronese Green* are artificial.

Carbuncle (Lat. *carbunculus*). A gem of a deep red colour. A jewel shining in the dark. (*Milton.*)

Carcaissum, Med. Lat. (Fr. *carquois;* It. *carcasso;* Mod. Gr. γαρκάσιον). A quiver.

Carcamousse, Med. A battering-ram. The name is onomatopoetic.

Carcanet, O. E. A necklace set with stones, or strung with pearls.

Carcass, Arch. The unfinished frame or skeleton of a building.

Carcer (akin to *arceo,* i. e. an enclosure [Gr. ἕρκος]). (1) A prison. (2) The circus. At Rome the prisons were divided into three stages: the first, which formed a story above ground (*carcer*

Fig. 137. Carceres. Roman prisons.

superior), was for prisoners who had only committed slight offences; the *carcer interior,* or

Fig. 138. Carceres. Stables in the circus at Rome.

stage on a level with the ground, served as a place
of confinement in which criminals were placed to
await the execution of their sentence ; lastly
there was the *carcer inferior*, or subterranean
dungeon called *robur*, for criminals condemned
to death. Fig. 137 represents the *carcer* built at
Rome by Ancus Martius and Servius Tullius ;
Fig. 138 the *carceres* of the circus.

Carchesium (καρχήσιον). (1) A drinking-cup
of Greek invention, and having slender handles
rising high over the edge, and reaching to the
foot. It was an attribute of Bacchus, and was
used in the religious ceremonies. (2) A scaffolding in the shape of the *carchesium* at the mast-
head of a ship. (Anglicè, " crow's-nest.")

Cardinalis. (See SCAPUS.)

Cardo. A pivot and socket used for the hinge
of a door. The term was also used in carpentry
to denote a dove-tailed tenon ; this was called
cardo securi-culatus, i. e. a tenon in the shape of
an axe, the dove-tail bearing some resemblance to
the blade of that tool.

Care-cloth, O. E. A cloth held over the
bride and bridegroom's heads at a wedding.

Carellus (Fr. *carreau*). A quarrel or arrow
for cross-bows, the head of which was either
four-sided or had four projections.

Carillon, Fr. A set of large bells, arranged to
perform tunes by machinery, or by a set of keys
touched by a musician. Antwerp, Bruges, and
Ghent are celebrated for the carillons in their
steeples.

Caristia (from χάρις, favour or gratitude). A
Roman feast, at which the members of a family
came together. It lasted three days : on the
first, sacrifices were offered to the gods ; the
second was consecrated to the worship of deceased
relations ; and on the third the surviving members of the family met at a banquet. Strangers
were not allowed in these gatherings.

Carminated Lakes. Also called *Lake of
Florence, Paris,* or *Vienna*. Pigments made from
the liquor in which cochineal and the other ingredients have been boiled to make *carmine*.
(See MADDER.)

Carmine. A beautiful pigment prepared from
the insect, cochineal. Carmine is the richest
and purest portion of the colouring matter of
cochineal. The various kinds of carmine are
distinguished by numbers, and possess a value
corresponding thereto ; the difference depending
either on the proportion of the *alumina* added,
or on the presence of *vermilion* added for the
purpose of diluting and increasing the quantity
of the colour : the alumina produces a paler tint,
and the vermilion a tint different to that of
genuine carmine. The amount of adulteration
can always be detected by the use of liquor
ammoniæ, which dissolves the whole of the carmine, but leaves the adulterating matter un-
touched. Carmine is chiefly used in miniature

painting and in water-colours. It is made in
large quantities in Paris.

Carmine-madder. (See MADDER.)

Carnarium, R. (*caro*, flesh). (1) A larder for
fresh or salted provisions. (2) The iron hooks on
which they were hung.

Carnificia or **Carnificina**, R. (*carnifex*, executioner). Subterranean dungeons, in which
criminals were put to the torture, and, in many
cases, executed.

Carnix or **Carnyx** (Celtic and Gaulish word).
A trumpet in the form of a long horn, of which
the mouth was curved so as to resemble the
mouth of an animal. This instrument gave out
a peculiarly loud strident sound, and was used
more particularly by the Celtic nations, notably
the Gauls. It is constantly found represented on
the coins of these nations, and on bas-reliefs.
Some archæologists have mistaken the *carnices*
on medals for *cornucopiæ*.

Carol, Chr. An enclosed place ; a circular
gallery. In old French, *carole* signified a round
dance, or a circle of stone. In the last century
the term was applied to the ambulatory, or circular gallery, behind the choir in churches.

Carpentum, R. A two-wheeled carriage of
Gaulish invention ; it was often covered with an
awning, resembling in form that of the CAMARA
(q.v.). The *carpentum funebre* or *pompaticum*
was a hearse. It was made to resemble a
shrine or small temple. Lastly, the term *carpentum* was used to denote a cart, with two
wheels, employed for agricultural purposes.

Carrago (i. e. formed of *carri* or carts). A
kind of intrenchment peculiar to certain barbarous nations. It was constructed by drawing
up waggons and war-chariots in a curved line,
approaching a circle as nearly as the nature of
the ground permitted. It formed a first line of
defence, behind which the combatants sheltered
themselves in order to defend the camp proper,
which lay in the centre of the *carrago*.

Carreaux, Med. Fr. Quarrels for cross-bows,
so called from their square form.

Carriolum. (See CARROCIUM.)

Carroballista or **Carrobalista** (*carrus*, a car).
A *ballista* mounted upon a carriage, to be trans-
ported from place to place. (See BALLISTA.)

Carrocium, Carrocerum, Med. Lat. A standard fixed on a carriage.

Carrotus. A quarrel. (See CARELLUS, &c.)

Carruca, Carrucha, or **Carucha.** A carriage
of costly description, richly ornamented with
bronze and ivory carvings and chased gold. It
differed widely from the ESSEDO and the RHEDA
(q.v.).

Carrus or **Carrum** (Celtic root). A cart or
chariot of Gaulish invention, on two wheels, used
in the army as a commissariat waggon. A *carrus*
occurs among the sculptures on the column of
Trajan.

Cartamera (Gaulish word). A Gaulish girdle made of metal, and used to support the *braccæ*, or trousers. It was made sometimes in the form of a serpent with its tail in its mouth, but more generally resembled a fringe of twisted hemp, like the *torques*, by which name accordingly it was known among the Romans. (See TORQUES.)

Cartibulum, R. (corrupted from *gertibulum*, i. e. that which bears or carries). A side-board, consisting of a square slab of stone or marble, supported in the middle by a pedestal or stem. The *cartibulum* always stood against a wall.

Fig. 139. Egyptian Cartouche.

Cartouche, Egyp. An elliptical tablet of scroll-like form, containing the names of the Pharaohs. Fig. 139 represents the cartouche of King Artaxerxes. Cartouches were applied to decorate columns, an illustration of which may be seen on the abacus and capital of the column in Fig. 140.

Caryatides (Καρυάτιδες, i. e. women of Caryæ). Female figures, in an upright posture, which were employed in lieu of columns to support entablatures or any other members of architecture. One of the finest instances of the application of caryatides to this purpose is to be found in the portico of the temple of Pandrosos, at Athens.

Caryatis. A festival in honour of Artemis Caryatis, which was celebrated at Caryæ, in Laconia.

Fig. 140. Egyptian Column with Cartouche.

Case Bags, Arch. The joists framed between a pair of girders, in naked flooring.

Cash. A Chinese coin.

Casque, Fr. Helmets of every description, from those of classical times to the present, have been called casques by the poets; but the head-piece specially so designated is first seen in English armour of the reign of Henry VIII.

The casque was generally without a visor, and worn more for parade than warfare. The en-

Fig. 141. Casque.   Fig. 142. Casque.

graving Fig. 141 represents a Gaulish and Fig. 142 an Oriental casque.

Casquetel. A small open helmet without beaver or visor, having a projecting umbril, and flexible plates to protect the neck behind.

Cassel Black. (See BLACK.)

Cassel Earth. A brown pigment.

Cassel Yellow. (See TURNER'S YELLOW.)

Cassida. (See CASSIS.)

Cassilden, O. E. Chalcedony.

Cassis or, rarely, **Cassida** (perhaps an Etruscan word). A casque or helmet made of metal, and so distinguished from GALEA (q.v.), a helmet made of leather. Figs. 141 and 142 represent respectively a Gaulish and an Eastern *cassis* (the latter, however, is considered by some antiquaries to be Gaulish). The war-casque of the Egyptian kings, although of metal, was covered with a panther's skin; it was ornamented with the URÆUS (q.v.).

Cassock signifies a horseman's loose coat, and is used in that sense by the writers of the age of Shakspeare. It likewise appears to have been part of the dress of rustics. (*Steevens.*) It was called a "vest" in the time of Charles II. Later on it became the distinguishing dress of the clergy.

Cassolette, Fr. A perfume box with a per-forated lid; the perforations in a censer.

Cassone. An Italian chest, richly carved and gilt, and often decorated with paintings, which frequently held the *trousseau* of a bride.

Castanets. Various peoples have employed flat pieces of wood to produce a certain kind of noise during religious ceremonies. The Egyptians seem to have had for this purpose "hands" of wood or ivory, which were struck one against the other to form an accompaniment to chants or rhythmic dances. (See CROTALA, &c.)

Castel Durante. An ancient manufactory of Urbino ware, established in the 14th century. Fig. 143, from a cup in the Louvre, is a fine specimen of Castel Durante majolica of the 16th century.

Castellum (dimin. of CASTRUM, q.v.; i. e. a small castle). A small fortified place or citadel; also a reservoir for water. The ruins of *castella* still existing are very few in number ; one of the

Fig. 143. Cup of Castel Durante (1525), in the Museum of the Louvre.

most perfect, as far as the basin is concerned, is that of the *castellum divisorium* or *deversorium*, at Nismes.

Casteria. A storehouse in which the rudder, oars, and movable tackle of a vessel were kept.

Castor. The beaver ; hence applied to beaver hats.

Castoreæ, R. Costly fabrics and dresses made of the fur of beavers.

Castra, R. (plur. of *castrum*, which, like *casa*, = the covering thing). This term was applied solely to an encampment, a fortified or intrenched camp, while the singular *castrum*, an augmentative of CASA (q.v.), denotes a hut, or strongly-constructed post, and consequently a fort, or fortress ; but for this last the Romans preferred to use the diminutive *castellum*.

Castula or **Caltula**, R. A short petticoat worn by Roman women, held up by braces.

Casula, R. (dimin. of *casa*). (1) A small hut or cabin. (2) A hooded cloak, or capote.

Cat. The Egyptian name for the cat (*maaou*) is evidently onomatopoetic. As a symbol, this animal played a part which has hitherto not been clearly determined. Certain papyri show us the cat severing the serpent's head from its body, a symbol which would seem to point out the cat as the destroyer of the enemies of the daylight and the sun. Again, the goddess *Bast* is represented with a cat's head, the animal being sacred to her.

Cat (Med. Lat. *cattus* or *gattus*). A covering

under which soldiers lay for shelter, while sapping the walls of a fortress, &c.

Cataclista, R. A close-fitting garment worn by Roman ladies, bearing a great resemblance to those which are to be seen on Egyptian statues.

Catacombs, Chr. This term, the etymology of which is uncertain, serves to denote disused stone quarries, made use of by the early Christians for their meetings, and as subterranean cemeteries. We meet with catacombs in several cities, but the most celebrated are unquestionably those of Rome. Catacombs also exist at Syracuse, Catana, Palermo, Naples, and Paris.

Catadromus, R. (from κατά and δρόμος, i. e. a running down). A tight-rope for acrobats in a circus or amphitheatre. The *catadromus* was stretched in a slanting direction from a point in the arena to the top of the building.

Catafaltus, Med. Lat. (See CAGASUPTUS.)

Catagrapha, Gr. and R. (κατα-γραφή, i.e. a drawing or marking down). A painting in perspective (rarely met with in the works of the ancient painters).

Cataphracta, Gr. and R. (κατα-φράκτης, i. e. that which covers up). A general term to denote any kind of breastplate worn by the Roman infantry. [Cataphracti were heavy-armed cavalry, with the horses in armour.]

Cataphracti. Decked vessels, in opposition to *aphracti*, open boats.

Catapirates, Gr. and R. (κατα-πειρατής, i. e. that which makes trial downwards). A sounding-lead, of an ovoid form, with tallow or a kind of glue at the end, by means of which sailors were able to ascertain the nature of the bottom.

Catapulta, Gr. and R. (κατα-πέλτης, i.e. that which hurls). A military engine for discharging heavy missiles. The *ballista* projected stones ; the *catapult*, darts ; the *scorpio* (uncertain). They were all called *tormenta*, from the *twisting* of the ropes of hairs or fibres which supplied the propelling force.

Catascopium, Gr. and R. (dimin. of CATASCOPUS, q.v.). A post of observation or sentry tower.

Catascopus, Gr. and R. (κατάσκοπος, i. e. that which explores or spies). (1) A post of observation. (2) A vessel employed as a spy-ship ; and by analogy (3) a scout, i. e. a soldier whose duty is to act as a spy on the enemy.

Catasta (from κατάστασις, i. e. a place of presentation). A platform upon which slaves were placed to be publicly sold. Some scaffolds of this kind were made to revolve, so that the purchaser might thoroughly inspect every part of the slave at his leisure. *Catasta arcana* was the name given to a gridiron, or iron bed, upon which criminals were laid to undergo torture. (See GRIDIRON.)

Cateja (Celtic word). A missile made of wood hardened in the fire. It was employed by the Gauls, Germans, and other barbarians in the way of a harpoon, a rope being fastened to one end of the weapon, by means of which it could be recovered after it had been launched.

Catella (dimin. of CATENA, q.v.). A term specially used to denote the finer sorts of chains made of bronze, silver, and gold. Chains made of the precious metals were worn as trinkets. [The use of the diminutive indicates elegance and delicacy.]

Catellus, R. (dimin. of CATENA, q.v.). A chain used to shackle slaves, or perhaps merely attached to them in the way of a clog.

Catena, R. (1) A chain, especially (2) a chain of gold or silver worn as an ornament round the body, like a *balteus* (shoulder-belt), by certain goddesses, dancing-girls, bacchantes, or courtezans.

Catenarius. The chained dog kept at the entrance of their houses by the Romans.

Catharmata (καθάρματα, from καθαίρω, i.e. that which is thrown away in cleansing). Sacrifices in which human victims were offered up, in order to avert the plague or similar visitations. [They were thrown into the sea.]

Cathedra (καθέδρα, from κατά and ἕδρα, i. e. a place for sitting down). A chair having a back, but without arms. There were various kinds of *cathedræ*: the *cathedra strata* was a chair furnished with cushions; *cathedra supina*, a chair with long sloping back; *cathedra longa*, a chair with long deep seat. The *cathedra philosophorum* was the equivalent of our modern term, a professor's chair.

Catherine Wheel. In Gothic architecture, a large circular window, filled with radiating divisions; called also rose window.

Cathetus, Arch. (1) The axle of a cylinder. (2) The centre of the Ionic volute.

Catillus and **Catillum** (dimin. of CATINUS,

Fig. 144. Catillus for grinding corn.

q. v.; i.e. a small bowl). (1) The upper part of a mill for grinding corn, which served both as grindstone and hopper or bowl. Fig. 144 represents an ancient mill, a fourth part of the

catillus being suppressed in order to show the reader the mechanism. (2) A small dish having much resemblance to the *catinus*, and so by analogy (3) a flat circular ornament employed to decorate the scabbard of a sword.

Catinus and **Catinum**, R. (akin to Sicilian κάτινον). Dishes used for cooking, and for the table. *Catina* might be of earthenware or metal, of glass or other precious material, and were employed as sacrificial vessels to hold incense, &c.

Catty. A Chinese weight = 1⅓ lb.

Catulus, R. When a slave ran away from his master, and was retaken, he was led back in chains, the *catulus* being the chain which was attached to an iron collar passing round his neck. A slave was thus said to be led back *cum manicis, catulo, collarique*, i. e. with manacles, leading chain, and neck-collar.

Caudex. (See CODEX.)

Caudicarius, Codicarius, R. (from *caudex*, a tree-trunk). A wide flat barge employed in river transport. It was of rough construction, and was broken up on arriving at its destination.

Caudicius, R. A vessel of the same kind as the *caudicarius*, employed on the Moselle.

Caughley-ware (Shropshire). A soft porcelain; 18th century.

Caul, O. E. A cap or network enclosing the hair.

Cauliculi or **Caulicoli**, R. (dimin. of *caulis*, a stalk). Acanthus leaves springing from the capital of a Corinthian column.

Caupolus. (See CAUPULUS.)

Caupona, R. (*caupo*, an innkeeper). An inn or hostel for the accommodation of travellers. The *cauponæ* bore a general resemblance to our roadside inns. [Also, a cooked-meat shop.]

Cauponula, R. (dimin. of *caupona*). A small tavern, or low wine-shop of mean appearance.

Caupulus, R. A kind of boat, classed by authors among the *lembi* and *cymbæ*.

Caurus, R. An impersonation of the North-West wind; represented under the form of an old man with a beard, pouring down rain from an urn.

Causia, Gr. and R. (καυσία, from καῦσις, i. e. that which keeps off heat). A broad-brimmed felt hat, of Macedonian invention, and adopted by the Romans. It was especially worn by fishermen and sailors.

Cauter (καυτήρ, i. e. that which burns). A cautery or branding-iron. The *cauter* was (1) an instrument used by surgeons; it was also used for branding cattle and slaves. (2) An instrument employed to burn in the colours in an encaustic painting.

Cauterium = CAUTER (q.v.).

Cavædium, R. (from *cavum* and *ædes*, i. e. the hollow part of a house). An open courtyard. In early times the Romans had an external courtyard to their houses. In course of time, however, the increase of luxury and comfort brought about a change in the *cavædium*, which was partially covered in with a roof supported by columns, a partial opening being left in the centre, which was called the *compluvium*. When thus altered, the *cavædium* went under the name of ATRIUM (q.v.).

Cavalherium. (See CABALLARIA.)

Cavallerius or **Cavallero**, Med. Lat. A knight or cavalier.

Cavea, R. (from *cavus*, i. e. a hollow place or cavity). (1) A wooden cage with open bars, of wood or, more generally, of iron, used for the transport and exhibition of the wild beasts of a menagerie. (2) A bird-cage. (3) A frame of wicker-work employed by fullers and dyers. (4) A palisade to protect young trees when growing up, and (5) the vast reversed cone formed by the successive stages of a theatre or amphitheatre. This might be divided, according to the size of the building, into one, two, or three distinct tiers, called respectively upper, lower, and middle (*summa, ima, media cavea*). (6) A warlike machine used in attacking cities.

Cavetto, Arch. (deriv. from Ital. *cavo*). A concave moulding formed of a segment of a circle.

Cavo-relievo. Intaglio-sculpture cut into the stone, as in Egyptian art.

Ceadas or **Cæadas** (κεάδας or καιάδας). A deep cave into which the Spartans thrust condemned prisoners.

Ceinture or **Ceint.** A girdle. (See CINCTUS.)

Celadon. A peculiar tinted porcelain, described by Jacquemart as the earliest tint of Chinese pottery.

Celebê (Κελέβη). A vase of ovoid form and with two handles. The lower part is shaped elegantly, like an amphora, but the upper part resembles a pitcher with a sort of projecting lip. Its peculiarity is in the *handles*, which are "pillared" and "reeded."

Celes, R. A racing or saddle horse, as opposed to a draught horse. The same term was also applied to a vessel or boat of a peculiar form, propelled by oars, in which each rower handled only a single oar. It was also called *celox*.

Fig. 145. Plan of temple showing the Cella.

Cella, R. (from *celo*, to hide). The interior of a temple, i. e. the part comprised within the four walls. In Fig. 145 *a* represents the portico, *b* the *cella*. The term is also used to denote a niche, store-room, or, in general, any kind of cellar ; e. g. *cella vinaria, cella olearia*, and even a tavern situated in a cellar.

The term was also applied to slaves' dormitories, the parts of the public baths, &c.

Cellatio. A suite of apartments in a Roman house set apart for various purposes, but especially as quarters for slaves.

Cellula (dimin. of CELLA, q.v.). A small sanctuary, i. e. the interior of a small temple, and by analogy any kind of small chamber.

Celox. (See CELES.)

Celt. A variety of chisels and adzes of the flint and bronze periods.

Celtic (Monuments) were usually constructed of huge stones, and are known, for that reason, as *megalithic monuments*. Such are STANDING STONES, DOLMENS, MENHIRS or PEULVANS, CROMLECHS, COVERED ALLEYS, TUMULI, &c. (See these words.)

Cembel. A kind of joust or HASTILUDE.

Cendal, Sandal, &c., O. E. The name, variously spelt, of a silken stuff used for vestments, and for banners, &c.; 13th century. We now call this stuff *sarcenet*.

Cenotaph (κενο-τάφιον, i. e. an empty tomb). A monument raised to a Roman citizen who had been drowned at sea, or who, from any other cause, failed to receive burial.

Censer. A sacred vessel used for burning perfumes.

Centaur (κένταυρος, according to some, from

Fig. 146. Centaur.

κεντέω and ταῖρος, i. e. herdsman ; but prob. simply from κεντέω, i. e. Piercer or Spearman). The Centaurs are represented with the body of a horse, and bust, head, and arms of a man. (Fig. 146.) In Christian archæology, the Centaur is a symbol of the swift passage of life, the force of the instincts, and in a special sense, of adul-

Fig. 147. Centaur and young.

tery. The war of the Centaurs and the Lapithæ is the subject of the frieze at the British Museum, from a temple of Apollo in Arcadia. *Hippocentaurs* were half-horse ; *Ono-centaurs*, half-ass ; and *Bucentaurs* or *Tauro-centaurs*, half-ox.

Cento (κέντρων, patchwork). A covering made of different scraps of cloth, and used as clothing for slaves. The same term denotes a coarse cloth which was placed beneath the saddle of a beast of burden, to keep the back of the animal from being galled by the saddle. In Christian archæology the term was used to denote a coarse patchwork garment, and, by analogy, a poem composed of verses taken from various authors, like the *Cento nuptialis* of Ausonius.

Centunculus (dimin. of CENTO, q.v.). A motley garment of various colours, like that of our harlequin. It was worn, according to Apuleius, by the actors who played in burlesques, and there are certain vases on which Bacchus is represented, arrayed in a similar costume.

Cepotaphium (κηπο-τάφιον). A tomb situated in a garden.

Cera (akin to κηρός). Wax, and, by analogy, any objects made of wax, such as images of the family ancestors (*imagines majorum*) ; or the wax tablets for writing on with the *stylus*. These were called respectively *ceræ duplices, triplices, quintuplices*, according as they had two, three, or five leaves. The first, second, third, and last tablet were called respectively *prima, secunda, tertia, ultima* or *extrema cera*.

Ceramic. Appertaining to POTTERY (q.v.).

Cerberus. The three-headed dog who guarded the gates of hell.

Cercurus (κέρκουρος, perhaps from Κέρκυρα, the island Corcyra). A Cyprian vessel propelled by oars. Its form is unknown.

Cerebrerium. An iron skull-cap, *temp.* Edward I.

Cere-cloth (*cera*, wax). Cloth saturated with wax, used for enveloping a consecrated altar-stone, or a dead body.

Cereus (*cera*, wax). A wax candle, made either with the fibres of cyperus or papyrus twisted together and dipped in wax, or with the pith of elder, or rush, covered with the same material.

Ceriolare (*cera*, wax). A stand, holder, or candelabrum for wax candles. There were a great variety of this kind of vessel. (See CANDELABRUM.)

Cernuus (from *cer* = κάρα, and *nuo*, i. e. with head inclined to the ground). A tumbler who walks upon his hands with his feet in the air. Women even used to turn series of summersaults, resting alternately on the feet and hands, among a number of swords or knives stuck in the ground. This exhibition was called by the Greeks εἰς μαχαίρας κυβιστᾶν, i. e. lit. to tumble head over heels between knives).

Cerōma (κήρωμα, a wax-salve). A room in which wrestlers rubbed themselves over with oil and fine sand. The room was so named from the unguent employed, which consisted of wax mixed with oil [which was also called *cerōma*].

Cero-plastic. The art of modelling in wax.

Cero-strotum or **Cestrotum**, Lat. A kind of encaustic painting upon ivory or horn, in which the lines were burnt in with the cestrum, and the furrows filled with wax.

Certosina Work. Florence, 15th century. Ivory inlaid into solid cypress-wood and walnut. The style is Indian in character, and consists in geometric arrangements of stars made of diamond-shaped pieces, varied with conventional flowers in pots, &c.

Certyl. Old English for kirtle.

Ceruse. A name for white lead. (See CARBONATE OF LEAD.)

Cervelliere. (See CEREBRERIUM.)

Cervi (lit. stags). Large branches of trees with the forks still left upon them, but cut down close to the stock, so that the whole presented the appearance of a stag's antlers. *Cervi* were employed to strengthen a palisade, so as to impede the advance of infantry, or resist attacks of cavalry.

Cervical (from *cervix*, a neck). A cushion or pillow for supporting the back of the head on a bed or dining-couch. (See PULVINAR.)

Cervus. (See STAG.)

Ceryceum (κηρύκειον, a herald's staff). It is a synonym of CADUCEUS (q. v.).

Cesticillus (dimin. of CESTUS, q.v.). A circular pad used as a rest by persons who had to carry burdens on their heads.

Cestra. (See CESTROSPHENDONE.)

Cestrosphendonê, Gr. (a dart-sling.) A dart fixed to a wooden stock with three short wooden wings, discharged from a sling.

Cestrotum. (See CEROSTROTUM.)

Cestrum or **Viriculum** (κέστρον, i. e. that which pricks or pierces). A graver used in the process of encaustic painting on ivory. It was made of ivory, pointed at one end and flat at the other. (See CEROSTROTUM, RHABDION.)

Cestus (κεστὸς, embroidered). (1) In general any kind of band or tie ; but specially the embroidered girdle of Venus. (2) A boxing gauntlet. (See CÆSTUS.)

Cetra (prob. a Spanish word). A small round shield in use among several barbarous nations, but never by the Romans.

Chaable, Old Fr. A large ballista. (See CABULUS.) Trees blown down by the wind are still called " caables" in France. (*Meyrick.*)

Chabasite (χαβὸς, narrow, compressed). A crystal of a white colour.

Chaconne, Fr. (Sp. *chacona ;* It. *ciacona*). A modification of the dance *chica* (q.v.).

Chadfarthing, O. E. A farthing formerly paid among the Easter dues, for the purpose of hallowing the font for christenings. (*Halliwell.*)

Chafer, O. E. (1) A beetle or May-bug. (2) A saucepan.

Chafer-house, O. E. An ale-house.

Chafery, O. E. A furnace.

Fig. 148. Chaffagiolo ware. Sweetmeat plate, with arabesques, about 1509.

Chaffagiolo, or **Caffagiolo**, is the place where Cosmo the Great established the first Tuscan manufactory of majolica, and where Luca della Robbia acquired his knowledge of the stanni-ferous enamel. Fig. 148 is a specimen of Chaffagiolo ware of the 15th century.

Chain-moulding, Arch. An ornament of the Norman period, sculptured in imitation of a chain.

Chain-timbers, Arch. Bond timbers, the thickness of a brick, introduced to tie and strengthen a wall.

Chair. (See SELLA.)

Chair de Poule (chicken's flesh). An ornamentation of the surface of pottery with little hemispheric points ; a Chinese method.

Chaisel, Old Fr. (1) An upper garment. (2) A kind of fine linen, of which smocks were often made.

Chalameau, Fr. Stem or straw-pipe. The lower notes of the clarionet are called the *chalameau* tone, from the ancient *shawm*.

Chalcanthum (χάλκ-ανθον, i. e. that which is thrown off by copper). Shoemaker's black or copperas, used for imparting a dark colour to boot-leather. (See ATRAMENTUM.)

Chalcedony. (See CALCEDONY.)

Chalcidicum (Χαλκιδικὸν, i. e. pertaining to the city of Chalcis). The exact meaning of this term is unknown. According to some, it was a portico ; according to others, a kind of long hall or transept.

Chalciœcia (χαλκι-οίκια, brazen house). A Spartan festival in honour of Athena under that designation.

Chalcography (χαλκὸς, copper). Engraving on copper. *Chalcography* was discovered in Florence, in the 15th century, and early introduced into England. Caxton's "Golden Legend," containing copper-plate prints, was published in 1483. The process is as follows :— A perfectly smooth plate of copper, having been highly polished, is heated in an oven, and then white wax rubbed over it until the whole surface is covered with a thin layer. A tracing is laid over the wax, with the black-lead lines downwards, which transfers the design to the wax. Then the tracing-paper is removed, and the engraver goes over the lines lightly with a fine steel point, so as just to penetrate the wax, and scratch a delicate outline upon the copper. The wax is then melted off, and the engraving finished with the *graver*, or *burin*, a steel instrument with a peculiar pyramidal point. Should the lines be cut too deeply, a smooth tool, about three inches long, called a *burnisher*, is used to soften them down, and to burnish out scratches in the copper. The *ridges* or *burrs* that rise on each side of the engraved lines are scraped off by a tool about six inches long, called a *scraper*, made of steel, with three sharp edges. This method has for printing purposes been generally superseded by other processes, principally *etching*.

Chalcus (χαλκοῦς). A Greek copper coin, somewhat less than a farthing.

F

Chalice, Chr. (deriv. from *calix*, a cup). A sacred vessel used in the celebration of the mass.

Fig. 149. Chalice, silver-gilt—14th century.

There were many different kinds, called *minis-teriaies, offertorii, majores,* and *minores.* The *ministeriales* served to distribute the wine ; the *offertorii* were employed by the deacons to hold the wine offered by the faithful. Lastly, they were distinguished according to their size, as large or small (*majores* and *minores*). Vessels called *calices* were also frequently suspended from the arches of the ciborium, and other parts of the church, as ornaments. In Christian symbolism the chalice and serpent issuing from it are an attribute of St. John the Evangelist.

Chalon, O. E. A coverlet. (*Chaucer.*)

Chamade, Fr. A beat of drum or trumpet inviting the enemy to a parley.

Chamber Music, as opposed to concert music. Madrigals were probably the earliest specimens of chamber music.

Chambers, O. E. Small cannon for firing on festive occasions.

Chamberyngs, O. E. Bedroom furniture.

Chameleon (χαμαὶ, on the ground, and λέων, a lion). In Christian symbolism, the emblem of inconstancy ; in Chemistry, manganate of potass is called *chameleon* from the changes of colour which its solution undergoes. The chameleon with a dolphin on its back (Fig. 150) was the device of Pope Paul III.

Chamfer, Arch. (1) The angle of obliquity (of the sides of a steeple, &c.). (2) A hollow channel or gutter, such as the fluting of a column.

Fig. 150. Chameleon and Dolphin.

Chamfron, O. E. (Med. Lat. *chamfrenum;* Fr.*champ-frein*). A frontal of leather or steel to a horse's bridle. (Fig. 151.)

Chamlet, O. E. (See CAMLET.)

Chammer, O. E. (Fr. *chamarre*). A gown worn by persons of rank, *temp.* Henry VIII.

Champ, Arch. A flat surface.

Champ-levé. A form of enamelling in which the pattern is cut out of the metal to be ornamented.

Fig. 151. Chamfron.

Chamuleus, R. and Gr. A heavy dray for the transport of building materials, such as blocks of marble, columns, obelisks, &c.

Chance, O. E. The game of hazard.

Chancel, Chr. (from *cancelli*, a lattice). A term anciently used to denote the *choir*. It derived its name from the *cancelli* or stone screen by which it was enclosed.

Chandaras (Sanscrit, *chanda-rasa*, lit. moon-juice). An ancient name for *copal*.

Chandeleuse, Fr. Candlemas Day.

Chandi (from *chand*, the moon). Indian name for silver.

Chand-tara (lit. moon and stars) is the name of an Indian brocade, figured all over with representations of the heavenly bodies.

Changeable Silk, O. E., was woven of two colours, so that one of them showed itself unmixed and quite distinct on one side, and the second appeared equally clear on the other; mentioned A.D. 1327, 1543, &c.

Changes. The altered melodies produced by varying the sounds of a peal of bells.

Chante-pleure, Fr. A water-pot, made of earthenware, about a foot high, the orifice at the

Fig. 152. Chante-pleure.

top the size of a pea, and the bottom full of small holes. Immersed in water, it quickly fills. If the opening at the top be then closed with the thumb, the vessel may be carried, and the water distributed as required. The widow of Louis I., Duke of Orleans, adopted this as her device, after the murder of her husband, in 1407.

Chantlate, Arch. A piece of wood under the eaves of a roof, by which two or three rows of overhanging slates or tiles are supported.

Chantry, Chr. (Fr. *chanter*, to sing). A chapel to which is attached a revenue as provision for a priest, whose duty it is to sing masses for the repose of the founder's soul.

Chape, O. E. (Spanish *chapa*, a thin plate of metal). (1) The transverse guard of a sword. (2) A metal plate at the end of a scabbard. (3) A catch by which a thing is held in its place.

Chapeau, Her. Also called a *cap of dignity, of maintenance,* or *of estate.* An early symbol of high dignity.

Fig. 153. Chapeau.

Chapeau Chinois, Fr. A set of small bells arranged in the form of a Chinese hat.

Chapel or **Chapelle de Fer.** Iron helmet of

knights of the 12th century. The diminutive is *chapeline.*

Chaperon, Fr. A hood or small cap for the head.

Chapiter, Arch. The upper part of a capital.

Chaplet, Arch. (Fr. *chapelet*). (1) A small cylindrical moulding, carved into beads and the like.

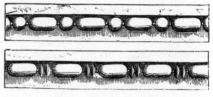

Fig. 154. Chaplet Moulding.

(See Fig. 154.) (2) *Chaplets of flowers,* which were worn in England, by both sexes, on festive occasions, during the Middle Ages, and chaplets of jewels in earlier times. (3) Chr. It was anciently the custom to crown the newly baptized with a chaplet or garland of flowers. (4) Chr. A succession of prayers recited in a certain order, regulated by beads, &c. (5) In Heraldry. A garland or wreath. (See CRANCELIN.)

Chapter, Chr. (Lat. *capitulum*). The body of the clergy of a cathedral, united under the bishop.

Chapter-house, Chr. A place of assemblage for a CHAPTER of the clergy. That of Westminster contains some fine wall-paintings of the middle of the 14th century.

Chaptrel, Arch. The capital of a column supporting an arch ; an impost.

Character, Gr. and R. Generally, any sign or mark impressed, painted, or engraved on any object. In a more restricted sense, it denotes the instrument of iron or bronze with which such marks were made. In Art, the expression means a faithful adherence to the peculiarities of objects represented.

Charbokull, O. E. A carbuncle.

Charcoal Blacks are made of ivory, bones, vine-twigs, smoke of resin, &c., burned in a crucible excluded from the air. The best charcoal *crayons* are made of box and willow ; the former produces a dense hard crayon, the latter a soft friable one. (*Fairholt.*) (See BLUE BLACK.)

Chare Thursday, O. E. Maundy Thursday.

Charge, Her. Any heraldic figure or device.

Charisia, Gr. (Χάριτες, the Graces). Nocturnal festivals held in honour of the Graces, at which cakes and honey were distributed to those present.

Charisteria, Gr. (χάρις, gratitude). Festivals

celebrated yearly at Athens, in remembrance of the Athenian general Thrasybulus, the saviour of his country.

Charistia. (See CARISTIA.)

Charistion. An instrument of Archimedes for weighing. Whether it bore most resemblance to the balance (*libra*), or the steelyard (*statera*), is uncertain, as its form is entirely unknown.

Charles's Wain (Anglo-Saxon, *carles-waen*, the churl's waggon). The seven stars forming the constellation generally called the Great Bear.

Charnel, O. E. Apex of the basinet.

Charnel-house. A small building attached to a cemetery, for a receptacle for the human bones disinterred when fresh graves were dug.

Charta, Gr. and R. Writing-paper in use among the ancients. There were eight different kinds, which were classed as follows in the order of their quality : (1) *Charta Augustana* or *Claudiana*; (2) *Liviana*; (3) *hieratica*; (4) *amphitheatrica*; (5) *Saitica*; (6) *leneotica*; (7) *fanniana*; (8) *dentata*. The last was so called from being polished by means of the tooth (*dens*) of some animal, or a piece of ivory. There was also a *charta emporetica* or packing-paper, and lastly a *charta bibula*. It is uncertain whether this last was blotting-paper, or a kind of transparent paper which had been steeped in oil or some other fatty substance.

Charter-room or **Charter-house.** A place in which the charters of a particular family or house were preserved.

Chartophylax, Chr. A man who had charge of the charters of a church.

Chasing. (See CÆLATURA.)

Chasse, Chr., Fr. A reliquary in the form of a box with a ridged top.

Chastelain, O. E. The lord of a castle.

Chastons, O. E. Breeches of mail ; 13th to 16th century.

Chasuble (Lat. *casula*, a cottage). Part of ancient ecclesiastical costume common to all the Roman Catholic clergy, from the priest to the Archbishop. It was originally made of wool, and in one piece throughout, without sleeves, and without slit or opening in front, and perfectly circular ; but the shape varied with the material ; and from the 6th cen-

Fig. 155. Chasuble.

tury downwards we hear of chasubles of brilliant colour and costly materials, such as silk or thickly-embroidered cloth of gold, and oval in form, hanging no longer in graceful folds as in the 11th century. The engraving (Fig. 155) shows a chasuble of the year 1387. (Compare PÆNULA, PLANETA.)

Chatai, Hindoo. Mats, a common manufacture all over India. Those of Midnapore, near Calcutta, are remarkable for their fineness and classical design of the mosaic, like patterns of stained glass.

Chat-faux, Med. A wooden shed—modern scaffold. (See CAGASUPTUS.)

Chatrang (Sanscrit *chatur-anga*, the four *angas* or soldiers ; or *chaturaji*, the four kings). The Persian name for a very ancient game of the " Four Kings," supposed to be the origin of the four suits of playing-cards. (*Rev. E. S. Taylor, " History of Playing-cards.*")

Chatzozerah, Heb. A Jewish trumpet mentioned by Moses, used chiefly for religious and warlike occasions.

Chauffault, Old Fr. A tower of wood.

Chausses, O. E. (1) Pantaloons of mail used by the Danes. (2) Tight pantaloons worn by the Normans and mediæval English.

Chaussetrap. (See CALTRAPS.)

Chaussons, O. E. Breeches of mail (or of cloth).

Chavarina, Med. Lat. A carbine.

Checkere, O. E. A chess-board.

Checkstone, O. E. A game played by children with small round pebbles.

Checky, Her. (See CHEQUÉE.)

Cheese, Chr. St. Augustine says that a sect called the Artotyrites offered bread and *cheese* in the Eucharist, saying "that the first oblations which were offered by men, in the infancy of the world, were of the fruits of the earth and of sheep." (*Aug. de Hæres.* c. xlviii.)

Chef-d'œuvre, Fr. A work of the highest excellence.

Chekelatoun. (See CICLATOUN.)

Chekere, O. E. Chess (q.v.).

Chêlè (χηλὴ, prob. from a root χα-, meaning cloven). This term is applied to a great variety of objects ; it signifies a cloven foot, a hooked claw, or anything presenting a notched or serrated appearance. Thus a breakwater, the irregular projections of which bore some resemblance to the teeth of an immense saw, was also called *chêlè*. There were, besides, various engines and machines which went under this name.

Chelidoniacus, sc. *gladius* (from the Greek χελιδών, a swallow). A broad-bladed sword with a double point like a swallow's tail.

Chelidonize, Gr. (lit. to twitter like a swallow). Singing the "Swallow Song" (χελιδόνισμα), a popular song sung by the Rhodian boys in the month Boedromion, on the return of the swallows, and made into an opportunity for begging. A similar song is still popular in Greece. (*Fauriel*, "*Chants de la Grèce*.") (See CORONIZE.)

Cheliform ($\chi\eta\lambda\grave{\eta}$, a claw). In the form of a claw.

Chelonium (a tortoise-shell, from $\chi\epsilon\lambda\acute{\omega}\nu\eta$, a tortoise). (1) A kind of cramp or collar placed at the extremities of the uprights of certain machines. (2) A part of a catapult, also called *pulvinus*. (See CATAPULTA.)

Chelys ($\chi\acute{\epsilon}\lambda\upsilon s$, a tortoise). (1) The lyre of Mercury, formed of strings stretched across a tortoise-shell. (2) In the 16th and 17th centuries, a bass-viol and division-viol were each called *chelys*. (See also TESTUDO.)

Chemise de Chartres, Fr. A kind of armour mentioned among the habiliments proper for knights who should engage in single combat. (*Meyrick*.)

Chenbele. (See CEMBEL [hastilude].)

Cheng, Chinese. A musical instrument, consisting of a box or bowl, into which a series of tubes of different length and pitch are inserted; the tubes have holes in them to be played upon with the fingers.

Chêniscus ($\chi\grave{\eta}\nu$, a goose). An ornament placed at the bow, and sometimes the stern of ships. In shape it resembled the neck of a swan or goose.

Chequée, Checky, Her. Having the field divided into contiguous rows of small squares; alternately of a metal (or fur) and a colour.

Chequers, O. E. (See CHECKSTONE.)

Cherub, pl. **Cherubim**, Heb. According to the classification of Dionysius, the first *hierarchy* of Angels consists of three *choirs* called SERAPHIM, CHERUBIM, and THRONES, and, receiving their glory immediately from Deity, transmit it to the second hierarchy. The first hierarchy are as councillors; the second as governors; the third as ministers. The SERAPHIM are absorbed in perpetual love and worship round the throne; the CHERUBIM know and worship; the THRONES sustain the throne. The SERAPHIM and CHERUBIM are in general represented as *heads* merely with two or four or six wings, and of a bright red or blue colour, &c. (Cf. *Mrs. Jameson's Legendary Art*.) (See ANGELS, SERAPHIM, DOMINIONS, &c.)

Cherubic Hymn, Chr. A hymn sung in the Greek Church before the great entrance (see ENTRANCE); so called from its first words, οἱ τὰ χερουβὶμ μυστικῶς εἰκονίζοντες, κ.τ.λ.

Chesible, for CHASUBLE (q.v.).

Chesnut Brown. A brown lake pigment prepared from the horse chesnut; very durable for oils and water-colour painting.

Chess. Writers immediately after the Conquest speak of the Saxons as playing at chess, which, they say, they learned from the Danes. The game of chess is very prominent in the romances of the Middle Ages. The Scandinavian navigators introduced some remarkable elaborately carved chessmen, of walrus ivory, from Iceland, in the 12th century. The castles are replaced by warriors on foot, called *hrokr*, from the Saracen *roc*, Persian *rokh*, our **rook**. In the Saracen game the *vizier* represented our queen, and the *elephant* our bishop, the *roc*, or hero, as aforesaid, our rook. Beautifully carved chessmen in the costumes of the 13th and 14th century exist in England. They were all very large, a king being four inches in height and seven in circumference. The *chess-boards* were of corresponding size, and made of all materials, including the precious metals, crystal, sapphires, and topazes. The pieces varied in form: the mediæval rook had a head like a *fleur-de-lis*, the knight was represented by a small upright column with the upper part bent on one side. The *aufin* or bishop was of the same shape, but the bent end was cleft to indicate a mitre. The figures of the 16th century much more nearly resemble those now in vogue.

Chesse, O. E. (Fr. *chasse*). A border, a circlet.

Chest of Viols, O. E. A set of instruments complete for a "consort" of viols, i.e. two trebles, two tenors, and two basses.

Chester, O. E. A person who places corpses in their coffins.

Chests and **Coffers**, in Norman times, were adorned with elaborate carving and richly inlaid. They were still the general depositories for clothes and treasures. *Cupboards* (armoires) were introduced by the Normans, and filled with household utensils.

Chevalet, Fr. The *bridge* of a violin or other stringed instrument.

Cheval-traps. (See CALTRAPS.)

Chevaucheurs. Anglo-Norman horsemen, or running messengers.

Chevaux-de-frize. An arrangement of iron spikes for the defence of a battlement against assault.

Cheveril, O. E. Kid leather, proverbially *elastic*; hence, a *cheveril conscience* (that will stretch).

Chevesaile, Old Fr. A necklace.

Chevetaine, Old Fr. A captain; hence the mediæval *cheuptanus*.

Chevron. (1) Arch. One of the mouldings frequently used in Norman architecture, usually called *zigzag* (q.v.). (2) A badge on the coat-sleeve of a non-commissioned officer. (3) Her. One of the ordinaries; the lower half of a SALTIRE (q.v.).

Chevronel, Her. A diminutive of the CHEVRON, of half the size.

Chevroter, Fr. A musical term: "to skip, quiver, to sing with uncertain tone, after the manner of goats," *alla vibrato.*

Chiaroscuro, It. (*chiaro*, light, and *oscuro*, dark). Light and shade.

Chiave of Pavia. One of the Italian literary academies, composed entirely of noble and illustrious persons, who wore a golden key suspended round the neck, and had for a motto, *Clauditur et aperitur liberis,* and the text from Rev. iii. 7.

Chica. A dance popular in Spanish South America, of a *jig*-like character; the origin of the *Fandango.* (See CHACONNE.)

Chief, Her. One of the ordinaries; the *chief* bounded by a horizontal line contains the uppermost third of the field of a shield. *In chief*, arranged horizontally across the upper part of the field.

Childermas, O. E. Innocents' Day.

Chilled (Fr. *chancissure*). Said of a moisture on the varnish of a picture by which the defect of cloudiness called *Blooming* is caused.

Chimæra, Gr. A monster described by Homer, with a lion's head, a goat's body, and a dragon's tail. In Christian art it is a symbol of cunning. (See also DOG OF FO.)

Chime. (1) To play bells by swinging the *hammers*, opposed to *ringing* by swinging the *bells*. (2) A chime of bells is a CARILLON.

Chimere, Chr. The outer dress of a Protestant bishop. It is made of black satin, without sleeves.

Chimneys (Gr. χιμήνη, winter), carried up in the massive walls of the castles, were first introduced into England by the Normans. The fire was still piled up in the middle of the hall, but fireplaces were built against the side walls in the more private apartments—the original of the well-known mediæval fireplace and "chymené." Leland, in his account of Bolton Castle, which was "finiched or Kynge Richard the 2 dyed," notices the *chimneys:* "One thynge I muche notyd in the hawle of Bolton, how chimeneys were conveyed by tunnells made on the syds of the walls, betwyxt the lights in the hawle, and by this means, and by no covers, is the smoke of the harthe in the hawle wonder strangely conveyed."

Chin-band, **Chin-cloth**. A muffler of lace worn by ladies, *temp.* Charles I.

China. (See POTTERY.)

China (or **Chinese**) **Ink.** (See INDIAN INK.)

Chinese Paper. A fine absorbent paper of a yellowish tint, used for proofs of engravings, &c. Japanese paper is now frequently preferred.

Chinese White. OXIDE OF ZINC (q.v.). It is more *constant* than white lead.

Chinny-mumps. A Yorkshire music made by rapping the chin with the knuckles.

Chints or **Chintz** (Hindoo, *chhint*, spotted cotton cloth). Cotton cloth printed in more than two colours.

Chiramaxium, Gr. and R. (χειρ-αμάξιον, i. e. hand-cart). An invalid's chair mounted upon two wheels, and drawn or pushed by slaves.

Chiridota, Gr. and R. (from adj. χειριδωτὸς, i. e. lit. having sleeves). Tunics with long sleeves, worn in especial by the Asiatic races and by the CELTS. The early Britons, before the Roman invasion, wore close coats checkered with various colours in divisions, open before and with *long close sleeves to the wrist.*

Chirimia, Sp. (from *chirimoya*, a pear). An oboe.

Chirography. The art of writing with the hands.

Chirology. The art of talking with the hands.

Chiromancy (μάντις, a soothsayer). Divination from the lines of the palms of the hands.

Fig. 157. Diana wearing the Greek chiton.

Chironomia, Gr. and R. (χειρο-νομία, i. e. measured motion of the hands). The mimetic art. By this term is expressed not only the art of speaking with gestures and by means of the hands, but also the action of speaking combined with gesticulation. This art dates from a high antiquity. It was originally part of the art of dancing,—clapping the hands in rhythm ; also a gymnastic exercise, for pugilists and others.

Chiroplast. An instrument for teaching fingering of musical instruments, invented by Logier in 1810.

Chirothecæ (Gr. χειροθήκη ; Lat. *gantus*). Gloves were unknown to the early Greeks and Romans, but in use among the ancient Persians. In Christian archæology they are first met with in the 12th century. (See GLOVES.)

Chisleu, Heb. The ninth month of the Jewish year. It begins with the new moon of our December.

Chiton (χιτών). The Greek tunic. (Fig. 157.)

Chitte, O. E. A sheet.

Chivachirs (Chevaucheurs). Old Fr. Running messengers.

Chlaina (Lat. *læna*). A kind of cloak, of ample size, worn by the Greeks in campaigning. In time of peace it served as a bed coverlet. The diminutive χλανίδιον appears to have been a woman's mantle.

Chlamyda. (See CHLAMYS.)

Chlamys, Gr. A short light mantle, which was worn by Greek youths (not by Romans) until they arrived at manhood. It was the regular equestrian costume, and was of an oblong square shape. (Fig. 159.) The chlamys is seen in representations of men hunting or fighting with beasts, as a shield wrapped round the left arm, the right poising the spear. (Fig. 158.) In Botany, the floral envelope.

Fig. 159.

Chœnix (χοῖνιξ). A Greek measure of capacity, variously valued from a pint and half to two quarts.

Choir, Quire, or **Quere,** Arch. The part of the church for the singers and *clerks,* i. e. the space between the NAVE (for the people), and the BEMA, or presbytery, for the celebrating clergy. But in mediæval writings the term includes the BEMA. (See CHANCEL.)

Choir Wall or **Choir Screen** (Fr. *clôture*). The wall or screen between the side-aisles and the choir.

Choosing-stick (a Somersetshire provincialism). A divining-rod.

Chopines, It. Clogs or high shoes, of Asiatic origin, introduced from Venice in the 16th century.

Choragic Monuments. Small pedestals or shrines erected by the winner of a choral contest to display the *tripod* which was his prize. At Athens there was a street lined with such monuments, called the " Street of the Tripods." The Choragic Monument of Lysicrates, still existing in Athens, is one of the most valuable remains of Greek architecture.

Choragium, Gr. and R. (χορηγὸς, or chorusleader). A large space in a theatre, situated behind the stage. It was here that the " properties " were kept and the rehearsals of the chorus took place. The term is also used to denote the furniture, costumes, decorations, and, in a word, all the accessories required in the production of a piece.

Chordaulodion. A self-acting musical instrument invented by Kauffmann of Dresden in 1812.

Chorea, Gr. and R. (χορὸς, q.v.). A choral dance, in which the dancers took each other by the hand and danced to the sound of their own voices.

Chorus, Gr. and R. (χορὸς, i. e. prop. a circle). (1) A choir of singers in a dramatic entertainment. (2) A band of dancers who went through their movements to the sound of their

Fig. 158. Apollo wearing the chlamys folded round his arm.

own singing. (3) A round choral dance ; in this last signification *chorea* may equally well be used.

Chorus or **Choron**, O. E.   An instrument somewhat resembling a bagpipe ; the name was also applied to certain stringed instruments. The word *choron* originally designated a horn. (Hebrew, *Keren.*)

Chous, Gr. and R. (χόos, contr. χοῦs, i. e. that from which one pours). An amphora, forming a measure of exact capacity. Another name for it was CONGIUS (q.v.). It held twelve COTYLÆ (q.v.).

Choutara, Hindoo.   A kind of guitar with four wire strings.

Chrism, Chr. (from χρίω, to smear). A composition of balsam and oil of olives used by Christians of various denominations at the administration of the sacraments.

Chrismal, Chrismatory, Chr. (1) The vessel made to contain the consecrated oil. (See LABARUM.) (2) A vessel for the reservation of the consecrated Host. (3) A cloth used to cover relics. (4) Old English *chrisom*, a white linen cloth put upon the child's head in baptism. (See FONT-CLOTH.)

Chrismarium, Chr.   (See CHRISMAL, 1.)

Chrisom, O. E. (1) See CHRISMAL, 4. (2) A child that dies within a month after birth.

Christ-cross, O. E. (1) The Alphabet; so named from a school lesson beginning "Christe Crosse me spede in alle my worke." (2) The mark made for his signature by a person who cannot write.

Christemporeia, Chr.   Literally, the selling of Christ, simony.

Christian Horses, O. E.   Bearers of sedan chairs.

Christmas-boxes.   So called from the old practice of collecting them in boxes.

Chromatic Scale (χρῶμα, colour).   In Music, the scale that proceeds by semi-tones ; so called from the practice of printing the intermediate notes in various colours.

Chromatics   The science of colours.

Chromatrope.   An optical instrument for assisting the invention of combinations of colours.

Chrome, Chromium.   An important mineral, the green oxide of which furnishes the *Chrome Green*.

Chrome Green.   A dark-green pigment prepared from oxide of chromium ; mixed with Prussian blue and chrome yellow it is called *Green Cinnabar*.

Chrome Ochre.   Oxide of chromium of a fine yellowish green.

Chrome Red.   A chromate of lead ; a durable pigment used in oil painting. (See RED LEAD.)

Chrome Yellow.   A chromate of lead, which makes a bad pigment for oil painting. It is very poisonous and not durable ; when mixed

with white lead it turns to a dirty grey. As a water-colour pigment it is less objectionable.

Chromite.   Chromate of iron ; a mineral consisting of protoxide of iron and oxide of chromium, used in the preparation of various pigments.

Chronogram (χρόνοs, time).   An inscription which includes in it the date of an event.

Chryselephantine Statues of ivory and gold. The most celebrated were that of *Minerva*, by Pheidias, which stood in the Acropolis at Athens, and was 40 English feet in height ; and that of Zeus, 45 feet high, likewise by Pheidias, in the temple of Olympia. A reproduction of this statue was shown in the Paris Exhibition of 1855.

Chrysendeta, R. (χρυσένδετα, i. e. set or inlaid with gold).   A very costly description of plate-service employed by wealthy Romans. Of its precise character nothing unfortunately is known, but to judge from the epigrams of certain authors, it must have been chased and embossed.

Chrysoberyl (βήρυλλοs, a beryl).   A gem of a yellowish-green colour ; a species of *corundum* (q.v.).

Chryso-clavus (Lat. *golden nail-head*).   All rich purple silks, woven or embroidered with the *clavus* in gold, were so named.   They were used for altar frontals, and the *clavi* were sometimes made so large that a subject was embroidered upon them ; they were then called *sigillata* or *sealed*. (See CLAVUS.)

Chrysocolla or **Gold Green** (χρυσόκολλοs, inlaid or soldered with gold). (1) Native verdigris. Its principal use was for the preparation of a solder for gold. (See SANTERNA.) (2) The Greek term for *Green Verditer* and *Armenian Green* (Latin, *Armenium*) ; a pigment obtained from *malachite* and green carbonate of copper. It was also called *pea green* or *grass green*.

Chthonia, Gr. and R. (χθών, the earth).   Festivals held every spring at Argos in honour of Ceres, at which four aged women sacrificed heifers.

Church, in Christian art, is the attribute of a founder thereof, who is frequently represented holding it in his hand.   The most ancient symbol of the Church is the *ark of Noah*, subsequently a *ship*, often covered with the waves, &c., very frequent in the catacombs.   On tombs it is held to imply that the dead expired in full communion with the Church.

Churcheard, Church-haw, Church-litten. Old English provincialisms for a churchyard or burial-ground.

Church-stile, O. E.   A pulpit.

Chymbe, O. E.   A cymbal :—

"As a *chymbe* or a brazen belle,
That nouther can undirstonde my telle."

Chymol, Gemell, O. E. A hinge, still called the eastern counties a "gimmer."

Chytra, Gr. and R. (from χέω, to pour). A common kind of pot, of Greek origin, made with red clay. It was used for cooking.

Chytria, Gr. An Athenian festival, which derived its name from the χύτρα, or common pot in which were cooked the vegetables or other provisions offered to Bacchus and Mercury in memory of the dead.

Chytropus, Chytropous, Gr. (χυτρό-πους, lit. a pot-foot). A *chytra* with three or four feet.

Cibilla. (See CILLIBA.)

Ciborium, Gr., R., and Chr. (κιβώριον, the pod of the καλοκασία, or Egyptian bean). (1) A drinking vessel so called because it resembled the Egyptian bean in shape. (2) In Christian archæology a kind of baldachino or canopy, supported by a varying number of columns, which forms the covering of the high altar in a church. Called also the *Tabernacle, Sacrament house, God's house,* or *holyroof.* (See SEVEREY.) (3) Ciborium also signifies a vessel in which the consecrated wafer is "reserved."

Ciclatoun or **Siklatoun.** The Persian name, adopted in England, for a textile of real gold thread ; 12th century.

Ciconia, R. (lit. a stork). (1) A sign made in dumb show by bending the forefinger into the form of a stork's neck. (2) An instrument, in shape like an inverted T, employed by farmers to make sure that trenches dug by the spade were of uniform depth. (3) *Ciconia composita* was the name given to a more elaborate instrument of the same kind invented by Columella.

Cicuta, R. (i. e. lit. the hemlock). A term used by analogy to denote anything made out of the hemlock plant, especially the *Pan's pipes.*

Cidaris, Gen. (κίδαρις or κίταρις, a Persian tiara). A sort of diadem or royal bonnet worn by Eastern princes. It was tall, straight and stiff in shape, and was ornamented with pearls or precious stones. The same name was also applied to the bonnet worn at ceremonies by the high priest of the Jews. (See TIARA.)

Cilery, Arch. Drapery or foliage carved on the heads of columns.

Cilibantum, R. (See CILLIBA.) A stand or table with three legs.

Cilicium, R. (1) A coarse cloth made of goat's hair, and manufactured in Cilicia. It was much used in the army and navy : in the former for making the soldiers' tents ; in the latter for clothes for the sailors or for sails. (2) During the time of mourning, or when suffering under any calamity, the Jews put on a kind of *cilicium* made of coarse canvas. (3) A cloth mattress stuffed with sea-weed or cow-hair, which was placed outside the walls of besieged cities to deaden the blows of the battering-ram or of projectiles. (4) In Christian archæology the *cilicium* or hair-shirt is a sleeveless jacket made with a material of horse-hair and coarse hemp. The Dominicans, Franciscans, and certain Carthusians wear the *cilicium* to mortify the flesh.

Cilliba, Gr. and R. (κίλλος, an ass). A trestle, and by analogy a dining-table supported by trestles. This form of table, which was commonly used by the early Romans, was replaced later on by the circular table.

Cimbal. An old name for the DULCIMER (q.v.).

Cimeter, Cymetar, Scimeter, &c. A short curved sword used by the Persians or Turks, mentioned by Meyrick as adopted by the Hussars, *temp.* Elizabeth.

Cincinnus, R. A long ringlet or corkscrew curl of hair produced with the curling-irons. (See HAIR.)

Cincticulus, R. (dimin. of CINCTUS, q.v.). A kind of short petticoat worn by youths.

Cinctorium, R. (from *cinctus,* a girdle). (1) A sword-belt worn round the waist, and thus distinguished from the BALTEUS or baldric, which passed over the shoulder. The *balteus* was worn by private soldiers, while the *cinctorium* was the distinctive badge of an officer. (2) The dagger, so called because it was suspended from or put into the girdle.

Cincture, Arch. The fillet, at each end of the shaft of a classical column (q.v.).

Cinctus, R. (from *cingo,* i. e. a girding). A short petticoat (or kilt) worn by men ; also in the same sense as *cingula* and *cingulum,* a *girdle. Cinctus gabinus* was a particular manner of arranging the toga, by throwing one end over the head, and fastening the other round the waist like a girdle. As an adjective, *cinctus* was applied to any individual of either sex who wore any kind of belt or girdle. (See DISCINCTUS.)

Cinerarium, R. (i. e. a place of ashes). A niche in a tomb, sufficiently roomy to hold an urn of large size, or a sarcophagus. The following was the disposition of one, or in many cases, three sides in a Roman tomb : in the centre of

Fig. 160. Cineraria.

the wall was a large niche (*cinerarium medianum*) for a sarcophagus, and on each side of this two small niches (*columbaria*), and above each of the latter was a much larger recess for large urns. (See also COLUMBARIUM, CUBICULUM, CUPELLA.)

Cinerarius. A hair-dresser (who heated his tongs in the *cinders*).

Cingulum, R. A girdle or other fastening round the waist. In modern archæology, *cingulo militari decorare* signifies to create a knight, from the practice of investing him with the military girdle ; and *cingulum militare auferre* is to degrade a knight. (See DISCINCTUS.)

Ciniflo, R. A synonym for CINERARIUS (q.v.).

Cinnabar. Sulphide of mercury ; an ancient red pigment used for sacred and imperial purposes. (See CHROME GREEN, DRAGON'S BLOOD, VERMILION.)

Cinnamon-stone. A variety of lime-garnet of a clear cinnamon-brown tint.

Cinque-cento (literally, 500). The Italian art of the 16th century.

Fig. 161. Heraldic Cinque-foil.

Cinque-foil, Arch. (Fr. *cinque* and *feuille*, a leaf). An ornamental foliation or feathering of the lanceolated style, consisting of five projecting points or cusps. (Fig. 161.)

Cinta, Med. Lat. (Fr. *enceinte*). The outside wall of a fortress.

Cinyra. An oid term for a harp.

Cippus, R. (1) A short stone pillar of cylindrical form, employed to mark the boundaries between adjoining estates or nations. (2) A pillar of cylindrical or rectangular form, and sometimes perfectly plain, sometimes richly ornamented, erected for a tomb-stone. (Fig. 162.) In some instances the cippus enclosed a cavity in which the urn containing the ashes of the dead person might be placed. A *cippus* was placed at the corner of a cemetery, and the measurements of the burying-ground were recorded upon it. In Med. Lat. the word is used for the keep of the castle.

Fig. 162. Cippus (Tomb-stone).

Circenses Ludi, R. Games in the circus. (See CONSUALIA.)

Circinate. Curled in the manner of the Ionic volute, or like the fronds of young ferns rolled inwards from the summit to the base.

Circinus, R. A compass ; an instrument employed, as now, by architects, sculptors, masons, and various other trades. The Romans were also acquainted with reduction compasses.

Circle. The emblem of Heaven and eternity.

Circumlitio. An ancient Greek varnish, with which the statues of the Greeks were tinted. (*Eastlake.*)

Circumpotatio, R. (from *circum* and *poto*, i. e. a drinking-around). A funeral feast in which the guests passed round the wine from hand to hand. It took place at the tomb of the person in whose memory it was held, and on the anniversary of his death.

Circumvallation. A fortification made round a blockaded place by a besieging army.

Circus, Gr. and R. (i. e. a circle). A flat open space near a city, round which were raised scaffoldings for the accommodation of the spectators. This was the form of the earliest circuses ; but as civilization advanced, they were regularly constructed of stone. The arena was in the form of a vast rectangle terminating at one extremity in a semicircle, and surrounded

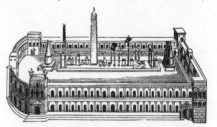

Fig. 163. Model of a Roman Circus.

by tiers of seats for the spectators. At the end fronting the semicircular part was a rectangular pile of buildings, underneath which were the *carceres* or stalls for the horses, and down the centre of the circus ran a long low wall called the *spina*, adorned with statues, obelisks, &c. This *spina* formed a barrier by which the circus was divided into two distinct parts, and at each end of it was a *meta* or goal, round which the chariots turned. (See META and OVUM.) The Romans constructed circuses in England, wherever they had a large encampment. The ruins exist at Dorchester, Silchester, Richborough, and other places.

Cirrus, R. (1) A lock of hair ; a ringlet curling naturally, and so distinguished from the *cincinnus*, a curl produced by means of the curling-iron. (2) A tuft ; the forelock of a horse when tied up above its ears. (3) A tuft of flowers forming a bunch or head, such as *phlox, calceolaria*, &c. (4) Light *curled* clouds in the sky, portending wind, are hence called *cirri*.

Ciselure, Fr. Chasing. (See CÆLATURA.)

Cissibium or **Cissybium**, Gr. and R. (κισσύβιον, i. e. made or wreathed with ivy). A drinking-vessel, so called because the handle was made of ivy-wood, or more probably because it had an ivy-wreath carved upon it.

Cissoid (lit. ivy-shaped). A celebrated curve, applied in the trisection of an angle, invented by Diocles the geometer.

Cissotomiæ, Gr. (κισσο-τόμοι, sc. ἡμέραι, i. e. the days of ivy-cutting). A festival held in Greece, in honour of Hebe, goddess of youth, and a youth called Cissos, who, when dancing with Bacchus, had fallen down and been changed into ivy. Accordingly at this festival youths and girls danced with their heads wreathed with ivy.

Cista, **Cistella**, **Sitella**, R. (κίστη, a chest). (1) A large wicker-work basket in which the voters deposited their voting-tablets at the comitia. It was of a cylindrical shape, and about four or five feet high. (2) A smaller basket into which the judges cast the tablets recording their sentence. (3) A wicker-work basket in which children carried about their playthings. (4) The cist which was carried in procession at the Eleusinian festival, and which might be either a wicker basket or a box of metal. It was filled with corn, rice, sesame, salt, and pomegranates. Richly ornamented chests or boxes, with bronze mirrors in them, found among Etruscan ruins, are called *cistæ mysticæ*. The *sitella*, or *situla*, was a different vessel ; viz. a *bucket* of water, into which the lots (*sortes*) were thrown. The situla had a narrow neck, so that only one lot could come to the surface when it was shaken. It was also called *Urna* or *Orca*.

Cistella, R. A dulcimer ; *lit.* a little box. (See CISTA.)

Cistellula, R. (dimin. of CISTA, q. v.). A very small *cista*.

Cistophorus, Egyp., Gr., and R. (κιστοφόρος, i.e. bearing a *cista* or *cistus*). A silver coin, current in Asia, and worth about four drachmæ. It was so called from bearing the impression of a *cista* (chest), or, more probably, of the shrub *cistus*. [Value four francs of French money.]

Cistula, R. Dimin. of CISTA (q.v.).

Citadel (It. *cittadella*, a little town). A fortress within a city.

Cithara, **Cither**, Gr. and R. (κιθάρα). A stringed instrument of great antiquity, resembling our modern guitar. It was played with a *plectrum*. The name was afterwards applied to many stringed instruments of varied form, power of sound, and compass. The mediæval *Rotta* was called *C. teutonica ;* the harp was called *C. Anglica.*

Cithara Bijuga. A guitar with a double neck.

Citole, O. E. A kind of guitar.

" A *citole* in hir right hand had sche." (*Chaucer.*)

Cittern. A stringed instrument, like a guitar, strung with wire instead of gut. The *cittern* was at one time a part of the furniture of every barber's shop, and customers played on it while waiting for their turns. (Niche 1 of Exeter Gallery. See CLARION.)

Civery, Arch. (See SEVEREY.) A bay or compartment of a vaulted ceiling.

Civic Crown, Her. A wreath of oak-leaves and acorns. (See CORONA.)

Ckuicui, Peruvian. One of the divisions of the temple of the Sun (*Inti*), so named as being dedicated to the rainbow (*Ckuichi*). (See INTI.)

Clabulare. (See CLAVULARE.)

Clack or **Clap-dish**, O. E. A box with a movable lid used and rattled by beggars to attract attention :—

" His tongue moves like a beggar's *clapdish*."

Cladeuteria. A Greek festival held in honour of Bacchus, at the time when the pruning of the vines took place.

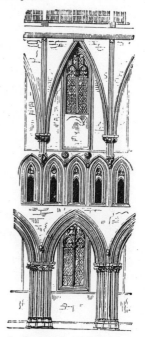

Fig. 164. Clerestory and Triforium in Worcester Cathedral.

Claire-voie (Anglicè, **Clerestory**), Arch. (i. e. clear-storey). A row of large windows, forming the upper storey of the nave of a church, rising clear above the adjoining parts of the building.

Clan (Gaelic, *klann,* children). A tribe of persons of one common family, united under a chieftain.

Clap-bene, O. E. *Bene* signifies a prayer, and children were invited by this phrase to *clap* their hands together, as their only means of expressing their prayers.

Clapdish. (See CLACKDISH.)

Clappe or **Clapper,** O. E. A wooden rattle used to summon people to church on the last three days of Passion Week, when the bells were not rung.

Clarenceux, Her. The title of one of the three kings of arms at Heralds' College. The others are called GARTER and NORROY.

Clarichord, O. E. A stringed instrument, in the form of a spinet, of mediæval times. At the marriage of James of Scotland with the Princess Margaret, A.D. 1503, " the king began before hyr to play of the *clarychordes,* and after of the lute. And upon the said clarychorde Sir Edward Stanley played a ballad, and sange therewith." (*Wharton,* "*History of English Poetry.*") It is identical with the *clavichord,* the origin of the spinet, harpsichord, and pianoforte.

Clarion, O. E. A small trumpet, with a shrill sound. (Represented in the third niche of the "Minstrels' Gallery" of Exeter Cathedral, of which there is a cast in the South Kensington Museum.)

Fig. 165, 166. Clarions (heraldic).

Classic Orders of Architecture. The *Grecian:*

Doric, Ionic, and Corinthian ;—and the *Roman :* Tuscan, Doric, Ionic, Corinthian, and Composite orders (q.v.) are generally thus distinguished.

Clathrate. Latticed like a grating (*clathri*).

Fig. 167. Clathri over bronze doors.

Clathri, R. A grating or trellis formed of wooden or metal bars ; *clathri* were employed to form the imposts over hypæthral doors, and to light the stables (*carceres*) under the circus, &c. Fig. 167 represents one of the bronze doors of the Pantheon at Rome with the grating above.

Claude Glass. A dark convex glass for studying the effect of a landscape in reverse.

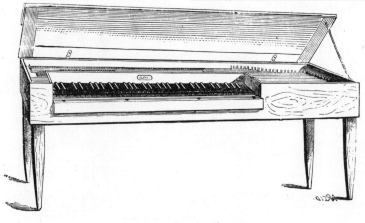

Fig. 168. Clavichord—18th century.

Its name is supposed to be derived from the similarity of the effects it gives, to those of a picture by Claude Lorrain.

Clausula, R. The handle of any instrument whatsoever, when made in such a way that the hand can be inserted into it, as for instance with a ring or sword-hilt. The STRIGILIS (q.v.) had a handle of this description. *Clausula* is thus to be distinguished from *capulus* (a straight handle), and *ansa* (a handle affixed to another object).

Clava, R. (1) A stout knotty stick, growing much thicker towards one end. (2) A very heavy club with which young recruits went through their exercises. (3) A club like that of Hercules, or a mace or war-club with an iron head, and studded with nails or (more commonly) sharp spikes.

Clavate. Club-shaped; tapering down from the top.

Clavesignati, Med. Lat. The Papal troops were so called, who had the keys of St. Peter on their standards and uniforms.

Claviary. In Music, an index of keys.

Clavichord. A stringed instrument in the form of a spinet. (Fig. 168.) (See CLARICHORD.)

Clavicula. Dimin. of CLAVIS (q.v.).

Clavier. Of a musical instrument, the keyboard.

Clavis, R. A key. The *clavis clausa* was a small key without a neck or lever; *clavis laconica*, a key of Egyptian invention, having three teeth; *clavis adultera*, a false key; *clavis trochi*, a curved stick made of iron and having a hook at the end, which was used by Greek and Roman boys for trundling their hoops.

Clavius. A walled plain in the moon, more than a hundred miles in diameter.

Clavulare or **Clabulare**, R. A large open cart used for carrying provisions, especially *dolia* (casks) filled with wine. The body of the carriage was formed by a wooden trellis-work (*clavulæ*)—whence its name—and was of a semi-cylindrical shape, adapted to accommodate wine barrels.

Clavus, R. A nail. In Christian archæology, a purple hem or band applied as an ornament to a dress, which was then called *vestis clavata*. (See CHRYSO-CLAVUS.)

Claymore (Gaelic, *claidheamb*, a sword, and *mor*, great). The highland broadsword.

Clechée, Her. (See UNDÉE.) A variety of the heraldic cross.

Clef or **Cliff**, Music. A figure indicating the pitch to be adopted for the key-note of a piece of music; an invention of the 13th century.

Clepsydra, Gen. (κλεψ-ύδρα, i. e. a stealing-away of water). A water-clock, and by analogy an hour-glass or *sand*-clock. The *clepsydra* was used as an hour-glass in the courts of justice at Athens, to measure out the time allowed to each orator.

Clerestory. (See CLAIRE-VOIE.)

Cleystaffe, O. E. A pastoral staff.

Clibanus, R. (1) A basket used for baking bread; the bread itself, when thus baked, being called *clibanicius*. (2) Med. Lat. A short hauberk, which the later Greeks called κλίβανον, because it covered the breast. (*Meyrick*.) (3) Med. Lat. A tower.

Clicket, O. E. A key.

> "With his *clicket*
> Damian hath opened this wicket." (*Chaucer*.)

Cliff. (See CLEF.)

Clipeolum. Dimin. of CLIPEUS (q.v.).

Clipeus and **Clipeum**, R. (akin to καλύπτω,

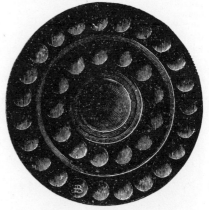

Fig. 169. Clipeus.

to cover or conceal). A large broad shield of circular shape and concave on the inside. It was of great weight, and formed part of the special equipment of the cavalry. The original *clipeus Argolicus* was circular, and often likened

Fig. 170. Ornamental Clipeus.

to the sun : in Roman sculpture it is often oval. The outer rim was termed *antyx ;* the *boss* in the centre, *omphalos,* or *umbo;* a leather strap for the arm, *telamon.* It was replaced, subsequently, by the SCUTUM (q.v.). Fig. 169 is an ornamented bronze *clipeus,* thought to be Gaulish. This term also serves to denote (1) a shield of metal or marble which was employed as an ornament (Fig. 170 represents an ornamental shield, such as was placed on the frieze of a building, and especially in the metopes of the Doric entablature) ; and (2) an apparatus employed in the *laconicum* (q.v.) to regulate the temperature. In the illustration to *Caldarium* a slave may be seen pulling the chains of the *clipeus.*

Cloaca, R. (from *cluo,* i. e. the cleanser). A subterranean sewer or canal constructed of masonry. The *Cloaca Maxima,* or Main Sewer

Fig. 171. Cloaca Maxima at Rome.

of Rome, was constructed by the elder Tarquin to drain a marsh lying at the foot of the Palatine and Capitoline Hills. Fig. 171 represents one of its mouths. It was formed of three tiers of arches, the innermost being fourteen feet in diameter.

Clocks, O. E., "are the gores of a ruff, the laying in of the cloth to make it round, the plaites ;" also ornaments on stockings and on hoods.

Clog-almanacks. The Anglo-Saxons calculated by the phases of the moon, set down on square pieces of wood, a foot or two long. These *clogs* are still common in Staffordshire. (Cf. *Plott's History of Staffordshire; Gough's Camden's Britannia,* ii. 379.)

Cloish, or **Closh,** O. E. A kind of nine-pins played with a ball. (*Strutt,* p. 202.) Cf. CLUB-KAYLES.

Cloisonné. A form of enamelling by incrus-

tation, in which the pattern is raised by strips of metal or wire welded on.

Cloister, Chr. (from Lat. *claustrum,* q. v.). A kind of court or quadrangle surrounded by a covered way, and having much analogy to the *atrium* of a Roman house. The cloister was an essential appendage to an abbey. One of its sides was usually bounded by the church, with which it easily communicated. The walls of the cloisters were often adorned with frescoes, and the court was occasionally planted with trees, the centre being occupied by a fountain. A monastery was often called a *cloister.* The sides of the cloister were anciently termed the PANES of it, and the walks its alleys or deambulatories. (Fig. 173.)

Fig. 172. Clustered column in Nave of Wells Cathedral.

Cloister Garth. The quadrangular space enclosed by the cloisters. The *cloister garth* at Chichester is still called the *Paradise,* and that at Chester the *Sprise* garden. (See PARADISE, SPRISE.)

Close, Her. With closed wings.

Close-gauntlets. Gauntlets with immovable fingers.

Closet, Her. A diminution of the BAR, one-half its width.

Cloths of Estate. Costly embroidered hangings for the canopy of a throne.

Clouée, Her. Fastened with nails, and showing the nail-heads.

Clouts. Old name for kerchiefs.

Clown, in pantomime. *Harlequin* is Mercury, the *Clown* Momus, and the painted face and wide mouth taken from the ancient masks ; *Pantaloon* is Charon, and *Columbine* Psyche. (*Clarke's Travels,* viii. 104-7.)

Club, Gr. and R. (Gr. φάλαγξ). This weapon being used in close fight gave its name to the compact body of troops so called. The Scythians united it with the mace, both being spiked. *Ducange* mentions the *vulgastus,* a crooked club ; the *plumbata,* loaded with lead,

Fig. 173. Cloisters in the Church of Mont St. Michel.

the *spontonus* with iron. In the army of Charles I. rustics untrained were called clubmen. (See CLAVA.)

Club-kayles, O. E. Skittles played with a club, instead of a ball. (See CLOISH.)

Clubs, at cards, are the ancient *trèfles*, the trefoil or clover-plant. (See TREFLE.)

Cluden, Gr. and R. A sword, the blade of which was contrived to recede into the handle. It was used for theatrical representations.

Fig. 174. Clunaculum.

Clunaculum, R. (1) A dagger so called because it was worn at the back; "*quia ad clunes pendet*," as Festus says. (2) The sacrificial knife with which the victim was ripped up. The dagger represented in Fig. 174, taken from the arch of Carpentras, was probably a Gaulish *clunaculum*.

Clustered Column, Arch. A pier formed of a congeries of columns or shafts clustered together, either attached or detached. It is also called a COMPOUND PIER. Fig. 172 is a specimen from Wells Cathedral.

Clypeate. Shaped like a shield.

Cnopstara. A weapon used by the Caledonians; a ball filled with pieces of metal swung at the heads of their lances, to frighten cavalry.

Coa Vestis, or simply **Coa** (i. e. the Coan robe). A very fine robe [made of silk, spun in *Cos*], of such light texture as to be almost transparent. It was worn by *hetairai* and singing and dancing girls, &c.

Coactilis, sc. *lana* (from *cogo*, i. e. that which is forced together). A kind of felted cloth made of wool closely pressed together. It formed a texture analogous to our felt. Another name for it was *coactus*.

Coal as an ancient pigment was used both in water-colours and in oil; it furnishes a brownish tint. " The shadows of flesh are well rendered by pit-coal, which should not be burnt." (*De Mayerne.*)

Coassatio (from *coasso*, to join planks together). A general term for planks joined together, such as the flooring of a room, the top of a table, the deck of a ship, the road-way of a wooden bridge, &c. (See CONSTRATUM.)

Fig. 175. Coat Armour.

Fig. 176. Coat Armour. Devices on shield.

Coat Armour, Med. Embroidery of heraldic devices upon costume; hence a term for heraldry in general. (Figs. 175 and 176.)

Coat Cards, O. E. Court cards and tens, so named from the *coat armour* worn by the figures.

Cob. Irish name of a Spanish coin formerly current in Ireland; value about 4*s.* 8*d.*

Cobalt. A metal found in various combinations, from which various colouring matters are obtained of great use in the arts. *Cobalt blue,* a beautiful blue pigment, is obtained by mixing a salt of pure cobalt with a solution of pure alum, precipitating the liquid by an alkaline carbonate, washing the precipitate with care, drying and igniting it strongly. A fine green, known as *Rinmann's green,* is similarly prepared. The chloride, the nitrate, and the sulphate of cobalt form *sympathetic inks,* which only become visible when the moisture is absorbed by the application of heat. From phosphate of cobalt a beautiful blue pigment is produced, called *Thenard's blue.* It is said to have all the characters of ultramarine. Oxide of cobalt has the property of colouring glass blue; hence a glass formed of this oxide under the name of *smalt* is the blue colouring matter used for ornamenting porcelain and earthenware, for staining glass, for painting on enamel, &c.

Cobalt-bloom. (See ERYTHRINE.)

Cobbards, O. E. The irons supporting a spit.

Cob-wall, Arch. A wall formed of unburned clay mixed with straw.

Cochineal. (See CARMINE.)

Cochineal Lakes. (See CARMINATED LAKES.)

Cochlea (κοχλίας, i. e. a snail with spiral shell). Any object of spiral shape, like a screw; and so a worm and screw as a mechanical power in oil-, wine-, &c. presses; the "Archimedean Screw," or " water-snail " for raising water; the revolving door through which the wild beasts were let out into the amphitheatre; and other contrivances similar to the Italian *ruota,* by which persons can be introduced through a wall without opening a door; also a spiral staircase, &c.

Cochlear, Cochleare (from κόχλος, a shell-fish). (1) A spoon having at one extremity a sharp point, and at the other a sort of small bowl. (2) A measure of capacity of very small size.

Cochlearium, R. A pond or nursery for fattening snails for the table. (English "cockles.")

Cochlis, sc. *columna* (κοχλìς, i. e. lit. a snail). A hollow monumental column, the interior of which was fitted with a cockle or spiral staircase, like the "Monument" of London.

Cock. In Christian art, the emblem of St. Peter, and of watchfulness.

Cockatrice. In Christian art, the emblem of sin; attribute of St. Vitus. (Her.: see the illustration to BASILISK.)

Cock-bead, Arch. A bead which projects from the surface of the timber on both sides.

Cockers, O. E. Ploughmen's laced boots.

Cocket, O. E. A seal formerly attached to goods which had paid customs dues. Ancient *cockets* bear such inscriptions on them as "*God willing,*" "*If God please,*" &c.

Cockle-stairs, O. E. Winding stairs. (Cf. COCHLEA.)

Coctilis, Cocta, Coctus, R. (prepared by fire). *Later coctilis* was a brick hardened artificially by fire, in contradistinction to one dried in the sun; *murus coctilis,* a wall built of hardened bricks. (See ACAPNA.)

Cocurra, Med. Lat. A quiver.

Cocytia (from Κωκυτὸς, the river of weeping). A festival held in honour of Proserpine, who had been carried off by Pluto. The latter, as king of the infernal regions, included in his sway the river Cocytus. The Cocytus and Acheron, two rivers of Epirus, remarkable for unwholesome and muddy water, and subterranean currents, were hence called the rivers of Hell. "Cocytia virgo" was Alecto, one of the Furies.

Cod, Scotch. A pillow (also *pod*).

Codex (*caudex,* the trunk of a tree). (1) A blank book for writing in, consisting of thin tablets of wood covered with wax; the term thus came to mean *code,* that is, a book containing laws, since these were inscribed in a book, the leaves of which were composed of thin leaves of wood. When parchment or paper was introduced, the term was still applied; and hence, later, became appropriate to any code of laws, e. g. the Gregorian, Theodosian, Justinian, &c. (2) An early manuscript book, such as the Codex of the Greek New Testament and of "Virgil" in the Vatican. (3) The term was also applied to the heavy logs attached to the feet of slaves; these were of various shapes, sometimes even serving the purpose of a seat.

Codicillus (dimin. of CODEX, q.v.). A small book, or small leaves of wood covered with wax. The plural *codicilli* denoted a number of such sheets put together so as to form a sort of memorandum-book for taking rough notes. Any supplemental note made on the margin of the leaves composing a will, or added to them, was also called *codicillus* (codicil).

Codon (Gr. κώδων). A bell; the bell of a trumpet; a trumpet with a bell-mouth.

Cod-piece (from O. E. "cod," a pillow or stuffed cushion; Fr. *braguette*); introduced *temp*. Henry VIII. An appendage to the taces over the os pubis, copied in the armour of the period. It continued in use to the end of Elizabeth's reign.

Cœlum. In Architecture, that part of a building which was placed over any other part, and so a ceiling, or soffit.

Cœmeterium, Cemetery, Chr. (κοιμητήριον, from κοιμάω, i. e. a sleeping-place; Lat *dormitorium*). This term is an exclusively Christian one; it signifies a field of rest or refuge; the last resting-place of man. (See HYPOGÆUM.)

Cœna (from Sanscr. *khad-*, to eat). The principal meal among the Romans, consisting of several courses termed respectively *prima, altera* or *secunda, tertia, quarta cœna*. The hour at which the *cœna* took place varied with the habits of the master of the house, but it was usually about four or five o'clock. It was the third meal of the day, being preceded by the *jentaculum* (breakfast), and the *merenda* or *prandium* (luncheon or early dinner). The corresponding Greek meal was called *deipnon*, which closed with a libation to Zeus; after which the drinking party that remained was called *Symposium*. (See LAST SUPPER.)

Cœnaculum. In early times this term was used for the TRICLINIUM (q.v.); later on it came to mean the upper stories of houses inhabited by the poor, our attic or garret. In the plural, *cœnacula* denotes the whole suite of rooms on the upper story of a house, and *cœnacula meritoria* such apartments let out on hire.

Cœnatio, like *cœnaculum*, a dining-room situated upstairs. It thus differed from the TRICLINIUM (q.v.), which was a dining-room on the ground floor; the former was used in

winter, the latter in summer. The *cœnatio*, or *diæta*, was a very magnificent apartment. Nero had one in his golden palace, constructed like a theatre, with a change of scenery for every course.

Cœnatoria, Cœnatoriæ Vestes. The garments worn by the Romans at the dinner-table.

Cœnobium (κοινό-βιον, i. e. a life in common). A monastery; a convent of monks who lived in common.

Cœur, Carreau, Pique, and **Trèfle.** The four French suits of cards, corresponding with our Hearts, Diamonds, Spades, and Clubs, probably introduced in the reign of Charles VII. of France (15th century). (*Taylor*.) Cœur is sometimes derived from *Chœur*. (See COPPE and CHATRANG.)

"The hearts are the ecclesiastics, whose place is in the *choir*; the pike the military, &c." (*Menestrier*.)

Coffer. (See ARCA.) (1) In Architecture, a sunken panel in a ceiling or soffit. (2) A chest.

Cognizance, Her. Synonym for *Badge*.

Cogware, O. E. A coarse narrow cloth like frieze; 16th century.

Cohors, Cohort, R. A body of infantry forming the tenth part of a legion. The number of men composing a cohort varied at different periods between 300 and 600 men, according to the numerical strength of the legion. The first cohort of a legion was called a military cohort; the prætorian cohort formed the general's body-guard, while to the city cohort was entrusted the protection of the city. The term was sometimes, though very rarely, applied to a squadron of cavalry.

Coif or **Quoif.** A close hood.

Coif de Fer, Coiffette. A skull-cap of iron of the 12th and 13th centuries.

Coif de Mailles. A hood of mail worn by knights in the 12th century.

Coiffe, Arch. A term employed during the 16th and 17th centuries to denote the vaulted ceiling of an apse.

Coillon. (See COIN.)

Fig. 177. Helmet with Cointise behind.

Coin or **Coigne,** Arch. The corner of a building. (See QUOIN.)

Coin-stones, Arch. Corner-stones.

Cointise or **Quintise.** (1) A scarf wrapped round the body, and sometimes attached to the helmet. (2) Quaintly-cut coverings for the helmet. Fig. 177 represents a helmet decorated with PANACHE, CORONET, and *cointise*. This is the origin of *mantling* in heraldry. (3) A garment worn over armour, *temp*. Edward II., was so termed. (4) Horses' caparisons.

Colatorium. A colander. (See COLLUM VINARIUM.)

G

Colayn Riban, O. E. An ecclesiastical textile, or *orphrey web,* for the manufacture of which Cologne was famous in the 15th century.

Colcothar of Vitriol. A red pigment formerly called *caput mortuum.*

Cold-harbour. This common topical name is the Anglo-Saxon *cealdherberga,* cold "*herberge,*"or shelter, and probably indicates a place where the ruins of a Roman villa or station were the only available shelter for travellers, in the ancient scarcity of inns.

Fig. 178. Collar of Lancaster.

Collar (of a shaft), Arch. The ANNULET (q.v.). (See also COLLAR-BEAM.)

Collar, Med. (1) A defence of mail or plate for the neck. (2) Generally. An ornament for the neck. The Egyptians, Persians, Greeks, Romans, and Gauls wore collars, which were named variously *streptos* (στρεπτὸς), *torquis, torques,* &c. Collars were ornamented with heraldic *badges* in the Middle Ages. (3) Heraldic. One of the insignia of the orders of knighthood. (See Fig. 178.)

Fig. 179. Collar of S.S.

Collar of S.S. Originally adopted by Henry IV., on the canopy of whose tomb it is employed as decoration over the arms of himself and his queen. Its significance is doubtful. Camden says the letters are the initials of Sanctus Simo Simplicius, an eminent Roman lawyer, and that it was particularly worn by persons of the legal profession.

Collar-beam, Arch. A horizontal tie, connecting a pair of rafters together, across the vault of a roof.

Collare, R. (*collum,* neck). A collar made of iron or leather, and studded with spikes. It was used both to confine slaves, and as a dog-collar. When a slave ran away from his master, an iron collar, with a leading-chain attached to it, was put round his neck.

Collarium, Med. Armour for the neck.

Collegium, R. A religious or industrial corporation in ancient Rome. The corresponding Greek institutions were the *Hetairiai.* The *collegia* included trade companies or guilds.

Collet. The setting which surrounds the stone of a ring. (See CRAMPON.)

Colliciæ, Colliquiæ. (1) Broad open drains through fields. (2) Gutters of hollow tiles (*imbrices*) placed beneath the roof of a house to receive the rain-water, and convey it into the IMPLUVIUM.

Colliciaris (sc. *tegula*). A hollow tile employed in the construction of *colliciæ.*

Collodion. A solution of gun cotton in ether, used in photography.

Collum Vinarium (from *collum,* a neck). A colander or wine-strainer. The custom of straining wine dates back beyond our era, and Christ made an allusion to it when he told the Pharisees that their *colla* allowed a camel to pass, while they kept back a gnat. Snow was put into a strainer or a bag, called respectively *collum nivarium, saccus nivarius,* through which the wine was allowed to filter, not only to cool it, but because the intense cold cleared the wine, and rendered it sparkling and transparent; it was then called *vinum saccatum.* The Christian Church from the first adopted this instrument in its liturgy; another name for it was *colatorium.* (See NASSA.) The colander for wine was made of silver, or bronze, or other metal. The linen cloth called *saccus* was not used for wine of any delicacy, as it spoiled its flavour.

Colluviarium, R. An opening made at regular intervals in the channel of an aqueduct, for ventilation. As this opening formed a kind of well, it was also called PUTEUS (q.v.).

Collyra, Gr. and R. A kind of bread made in a special manner, which was eaten with soup or sauce; there was also a cake so called.

Collyris (κολλυρὶς, synonym of κολλύρα, q.v.).

Fig. 180. Collyrium or unguent Vase; Egyptian. Museum of the Louvre.

A head-dress worn by Roman ladies, resembling in shape the bread called κολλύρα; the latter was called κολλυρὶς as well.

Collyrium (κολλύριον, dimin. of κολλύρα, q.v.). (1) A term denoting anything we should now call an unguent, but especially the salve *collyrium*, which was a liquid medicament. (2) *Collyria* was a term applied to Egyptian vases of terracotta, with or without enamel; to small quadrangular boxes of wood or pottery; and, lastly, to small cylindrical cases of wood or bronze divided into compartments. There were three prevailing forms of the vases. The Egyptians used antimony to make their eyes look larger, and had some medicament for the relief of tooth-

Fig. 181. Roman Plebeian wearing the Colobium.

ache; and inscriptions indicating these uses may be read upon vessels of this kind. (Fig. 180).

Colne, O. E. A basket or coop.

Colobium (from κολοβὸs, docked or curtailed). A tunic with short sleeves, which scarcely covered the upper part of the arm. At Rome it was worn by men of free birth. The *colobium* appears to have been the first dress adopted by Christian deacons, and in the liturgical writings it is often met with under the name of *levitonarium;* when it was of fine linen, it was also called *lebiton* and *lebitonarium*. (Fig. 181.) Later on the sleeves were lengthened, and it became known as the DALMATIC (q.v.).

Cologne Black. (See BLACK.)

Cologne Earth. A bituminous earth of a violet-brown hue, transparent and durable in water-colour painting.

Colonica. Synonym of *villa rustica*. A farmhouse.

Color, Lat. (1) The term is used in several senses in mediæval treatises upon music, with a general idea of a quality of tone obtained by striking variations. (2) The coloured lines used in transcribing music. (See NEUMES.)

Colores Austeri. Ancient pigments, not *floridi*.

Colores Floridi. Ancient expensive and brilliant pigments. They were chrysocollum, indicum (or indigo), cæruleum (smalt), and cinnabar.

Colossus (κολοσσός). The word was used for all statues larger than life; that at Rhodes was ninety feet high. The Minerva and Jupiter Olympus of Pheidias, the Farnese Hercules, and the Flora of the Belvidere, were all colossal.

Colours, in Heraldry, are five: Blue or Azure, Red or Gules, Black or Sable, Green or Vert, Purple or Purpure. In French heraldry Green is Sinope. The uses and general symbolism of each colour are described under its own heading. The best work on *symbolic colours* is the "Essay" of M. Portal. One of the best on the *theory of colours* is that of Chevreuil.

Colubrina, Med. Lat. (from *coluber,* a snake). A culverin.

Columbar, R. A kind of pillory used for punishing slaves. The instrument derived its name from the holes in it, which bore some resemblance to pigeon-holes.

Columbarium. A dove-cote or pigeon-house, often constructed to hold as many as 4000 or 5000 birds. In the plural the term has many meanings. (1) It denotes the pigeon-holes or cells for the nests in a pigeon-house. (2) In a sepulchral chamber, the niches for holding the cinerary urns (*ollæ*). Fig. 182 represents the numerous *columbaria* in the tomb of the freedmen of Octavia. In the sepulchral architecture of the Jews, the rock-hewn walls forming the vestibules of certain tombs were honey-combed with minute *columbaria*, in which only lamps were placed. Fig. 183 represents cells of this character taken from the tomb of *Quoublet-el-*

Fig. 182. Columbarium.

Endeh. (3) The openings in the side of a ship through which the oars passed. (4) The holes

Fig. 183. Columbaria in rock-hewn walls.

made in a wall to receive the head of a tie-beam. (5) The openings of the scoops in a particular kind of hydraulic wheel called TYMPANUM (q. v.).

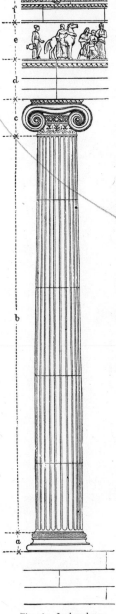

Fig. 184. Ionic column.

Columella. Dimin. of *columna*. (See COLUMN, CIPPUS.)

Columen, Gr. and R. The highest timber in the framework of a roof, forming what is now called the ridgepiece.

Column, Arch. A column consists of three principal parts: the base (*a*), the shaft (*b*), and the capital (*c*). In the *Doric*, or most ancient style, the columns in a row rest upon a common base (*podium*). In the Ionic and Corinthian, each column has its own base (*spira*). The shaft of all columns *tapers* gradually from the base to the capital. Any swelling introduced to modify the straightness of the line was called *entasis*. On the summit of a row of columns rests the *architrave*, or chief beam (*d*); above this the *frieze* (*e*), and the *cornice* (*f*) projects above the frieze. These three together are called the *entablature*. The triangular gable-end of the roof, above the entablature, is called the *pediment*. A circuit of columns, enclosing an open space in the interior of a building, was called a *peristyle*. A temple of two stories, with one peristyle upon another (Ionic or Corinthian columns over the heavier Doric), was called *hypæthral.* In Christian archæology the column is a symbol of the Church, which was called, so early as St. Paul, *columna et firmitatum veritatis* (the column and support of truth).

Colures. In Astronomy, the two circles which pass through the four cardinal points of the ecliptic—the equinoctial and solstitial points.

Coluria, Arch. Circular segments of stone, in the construction of a column, such as are now called tambours or disks.

Colus. A distaff. With the Romans it consisted of a thick cane (*arundo, donax*), split at the end in such a way that the opening formed a basket. *Compta, plena,* or *lana amicta* were the epithets applied to a *colus* when filled with wool. The thread obtained from it was called *stamen.* The ball of loose wool at one end, prepared for spinning, was called *glomus.* The lower end of the distaff rested under the left arm; the right hand spun and wound the thread on to the spindles (called *fusus*). (See DISTAFF.)

Colymbion, Chr., Med. A vessel for holy water at the entrance of a church.

Colymbus, Gr. and R. A basin or reservoir used either as a swimming-bath or for washing linen in.

Coma (κόμη). (1) The hair; hair of the head. (2) The mane of animals. (See CÆSARIES, CINCINNUS, HAIR, &c.)

Comatorius or **Comatoria** (sc. *acus*). A long pin or bodkin of gold, silver, bronze, or ivory, used by the Roman ladies to keep up their hair when plaited. It was also called ACUS CRINALIS (q.v.). (Compare DISCERNICULUM.)

Combattant, Her. Said of lions, or other animals of prey, rampant and face to face.

Combs (Lat. *pecten*, Gr. κτείς), as used for combing the hair, but not for wearing upon the head, are found in Pompeian and Egyptian tombs, and in the early British, Roman, and Saxon barrows. In the Middle Ages ivory combs were richly carved, and the ceremonial combs for use in ecclesiastical ceremonies are especially splendid. Greek and Roman combs were of boxwood; Egyptian combs were of ivory. Uncombed hair was a general sign of mourning. (See DISCERNICULUM.)

Commentaculum (from *commento,* to strike on the face). A staff or wand carried in sacred processions by the Roman priests to assist them in clearing a way and preventing the people from pressing in on them too closely. *Commotaculum* was also used.

Commissatio (from *commissor,* to revel). A revelling or feasting which began after the CŒNA (q.v.), and lasted far on into the night. (See SYMPOSIUM.)

Commistio or **Commixtio,** Chr. The placing of a portion of the bread into the chalice of wine, during the ceremony of consecration.

Common-house. The part of a monastery in which a fire was kept for the monks during winter.

Communicales, Chr. Communion vessels, made especially to be carried in procession in Rome.

Compass. In Music, the whole range of sounds capable of being produced by a voice or instrument.

Compass-headed, Arch. A semicircular arch.

Compass Roof, Arch. An open timber roof.

Compass Window, Arch. A bay-window on a circular plan.

Compes. (1) A ring of gold or silver worn by the Romans round the leg, just above the ankle. (2) The chains or shackles worn round the ankle by slaves or prisoners.

Compitalia, Compitales. A festival held by the Romans in honour of the *Lares compitales,* celebrated in the cross-roads, *compitia,* where the images of those deities were often placed in niches.

Fig. 185. Ancient Carved Ivory Comb.

Complement, Her. Applied to the moon, when full.

Complement. In Music, the interval to be added to another interval to make an octave; e.g. a third to a sixth; a fourth to a fifth, &c.

Complementary Colours. If the whole of the

light which is absorbed by a coloured body were reunited with the whole of the light which it reflects, white light would result ; in this case the absorbed colours are complementary to those which are reflected. The colour given by a mixture of the colours of any portion of a spectrum is the *complement* of the remaining portion. *Red* is complementary to *Green, Orange* to *Blue, Greenish Yellow* to *Violet, Indigo* to *Orange Yellow,* and, in each case, *vice versâ.*

Completorium, Chr. The last of the *Hours of Prayer.*

Compline, Chr. Short evening prayers completing the daily round of devotion prescribed by the *Hours of Prayer.*

Compluvium, R. An opening in the roof of the *atrium,* furnished with gutters all round, which collected the rain-water from the roof, and conveyed it into the basin (*impluvium*) in the middle of the atrium.

Compon-covert, O. E. A kind of lace.

Fig. 186. Capital of the Composite Order.

Composite Order of Architecture. The last of the five Roman orders, composed of the Ionic grafted upon the Corinthian order. The examples at Rome are in the arch of Septimus Severus, the arch of the Goldsmiths, the arch of Titus, the temple of Bacchus, and the baths of Diocletian.

Compound Arch, Arch. A usual form of mediæval arch, which " may be resolved into a number of concentric archways, successively placed within and behind each other." (*Prof. Willis.*)

Compound Pier, Arch. A clustered COLUMN (q.v.).

Compounded Arms, Her. Bearings of two or more distinct coats combined, to produce a single compound coat.

Comus (Gr. κῶμος). (1) A revel, or carousal which usually ended in the guests parading the streets crowned with garlands, &c. (2) Festal processions instituted in honour of Bacchus and

other gods, and of the victors at the games. (3) Odes written to be sung at such processions, e. g. those of Pindar.

Comus (Gr. κομμός, from κόπτω, to strike). (1) A beating of the head and breast in lamentation ; a dirge. (2) A mournful song sung in alternate verses by an actor and a chorus in the Attic drama.

Concædes. A barricade constructed of trees which have been cut down and placed across the road (to impede the enemy's march).

Concamerate, Arch. To arch over ; to vault.

Concave. Hollowed in ; opposed to *convex,* bulging out.

Concha (lit. a muscle or cockle). (1) A shell or shell-fish. (2) A Triton's conch. In works of art, the Triton, or sea-god, has for a trumpet the *buccina,* remarkable for a spiral twist, long and straight ; or the *murex,* equally twisted, but short and wide-mouthed. (3) The term was applied, by analogy, to various objects having the shape of a shell, such as cups or vases used for holding perfumes or for other purposes. (4) In Architecture, an apse, or a plain concave of a dome, is so called.

Conchoid. A mathematical curve in the form of the outline of a shell.

Conclave (with a key), Chr. (1) A meeting of cardinals assembled to elect a pope ; and (2) the hall or apartment in which such meeting is held. The institution of the conclave dates from Gregory X.

Concrete, Arch. A mixture of gravel, pebbles, or broken stone with cement.

Condalium (κονδύλιον, dimin. of κόνδυλος, a knob or joint). A ring generally worn upon the first joint of the forefinger on the right hand.

Conditivium, Conditorium. (1) An underground vault in which were chests or coffins for holding bodies which had not been reduced to ashes. (2) A sarcophagus in which the body was placed. (3) A kind of arsenal or magazine in which military engines were kept.

Condrak, O. E. A kind of lace.

Condyle. A knuckle ; the rounded end of a bone ; hence—

Condyloid. Shaped like a *condyle ;* and

Condylus. Synonym of CONDALIUM (q.v.).

Cone. A figure broad and round at the base, tapering upwards regularly towards a point.

Coney, Cony, O. E. (1) A variety of the rabbit. (2) A beehive.

Confessio, Chr. Originally the place where a saint or martyr was buried ; thence the altar raised over his grave ; and subsequently the chapel or basilica built there.

Congé, Arch. The cavetto (hollow moulding) which unites the *base* and *capital* of a column to its shaft.

Congius (deriv. doubtful). A Roman measure

containing six *sextarii* or twelve *heminæ*. It was used especially for measuring liquids. *Angl.* a pint and a half.

Conic Sections. Curves formed by the intersection of a *cone* and a *plane;* the circle, the ellipse, the hyperbola, and the parabola.

Conisterium, Gr. and R. A room in which wrestlers, after having had oil applied to their bodies, were rubbed over with fine sand (κόνις). The *conisterium* was an appendage to a palæstrum, gymnasium, &c.

Conopeum, Canopium, Gr. and R. (from κώνωψ, a gnat). A musquito-net, of very light material, introduced into Rome from Egypt. [This is the origin of the English word *canopy.*]

Consecratio, R. A kind of apotheosis or deification by which a mortal was enrolled in the number of the gods. It was unknown under the republic, and was only instituted in the time and on behalf of the emperors. The ceremony was solemnized in the Field of Mars, and with

Fig. 187. Consecrated pyre on Roman medal.

the greatest splendour. A magnificent pyre was raised, from the top of which, when kindled, an eagle was let fly, which was supposed to carry up to the skies the soul of the deified emperor. Fig. 187, taken from a medal, represents one of these pyres.

Consentiæ, Gr. and R. Festivals held in honour of the twelve principal divinities of Rome or Greece.

Consignatorium Ablutorum, Chr. In early times there were baptisteries near churches, with a place closely adjoining in which to administer the rite of confirmation; it was the place specially set apart for the administration of this rite that was called *consignatorium ablutorum.*

Console. A projecting ornament, in wood or stone, used as a bracket.

Constant White. SULPHATE OF BARYTES (q.v.).

Constellations. Groups of stars, mostly with classical names. *Ancient C.*, forty-eight formed by Ptolemy in A.D. 150, with two others added by Tycho Brahe; *Modern C.*, fifty-nine others since formed, many by Helvetius at the end of the 17th century. (*Rossiter.*)

Constratum, R. A flooring constructed of planks. (See COASSATIO.)

Consualia, R. A festival of ancient Rome held in honour of the god *Consus.* It was from this festival that the games of the circus took their rise. Livy calls the god Neptunus Equestris. The feast was held with horse and chariot races. Horses and mules did no work, and were crowned with garlands during its celebration. The Rape of the Sabines took place at the first Consualia.

Contabulatio, R. The long parallel folds formed in any garment of ample size, such as the *toga, palla,* and *pallium.*

Contignatio, R. (a joining together of beams). The woodwork of beams and joists supporting the flooring in a building of several stories. The term is also used to denote the flooring and sometimes the story itself.

Continuous Impost, Arch. In Gothic architecture, the mouldings of an arch, when carried down to the ground without interruption, or anything to mark the impost-joint. (*Newlands.*)

Contoise, Fr. A flowing scarf worn attached to the helmet before 1350. (See COINTISE.)

Contomonobolum, R. A game which consisted in leaping over a wide space by aid of a pole (*contus*) which was used as a fulcrum.

Contorniate. A class of antique medals having the *contour*, or edge, marked with a deep cut. They generally have monograms on the obverse, and scenes of mythology on the reverse.

Contour, Fr. Outline.

Contournée, Her. Facing to the sinister.

Contra, in compound words in music, signifies *an octave below : contra-basso,* a double bass, &c.

Contra Votum, Chr. (i. e. against one's desires). A formula of grief, placed by the ancients on tombs, columns, and other sepulchral monuments, and adopted by Christians in the 5th century. (See ACCLAMATIONS.)

Contractura, R. The tapering of the column, which begins from the upper part of the shaft, and gradually widens as it reaches the base. (See ENTASIS.)

Contralto, It. In Music, the voice of deepest tone in females, allied to the tenor in men.

Contrapuntal, Mus. Relating to COUNTERPOINT (q.v.).

Contre - imbrications. An ornament cut in the form of fishes' scales overlapping one another, the scales being indented. In the *imbrications* they stand out.

Contrepoint, O. E. (See POURPOINT.)

Contubernium, R. (1) A tent capable of accommodating ten soldiers and their corporal (*decanus*). (2) A dwelling-place, especially for slaves. Hence *contubernales* came to mean comrades, and generally persons living in intimacy under one roof together.

Contus (κοντὸs), Gr. and R. (1) A punting-pole, used also for taking soundings; each trireme was furnished with three poles of different lengths. (2) A cavalry pike or lance.

Conus, Gen. (κῶνοs, a cone). (1) In general, any object of a conical form. (2) A kind of sun-dial described upon a hollow cone. (3) The metal ridge at the top of a helmet, to which the plume was attached. (See Fig. 252.)

Convivium, R. A banquet which generally took place at about the same hour as the *cœna*, but which was never followed by a *commissatio*. (See CŒNA, COMMISSATIO.)

Coopertorium, R. (that which covers). A rug of coarse cloth; a kind of blanket.

Cop, O. E. Generally the top of anything; a mound or heap. (See BATTLEMENT.)

Copal. A hard resin, which, dissolved in boiling linseed oil, forms an excellent varnish for pictures. It is also used as a vehicle for painting. The South African copal is the finest in quality. (See VARNISH.)

Copatain, O. E. A sugar-loaf hat; "a copped-crown hat."

Cope, Chr. A sacerdotal garment, also called a *pluvial*, because it was originally worn by priests in processions as a protection against the rain. It was open in the front, and fastened on the breast by a "morse" or clasp. In the primitive Church the cope was furnished with a hood, and hence mentioned as CUCULLA.

Cope, Arch. To top a wall with thin bricks or stone.

Coperone, O. E., Arch. A pinnacle.

Cop-halfpenny, O. E. The game of "heads and tails."

Cop-head, O. E. A crest of feathers or hair on an animal's head.

Coping, Arch. The capping or covering of a wall, generally sloping to throw off rain. In Fig. 77 two of the merlons are coped.

Cophinus, Gr. and R. A large shallow wicker basket used for agricultural purposes. *Cophinus et fœnum*, "a basket of hay," is Juvenal's word for the poor man's bed. Compare English *coffin*.

Coppa Puerpera, It. Caudle-cup.

Coppe (It.), **Cups** (Sp. *copa*). The early Italian suit of playing cards corresponding to hearts. The *Rev. E. S. Taylor* suggests, "The notion of hearts, as the seat of the affections, &c., is in connexion with the office of the *clergy*;" hence the *chalices*. (See CŒUR.)

Copped, O. E. Crested. (For COP-HEAD, q.v.)

Copperas (white) is considered the safest metallic *drier* for pigments and varnish.

Copper-enamelling. (Fig. 188.) (See ENAMELS.)

Copper-plate Engraving. (See CHALCOGRAPHY.)

Coppet, O. E. Saucy.

Coppid, O. E. Peaked; referring to the fashion of the long peaked toe.

Copple-crowned, O. E. With a head high and rising up, said of a boy "with his hair on end."

Coppull, O. E. A hen's name (in the Turnament of Tottenham).

Cops or **Merlons**, Arch. The raised parts of a battlement. (See Fig. 77.)

Fig. 188.   Ewer and basin of enamelled copper (Turkish).

Coracle, O. E. A boat of wicker-work covered with hides.

Coracoid (κόραξ, a crow). In the form of a crow's beak, e. g. a bone in the shoulder-blade.

Coral (see AMULETS) is mentioned in the Lapidarium of Marbodus as a very favourite and potent amulet.

> "Wondrous its power, so Zoroaster sings,
> And to the wearer sure protection brings.
> And, lest they harm ship, land, or house, it binds
> The scorching lightning and the furious winds.
> Sprinkled 'mid climbing vines or olives' rows,
> Or with the seed the patient rustic sows,
> 'Twill from thy crops avert the arrowy hail,
> And with abundance bless the smiling vale."
> (KING, *Antique Gems*.)

Coranach, Coronach, Gaelic (*corah-rainach*, a crying together). A dirge.

Coranto, It. An Italian form of the country dance or jig.

Corazza, O. E. A cuirass.

Corbel, Arch. A projecting bracket supporting a pier, cornice, or column.

Corbel Steps, Arch. Steps into which the outlines of a gable are sometimes broken ; also called CORBIE STEPS.

Corbel Table. A term in mediæval architecture, applied to a projecting course and the row of corbels which support it.

Corbie, Scotch. A raven ; hence a "corbie messenger," one that is long upon his errand, like the raven sent from the ark, who returned not again.

Corbie Steps. (See CORBEL STEPS.)

Corbis, R. A wicker basket of conical shape, used especially for agricultural purposes. A similar basket in every-day use in parts of Italy is still called "la corbella." Cf. the German "Korb."

Corbita, R. A merchantman of the larger class, so called because it hung out a basket at the mast-head. These vessels were also called *onerariæ*.

Corbona Ecclesiæ, Chr. The treasure of a church, accumulated from the offerings of communicants at the Sacrament. The Greek synonym for this term is *gazophylacium*.

Corbula. Dimin. of CORBIS (q.v.).

Corce, O. E. The body, stomach.

> "He start to hym with gret force,
> And hyt hym egurly on the *corce!* "
> (*Old MS*.)

Cordate, Cordiform. Heart-shaped.

Coráax, Gr. and R. A dance of the ancient Greek comedy of a ridiculous and indecent character. Fauns and satyrs are constantly represented dancing the *cordax*.

Cordeliers, Fr. The Franciscan friars are so called from the *rope* girdles they wear.

Cordevan, O. E. A leather of goat-skin, originally from Cordova in Spain. Spelt also *Cordewayne ;* hence *cordwainer* or *cordiner,* a shoemaker.

Cordigard, Med. (from the French *corps de garde*). A detachment of troops appointed for a particular service.

Corean Porcelain, from a country intermediate between China and Japan, combines the qualities

Fig. 189. Corean tea-pot. (About A.D. 1562.)

of the most ancient art of each. The tea-pot represented in Fig. 189 is covered with gravings in the paste imitating the waves of the ocean, and shows four times repeated an imperial Japanese device, by which it appears that the piece was destined for the Mikado.

Corinthian Order of Architecture. This order originated in Greece, and the capital is said to have been suggested by observing a tile placed

Fig. 190. Capital of the Corinthian Order.

on a basket left in a garden, and an acanthus growing round it. The principal distinction of this order is its capital, richly ornamented with leaves and flowers. Among the principal Corinthian examples are the temple of Vesta, the basilica of Antoninus, and the temples of Jupiter Tonans and Jupiter Stator ; all at Rome.

Corium, R. Leathern body-armour cut into scale form.

Cork burned forms the pigment called *Spanish Black*.

Corn. In pagan art, the attribute of Ceres and Justitia and Juno Martialis.

Cornal. The head of a tilting-lance. (See CORONEL.)

Cornelian, Carnelian, Gen. A variety of chalcedony of a horny transparency and a more or less deep red. Engraved cornelians have perpetuated much information about the manners and customs of the ancient Greeks and Romans. (See SARDS.)

Cornemuse. A French form of the bagpipe.

Cornet. (1) A kind of heraldic banner. (2) The bearer of the colours of a regiment. (3) Square caps worn in the Universities. (4) Any object having *corners*, or angular extremities. (5) An obsolete musical instrument, once in common use in Germany and in England, something like a HAUTBOY, but larger and of a coarser tone. (See WAITS.)

Cornice. (See CORONIS.)

Cornichon, Fr. A kind of game at "quoits."

Fig. 191. Coin showing the Corniculum.

Corniculum, R. (dimin. of *cornu*, and so a small horn). It was a mark of distinction conferred on a soldier who had distinguished himself by his conduct or courage, and was worn on his helmet. On Thracian and other coins we find representations of this horn as part of the royal head-dress.

Cornish, O. E. The ring placed at the mouth of a cannon.

Cornlaiters, O. E. Newly-married peasants begging corn to sow their first crop with.

Cornu, Cornus, and **Cornum**, R. (1) The horn of an animal. (2) Any object made of horn or of a horn-like shape. The musical *cornu* was curved ; the straight horn was called *tuba*.

Cornu Altaris (horn of the altar), in Christian archæology, means merely the *corner* or *angle* thereof. *Cornu Evangelii* is the angle to the left, *c. Epistolæ* that to the right, of the celebrating priest.

Cornu-copiæ, R. Horn of abundance, a symbol of concord, prosperity, and good fortune. It was represented as a wreathed horn, filled to overflowing with corn and fruit.

Corolla, R. (dimin. of CORONA, q.v.). The *corolla* denoted in a general sense a small crown or even a garland ; in a more restricted acceptation it was a garland of artificial flowers made of horn shavings and painted various colours. Women used to wear this kind of wreath during winter.

Corollarium, R. (dimin. of CORONA, q.v.). It denoted especially a wreath made out of thin metal leaves, which the audience in a theatre presented to their favourite actors.

Corona (κορώνη), R. A crown or garland made with natural or artificial leaves and flowers (of horn, parchment, &c., or metal). There were many different kinds of *coronæ*, of which the principal were the following : *corona civica; corona classica, navalis*, or *rostrata; corona castrensis* or *vallaris; corona longa; corona muralis; corona obsidionalis; corona natalitia; corona oleagina; corona ovalis; corona pactilis, plectilis*, or *plexilis; corona triumphalis; corona sutilis*, &c. The most honourable was the *c. obsidionalis*, presented by a beleaguered army, after its liberation, to the general who raised the siege. It was made of grass, or wild flowers plucked on the site. The *c. civica* was presented to a Roman soldier who had saved the life of a citizen in battle. It was made of oak leaves. The *c. navalis* was made of gold.

Fig. 192. Mural crown.

The *c. muralis*, presented to the first man over the wall of a besieged city, was also made of gold, and it was ornamented with turrets. The *c. castrensis*, presented to the first soldier who forced an entrance into an enemy's camp, was of gold ornamented with palisades. Of the *c. triumphalis* there were three kinds : one of laurel or bay leaves, worn by the commanding officer during his triumph ; one of massive gold held over his head ; and a third of still greater value, also of gold. The *c. ovalis*, to commemorate an ovation to an officer, was made of myrtle leaves. The *c. oleagina*, of olive leaves, was given to common soldiers. Besides these, there were the various sacerdotal *coronæ*, emblematical of their functions : the funereal

Fig. 193. Naval crown.

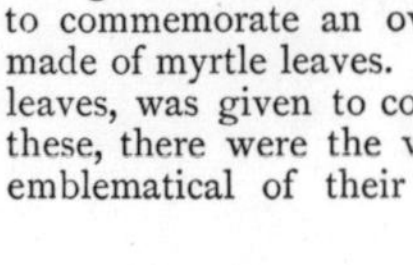

Fig. 194. Celestial crown.

chaplets of leaves and flowers for the dead, called *c. funebres* or *sepulchrales;* the wreaths of roses, violets, myrtles, ivy, &c., worn at convivial meetings, *c. convivialis;* and the bridal wreath, of Greek origin, made of flowers not bought, but plucked by the bride herself, the verbena being the chosen flower among the Romans, *c. nuptialis;* and finally the *c. natalitia* suspended over the door of a house where a child was born. At Athens this was of olive for a boy, and of wool for a girl. At Rome the wreath was made of laurel, ivy, or parsley. The various crowns used in heraldry are described under their respective headings. (See CROWN.)

Corona or **Drip-stone**, Gen. A moulding forming part of a cornice, the lower part or drip of which is grooved, so as to throw off the rain-water from the structure. Drip-stones are sometimes plain, sometimes decorated with rich sculptures.

Corona Lucis, Chr. A lamp or chandelier suspended above the altar of a church, from which usually depended a jewelled cross.

Coronach, Scotch. A dirge.

Coronarium (aureum), R. The gold for a triumphal crown (*corona triumphalis*) : it was sent by the provinces to a victorious chief or general.

Coronarium (opus), R. Stucco-work applied to the decoration of a cornice or projecting moulding.

Coronel, Med. The head of a jousting-lance, so called from its resemblance to a little crown. Twelve were allowed to a tilter in the time of Henry VI. (*Meyrick.*)

Coronell, O. E. A colonel.

Fig. 195. Prince of Wales's coronet.

Coronets. Ensigns of nobility worn upon the head, introduced into England about the middle of the 14th century. (See BARON, DUKE, EARL, &c.) Ladies also wore them surmounting the horned head-dress of the reign of Henry V. The engraving (Fig. 196) represents Beatrice, Countess of Arundel, with coronet.

Coronis (κορωνίς). Anything curved ; the *cornice* of an entablature.

Coronize (Gr. κορωνίζω, from κορώνη, a crow). To beg for the crow ; said of strollers who went about begging with a crow, singing begging songs. (See CHELIDONIZE.)

Corporal, O. E. The fine linen cloth or veil for the pyx, sometimes embroidered with golden thread and coloured silks. With such a "corporal" Mary, Queen of Scots, bandaged her eyes for her execution.

Fig. 196. Coronet of Countess of Arundel, *temp.* Henry V.

Corpse-candle, O. E. A thick candle used formerly at *lake-wak-s.*

Fig. 197. Corpse or Lich-gate.

Corpse-gate or **Lich-gate.** A shed over the gate of a churchyard to rest the corpse under. (Fig. 197.)

Corrugis, R. (*corrugo*, to wrinkle). Literally, wrinkled ; a loose garment which was wrapped round the body, and fell into numerous folds, so as to present the appearance of a wrinkled surface.

Cors, Arch. The shaft of a pinnacle.

Corsæ, R. The mouldings decorating the surface of a marble door-post.

Corse, O. E. (See CORCE.)

Corse of Silk, O. E. Probably a silk ribbon.

Corselet, Fr. A light breastplate ; 16th and 17th centuries.

Corspresant, Med. A mortuary.

Fig 198. Cortina.

Cortina, R. (1) A deep circular vessel in the shape of a saucepan, used for various purposes. (2) The snake's skin spread over the tripod of the Pythoness at Delphi. (3) An altar of marble, bronze, or the precious metals, in the form of a tripod. (4) The vault over the stage in a theatre was called *cortina*, from its resemblance to the lid of a tripod. (5) Tables of marble or bronze, made to imitate the slab upon which the Delphic priestess sat, were also called *cortinæ* Delphicæ. (See Fig. 199.)

Fig. 199. Cortina (Etruscan).

Cortinale, R. A cellar in which wine was boiled in caldrons (*cortinæ*) to preserve it.

Corundum. The Indian name for a very hard mineral called adamantine spar. The ruby and sapphire are varieties of *corundum*.

Corven. O. E. for carven, cut.

> "*Corvene* wyndows of glase,
> With joly bandis of brase."
> (*Lincoln MS.*)

Corvus, R. (lit. crow). A crane or *grappling-iron*, used in naval warfare. It was a strong piece of iron with a spike at the end, which, being violently let down upon a ship from the yard-arm, or a special mast made for the purpose, went through the bottom and sank it, or at any rate grappled it fast. A variety of *corvus* was also made use of in the assault of fortified places.

Corybantica, Gr. and R. Festivals celebrated at Cnossus, in Crete, by the Corybantes, in honour of Atys and his mother Cybele. The priests ran through town and country carrying torches and uttering savage cries to the accompaniment of drums and cymbals. They performed frenzied dances known under the name of *Corybantic dances*.

Corycæum, Gr. and R. A large apartment in a gymnasium or a large bathing establishment, for the CORYCOBOLIA or sack-throwing, a game which consisted in suspending from the ceiling of the *corycæum*, at the height of about a yard from the ground, a sack filled with sand, bran, or seeds, to be thrust away with blows of the fist, and when it was in full swing to be stopped with the hands, back, or breast. The exercise was also called *Corycomachia*.

Corymbus, R. (κόρυμβος, a cluster). (1) A bunch of any fruit that grows in clusters, such as ivy-berries. (2) A head-dress or wig arranged in the form of *corymbi*, in a knot at the top of the head, as that of Venus is represented in the Medici statue. (3) The term is also sometimes used as a synonym of APLUSTRE (q.v.).

Corynalle, Arch. (See CORNAL.)

> "The schafte was strong over alle,
> And a well-shaped *corynalle*."

Coryphæus, Gr. (lit. at the head). (1) Any leader. (2) Esp. the leader of the chorus of the Attic drama. (3) An epithet of Jupiter Capitolinus.

Corytus, Gr. and R. A bow-case. The quiver for arrows was called *pharetra*.

Fig. 200. Cos—a Roman Grindstone.

Cos, R. A hone, whetstone, or grindstone. Fig. 200 is taken from an engraved gem.

Cosmi (κόσμοι). The supreme magistrates in Crete.

Costanti. One of the Italian literary academies. They had for their device the sun shining on a column, with the motto *Tantum volvitur umbra* (the shadow only revolves).

Cote, O. E. A woman's gown ; 15th century.

Cote Armour. (See COAT ARMOUR, TABARD.)

Cote-hardie. A tight-fitting gown ; 14th century.

Cothurnus, Gr. and R. The Buskin ; a high boot of Greek invention, met with on representations of certain divinities and of some of the emperors covered with rich ornamentation. It is an attribute of the huntress Diana. The sole was thickened with cork for tragic actors, to make them taller. Horsemen wore it as high as the knee.

Cotillion (Fr. *cotte*, an under-petticoat). A dance introduced from France, where it usually terminated a ball.

Cotise, Her. A diminutive of the Bend, being one-fourth of its width.

Cotta. A short surplice.

Cottabus, Cottabê, Cotabos, Gr. and R. A game of Greek origin, played in various manners, by throwing wine into empty cups swimming on a basin of water, or into scales suspended above a bronze ornament. The man who drowned most cups won a prize, or he who made the best sound had a good omen. There were other methods.

Cotyla, Gr. and R. A measure of capacity equal to half a pint English.

Cotyttia (κοττύτια). Nocturnal festivals celebrated by the Edonians of Thrace in honour of a goddess called Cotytto (Cybele).

Fig. 201. Hart *couchant.*

Couchant or **Dormant,** Her. In repose. The illustration gives the device of King Richard II., a white hart *couchant* on a mount, &c. (Fig. 201.)

Coucher, O. E. A book kept *couched* or lying on a desk, e. g. books of the church services left in the places where they were used.

Coudières. (See COUTERE.)

Coufic. (See CUFIC.)

Coulisse, Tech. A piece of timber with a channel or groove in it, such as that in which the side-scenes of a theatre move.

Counter, Her. Reversed or opposite.

Counterfort, Arch. A buttress.

Counterpoint, Music. The art of combining melodies, or rather of adding to a melody harmonious parts. *Double Counterpoint* is "a kind of artificial composition, where the parts are inverted in such a manner that the uppermost becomes the lowermost, and *vice versâ.*" (See *Stainer and Barrett, Dic. of Musical Terms.*)

Counter-proof. An impression of an engraving printed from a wet proof.

Counter-seal or **Secretum.** A seal on the reverse or back of another seal. Early seals were generally impressed on both sides.

Countess, Arch. A roofing slate, 20 inches by 10 inches.

Couped, Her. Cut off smoothly. The reverse of *erased.*

Coupled (columns), Gen. Two columns are said to be *coupled* when they are placed quite close to each other without touching. *Coupled heads* is the term applied to two heads placed back to back upon the same pedestal or the same trunk. Many pedestals ornamented with HERMÆ (q.v.) are surmounted by coupled heads.

Courant, Her. Running.

Course, Arch. One range, or stratum, of

bricks, stones, or other material in the construction of a wall.

Court Cards. The king, queen, and knave of a suit. They were originally *named* in France; e. g. the four *kings* were Charlemagne, Cæsar, Alexander, and David; the four *queens,* Judith, Rachel, Argine, and Pallas; and the *valets,* Lahire, Hector, Lancelot, and Hogier. Of these the *kings* were said to represent the four ancient monarchies of the Jews, Greeks, Romans, and Franks; and the *queens,* wisdom, birth, beauty, and fortitude. (*Taylor.*) (See CHAT-RANG.)

Court Cupboards, O. E. Richly carved and large cupboards for plate and other valuables, *temp.* Charles I.

Court Dish, O. E. A kind of drinking cup.

Courtepy (Teutonic). Short cloak or gown.

Coussinet, Arch. The crowning stone of a pier, lying immediately under the arch.

Coutel, Fr. A short knife or dagger in use in the Middle Ages.

Coutere or **Coutes.** The elbow-piece in armour.

Fig. 202. Couvre-feu (Curfew).

Couvre-feu, Angl. **Curfew.** A screen used, as its name implies, for covering the fire; introduced with the famous Curfew-bell, *temp.* William Rufus. (Fig. 202.)

Cove, Arch. A name for concave mouldings or other concavities.

Coved Ceiling, Arch. A ceiling springing from the walls with a cove.

Coventry Blue. A celebrated "blew threde" made at Coventry, *temp.* Elizabeth.

Covert, Her. Partly covered.

Covinus, R. (Celtic, *kowain*). A war-chariot. The spokes of its wheels were armed with scythes. [It was used by the ancient

Britons. The Romans gave the name to a close travelling carriage covered in all round.] (Compare CURRUS, CARPENTUM.)

Coward or **Cowed,** Her. An animal with its tail between its legs.

Cow-lady, O. E. The lady-bird.

> " A paire of buskins they did bring
> Of the *cow-ladye's* corall wyng."
>   (*Musarum Deliciæ.*)

Cowl, Mod. (from *cuculla,* CUCULLUS, q.v.). A priest's hood.

Cox or **Cokes,** O. E. A fool; hence *Coxcomb,* for the top of a fool's cap.

Crackle Porcelain or **Cracklin.** A kind of china, the glaze of which has been purposely cracked all over in the kiln. The Chinese have many kinds of this manufacture, some of which are extremely rare and valuable. White and grey are the common colours amongst modern crackle. The yellow and cream-coloured specimens are much prized : these are seldom seen in Europe. The greens, light and dark, turquoise, and reds are generally finely glazed, and have the crackle lines small and minute. In colouring, these examples are exquisite, and in this respect they throw our finest specimens of European porcelain quite into the shade. The green and turquoise crackle made in China at the present day are very inferior to the old kinds. Perhaps the rarest and most expensive of all ancient crackles is a yellowish stone-colour. (*Fortune.*)

Crackled Glass. (See GLASS.)

Cracowes. Long-toed boots and shoes, introduced in 1384.

Cradle Vault, Arch. A cylindrical vault.

Cradling. A builder's term for a timber frame for a ceiling, &c.

Craig, Scotch. (1) A rock. (2) The neck ; throat.

Crampet. The decorated end of a scabbard.

Crampon. The border of gold which keeps a stone in a ring. (See COLLET.)

Cramp-ring, O. E. A ring consecrated on Good Friday, an amulet against cramp.

Crancelin, Her. (from the German *Kranzlein,* a small wreath). The chaplet that crosses the shield of Saxony. It is said to be an augmentation conferred by the Emperor Barbarossa, who took from his head his own chaplet of rue, and threw it across the shield of the Duke of Saxony. (*Boutell.*)

Crane's-bills. Geraniums, so called from the shape of their seed-vessels.

Crannogs, Irish. Lake fortresses constructed on artificial islands.

Crapaudine Doors. A technical name for doors that turn on pivots at top and bottom, or are hung with so-called *centre-pin* hinges.

Crash. The grey linen used for the kind of embroidery called *crewel-work.*

Crater, Gr. and R. (κρατήρ, from κεράννυμι, to mix). (1) A large and beautiful vase with a wide open mouth, in which the wine and water was mixed which was handed round at banquets and sacrifices. It was into vases of this description that slaves dipped a ladle (*cyathus*), with which they filled the cups. The beautiful silver *crater* shown in the illustration (Fig. 203), of a date not later than the 1st century, was found with other treasures of a similar kind at Hildesheim, near Hanover, in 1869. It is now in the Berlin Museum. (2) The mouth of a volcano is named from its resemblance to the Greek crater. (3) A small constellation of the southern hemisphere called the Cup.

Crates, R. A frame or basket made of hurdles, and so a hurdle itself. (English, "*crate.*")

Craticula, R. (dimin. of *crates*). A

Fig. 203. Silver Crater (Roman). Found at Hildesheim.

small hurdle, and by analogy, a gridiron, which looks like a small hurdle.

Creag, O. E. The game of ninepins.

Creagra, Gr. (κράγρα, from κρέας and ἀγρέω, i. e. a flesh-hook). A synonym of the Latin term HARPAGO (q.v.).

Creasing. A builder's word for a row of tiles under the coping of a wall.

Credence Table. The small table beside an altar, on which the communion was placed before consecration.

Creme-box, O. E. A chrismatory (q.v.).

Cremesyn, O. E. Crimson velvet.

Cremium, R. (cremo, to burn). Small wood, made up into bundles, used by bakers, and for lighting the hypocausts under the baths.

Crenel. The peak at the top of a helmet.

Crenellated, Her. Embattled. (See BATTLEMENT.)

Crenelle, Fr. A cutting or indentation of the walls of a fortress or tower, &c. The spaces between the solid masonry are called *embrasures*, and the solid portions themselves *merlons*; usually the tops of the merlons are coped to throw off rain. (See COPING.) Fig. 204 shows

Fig. 204 Crenellated walls at Pompeii.

a portion of the crenellated walls of Pompeii restored. (See Fig. 77.)

Crepida, Gr. and R. (κρηπίς). A slipper made of a strong leather sole, to the edges of which was fixed a piece of leather with eyelet-holes (*ansæ*) for the laces (*corrigiæ*) or a strap (*amentum*). This shoe was of Greek origin. *Crepida carbatina* was the name given to a shoe of the simplest and plainest description. (See CARBATINA.) [This shoe is only found represented on figures clothed with the *pallium*, not the *toga*.]

Crepido, Gr. and R. (κρηπίς). In a general sense, any kind of base or stand upon which another object rests, and by analogy the em-

bankment of a quay, a dike, or jetty. The term is also applied to the raised causeway for foot passengers at the side of a road or street. Fig. 204 represents a *crepido* on a high road near

Fig. 205. Crepido in a street in Pompeii.

Pompeii, and Fig. 205 a *crepido* in the streets of the same town.

Crepitaculum, R. (crepo, to creak). A child's rattle, made in the form of a circle to which bells were attached. These rattles have been found in the excavations of Pompeii. Some authors apply the term to the SISTRUM of the Egyptians.

Crepitus (sc. *digitorum*), R. A snapping of the fingers made by pressing the tip of the thumb firmly against the tip of the middle finger.

Crepundia, R. A general term for playthings for children, as well as for necklaces of various ornaments, or amulets. These were in some instances of great length, and were worn by the children like shoulder-belts.

Créquier, Her. The wild plum-tree: the device of the Créquy family.

Fig. 206 Crescent.

Crescent, Her. The *difference* of the second son. The moon is a crescent when she appears as in Fig. 206. (Compare DECRESCENT, INCRESCENT.)

Cresolite, O. E. Crystal.

Crespine, Fr. A network to confine the hair of ladies; the *calantica* of the ancients. It is found in mediæval monuments in a variety of forms.

Cressets. A small pan or portable fireplace, filled with combustibles, used for illuminating purposes; 16th century. Her., a beacon. (See Fig. 54.)

Crest, Arch. (crista). A running ornament, more or less incised and perforated, which is placed on the ridge of roofs. Many monuments of antiquity have been adorned with terra-cotta crests; in the Romano-Byzantine architecture examples occur which are made of stone, while in Pointed or Renaissance art they were made of lead.

Fig. 207. Royal crest of England.

Crest, Her. (Lat. *crista*). This word, familiar to us as the name of an ornament surmounting the helmet and the insignia of a gentleman of coat armour, signified in classic times a comb terminating in a peak in front of the casque decorated with horsehair or plumes. (See CRISTA, Fig. 252.) The earliest appearance of a crest in England is on the second seal of Richard I. Fig. 207 illustrates the manner in which the crest is worn upon the royal crown of England. Crests are not worn by ladies, excepting by the Sovereign. (See PANACHE.)

Fig. 208. Crest-coronet.

Crest-coronet, Crest-wreath, or **Orle,** Her. A coronet or wreath to support a crest. (Fig. 208 and 209.)

Fig. 209. Crest-wreaths.

Crest-tiles. Tiles used for covering the ridge of a roof.

Creta Lævis. A crayon of permanent colour for chalk drawing.

Crewel-work. (See CRASH.)

Crewels. A worsted of two plies adapted for embroidery.

Crewetts. Small vessels used at the altar, to hold the wine and water for consecration.

Crimson (Arab. *cremisi*, the cochineal insect). A deep tone of red, tinged with blue.

Crinale, R. (*crinis*, the hair). A large convex comb worn by women and children at the back of the head.

Crined, Her. Having a mane or hair.

Crinetts, O. E. The long small black feathers on a hawk's head. (*H.*)

Crinze, O. E. A drinking cup. (*H.*)

Criobolè, Gr. (κριοβόλη). A sacrifice to Cybele, so called because the victim was a ram (κριός).

Crista, R. The crest of the helmet, which

was attached to an elevated ridge (generally of horsehair). A fine example is given in the head of "Rome," on the Tazza of Diruta. (Fig. 252.) (See CREST.)

Cristatus, R. (*crista*). Having a ridge and a crest. (Fig. 252.)

Cristendom, O. E. Baptism.

"And that bastard that to the ys dere.
Crystyndome schalle he none have here." (*H.*)

Cristygrey. A kind of fur much used in the 15th century.

"Of no devyse embroudid hath hire wede,
Ne furrid with ermyn ne with *cristygrey*."

Crites (κριτής). A judge in *equity*, as opposed to DIKASTES, a judge in *law*.

Croakumshire. An ancient name for the county of Northumberland. (*H.*)

Crobbe, O. E. Knops of buds hung as ornaments from a roof.

Crobylus, Gr. and R. (κρωβύλος). A method of arranging the hair peculiar to the inhabitants of Athens. The hair, rolled up in a knot on the top of the head, was fastened with golden clasps in the shape of grasshoppers. The name applies only to men's hair; the same fashion for women was called *Corymbus*.

Croc or **Crook.** A curved mace.

Crocea. A cardinal's cloak.

Crochet. Knitting done with linen thread, and used under the name of *nun's lace* from the 16th century for bordering altar-cloths, albs, &c.

Fig. 210. Crocket.

Crocket. (1) An architectural enrichment, generally of leaves or flowers; an ornamentation peculiar to the pointed style of architecture. (Fig. 210.) (2) A large roll of hair, much worn in the time of Edward I.

"His *crocket* kembt,
and thereon set
A nouche with a
chapelet."

Crocota, Gr. and R. (from κρόκος, crocus). A very rich robe of saffron colour, whence its name. It was worn by Greek and Roman women as a gala dress, especially at the Dionysia.

Cromlec'h, Celtic (from *cromm*, curved, and *lec'h*, place). An enclosure formed by *menhirs*, or huge stones planted in the ground in a circle or semicircle. These enclosures (Fig. 211) were consecrated places used as burying-grounds. (See STANDING-STONES, DOLMENS, MENHIRS, &c.)

Fig. 211. Cromlech.

Fig. 212. Cross *Recercelée*.

Cross, Chr. (*Crux*). The symbol of the Christian religion. The ordinary or primitive type of cross has no summit. It is called *commissa* or *patibulata*, and sometimes the *Tau* cross, from its resemblance to the Greek letter so named (T). Fig. 121 represents a stone cross of the Romano - Byzantine period, at Carew, in England. The St. Andrew's cross has the form of an X. The Greek cross is of four equal parts. The Latin cross has the foot longer than the summit or arms. The Maltese cross and the cross of Jerusalem are varieties of the Greek cross. The Patriarchal cross (heraldic) has two cross pieces, the triple cross has three, &c. PER CROSS, in heraldry, is the division of a shield *quarterly* (a combination of pale and fesse). (Figs. 212 to 215.)

Fig. 213. St. Andrew's Cross (*Saltire*).

Cross and Pile, O. E. The game of "heads and tails."

Cross-aisled, Arch. Having TRANSEPTS.

Fig. 214. St. George's Cross *fimbriated*.

Cross-bows were brought to England by the Crusaders. They were frequently richly carved and inlaid.

Cross-days, O. E. The three days before Ascension Day.

Cross-gartered. Having the garters crossed on the leg. (*H.*)

Cross-hatching. A term in engraving applied to lines which intersect at regular angles, to increase depth of shadow.

Crossos, Gr. (κρωσσός). A wide-bodied vessel narrowing towards the mouth; it is furnished with a stand and two handles or ears (δίωτοι).

Cross-row, O. E. The alphabet. (See CHRIST-CROSS.)

Fig. 215. Victoria Cross.

Cross-springer, Arch. In vaulting, the diagonal rib of a GROIN.

Cross - vaulting, Arch. That which is formed by the intersection of two or more simple vaults. When the vaults spring at the same level, and rise to the same height, the cross vault is termed a GROIN. The illustration (Fig. 173), the cloisters of the church of Mont St. Michel in France, shows the cross-vaulting.

Fig. 216. Crotalia. Greek necklace.

Crotalium, Gr. and R. (from κροτέω, to rattle). A small rattle. The Greek and Roman ladies gave this name to their pendants formed of two or four pear - shaped pearls (*elenchi*), which rattled softly as the wearer moved about. (Fig. 216.)

Crotalum Gr. and R. (κρόταλον). Castanets made of slit cane, used by dancers in the worship of Cybele. The Middle Ages also had their *crotala*, which consisted of a metal rod, in which were inserted rings, which sounded when the instrument was shaken.

Crow or Raven. The attribute of St. Vincent.

Crowde or Croud, O. E. (1) The crypt of a church. (2) A fiddle.

Crown. (See CORONA. See also MURAL CROWN, NAVAL CROWN, CREST, &c.)

Fig. 217. Crown of Her Majesty the Queen.

Crown (of a bell). The top of the inside of

H

a bell, in which the ring is fixed from which the clapper is suspended. In architecture the spire of a steeple is said to *crown* the tower, or a fleuron to crown a gable, &c.

Crown. An old English coin, the value of which has varied at different periods. The

Fig. 218. Crown of the Rose.

illustration represents the gold crown of Henry VIII., dated 1462, called a crown of the Rose, value 4*s*. 6*d*. Other crown pieces were called, from the mint-mark, crowns of the Sun.

Croyle, O. E. Crewel; tightly-twisted worsted.

Crozier, Chr. The name is often *improperly* applied to the bishop's crooked pastoral staff; it belongs to the staff surmounted by a cross which is borne before an archbishop. The Byzantine crozier was that of the T-shaped cross; it had sometimes curved serpents on both sides.

Crucifix. The representation of the Saviour on the Cross was first introduced in the time of Constantine. It has undergone considerable variation at different periods.

Fig. 219. Porcelain Cruciform Box (Egyptian).

Cruciform. Shaped to form a cross. The illustration represents a specimen of ancient Egyptian porcelain, of this shape, ornamented with the lotus. (See EGYPTIAN POTTERY.)

Crumata. (See CRUSMATA.)

Crumena, R. A leather pouch for carrying money. The *balantion* of the Greeks was worn suspended from the neck by a strap.

Crumenal, O. E. A purse.

Crupezia, Gr. (κρούω, to strike). A kind of sandal with a double sole, in the middle of which were castanets with springs. (See CROTALUM.) Greek flute-players used them in the theatre to beat time to the singing and declamation of the chorus.

Crusca, Accademia della. A literary academy established in Florence in the 15th century

by Cosmo de' Medici; their device, a bolting-mill, represented in Fig. 220, was symbolical of

Fig. 220. Device of the Della Cruscan Academy.

their object to cultivate the Italian language by winnowing the flour from the bran; and in allusion to it, the members called themselves by appropriate names, as Infarinato, Rimenato, Gramolato, Insaccato, &c. On the top of the shield is the Marzocco, or Lion of Florence, the emblem of the city.

Crusilée, Crusily, Her. Having the field semée of small crosses.

Cruske, O. E. An earthen vessel; cf. the Irish *cruishkeen*.

Crusmata, Crumata, Gr. and R. (κρούω, to strike). Castanets.

Crustæ, R. In the finest works of the chaser, the ornamental pattern was frequently distinct from the vessel, to which it was either fastened permanently, or so that it could be removed at pleasure, the vessel being of silver, and the ornaments of gold, which were called *crustæ* or *emblemata* (Dr. Smith). Of these the former were the figures embossed in low relief, and the *emblemata* were those in high relief. (See DAMASCENING, EMBLEMATA.)

Crustulum, R. (dimin. of *crustum*). Anything baked ; plaster mouldings ; a cheap kind of decoration in bas-relief.

Crutch. An attribute of St. Anthony, to denote his age and feebleness.

Crux. The Latin equivalent for CROSS (q. v.).

Crwth (A.S. *crudh*, Eng. *crowd*). A Welsh instrument, a sort of violin, similar to the *rébek* of the Bretons.

Crypta, Crypt, Chr. (κρύπτω, to bury). In ancient times the crypt was really a cloister ; it formed, in fact, a long and narrow gallery surrounded by buildings, and itself surrounding a building, garden, or court. The courtyards of *villæ* were surrounded by crypts ; the ruins of Diomed's *villa*, at Pompeii, afford a curious

Fig. 221. Crypt at Lanmeur (France).

instance of the kind. In modern archæology the term crypt is applied to a subterranean chapel underneath a church. (Figs. 221 and 222.)

Fig. 222. Crypt of St. Mary's Church, Warwick.

Among the Romans the word meant (1) a covered portico, or arcade, called *crypto-porticus.*

(2) A grotto, or more accurately a tunnel. (3) A subterranean vault used for secret worship. (4) In the catacombs, a tomb in which a number of bodies were interred together.

Crypteia (κρυπτεία). A systematic massacre of Helots at night, by young Spartans, who hid themselves during the day.

Crystal. Rock crystals are frequently found large enough to make vessels of. The Romans had crystal drinking-cups of extraordinary size and beauty. Crystal ornaments were especially chosen for ecclesiastical purposes, and for mediæval bookbinding, &c., and are frequently found in early British graves.

Crystalotype. A sun-picture taken and fixed on glass by the collodion process.

Cubiculum, R. and Chr. (*cubo*, to recline). (1) A bedroom. (2) The emperor's pavilion or tent at the amphitheatre or circus. (3) In Christian archæology, the sepulchral chambers of the catacombs. (See CINERARIUM.)

Cubile, R. (*cubo*). A bed, or chamber containing a bed.

Cubit (Gr. πῆχυς, Lat. *cubitus*, an elbow). A measure of length among the Egyptians, Greeks, and Romans. In Egypt there were two cubits ; the *natural cubit*, or small cubit, was equal to 18 inches (6 palms or 24 fingers) ; the *royal cubit* to 21 inches (7 palms or 28 fingers). Each of the subdivisions of the cubit was consecrated to a divinity. The Greek cubit was equal to about $18\frac{1}{4}$ inches ; the Roman cubit to very nearly $17\frac{1}{2}$ inches.

Cubital, R. A bolster or cushion used by the Romans to rest the elbow on when reclining.

Cubit-arm, Her. A human arm couped at the elbow.

Cubitoria, —æ (sc. *vestimenta, vestes*). (See CŒNATORIA.)

Cucullus, R. Literally, a piece of paper rolled into the shape of a funnel, used at Rome by apothecaries and other tradespeople for wrapping up certain kinds of goods ; and hence, by analogy, the hood affixed to certain garments, such as the *lacerna, pænula, sagum*, &c. (See COWL.)

Cucuma, R. A term applied to various earthenware or metal vessels, when they were used to heat water or any other liquid.

Cucurbita, R. A pumpkin or gourd, and thence a cupping-glass.

Cudo, Cudon, R. A skull-cap made of soft leather or furs.

Cuerpo (Span.). Body clothing, i. e. a jacket.

Cufic (characters), Arab. The Cufic is the most ancient form of Arabian writing, and bears a great resemblance to the Syriac writing called *estranghelo ;* it appears to have originated in the city of Cufa or Coufa, whence the name.

Cuirass. (See CINGULUM, LORICA, PEC-
TORALE, THORAX.)

Cuir-boulli, Fr. Boiled leather, frequently
mentioned by mediæval writers. It has lately
been revived under the name of *impressed leather*,
and brought to a high state of perfection. (*Fairholt.*) Hence :—

Cuirbouly, O. E. Tanned leather.

Fig. 223. Cuisse.

Cuisses, Fr.
Armour for
the thighs, in-
troduced a-
bout the mid-
dle of the 14th
century. In
earlyexamples
they consisted
of one, two,
or three pieces
of plate over-
lapping ; later
on they were
formed of one
piece only,and
finally were
finished with
a back piece,
enclosing the
whole of the
thigh in armour.

Cuitikins, Cutikins, Scotch. Guêtres, gaiters.

Cuker, O. E. Part of a woman's horned head-
dress, "furred with a cat's skin."

Culcita, R. A mattress of horsehair, wool,
wadding, or feathers.

Culettes, Fr. Plates of armour protecting the
back, from the waist to the saddle.

Culeus or **Culleus,** R. The largest liquid
measure of capacity used by the Romans, containing 20 amphoræ, or about 119 gallons. The
same name was also applied to a very large sack,
of skin or leather, used for oil or wine. It was
in the *culei* that parricides were sewed up.

Culigna, R. A vessel for holding wine. It
was a kind of amphora of a broader form, its
width exceeding its height.

Culina, R. A kitchen.

Cullis, Arch. Same as COULISSE (q.v.).

Culme, O. E. The summit.

Cultellus, R. (dimin. of CULTER, q.v.). A
knife. *Cultellus ligneus*, a wedge of wood.

Culter or **Culta,** R. A knife. *Culter coquinaris*
was a kitchen-knife; *culter venatorius*, a hunting-
knife ; *culter tonsorius*, a razor ; *culter vinitorius*,
or *falx vinitoria*, a vine-dresser's pruning-knife.
The term denoted as well (1) the knife with
which the officiating priest cut the victim's
throat ; (2) a knife for carving, also called
cultellus; (3) the *coulter* of a plough fixed in
front of the plough-share.

Culullus, R. (*culeus*, q.v.). Generally,
any drinking-vessel, and more particularly any
earthenware vessel used by priests and vestals at
sacrifices.

Culver, A.S. A dove.

Culver-house. A pigeon-house.

Cumera, R. A kind of large box or basket
employed by country people for keeping their
seed-wheat in.

Cumerum, R. A bridal basket containing the
presents of the bride and bridegroom ; it was
carried by a *camillus* in the bridal procession.

Cumpi-coptra, Peruv. One of the divisions
in the royal arsenals of the ancient Peruvians.
It contained lama-wool, and textures of alpaca,
embroidered in the college of the Virgins of the
Sun (PASUA-HUASI, (q.v.).

Cunabula, R. Literally, a child's cradle, and
thence a bird's nest, a beehive, a native city ;
any place, in short, in which a living thing is
born. A synonym for this term is CUNÆ.
Bibliologists call early specimens of printing by
this name, or INCUNABULA (q.v.).

Cuneiform (characters). Oriental characters
formed by a single symbol, which is in the shape
of a wedge (*cuneus*). This kind of writing has
been in use among many nations ; more particularly the ancient Persians, Persepolitans, Baby-

Fig. 224. Cuneiform characters.

lonians, and Ninevites. Fig. 224 represents the
first cuneiform characters which found their way
to Europe.

Cuneus, R. (1) A wedge of wood, iron, or
any other metal. (2) In a theatre or amphitheatre, a set of tiers comprised within two
staircases (*scalæ*), so called from its wedge-like
form. (3) A body of soldiers drawn up in the
form of a wedge to break through the enemy's
line. The common soldiers called the formation *caput porcinum*, a pig's head.

Cuniculus, R. (*cuneus*). An underground
passage to a fortified place.

Cupa, R. A barrel or hogshead. *Vinum de
cupâ* was wine which had not been drawn off
in amphoræ ; it was wine from the cask, new
wine. The cupa was sometimes made of earthenware like the dolium. It was used for many
purposes besides that of a wine-vat. (See
CUPELLA.)

Cupel. A melting-pot for gold.

Cupella, R. and Chr. (dimin. of CUPA,
q.v.). In Christian archæology, a tomb.
The word occurs on a catacomb marble, in-

scribed with grotesque Latin : "I, Secunda, erected this *cupella* to my two children," &c. [The cupa was sometimes used by the Romans as a sarcophagus.] (See CINE-RARIUM.)

Cupola, It. A concave roof, circular or polygonal.

Cups. (See COPPA.)

Curb Roof, Arch. A Mansard roof; a roof with a double set of rafters on each side, of peculiar construction.

Curch, Gael. A kerchief.

Curfew. (See COUVRE-FEU, Fig. 202.)

Curia, Curiæ, R. (1) A building in which the people met together to offer sacrifices and take part in the festivities on certain days of festival. (2) The *senatorial curiæ* were buildings in which the senate usually assembled.

Fig. 225. Currus. The Chariot of the Sun. The device of Philip II. of Spain.

(3) The *Salian curia* was a place situated on the Palatine Hill, which formed the place of assembly for the *Salian* priests who guarded the *anciles* or sacred shields. (4) *Curia calabra* was a small temple founded, almost simultaneously with the building of Rome, on the Palatine ; it formed the observatory for the petty pontiffs whose duty it was to watch the appearance of the new moon. In Christian archæology the *Roman curia* denotes the pontifical tribunals collectively.

Curliewurlies, Scotch. Fantastical circular ornaments.

Currach, Scotch. A coracle or small skiff ; a boat of wicker-work covered with hides.

Currus, Chariot (Gr. ἅρμα). A two-wheeled car or carriage in use among nearly all the nations of antiquity. There were racing-chariots, riding-chariots, and triumphal chariots. Some of these were profusely decorated with ivory (*currus eburnei*). War-chariots armed with scythes or sharp blades were called *falcati*. (See COVINUS.) The illustration (Fig. 225), a device of Philip II. of Spain, represents Apollo driving the chariot of the Sun.

Cursores. " Runners " before their masters' carriages ; messengers generally.

Curtail Dog, O. E. A dog belonging to a person not qualified to hunt game, which, by the forest laws, must have its tail cropped.

Curtail Step, Arch. The first step of a stair, when its outer end is finished in the form of a scroll ; when it has a circular end, it is called a round-ended step.

Cushat, Scotch. A wood-pigeon.

Cushion-capital, Arch. (1) A capital resembling a cushion pressed by a weight. (2) A

cube rounded off at its lower angles ; the capital most prevalent in the Norman style.

Cusp. In Astrology, the "entrance" of a "house."

Cuspis, R. A point, more particularly the

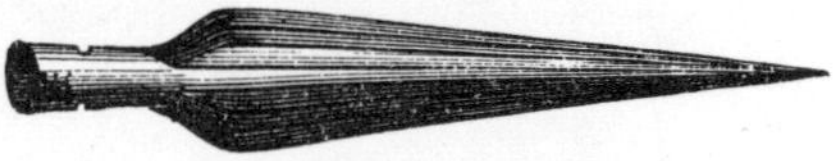

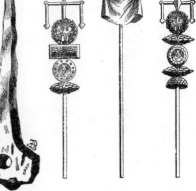

Fig. 226. Cuspis.

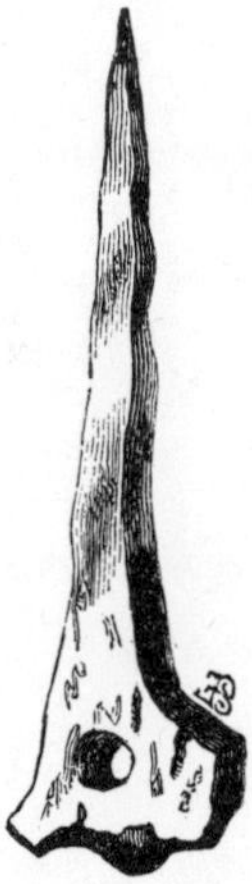

Fig. 227. Cuspis— Flint lance.

Figs. 228, 229, 230. Cuspides— Roman lances.

point of a lance, or javelin, since these were not barbed. Fig. 226 represents a javelin-head which gives a complete idea of the character of the point called *cuspis*; Fig. 227 shows a flint lance ; and Figs. 228 to 230 the lance-headed *cuspides* affixed to the top of the Roman ensigns. (See SPICULUM.)

Cusps. The foliations of architectural tracery, such as are formed by the points of a trefoil.

Custodia. The shrine or receptacle for the host in Spanish churches.

Cutlass, Coutel-hache, or **Coutel-axe,** O. E. This weapon was introduced at the end of the 15th century.

Cut-work. Also called "opus consutum ;" *Ital.* " di commesso." Open-work embroidery came into universal use in England in the 16th century. In the reign of Richard II., however, we are told,—

" Cut werke was greate both in court and townes,
  Bothe in mene's hoddies, and also in their gownes."

(See APPLIQUÉ.)

Cyanogen. A gaseous compound of carbon and nitrogen, necessary to the formation of *Prussian blue.*

Cyathus, Gr. and R. A vase or ladle with one handle, used for taking wine from the crater (κρατήρ), in order to fill the cups (*pocula, calices*) of the guests, at feasts and banquets. The term was also used to denote a small measure containing the twelfth part of the *sextarius,* or ·0825 of a pint. The cyathus was used in medicine to measure drugs with accuracy. [It is often represented, on vases, in the hands of Bacchus, in place of his proper goblet the Cantharus.]

Cybistic (dance), R. (κυβιστάω, to tumble). A part of the military exercises in which the performer threw himself at intervals on his hands, so as to rebound on his feet.

Cyclas, R. (κυκλὰς, circular). A long and loose piece of drapery, of a very fine texture ; it was hemmed with purple or gold embroidery. The *cyclas* formed part of a woman's costume, but it was also worn by men of an effeminate or dissolute character ; hence—

Cyclas, O. E. The name of a long sleeveless gown worn by knights over their armour (from *ciclatoun,* q. v., of which it was made).

Cyclopean (masonry, monuments), Gr. and R.

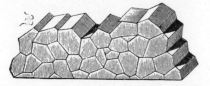

Fig. 231. Cyclopean Masonry.

(κυκλώπειον). Ancient structures, also known

as *Pelasgian,* as being the work of Pelasgians who had learned in the school of Phœnician workmen called Cyclopes. These ancient structures are formed of enormous irregularly-shaped stones (Fig. 231), placed one above the other without cement or mortar. Remains of them are found in Asia Minor, Greece, and Italy ; they consist chiefly of the walls of acropoles.

Cylix, Gr. and R. A vase also known as a *calix* or *cup.* It was a wide flat drinking-cup,

Fig. 232. Cylix. A Gallic drinking-cup.

very shallow, of a circular form, with two handles, and mounted on a tolerably tall foot. Fig. 232 shows a silver cylix or Gaulish cup, found in the ruins of Alisia.

Cyma, Cymatium (Eng. **Ogee,** Gr. κυμάτιον). An architectural moulding, named from the Greek κῦμα (wave or billow), the moulding consisting of an undulation. A cyma, the outline of which is convex at the top and concave below, is called *cyma reversa ;* when it is hollow in the upper part, it is called a *cyma recta.* (Fig. 233.)

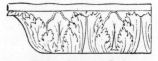

Fig. 233. Decorated Cyma.

Cymatile, R. (κῦμα). A Roman female dress, of a changing sea-green colour, like the waves.

Cymba, R. (κύμβος, a hollow). (1) A small boat. (2) A vase of metal or clay in the form of a small boat. (See CYMBIUM.)

Cymbals, O. E. A contrivance of a number of metal plates, or bells, suspended on cords. .

Cymbalum, R. (from κύμβος). The cymbals ; a musical instrument made of two disks of bronze or brass. (See CROTALUM, FLAGELLUM.)

Cymbe, Gr. An ointment-pot, similar in shape to the *Ampulla* (q.v.).

Cymbium, R. (κυμβίον). A boat-shaped drinking-cup with two handles. (See CYMBA.)

Cynocephalus, Egyp. An ape with a dog's head ; a sacred animal, representing Anubis in the Egyptian mythology.

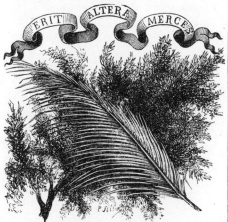

Fig. 234. Branch of Cypress and of Myrtle. Device of M. A. Colonna.

Cynophontis (sc. ἑορτὴ), Gr. (derived from the Greek κύων, dog, and φόνος, slaughter). Festivals held at Argos during the dog-days, when dogs found straying in the city were killed.

Cynopolites, Egyp. (κυνοπολίτης). A nome of Upper Egypt.

Cypress. In Persian art, this tree is the frequently-occurring emblem of the religion of Zoroaster. and of the soul aspiring to Heaven. In Christian and modern symbolism it is the emblem of mourning. The device of *cypress* and *myrtle* assumed by Marc Antonio Colonna on the occasion of the defence of Ravenna is emblematic of "*death* or *victory*." The wood of the cypress-tree was much used for statuary by the ancients. Carved chests of cypress were especially used, in the Middle Ages, for keeping clothes and tapestry ; its aromatic properties were considered a specific against moth. (Fig. 234.)

Cyprus. Thin stuff of which women's veils were made.

Cyprus or **Verona Green**. A pigment mentioned by Pliny as *Appian Green* : it is prepared from green earths found at Cyprus or Verona, which are coloured by oxide of copper. (See APPIANUM.)

Cysts or **Cists**, Etrus. (κίστη, a chest). Offerings dedicated by women in the temple of Venus, of cylindrical caskets of enchased bronze. The handles of these caskets represent small figures, and the feet the claws of animals. Those which have been found in Etruscan tombs, chiefly at Præneste, are in many cases decorated with *a graffito* designs.

Cyzicenæ, Gr. (κυζικηναί). Large and richly-decorated apartments, built for the first time at Cyzicus, which had their principal fronts to the north, and were situated in a garden.

D.

Dabber. A tool used in etching to distribute the etching-ground over a plate of metal in the first process of engraving, and, in printing from copper-plate engraving and woodcuts, to spread the ink.

Dactyliography or **Dactyliology**, Gen. (δακτύλιος, a ring). The study of rings.

Dactyliotheca, Gr. (δακτυλιο-θήκη, a ring-box). (1) A glass case or casket containing rings. (2) A collection of rings, engraved stones, or precious stones. (See GLYPTOTHECA.)

Dactylus, Gr. (δάκτυλος, a finger). The Roman *digitus ;* a finger-breadth, the 16th part of a foot.

Dado, Arch. (1) The part of a pedestal between the base and the cornice. (2) In apartments, an arrangement of moulding, &c., round the lower part of the wall.

Dædal. A fanciful word coined by the poet Spenser, for "variegated in design."

Dædala, Gr. Ancient images preserved in sanctuaries in memory of Dædalus, to whom were attributed the greater number of those works of art the origin of which was unknown. Hence the name was especially attributed to certain wooden statues, ornamented with gilding, bright colours, and real drapery, which were the earliest known form of images of the gods.

Dædala, Gr. (δαίδαλα). Festivals in honour of Hera, celebrated in Bœotia.

Dæmon, **Daimon**, Gr. (δαίμων). The good genius who watched over an individual during his whole life, like the Latin *Lar* and *Genius*. It was the belief of Socrates that he was guided by his Daimon in every important act and thought of his life. The word has a general meaning of "Divinity."

Dag or **Dagge**. Old English name of a pistol.

Dagges, O. E. Ornamental cutting of the edges of garments, introduced into England about 1346. (See the illustration to COINTISE, Fig. 177).

Dagob, Hindoo. A conical tumulus or shrine in which relics and images of Buddha were worshipped.

Dag-swain, O. E. A sort of rough material of which coverlets for beds, tables, or floors were made.

Daguerreotype. A kind of photography on plates of silver, named after M. Daguerre, the inventor.

Daidies, Gr. (from δαίω, to kindle). A festival held at Athens, during which torches were lit; it lasted three days.

Dais, Chr. An architectural structure, decorated with sculptures and ornaments, which serves as a canopy for an altar, throne, pulpit, chair (*cathedra*), statue, or group. Fig. 235 represents a stone dais of the St. Anne door in the cathedral of Paris.

Fig. 235. Dais.

Dais. In Anglo-Saxon houses, and generally; a covered seat of honour, at the upper end of the hall, on a raised floor. ("In all the houses of the wealthy *in China* there are two raised seats at the end of the reception-room, with a table between them." *Fortune.*) (See DEAS.)

Dalmahoy, O. E. A kind of bushy bob-wig, worn especially by chemists; 18th century.

Dalmatic. A long robe or upper tunic partly opening at the sides, so named from its being of Dalmatian origin; an ecclesiastical vestment; also a portion of the coronation robes of sovereign princes. It was usually made of white silk with purple stripes, occasionally of other colours, the left sleeve only being ornamented; the right was plain for convenience. As early as the reign of Richard I., the dalmatic is mentioned amongst the coronation robes. (Fig. 236.) (See COLOBIUM, DEACON.)

Damara or **Dammar**. A resin used for varnishes. It is a valuable substitute for mastic.

Damaretion. A Sicilian coin, supposed to have been of gold, equal in value to a half-*stater*.

Damas (or **Damascus**) **Pottery Ware.** The commercial name in the 16th century for a large class of wares, now generally known as Persian.

Damascening, or **Damaskeening**, is the art of incrusting one metal on another, not in *crusta*,

Fig. 236. Ecclesiastical Dalmatic.

but in the form of wire, which by undercutting and hammering is thoroughly incorporated with the metal it is intended to ornament. (See DAMASK, DAMASCUS BLADES.) The process of etching slight ornaments on polished steel wares is also called Damascening. (Fig. 237.)

Damascus Blades are prepared of a cast steel highly charged with carbon, which, being tempered by a peculiar process, assumes the many-coloured *watered* appearance by which they are known. The process is called DAMASCENING (q.v.).

Damask. A rich fabric, woven with large patterns, in silk, linen, wool, or even cotton, originally made at Damascus. (See Fig. 88.)

Dames, O. E. The old name for the game of draughts, represented early in the 14th century. The pieces were originally square.

Danace (δανάκη). The *obolus* which was placed in the mouth of the dead to pay the passage of the Styx.

Dance of the Corybantes. (See CORYBANTICA.)
Dance of Death, Danse Macabre, Chr. Paintings,

Fig. 237. Specimen of Arabic Damascening (full size).

illuminations, or sculptures in bas-relief, representing men dancing under the eye of Death, who presides at this dance. In some instances the performers are skeletons and corpses. The most celebrated Dance of Death was that painted in fresco by Holbein in the cloister of the Dominicans at Basle. It has been destroyed by fire, but the etching-needle has preserved it for us. Other examples that may be named are, that in the new church at Strasburg, that of Lucerne, that in the palace at Dresden, and —most ancient of all—that at Minden, in Westphalia, which dates from 1380.

Dancette, Arch. The chevron or zigzag moulding peculiar to Norman architecture. (See CHEVRON.)

Dangu Faience. Pottery from a manufactory near Gisors in France, established in 1753.

Daphnephoria (δάφνη, a laurel). A festival held in honour of Apollo every ninth year at Thebes, in which the assistants carried laurel branches.

Dara, Ind. A kind of tambourine.

Darabukkeh. An Egyptian drum, unaltered from ancient times.

Daric Money. A Persian gold coin, stamped on one side with the figure of an archer kneeling, and on the other with a deep cleft, and to which the name of *Daric money* has been given by numismatists. Its proper name is the Stater of Dareius I., king of Persia. Its value is about 1l. 1s. 10d.

Darned Netting (needlework). (See LACIS.)

Datatim ludere, R. To play with a ball (*"catch-ball"*).

Davenport Pottery is the produce of a manufactory of fine faience established at Longport in England by John Davenport in 1793.

Day, Arch. Part of a window: the same as BAY.

Deacon, Chr. A dalmatic, or an alb; i. e. a *deacon's* vestment.

Dead-boot, O. E., Chr. Prayers for the dead.

Dealbatus, R. (*dealbo*, to whiten over). Covered with a coating of stucco (*albarium opus*). The builders of antiquity made great use of stucco, both in the interior and exterior of buildings. All the buildings of Pompeii are stuccoed.

Deambulatory, Arch. (*deambulo*, to walk about). The lateral nave which surrounds the choir of a church; it is usually separated from the aisles by a grating (*cancelli*).

Deas, Dais, Dees, Scotch. (1) A table, especially the great hall table. (2) A pew in a church. (3) A turf seat erected at the door of a cottage. (See DAIS.)

Death's-man, O. E. The executioner.

Debased, Her. Reversed.

Decadence. The term in ancient art is applied to the period after the fall of Rome, and before the *Renaissance* in the 14th century; in modern art to the period of the *rococo* style of Louis XV.

Decaduchi (δεκα-δοῦχοι), Gr. A council of ten, who ruled Athens from B.C. 403 until the restoration of democracy.

Decan, Egyp. A period of ten days, which was ruled by a star called its *Decan*. The month was divided into three decans, and the year into thirty-six, each being presided over by its own inferior divinity. On zodiacs they are arranged in groups of three above the twelve superior gods. The decans were the tutelary genii of the horoscope.

Decarchia (δεκ-αρχία). A council of the Lacedæmonians.

Decastellare, Med. Lat. To dismantle.

Decastylos, Arch. A building of which the portico has ten columns; a decastylic pediment is a pediment supported by ten columns.

Decemjugus (sc. *currus*), R. A chariot drawn by ten horses abreast; represented on the medals of the later emperors.

Decempeda, R. A ten-foot measuring-rod used by architects and surveyors.

Decemremis, R. (*remus*, an oar). A vessel with ten banks of oars. It is certain that the different ranks of rowers, who had each his own seat, sat one above the other; the lowest row was called *thalamos*, the middle *zuga*, and the uppermost *thranos;* but it is very difficult to understand in what manner so many ranks could have been arranged, and the question has been the subject of infinite discussion.

Decennalia or **Decennia.** A festival at Rome in commemoration of the refusal of Augustus to become emperor for a longer period than ten years at a time.

Decollation (= beheading). An ecclesiastical expression applied to St. John the Baptist and other martyrs.

Decorated Style of Architecture. The second of the POINTED or GOTHIC styles of architecture used in England. It was developed from the EARLY ENGLISH at the end of the 13th century,

Fig. 238. Decorated window.

and gradually merged into the PERPENDICULAR during the latter part of the 14th. Its most characteristic feature is the geometrical traceries of the windows.

Decrescent, In Detriment, Her. A half-moon having its horns to the sinister.

Decursio, R. (*decurro*, to run or march). Military manœuvres; a review, sham fight, or any exercise for training soldiers; the term *decursus* was also used.

Fig. 239. Decrescent.

Decussis, R. (*decem*, ten, and *as*). A piece of money marked with the numeral X (10), and which was worth ten asses (post-Augustan; see DENARIUS).

De Fundato or **Netted.** A name given to certain silks, which were dyed of the richest purple, and figured with gold in the pattern of netting.

De-gamboys, O. E. A musical instrument. (See VIOL DE GAMBO.)

Degradation, Gen. The diminishing of the tones of colour, light, and shade, according to the different degrees of distance. (A term used especially in reference to glass painting.)

Degreed, Degraded, Her. Placed on steps.

Deice, Deas, or **Deis,** O. E. (See DAIS.)

Deinos, Gr. A vessel with a wide mouth and semi-spherical body, something like the *cacabus*.

Delf. Common pottery from Delft in Holland.

Delft Faiences are remarkable for the beauty of their paste and of their enamel, but spurious

Fig. 240. Oil cruet, Delft ware.

imitations are said to be abundant. Fig. 240 is a representative specimen of the real Delft ware. The date of the establishment of this manufacture is uncertain, but earlier than 1614; the ornamentation is inspired by Japanese art. (Consult *Jacquemart's History of the Ceramic Art*.)

Delia, Gr. Festivals and games at Delos.

Delphica (sc. *cortina*), R. A table of a very costly description, made of white marble or bronze. It was used as a drinking-table, and had only three feet richly ornamented. [Explained under the heading CORTINA.]

Delphinia. A Greek festival in honour of Apollo.

Delphinorum Columnæ, R. The two columns at one end of the *spina* of a circus, on which marble figures of dolphins were placed. The seven *ova* (eggs) on similar columns at the end of the *spina* opposite to these dolphins, served to indicate the number of turns made by the chariots round the goal. (See OVUM.) [The figure of the dolphin was selected in honour of Neptune.] (Cf. CIRCUS.)

Delphinus, Dolphin, Gen. (δελφίν). The dolphin was often used as an ornament, and especially as a hand-rest or banister to the *vomitoria* or entrances of the theatres and amphitheatres. Fig. 241 represents a dolphin utilized

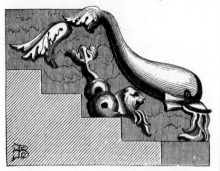

Fig. 241. Dolphin. Used as an ornament.

in this manner at the theatre of Puzzoli. Many

Fig. 242. Dolphin. Medal of Syracuse.

medals, as for instance those of Syracuse (Fig. 242), are stamped with a dolphin. (See also DOLPHIN.)

Delphis, R. A heavy mass of iron or lead used in naval warfare, to drop on board of a hostile ship and sink it. (Compare CORVUS.)

Delubrum, R. (*deluo*, to cleanse). A shrine; the part of a temple which contains the altar or statue of the deity, and thence a temple containing an altar.

Demembered, Dismembered, Her. Cut into pieces, but without any alteration in the form of the original figure.

Fig. 243. Demilion, *rampant*.

Demi, Her. The half; the upper, front, or dexter half, unless the contrary is specified.

Demi-brassarts, Vambraces, or **Avant-braces.** Half-armour for the arm.

Demi-culverin. A cannon of four inches' bore. (*Meyrick.*)

Demi-hag. A smaller kind of hackbut (arquebus).

Demi-haque, O. E. A fire-arm, smaller than the arquebus; 16th century.

Demi-jambes. Armour for the shins.

Demi-placcate. The lower part of a breast-plate.

Demi-relievo. Sculpture in relief, in which one-half of the figure projects; generally called *Mezzo-relievo.* (See BASSO-RELIEVO.)

Demiurgi (δημι-ουργοί). Popular magistrates.

Demosii. Slaves belonging to the state, at Athens.

Demotic (writing), Egyp. (δημοτικὰ, sc. γράμματα, i. e. popular writing). A mode of writing among the ancient Egyptians, differing from the *hieroglyphic* or sacred writing. This writing, which was employed for civil records, was introduced under the twenty-fifth dynasty, being derived from the *hieratic writing*, the first abbreviation of the hieroglyphics.

Demster, O. E. A judge.

Demyt, O. E. An old [word for dimity; a kind of fustian. Perhaps so called because first manufactured at Damietta.

Denarius, R. (*deni*, by tens). The silver coin principally in use among the Romans. Until the reign of Augustus the denarius was worth ten asses, and afterwards sixteen. *Denarius aureus* was a gold denarius, equal in value to twenty-five silver denarii.

Denia. A city of Valencia in Spain, which disputes with Alcora the production of a remarkable kind of pottery, of which Jacquemart mentions a vase with two handles of Arab form, resembling the alcarazas, upon a smooth white enamel decorated with birds and flowers coarsely painted.

Dens, R. Literally, a *tooth;* hence the prongs of a fork, the flukes of an anchor, the barbs of a lance, the teeth of a saw or rake.

Dentale, R. (*dens,* a tooth). The piece of wood in a plough on which the plough-share (*vomer*) is fastened.

Dentatus, R. Armed with teeth.

Dentelle Decoration. Of French pottery, a light lace pattern, more delicate than the "*lambrequin.*"

Dentels, Fr. (See DENTILE.)

Dentile, Dentils (Latin, *denticuli*), Arch. Ornaments in the form of small cubes or teeth, used in the moulding of cornices, in the IONIC, CORINTHIAN, and COMPOSITE orders. (See TOOTH-ORNAMENT, DOG'S-TOOTH.)

Depas, R. A bowl with two handles, the foot of which is made of a low flat moulding like the Doric fillet.

Depressed, Her. Surmounted, placed over another.

Derby Porcelain. Manufactory established in 1750. Jacquemart says, " Derby has made fine porcelains and statuettes which have nothing to fear by comparison with the groups of Saxony or Sèvres."

Dere, O. E. Noble, honourable.

" Syr Cadore with his *dere* knyghttes."

Derring do, O. E. Deeds of arms.

Deruncinatus, R. Smoothed and polished with the *runcina* or carpenter's plane.

Desca, Lat. A stall or desk in a church.

Descobinatus, R. Rasped with the SCOBINA or carpenter's rasp.

Destrere, Anglo-Norman. A war-horse.

Desultorius (sc. *equus*), R. (*desilio*, to leap off). A horse trained for equestrian performances in a circus by the *desultor*. *Desultorius* is itself sometimes used as a synonym for *desultor*. The *desultor* rode two horses at once, and got his name from his *leaping* or vaulting from one to the other.

Desvres, Pas de Calais, France. An interesting manufactory of faience established in the 17th century, of a style originating in Flanders. (*Jacquemart.*)

Detached. A term in painting applied to figures which stand out well.

Detriment, Her. (See DECRESCENT.)

Deunx, R. (*de* and *uncia*, a twelfth part off). A nominal value not represented by any coin. The term means literally eleven *unciæ*, or eleven-twelfths of anything [i.e. ounces or twelfths of a pound].

Developed, Her. Displayed, unfurled.

Devil, Chr. Mediæval representations of the devil (especially in painting) were taken from those of the satyrs of the ancients. They were, however, subject to no canon of symbolism at all, and varied from the likeness of a beautiful woman to every imaginable variety of the grotesque and repulsive.

Fig. 244. Old Devonshire Lace.

Devonshire Lace (Old). This lace is said to have been first introduced into England by the Flemings in 1567-73, and it long preserved its Flemish character. The engraving shows a specimen of old Devonshire lace, made at the beginning of the last century.

Devs, Pers. Evil genii, servants of Ahriman, in the religion of Zoroaster; they were twenty-eight in number, and were opposed to the ministers of the amchaspands or IZEDS (q. v.).

Dextans, R. (*de* and *sextans*, i. e. a sixth part off). A nominal value not represented by any coin. The literal meaning of the term is ten *unciæ*, or ten-twelfths of anything [ounces].

Dexter, Her. The right side, i. e. to the spectator's or reader's left.

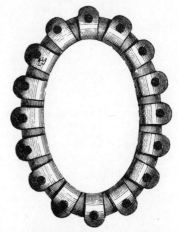

Fig. 245. Dextrochere or bracelet.

Dextrale, R. (*dexter*, right). A bracelet worn by Greek and Roman women on the right arm, and differing from the *dextrocherium* (Fig. 245), which was worn on the wrist. The latter ornament was often of gold. (See ARMILLA.)

Dholkee, Hindoo. A kind of tom-tom, or small drum. (See TOM-TOM.)

Diabathrum, Gr. and R. (βάθρον, that on which one stands). A sandal or light shoe worn by women, especially such as were tall. The comic poet Alexis, talking of courtesans, says, "One is too short, and so she puts cork in her *baukides;* another is too tall, and she puts on a light *diabathrum.*"

Diaconicum, Scevophylacium, and **Bematis Diaconicon**, Chr. A room in an ancient basilica near the altar, where the priests put on and took off their vestments, and the deacons (διάκονοι) prepared the vessels and sacred ornaments to be used in the service. *Diaconicum majus* was the sacristy.

Diadema, R. (διαδέω, to bind round). Originally the white fillet worn by Eastern monarchs round the head. It was made of silk, wool, or yarn, narrow, but wider in the centre of the forehead. The Greeks presented a diadem to every victor in the public games, and it was worn by priests and priestesses. As the emblem of sovereignty it is an attribute of Juno. Afterwards the term came to mean a diadem.

Diæta, Gr. and R. (i. e. a living-place). That part of a house in which a Roman received his guests. The same term was applied to a captain's cabin in the after-part of a ship.

Diætæ, R. Summer-houses. (See HORTUS.)

Diaglyph, Gr. and R. (διαγλύφω, to carve through). An intaglio, or design cut into the material on which it is executed. (See INTAGLIO.)

Diaglyphic. (Sculpture, engraving, &c.) in which the objects are sunk below the general surface.

Diagonal Rib, Arch. A cross formed by the intersection of the ribs which cut one another according to the groins of a groined roof.

Dialia, Gr. and R. (διάλια, from Δὶς, old form for Ζεύς). Festivals held in honour of Jupiter by the Flamen Dialis (the priest of Jupiter).

Diamastigosis, Gr. (διαμαστίγωσις, i. e. a severe scourging). A festival held at Sparta in honour of Artemis Orthia, during which boys were flogged at an altar in order to harden them to the endurance of pain.

Fig. 246. Diamicton.

Diamicton, Gr. and R. (διαμίγνυμι, to mix up). A wall, of which the outside surface was made of brickwork or regular layers of masonry, and the centre was filled up with rubble. (Fig. 246.)

Diamond, for glass-cutting, was not used till the 16th century, although suggested in a Bolognese MS. of a century earlier. Its discovery is attributed to Francis I., who, to let the Duchesse d'Estampes know of his jealousy, wrote on the palace windows with his ring,—

"Souvent femme varie ;
Mal habil qui s'y fie."

The art of cutting and polishing diamonds with diamond powder was discovered by Louis de Berquem in 1476.

Diamond, in Christian art. (See WHITE.)

Diamond Fret, Arch. The descriptive name for a decorated moulding in Norman architecture.

Diamond Rings were used as seal and bearings on his escutcheon (represented in Fig. 100) by Cosmo de' Medici, the founder of the famous Florentine family. The device in various forms was invariably adopted by his descendants. Fig. 247 is the device of Pietro de' Medici († 1470), the son of Cosmo : a falcon with a ring, and the punning motto, "Semper," forming

with the device the words "*Semper fa-'l-con di* (Dio) *amante.*"

Fig. 247. Di-amante, Punning device of Pietro de' Medici.

Diapasma, Gr. and R. (διαπάσσω, to sprinkle). A powder made of dried flowers and odoriferous herbs, which was put in a sachet for use as a perfume, or rubbed over the body.

Diaper, Arch. Ornament of sculpture in low relief, sunk below the general surface.

Diaper, O. E. A mode of decoration by a repeated pattern, carved or painted, generally in squares, representing flowers and arabesques.

Diaper or **Damask**, a name given to a fine

Fig. 248. Diapered surcoat of a Herald, with the clarion.

linen cloth made at Ypres, is spoken of as early as the 13th century.

> "Of cloth making she had such a haunt,
> She passed hem of Ypres and of Gaunte."
> *(Prologue of Canterbury Tales.)*

The peculiarity of this cloth, as of that of Damascus, was in the pattern. "*To diaper*" is, in heraldry, to cover the field of an escutcheon with devices independent of the armorial bearings. The engraving shows a surcoat diapered, on which are embroidered armorial bearings. (Fig. 248.)

Diasia, Gr. Festivals in honour of Zeus, held at Athens, outside of the walls of the city, for the purpose of averting epidemics and other ills (ἄση).

Diastyle, Arch. An intercolumniation, in which the columns are separated from each other by a space of three diameters.

Diathyrum, Gr. A passage leading at one end to the street-door of a house, and at the other to the door of the courtyard. The Romans called this space PROTHYRUM (q.v.).

Diatoni, Diatonoi, Gr. and R. (διατείνω, to extend through). Long stones extending from one face of a wall to the other (to which modern architects give the name of *perpenders* or *perpend-stones*), and which were employed in the method of construction called EMPLECTON (q.v.). In Fig. 249 one is represented by the stone placed between b and c.

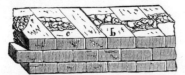

Fig. 249. Diatonoi.

Diatreta, Gr. (διάτρητα, i. e. bored through). A drinking-cup made of glass, cut in such a way that the designs or ornaments upon it stand out completely from the body of the vase, and form a tracery, which is only united to the vase itself by small ties or pins left for the purpose.

Diatriba, Gr. and R. (διατρίβω, to spend time). Places in which learned discussions were held, such as lecture or assembly rooms.

Diaulos, Gr. The double flute. (See AULOS, FLUTE.) One in the British Museum, found in a tomb at Athens, is of cedar-wood, with tubes fifteen inches in length.

Diazoma, Gr. (διάζωμα, that which girdles). A Greek synonym of the Latin term PRÆCINCTIO (q.v.).

Dicasterion, Dicastery, Gr. (δικαστήριον ; δίκη, justice). A tribunal at Athens in which the people themselves administered justice without the intervention of the magistrates.

Dicastes. A judge, or rather juryman, chosen annually from the citizens at Athens.

Dicerion, Chr. (δι-κέραιον, with two horns). A candlestick with two branches, holding which in their hands the Greek priests bless the people. The *dicerion* is symbolical of the two-fold nature of Christ. (See TRICERION.)

Dichalcon, Gr. (δίχαλκος, i. e. double-chalcos). A small Greek copper coin worth only one-fourth or one-fifth of an obolus.

Dichoria, Gr. (δι-χορία, i. e. division of chorus). When the ancient choruses divided into two, to recite in turn a part of the action of a play, or mutually to interchange sentiments, this action was called *dichoria;* each half of the chorus was called *hemichoria* (ἡμιχορία), and each stanza *antichoria* (ἀντιχορία).

Dicken, O. E. The devil. "Odds dickens !"

Dicker, O. E. Half a score.

Dicomos, Gr. (κῶμος, a feast). A banqueting-song, which was sung at the second course of the feast at the festivals of Bacchus.

Dicrotos, Dicrotus, Gr. (δί-κροτος, lit. double-beating). The Greek name for a vessel with two banks of oars, the Roman *biremis*.

Dictynnia (δίκτυον, a hunter's net). A Cretan festival in honour of Artemis.

Dictyotheton, Gr. (from δίκτυον, a net). A kind of masonry composed of regularly-cut square stones, forming, in a wall so constructed,

Fig. 250. Dictyotheton.

a net-work or chess-board pattern. It answered to the *opus reticulatum* of the Romans.

Didrachma, Didrachmum, Gr. (δί-δραχμον). A double silver drachma of the Greek coinage, which was worth about two shillings.

Die. In Architecture, for *dado*, or the part of a pedestal that would correspond to the *dado* (q.v.).

Die-sinking. The art of engraving on steel moulds, medals, coins, and inscriptions.

Difference, Differencing, Her. An addition to, or some change in, a coat-of-arms, introduced for the purpose of distinguishing coats which in their primary qualities are the same. Differencing is sometimes used in the same sense as Cadency; but, strictly, it is distinct, having reference to alliance and dependency, without blood-relationship, or to the system adopted for distinguishing similar coats-of-arms. (*Boutell.*)

Digitale, R. (*digitus,* a finger). A kind of glove worn by the Sarmatians, an example of which may be seen on Trajan's Column.

Diglyph, Gr. and R. (δί-γλυφος, doubly indented). An ornament consisting of two *glyphæ* (γλυφαί) or grooves channelled out on consoles. (See TRIGLYPH.)

Diipoleia (πολιεὺς, of the city). A very ancient Athenian festival, celebrated annually on the Acropolis, in honour of Zeus Polieus.

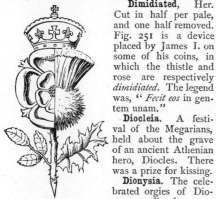

Fig. 251. Rose dimidiated. Device of James I.

Dimidiated, Her. Cut in half per pale, and one half removed. Fig. 251 is a device placed by James I. on some of his coins, in which the thistle and rose are respectively *dimidiated.* The legend was, "*Fecit eos* in gentem unam."

Diocleia. A festival of the Megarians, held about the grave of an ancient Athenian hero, Diocles. There was a prize for kissing.

Dionysia. The celebrated orgies of Dionysus or Bacchus, suppressed B.C. 186, and substituted by the Liberalia. (See BACCHANALIA.)

Dioptra, Gr. and R. (δίοπτρα; διοράω, to see through). An instrument used in surveying to measure distances and to take levels.

Dioscuria, Gr. and R. (Διοσκούρια). Games instituted at Rome in honour of the Dioscuri (Castor and Pollux), who, at the battle of Lake Regillus against the Latins (496 B.C.), were supposed to have fought on the side of the Romans.

Diospolites, Egyp. One of the nomes or divisions of Lower Egypt.

Diota, Gr. (δί-ωτα, with two ears). A name applied indifferently to any kind of vase furnished with two handles, such as *lagenæ, amphoræ, canthari,* &c.

Diplinthus, R. (πλίνθος, a brick). Masonry two bricks thick.

Diploïs, Gr. and R. Folded in two; an upper garment which was doubled in the same manner as a woman's shawl at the present day; it was much worn among the Greeks.

Diploma, Gr. and R. (δίπλωμα, i. e. double-folded). A passport consisting of two leaves (whence its name). The term is also used to denote a diploma by which any right or privilege is conferred.

Dipteral, Arch. A building having double wings. The term is applied to any building having a double intercolumniation all round it.

Diptheræ, Gr. and R. (διφθέραι; δέφω, to make supple). (1) Prepared skins for writing on. (2) A kind of garment; an overcoat of skin or leather which Greek slaves put on over their tunic.

Diptych, Gr. (δί-πτυχα, i.e. double-folded). Double tablets united by means of strings or hinges. *Diptycha consularia, ædilitia, prætoria* had engraved on them portraits of consuls, ædiles, prætors, and other magistrates. These consular diptychs were a part of the presents sent by new consuls on their appointment to very eminent persons. The series of them is a very valuable record of the progress of the art of ivory carving. In Christian archæology diptychs were decorated with scenes from biblical history. There were also diptychs of the baptized; of the bishops and benefactors of a church, living or dead; of saints and martyrs; and, lastly, of deceased members of the congregation, whose souls were to be remembered at mass. (See TRIPTYCH.)

Directors, or **Triangular Compasses.** A mathematical instrument adapted for taking three angular points at once.

Diribitorium, R. (*diribeo,* to sort or separate). A place or building in which a public officer inspected the troops, distributed the pay, and enrolled the conscripts in their respective regiments.

Dirige, Chr. A psalm forming part of the burial service, "Dirige gressus meos," &c.; hence **Dirge,** for funereal music or hymns in general.

Dirk. A Scotch dagger.

Diruta. An important porcelain manufactory in the Papal States, established by a pupil of Luca della Robbia in 1461.

Discerniculum, R. (*discerno,* to divide). A bodkin used by Roman women in the toilet to part their hair. (See COMBS.)

Discharging Arch. An arch built into the structure of a wall, to relieve the parts below it of the pressure of those above it; such arches are common over flat-headed doors or other openings.

Discinctus, Gr. and R. (*discingo,* to ungird). A man who is *ungirt,* that is, who does not wear a girdle round the waist of his tunic; for a man, this was a mark of effeminate manners. *Discinctus miles* denoted a soldier who had been stripped by his commander of his sword-belt, as a mark of disgrace. (Compare CINGULUM.)

Fig. 252. Tazza of Diruta, with head of "Rome."

Disclosed, Her. With expanded wings, in the case of birds that are not birds of prey. The contrary to CLOSE.

Discobolus, Gr. and R. (δισκο-βόλος, i.e. discus-throwing). A man throwing the DISCUS (q.v.). [A celebrated statue of the sculptor Myron so called.]

Fig. 253. Discobolus of Myron copied on a gem.

Discus, R. (δίσκος; δικεῖν, to throw). This term denoted (1) the discus hurled by the DISCOBOLUS (q.v.); that is, a circular plate of metal or stone, about ten or twelve inches in diameter. (2) A sun-dial. (3) A shallow circular vessel for holding eatables.

Disk. (See WINGED DISK.)

Disomum, Chr. (δί-σωμον, double-bodied). An urn or tomb which held the ashes or bodies of two persons; *bisomum* was also used. Both terms are met with in Christian inscriptions.

Displayed, Her. Birds of prey with expanded wings. Fig. 254 represents the crest of Edward IV., the falcon and fetterlock.

Fig. 254. Falcon Displayed.

Displuviatus, Displuviatum, R. An atrium, the roof of which was sloped outwards from the COMPLUVIUM(q.v.), instead of being sloped towards it. (See IMPLUVIUM and ATRIUM.)

Disposed, Disposition, Her. Arranged, arrangement.

Distaff. A common object in ancient art. It is an attribute of the Fates, and generally distaffs of gold were given to the goddesses. It was dedicated to Minerva. (See COLUS.) The name of St. Distaff's Day was given to the day after Twelfth Day in England.

Distance. In a picture, *the point of distance* is that where the visual rays meet; *middle distance* is the central portion of a picture, between the *foreground* and the *extreme distance*.

Distemper. A kind of painting in which the pigments are mixed with an aqueous vehicle, such as *size*. Distemper is painted on a dry surface. (See FRESCO-PAINTING.)

Ditriglyph, R. (δὶς, twice, and τρίγλυφος). The space between two triglyphs in the Doric order. The term is therefore a synonym of METOPE (q.v.).

Dividers. Ordinary compasses for taking off and transferring measurements.

Dividiculum, R. A reservoir in the form of a tower, in which the water of an aqueduct was collected, and whence it was afterwards distributed. (See CASTELLUM.)

Docana (δοκὸς, a beam). An ancient Spartan symbol of Castor and Pollux. It consisted of two upright beams, with cross pieces.

Doccia. An important Italian manufactory of soft porcelain founded in 1735. Jacquemart says, "Doccia now inundates Europe with spurious majolica of the 16th century, and with false porcelain of Capo di Monte, of which she possesses the moulds."

Dodecahedron, Gr. A solid figure of twelve equal sides.

Dodecastyle, Gr. and R. (δώδεκα, twelve, and στῦλος, pillar). A building, the arrangement of which admits of twelve columns in front. A dodecastyle pediment is a pediment supported by twelve columns.

Dodra, R. (*dodrans*, nine parts). A kind of beverage, or rather soup, composed of nine ingredients. We learn from Ausonius that it was made of bread, water, wine, oil, broth, salt, sweet herbs, honey, and pepper.

Dodrans, R. (i. e. three-fourths). Nine *unciæ*, or three-quarters of an *as*. There was no coin of this value. As a measure of *length*, nine inches. (See As.)

Doff or **Deff**, Egyp. The square tambourine of the ancient Egyptians; the *toph* of the Hebrews, still in use among the Arabs, especially in the Barbary States.

Dog. An emblem of fidelity and loyalty. In mediæval art, the attribute of St. Roch; also of St. Dominic, the founder of the Dominican order; of St. Bernard, St. Wendelin, and St. Benignus. As an emblem of fidelity, it is placed at the feet of the effigies of married women upon sepulchres. It was common to represent, in painting or mosaic, a chained watch-dog at the doors of Roman houses. The DOG OF FO is a sacred emblem in China, sometimes called a *Chimera*; it is placed as the guardian of the thresholds of temples, and of the Buddhist altars. In the Chinese zodiacal system the dog is the sign for the month of September.

Dog Latin. Barbarous Latin; e. g. "Verte canem ex" (turn the dog out).

Dog's-nose, O. E. A cordial used in low life, composed of warm porter, moist sugar, gin, and nutmeg. (*Halliwell*.)

Dog's-tooth Moulding, Arch. A characteristic ornament of Early English architecture, formed of four leaves with small spiral fillets,

which bear some resemblance to teeth. (See TOOTH-ORNAMENT.)

Dolabra, R. (*dolo*, to hew). An instrument like a pick or hatchet, which varied in form according

to the different purposes for which it was employed. The *dolabra* was used for digging, cutting, breaking, and chopping, and was thus a pick, a hatchet, an adze or *ascia*, &c. Dolabra of flint or other hard stone, called Celts, are of remote antiquity. (See CELT.) (Figs. 255 to 257.)

Fig. 257.
Gallic hatchet.

Doliolum. Dimin. of DOLIUM (q.v.).

Dolium or **Culeus**, Gr. and R. A large earthenware vessel with a wide mouth, and of rounded, spherical form. It was used to contain wine and oil when first made, before they were transferred into smaller vessels for keeping.

Dolmen, Celt. A term which, in the Celtic

Fig. 258. Dolmen.

Fig. 259. Dolmen, in the forest of Rennes.

language, means literally a stone table. It consists of a number of stones, of which some are fixed in the ground, and the others laid transversely over them. These structures were used as sepulchres. Figs. 258 and 259 represent two different types of dolmens. (See CROMLECH.)

Dolon or **Dolo**, R. (δόλων). (1) A long stick armed with an iron point. (2) A cane, in the hollow of which a poniard was concealed. (3) The fore-topsail of a vessel.

Dolphin, Her. A favourite fish with heralds. It is best known as the armorial ensign of the Dauphin, the eldest son and heir apparent of the kings of France—Or, a Dolphin *az.* In Chris-

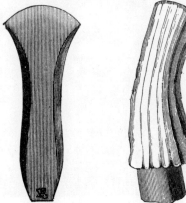

Fig. 255. Bronze Dolabra or hatchet (Celtic).

Fig. 256. Hatchet, flintstone.

I

tian archæology the dolphin is the symbol of swiftness, diligence, and love; it is often met

Fig. 260. Heraldic Dolphin.

with entwined with an anchor. The first Christians often wore these two symbols united in a ring. which was known as a *nautical anchor*. (See also DELPHIN.)

Dome, It. (1) Literally, the *house* of God. When a city possesses several churches, the name is applied to the

Fig. 260. Heraldic Dolphin.

cathedral only. (2) The interior of a *cupola*.

Dominions, in Christian art. (See ANGELS.)

Domus, Gr. and R. (Gr. δόμος, οἶκος). A house, in contradistinction to *insula*, a group of houses. The Greek house is divided into two parts by the central chambers. The external, the ANDRONITIS, contains the men's, and the inner, or GYNÆCONITIS, the women's apartments. The whole building was generally long and narrow, occupying a comparatively small frontage to the street, and the outside wall was plain without windows. Outside the door was often an altar of Apollo Agyieus, or an obelisk, or sometimes a laurel-tree, or a bust of the god Hermes. A few steps, called ANABATHMOI, led up to the house door (αὐλεία θύρα), over which there was generally a motto inscribed: the passage (θυρωρεῖον, πυλὼν, θυρὼν) (A B in the plan) had the stables on one side, and the porter's lodge opposite, and led to C, the PERISTYLE or AULA of the men's quarters, a HYPÆTHRAL, or open-air court, surrounded by porticoes called STOAI, and by the men's apartments, which were large banqueting-rooms (οἶκοι, ἀνδρῶνες), smaller sitting-rooms (ἐξέδραι), and sleeping-chambers (δωμάτια, κοιτῶνες, οἰκήματα). The door to the passage D was called μέταυλος or μέσαυλος (i.e. the middle of the aulæ), and gave admission to E, the peristyle or aula of the Gynæconitis. The rooms numbered 10 to 17 were the chambers

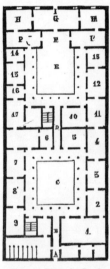

Fig. 261. Plan of a Greek house.

of the women; P P were called the Thalamos and Amphithalamos; H H and G were the ἱστῶνες, or rooms for working in wool; and at I was the garden door (κηπαία θύρα). There was usually an upper story where guests and slaves were lodged (ὑπερῷον, διῆρες), the stairs leading to which were outside the house. The roofs were flat, and it was customary to walk upon them. The floors were of stone, in later times ornamental or coloured. The construction and decoration varied with the ages; painted ceilings were a late introduction.

Fig. 262. Plan of a Roman house.

Of a Roman house, the principal parts were the VESTIBULUM, or court before the door, open to the street; the OSTIUM, JANUA, or FORES, the entrance; the ATRIUM, CAVUM ÆDIUM, or CAVÆDIUM, with the COMPLUVIUM open over the central tank (termed the IMPLUVIUM); the

Fig. 263. Atrium with Doric columns. (*See also* Fig. 49.)

ALÆ (wings\), TABLINUM, FAUCES, and PERI-
STYLIUM : of each of which a notice will be found
in its alphabetical place in this work. (See also
CUBICULA,TRICLINIA, EXEDRÆ, PINACOTHECA,
BIBLIOTHECA, BALNEUM, CULINA, CŒNACULA,
DIÆTA, SOLARIA, &c.) The floors of a Roman
house were either of the composition called RU-
DERATIO, and, from the process of beating down
pavita, were then called PAVIMENTUM, or
of stone or marble or mosaics (MUSIVUM OPUS).
The inner walls were usually covered with
frescoes. The ceilings left the beams visible,
which supported the roof, and the hollow or
unplanked spaces (LACUNARIA or LAQUEARIA)
were often covered with gold and ivory, or with
paintings. (See CAMARA.) The principal apartments had no windows, deriving their light from
the roof; in the upper stories there were
windows either open or latticed, or later filled
with mica, and finally glass.

Don Pottery. A name given to the productions
of a porcelain manufactory established in 1790
at Swinton on the Don.

Donjon, Mod. The principal tower of a
Norman or mediæval
castle. It was gene-
rally separate from
the other parts of the
building. The greater
number of feudal
fortresses originally
consisted merely of a
donjon erected on
an artificial earth-
work. This donjon
was surrounded by
an open space wall-
ed, called the Inner
Bailey, and another
beyond called the
Outer Bailey. Be-
neath were the dun-
geons. Fig. 264 re-
presents a donjon
called the Tower of
Loudun. The White
tower is the donjon of
the Tower of London.

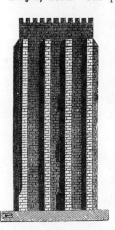

Fig. 264. Donjon.

Doom. In Christian art, the Last Judgment ;
a subject usually painted over the chancel arch
in parochial churches.

Dorelot. A network for the hair, worn by
ladies in the 14th century. (See CALANTICA,
CRESPINE, &c.)

Doric Order of Architecture. The earliest
and simplest of the three Greek orders. "The
Grecian Doric order, at its best period, is one
of the most beautiful inventions of architecture—
strong and yet elegant, graceful in outline and
harmonious in all its forms, imposing when on
a great scale, and pleasing equally when reduced

in size, by the exquisite simplicity of its parts."
(*Newlands.*) The columns of this order had no
pedestal, nor base ;
the capital, which
was half a dia-
meter in height,
had no *astragal*,
but a few plain
fillets, with chan-
nels between
them, under the
ovolo, and a small
channel below the
fillets. The *ovolo*
is generally flat,
and of great pro-
jection, with a
quirk, or return.
On this was laid
the ABACUS,
which was only a
plain tile, without
fillet or ornament.
A peculiarity of
this order was the
flutings of the co-
lumn, twenty in
number, shallow,
and with sharp
edges. The best
examples of the
Grecian Doric of
which we have
descriptions and
figures are the
temples of Miner-
va (called the Par-
thenon) and of
Theseus at Athens,
and that of Mi-
nerva at Sunium.

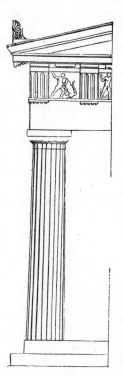

Fig. 265. Column and Capital
of the Doric Order.

The ROMAN DORIC differs in important particulars from the Grecian. (See ROMAN DORIC.)

Dormant or **Couchant,** Her. Asleep. (See
COUCHANT.)

Dormer (Fr. *dormir*, to sleep). The top story
in the roof of a house.

Dormer Window. A gabled window in the
sloping side of a roof, projecting *vertically* ; when
it lies in the slope of the roof, it is a *skylight*.

Dorneck, Dornex, or **Dornyks,** O. E. An inferior damask, wrought of silk, wool, linen thread,
and gold, at Tournay or *Dorneck* ; 15th century.

Dorsale, Dosser, Dossier, Chr. (*dorsum*, the
back). Pieces of tapestry or hangings put up
in the arches or bays surrounding the choir of a
church in order to screen the clergy and choristers
from draughts of air. Also pieces of tapestry hung
upon parapets, the panels of pulpits and stalls, and
sometimes the backs of side-boards. It was the
custom to hang tapestry, cloth of Arras, or

needlework round the lower half of all the ancient dining-halls to a height of about five feet above the basement.

Dorsualia, R. (*dorsum*). An embroidered saddle-cloth, which was laid across the back of a horse on the occasion of a triumphal entry, or on the backs of victims for sacrifice. Examples of *dorsualia* occur on several monuments, in especial on a bas-relief of the arch of Titus, at Rome.

Doryphorus, Gen. (δορυ-φόρος). Literally, spear-bearer. Fig. 130 represents a Persian spearman. A celebrated statue of Polycleitus (of the Argive school) is called the *Doryphorus.* "Polyclitus advanced his art in several respects, chiefly by fixing a law of proportion, of which his Doryphorus, a youth bearing a spear, was called the CANON (q.v.); and also by his making the weight of the body rest on one foot, in contradistinction to the ancient practice, thereby producing a contrast between the supporting, weight-bearing side of the body, and the supported, freely-resting side." (*Butler's Imitative Art.*) The statue by Polycleitus is lost. The proportions handed down to us by Vitruvius are thus described by Bonomi:—

(1) The length of the horizontally extended arms equals the height of the figure.
(2) The head is an *eighth*, the face a *tenth* of the whole height.
(3) From the top of the scalp to the nipples is *one-fourth*.
(4) From the nipples to horizontal line across the centre of the square—the pubes—is *one-fourth*.
(5) From that line to one just below the knee-cap is *one-fourth*.
(6) From that line to the ground is *one-fourth*.
(7) The fore-arm (from the elbow) is a *fourth* of the height ; the hand a *tenth*.

Dose or **Dosall,** O. E. (Lat. DORSALE, q.v.).

Dossar. (See DORSALE.)

Douai. A manufactory of modern faience established in 1784, producing stone-wares and "cailloutages."

Doublé, Fr. (1) The term is applied to precious stones, when cemented upon glass. (2) The inside lining of a well-bound book.

Doublet, although deriving its name from the French word *doublée* (lined), is in that language more generally known as "Pourpoint," of which, in fact, it is merely a variety. It first appeared in England in the 14th century made without sleeves, which for convenience were afterwards added ; and being universally adopted, it superseded the tunic. The engraving shows a doublet with stuffed sleeves of the time of Elizabeth. They were worn of varied forms till the reign of Charles II. (Fig. 267.)

Doubling, Her. The lining of a mantle or mantling.

Dove. A Christian symbol of frequent occurrence ; it expresses candour, gentleness, innocence, faith, and, in especial, the Holy Spirit. It is also a symbol of martyrdom and grief, and in this signification appears frequently represented on tombs and sarcophagi. With an olive-bough in its mouth it is a symbol of peace, and accordingly the inscription PAX (Peace) is often found accompanying representations of the dove, more particularly in the catacombs.

Fig. 267. Doublet costume, *temp.* Elizabeth.

With the Assyrians and Babylonians the dove was the symbol of Semiramis, who, according to them, took this shape on leaving earth. The dove was the favourite bird of Venus. As a symbol of conjugal fidelity, the device of two turtle-doves was adopted by Giovanna of Austria on her marriage with Francesco de' Medici. (Fig. 268.)

Dove-tail or **Swallow-tail,** Gen. A method of joining employed for wood, stone, or iron, and so called because the tenon by which the joint is effected is cut in the shape of a dove-tail or swallow-tail. This tail fits into a notch (Fig. 269). The ancients employed double dove-tails for joining stones together ; this method of construction was called *Opus* REVINCTUM (q.v.).

Dove-tail Moulding, Arch. (Norman ; called

also TRIANGULAR FRETTE). Decorated with running bands in the form of dove-tails.

Fig. 268. Two Doves. Device of Giovanna de' Medici.

Doves, the Eucharistic. Sacred vessels of gold, silver, gilded bronze, or ivory, in the

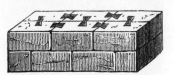

Fig. 269. Dove-tailed Masonry.

form of a dove, a tower, &c., which served as receptacles for the reserved Host ; they were hung up in the middle of the CIBORIUM (q.v.). At the Amiens Museum a dove of this kind is to be seen dating from the 12th century, and at the church of St. Nazaire at Milan there is one of silver, gilded within and enamelled without, which is also very ancient.

Dowlas, O. E. Coarse linen cloth made in Brittany ; "*filthy dowlas !* "

Drachma, Gr. (δραχμή; δράσσομαι, to hold in the hand). A drachm, the principal silver coin of the Greeks. There were two kinds of *drachmata*, which differed in value : the Attic drachm and the Æginetan. The Attic *drachma* was equal in value to a franc, equal to six *oboloi*. The piece of four drachmas was called a *stater*. As a weight the drachma was the eighth of an *uncia ;* about = our modern *drachm.*

Draco, Gen. (1) A dragon ; the ensign of the Roman cohort in the time of Trajan, adopted from the Parthians. (2) A fantastic animal of Pagan mythology : the garden of the Hesperides, the Golden Fleece, and the fountain of Castalia were all guarded by dragons. (3) In Christian archæology the dragon symbolizes sin, especially idolatry. (4) The Chinese give to several immortals the figure of a dragon. They distinguish the long dragon of heaven, a being especially sacred; the Kau, dragon of the mountain ;

and the Li, dragon of the sea. The dragons are represented as "gigantic saurians, with powerful claws, and terminated by a frightful head, scaly and strongly toothed." There are the scaly dragon, the winged dragon, the horned and the hornless dragons, and the dragon rolled within itself which has not yet taken flight to the upper regions. In their zodiacal system the dragon is the sign for the month of March. (See TCHY.)

Draconarius, R. The standard-bearer who carried the *draco.*

Dracontarium, R. A band for the head, so called because it was twisted in imitation of the *draco* which was used as an ensign.

Fig. 270. Heraldic Dragon.

Dragon, Her. A winged monster having four legs. (See DRACO.)

Dragon. A short carbine (hence "dragoons").

Dragon's Blood. A resinous astringent extract of a deep red colour, used as a colouring ingredient for spirit and turpentine varnishes and paints, &c. The Roman *cinnabar* was Dragon's Blood.

Draught (or **Drawte**) **Chamber,** O. E. The with-*drawing room.*

Draughts, Game of. (See DAMES, LATRUNCULI.)

Dravid'ha, Hind. A Hindoo temple constructed on an octagonal plan. (See NAGARAS, VIMANA, VESARA.)

Dresden Porcelain, made at the Royal Manufactory established at Meissen in Saxony in 1709, is most excellent anterior to 1796, since when its ancient perfection has been lost. The mark of the best period is two crossed swords, with a sloped cross or a small circle beneath. The later mark has a star beneath the swords. On rejected pieces the swords were cut across with a line ; but the manufactory at the present day counterfeits its old marks. Fig. 271 is a specimen of the best period, later than 1720 and before 1778.

Dressoir or **Dressouer** (the *buffet* of the 15th century, the *évidence* of the 16th) was the principal object of the dining-room, on which were displayed all the ornamental plate of the owner of the house, costly vases, &c. Kings had often three dressers, one for silver, another for silver-gold, and the third for gold plate. In form they varied ; but they were made of the most valuable woods, and enriched with the finest carving. They were sometimes covered over with cloth of gold : the city of Orleans offered one in gold to Charles IV., which was valued at 8000 livres Tournois.

Drilbu, Hind. A bell used in Buddhist worship.

Drinking-cups of Glass are frequently found in the Saxon barrows or graves in England. They are ornamented in various patterns, and

Fig. 271. Dresden milk-jug.

rounded at the bottom. The Anglo-Saxons were also rich in cups of the precious metals.

Fig. 272. Pot-pourri vase, Dresden china.

They used horn cups also, as did the Normans. In the 15th century flat-shaped cups or bowls were used.

Drip, Arch. The edge of a roof ; the eaves ; the corona of a cornice.

Drip-stone, Arch. The moulding in Gothic architecture which serves as a canopy for an opening and to throw off the rain. It is also called *weather-moulding* and *water-table*. (See also CORONA.)

Dromo, Dromon, R. (δρόμων ; δραμεῖν, to run). A vessel remarkable for its swift sailing ; hence—

Dromon or **Dromound,** O. E. A mediæval ship, propelled by oars and one sail, used for the transport of troops. The Crusaders called it a *dromedary*.

Dromos, Gr. and Egyp. (δρόμος). (1) The Spartan racecourse. (2) An avenue leading to the entrances of Egyptian temples ; that leading to the great temple of Karnac contained 660 colossal sphinxes, all of which were monoliths.

Drop Lake is a pigment obtained from Brazil wood, which affords a very fugitive colour.

Drops, Arch. (Lat. *guttæ*). Ornaments resembling drops, used in the Doric entablature, immediately under the TRIGLYPH and MUTULE.

Druidic (Monuments), Celt. Celtic monuments, also known by the name of *Megalithic*. (See STANDING-STONES, DOLMENS, MENHIRS, CROMLECHS, &c.). The most ancient and probably the largest Celtic or Druidical temple was at Avebury in Wiltshire. *Dr. Stukeley,* who surveyed it in 1720, says that "this may be regarded as the grand national cathedral, while the smaller circles which are met with in other parts of the island may be compared to the parish or village churches."

Drum, Arch. (1) Of a dome or cupola, the STYLOBATE (or vertical part on which the columns rest). (2) Of the Corinthian and Composite capitals, the solid part ; called also BELL, VASE, BASKET.

Dry Point. Direct engraving upon copper with the sharp etching-needle itself, without the plate being covered with etching-ground, or the lines bit in by acid. This method produces very soft and delicate work, but it is not so durable in printing as the etched line.

Dryers. In painting, substances imparted to oils to make them dry quickly. The most general in use is OXIDE of LEAD, but white copperas, oxide of manganese, ground glass, oxide of zinc, calcined bones, chloride of lime, and verdigris have all been used at various times.

Drying Oil. Boiled oil, used in painting as a vehicle and a varnish. It is linseed oil boiled with litharge (or oxide of lead).

Dryness. A style of painting in which the outline is harsh and formal, and the colour deficient in mellowness and harmony.

Duck-bills, O. E. Broad-toed shoes of the 15th century.

Duke, Her. The highest rank and title in the British peerage; first introduced by Edward III. in the year 1337, when he created the Black Prince the first English duke (in

Fig. 273. Duke's coronet.

Latin "dux"). The coronet of a duke, arbitrary in its adornment until the 16th century was far advanced, is now a circlet, heightened with eight conventional strawberry-leaves, of which in representation three and two half-leaves are shown. (*Boutell.*)

Dulcimer. A musical instrument, the prototype of our pianoforte. It was very early known to the Arabs and Persians, who called it *santir.* One of its old European names is the *cimbal.* The Hebrew *nebel*, or perhaps the *psanterin* mentioned by Daniel, is supposed to have been a dulcimer; the *psalterion* of the Greeks also. A hand organ of the Middle Ages was called a dulcimer.

Dunkirk. A manufactory of modern faience which only existed for a short time in the 18th century, and was closed within a year. The works are therefore very rare. Jacquemart mentions a clock bearing a close resemblance to certain Dutch products, inscribed *Dickhoof* and *A. Duisburg*, and by the latter name identified as Dunkirk work.

Duns, Celtic. Ancient hill forts of the simplest kind, consisting of a round or oval earthen wall and ditch on a rising ground, probably contemporary with the pit dwellings.

Dunster, O. E. Broad-cloth made in Somersetshire, *temp.* Edward III.

Dutch Pink. (See PINKS.)

Dutch White. (See CARBONATE OF LEAD, BARYTES.)

Dwararab'ha, Dwaragopouras, Dwaraharmya, Dwaraprasada, Dwarasala, Ind. (See GOPOURAS.)

E.

Eagle, Her. The eagle (called in heraldry *Alerion*)appears in the earliest English examples of arms, and his appearance often denotes an alliance with German princes. Both the German emperors and Russian czars adopted the eagle for their heraldic ensign in support of their claim to be considered the successors of the

Fig. 274. Eagle—Ensign of France.

Roman Cæsars. The eagle borne as the ensign of Imperial France sits, grasping a thunderbolt, in an attitude of vigilance, having its wings elevated, but the tips of the feathers drooping, as they would be in a living bird. In remote antiquity the eagle was an emblem of the sun, and the double-headed eagle typifies the rising and the setting sun. The eagle was the attribute of Jove as his messenger. The eagle killing a serpent or a hare is an ancient symbol of victory. In Christian art the eagle is the attribute of St. John the Evangelist, the symbol of the highest inspiration. St. John is sometimes represented with human body and eagle head. The lectern in Christian churches is commonly in the form of an eagle. Elisha the prophet is represented with a two-headed eagle. (See AQUILÆ.)

Earl, Her. (from the Gaelic *iarflath*, "a dependent chief" = *iar*, "after," and *flath*, "lord"; pronounced *iarrl*). Before 1337 the highest, and now the third degree of rank and dignity in the British peerage. An earl's coronet has eight lofty rays of gold rising from the

Fig. 275. Earl's coronet.

circlet, each of which supports a large pearl, while between each pair of these rays there is a golden strawberry-leaf. In representation five of the rays and pearls are shown. Elevated clusters of pearls appear in an earl's coronet as early as 1445; but the present form of the coronet may be assigned to the second half of the following century.

Earl Marshal. In England, one of the great officers of state, who regulates ceremonies and takes cognizance of all matters relating to honour, arms, and pedigree.

Early English Architecture. The first of the pointed or Gothic styles of architecture used in England. It succeeded the NORMAN towards the end of the 12th century, and gradually

merged into the DECORATED at the end of the
13th. Its leading peculiarity is the long narrow
lancet window.

Earn, Scotch. An eagle

Fig. 276. Greek or Etruscan ear-rings in gold.

Ear-rings (Lat. *inaures,* Gr. ἐνώτια) were
a common ornament for ladies in Greece and
Rome, and among the early Saxons : they were
worn by men during the reigns of Elizabeth and
James I.

Earth Tables, Arch. The projecting course of
stones in a wall, immediately above the surface
of the ground, now called the plinth. (*Parker.*)

Earthenware. (See POTTERY.)

Easel (from the German *esel,* an ass). A
frame with movable rest for resting pictures on.

Easel-picture. A small portable picture.

Easter, Chr. (A.S. *eastre*). From the goddess
"Eostur," whose festival fell in April. The
Latin name "Paschal" refers to the Jewish
feast of the Passover. The Paschal season
originally extended over fifteen days, from Palm
Sunday to Low Sunday. (See *Smith and
Cheetham's Dict. of Christian Ant.*)

Eaves (A.S. *efese,* the edge). The overhanging "edge" of the roof of a house.

Ebénistes, Fr. Workers in fine cabinet-
making.

Ebony. A heavy, hard, black wood, obtained
from the Diospyrus ebenus. Ebony and other
exotic woods came into general use in Europe
from the end of the 17th century—subsequently
to 1695, when the Dutch settled in Ceylon. The
black ebony is the most valuable, but there are
green and yellow varieties. Old carved ebony
furniture found in English houses dates generally from the early years of the Dutch occupation of Ceylon.

Eburnean. Made of ivory.

Ecbasios (ἐκβαίνω, to disembark). A sacrifice
offered to Apollo after a favourable voyage.

Ecclesia, Gr. General assembly of the citizens
of Athens. (See *Smith and Cheetham's Dict.
of Christian Ant.*)

Echea, Gr. and R. (ἦχος, sound or noise).
Earthenware or bronze vessels used to strengthen
the sound in theatres. (See ACOUSTIC VESSELS.)

Echinate. Armed with spines or bristles
like a hedgehog.

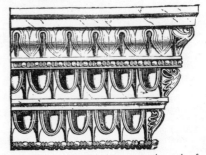

Fig. 277. Echinus or egg and tongue on the ovolo of a
Greek cornice.

Echinus, Arch. (Gr. ἐχῖνος, a hedgehog).
The *egg and dart* or *egg and tongue* ornament
frequently carved on the round moulding, much
used in classic architecture, called the *ovolo.*
(Fig. 277.)

Echometry (μέτρον, a measure). The art of
measuring the duration of sounds.

Ecorchée, Fr. (lit. flayed). Said of an anatomical model specially prepared for the study
of the muscular system.

Ecphonesis, Chr. That part of a devotional
office which is said *audibly,* in contrast with that
said *secreté.*

Ectypus, R. A hollow mould which produces an impression in relief which is called
ectypum.

Fig 278. Ecuelle, Venetian porcelain.

Ecuelle, Fr. A porringer. Fig. 278 is a
specimen in the best style of Venetian porcelain.

Edward-Shovelboards, O. E. Broad shillings
of Edward VI., formerly used in playing the
game of shovelboard. (*Halliwell.*)

Effeir of War, Scotch. Warlike guise.

Effigies, R. An image or effigy. The word is
usually applied to the heads upon coins or medals.

Egg and Dart, or **Egg and Tongue, Ornament,** Arch. (Fr. *aards et oves*). A carving

commonly inserted on the ovolo moulding. (See ECHINUS.)

Egg-feast or **Egg-Saturday**, O. E. The Saturday before Shrove Tuesday.

Egg-shell Porcelain. A very thin white porcelain of the "Rose family," to which the Chinese have given the name of "porcelain without embryo."

Eggs, as a Christian emblem, are supposed to represent "the immature hope of the resurrection." (*Martigny*.)

Egret (Fr. *aigrette*). A small white heron, marked by a *crest* on his head.

Egyptian Architecture and **Sculpture** can be studied in the monuments remaining from remotest antiquity to about A.D. 300. Great varieties of style occur, which can be easily attributed to their respective periods by the hieroglyphical inscriptions. The three primitive motives of all Egyptian buildings are the *pyramid, caves,* and *structures of timber;* all contemporary with the most ancient relics. In sculpture, the most ancient works of all are also those most remarkable for fidelity to nature. The conventionality introduced afterwards with the *canon of proportions* is still combined with a close imitation of Nature in the details. The Grecian or Ptolemaic period begins B.C. 322. [See *Wilkinson's Ancient Egyptians, Canina's Egyptian Architecture;* and the works of *Brugsch, Marriette, Soldi, Ebers,* &c.]

Egyptian Blue, the brilliant blue pigment found on the monuments, is found by analysis to consist of the hydrated protoxide of copper, mixed with a minute quantity of iron. The green colour was derived from another oxide of copper; violet from manganese or gold; yellow from silver, or perhaps iron; and red from the protoxide of copper.

Fig. 279. Oviform bottle. Egyptian.

Egyptian Pottery of great beauty is found in great quantities along with the costly ornaments in the tombs. It is intermediary between porcelain and stoneware, and its colouring demonstrates a high degree of skill, science, and precision of execution. Among the forms frequently found are the oviform, long-necked bottles (Fig. 279), lenticular phials

with royal cartouches (Fig. 280), lamps (Fig. 281), &c. (See also Fig. 219.)

Fig. 280. Lenticular Phials. Louvre Museum.

Eikon, Gr., or **Icon**, Lat. An image; hence iconoclasts or image-breakers.

Eileton, Chr. (from εἴλω, to wind or

Fig. 281. Lamp in blue enamelled earthenware. Egyptian.

fold). The cloth on which the elements are consecrated in the Eucharist. "The *eileton* represents the linen cloth in which the body of Christ was wrapped when it was taken down from the cross and laid in the tomb." (*Germanus*).

Eisodos, Chr. A ceremony of the Greek Church, of two parts. (1) The bearing into the church in procession of the book of the Gospels is called the *Lesser Entrance.* (2) A similar bearing in of the elements of the Eucharist is called the *Greater Entrance.*

Elæolite (lit. oil-stone). A mineral having a fatty resinous lustre.

Elæothesium, Gr. and R. A room in a suite of baths where oils, perfumes, and essences were kept, and the bathers were anointed and rubbed.

Elaphebolia, Gr. Athenian festivals held in the month called *Elaphebolion*, or the ninth month of the year, when a stag (ἔλαφος) was sacrificed to Diana.

Elbow-gauntlet. A long gauntlet of plate armour, adopted from the Asiatics in the 16th century.

Elbow-pieces (Fr. *coudières*). Plate armour to cover the joint at the elbow.

Elbows, Mod. (Fr. *accoudoirs*). The divisions between the stalls in a church, also called by the French "museaux," from the fact of their ends being ornamented with an animal's head.

Electoral Bonnet, Her. A cap of crimson velvet guarded with ermine, borne over the inescutcheon of the arms of Hanover from 1801 to 1816.

Electrotint. A method of preparing engraved copper plates for the printing-press by the electrotype process. (See *Art Journal*, 1850.)

Electrotype. The process whereby works in relief are produced by the agency of electricity, through which certain metals, such as gold, silver, and copper, are precipitated from their solutions upon moulds in so fine a state of division as to form a coherent mass of pure metal, equal in toughness and flexibility to the hammered metals. (*Fairholt.*) At the present day electrotypes are generally taken from engravings on wood for printing from.

Electrum (ἤλεκτρον). In Homer and Hesiod this word means *amber*. Pliny says that when gold contains a fifth part of silver, it is called electrum. Its colour was whiter and more luminous than that of gold, and the metal was supposed to betray the presence of poison. Specimens are rare. A beautiful vase of electrum is preserved in the St. Petersburg Museum. Some coins in electrum were struck by the kings of Bosporus, and by Syracuse and some Greek states.

Elements, Chr. The bread and the wine in the Lord's Supper. In the Eastern liturgies the unconsecrated elements are called "the MYSTERIES," and the bread alone the SEAL (σφραγὶς), from its being divided by lines in the form of a cross. The interesting subject of the composition and form of the elements in the early churches is fully discussed in the "Dictionary of Christian Antiquities" (Smith and Cheetham).

Elemine. A crystallized resin used to give consistency to the varnish which forms part of the composition of lacquer.

Elenchus, R. (ἔλεγχος). (1) A pear-shaped pearl highly esteemed by the Roman ladies, who wore such pearls mounted as drops or pendants to brooches and rings. (See the illustration to CROTALIUM.) (2) An index to a book.

Elephant. In mediæval heraldry this animal is a symbol of piety, from an ancient legend, mentioned by Ælian, Pliny, and others, that it has in religious reverence, with a kind of devotion, not only the stars and planets, but also the sun and moon.

Elephant Paper. Drawing-paper manufactured in sheets, measuring 28 inches by 23. *Double Elephant Paper* measures 40 inches by 26¾.

Eleusinian Mysteries. The holiest and most venerated of the Greek festivals. The Lesser Eleusinia, held at Agræ in the month Anthesterion, were a preparation for the Greater, which were celebrated at Athens and Eleusis. The *Mystæ* were the initiated at the Lesser, of which the principal rite was the sacrifice of a sow, previously purified by washing in the Cantharus. The Greater were celebrated every year in the month Boedromion, and lasted nine days. On the first day the Mystæ assembled at Athens; on the second they went through a ceremony of purification at the sea coast; the third was a day of fasting; on the fourth there was a procession of a waggon drawn by oxen, followed by women who had small mystic cases in their hands; on the fifth, or torch day, the Mystæ went in the evening with torches to the temple of Demeter, where they passed the night; on the sixth, which was the most solemn of all, a statue of Iacchos, the son of Demeter, was borne in procession to Eleusis, and the Mystæ were there initiated in the last mysteries during the following night. There was something in the secrets of this part of the ceremony which excited greatly the imagination of the ancient writers, especially Christians, who describe them "in an awful and horrible manner." Each of the initiated was dismissed by the *mystagogus* with the words κόγξ, ὄμπαξ. On the next day they returned to Athens, and resting on the bridge of Cephisus engaged in a contest of ridicule with the passers-by: the eighth and ninth days were unimportant.

Eleutheria. A Greek festival in honour of Zeus Eleutherios (the Deliverer).

Elevati of Ferrara. One of the Italian literary academies. Their device was from the fable of Hercules and Antæus, with the motto from Horace, "*Superat tellus, sidera donat*" (Earth conquers us, but gives us Heaven).

Elevation. (1) In Architecture, &c., a perpendicular plan drawn to a scale. (2) In Christian archæology, the *lifting up* of the elements at certain points in the Eucharistic service, universally prescribed in the early Oriental liturgies, and introduced into the Western Church with the doctrine of transubstantiation.

Elgin Marbles. Friezes and metopes from the Parthenon at Athens, brought to the

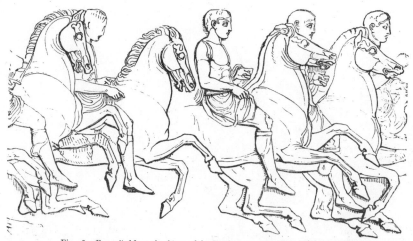

Fig. 282. Bas-relief from the frieze of the Parthenon. One of the Elgin Marbles.

British Museum by Lord Elgin. They are adorned with sculptures in relief; those on the frieze represent the Panathenaic procession in honour of Athena; those on the metopes, chiefly the contests of the Centaurs and Lapithæ. There are also statues and friezes, especially from the temple of the Wingless Victory and the CHORAGIC MONUMENT of Lysicrates. They are admirably described by Mr. Newton in his "Guide" to these sculptures published by the authorities of the British Museum. (Fig. 282.)

Elizabeth, Queen. The costume and the royal appurtenances of this monarch are well illustrated by the Royal Seal. In the Royal Arms we see the lions and the lilies (*France modern and England quarterly*). On the reverse (Fig. 284) the Tudor Rose, fleur-de-lis, and harp appear separately crowned for England, France, and Ireland. Elizabeth was fond of allegory and devices. In her portrait by Zoffany "the lining of her robe is worked with eyes and ears, and on her left sleeve is embroidered a serpent—all to imply wisdom and vigilance." In her other hand is a rainbow with the motto, "*Non sine sole iris*" (no rainbow without the sun).

Elizabethan. The style of architecture and decoration gradually developed during the reign of the Tudors in England. Its characteristics are a mixed revival of classical forms with quaint and grotesque relics of the Gothic. Typical examples are Crewe Hall, Speke, in Lancashire, Haddon Hall, Kenilworth Castle, Raglan Castle, &c.

Ellipsis, Ellipse. A figure formed by cutting a cone obliquely across its length; hence—

Ellipsograph. An instrument for describing a semi-ellipse.

Ellotia or **Hellotia.** A Corinthian festival with a torch-race, in honour of Athena as a goddess of fire.

Fig. 283. Great Seal of Queen Elizabeth.

Ellychnium, R. (λύχνος, a light). The wick of an oil lamp ; it was made of flax fibres or papyrus.

Fig. 284. Great Seal of Queen Elizabeth.

Emarginated. Having the *margin* broken by a notch or notches.

Embalming was frequently practised by the early Christians, especially with the bodies of martyrs. The practice was derived from the Jews. As a pagan ceremony embalming was intended to facilitate *cremation.*

Embalon, Gr. and R. A beak, corresponding to the modern *ram,* under the bows of a war galley, for the purpose of sinking the enemy.

Embas, Gr. A shoe of white felt, used esp. by the Bœotians.

Ember Days, Chr. (in Anglo-Saxon, *ymbren dagas,* "recurrent days ;" in Latin, *jejunia quatuor temporum;* in French, *les quatre temps,* &c.). Special fasts appointed to be observed at

Fig. 285. Emblemata.

the commencement of each of the *four seasons* of the year. In the Eastern Church there is no trace of such an observance. (The word has no connexion with *embers* in the sense of ashes.)

Emblazon, Her. (See BLAZON.)

Emblemata, Gr. (ἐμβάλλω, to put in). INLAID WORK, or (1) Mosaic made of coloured cubes of glass or vitreous enamel. (See SECTILE, TESSELLATUM, VERMICULATUM.) Fig. 285 represents *emblemata* of different kinds of glass. (2) *Crusts* exquisitely wrought on the surface of vessels or other pieces of furniture ; as, for instance, alabaster on marble, gold on silver, silver on bronze. The Romans generally used the term *crustæ* for this kind of work. From EMBLEMATA is derived our word EMBLEM, the true meaning of which is "a symbolical figure or composition which conceals an allegory." Thus an *ape* symbolized malice and lust ; a *pelican* piety, and the Redeemer's love for the world, &c. The most important books of Emblems are by Alciati, Paradin, and Sambuco.

Embolismus, Embolis, or **Embolum,** Chr. (1) An inserted or intercalated prayer in a liturgy. (2) The number of days required to make up the lunar year to the solar. (See EPACT.)

Embolium, Gr. and R. (lit. something thrown in). An interlude or comic piece recited by an actress (*emboliaria*) between the acts of a drama.

Embolos, Arch., Chr. A covered portico or cloister surrounding the external walls of a church.

Embolum, Gr. The Greek term answering to the Latin ROSTRUM (q.v.). (See also EMBOLISMUS.)

Embolus, R. (ἔμβολος). The piston in the chamber of a pump.

Embossing, Embossment. A prominence like a boss ; raised ornamental work.

Embowed, Her. Bent. An arm embowed has the elbow to the dexter.

Embrasure, Arch. (1) The interval between the COPS of a battlement. (2) An expansion of doorways, windows, &c., given by slanting the sides. (See SPLAY.)

Embroidery is one of the oldest of the ornamental arts. Some specimens of ancient *Egyptian* embroidery are exhibited in the Louvre, and Herodotus mentions the embroidered vestments of the gods in Egypt. The *Israelites* appointed Aholiab, "a cunning workman, and an embroiderer in blue, and purple, and scarlet, and fine linen," to be *chief embroiderer* to the sacred ark. The prophet Ezekiel mentions the embroidery of *Tyre.* It was the principal domestic occupation of ladies in *Greece,* from the days when Penelope embroidered a garment for Ulysses, representing a dog chasing a deer. The *Romans* called embroidery "Phrygium," and imported it largely from the East. In later times *Byzantium* was celebrated for its embroidered ecclesiastical vestments.

Fig. 236. Indian Embroidery. In the Indian section of the South Kensington Museum.

siastical vestments. Pope Paschal, in the 9th century, was the greatest patron of the art. When the Caliph Omar pillaged the *Persian* palace of Khosroes, he found there a carpet of silk and cloth of gold, sixty cubits square, having a garden depicted upon it, and rubies, emeralds, sapphires, beryls, topazes, and pearls arranged with consummate skill to represent trees, fruit and flowers, rivulets, fountains, roses and shrubs. Our English word "embroidery" is derived from the Celtic "brouda," to prick. Anglo-Saxon embroidery was celebrated throughout Europe as *Opus Anglicanum*. The celebrated Bayeux tapestry is attributed to the 12th century. A copy of it may be seen in the South Kensington Museum. The art decayed in England during the Civil War of the 17th century.

Embrued, Her. Stained with blood.

Embu. A French term for the *loss of tone* in an oil sketch, caused by the absorption of the oil whilst it is drying. It is easily corrected by a glaze.

Emerald. A precious stone of various shades of green, much used by the ancients for gem-engraving. The less brilliant varieties are known as beryls. For its significance in Christian art, see GREEN.

Emerald Green. A vivid bright green pigment, prepared from the arseniate of copper, and used both in oil and water-colours; called also *Paul Veronese Green.*

Emissarium, R. (*emitto*, to send forth). A channel, natural or artificial, for letting off stagnant water. Some of these channels are the most wonderful monuments of Roman ingenuity. The lakes of Trasimene, Albano, Nemi, and Fucino were all drained by EMISSARIA. The last is open to inspection, and is described as "a stupendous work of engineering, planned by Julius Cæsar, and completed by the Emperor Claudius.'

Empaistic, Gr. *Damascening* (q.v.) or *in crusta* work practised by the ancients, as opposed to TOREUTIC ART (q.v.).

Emperor Paper. The largest kind of drawing-paper manufactured : in sheets measuring 66 inches by 47.

Emphotion, Chr. (from ἐμφωτίζω, to enlighten). A name given in the early Church to the white robe with which persons were invested in baptism ; as it were, "a robe of light."

Emplecton, Gr. and R. (lit. inwoven). A method of building, originating in Greece and adopted by the Romans, in which a space left in the interior of the wall was filled in with rubble, the whole block of masonry being bound together at intervals by ties (*diatonoi*). In the engraving, *c* and *b* are the *square stones*, the parts between them being the ties or diatonoi, and *o* the rubble. (See Fig. 249.)

Emporium, Gr. and R. (ἔμπορος, a passenger in a ship). A place at a sea-port where imported merchandise was warehoused and exposed for sale. The remains of the ancient *emporium* of Rome have been discovered on the banks of the Tiber. The name is sometimes applied to a town, but applies properly only to a certain place in a town.

Enafota or **Enafodia,** Chr. (Gr. ἐννεάφωτα). A corona or chandelier of "nine lights."

Enaluron, Her. (See ENTOIRE.)

Enamel (Fr. *esmail;* Ital. *smalto*). A glassy substance of many brilliant colours, melted and united to gold, silver, copper, bronze, and other metals in the furnace. Enamel is coloured *white* by oxide of tin, *blue* by oxide of cobalt, *red* by gold, and *green* by copper. Different kinds of enamel are (1) inlaid or incrusted. (2) Transparent, showing designs on the metal under it. (3) Painted as a complete picture. "Many fine specimens of ancient Chinese enamel were seen in the Exhibition of 1851. They have the enamel on copper, beautifully coloured and enlivened with figures of flowers, birds, and other animals. The colouring is most chaste and effective. The Chinese say that no good specimens of this manufacture have been made for the last six or eight hundred years." (*Fortune.*) Beautiful transparent enamels are made in India. They look like slices of emerald or sapphire laid in beds of gold, having tiny figures of beaten gold let into their surfaces. (See also CLOISONNÉ, CHAMP-LEVÉ, BASSE-TAILLE, &c.) The beautiful example of enamel-work, Fig. 287, is attributed to Benvenuto Cellini. (See Fig. 188.)

Enamel. Painting in enamel is done by means of colours that are vitrifiable, a quality that is communicated to them by combining them with a vitreous base, which is called their flux. These are fused and fixed on the enamel by the action of fire, which produces in the colours applied such changes as the artist has previously learned to calculate. (*Bouvier.*)

Enamelled Glass. (See GLASS.)

Enamelled Wares. (See GLAZED WARE.)

Encænia, Chr. A dedication festival.

Encarpa, Gr. An architectural decoration formed of festoons or garlands of flowers and fruits (καρποί), whence its name. Fig. 288 shows an example from the temple of Vesta at Tivoli.

Encaustic, R. (lit. burning in). The art of painting in encaustic. Pliny says, "The colours were applied with wax on marble, and transparent gum on ivory. Coloured wax was applied to the wall in the form of a paste, and in the manner of mosaic or enamels. This was then melted or fused with hot irons (*cauteria*), a small fillet of a different tint being inserted between each flat tint." Fairholt says, "There is no antique painting extant which is properly called ENCAUSTIC; all those supposed to be so have, on closer examina-

Fig. 287. Pendant of gold, enamelled and enriched with jewels.

tion, proved to be in FRESCO or in TEMPERA."

Encaustic Tiles. Ornamental tiles for floorings, extensively used in the Middle Ages.

Encheirion, Chr. The napkin with which the priest wipes his hands; worn at the girdle.

Encoignure, Fr. A table made with an angle to fit into a corner.

Encolpia, Chr. (lit. worn on the breast, or from the Gr. ἐγκυλπίζω, to contain in the womb). (1) Small caskets containing relics or a copy of the Gospels, worn by the early Christians suspended from the neck. (See EPOMADION.) Their use is of the highest antiquity, and specimens have been found in the tombs of the ancient cemetery of the Vatican, belonging to the 4th century. These were square in form, having on one side the sacred monogram IXP for IHΣΟΥΣ ΧΡΙΣΤΟΣ between the letters A and Ω. (2) The pectoral crosses worn by bishops are also called *encolpia.* Reliquaries in the form of a cross are first mentioned by Gregory the Great. He sent one of them to Queen Theodelinda. (*Martigny.*)

Encomboma, Gr. (i. e. girt on). A Greek apron, tied round the waist, worn chiefly by young maidens and by slaves to keep the tunic clean.

Encyclical Letters. (1) Chr. Letters "sent round" to all who should read them, and not addressed to any particular person (from the members of a council, &c.). (2) Gen. The same words, γράμματα ἐγκύκλια, apply to the subjects which the Greeks included in the "circle of the sciences," or encyclopædia.

Encysted. Enclosed in a cyst.

Endecagon (ἔνδεκα, eleven; γωνία, an angle). A plane figure having eleven sides and eleven angles.

Endorse, Her. A diminutive of the PALE (q.v.), one-fourth of its width.

Endo'hys. (See ENDYTIS.)

Endromis, Gr. and R. (δρόμος, a course or running). In Greek this name is given to hunt-

Fig. 288. Encarpa (Festoons) on the Temple of Vesta at Tivoli.

ing boots of Cretan origin, such as Diana is represented wearing by the Greek sculptors. Among the Romans the *endromis* was an ample blanket of coarse wool, introduced from Gaul, in which athletes wrapped themselves when they were heated with the exercises. *Endromis Tyria* was the name given to a large woollen wrap much finer than the ordinary *endromis*, and which was worn by the Roman ladies after their gymnastic exercises.

Endytis, Chr. (ἐνδύω, to put on). This term, in the Middle Ages, denoted an altar-covering; other terms for it were *endothis* and *endothys*.

Energumens, Chr. Men possessed with devils.

Enfeu, Fr. A sepulchral vault usually placed under the choir of a church; it assumed the form of a large niche. Originally bishops were interred by "droit d'enfeu" in tombs of this kind. The term is derived from the Latin *infodere* (to dig).

Enfiled, Her. Pierced with the sword.

Engageants, Fr. "Double ruffles that fall over the wrists." (*Ladies' Dictionary,* 1694.)

Engineer's Cartridge. Drawing-paper manufactured in sheets measuring 30 by 22 inches. *Double Engineer's Cartridge* measures 46 inches by 30.

Engobe, Fr. A "slip" or thin coating of white clay used to coat pottery before the invention of the tin glaze.

Engrailed, Her. A border-line indented in semicircles.

Engraving. Copper-plate engraving is called CHALCOGRAPHY (q.v.) (Gr. χαλκὸς, copper); wood engraving, XYLOGRAPHY (q.v.) (Gr. ξύλον, wood); and engraving on stone, LITHOGRAPHY (q.v.) (Gr. λίθος, a stone). [Each process is described under its own heading. See also ETCHING.]

Enhanced, Her. Raised towards the CHIEF, or upper part of the shield.

Enneapylæ, Pel. (ἐννέα and πύλαι). Literally, nine gates; a fortified enclosure constructed by the Bœotian Pelasgians round the Acropolis of Athens, some years after the Trojan war. Xerxes destroyed the *enneapylæ* after the capture of Athens. A few fragments of it remain to this day, not far from the temple of the Wingless Victory.

Figs. 289, 290. Gallic Ensigns.

Enotia, Gr. (Lat. *inaures*). EAR-RINGS (q.v.).
Enseniator, Med. Lat. (from the Italian *insegna,* an ensign). A mounted ensign-bearer.
Ensiculus, R. A small sword, or child's sword, used as a plaything. It is the diminutive of ENSIS.
Ensigned, Her. Adorned; having some ensign of honour placed above, as a coronet above a shield.

Fig. 291. Gallic Ensign.

Ensigns, Gen. (Lat. *signa militaria;* Gr. σημεῖα). Military symbols beneath which soldiers are ranged according to the different regiments to which they belong. The most ancient Roman ensign was a bundle of straw, hay, or fern. Then came the eagle, the wolf, the minotaur, the horse, and the boar.

Afterwards the eagle alone was displayed (B.C. 104) ; it was made of silver or bronze,

Fig. 292. Entablature with leaf ornament.

Fig. 293. Entablature with honeysuckle ornament.

with expanded wings. The serpent or dragon was used as a particular ensign by the several *cohorts*, and the centuries had also each its ensign; but these were cloth flags. Under Constantine the LABARUM (q.v.) was introduced. (See CUSPIS, Figs. 228 to 230.)

Fig. 294. Egyptian Column, showing entasis.

Ensiludium, Med. Lat. A contest in sport with swords. (See CEMBEL, HASTILUDIUM.)

Ensis, Sword. A synonym of GLADIUS (q.v.).

Ensis a Estoc, Med. A stabbing-sword, usually carried at the saddle-bow.

Entablature. A member of architecture placed as a crown to another. The entablature is composed of *architrave*, the part immediately above the column; *frieze*, the central space; and *cornice*, the upper projecting mouldings. (See Fig. 184.)

Entalma, Chr. The document by which a bishop confers the right of hearing confessions.

Entasis, Gr. and R. (*ἔντασις*, a stretching tight). The *swelling* of a balustre or of the shaft of a column. The narrowing of the shaft is called CONTRACTURA (q.v.).

Enterclose, Arch. A passage between two rooms in a house.

Enthronisation, Chr. (Lat. *incathedrare*). (1) The ceremony of placing a newly-ordained bishop upon his throne. (2) That of placing the relics in the altar of a church on consecration. (3) The installation of a presbyter in his church is sometimes called *enthronisation*.

Entire, Her. Said of a charge when it extends to the border-lines of a shield, coat, or banner; also of a shield, coat, or banner of arms, when borne without any difference or mark of cadency.

Entoire, Entoyre, Her. A bordure charged with a series of inanimate figures or devices, as crosslets, roundles, &c. To a similar bordure of living figures the term ENALURON is applied.

Entrance, Chr. (See EISODOS and INTROIT.)

Entrecoupe, Fr. When two vaults are superimposed, and both spring from the same walls, "entrecoupe" is the term applied to the arched interval—if any—between them.

Enveloped, Environed, Her. Surrounded.

Eolian (Æolian) Harp. A musical stringed instrument arranged to be played upon by the wind (from Eolus [or properly Æolus], the ruler of the winds).

Eolodicon. A musical instrument similar to a harmonium, invented in the last century by Eschenbach.

Eolophone. A musical instrument similar to a harmonium.

Eōra, Gr. (*ἐώρα*). A festival held at Athens in honour of Icarius and his daughter Erigonê. It was known also by the names of *Æora* (*αἰώρα*) and *Aletis* (*Ἀλῆτις*). The last appellation originated in a hymn which was sung at the festival, and which had been composed by Theodorus of Colophon. It was sometimes called "Eudeipnos," from the rich banquets usually given during its celebration.

Epact (Gr. *ἐπακταί*, sc. *ἡμέραι*; in Med. Lat. *adjectiones Lunæ*). The number of days required at the end of a lunar year to complete the solar year. (See EMBOLISMUS.)

Epagomenæ (sc. days), Gen. (*ἐπαγόμεναι ἡμέραι*, i.e. intercalated days). The name given to the five supplementary days of the year among those nations who divided the year into twelve months of thirty days each.

Epaullière or **Epaullèts**, Fr. Shoulder-plates; also the shoulder-knots formerly worn by gentlemen, but now restricted to domestic servants. (See AIGLET.)

Ependytes, Chr. (*ἐπενδύτης*, i.e. worn above). The "fisher's coat" of St. Peter. A coarse cloak worn by the monks of the Middle Ages over another garment; it is also called, in the ancient MSS., *superaria, superindum*, and *sagus rusticus*. It is frequently described, especially in the East, as made of skins (*μηλωτὴς*, *pelliceus*).

Epergne (Fr. *épargne*, economy). An ornamental stand, with dish and branches, for the centre of a table.

Epernay Ware. At Epernay were specially made glazed wares in relief for the service of the table, in shapes such as a hare, a fowl, &c., in half relief; also surprise or puzzle jugs.

Epha or **Ephah**, Heb. A measure of capacity, about 3 pecks and 3 pints.

Ephebeum, Gr. (ἐφηβεῖον). The large hall of a gymnasium, situated in the centre of the building, in which the youths (*ephebi*) practised gymnastic exercises.

Ephippium, Gr. (ἐφίππιον, i. e. for putting on a horse). A saddle. Among the Greeks and Romans it was a kind of pad, square or round in shape, and regularly stuffed. Saddle-cloths hung from it, but it had no stirrups. The word *sella*, or *sella equestris*, became common in later times.

Ephod, Hebrew. A short upper garment worn by the Jewish priests. The ephod, which was also worn by the Jewish judges and kings, was made of fine linen; that of the high priest consisted of a sleeved tunic, woven with gold thread, purple, hyacinth, and twisted flax. Two sardonyx stones set in gold adorned the clasps by which this tunic was fastened round the shoulders.

Epi or **Girouette,** Fr. The complicated iron ornament with which steeples and pointed roofs were surmounted in the architecture of the Renaissance period, replaced in modern times by the weather-cock. A similar spiked ornament, of pottery or metal, is still common on the gables of houses in Normandy.

Epic. In Art, the graphic representation of an "epos," or event, cardinal in history.

Epichysis, Gr. and R. (ἐπίχυσις, i. e. that which pours in). A Greek pitcher with a long neck and a handle; it was used for pouring wine into cups.

Epicopus, Gr. and R. (ἐπίκωπος, i.e. furnished with oars). A vessel with oars. (See NAVIS.)

Epicrocum, Gr. and R. A woman's garment, of a saffron yellow (crocus), whence its name.

Epicycloid. "A curve described by the movement of the circumference of one circle on the convex or concave part of the circumference of another." (*Stormonth.*)

Epideipnis, Gr. (i.e. following the dinner). The last course of a dinner or any kind of banquet.

Epidemia, Gr. (lit. among the people). Festivals held at Argos in honour of Juno, and at Delos and Miletus in honour of Apollo. They received their name from the fact that these deities were supposed to be present at them, and to mingle with the people (ἐπί, among; δῆμος, people).

Epidote. A mineral of a green or greyish colour: of the garnet family.

Epidromos, Gr. (1) The mizen, or sail on the mast nearest to the stern, in vessels with several masts. (2) A part of the oil-press. (3) A running rope passing through the rings of a large net for catching birds, by means of which the huntsman, who was on the watch, closed the net when the game had found their way into it.

Epigonation, Gr., Chr. An ornament peculiar to the Eastern Church; a lozenge-shaped piece of some stiff material, hanging from the girdle on the right side as low as the *knee* (whence its name).

Epigrus. (See EPIURUS.)

Epiphany, Chr. This festival is known by various names in the different European languages; and the names are either (1) mere reproductions of the Latin name, or renderings of it; or (2) refer to the manifestation to the Magi as the three Kings, as the Dutch Drie-Koningendag, &c.; or (3) indicate it as the final day of the Christmas festivity, *Twelfth Day*, &c. (See *Smith and Cheetham's Dictionary of Christian Antiquities.*)

Epiphi, Egyp. The third month of summer, called the season of harvests.

Epirhedium, R. (ἐπί Gr., and *rheda* Gallic). A kind of chariot. The word was formed by the Romans as above, and is explained as *Ornamentum rhedarum, aut plaustrum.* (See RHEDA, PLAUSTRUM.)

Episcenium, Gr. and R. (ἐπι-σκήνιον, i. e. above the stage). A room situated above the stage, in ancient theatres, for the machinery.

Episcopalia, Chr. The ring and the pastoral staff, the distinctive marks of the authority of a bishop.

Episotron (ἐπί-σωτρον). (See CANTHUS.)

Epistle Side (of a church). The south side.

Epistomium, R. (στόμα, a mouth). The cock of a vessel or water-pipe, which let out only a little water at a time.

Epistylium, Gr. and R. (ἐπι-στύλιον). An epistyle; literally, on the column (ἐπί, on, and στῦλος, a column); that is, the architrave or lower beam of an entablature laid horizontally upon columns. By analogy the term is used to denote the entire ENTABLATURE (q.v.).

Epitaph (ἐπιτάφιος). (1) A eulogy pronounced at a funeral. (2) Memorials of art in churches, in remembrance of the dead. (3) Inscriptions on tombs.

Epithalamium, Gr. A nuptial song. A fragment of verses from one of these songs, written by Hesiod, has come down to us.

Epithedes or **Sima,** Arch. The upper member of the cornice of an entablature.

Epitoga, R. A cloak worn over the toga.

Epitoxis, Gr. and R. That part of the catapult in which the missile was laid.

Epitrachelion, Chr. (i. e. on the neck). The Greek name for the stole. (See STOLE.)

Epiurus, R. (ἐπίουρος). A wooden peg used as a nail.

K

Epoch. A fixed and important period of novelty or change, which gave a new and distinctive character to Art. (*Fairholt.*)

Epomadion, Gr., Chr. The cord or ribbon by which relics, or crosses (ENCOLPIA), were suspended from the neck.

Eques, R. Generally, any one on horseback, a rider, and by analogy a knight, that is, a patrician or man of distinguished family. *Eques alarius* was the name given to the cavalry of the allies; *eques cataphractus* was a knight whose horse, as well as himself, was clad in complete armour; *eques extraordinarius* were the picked cavalry in the service of the consuls; *eques legionarius, eques prætorianus,* the prætorian cavalry; *eques sagittarius,* the mounted archers

Equipped, Her. Fully armed, caparisoned, or provided.

Equiria, R. (*equus*). Games instituted by Romulus, and celebrated at Rome in the Field of Mars on the third of the calends of March (27th February). These games, held in honour of Mars, consisted of chariot-races. There were two festivals of this name; the second was on the eve of the ides of March (14th March).

Equuleus or **Eculeus,** R. (lit. a colt, a young horse). This was an instrument of torture on which slaves were placed astride. The law prescribed that all slaves called as witnesses should be examined under torture.

Equus, R. A horse; properly a stallion, as opposed to *cauterius,* a gelding, and *equa,* a mare.

Eradicated, Her. Torn up by the roots.

Erased, Her. Torn off with a ragged edge.

Eremites, Gr., Chr. Hermits.

Ergastulum, R. (ἐργάζομαι, to work). A private prison attached to a farm or *villa rustica,* in which insubordinate and ill-conducted slaves were kept in chains; they were under the superintendence of a gaoler, who was himself a slave, and who was called ERGASTULARIUS. *Ergastula* were built underground, and thus formed subterranean dungeons.

Ergata, Gr. and R. (ἐργάτης, i.e. worker). A strong capstan used for moving heavy weights; among other things, for hauling vessels on shore.

Ericius, R. (lit. hedgehog). A military engine, a cheval-de-frise or long beam studded with iron spikes, whence its name. It was placed across a door or other opening to which it was desired to bar ingress.

Ermine, Ermines, Erminois, Her. The animal, the ermine, sometimes appears in blazon, and an ermine spot is borne as a charge. Generally the ermine is an emblem of royalty, purity, and honour. The illustration (Fig. 295) is of the arms of Anne of Bretagne, the Queen of Charles VIII.

Erotidia, Gr. (ἐρωτίδια). Festivals held every fifth year at Thespiæ in Bœotia, in honour of Eros, the principal divinity of the Thespians.

Erpa, Egyp. A title in use among the Egyptians implying authority generally; the crown

Fig. 295. The Ermine. Arms of Anne of Brittany.

prince was so designated, and the high priest was, in the same manner, called *erpa* of the priests.

Escallop or **Scallop Shells** were emblems worn by pilgrims, and of St. James the Great, from the 13th century.

Fig. 296. Escallop.

Escape, Arch. (or Apopyge). The small curvature given to the top and bottom of the shaft of a column where it expands to meet the edge of the fillet above the torus of the base, and beneath the astragal under the capital.

Fig. 297. Escaufaille, or portable brazier.

Escaufaille, Fr. A small portable brazier on wheels, which was taken from room to room as required.

Eschelles, Fr. "A stomacher laced or ribboned in the form of a ladder." (*Ladies' Dict.,* 1694.)

Escoinson, Med. Fr. The interior edge of the window-side or jamb. This was often decorated with a pilaster called the "pilastre des écoinsons."

Escroll, Her. A ribbon charged with a motto; also a ribbon, coiled at its extremities, borne as a charge.

Escutcheon. (1) The heraldic shield. (2) Metal plates on doors. Escutcheons are abundantly used in Gothic architecture, and are frequently carved on the bosses of ceilings and

Fig. 298. Escutcheon of the Sforzas.

at the ends of weather mouldings, &c. Sometimes, instead of armorial bearings, escutcheons have the instruments of the Crucifixion or other devices carved on them.

Escutcheon of Pretence, Her. A shield charged upon the field of another shield of larger size, and bearing a distinct coat of arms.

Espadon. A long Spanish sword. It was the weapon used for decapitation of criminals.

Espietus, Expiotus, Med. Lat. A dart (1361).

Espringale, Springale, Espringold. A machine for throwing darts.

Esquire, Her. A rank next below that of knight.

Esseda, Essedum, R. (from the Celtic *ess*, a carriage). A chariot of Gaulish origin, drawn by two horses, which was used by the Britons and the Germans in war. It was mounted on two wheels, and was open in front, but closed behind. The pole was broad, and the rider used to run to and fro upon it in the battle. The Romans constructed carriages of a similar kind. A similar chariot drawn by one horse was called the *cisium*. (See CURRUS.)

Essonite. The cinnamon stone, a variety of the garnet. It is of a reddish yellow tint, resembling the colour of cinnamon. These stones come principally from Ceylon, and are frequently sold for hyacinths or jacinths, from which, however, they differ in many important peculiarities. (*H. Emanuel.*)

Este. A manufactory in Italy of soft porcelain ; also of fine faience and pipe-clay.

Estivation, Bot. The arrangement of the un-expanded leaves of the flower-bud which burst in Summer ; as opposed to VERNATION, the arrangement of the leaves of the bud which burst in Spring.

Estoc, Fr. (Med. Lat. *estoquum*). A short sword worn at the girdle ; also called a "tuck " (*temp.* Elizabeth).

Estoile, Her. A star with wavy rays or points, which are six, eight, or sometimes more in number.

Estrade, Fr., Arch. A platform raised three or four inches above the rest of the floor of a chamber, upon which to place a bed or a throne, &c.

Estrif or **Estref**, Med. A kind of arrow for the balista.

Etching. In this process the copper plate is covered with an *etching-ground*, which is a preparation of bees'-wax, Burgundy pitch, black pitch, and asphaltum (or other ingredients) ; and the lines of the design are traced out with *etching-needles*, which remove the etching-ground from the copper wherever they pass, and slightly scratch the surface of the plate. Next, a border of *banking-wax* is put round the sides of the plate, making a trough of it. The *banking-wax* is made of bees'-wax, common pitch, Burgundy pitch, and sweet oil melted in a crucible and poured into cold water. The next operation is to pour in nitrous acid reduced with water to a proper strength (about one part acid to four parts water). When the acid has been on a sufficient time to corrode the fainter parts of the subject, it is to be poured off, the plate washed with water, and left to dry. These fainter parts are then to be varnished with a mixture called *stopping-ground*, made of lamp-black and Venice turpentine, applied with a camel's-hair pencil. This stops the further action of the acid on these parts. When the surface is dry, fresh acid is poured on to *bite in* the bolder parts, and the processes of *stopping* and *biting in* are alternated for every gradation of tint. The wax is removed from the plate by heat, and cleaned away with a rag moistened with olive oil ; and the work is then complete, or it may be finished off with the *graver*. *Etching-points* or *needles* resemble common needles, fixed in handles four or five inches long ; some are made oval to produce broader lines. The *dry point* is only a very fine-pointed needle for the delicate lines. Imitations of chalk and pencil drawings are sometimes produced by *etching on soft ground*. *Etching on steel* is done in the same way as on copper. For *etching on glass*, a ground of bees'-wax is laid on, and the design traced as above. Sulphuric acid is then poured on, and fluor-spar sprinkled on it, or fluoric acid may be at once used ; this is allowed to remain four or five hours, and is then removed with oil of turpentine. (See also STIPPLE, MEZZOTINTO, AQUATINTA.)

Eterea of Padua. One of the Italian literary academies. Their device, a charioteer in his car in the air, drawn by a white and black horse, the one endeavouring to touch the earth, the other to ascend. Motto, " *Victor se tollit ad auras.*"

Etiolation. The process of blanching to which plants are subject in dark places.

Ettwee. O. E. for ETUI (q.v.).

Etui, Fr. (by contraction *Twee,* Boyer). A case formerly worn at the girdle by ladies. They were made of gold or silver, or ornamented with paintings in enamel. The richly-decorated example represented in Fig. 299 was the property of a granddaughter of Oliver Cromwell.

Euripus, R. (εὔ-ριπος). An artificial canal or watercourse in the gardens of a Roman villa, generally stocked with fish and aquatic or amphibious animals. The same term was applied to a moat dug at the foot of the *podium* in an amphitheatre or circus, which was intended, in

Fig. 299. Etui.

conjunction with the metal railings or trellis-work placed at the top of the *podium*, as a protection to the spectators, when wild beasts were exhibited in the arena. *Euripus* is also applied by Tertullian and other authors to the *spina* of a circus.

Eustyle, Arch. (εὔ-στυλος). An intercolumniation in which the columns are separated by a width of two diameters and a quarter, measured at the lower part of the column, excepting the central intercolumn, which is of three diameters. It is the form of columniation which, according to Vitruvius, satisfied the demands at once of solidity of structure, beauty of appearance, and general harmony of effect.

Euterpean. Pertaining to music : from the Muse Euterpe.

Everriculum, R. (*everro,* to sweep out). A fishing-net.

Ewery, Med. An office of household service, where the ewers, &c., were kept : our modern *scullery.*

Exacisculatus, R. Destroyed by means of a pick (*acisculus*). The term is of frequent occurrence in sepulchral inscriptions, its purpose

being to serve as a notice to the thieves who broke into tombs.

Examen, R. (*exigo,* to examine). The tongue or index on the beam of a balance.

Exasciatus, R. Hewn or fashioned with the adze (*ascia*) ; whence the expression *opus exasciatum* for work which only required to be finished or polished.

Excalceatus, R. (lit. without shoes or boots). A comic actor or comedian who wore sandals. The tragic actor, on the other hand, who wore on the stage the laced boot or *cothurnus,* was called *cothurnatus.*

Excubitorium, R. The post or guard of the *excubitores ;* of these there was one in each quarter of the city, or fourteen in all.

Fig. 300. Exedra.

Exedra, Gr. and R. An assembly-room or hall for discussion or conversation, forming part of a gymnasium, palæstra, or private house. In many cases *exedræ* were in the open air, consisting merely of circular marble benches. (Fig. 300.) When an exedra was covered in, one of the sides often terminated in a circular apse (*absis*). [Larger rooms were called " *Leschai.*"]

Exedrium, R. Diminutive of EXEDRA (q.v.).

Exequiæ. (See EXSEQUIÆ.)

Exergue. The bottom space on a coin, where the date is engraved.

Exiteria, Gr. and R. (ἐξιτήρια, concerning departure or result). Sacrifices offered to propitiate the gods on the eve of an important enterprise, or in gratitude for success.

Exomis, Gr. and R. (ἐξ-ωμίς, i. e. off the shoulders). A short tunic, of Greek origin, adopted by the Romans. It left the right shoulder and arm exposed, and had only a short sleeve for the left arm. The term was also applied to the *pallium,* when so arranged upon the person as to resemble the tunic just described.

Exonarthex. (See NARTHEX.)

Exostra, Gr. and R. (ἐξώστρα). (1) A flying bridge thrown from a movable tower (*acrobaticon*) on to the walls of a besieged town, by means of which the assailants made their way into the place. (2) A theatrical machine which was pushed to the front of the stage from behind a curtain which concealed it until it was wanted.

Expeditus (opposed to *impeditus*), R. Free, unencumbered ; light-armed troops (*velites*) were thus called (*expediti*), [or any other troops, when they left their *impedimenta* behind for a forced march, &c.]

Expositories. (See MONSTRANCES.)

Exsequiæ, R. (*exsequor*, to follow after). A funeral conducted with great pomp. (See FUNUS.)

Extispicium, R. (*exta* and *inspicio*, to inspect). Divination by inspection of the entrails of victims sacrificed on the altar ; called also *haruspicina.*

Extra-dos, Arch. The exterior curve of an arch ; opposed to the SOFFIT or INTRA-DOS.

Extremities. In Art, the head, feet, and hands : compare *acrolithes.*

Ex-voto, Gen. Offerings of any kind in fulfilment of a vow (*ex voto*).

Eye. In Christian art, the emblem of Providence. Attribute of St. Lucia, as a symbol, *not* of her martyrdom, but of the meaning of her name ("light"). (See OUDJA, OCULUS.)

F.

Fabaria, R. Offerings of bean-flour (*faba*) made by the Romans on the 1st of June to the goddess Carna ; from these offerings the calends of June took the name of *fabariæ.*

Fabatarium, R. A large earthenware vessel in which bean-flour (*puls fabacia*) was served. boiled up with water or broth. It formed a kind of *polenta.*

Fig. 301. Faenza sweetmeat-dish.

Fabrica, R. (*faber*, an artisan). The shop in which an artisan works, chiefly a joiner's or carpenter's shop.

Fabrilia, R. A general term, including all the different kinds of tools used by an artisan.

Façade, Arch. The *face* or front of a building.

Face-guard. On a helmet, a bar or bars of iron protecting the face.

Face-painting, O. E. Portrait-painting.

Facets (Fr. *facette*, a little face). The flat surfaces cut upon precious stones.

Facial Angle. The angle formed by two lines, one horizontal from the nostrils to the ear, the other perpendicular from the nostrils to the forehead.

Fac-simile (from Latin *factum*, made, and *simile*, like). A perfectly exact copy.

Factorium (sc. *vas*), **R.** A vessel containing exactly a *factum*, or quantity of grapes or olives proper to be placed under the press (*torcular*) at one *factum* or making.

Faculæ, R. Little torches.

Faenza. A manufacture of pottery considered by some writers to be the most ancient in Italy. *Garzoni*, writing in 1485, says, "The majolicas of F. are white and polished, and one can no more confound them with those of Treviso, than one would take puff-balls for truffles." *Vincenzo Lazari* says they are distinguished by the softness of the tints, the correctness of the drawing, and the whiteness of the enamel at the back. For a long and interesting account of this most important botega, see *Jacquemart, Hist. of the Ceramic Art.* The name of *Fayence* is derived from Faenza, and *not* from the little town of Fayence in France. (Fig. 301.)

Faience. (See FAYENCE.)

Fairy Butter, O. E. (1) A fungous excrescence about the roots of trees, and (2) a species of *tremella* found on furze and broom are so called.

Fairy Circles. Circles of coarse green grass common in meadows, and attributed to the dancing of the fairies.

Fairy Dances = FAIRY CIRCLES (q.v.).

Fairy Darts. Small flints in the form of arrow-heads, possibly of the stone age.

Fairy Faces. Fossil *echini* or sea-urchins.

Fairy Groats. A country name for certain old coins. (See *Harrison's England*, p. 218.)

Fairy Loaves. Fossils found in the chalk, called also *fairy faces*.

Fairy Money. Treasure trove was so called.

Fairy Pipes. Small old tobacco-pipes, frequently found in the north of England.

Fairy Rings. (See FAIRY CIRCLES.)

Fairy Sparks. Phosphoric light seen on various substances in the night time. (*Halliwell*.)

Fairy Stones. (See FAIRY LOAVES.)

Faith, in Christian art, is represented by a female figure holding the Eucharistic cup.

Fala, R. A wooden tower used in the siege of a fortified place, but the exact form of which is unknown; it differed from the ACROBATICON.

Falarica or **Phalarica, R.** A heavy spear, used by the Saguntines, which was generally discharged from a *balista*. Its shaft was sometimes enveloped with sulphur and resin, and with tow steeped in oil; and it was launched blazing against wooden towers for the purpose of setting them on fire.

Falbala. (See FURBELOW.)

Falcastrum, R. (*falx*, a sickle). An agricultural tool with a curved blade for tearing up weeds.

Falcatus, R. Furnished with scythes (*falces*). (See CURRUS.)

Falchion. A broadsword, spelt "fawchon;" 14th century. (See FALX.)

Falcicula. Dimin. of *falx*.

Falcon, in mediæval art, is the attribute of a gentleman, in allusion to the restrictions of the sumptuary laws.

Falcula. Dimin. of *falx*.

Faldestol, O. E. An elbow-chair of state; modern "*fauteuil.*" (See FALDSTOOL.)

Falding (A.S. *feald*). A kind of coarse cloth, like frieze.

Faldstool, Faldistory, O. E. A folding-stool, like a modern camp-stool, used in cathedral church services in Saxon times.

Fall or **Falling-band.** A large collar falling on to the shoulders; 16th and 17th centuries. (See BANDS.)

Fallals, O. E. The falling ruffs of a woman's dress.

False, Her. Said of any charge when its central area is removed; thus an annulet is a "false roundle."

False Roof, Arch. The space between the ceiling of the garret and the roof.

Fig. 302. Feather Fan—Italian.

Falx, R. A scythe, sickle, bill-hook, &c.; any instrument with a curved edge used for cutting grass, wood, or other objects. There were many different kinds, which were called respectively *arboraria* and *sylvatica, denticulata,*

Fig. 303. Venetian lady, with a square fan of the 16th century.

fœnaria or *veruculata, vinitoria, vineatica,* and *putatoria.* The term *falx* was also applied to a falchion strongly curved at the end. *Falx supina* was a dagger with a keen and curved blade ; *falx muralis* was an instrument employed in warfare, both by sea and land, either to cut the masts and rigging of a vessel, or to sweep

the ramparts clear of defenders. [*Culter* is a knife with one straight edge ; *falx*, one with the edge curved. Hence our *falchion,* &c.]

Familia, Med. Lat. An old term for a set of chessmen. Among the jewels in the wardrobe-book of Edward I. occur "una *familia* de ebore, pro ludendo ad scaccarium," and "una familia pro scaccario de jaspide et crystallo."

Fan, Egyp. With the *Egyptians*, the fan of ostrich feathers for brushing away flies was looked upon as the insignia of princes and chieftains ; the *flabellum* or *umbellum* (parasol) was carried by inferior officers. Both kinds of fan are frequently represented on the sacred barges. The use of the fan was first introduced into England in the 16th century ; they were first made of feathers with long handles of gold, silver, or ivory of elaborate workmanship, and sometimes inlaid with precious stones. The engraving shows one from a portrait of Queen Elizabeth. The *Greeks* and *Romans* had fans of various elegant materials, often of peacock's feathers ; sometimes of wings of birds, or of linen stretched on a frame. *Italian* fans, mediæval, were square flags, as in Fig. 303. Folding fans were first introduced in the 17th century. Inventories of churches and monasteries of the 14th century include ecclesiastical fans or *flabella.* These are still used in the Catholic Church in the East. An illumination at Rouen represents the deacon raising the flabellum, a circular fan with a long handle, over the head of the priest at the altar. In the accounts of the churchwardens of Walberswick, Suffolk, of 1493, is the entry "for a bessume of pekok's fethers, IVd." (Figs. 302, 303.)

Fan-crest, Her. An early form of decoration for the knightly helm.

Fandango. A Spanish dance.

Fane. (1) A vane or weathercock ; "a fayne of a schipe," i. e. a vane on the top of a mast. "Of sylver his maste, of golde his *fane*." (2) *Anglo-Saxon.* A banner. (3) The white flower - de - luce. (*Gerard.*) (4) Enemies. (*Halliwell.*) (See also FANUM.)

Fanfare, Fr. A flourish of trumpets.

Fannel or **Phannel**, O. E. The FANON (q.v.).

Fanon, Chr. The maniple or napkin worn by the priest at mass. It was originally nothing but a plain strip of linen worn on the left wrist. In later times it was highly decorated, and often made of the richest materials.

Fan-tao, Chinese. A fabulous peach-tree, which blossoms every 3000 years ; represented on pottery as an attribute of Cheou-Lao, the god of longevity, who holds in his hand a fruit of it.

Fan-tracery. In Gothic architecture, elaborate carved work spread over an arched surface, like a fan with the handle resting on a corbel or stone bracket below.

Fanum, R. (*fari*, to speak) ; Eng. **Fane.** A term synonymous with TEMPLUM (q.v.), but implying also the idea of a place which had been consecrated by the solemn formula of the augurs. The *fanum* thus comprised not only the building itself, the temple, but also all the consecrated ground surrounding it ["*locus liberatus et effatus.*"]

Farrago, R. (i. e. made of *far*, spelt). Fodder for horses and cattle, consisting of the green ears of different kinds of grain.

Farthingale (Fr. *vertugale*) is first spoken of in 1547. It was a sort of cage made of whalebone worn under the petticoat, increasing the size of the hips. In Elizabeth's reign it reached to a preposterous size, giving the wearer the appearance of "standing in a drum," according to "Sir Roger de Coverley." There were *wheel-farthingales* and *tub-farthingales*. Farthingales

bandage ; such as (1) the swathes (Gr. σπάρ-γανον) in which newly-born children were wrapped ; (2) a white band, or for women, a purple, worn as a diadem (DIADEMA) ; (3) (*f. pectoralis*) a bandage worn by young Roman girls to prevent excessive development of the breast ; (4) (*f. cruralis*) a bandage wound closely round the leg from the ankle to the knee, &c.; these were adopted in Europe in the Middle Ages ; (5) (*f. pedulis*, Gr. ποδεῖον) a sock ; (6) see ZONA. (7) In *architecture* the term *fascia* or *facia* is applied to three flat parallel *bands* of stone, introduced to break the monotony of architraves, more especially of the Ionic, Corinthian, and Composite Orders.

Fig. 304. Farthingale of the time of Elizabeth.

Fig. 305. Roman lictor carrying the fasces.

were worn during the reign of Charles I., but of more moderate dimensions; and in Charles II.'s reign the fashion vanished to reappear in the hoop of the 18th century. The engraving gives an example of a moderate farthingale. (Fig. 304.)

Fartura, R. (*farcio*, to stuff). The act of fattening poultry ; and thence applied to a kind of structure, the centre of which was filled with rubble.

Fasces. (See FASCIS.)

Fascia, R. Any strip of cloth used for a

Fasciculus, R. (dimin. of *fascis*). A small bundle, or number of objects tied up into small bundles.

Fascina (*fascinum* = fascination). Amulets worn to avert the "evil eye." "Nescio quis teneros oculus mihi fascinat agnos." (*Virgil.*)

Fasciola (dimin. of *fascia*). A small bandage. (See FASCIA.)

Fascis, R. A bundle ; a small packet ; a small faggot of wood, or fascine. In the plural *fasces* denoted the bundle of rods, with an axe in the middle, carried by the lictors before certain of the Roman magistrates. (See Fig. 305.) *Fasces laureati* were the fasces crowned with laurel leaves, which were carried before a victorious general ; *fasces versi*, the reversed fasces, which were carried axe downwards, in token of mourning, at funerals. The fasces were carried by the lictors on their shoulders, as shown in Fig. 305 ; and when an inferior magistrate met a superior one, the lictors of the former lowered their fasces to him ; hence the expression *submittere fasces*, to yield or confess inferiority.

Faselus. (See PHASELUS.)

Fasti, R. (*fas*, divine law). Archives or calendars engraved on stone or marble; they were of two kinds. (1) The *fasti sacri* or *kalendares*, a kind of almanack or calendar, setting out the *dies fasti*, or lawful days on which certain kinds of business might be transacted without impiety ; also the religious festivals, &c. The calendars were entirely in the keeping of the priests. (2) The *fasti annales* or *historici*, which contained the names of the consuls and magistrates, and a short account of the most remarkable events. Some important lists of this kind of the time of Tiberius are preserved in the capitol at Rome, and called the Fasti Capitolini.

Fastigium, R. (*fastigo*, to raise to a point). The top of a pediment, and thence the entire pediment itself. In a building this term also signifies the *ridge*, or top of a roof whose two sides rise up to a point.

Faun (Lat. *Faunus*). A woodland god, frequently represented with sharp ears and with the feet of a goat.

Fauteau, Fr. A military engine used in the Middle Ages ; it was a kind of battering-ram suspended in a tower. (See ARIES.)

Faux, R. Any narrow passage, lobby, corridor, or entrance to a house, in especial the passage which formed the communication between two blocks of a house. In the plural, *fauces*, like *carceres*, denoted stalls or stables for horses. (See CARCER.)

Favissæ, R. Pits or cellars under a temple, in which all the furniture and sacred implements which had become unfit for use were kept.

Favour, O. E. A love-gift ; a ribbon or glove, &c., worn on the crest of the favoured knight at a tournament, &c.

Favourite, O. E. A lock of hair : "a sort of modish lock, dangling on the temples." (*Ladies' Dictionary*, 1694.)

Favus, R. A flagstone or tablet of marble cut into a hexagon, like the cell of a honeycomb (*favus*), whence its name. [Pavements of this pattern were called Sectilia.]

Fax, R. A torch. This consisted either of pieces of wood joined together and steeped in resin, or a metal tube filled with inflammable materials, such as resin, pitch, tallow, tow impregnated with wax, &c. [The early evening was hence called *prima fax*, and as marriages were celebrated at that time of day, the *torch* was made an attribute of Hymen, and a symbol of marriage. The torch was also carried at funerals to fire the pile with.]

Fayence. Pottery.

Feather. In Christian art (German) an attribute of St. Barbara ; it is generally a peacock's feather. This refers to an old German version of her legend, which relates that when St. Barbara was scourged by her father, angels changed the rods into feathers.

Featherings, in Architecture, are lacelike ornaments along the edges of arcs in windows, canopies, &c.

Feathers, Her. The feathers borne as crests and badges are generally those of the ostrich, sometimes of the swan,

Fig. 306. Ostrich feathers. (An escroll for a coronet.)

the turkey, and a few other birds. Fig. 306 is a representation of an early plume of ostrich feathers, as they are carved, with an escroll in place of a coronet, in the Abbey Church of St. Albans. From the time of the accession of the House of Stuart to the crown of the United Kingdom, the coroneted plume of three ostrich feathers appears to have been regarded, as it is at this present day, as the special badge of the Princes of Wales.

Februa, Februales, R. A festival in honour of the dead instituted by Numa ; it was celebrated every year on the ides of February.

Feet. In Christian art the feet of Our Lord, also of angels and of the Apostles, should always be represented naked, without shoes or sandals. (*Fairholt.*)

Felt (Fr. *feutre*). A sort of coarse wool, or wool and hair. Felt hats were first made in England by Spaniards and Dutchmen, in the beginning of the reign of Henry VIII. Felt was also used for the stuffing of garments.

Feminalia or **Femoralia,** R. (*femur*, the thigh). Short breeches or a kind of drawers

R. Dudley del.

Fig. 307. Silver Feretory or Reliquary, of good English work,
for the most part in repoussé.

which reached from the waist to about the knee.
[Worn by Augustus Cæsar, who was very
susceptible to cold.]

Fendace (armour). The old name for the
gorget.

Fenestella, Chr. (lit. a small window). A
niche made in the wall of a church, near the
altar, and containing the stone basin in which
the priest poured away the water in which he
had washed the chalice.

Fenestra, Window. *Fenestra biforis* is a *Ge-
mel-window,* formed by a double bay. *Fenestra*
was the name given to the hole pierced in the
ears to receive the earrings, as also to the
loop-holes made in the walls of a fortress.

Fenestration, Arch. A term which expresses
the disposition and arrangement of all the
windows in a house.

Fengite. Transparent alabaster used for glass
in windows.

Ferculum, R. (*fero,* to carry). Contracted
form of *fericulum,* a tray, and thence the
dishes carried upon a tray ; a *course* or *remove.*
In a triumphal procession the term was applied
to a platform for displaying an enemy's spoils,
a rich booty, images of the gods, &c.; or the
ashes of the dead in a funeral.

Feretory, Chr. (1) A richly-ornamented
shrine, often of solid gold and set with jewels,
in which the relics of saints are carried in
Roman Catholic processions. (2) The enclosure or chapel in which the shrine was
kept.

Feretrum or **Pheretrum,** Gr., R., and Chr.
(Lat. *capulus*). A bier ; sometimes a shrine.
The term was used at a period when coffins were
uncommon ; more properly the **FERETORY, 1**
(q. v.).

Feriæ, R. Days of festival among
the Romans ; they were classed as follows : (1) *Feriæ statæ* or *stativæ,*
which were held regularly on the
days indicated in the calendar ; these
were the *immovable festivals,* such as
the Agonalia, Carmentalia, Lupercalia, &c. (2) *Feriæ conceptæ* or *con-
ceptivæ,* which were held every year,
but at uncertain intervals ; these were
the *movable festivals,* such as the
Latinæ, Sementivæ, Paganalia, and
Compitalia. (3) Lastly, there were
the *feriæ imperativæ* or *official festivals,* which were held by order of the
dictators, consuls, or prætors. All
feriæ were *dies nefasti,* on which
lawsuits, political transactions, &c.
were impious, and slaves were re-
lieved of their labour. The *feriæ
Latinæ* were the most important of
all Roman festivals.

Fermail, Her. A buckle.

Ferr, Her. A horse-shoe.

Ferrara. A manufactory of majolica in
North Italy, described by Jacquemart as "one
of the most brilliant in Italy;" established
by Alfonso I. with artists imported from Faenza,
circa 1495. (*Jacquemart.*)

Fig. 308. Fesse.

Ferrea Solea. A horse-
shoe. (See SOLEA and
HIPPOSANDALIUM.)

Ferriterium. A prison
for slaves. Synonym of
ERGASTULUM (q.v.).

Ferula, R. The fen-
nel ; a plant with which
children were beaten for
slight faults, and thence a
cane or stick with which
slaves were chastised.

Fesse, Her. One of the ordinaries. A broad
band of metal or colour crossing the shield
horizontally.

Fig. 309. Festoon of foliage.

Fesse-point, Her. The central point of an
escutcheon.

Fesse-wise, In Fesse, Her. Disposed in a
horizontal line, side by side, across the centre
of a field, and over the fesse-point of a shield.

Festoon, Arch. Garland of flowers. (Fig. 309.) (See ENCARPA.)

Festra, R. An abbreviation anciently employed for FENESTRA (q.v.).

Festuca or **Vindicta,** R. The rod which the lictor held over the head of a slave during the ceremony of *manumissio*, by which he was given his freedom. (See MANUMISSIO.)

Fetter-lock, Her. A shackle, padlock; a Yorkshire badge.

Fibrinæ (vestes), **Fibrinæ** (lanæ). (See CASTOREÆ.)

Fibula, Gen. (*figo*, to fix). (1) A clasp, buckle,

Fig. 310. Fibula. Gallic.

or brooch; any contrivance made of gold, silver, bronze, ivory, &c., used for fastening male or female attire. (2) The buckle of a head-band (*tænia, vitta*). Figs. 310 and 311 represent buttons and clasps belonging to the Gaulish and Merovingian periods. [The girdles of the *Franks* and *Saxons*, found in English tombs, were usually ornamented most profusely. Not only were the buckles (*fibulæ*) of the richest workmanship, and conspicuous for size and decoration, but they are sometimes supplemented by enchased plates, or plates set with precious stones. (*Roach Smith.*)] (See Figs. 105 to 113.)

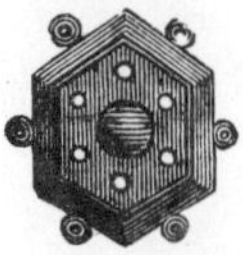

Fig 311. Fibula. Gallic.

Fictile Ware, Keremania, R. (*fingo,* to mould). Any object made of terracotta or pottery, such as tiles, bricks, vases, &c. (See POTTERY.)

Fiddle (A.S. *fithele*), or **Viol,** is represented in an Anglo-Saxon MS. of the 11th century, of a pear-shape, with four strings. The fiddle-bow probably originated in Hindustan, where the *Hindus* claim that the ravanastron was invented about 5000 years ago by Ravanon, a king of Ceylon. Almost identical with this is the *Chinese* fiddle called *urheen,* which has only two strings, and its body consists of a small block of wood, hollowed out and covered with a snake-skin. A German fiddle of the 9th century, called *lyra,* has only one string. In the Nibelungen Lied Volker is described as dexterous in playing the fiddle. Interesting representations of performers on the fiddle are painted on the roof of Peterborough Cathedral. They are attributed to the 12th century.

Fidelia, R. An earthenware vessel or jar used as a receptacle for cement.

Fides or **Fidis,** R. A general term comprising all stringed or gut instruments (from *sphidé,* catgut).

Fidicula, R. (dimin. of *fides*). A very fine catgut string, a *treble-string.* The plural *fidiculæ* denotes an instrument of torture for slaves, the form of which is unknown.

Field. In Numismatics, the surface of a coin on which objects were engraved; in Heraldry, the entire surface of a shield or banner.

Figure-paintings. Paintings of the human figure.

Filagree, Filigree, or **Filigraine** (It. *fili-*

Fig. 312. Silver Filigree. Reliquary, belonging to Lord Hastings, said to have been dug up in the foundations of St. Paul's, London.

grana=filum and *granum,* or granular net-work; so called because the Italians, who first introduced this style of work, placed beads upon it. [*Ure.*]). This work is of gold or silver wire plaited and soldered into delicate arabesques and flower patterns. In the 15th century the Spanish Moors "made admirable chiselled, enamelled, and gilt work, and applied filigree work on the surface, a system kept up at Salamanca and Cordova to the present day." The Eastern nations have always been famous for filigree work.

File, Her. A label (from the Latin *filum,* a narrow ribbon).

Filfot, called also the **Gammadion.** (See FYLFOT.)

Filigree Glass. (See GLASS.)

Fillet, Her. A diminutive of a chief.

Fillets, Gen. Strips of linen employed for

various purposes. The victims which were conducted by priests to sacrifice were adorned with
sacred fillets. Among the Egyptians fillets were
employed to swathe mummies, the strips being
repeatedly wound by the embalmers round the
corpse, till it reassumed the appearance it had
presented before being dried. (See DIADEM,
FASCIA.) In Architecture, a small round or
rectangular moulding which separates two others
which are larger and more prominent; the
fillet also separates the flutings of columns.
(See TÆNIA.)

Fig. 313. Cross
fimbriated.

Fimbria, R. The border
or fringe of a cloth or garment. [These were more
common among the Egyp-
tians and Assyrians than
the Greeks and Romans, and
are mentioned in the
Bible.]

Fimbriated, Her. Bor-
dered; the border (which
is narrow) lying in the same
plane with the object bordered. (Fig. 313.)

Finial. In Gothic architecture, an ornament
of carved work represent-
ing foliage, on the apex
of a spire or pinnacle.
(See CROCKET.) (Fig.
314.)

Fir-cone upon a stem
was the form of vases special to the majolica manufactory of Deruba; "a
form," says Jacquemart,
"quite special to that
manufactory, and directly
imitated from the extreme
East and from Asia Minor."

Fire. Flames of fire
placed near St. Anthony
signify his spiritual aid as
patron saint against fire
in all shapes, in the next
world and in this. *Tongues
of fire* are, of course, de-
picted on the heads of the Apostles, in representations of the Day of Pentecost.

Fire-dog. (See ANDIRON.)

Fire-lock. The musket fired by flint and
steel, invented in France about the year 1630.
(See MATCH-LOCK.)

Fire-stommer, O. E. A poker.

Fiscus, R. A wicker-work basket used for
gardening purposes, especially for gathering in
the olive and grape crops. The Romans also
made use of this basket for transporting sums of
money; hence *fiscus* came to mean a money-
chest, and was the name given to that part of
the revenue which was applied to the civil list
of the emperors [opposed to *ærarium*, the pro-

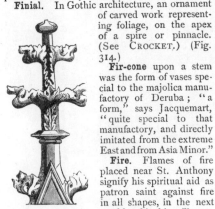

Fig. 314. Finial.

perty of the senate]; but at last the word was
used to signify generally the property of the state.

Fish. In Christian art, the symbol of water
and the rite of baptism. (See ACROSTIC and
VESICA PISCIS.)

Fistuca, R. A pavior's ram or beetle; a
wooden bar or pile used to consolidate floorings,
masonry, and pavements.

Fistula, R. (1) A water-pipe of lead or
earthenware. (2) A writing-pen made of reed,
and thence a Pan's pipe. (3) A rolling-pin for
making pastry. (4) A probe. (5) A machine
for bruising corn, which was called *fistula
farraria.*

Fitch. The best of paint-brushes are made
of the hair of the *fitch* or polecat. They are
black, elastic, and firm though soft. They are
made flat or round, and are used also for varnishing.

Fitchée, Her. Pointed at the base.

Flabelliform, Arch. (*flabellum*). Fan-shaped.
The term is usually applied to an ornament
composed of leaves and palms, which is of frequent occurrence on Romano-Byzantine monuments.

Flabellum, Gen. (*flo*, to blow). A fan.
(See FAN.)

Flagellum, Gen. (*flagrum*). A whip or
scourge made with thongs of leather, especially
thongs of the ox's hide, or twisted or knotted
cords, &c., used in antiquity for punishing slaves
or culprits. It was a terrible weapon, and the
lash was often knotted with bones, or heavy
metal *hooks* to tear the flesh (*scorpio*). Gladiators used to fight in the arena with *flagella*.

Flagon. A vessel with a long neck covered
at top, and a spout. The flagons of the 15th
and 16th centuries are the best in design and
ornamentation.

Flail. A weapon like a flail, of wood and
iron armed with spikes, *temp.* Henry VIII.

Flake-white. So called from its form, in
commerce, of *flakes* or scales. As a pigment it
possesses great body, and enters largely into
numerous compound tints. (*Fairholt.*) (See
CARBONATE OF LEAD.)

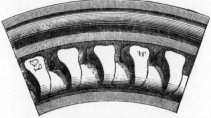

Fig. 315. Flat-heads.

Flamboyant (style), Mod. The style of
French architecture peculiar to the 15th cen-

tury, so called because the mullions and tracery of the windows in the monuments belonging to that period are curved and twisted like the waving of flames. This style was contemporary with that called "the perpendicular" in England.

Flamen, R. A priest devoted to the service of any one god; e. g. *Flamen Martialis*, the priest of Mars. Their characteristic dress was the APEX, the LÆNA, and a laurel wreath.

Fig. 316. Projecting-heads.

Flaming Heart, in Christian symbolism, expresses fervent piety and love.

Flammeolum (dimin. of *flammeum*). A term denoting a texture much finer than that of the *flammeum*.

Flammeum, R. A bridal veil worn by the

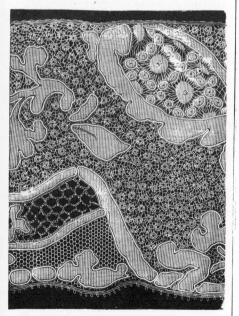

Fig. 317. Old Flemish Lace.

bride on the day of her marriage ; it was of light gauze, and in colour of a vivid and brilliant yellow, like a flame ; whence its name. It covered the lady from head to foot, and was removed by the bridegroom on their arrival home after the ceremony.

Flammula, R. A small flame ; a small banner borne by light cavalry regiments ; it was of a vivid and brilliant yellow colour, like the bridal *flammeum*; whence its name. (Modern ORIFLAMME, q.v.)

Flanches, Flasques, Her. Subordinaries.

Flat-heads, Projecting-heads, Mod. An ornament peculiar to the Romano-Byzantine period, which decorates archivolts. Fig. 315 gives an example of flat-heads ; Fig. 316 of projecting-heads.

Flaying-knife. An attribute of St. Bartholomew, signifying the manner of his martyrdom. In Croyland Abbey it was anciently the custom to present all members of the community with small flaying-knives on St. Bartholomew's Day (Aug. 24).

Flemish Lace. Flanders and Italy dispute the invention of pillow lace. It is certain, however, that lace of home manufacture was worn in the 15th century in the Low Countries, and from that time to the present lace-making has formed a source of national wealth to Belgium. The engraving shows a fine specimen of old Flemish lace composed of six different designs joined together, commonly known as "Trolle Kant." A similar lace is made in some of our own counties, and called " Trolly." (Fig. 317.)

Fleur-de-lis (Fr.), the royal insignia of France, was first adopted by Louis VII. (about A.D. 1137) *semée*, or scattered over the field. This shield is blazoned as " France Ancient." On the occasion of his marriage, in 1234, St. Louis instituted the order of the " Cosse de Genest" (Fig. 318), and, as an emblem of his humility, took for his badge the broom-flower with the motto *Exaltat humiles*. The collar of the order was composed of broom - flowers enamelled, intermixed with fleurs-de-lis. In the reign of Charles VI. four collars of the order of the Cosse de Genest were sent as presents to King Richard II. and

Fig. 318. " Cosse de Genest," showing a Cross fleurettée

his uncles the Dukes of Lancaster, Gloucester, and York. The fleur-de-lis entered the English insignia in 1275 with the marriage of Edmund with Blanche of Artois, and was erased on January 1, 1801.

Fleurettée, Her. Terminating in, or bordered with fleurs-de-lis, like the cross in Fig. 318.

Fleuron. A small full-blown rose placed in the centre of the abacus of the capital in certain orders of architecture.

Flexed, Her. Bowed, bent.

Flighted, Her. Feathered, as arrows are.

Flo, O. E. An arrow.

"Robin bent his joly bowe,
Therein he set a *flo.*"
(*Wright's Songs and Carols.*)

Floralia, or **Florales Ludi.** A Roman festival in honour of Flora, said to have been instituted B.C. 238, to invoke the protection of the goddess upon the spring blossoms.

Florentine Fresco. A peculiar method of fresco-painting, by which the lime is kept moistened during the process.

Florentine Lake. (See CARMINATED LAKES.)

Florentine Mosaic. Inlaid work in coloured stones, and precious stones combined into beautiful patterns.

Florid (style), Arch. This term, now disused, has been replaced by that of FLAMBOYANT style (q.v.).

Florimontana. A literary society established at Annecy in 1606. They took for their device an orange tree, with the motto, "*Flores, fructusque perennes.*"

Fluor-spar or **Derbyshire-spar.** A mineral rock very common in Derbyshire, where it is made into ornaments, &c., with the lathe.

Flute, Gen. Said to have been invented by Apollo or Mercury. The simplest form of flute was made with an oat-stalk (*avena*) or a hollow reed (*calamus*); in the course of time it was made of ivory, bone, or the shin-bones of animals; whence its Latin name of TIBIA (q.v.). The Greek flute (*aulos*) was held like a flageolet, and a vibrating reed was inserted into the mouthpiece. The single flute was called *monaulos*; the double one *diaulos*. A specimen of the last in the British Museum was found in a tomb at Athens. It is made of cedar, and the tubes, which are fifteen inches in length, have each a

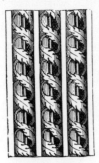
Fig. 319. Flutings.

separate mouthpiece and six finger-holes, five of which are at the upper side, and one underneath. The flutes of the *Etruscans* were often of ivory; those used in religious ceremonies were of boxwood, ass's bone, bronze, and silver. The *Persian* flute called "*nay*," and the "*surnay*," a kind of oboe, are still popular in the East. In *Mexico*, the young man sacrificed to the god was taught to play the flute, and as he went to his death he broke a flute on each of the steps of the temple. The practice of making flutes of the bones of their enemies was common with many Indian tribes in America.

Fig. 320. Foculus.

Flutings or **Flutes,** Arch. Small semicircular indents or grooves cut perpendicularly, by way of ornament, in the shafts of columns and pilasters. Flutings may be either decorated or plain. When filled with a bead-moulding, they are said to be *cabled*. Fig. 319 represents flutings decorated with leaves twined round a reed.

Fly, Her. The length and also the side of a flag furthest from the mast.

Fo, Chinese. (See DOG OF FO.) The "Hand of Fo" is a fragrant fruit, a kind of *cédrat*, generally styled the Chinese hand-plant, used to perfume apartments.

Focale, R. (*fauces,* the throat). A square piece of cloth which was wrapped round the neck, and covered the ears.

Foculus, R. (dimin. of *focus*). A portable fireplace; a brazier or chafing-dish. (Fig. 320.)

Focus, R. The hearth or fireplace of a house, consecrated to the Lares or household gods.

Foil, in Architecture. (See TREFOIL, QUATREFOIL, &c.)

Fig. 321. Foliage of the Acanthus.

Foliage, Gen. Nearly every style of architecture has made use of foliage for purposes of ornamentation. In antiquity, the leaves of the acanthus, palm, laurel, olive, ivy, &c., were thus employed; the Romano-Byzantine, Byzantine, and Pointed styles utilized for the same purpose the vine, oak, cinquefoil, parsley, mahonia, mullein, thistle, &c. Foliage has been applied to the decoration of capitals, archivolts, bands, cornices, and friezes ; and it has also been used to form CROCKETS (q.v.), crownings, pinnacles, &c. Architectural work thus enriched is said to be FOLIATED, and the ornament itself is called FOLIATION.

Fig. 322. Foliage on moulding.

Folliculus, R. A leather cap encircling the hole by which an oar protruded from a ship. The term is a diminutive of FOLLIS (q.v.).

Follis, R. A small ball of leather inflated with air, which also went by the name of *folliculus;* used for a plaything.

Fong-hoang, Chinese. A fabulous bird which is immortal, lives in the highest regions of the air, and only approaches men to announce to them happy events and prosperous reigns. It is easily recognized (on pottery, &c.) by its carunculated head, its neck surrounded by silky feathers, and its tail partaking of the Argus pheasant and the peacock. (*Jacquemart.*)

Fig. 323. Pompeian fountain.

Fons, Fountain, Gen. In antiquity, natural springs and fountains were objects of religious worship. Fig. 323 represents a Pompeian fountain known as the Fountain of Abundance.

Font, Chr. The vessel which contains the consecrated water used in the administration of baptism, by sprinkling or aspersion (Fig. 324), introduced in lieu of the original mode of immersion (Fig. 325). (Compare PISCINA.)

Fontange, Fr. "A modish head-dress," deriving its name from Mademoiselle de Fontange, a lady of the court of Louis XIV., who invented it. (Fig. 326.)

Fig. 324. Baptismal font (Romano-Byzantine).

Font-cloth, O. E. (1) The hanging with which the font was ornamented. (2) The CHRISMALE (q.v.).

Fools. In Church architecture and decoration, grotesque figures of men with fool's cap and bells are frequently seen under the seats of choir-stalls and *miserere* seats. (See the article OBSCŒNA.)

Foolscap. A fool's cap was the device of the Italian society called the Granelleschi, formed at Venice in 1740 to oppose the corruption of the Italian language. A sheet of foolscap paper is 17 in. by 13½ in.

Foreceps. Tongs or pincers, the attributes of some of the martyrs. (See FORFEX.)

Fig. 325. Early English Font.

Foreshortening. The art of representing objects on a plane surface as they appear to the eye in perspective.

Forfex, R. (1) Large scissors or shears used to cut hair or shear animals. (2) A clip, in the form of shears, for raising weights. (Fig. 327.) Fig. 328 represents a shears described by Vitruvius, which was used to raise stones.

Fig. 326. The Fontange Head-dress.

Fig. 327. Roman Forfex.

Fig. 328. Forfex.

ral, *fores* denotes a folding-door with two leaves, as, for instance, *fores carceris*, the door of the stalls in a circus.

Forks were not in general use earlier than the 14th century. One of the earliest occasions on which a fork is mentioned informs us that John, Duke of Brittany in 1306, had one "to pick up soppys."

Forlon. A Spanish carriage with four seats.

Forma, R. (*fero*, to produce). A mould, form, or model; a mould for making bricks or other objects in clay, such as (1) antefixa, masks, &c.; (2) a shoemaker's last; (3) the water-way of a subterranean aqueduct. *Diminutive*, **Formella,** R. A small shape or mould used especially by the Romans to give an artificial form to the fish which was served as one of the courses at dinner.

Fornacalia, R. A festival of bakers in honour of the goddess *Fornax* (oven-goddess). It took place in February, the day being given out by the *curio maximus*, who announced, in tablets which were placed in the forum, the part which each *curia* had to take in the festival. Those persons who did not know to which curia they belonged, performed the rites on the last day, called *Stultorum feriæ* (the feasts of fools).

Fornacula (dimin. of FORNAX, q.v.). (1) A small furnace for smelting metals. (2) A small furnace for a bath-room.

Fornax, R. A furnace; an oven; a kiln for baking pottery: *fornax calcaria*, a lime-kiln; *fornax æraria*, a blast-furnace for smelting metals; *fornax balnei*, a hypocaust or bath-furnace; this was also called FORNACULA (q.v.). FORNAX is also the name of the goddess of *ovens*.

Fornix, R. A term having the same meaning as ARCUS (q.v.). It also denotes (1) a triumphal arch (*arcus triumphalis*); (2) a vault or vaulted room; (3) a vaulted gate.

Forril. A kind of parchment, specially prepared for bookbinding.

Forulus, R. (dimin. of *forus*, a shelf). A cupboard, cabinet, or dwarf bookcase.

Fori, R. This term, which is the plural of *forus*, denotes (1) the flooring of a ship; (2) the flooring of a bridge; (3) the standing-places on a temporary platform; (4) the shelves forming the divisions or different stories of a beehive; (5) the narrow parallel furrows drawn in a garden by means of the hoe.

Foricula. A little door. Dimin. of FORIS (q.v.).

Foris, R. The door as distinguished from the frame in which it hung. In the plu-

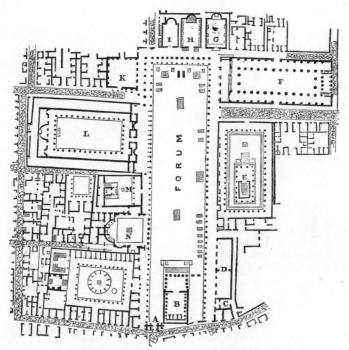

Fig. 329. Ground-plan of the Forum at Pompeii.

Forum, R. A large open space used by the Romans as a market ; it answered to the Greek AGORA (q.v.). Fig. 329 represents the *forum civile* of Pompeii, unquestionably one of the most complete examples bequeathed to us by antiquity. *A* is the principal entrance ; *B*, a Corinthian temple ; *C*, the public prison (*carcer publicus*) ; *D* is supposed to have been a *horreum*, or public granary ; *E*, the temple of Venus, the guardian goddess of the city ; *F*, the basilica ; *G*, *H*, *I*, the curiæ, which were a kind of civil and commercial tribunals ; *K* is a rectangular building which probably served the purpose of a shop for money-changers ; *L*, a portico terminating in an absis ; *M*, the temple of Mercury or Quirinus ; *N*, a building with a large semicircular tribune, which probably formed the residence of the AUGUSTALES.

Forus. A synonym of FORUM (q.v.). *Forus aleatorius* was the term applied to a dice-table.

Fossil Ivory. The tusks of the mammoth—the extinct *elephas primigenius*—found in great quantity in Siberia, are the material of which nearly all the ivory-turner's work in Russia is made. The ivory has not undergone any petrifying change like other fossils, and is as well

adapted for use as that procured from living species.

Fote (or **Foot**) **Mantel.** An outer garment of the petticoat kind, bound round the hips (of a woman on horseback) "to keep her gown or surcoat clean." (*Strutt.*)

"A *fote-mantel* about hir hips large." (*Chaucer.*)

Fountain, Her. A circular figure or ROUNDLE that is *barry wavy* arg. is so blazoned.

Fourchée, Her. Divided into two parts ; said of a lion with a double tail.

Fraces, R. A kind of fuel made of the tan obtained from the residuum of oil-presses ; it was thus the pulp of olives.

Frænum, Frenum, R. A horse's bridle, including the bit and the reins. [The bit was called *orea* or Greek στόμιον.]

Framea, R. (1) A German spear, the iron head of which was short but very sharp ; it was employed by them as a pike. (2) A weapon used by the Franks.

Franᴄisᴄa. A kind of battle-axe used by the Franks.

Frankfort Black. A German pigment prepared like *blue black* (q.v.).

L

French Ultramarine. (See GUIMET'S ULTRA-MARINE.)

Fresco Painting (i.e. *al fresco*, upon fresh or wet ground), generally employed for large pictures on walls and ceilings, is executed with mineral and earthy pigments upon a freshly-laid

Fig. 330. Greek Fret.

ground of stucco. It was known to the ancients, and must be distinguished from DISTEMPER PAINTING (q.v.) on plaster, which is a different

Fig. 331. Greek Fret.

process. "*Buon* (or genuine) *fresco*," painted on the fresh surface of plaster, is distinguished from "*fresco secco*," or a process of painting on

Fig. 332. Greek Fret.

dry plaster commonly practised in Italy and Munich. It is argued that the latter was the process used at Pompeii, and generally by the ancients, because (1) lime is found in nearly all the

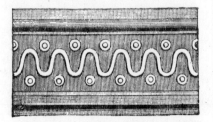

Fig. 333. Undulated Fret.

colours, and (2) the nature of the joinings in the work indicates that each compartment does

not contain only one day's work, as it must in *buon fresco*.

Fret, Arch.   An angular, interlaced archi-

Fig. 334. Scroll Fret.

tectural ornament of the Greek and Romano-Byzantine period, also known as *broken batoon* and *Vitruvian scroll*, and presenting some analogy with *chevron* or zigzag. There are *crenelated* or *rectangular frets*, *triangular*, *nebulated*, *undulated frets*, &c.

Fret, O. E.   A *caul* of gold or silver wire.

"A *fret* of golde she had next her hair." (*Chaucer.*)

Fret or **Frette,** Her.   One of the sub-ordinaries.   The illustration is one of the badges of the Arundel family: a chapeau or and gules, surmounted by a *fret* or, and an acorn leaved vert.

Fig. 335. Badge of the Arundel family, with fret.

Frieze, Arch. That part of the entablature which is included between the architrave and the cornice. (See Fig. 184.) Another name for it is ZOOPHORUS (q.v.).   It was generally richly sculptured. The finest frieze ever found is that of the Parthenon, the ornamentation of which may be studied in the Elgin-marble room at the British Museum. (See Fig. 282.)

Frieze, Frize.   A coarse woollen cloth, first mentioned 1399.

"Cloth of gold, do not despize
To match thyself with cloth of frize.
Cloth of frize, be not too bold,
Though thou be matched with cloth of gold."

Frigidarium, R. (*frigidus*, cold). (1) A cool apartment in a bathing establishment. (2) A cool place used as a larder.

Frisquet.   In wood engraving, a piece of paper laid over the proof-paper in the act of printing, to keep clean the parts not intended to be exposed to the ink.

Fritillus, R.   A dice-box of a cylindrical form, called also *turricula* or *pyrgus* (Greek φιμός).

Frog. An ancient emblem of silence and secrecy, from a legend quoted by Ælian that

Fig. 336. Frog. The device of Mæcenas.

the frogs of Syriapha never croak in their own marshes. Hence it was adopted by Mæcenas, the friend of Augustus, for his device. (Fig. 336.)

Fig. 337. Frontale of a bridle.

Frontale, Gen. (*frons*, the forehead). (1) A frontlet or head-band worn by Greek women, and to be seen principally on the statues of goddesses. (2) A plate or band of metal placed across the forehead of horses (Fig. 337) as a protection for the frontal bone. The Medes, Persians, Greeks, and Romans made use of the *frontale* for their cavalry horses. For the ecclesiastical **Frontal,** Mediæval, see ANTE-PENDIUM. Henry III. gave a FRONTAL to the high altar at Westminster Abbey, upon which, besides carbuncles in golden settings, and several large pieces of enamel, were as many as 866 smaller pieces of enamel.

Frontispiece. In Architecture, the façade or face of a building. The engraved title-page of a book was originally called the frontispiece.

Frote, O. E. To rub; to stir.

Frountere, O. E. FRONTAL (q.v.).

Fucus, Gr. Cosmetic paint, much used by the Greek and Roman ladies. They stained their eyebrows black with a preparation of sulphuret of antimony called *stimmi*, or of soot, *asbolos*. The Roman ladies, in addition to rouge and white for the complexion, used to trace out the veins on their temples with a blue paint, and they wore the patches of Queen Anne's time (*splenia*). "From beef without mustard, a servant which overvalues himself, *and a woman which painteth*,—good Lord deliver us!" (*Stubbes.*)

Fuller's Bat or Club. Attribute of St. James the Less, who was killed with such an implement.

Fullonica, Fullonum, R. (*fullo*, a fuller). A fuller's establishment. An example of one, in perfect preservation, is preserved at Pompeii. The *fullones* acted as laundrymen to Greek and Roman families, washing linen as well as woollen clothes by treading in tubs (using urine for soap, which was unknown to them); hence *saltus fullonicus*, a fuller's dance.

Fulmen. The thunderbolt of Jove. (See also ILLAPA.) It is generally represented as a double cone of flame, with lightnings on each side, or frequently with wings.

Fumarium, R. (*fumus*, smoke). A chamber in the upper part of a Roman house, into which the smoke from the fires was conducted. The smoke-room was used for drying wood and ripening wine. The "Rauchkammer" or smoke attic is still a common institution in good houses in Germany.

Funale, R. (*funis*, a rope). A link or torch made of various materials.

Funalis or Funarius (sc. *equus*). The trace-horse, so called because its traces, instead of being of leather, were of rope (*funis*).

Funarius. (See FUNALIS.)

Funda, Sling, Gen. The sling has been employed by most of the peoples of antiquity as a weapon of warfare for hurling stones, chiefly flints or leaden bullets (*glandes*). The slings of the Egyptians were made of leather thongs or plaited cord. The *funaitores*, or slingers, of the Greek and Roman armies carried each a provision of stones in the folds (*sinus*) of his pallium, a shield on his left arm, and brandished his sling in the right hand. The most celebrated slingers were the inhabitants of the Balearic Islands, which took their ancient name from this circumstance.

Fundibalus, Fundibalum, R. (βάλλω, to throw). A machine for hurling stones; a kind of *balista* (q.v.). (Fig. 338.)

Fig. 338. Fundibalus—Onager.

Fundula, R. A blind alley or *cul-de-sac.*
Fig. 339 represents one of the kind at Pompeii.

Fig. 339. Street at Pompeii.

Fundulus, R. The piston of a hydraulic machine.

Funeral Ceremonies. 1. Greek. The expressions τὰ δίκαια, νομιζόμενα, or προσήκοντα, the just and lawful rites, are expressive of the Greek idea that the proper burial of the dead was a most sacred duty to them. The first act was to place in the mouth of the corpse an *obolus,* with which the spirit would pay the ferryman in Hades. This coin was then called *danaké.* The body was then washed and anointed, the head crowned with flowers, and the handsomest robes put on. All this was done by the women of the family. By the side of the bed upon which the corpse was then laid (πρόθεσις) were placed painted earthen vessels (*lecuthoi*; see LECYTHUS), which were afterwards buried with the corpse. (These vases are frequently disinterred in modern excavations.) A honey-cake (*melittouta*) to throw to the dog Cerberus was laid on the bed. Before the door a vessel of water (*ostracon* or *ardalion*) was set, to be used, like the holy water of Catholic times, by persons *leaving* the house, for purification. On the third day after death, the *ecphora,* or carrying out for burial, took place in the morning before sunrise. The men walked before the corpse, and the women behind. Hired mourners (*threnodoi*) accompanied the procession, playing mournful tunes on the flute. The bodies were either buried or burned, until cremation gave way to a Christian prejudice. The body was placed for burning on the top of a *pyre* (Gr.

πῦρ, fire); and, in remote ages, animals, prisoners, or slaves were burned with it. Oils and perfumes were thrown into the flames. Finally, the smouldering ashes were quenched with wine, and relatives and friends collected what remained of the bones. The bones were then washed with wine and oil, and placed in urns, often golden.

2. Roman. *Funera justa* conveys the same idea as the Greek *dicaia* of the right and title of the dead to a proper observance. With the Romans, the washing, anointing, &c. of the body was done by slaves (*pollinctores*) of the undertakers, who were called *libitinarii,* because they dwelt near the temple of Venus Libitina, in which all things requisite for funerals were sold and a mortuary register was kept. The coin having been duly placed in the mouth, the body was laid out in the vestibule dressed, of ordinary citizens in a white toga, and of magistrates in their official robes, and the couch was strewn with flowers, and a branch of *cypress* was placed at the door of the house. All funerals were, in ancient times, performed at night, but afterwards only those of the poor. At a great funeral the corpse was carried out on the eighth day, preceded by musicians (*cornicines,* &c.) and mourning women (*præficæ*), who chanted a funeral hymn (*nænia*)*;* players and buffoons (*histriones, scurræ*) followed, and a procession of the freed slaves wearing the cap of liberty (*pileati*). Images of the deceased and of his ancestors were borne before the corpse, which was carried on a litter (*feretrum*). The common bier of the poor was called *sandapila,* and its bearers *vespillones,* because they bore it forth in the evening (*vespere*). The couches of the rich were of ivory, richly ornamented with gold and purple. The relations walked behind in mourning, sons with the head veiled, and daughters with dishevelled hair. At the forum a funeral oration (*laudatio*) was delivered, and thence the procession went to the place of burial or cremation. Those who were buried (as all were subsequently to the 4th century A.D.) were placed in a coffin (*arca* or *loculus*), often of stone. The Assian stone, from Assos in Troas, was said to consume all the body, with the exception of the teeth, in forty days, whence it was called sarcophagus (q.v.). For cremation the pyre, or *rogus,* was built like an altar, and the corpse in its splendid couch being placed on the top, the nearest relation, with averted face, fired a corner of the pile. Perfumes were forbidden by the Twelve Tables. Sometimes animals were slaughtered, and in ancient times, captives and slaves, but afterwards gladiators were hired to fight round the blazing pile. (Compare BUSTUM.) When the pyre was burnt down, the embers were soaked with wine, and the bones and ashes collected into urns. (See URNA.) The solemnities continued for nine days after the funeral, at the end of which time a sacrifice was performed called the *novemdiale*. Men wore *black* for mourning, and women white ; but at all banquets given in honour of the dead the guests were clothed in white.

Funeral Urns of Indian pottery are found of extremely ancient date. That represented in Fig. 340 is a covered jar, of primitive make, with an inscription in ancient characters ; its date is probably from 260 to 240 B.C. (*Jacquemart.*)

Fig. 340 Covered urn of red pottery. Ohojepore.

Fur. *Strutt* says that " the furs of sables, beavers, foxes, cats, and lambs were used in England before the Conquest ; to which were afterwards added those of ermines, squirrels, martens, rabbits, goats, and many other animals." In the Middle Ages the more precious furs, as ermine and sable, were reserved for kings, knights, and the principal nobility of both sexes. Inferior ranks used " vair" and "gris," or gray; while citizens, burgesses, and priests wore the common squirrel and lamb-skins. The peasants wore cat-skins, badger-skins, &c. In after times were added the skins of badgers, bears, beavers, deer, fitches, foxes, foynes (or martens), grays, hares, otters, sables, squirrels, weasels, wolves, &c. The mantles of our kings and peers, and the furred robes of municipal officers are the remains of this fashion, which in the 13th century was almost universal.

Fur, Her. The *furs* are of comparatively rare appearance in heraldry, and do not appear in the best ages. *Vair* and *ermine* are common. In Fig. 341 is an example of the treatment of ermine from the monument of Edward III.

Fig. 341. Shield with Ermine.

Furbelow, O. E. An ornament on the petticoat of a woman's dress, described as a " puckered flounce," to display which it became the fashion to roll back the skirts of the gown. " The Old Mode and the New, or the Country Miss with her Furbelow," is the title of an old play, *temp.* William and Mary.

Furca, R. A fork with two teeth (*bidens*), or two prongs ; a hay-fork : *furca carnarii*, a fork used for taking down the meat hung up in the *carnarium*. The term *furca* was further applied to a kind of fork by aid of which a foot-traveller carried his baggage, but the more usual name for this kind of fork was *ærumna* (q. v.). Also, a wooden fork placed for punishment across the shoulders of slaves and criminals, to the prongs of which the hands were tied. Reversed it formed a cross upon which criminals were executed, either by scourging or by crucifixion with nailing. The patibulum was a similar instrument of punishment formed like the letter H.

Furgon, O. E. (Fr. *fourgon*). A fork for putting faggots and sticks on to the fire.

Furnus, R. (1) A baker's oven. (2) A baker's shop. (See FORNAX.)

Fuschan in Appules, O. E. Fustian of Naples. (See FUSTIAN.)

Fuscina, R. (1) A fork with three prongs used for spearing fish. (2) The trident of the *retiarius.* Originally it was called *tridens*, and used as a goad to drive horses. Neptune always carries one.

Fuscinula (dimin. of FUSCINA, q.v.). A carving-fork.

Fusée, Fr. A gun with a wide bore, like a blunderbuss.

Fusiform (*fusus*, a spindle). In the form of a spindle.

Fusil, Fr. The steel for striking fire from a flint ; an ancient device of the Dukes of Burgundy, the motto inculcating the worthlessness of latent virtues never brought into action.

Fig. 342. Fusil. Device of Philip of Burgundy (D. 1467).

Fusi-yama. The sacred mountain of the Japanese, often depicted on their porcelain.

Fustian. "A species of cotton cloth much used by the Normans, particularly by the clergy, and appropriated to their chasubles." (*Strutt.*) It was originally woven at Fustat, on the Nile, with a warp of linen thread, and a woof of thick cotton, so twilled and cut that it showed on one side a thick but low pile. In the 14th century Chaucer says of his knight,—

"Of fustian he wered a gepon."

In the 15th century Naples was celebrated for fustian. An old English account of this date has "Fuschan in Appules" (for Fustian from Naples).

Fustibalum, R. A pole about four feet long, furnished with a sling (*funda*) in the middle. It was wielded by both hands, and was used to hurl huge stones to a distance.

Fusus (Gr. ἄτρακτος). A spindle. It was generally made of wood; but some nations, as for instance the Egyptians, had spindles of pottery.

Fygury, O. E. An old name for silks *dia-pered* with *figures* of flowers and fruit. A cope in the York fabric rolls is described "una capa de sateyn fygury."

Fylfot or **Filfot.** This mysterious ornament exactly resembles the Hindu *arani* of remote antiquity, i. e. the instrument of wood by which fire was obtained by friction; which is the symbol of *Agni*. This symbol has never been lost, and occurs sixty times on an ancient Celtic funereal urn; also on monumental brasses and church embroidery of the Middle Ages. It is generally called the GAMMADION.

Fig. 343. Fylfot.

G.

Gabardine or **Gallebardine,** It. "A rough Irish mantle, or horseman's coat; a long cassock." It was, and is, a favourite outer garment of the Jews.

Gabion, Fortification. A basket filled with earth, used in the construction of earthworks for defensive purposes.

Gable, Arch. (German *Giebel*, point). The triangular end of a house from the eaves to the top.

Gablet. Diminutive of gable—applied to furniture and niches.

Gadlyngs, O. E. Spikes on the knuckles of gauntlets, like the modern "knuckle-dusters."

Gæsum, R. A weapon of Celtic origin. It was a strong, heavy javelin with a very long barbed iron head, used rather as a missile than a spear.

Gage, Med. A glove or cap thrown to the ground as a challenge to combat.

Galages, O. E. (modern, *goloshes*). Clogs fastened with *latchets*.

Galaxia, Gr. (Γαλάξια). Festivals in honour of Apollo, who was surnamed *Galaxios;* they were so called because the principal offering consisted of a barley cake cooked with milk (γάλα).

Galaxy (Gr. γάλα, milk). In Astronomy, the Milky Way. It passes between Sagittarius and Gemini, dividing the sphere into two parts.

Galbanum, R. (*galbus*, yellow). A yellow garment worn by women; men who adopted this kind of dress were looked upon as foppish and effeminate.

Galbe, Fr. The general contour or outline of any member of architecture; in especial, the shaft of a column. (See CONTRACTURA.) It also denotes the lines of a vessel, console, baluster, &c.

Galea, R. A helmet; especially one of skin or leather, in contradistinction to CASSIS, which denoted a metal helmet.

Galeated. In Heraldry, wearing a helmet.

Galeola, R. A very deep vessel in the shape of a helmet. It was used for holding pure wine, and was a kind of ACRATOPHORUM (q.v.).

Galerus, Galerum, R. A peasant's cap made of fur, and thence a wig. It was a round leather cap, ending in a point, originally peculiar to the priesthood.

Galgal, Celt. A Celtic or megalithic monument, more commonly called TUMULUS.

Galiot, Galliot (dimin. of *galère*). A ship moved by both sails and oars.

Gall (A.S. *gealla*). In an animal, a bitter yellowish-green fluid secreted by the gall-bladder. Ox-gall, clarified by boiling with animal charcoal and filtering, is used in water-colour and in ivory painting to make the colours spread more evenly upon the paper, ivory, &c.: mixed with gum-arabic it thickens, and fixes the colours. A coating of it *sets* black-lead or crayon drawings. This word is also applied to anything exceedingly bitter, especially to the bitter potion which it was customary among the Jews to give to persons suffering death under sentence of the law, for the purpose of rendering them less sensible to pain. ὄξος μετὰ χολῆς, "vinegar to drink mingled with gall." (Matt. xxvii. 34.)

Galle (Tours de), Celt. A name applied to certain ancient monuments in France, built by the Gauls.

Galleon (Sp. *galeon*). A large Spanish ship, formerly used in trading to America as a war vessel.

Gallery, Gen. A covered place much longer than it is wide. In Christian archæology it is a kind of tribune situated above the side aisles, and having bays over the nave; it is also called TRIFORIUM (q.v.).

Galley (Icelandic *galleyda*). A one-decked vessel, navigated with sails and oars, in Heraldry called a LYMPHAD (q.v.). The prow of a galley (Fig. 344), one of the devices adopted by Cardinal Richelieu, may still be seen among the architectural decorations of his palace.

Galloon (Sp. *galon*). A narrow kind of lace made of silk woven with cotton, gold, or silver; or of silk only.

Gallow-balk, O. E. (See GALOWS.)

Gally-gascoynes, O. E. Broad loose breeches; 16th century.

Fig. 344. Device of Cardinal Richelieu, from the Galerie d'Orléans, Palais Royal.

"His galligaskins were of corduroy,
And garters he had none."
(*The Weary Knife-grinder.*)

Galows, O. E. An iron bar fastened inside an open chimney, from which the *reeking-hook* was hung, for suspending pots and vessels over the fire.

Fig. 345. Garde de Bras.

Galvanography. (See ELECTROGRAPHY, ELECTROTYPE.)

Gamashes. "High boots, buskins, or startups." (*Holme*, 1688.)

Gambeson (Saxon *wambe*, the belly). A quilted tunic, stuffed with wool. It answered the purpose of defensive armour, and was subsequently called a *pourpoint.*

Gamboge. A gum resin of a forest tree called Garcinia Cambogia, generally imported in cylindrical rolls. It forms a beautiful yellow pigment, used for water-colour; it is used to stain wood in imitation of box, and the tincture enters into the composition of the gold-coloured varnish for lacquering brass; it also gives a beautiful and durable stain to marble. (*E. B.*)

Gamelion. The seventh month of the ancient Athenian year, corresponding to our January. It was so called because it was a favourite season for marriages (γάμη).

Fig. 346. Gargoulette. Arab.

Gammut. (See GAMUT.)

Gamut. The musical scale; so called from the first tone, UT (our DO), of the model scale of Guido, which was represented by the Greek *gamma.*

Ganoid (γάνος, brightness). A name applied to an order of fishes, having angular scales, composed of bony plates, covered with a strong shining enamel.

Gantlet. (See GAUNTLET.)

Garb, Her. A sheaf of wheat, or of any other grain to be specified.

Garde de Bras. An additional protection for the left arm, to the elbow-piece of which it was fastened by straps and a screw. It was used only for jousting, and first appears at the end of the 15th cent. The example shown is of the 16th cent., from the Meyrick collection. (Fig. 345.)

Gargoulette. An Arab vase, or water-cooler, with one handle, furnished with a spout adapted for drinking through. The piece in the illustration is from the Arabian potteries of Maghreb in Africa. This pottery is described by M. Jacquemart as "covered with a pinkish grey enamel of rose colour, and heightened by a polychrome decoration in zones, generally consisting of bands of scrolls, flowers, denticulations, rosettes, &c.; where citron, yellow, manganese-brown, green, and blue form the most charming harmony."

Gargoyle, Mod. The projecting extremity of a gutter. In antiquity terra-cotta masks were used for the purpose. (Fig. 347.) During

Fig. 347. Gargoyle, Antique.   Fig. 348. Gargoyle, Gothic.

the Gothic period any kind of representation was employed. Fig. 348 shows an upright gargoyle from the church of St. Remy at Dieppe.

Garland, Arch. A term employed by some authors as synonymous with foliage; but it denotes rather heavy festoons tied with fillets, and consisting of leaves, fruits, and flowers, as shown in Figs. 287 and 309, taken from the temple of Vesta at Tivoli. (See ENCARPA, FESTOONS.)

Garnet. This gem, on account of its brilliant colour and hardness, is much used in jewellery, and although an abundant supply renders it of

little value, the gem nevertheless possesses every quality necessary for ornamental purposes. It occurs in many colours—red, brown, yellow, white, green, black; the streak is white; the diaphaneity varies from transparent to sub-translucent, or nearly opaque, and it has a sub-conchoidal or uneven fracture. The varieties used in jewellery are called *carbuncle, cinnamon-stone* (or *essonite*), *almandine,* and *pyrope* or Bohemian garnet. *Garnets* are not much used for engraving, being of splintery, bad grain under the tool. (*A. Billing, Science of Gems,* &c.; *H. Emanuel, Diamonds and Precious Stones.*)

Garnished, Her. Adorned in a becoming manner.

Garter, Order of the, instituted by Edward III. in 1350, consists of the Sovereign and twenty-five knights companions, of whom the Prince of Wales always is one. Knights of the Garter place K.G. after their names; and these letters take precedence of all other titles, those of royalty alone excepted. The stalls of the knights are in the choir of St. George's Chapel, Windsor Castle, where their garter-plates are fixed and their banners are displayed. The insignia are the garter itself, the badge of the order; the collar, and the Lesser George or jewel. (Fig. 349.) It was this jewel that Charles I., immediately before he suffered, delivered to Archbishop Juxon, with the word

Fig. 349. Order of the Garter. Lesser George.

"Remember!" The ribbon of the order is dark blue; it passes over the left shoulder, and the Lesser George hangs from it under the right arm.

Garter King of Arms, Her. The chief of the official heralds of England, and officer of arms of the Order of the Garter.

Gastrum, R. An earthenware vessel with a round *belly;* whence its name.

Gaulus, R. A vessel used for drinking and other purposes. The same term was also applied to a broad-built ship employed by the Phœnicians and by pirates.

Gauntlet. The knight's gauntlet was made of leather covered with plates of steel. It was not originally divided into fingers. (Fig. 350.)

Gausapa, Gausape, Gausapum, R. (γαυσάπης). (1) A garment introduced from Egypt into

Rome, in the time of Augustus ; it was made of a woollen cloth with a long nap on

Fig. 350. Gauntlet.

one side, and was worn on leaving the bath ; it was white or dyed purple. Gausapa was used not only for articles of dress, but for table linen, napkins, dusters, and mattings. (2) A wig made of human hair, worn at Rome during the Empire.

Gauze. A light, transparent silk texture, supposed to have been invented at Gaza in Palestine ; whence the name.

Gavotte (It. *gavotta*). A lively dance-tune in two-fourth time, consisting of two sections, each containing eight measures.

Gehenna (Heb. *Ge-hin-nom*, i. e. the valley of Hinnom). In this place, on the north of Jerusalem below Mount Zion, is a place called Tophet, where children were sacrificed to Moloch. King Josiah made it the common receptacle for rubbish and carcases, and a fire was kept constantly burning there ; hence the Jews used this term to signify "hell." (Compare HADES.)

Gemellar, R. (*gemellus,* twin). A case for holding oil ; it was called *gemellar* from the fact of its being divided into two compartments.

Gemelled, Arch. Double ; thus a *gemelled bay* is one divided into two parts; *gemelled arches,* those which are joined two and two.

Gemelles, Her. In pairs. (See BARS-GE-MELLES.)

Gemmæ, Lat. (1) Precious stones, esp. cut or engraved. (2) Drinking-vessels or objects made of precious stones. (3) Pearls. (4) The eyes of a peacock's tail. The original meaning of the word is a *bud, eye,* or *gem* on a plant ; anything *swelling* and bright.

Gemoniæ, or **Gemoniæ Scales,** R. (i.e. steps of sighs). Steps leading to the prison in the forum, on the stairs of which the corpses of criminals were exposed for several days.

Gems. Precious stones, especially when carved. (See CAMEOS.)

Genet, Her. A spotted animal, something like a marten.

Genethliaci, Gr. and R. (γενέθλη, birth). Astrologers who cast "*nativities.*"

Genius, R. (*geno,* to beget). The Romans

believed the existence of a good genius, or guardian angel, born with every mortal, and which died at the same time with him. *Genius loci* was the name given to the guardian spirit of a place. [See JUNONES, LARES, PENATES, &c. The superstition has many forms in Christian as well as in pagan art.]

Genoa Lace. Mention is made of Genoa Lace as early as the 15th century. Genoa was as celebrated for its pillow lace as Venice for its

Fig. 351. Genoa Point Lace—Pillow-made.

needle-made. The characteristic of this lace was its design, a kind of barleycorn-shaped pattern, radiating into rosettes from a centre. It was particularly adapted for the large turnover collar of Louis XIII., and was produced by plaiting, and made entirely on the pillow.

Genouillières, Fr. (1) Steel coverings for the knees. From the 13th century. They were often richly ornamented. (2) In *Fortification,* the sill of the embrasure.

Genre Pictures. Those representing scenes of every-day life and manners.

Fig. 352. "George" Gold Noble, Henry VIII.

Geodes. In Mineralogy, hollow lumps of chalcedony found deposited in the cavities of flints, formed by the chemical action of water.

George. A gold noble of the time of Henry VIII. (Fig. 352.)

George, Saint, Her. The patron saint of England. His red cross on a silver field first appears in English heraldry in the 14th century. (See Fig. 349.)

George, The, Her. A figure of St. George on horseback, worn as a pendant to the collar of the Order of the Garter. (See GARTER.)

Georgic (γεωργικὸς, rustic ; from γῆ, earth, and ἔργον, work). Poems on the subject of husbandry.

German Silver. An alloy of nickel, zinc, and copper. The proportions recommended are nickel 25, zinc 25, copper 50.

Gerrhæ. Persian shields made of wicker-work.

Ghebres, Pers. Fire-worshippers.

Ghibellines. An Italian faction, 13th century, who supported the German Emperors against the *Guelphs*, who stood by the Pope. The war-cry of the Guelphs was taken from the name of Henry the Lion, Duke of Saxony, of the house of *Wölf;* that of the Ghibellines from *Weiblingen,* a town of Würtemberg, the seat of the Hohenstauffen family, to which Conrad, Duke of Franconia, belonged. These two dukes were rivals for the imperial throne of Germany.

Ghoul, Ghole, Pers. A demon who fed on dead bodies of men.

Giallo, Giallolino, Gialdolino, It. Pale yellow. (See MASSICOT.)

Giaour, Turkish. An unbeliever in Mohammed.

Gigantomachia, Gr. A favourite subject of

Fig. 353. Gimmel Rings. The device of Cosmo de' Medici.

Greek art, representing the War of the Giants, sons of Cœlus and Terra, against Jupiter. They "heaped Ossa on Pelion" to scale heaven, and were defeated by Hercules. They are represented as of vast stature and strength, having their feet covered with scales. A beautiful cameo in the Naples Museum represents Jove in his chariot subduing the giants. In 1875 the German expedition found among the ruins of a temple at Pergamus a series of sculptures of almost colossal proportions, representing, as Pliny describes them, the Wars of the Giants. These sculptures are now in the Berlin Museum.

Gillo, R. A wine-cooler, of earthenware.

Gimmel Ring, Her. Two, sometimes three annulets interlaced. (Fig. 353.)

Gingham (Javanese *ginggan*). Cotton cloth, woven from dyed yarns ; distinguished from cloth printed or dyed *after* weaving.

Ginglymus, R. (γίγγλυμος). A hinge moving in a socket.

Gingrinus, R. (γίγγρας). A flute used at funerals.

Gipcières. Richly-ornamented leather purses of the 14th and 15th centuries. They were often engraved with religious mottoes. (Fig. 354.)

Gipon. Probably the same as *gambeson.*

Girandole. A large kind of branched candlestick.

Fig. 354. Gipcière.

Girdled, Girt, Her. Encircled or bound round.

Girdles. These were the most beautiful and costly articles of dress during the Middle Ages. They were frequently made entirely of gold or silver, decorated with cameos, precious stones, &c. Besides the knightly sword ; the purse, dagger, rosary, or penner and ink-horn and other objects were suspended from the girdle. From this word the waist was called the *girdlestead,* or place (*sted*) of the girdle. The girdles of ladies were equally splendid, and frequently depended nearly to the ground, as in Fig. 355. The girdle is an attribute of St. Thomas, from a legend that the Virgin, pitying his weakness of faith, threw down to him her girdle, after her assumption into heaven.

Girgillus, R. A roller turned by a windlass, for drawing up the bucket of a well. (See JACK.)

Girouette. (See EPI.)

Girt, Her. (See GIRDLED.)

Gisarme. A scythe-shaped weapon with a pike, fixed on a long staff.

Gittern, O. E. A small guitar, strung with catgut.

Givre. (See WYVERN.)

Glabrous (Lat. *glaber*). Smooth, bald.

Glade (Norman *glette*, a clear spot among clouds). An opening or passage in a wood through which the light may shine.

Gladiators were first exhibited at Rome, B.C. 264, at a funeral. The practice had its origin in that very ancient one of slaughtering slaves and captives on such occasions. Subsequently it became more general. The different classes of gladiators, distinguished by their arms and other circumstances, were : *Andabatæ,* who wore helmets without any opening for the eyes, and therefore fought blindfold; *Essedarii*, who

Fig. 355. Girdle of a Flemish lady of the 15th century.

fought from chariots (ESSEDÆ); *Hoplomachai*, who wore heavy defensive armour; *Laqueatores*, who carried a sort of lasso or noose; *Meridiani*, who fought in the middle of the day, and were very slightly armed; *Mirmillones*, so called from their having the image of a fish (mormyr) on their helmets; *Retiarii*, armed with a trident and a net. Others, as *Samnites, Thraces*, &c., were named from the nation whose fashion of armour they adopted. The fights of gladiators were favourite subjects of Roman art, and it is assumed that in cases where no actual combats took place at a funeral, they were represented

on the walls of tombs in sculpture or paint. The most celebrated statues of the kind are the

Fig. 356. Roman sword.

so-called "Dying Gladiator" in the museum of the capitol at Rome, and the Gladiator of the Borghese collection.

Gladiolus. Diminutive of GLADIUS, and synonym of LIGULA. (See both words.)

Gladius, R. A general term, including all the different kinds of swords or glaives, but denoting more particularly the two-edged swords used by the Greeks, Romans, and Gauls. Fig. 357 represents two Gaulish swords, the form of which may easily be guessed, even though they are in the scabbard; Fig. 356 is a Roman *gladius*.

Fig. 357. Gallic swords.

Glaive. A blade on a pole having its edge on the outside curve, used by foot-soldiers in the 15th century.

Glans, Gr. and R. (lit. an acorn). A large leaden slug, of long oval form, which was hurled by a sling in place of stones.

Glass. The discovery is lost in remote antiquity. Pliny gives a legend which ascribes it to chance. Glass bottles in Egypt are represented upon monuments of the 4th dynasty (at least 2000 years B.C.). A vase of greenish glass found at Nineveh dates from B.C. 700. Glass is found in the windows at Pompeii; and the Romans stained it, blew it, worked it on lathes, and engraved it. Pliny mentions, as made by the Romans in his time, glass coloured opaque, red, white, black (like *obsidian*), or imitating jacinths, sapphires, and other gems; also *murrhine glass.* This last was either an imitation of fluor spar, or a kind of agate, or fluor spar. The Romans also made *mosaic* or *mille-fiori*, in which the threads of colour are melted into a rod, so that at every section the whole pattern appears; and *cameo glasses*, in which a paste of one colour is laid over another, and the whole then carved into the required design; *gold leaf* was also worked into the substance or fixed on the surface. A gate at Constantinople took its name from the glass works near it, but

Fig. 358. Venetian Glass Vase, 16th century.

chalcedony ; other varieties are imitations of lapis lazuli and tortoise-shell ; and *avanturine*, which is obtained by mingling metallic filings or fragments of gold leaf with melted glass. (5) *Millefiori*, or *mosaic glass*, in imitation of the old Roman process. (6) *Reticulated, filigree*, or *lace glass*. The varieties contain fine threads of glass, generally coloured, but sometimes milk-white, included in their substance. The lightness and strength of the Venetian glass are due to its not containing lead like our modern flint glass. Venetian *mirrors* were for a long period widely celebrated. The oldest example of the German *drinking-cups*, ornamented with paintings in enamel, is of the date of 1553. The designs are commonly armorial bearings. From the beginning of the 17th century the Bohemian manufactories supplied *vases* enriched with ornamental subjects, particularly with portraits engraved upon the glass. The art of *wheel engraving upon glass* flourished in France under Louis XVI. In modern times this kind of ornamentation is produced by the agency of hydrofluoric acid. "Coarse glass-making in England was, in Sussex, of great antiquity." (*Fuller.*) "The first making of Venice glasses in England began in London, about the beginning of the reign of Queen Elizabeth, by one Jacob Vessaline, an Italian." (*Stow.*)

Glass-glazed Wares. (See GLAZ-ED WARES.)

Glaucous (γλαυκός). Of a sea-green colour, or a greyish blue.

Glazed Wares. Almost immediately after the invention of Ceramic manufacture, the application of *glaze* or *coloured enamel* must have improved it. What we term *glaçure* is a light varnish which enlivens and harmonizes the porous surface of terra-cotta. In its simple state it is a mixture of silex and lead, and in this state it is transparent, as we find it on *antique vases* ; when vitrifiable, and mixed with tin, as in the case of *majolicas*, it is called enamel ; and when of vitrifiable and earthen substance, such as can only be melted at the temperature required for the baking of the paste itself, it is known as GLAZE, or *couverte*, and can be identified in the Persian faiences and Flemish stone-ware. (Figs. 359, 360.) (See Burty, *Chefs-d'œuvre of the Industrial Arts.*)

Glazing. In oil painting, the application of

little is known of the Byzantine art, nor of earlier European art than the 13th century. In mediæval times stained glass windows, in leaden frames, were constructed with great success in England, France, and Flanders. In the 13th century they appear in Italy. The Venetian art took its impulse from the capture of Constantinople in 1204. Its peculiar beauty is derived from the curved forms and tenuity of substance obtained in blowing. (Fig.358.) There are six kinds of Venetian glass. (1) Vessels of colour-less or *transparent glass*, or of single colours, generally blue or purple. (2) *Gilt* or *enamelled glass*. (3) *Crackled glass*, having a surface rough and divided irregularly into ridges. (4) Variegated or *marbled opaque glass*, called *schmeltz* ; the most common variety is a mixture of green and purple, sometimes resembling jasper, sometimes

thin layer of colour to finally modify the tone. In pottery, a vitreous covering over the surface. (See GLAZED WARES.)

Virgin, or saints who are in the act of ascending into heaven. When used to distinguish one of the

Fig. 359. Flemish stone-ware Cruche, 17th century.

Fig. 360. German enamelled stone-ware Cruche, date first half of the 16th century.

Globe, held in the hand, is the emblem of power.

Globus, R. A military manœuvre employed by a body of Roman soldiers when surrounded by superior forces ; it consisted in forming a circle facing in every direction.

Glory, Nimbus or **Aureole,** the Christian attribute of sanctity, is of pagan origin, common to images of the gods, and Roman, even Christian, emperors. Satan in miniatures of the 9th to 13th century wears a glory. The earliest known Christian example is a gem of St. Martin of the early part of the 6th century. The glory round the head is properly the nimbus or aureole. The oblong glory surrounding the whole person, called in Latin "vesica piscis" (Fig. 361), and in Italian the "mandola"(almond) from its form, is confined to figures of Christ and the

three divine Persons of the Trinity, the glory is often cruciform or triangular : the square nimbus designates a person living at the time the work was executed. In other instances it is circular. Coloured glories are variously symbolical. (*Mrs. Jameson,* " *The Poetry of Sacred and Legendary Art.*")

Gloves. In the 14th century already *gloves* were worn, jewelled on the back, as a badge of rank. "They were worn in the hat," says Steevens, "as the favour of a mistress, or the memorial of a friend, and as a mark to be challenged by an enemy." A glove of the 17th century is described "of a light buff leather, beautifully ornamented with spangles and needlework in gold and silver threads, with a gold lace border, and silk opening at the wrist." Gloves were called "cheirothecæ," hand-coverers, by the Greeks and Romans ; they were made without separate fingers, the thumb only being free. A legend current at Grenoble affirms that St. Anne, the mother of the Virgin Mary, was a knitter of gloves.

Gluten. In wax painting, the compound with which the pigments are mixed.

Glyphs, Arch. The flutings of an ornament or grooving forming the segment of a circle. (See DIGLYPH, TRIGLYPH.)

Glyptics. The art of engraving on precious stones.

Glyptotheca, Gr. and R. (1) A gallery for sculpture. (2) A collection of engraved stones.

Gnomon, Gr. and R. The iron pin or index, which, by the projection of its shadow, marks the hour upon a sun-dial.

Goal. (See META.)

Goat. The

Fig. 361. Glory. Vesica Piscis in Ely Cathedral.

emblem of lasciviousness.

Gobelins. Celebrated Royal French manufactory of tapestry, named from the successors of Jean Gobelin, who brought the art to Paris in the 15th century from Rheims. [See *Burty, Chefs-d'œuvre of Industrial Art.*]

Godenda, O. E. A pole-axe, having a spike at its end; 13th century.

Goderonné, Gouderonné (Needlework). A fluted pattern of embroidery in vogue in the 16th century.

Fig. 362. Egyptian Diadem of gold and lapis lazuli of the ancient Empire, found in the tomb of Queen Aah-Hotep.

Gold. It is probable that the earliest recorded mark upon units of value was the image of a sheep or an ox ; hence money in Latin is called *pecunia,* from *pecus,* cattle, the original form of barbaric wealth, for which gold was the substitute. The wealth of Abraham in silver and gold, as well as in cattle, is mentioned in Genesis. No coins of gold or silver have been found in EGYPT or NINEVEH, although beautiful specimens of the goldsmith's art have been

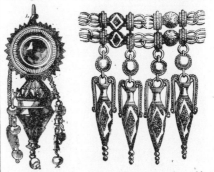

Fig. 363. Greek Ear-ring of gold, and part of a necklace. (*See also Fig.* 276.)

recovered from the tombs of both countries. The HEBREWS, taught by the Egyptians, made their ark, mercy-seat, altar of incense, seven-branched candlestick, and other golden ornaments, even in the desert of Sinai. The seven-branched candlestick is represented in sculpture on the arch of Titus at Rome. At BABYLON and NINEVEH gold is said to have been lavishly applied in gilding sculpture, and even walls ; but it is suggested that an alloy of copper, the *aurichalcum* of the Greeks, was the metal in reality used for this purpose. The heroes of the Greek epic had golden shields and helmets ; breastplates and other large pieces of golden armour are among the recent discoveries at Mycenæ; at Kourioum in the island of Cyprus also great stores of golden ornaments of a very early age have been discovered. In SCYTHIAN tombs in Russia also, about Kertch, beautiful relics of Grecian work in gold have been found, showing that in the very earliest ages the skill and taste applied to this art were not less than those of later times. The gold jewellery of ancient India also excelled that of modern date, but none, before or since, ever equalled the great age of GREEK art. Pausanias describes a statue of Athene, made by Pheidias, and kept in the Parthenon at Athens, of ivory and gold—*chryselephantine*—delicately worked all over ; and a still larger statue of Jupiter, of the same materials. Native gold alloyed with one-fifth silver was greatly prized by the Greek artists, who gave it the name of *electrum*. Examples of this electrum are rare; there is a vase at St. Petersburg. The ROMANS used to pay enormous prices for their household plate; for an example, the bowl of Pytheas, on which were represented Ulysses and Diomed with the palladium, fetched 10,000 denarii, or about 330*l.* *per ounce*. Few specimens of Roman art have escaped destruction. (Fig. 7.) Of the age of BYZANTINE splendour we are told that the Emperor Acadius, early in the 5th century, sat on a throne of massive gold, his chariot being also of gold, &c. In the 9th century the throne of Theophilus was overshadowed by a tree of gold, with birds in the branches, and at the foot two lions all gold. The lions roared and the birds piped in the branches. A remarkable wealth of ancient goldsmith's work has been found in IRELAND, consisting principally of personal ornaments. In the 9th and 10th centuries the Irish workmanship was unsurpassed in Europe. It consisted principally of objects for religious use, and is characterized by a filagree of extraordinary richness, akin to the intricate traceries of the Irish illuminated work on MS. of the same date and derivation. In the 10th and 11th centuries there was a great revival of art throughout Europe. In GERMANY, the abbey of Hildesheim, under Bishop Bernward, became the centre of a school of goldsmiths, and some beautiful specimens of hammered gold, by the bishop's hand, are preserved.

Gold, in Christian art. (See YELLOW.)

Gold, Cloth of, is mentioned in the Pentateuch, and was common throughout the East in all ages. It was originally wrought, not in rounded wire but flat, as the Chinese, the Indians, and the Italians (their *lama d'oro*) weave it now. The early Roman kings wore tunics of gold, and the Romans used it as a shroud for burial. King Childeric, A.D. 482, was buried at Tournai in a mantle of golden stuff. It was much favoured in England for church vestments, and by royalty, especially by Edward IV. and Henry VIII. and the nobility of their time. (The different varieties are described in their order. See ACCA, ARESTE, BATUZ, CHRYSO-CLAVUS, CICLATOUN, DORNECK, SAMIT.)

Goldbeater's Skin, prepared from a membrane found in the stomach of the ox, is used to separate leaf-gold in the process of gold-beating.

Golden Fleece. An Order of Knighthood instituted on the 10th of January, 1429, by Philip, Duke of Burgundy. The COLLAR is composed of double steels, interwoven with flint-stones, emitting sparks of fire; at the end whereof hangs on the breast a Golden Fleece. The fusils are joined two and two together, as if they were double BB's (the cyphers of Burgundy). The *flint-stones* are the ancient arms of the Sovereigns of Burgundy, with the motto " *Ante ferit quam flamma micet.*" (See Fig. 342.) The motto of the Order is "*Pretium non vile laborum.*" There are four great officers, viz. the Chancellor, Treasurer, Register, and a King of Arms, called *Toison d'Or*. The BADGE consists of a Golden Fleece, suspended from a flint-stone, which is surrounded with flames of gold.

Golden Spur. An Order of Knighthood said to have been instituted by Pius IV., at Rome, in 1559. They are sometimes spoken of as the CHEVALIERS PIES or PIORUM, and must be distinguished from those who are created knights on the coronation or marriage days of Emperors and Kings, and who receive at the same time the *Spurs of Honour*. These alone are entitled to the appellation of EQUITES AURATI. [Cf. *Peter de Bellet, Favin*, &c.]

Golden Stole of Venice. (See STOLA D'ORO.)

Golione, O. E. A kind of gown.

Gondola, It. A Venetian pleasure-boat or barge.

Gonfalon or **Gonfanon,** Fr. (1) A richly-worked pointed banner carried upon a lance; 13th century. (2) An ecclesiastical banner.

Gonfalonier. The bearer of a gonfalon.

Goniometer (γωνία, an angle, &c.). An instrument for measuring the angles of crystals.

Gonjo, O. E. (14th century). Said to be the *gorget*.

Gopouras, Hind. The pyramid-shaped door of the Hindoo temples. *Dwararab'ha*, or door of splendour, was the name given to a door with one or two tiers; *dwarasala*, or door of the dwelling, a door with two or four tiers; *dwaraprasada*, or propitious door, a door with three to five tiers; *dwaraharmya*, or door of the palace, a door with five to seven tiers; lastly, *dwaragopouras*, or door-tower with seven to sixteen tiers.

Gorged, Her. Wearing a collar.

Gorget, Fr. A defence or covering for the neck.

Fig. 364. Gorgoneia.

Gorgoneia. Masks of the Gorgon's head, which were fixed as bosses upon walls or shields.

Gossamer, O. E. (properly *God's summer*). The name is attributed to an old legend that the fine filaments so called are the fragments of the winding-sheet of the Virgin Mary, which fell away from her as she was taken up to heaven.

Gothamites, O. E. The inhabitants of the village of Gotham in Northumberland, renowned for their stupidity. A reprint of the tale called "The Wise Men of Gotham" appeared in 1840.

Gouache, Fr. This term is applied to the use in water-colour painting of opaque colours more or less mixed and modified with white. The process is extremely ancient, known to the Chinese and Indians of the earliest times, and to the Greeks and Romans. It was the method used by mediæval illuminators. Its result is a velvety reflection of the light.

Gourd of Noah.

A piece of ancient blue faience from Asia Minor. According to the tradition current in the country, these vessels, which are in great veneration, would go back to such remote antiquity that it was by one of them that Noah was betrayed into the first act of inebriety recorded in history. (*Jacquemart.*)

Fig. 365. Gourd-shaped bottle. Anatolian.

Gouttée, Guttée, Her. Sprinkled over with drops of gold, silver, blue (tears), red (blood), or black (*poix*).

Gown (British *gwn*, Norman *gunna*). The men wore gowns in the Middle Ages, the women at all times.

Grabatus, R. (κράβατος). A sort of low framework, consisting of a network of cords, used to support a mattress; it was the least comfortable kind of bed; whence the French word *grabat* to denote a sorry kind of bed.

Gradient, Her. Walking.

Gradus, R. A flight of steps leading to a temple; the tiers of seats in a theatre or amphitheatre, &c.

Græcostasis. A part of the Roman forum, where the Greek ambassadors stood to hear the debates.

Graffiti, It. Lines drawn with a graver upon clay or plaster. (See SGRAFFITI.)

Grafted, Her. Inserted and fixed.

Grand-garde. Plate armour to cover the breast and left shoulder, worn outside the usual armour in jousting at tournaments.

Grand Quarters, Her. The four primary divisions of a shield when it is divided per cross or quarterly.

Graphite. Plumbago.

Graphometer. A mathematical instrument, called also a semicircle

Graphotype. A method of producing book illustrations for printing along with type, without the art of an engraver.

Grass-green. (See CHRYSOCOLLA.)

Graver or **Burin.** An engraving-tool. (See CHALCOGRAPHY.)

Grazioso, It. In Music, an intimation to perform the music smoothly and gracefully.

Greaves. Plate armour for the legs.

Grece, O. E. A step, or flight of stairs. (See GRYSE.)

Greeces, Her. Steps.

Greek Lace. A kind of cutwork, described under LACE (q.v.).

Green, in Christian art, or the emerald, is the colour of spring; emblem of hope, particularly hope in immortality; and of victory, as the colour of the palm and the laurel.

Green. (See CARBONATES OF COPPER, OXIDES OF COPPER, SCHEELE'S GREEN, SAP GREEN, CHROME GREEN, &c.)

Green Bice. Green cinnabar. (See CHROME GREEN.)

Green Earth (burnt terra-verde) is a brown pigment, very useful for landscape painting in oil colours; it is not affected by exposure to strong light or impure air.

Green Lakes. (See PURPLE LAKES.)

Green Verditer. (See VERDITER.)

Gregorian Calendar. The calendar as reformed by Pope Gregory XIII. in 1582.

Gregorian Music. A collection of chants, originally compiled by Gregory I. (the Great), A.D. 600. "It was observed by St. Gregory, a great musician of his time, that the *Ambrosian Chants,* handed down traditionally to a great extent, had become corrupted; he therefore subjected them to revision, and added other modes and scales to those four which Ambrose had retained. This was done by taking away the upper tetrachord from the Ambrosian scales, and placing it below the lower tetrachord." (See *Music,* by the Rev. J. R. Lunn, B.D., in *Dictionary of Christian Antiquities.*)

Grey, in Christian art, the colour of ashes, signified mourning, humility, and innocence accused.

Greybeards, O. E. Stone-ware drinking-jugs, with a bearded face on the spout.

Gridiron (It. *la graticola*). The attribute of St. Lawrence.

Griffin. (See GRYPHUS.)

Grinding. Pigments are generally ground in poppy or nut oil, which dry best and do not deaden the colours. It is essential that these oils be in the purest state, bright and clear. A good oil ought to be so dry in five or six days that the picture can be repainted.

Griphus, Gr. and R. (γρῖφος). Literally, a fishing-net, and thence a riddle propounded by guests at a banquet.

Grisaille, Fr. A style of painting *in grey*, by which solid bodies are represented as if in relief; adapted for architectural subjects.

Groat. An old English silver coin, equal to 4*d.* In England, in the Saxon times, no silver coin larger in value than a penny was struck, nor after the Conquest till the reign of Edward III., who

Fig. 366. Groat of Edward III.

about 1351 coined *grosses* or great pieces, which went for 4*d.* each ; and so the matter stood till the reign of Henry VII., who in 1504 first coined shillings.

Grogram (Fr. *gros-grains*). A coarse woollen cloth with large woof and a rough pile. Grogram gowns were worn by countrywomen, 15th to 17th centuries. *Fairholt* says that the mixed liquor called *grog* obtained its name from the admiral who ordered it to be given to the sailors ; who from wearing a grogram coat was called " Old Grog."

Groin, Arch. The angular curve formed at the intersection of a vaulted roof ; the line made by the intersection of arched vaults crossing each other at any angle. (See Fig. 173.)

Grolier Scroll. A beautiful and elaborate style of decoration for bookbinding, introduced by *Grolier*, a celebrated patron of bookbinding, in the 15th century.

Gruma and **Gruma,** R. A quadrant ; an in-

Fig. 367. Grotesque from a stall in Rouen Cathedral.

strument used by land-surveyors. In the plural, *grumæ* denotes the intersection of two roads cutting each other at right angles.

Fig. 368. Grotesque decoration from the Cathedral at Rouen.

Grotesques, Arch. (It. *grottesco*, the style in which grottoes were ornamented). Figures of a monstrous, comic, or obscene character, which were spread in profusion over the façades of churches by mediæval artists (*ymaigiers*) ; in stone and in wood ; on choir-stalls and the wood-work and wainscoting of interiors. Figs. 367, 368 represent figures upon the stalls and columns in Rouen Cathedral.

Grounds or **Priming.** In painting, the first coat of colour laid all over the canvas, upon which the picture is to be painted.

Grus, Lat. (*a crane*). A constellation of the southern hemisphere.

Gry. A measure containing $\frac{1}{10}$ of a *line*. A *line* is $\frac{1}{10}$ of a *digit*, a *digit* is $\frac{1}{10}$ of a foot, and a (philosophical) foot is $\frac{1}{3}$ of a pendulum whose vibrations, in the latitude of 45°, are each equal to one second of time, or $\frac{1}{60}$ of a minute.

Fig. 369. Heraldic Griffin.

Gryphus, Griffin, Gen. (γρύψ). A fabulous animal, represented with the body of a lion, and the head and wings of an eagle. In ancient art it was applied in the decoration of friezes, one of the finest specimens being that at the temple of Antoninus and Faustina at Rome. It was a heraldic symbol among the Scythians, and is

M

the ancient crest of the city of London. As an emblem this monster symbolizes the destroying power of the gods.

Gryse, Grece, Tredyl, or **Steyre,** O. E. A step, a flight of stairs.

Fig. 370. Passant guardant.

Guacos or **Huacos,** Peruv. The consecrated burial-places of the ancient Peruvians.

Guardant, Her. Looking out from the field, as the lions in Fig. 370.

Guazzo, It. A hard and durable kind of distemper painting, used by the ancients, calculated to resist damp and to preserve the colours.

Gubbio. A celebrated Italian botega of ceramic art, founded in 1498 by Giorgio Andreoli, the reputed inventor of the secret of metallic lustres. Fig. 371 is a cup bearing upon

Fig. 371. Gubbio Cup, 1519. Louvre Museum.

a fillet the inscription "*Ex o Giorg.,*" "of the fabric of Giorgio."

Gubernaculum, R. (*guberno,* to direct). A rudder ; originally an oar with a broad blade, which was fixed, not at the extremity, but at each side of the stern. A ship had commonly two rudders joined together by a pole.

Guelfs or **Guelphs.** (See GHIBELLINES.)

Gueux, Badge of the. The celebrated Netherlandish confraternity of the Gueux (or Beggars), which had its origin in a jest spoken at a banquet, assumed not only the dress, but the staff, wooden bowl, and wallet of the professional

beggar, and even went so far as to clothe their retainers and servants in mendicant garb. The

Fig. 372. Badge of the Gueux.

badge represents two hands clasped across and through a double wallet.

Guidon, Fr. (1) The silk standard of a regiment ; (2) its bearer.

Guige, Her. A shield-belt worn over the right shoulder.

Guild, O. E. (Saxon *guildan,* to pay). A fraternity or company, every member of which was *gildare,* i. e. had to pay something towards the charges. Merchant guilds first became general in Europe in the 11th century. (See *Anderson's History of Commerce,* vol. i. p. 70.)

Fig. 373. Base ornamented with guilloche.

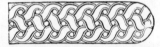

Fig. 374. Band with the guilloche ornament.

Guilloche. A series of interlaced ornaments on stone, resembling network.

Guilloched. Waved or engine-turned.

Guimet's Ultramarine. A valuable substitute for the more costly preparation. It is transparent and durable.

Guimet's Yellow is the deutoxide of lead and antimony, useful in enamel or porcelain painting.

Guinea. An English coin first struck *temp.* Car. II., and so called because the gold was brought from the coast of *Guinea* (the Portuguese *Genahoa*). It originally bore the impress of an elephant. The sovereign superseded it in 1817.

Guisarme. An ancient weapon of the nature of a pike or bill. (See *Meyrick.*)

Guitar (Spanish *guitarra*). A stringed musical instrument, played as a harp with the fingers.

Gules, Her. (Fr. *gueules*). Red, represented in engraving by perpendicular lines.

Gum-arabic dissolved in water constitutes the well-known vehicle for water-colour painting—*gum water*.

Gunter's Line. A line of logarithms graduated on a ruler, for practical use in the application of logarithms to the ordinary calculations of an architect, builder, &c. Other similar instruments invented by the great mathematician (+ 1626) are *Gunter's Quadrant* and *Gunter's Scale*, used by seamen and for astronomical calculations.

Gurgustium, R. A cave, hovel, or any dark and wretched abode.

Gussets were small pieces of chain mail at the openings of the joints beneath the arms.

Guttæ, Arch. (drops). Small conical-shaped ornaments, used in the Doric entablature immediately under the mutule beneath the triglyph. (See Fig. 265.)

Guttée, Her. (See GOUTTÉE.) Sprinkled over.

Gutturnium, R. (*guttur*, the throat). A water-jug or ewer; it was a vessel of very elegant form, and was used chiefly by slaves for pouring water over the hands of the guests before and after a meal. (See ABLUTIONS.)

Guttus, R. (*gutta*, a drop). A vessel with a very narrow neck and mouth, by means of which liquids could be poured out drop by drop; whence its name. It was especially used in sacrifices, and is a common object upon coins of a religious character.

Gutty, Her. Charged or sprinkled with *drops.*

Gwerre, O. E. The choir of a church.

Gymmers, O. E. Hinges. (The word is still used.)

Gymnasium, Gr. (γυμνάσιον; γυμνὸς, stripped). A large building used by the Greeks, answering to the Roman *palæstra*, in which gymnastics were taught and practised. There were also attached to it assembly rooms for rhetoricians and philosophers.

Gynæceum, Gr. (from γυνή, a woman). That part of the Greek house which was set apart for the women. (See DOMUS.)

Gypsum (Gr. γύψος). The property of rapid consolidation renders gypsum very available for taking casts of works of art, &c. It is much employed in architectural ornaments. The gypsum of Paris is called *Montmartrite,* and forms the best *Plaster of Paris,* as it resists the weather better than purer sorts. It contains 17 per cent. of carbonate of lime. (See also ALABASTER.)

Fig. 375. Gyronny.

Gyron, Her. A triangular figure, one of the subordinaries.

Gyronny, Her. A field divided into gyrons.

H.

H, as an old Latin numeral, denotes 200, and with a dash above it (H̄) 200,000.

Habena, R. (*habeo*, to hold). A term with numerous meanings, all of which were connected more or less with the idea of a thong or strap. In the singular, it signifies a halter; in the plural, *habenæ*, reins.

Habergeon. A coat of mail, or breastplate.

Habited, Her. Clothed.

Hackbut or **Hagbut.** Arquebus with a hooked stock.

Hackney Coach (from the French *coche-à-haquenée*). The *haquenée* was a strong kind of horse formerly let out on hire for short journeys.

Hadrianea, R. Small buildings in which Christians were allowed to meet, in virtue of an edict granted in their favour by the Emperor Hadrian.

Hæmatinon, R. (αἱμάτινον, of blood). A kind of glassy substance of a beautiful red, and susceptible of taking a fine polish. It was used to make small cubes for mosaic or small works of art.

Hagiographa (*sacra writings*). A name applied to those books of Scripture which, according to the Jewish classification, held the lowest rank in regard to inspiration. These are the books of Ruth, Psalms, Job, Proverbs, Ecclesiastes, Song of Solomon, Lamentations, Daniel, Esther, Ezra, and Chronicles.

Hair. The *Assyrian* monarchs are represented with beard elaborately plaited, and hair falling in ringlets on the shoulder, which may have been partly artificial, like that of the Persian monarchs, who, according to Xenophon, wore a wig. Both the hair and beard were dyed, and the eyes blackened with kohl, &c.

(*Layard.*) The *Egyptians* kept the head shaved, and wore wigs and beard-boxes. The *Hebrews* generally wore the hair short, but the horse-guards of King Solomon "daily strewed their heads with gold dust, which glittered in the sun." (*Josephus.*) The ancient *Greeks* wore their hair long. The *Athenians* wore it long in childhood, had it cut short at a solemn ceremony when they became eighteen years of age, and afterwards allowed it to grow, and wore it rolled up in a knot on the crown of the head, fastened with golden clasps (*crobylus, corymbus*). Women wore bands or coifs (*sphendone, kekryphalus, saccus, mitra*). Youths and athletes are represented with short hair. The favourite colour was blonde (*xanthus*); black was the most common. The ancient *Romans* also wore long hair; about 300 B.C. the prac-tice of wearing it short came in (*cincinnus, cirrus*). The Roman women anciently dressed their hair very plainly, but in the Augustan period adopted some extravagant fashions. Each of the gods is distinguished by his peculiar form of hair: that of Jupiter is long and flowing; Mercury has close curling hair, &c. The *Danes, Gauls,* and *Anglo-Saxons* wore long flowing hair, and the shearing of it was a punishment: when Julius Cæsar conquered the Gauls, he cut off their long hair. Among the early *Frankish* kings long hair was the privilege of the blood royal From the time of *Clovis* the French nobility wore short hair, but as they grew less martial the hair became longer. François I. introduced short hair, which prevailed until the reign of Louis XIII., which was followed by the period of periwigs and perukes of Louis XIV. The variations from the Conquest to the last generation in *England* are so striking and fre-quent that each reign may be distinguished by its appropriate head-dress. (Consult *Fairholt's Costume in England, Planché's Cyclopædia of Costume,* &c.)

Hair-cloth. (See CILICIUM.)

Hair Pencils or **Brushes** are made of the finer hairs of the marten, badger, polecat, camel, &c., mounted in quills or white iron tubes. The round brushes should swell all round from the base, and diminish upwards to a fine point, ter-minating with the uncut ends of the hair. (See FITCH.)

Halbert. A footman's weapon in the form of a battle-axe and pike at the end of a long staff.

H lcyon. The ancient name of the *Alcedo* or king-fisher; hence—

Ha cyon Days, i. e. the calm and peaceful season when the king-fisher lays its eggs in nests close by the brink of the sea; i. e. seven days before and as many after the winter solstice.

"Seven winter dayes with peacefull calme possest
Alcyon sits upon her floating nest."
          Sandy's Ovid, Met. b. xi.)

Hall-marks. The Goldsmiths of London formed their company in 1327, and were incor-porated by charter in 1392. The hall-marks, in the order of their introduction, are as fol-lows:—1. The leopard's head, called the king's mark. 2. The maker's mark, originally a rose, crown, or other emblem with or without initials. 3. The annual letter, in the order of the alphabet from A to V, omitting J and U. This mark is changed every twenty years. 4. The lion *passant*, added in 1597. 5. Instead of the leopard's head (1) for the king's mark, the lion's head *erased*, introduced in 1697 when the standard was changed, and, 6, a figure of Britannia substituted for the lion *passant* (4) at the same time. Plate with this mark is called *Britannia* plate. The old standard (of 11 oz. 2 dwt. pure gold in the lb.) was restored in 1719. 7. The head of the reigning sovereign in profile, ordered in 1784, when a fresh duty was laid upon plate.

Halling, O. E. Tapestry.

Hallowmas, Chr. The feast of All Souls, or the time about All Souls' and All Saints' Days, viz. the 1st and 2nd of November; and thence to CANDLEMAS, or the 2nd of February.

Halmos, Gr. and R. A vessel of round form, supported on a raised stand entirely distinct from the vessel itself; it was used as a drinking-cup.

Halmote or **Halimote.** The Saxon name for a meeting of tenants, now called a *court baron.*

Halteres (Gr. ἁλτῆρες), in the gymnastic exer-cises of the Greeks and Romans, were masses of lead, iron, or stone held in the hands to give impetus in leaping, or used as dumb-bells.

Ham (Scotch *hame*). A Saxon word for a place of dwelling, *a home;* hence "HAMLET." "This word," says Stow, "originally meant the seat of a freeholder, comprehending the mansion-house and adjacent buildings."

Fig. 376. Hanaper.

Hama, Gr. and R. (ἄμη or ἅμη). A bucket used for various purposes.

Hamburg White. (See CARBONATE OF LEAD, BARYTES.)

Hames or **Heames**, Her. Parts of horses' harness.

Hammer or **Martel**, Her. Represented much like an ordinary hammer.

Hamus or **Hamulus.** A fish-hook.

Hanaper, O. E. (Mod. *hamper*). A wicker basket. (Fig. 376.) Writs in the Court of Chancery were thrown into such a basket (*in hanaperio*), and the office was called from that circumstance the Haniper Office. It was abolished in 1842.

Handkerchiefs embroidered in gold were presented and worn as favours in the reign of Elizabeth. Paisley handkerchiefs were introduced in 1743.

Handle, Gen. In antiquity the leaves of a door were fitted with handles like those of our own day. Fig. 377 represents a bronze handle

Fig. 377. Bronze door-handle. Roman.

consisting of a double ring. Of these, the inner one could be raised so as to allow a person's hand to take hold of it, and draw the door his own way. This work of art is at the present time in the Museum of Perugia.

Handruffs, O. E. Ruffles.

Handseax. The Anglo-Saxon dagger.

Hanger, O. E. A small sword worn by gentlemen with morning dress in the 17th century.

Hangers or **Carriages**, O. E. Appendages to the sword-belt from which the sword hung, often richly embroidered or jewelled.

Hanselines (15th century). Loose breeches. (See SLOP.)

Haphe, Gr. and R. (ἁφή i.e a grip). The yellow sand with which wrestlers sprinkled themselves over after having been rubbed with oil. The object of this sprinkling was to enable the wrestlers to take a firmer grasp one of the other.

Hara, Gr. and R. A pig-sty, especially for a breeding sow. The term also denoted a pen for geese.

Hare, Chr. In Christian iconography the hare symbolizes the rapid course of life. Representations of this animal are met with on lamps, engraved stones, sepulchral stones, &c.

Harlequin (It. *Harlequino*, or little Harlay). The name is derived from that of a famous Italian comedian, who appeared in Paris in the time of Henri III., and from frequenting the house of M. de Harlay was so called by his companions. (*Ménage.*)

Harmamaxa, Gr. and R. (ἁρμ-άμαξα). A four-wheeled carriage or litter covered overhead, and enclosed with curtains. It was generally large, and drawn by four horses, and richly ornamented. It was principally used for women and children.

Harmonica. A musical instrument consisting of a number of glass cups fixed upon a revolving spindle, and made to vibrate by friction applied to their edges. These "musical glasses" are described in a work published in 1677. A *harpsichord-harmonica* is a similar instrument. in which finger keys like those of a pianoforte are used. (See the article in *Encycl. Brit.*, 8th edition.)

Harmonium. A musical instrument having a key-board like a pianoforte, and the sounds (which resemble those of organ pipes) produced by the vibration of thin tongues of metal.

Harp. The EGYPTIANS had various kinds of harps, some of which were elegantly shaped and tastefully ornamented. The name of the harp was *buni*. Its frame had no front pillar. The harps represented on the monuments varied in size from 6½ feet high downwards, and had from 4 to 28 strings. A beautiful Egyptian harp, in the Louvre collection, is of triangular shape with 21 strings, but, like all the harps represented on the monuments, it has no fore-pillar. The strings were of catgut. ASSYRIAN sculptures also represent harps. These also had no front pillar, and were about 4 feet high, with ornamental appendages on the lower frame. The upper frame contained the sound-holes and the tuning-pegs in regular order. The strings are supposed to have been of silk. The GREEK harp, called *kinyra*, resembled the Assyrian, and is represented with 13 strings : it is an attribute of Polyhymnia. The ANGLO-SAXONS called the harp the *gleo-beam*, or "glee-wood ;" and it was their most popular instrument. King David playing a harp is represented on an A.S. monument of the 11th century. It was the favourite instrument of the GERMAN and CELTIC bards, and of the SCANDINAVIAN skalds. It is represented with 12 strings and 2 sound-holes, and having a fore-pillar. A curious IRISH harp of the 8th century, or earlier, is represented in Bunting's "Ancient Music of Ireland," having no fore-pillar. The FINNS had a harp (*harpu*, *kantele*) with a similar frame, devoid of a front pillar. In CHRISTIAN ART a harp is the attribute of King David and of St. Cecilia. St. Dunstan is also occasionally represented with it. In Heraldry the harp is the device and badge of Ireland. The Irish harp of gold with silver strings on a blue field forms the third quarter of the royal arms.

Harpaga, Harpago, Gr. and R. A general term, including any kind of hook for grappling; more particularly a military engine invented by Pericles, and introduced into the Roman navy by Duillius. It consisted of a joist about two yards and a half long, each face of which was coated with iron, and having at one end a harpoon of iron or bronze; the other end was fitted with an iron ring, to which a rope was attached, so as to enable it to be drawn back when it had once grappled a ship or its rigging. *Harpago* or *wolf* was the term applied to a beam armed with a harpoon, which was employed to break down the tops of walls, or widen a breach already made. [A flesh-hook used in cookery to take boiled meat out of the caldron.]

Harpastum, R. A small ball employed for a game in which the players formed two sides. They stationed themselves at some distance from a line traced on the ground or sand where the *harpastum* was placed. At a given signal each player threw himself upon the ball, in order to try and send it beyond the bounds of the opposite party.

Harpies, Gen. ("Αρπυιαι, i.e. the Snatchers). Winged monsters, daughters of Neptune and Terra, three in number, viz. *Aëllo* (the tempest), *Ocypetê* (swift-flying), and *Cêlêno*; representing the storm-winds. They had the faces of old women, a vulture's body, and huge claws; they were the representatives of the Evil Fates, and the rulers of storms and tempests. In Christian iconography the Harpies symbolize the devil and repentance. [In the so-called "Harpy tomb" in the British Museum they are represented carrying off Camiro and Clytia, the daughters of Pandarus of Crete, as a punishment for his complicity with Tantalus in stealing ambrosia and nectar from the table of the gods.]

Harpsichord. A musical instrument intermediate between the *spinet*, *virginals*, &c., and the *pianoforte*, which supplanted it in the 18th century. It may be described as a horizontal harp enclosed in a sonorous case, the wires being struck with jacks armed with crow-quills, and moved with finger keys.

Harquebus. An improvement of the handgun introduced in the 15th century, applying the invention of the *trigger*.

Hart. A stag in its *sixth* year.

Hart or **Hind**, in Christian art, originally typified solitude and purity of life. It was the attribute of St. Hubert, St. Julian, and St. Eustace.

Fig. 378. Heraldic Hart.

Hart, Her. A stag with attires; the female is a hind.

Hasta (Gr. ἔγχος). A spear used as a pike for thrusting, or as a missile for hurling from the hand, or as a bolt from an engine. Homer defines the spear as "a pole heavy with bronze." The *hasta amentata*, for hurling, had a leathern thong for a handle (*amentum*) in the middle; *hasta pura* was a spear without a head, and was a much-valued decoration given to a Roman soldier who had saved a citizen's life; *hasta celibarium* was a spear which, having been thrust into the body of a gladiator as he lay dead in the arena, was afterwards used at marriages to part the hair of the bride. A spear was set up before a place where sales by auction were going on, and an auction-room was hence called HASTARIUM. Different kinds of spear were the *lancea* of the Greeks; the *pilum*, peculiar to the Romans; the *veru*, *verutum*, or "spit," of the Roman light infantry; the *gæsum*, a Celtic weapon adopted by the Romans; the *sparrus*, our English spar or *spear*, the rudest missile of the whole class; and many others mentioned under their respective headings in this work.

Hasta Pura. In Numismatics, a headless spear or long sceptre, an attribute of all the heathen deities; a symbol of the goodness of the gods and the conduct of providence, equally mild and forcible.

Fig. 379. Hasta— Roman ceremonial spear.

Hastarium, R. A room in which sales were made *sub hasta publica*, that is, by public auction, under the public authority indicated by the spear. The term also denoted a list or catalogue of sale.

Hastile, R. (*hasta*). The shaft of a spear, and thence the spear itself, a goad, &c.

Hat (A.S. *haet*, a covering for the head). Froissart describes hats and plumes worn at Edward's court in 1340, when the Garter order was instituted. Hats were originally of a scarlet-red colour, and made of "a fine kinde of haire matted thegither." A remarkable series of changes in the fashion of hats is given in *Planché's Encyclopædia of Costume.* Our illustration represents a young Venetian noble of the Middle Ages. (See also the illustrations to POURPOINT, BIRETTA, BOMBARDS, CALASH, CAPUCHON, CHAPEAU, CORONETS, &c.)

Fig. 380. Costume of a nobleman in Venice (16th century), showing the Hat of the period.

Hatchment, Her. (for *atchievement*). An achievement of arms in a lozenge-shaped frame, placed upon the front of the residence of a person lately deceased, made to distinguish his rank and position in life.

Hauberk (Germ. *Hals-berg*, a throat-guard).

A military tunic of ringed mail, of German origin, introduced in the 12th century.

Haumudeys, O. E. A purse.

Fig. 381. Hauriant.

Hauriant, Her. Said of fishes upright, "sucking the air." (Fig. 381.)

Hautboy. A wind instrument of the reed kind.

Haversack (Fr. *havre-sac*). A soldier's knapsack.

Hawk, Egyp. This bird symbolizes the successive new births of the rising sun. The hawk is the bird of Horus. It stood, at certain periods, for the word *God*, and, with a human head, for the word *soul*. The sun (*Ra*) is likewise represented with a hawk's head, ornamented with the disk.

Head-piece. An ornamental engraving at the commencement of a new chapter in a book.

Head-rail. The head-dress worn by Saxon and Norman ladies.

Healfang, A.S. The pillory, or a fine in commutation. " *Qui falsum testimonium dedit, reddat regi vel terræ domino* HEALFANG."

Heang-loo, Chinese. An incense-burner.

Heart. On numerous Christian tombs hearts may be seen sculptured. Many archæologists have

Fig. 382. Inscription, with hearts, found at Alise.

attempted to explain their meaning as symbols, but without entering on an unprofitable discussion of that question, it may be noticed that, in many cases, what archæologists have supposed to be hearts were nothing but ivy-leaves, which served as marks of separation between different words or sentences. Fig. 382 represents an inscription at Alise in which ivy-leaves figure, together with an ornament which some would insist were flames, if they were to take the leaves for hearts. When inscriptions, however, are defaced, the shape of the leaves is not nearly so distinguishable as in the figure. [One of the most frequent methods in which this emblem is introduced in Christian art is that the Saviour, or the Virgin Mary, is represented opening the breast to display the living heart—the natural symbol of Love, Devotion, or Sorrow. The Heart is an attribute of St. Theresa, St. Augustine, and other saints. The flaming heart is the emblem of charity. The heart pierced by seven daggers symbolizes the "seven sorrows" of Mary.]

Hecatesia, Gr. ('Εκατήσια). Festivals held at Athens in honour of Hecatê.

Hecatomb, Gr. and R. (ἑκατόμβη). A sacrifice offered in Greece and Rome under special circumstances, and at which a hundred head of cattle (ἑκατὸν) were slain; whence the name of the festival. [The term was generally applied to *all* great sacrifices, of much less extent than that implied by its etymological meaning.]

Hecatompylæ, Gr. (ἑκατόμ-πυλαι). The city with a hundred gates; a name given to the Egyptian Thebes.

Hecatonstylon, Hecatonstyle, Gr. and R. (ἑκατὸν and στῦλος). A portico or colonnade with a hundred columns.

Hecte or **Hectæus**, Gr. = a sixth (R. *modius*). In dry measure, the sixth part of the medimnus, or nearly two gallons English. Coins of uncertain value bore the same name; they were sixths of other units of value.

Hegira (Arabic *hajara*, to desert). The flight from Mecca, 16th July, A.D. 622, from which Mohammedan chronology is calculated.

Helciarius, R. One who tows a boat. He was so called because he passed a rope round his body in the way of a belt, the rope thus forming a noose (*helcium*).

Helepolis, Gr. and R. (ἑλέ-πολις, the taker of cities). A lofty square tower, on wheels, used in besieging fortified places. It was ninety cubits high and forty wide; inside were nine stories, the lower containing machines for throwing great stones; the middle, large catapults for throwing spears; and the highest other machines. It was manned with 200 soldiers. The name was afterwards applied to other siege engines of similar construction.

Helical, Arch. (ἕλιξ, a wreath). A spiral line distinguished from *spiral*. A staircase is *helical* when the steps wind round a cylindrical newel; whereas the *spiral* winds round a cone, and is constantly narrowing its axis. The term is applied to the volutes of a Corinthian capital. (See HELIX.)

Heliochromy (Gr. ἥλιος, the sun, and χρῶμα, colour). Process of taking coloured photographs.

Heliopolites, Egyp. One of the nomes or divisions of Lower Egypt, capital An, the sacred name for Heliopolis near Cairo.

Heliotrope. The *Hæmatite* or *blood-stone*; a siliceous mineral of a dark green colour, commonly variegated with bright red spots.

Heliotropion, Gr. A kind of sun-dial. (See HOROLOGIUM.)

Helix, Arch. (ἕλιξ, anything spiral). A small volute like the tendril of a vine placed under the Corinthian abacus. They are arranged in couples springing from one base, and unite at the summit.

Hellebore. A famous purgative medicine among the ancient Greeks and Romans. Philosophers prepared for work by drinking an infusion of the black hellebore, like tea. The best grew in the island of Anticyra in the Ægean Sea, and the gathering of it was accompanied by superstitious rites.

Helm, Helmet, Her. Now placed as an accessory above a shield of arms. Modern usage distinguishes helms according to the rank of the wearer. The term *helm* was applied by both Saxons and Normans, in the 11th century, to the conical steel cap with a nose-guard, which was the common headpiece of the day, and is depicted in contemporary illuminations, sculptures, and tapestries. Afterwards it was restricted to the *casque*, which covered the whole head, and had an aventaile or vizor for the face. The use of the *helm* finally ceased in the reign of Henry VIII.

Fig. 383. Helm of a Gentleman or Esquire.

Helmet. The diminutive of HELM, first applied to the smaller head-piece which superseded it in the 15th century. (See GALEA, ARMET, BASCINET, BURGONET, CASQUE, CHAPELLE LE FER, &c.)

Fig. 384. Helmet or Burgonet of the 16th century.

Hemi- (Gr. ἡμι-). Half; used in composition of words like the Latin *semi* or *demi*.

Hemichorion (ἡμιχόριον). (See DICHOREA.)

Hemicyclium, Gr. and R. (ἡμι-κύκλιον). A semicircular alcove, to which persons resorted for mutual conversation. The term was also used to denote a sun-dial.

Hemina, Gr. and R. (ἡμίνα, i. e. half). A measure of capacity containing half a sextarius (equal to the Greek *cotyle* = half a pint English).

Hemiolia, Gr. and R. (ἡμι-ολία, i. e. one and a half). A vessel of peculiar construction employed especially by Greek pirates.

Hemisphærium, R. A sun-dial in the form of a hemisphere; whence its name. (Fig. 385.)

Fig. 385. Sun-dial (Hemisphærium).

Hemlock, the *Conium maculatum* of botanists, was the poison used by the ancient Greeks for the despatch of state prisoners. Its effects are accurately described in Plato's description of the death of Socrates.

Heptagon (Gr. ἑπτὰ, seven, and γώνη, an angle). A seven-sided figure.

Hepteris, Gr. and R. (ἑπτ-ήρης). A ship of war with seven ranks of oars.

Heræa. Important Greek festivals, celebrated in honour of Hera in all the towns of Greece. At Argos, every fifth year, an immense body of young men in armour formed a procession, preceded by a HECATOMB of oxen, to the great temple of Hera, between Argos and Mycenæ, where the oxen were slaughtered, and their flesh distributed to the citizens.

Herald (Germ. *Herold*). An officer of arms. The heralds of England were incorporated by Richard III. The college now consists of three kings of arms, six heralds, and four pursuivants. The office of Earl Marshal, the supreme head of the English heralds, is hereditary in the family of the Duke of Norfolk. There is another herald king styled "Bath," who is specially attached to that order; he is not a member of the college. The chief herald of Scotland is styled Lord Lyon King of Arms; that of Ireland, Ulster King of Arms. *Chester herald* is mentioned in the reign of Richard II., *Lancaster king of arms* under Henry IV. (See MARSHAL, KINGS OF ARMS, &c.)

Heralds' College. A college of heralds was instituted in Rome by Numa Pompilius, and the office was held sacred among the most ancient Oriental nations. The institution was imported into England in the Middle Ages from Germany, a corporation of heralds, similar to the *collegium fetialium* of Rome, having been established in England in 1483 by Richard III. (See *Puiscus*, tom. i., and *Hofmann*, tom. ii.)

Hermæ, Gr. and R. ('Ερμαῖ). Hermæ, a kind of pedestals surmounted only by the head, or, in some cases, the bust of Hermes. Great reverence was felt for these statues. Houses at Athens had one before the doors; they were also placed in front of temples, near tombs, at street corners, or as mile-stones on the high roads. *Hermuli*, or small *Hermæ*, were a common ornament of furniture, as pilasters and supports. The same name is applied to similar statues having a man's head. This statue was probably one of the first attempts of art at plastic representation. The *phallus* and a pointed beard originally were essential parts of the symbol. In place of arms there were projections to hang garlands on. Then a mantle was introduced from the shoulders. Afterwards the whole torso was placed above the pillar; and finally the pillar itself was shaped into a perfect statue. All these gradations of the sculptor's art are traceable in existing monuments.

Hermæa. Festivals of Hermes, celebrated by the boys in the gymnasia, of which Hermes was the tutelary deity.

Hermeneutæ, Chr. (ἑρμηνευταί). Literally, interpreters. In the earliest ages of the Church, these were officials whose duty it was to translate sacred discourses or portions of Holy Scripture.

Herne-pan, O. E. (for *iron-pan*). Skull-cap worn under the helmet.

Heroum, Gr. (ἡρῷον, i. e. place of a hero). A kind of ÆDICULA (q.v.), or small temple, which served as a funeral monument. Several representations of Roman HEROA may be seen in the British Museum, representing funeral feasts in a temple, carved on the face of a sarcophagus (in the Towneley collection).

Herring-bone Masonry. Common in late Roman or early Saxon walls, where the ornamental lines take a sloping, parallel, zigzag direction.

Herygoud, O. E. A cloak with hanging sleeves.

Heuk or **Huque**, O. E. (1) Originally a cloak or mantle worn in the Middle Ages; then (2) a tight-fitting dress worn by both sexes. (*Fairholt;* see also *Planché, Encyclopædia.*) There appears to be great uncertainty as to the character of this garment.

Hexaclinon, Gr. and R. (ἑξά-κλινος). A dining or banqueting couch capable of holding six persons.

Hexaphoron, Gr. and R. (ἑξά-φορον). A litter carried by six porters.

Hexapterygon, Chr. (ἑξα-πτέρυγον). A fan used by Greek Catholics, and so named because it has on it figures of seraphim with six wings. (See FAN and FLABELLUM.)

Hexastyle, Arch. (ἑξά-στυλος). A façade of which the roof is supported by six columns.

Hexeris, Gr. (ἑξ-ήρης). A vessel with six ranks of oars.

Hiberna or **Hyberna**, R. A winter apartment. The halls in a Roman country house were built to face different ways according to the seasons; *verna* and *autumnalis* looked to the east; *hyberna*, to the west; *æstiva*, to the north.

Hidage, Hidegild, A.S. A tax payable to the Saxon kings of England for every *hide* of land. The word is indifferently used to signify exemption from such a tax.

Hidalgo (Span. *hijo d'algo*, son of somebody). An obsolete title of nobility in Spain.

Hieroglyphics, Egyp. (ἱερὸς, sacred, and γλύφω, to carve). Characters of Egyptian writing, the letters of which are figurative or symbolic. There are three kinds of Egyptian writing, the *hieroglyphic*, the *hieratic*, and the *demotic*. Clement of Alexandria says that in the education of the Egyptians three styles of writing are taught: the first is called the epistolary (*enchorial* or *demotic*); the second the *sacerdotal* (*hieratic*), which the sacred Scribes employ; and the third the *hieroglyphic*. Other nations, as for instance the ancient Mexicans, have likewise employed hieroglyphics.

Hieromancy, Gr. and R. Divination from sacrifices.

Hieron, Gr. (ἱερὸν, i. e. holy place). The whole of the sacred enclosure of a temple, which enclosed the woods, the building, and the priests' dwelling-place.

High-warp Tapestry. Made on a loom, in which the warp is arranged on a vertical plane, as the Gobelins. *Low-warp tapestry* is made on a flat loom, as at Aubusson, Beauvais, and other places. It is made more rapidly, and is inferior in beauty to the former.

Hilaria. A great Roman festival in honour of Cybele, celebrated at the vernal equinox. It consisted chiefly of extravagant merry-making to celebrate the advent of spring.

Hippocampus, Gr. and R. A fabulous animal, which had the fore-quarters of a horse ending in the tail of a dolphin. [It is imitated from the little " sea-horse " of the Mediterranean, now common in aquariums ; and in mural paintings of Pompeii is represented attached to the chariot of Neptune.]

Hippocentaur. A fabulous animal, composed of a human body and head attached to the shoulders of a horse. (See also CENTAUR.)

Hippocervus, Chr. A fantastic animal, half horse and half stag ; it personifies the pusillanimous man who throws himself without reflection into uncertain paths, and soon falls into despair at having lost himself in them.

Hippocratia, Gr. Festivals held in Arcadia in honour of Neptune, who, by striking the earth with his trident, had given birth to the horse.

Hippodromus, Gr. and R. The Greek name for an arena for horse and chariot races, in contradistinction to the stadium, which served for foot-racing. Fig. 386 represents the hippodrome at Olympia, taken from Gell's *Itinerary of the Morea.* The following is the key to the plan :— 1, 2, and 3 are *carceres*; A, the space included between the stalls or *carceres*; B, starting-place for the chariots ; C, the colonnade ; D, the arena ; E, the barrier ; F, the goal; G, the

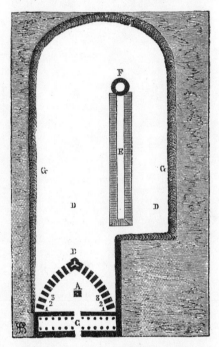

Fig. 386. Ground-plan of a Hippodrome.

space occupied by the spectators. [The word was also applied to the races themselves.] (See also CIRCUS.)

Hippogryph. A mythical animal represented as a winged horse with the head of a *gryphon.*

Hippopera, Gr. and R. (ἱππο-πήρα). A saddle-bag for travellers on horseback. (See ASCOPERA.)

Hippotoxotes (ἱππο-τοξότης). A mounted archer. The Syrians, Persians, Medes, Greeks, and Romans had mounted archers among their light cavalry.

Histrio. An actor. The GREEK dramas were originally represented on the stage by one performer, who represented in succession the different characters. Æschylus introduced a second and a third actor. The actors were all amateurs, and it was not until a later period that the histrionic profession became a speciality. Sophocles and Æschylus both probably acted their own plays. The ROMAN name for an actor, *histrio*, was formed from the Etruscan *hister*, a dancer. The earliest *histriones* were dancers, and performed to the music of a flute ; then Roman youths imitating them introduced jocular dialogue, and this was the origin of the drama. After the organization of the theatres, the *histriones* were subjected to certain disabilities ; they were a despised class, and excluded from the rights of citizenship. The greatest of *histriones* in Rome were Roscius and Æsopus, who realized great fortunes by their acting.

Hobelarii, Med. Lat. (See HOBLERS.)

Hoblers, A.S. Feudal tenants bound to serve as light horsemen in times of invasion.

Hob-nob, O. E. (Saxon *habban*, to have ; *næbban*, not to have). "Hit or miss ;" hence a common invitation to reciprocal drinking.

Hock-day, Hoke-day, or **Hock Tuesday.** A holiday kept to commemorate the expulsion of the Danes. It was held on the second Tuesday after Easter. *Hocking* consisted in stopping the highway with ropes, and taking toll of passers-by.

Hocus-pocus. Probably a profane corruption of the words *hoc est corpus* used in the Latin mass.

Holocaust. A sacrifice entirely consumed by fire.

Holosericum (Gr. ὅλον, all ; σηρικόν, silk). A textile *all silk*.

Holy Bread, Holy Loaf, or **Eulogia** (Lat. *panis benedictus*). This was not the eucharistic bread (which was used in the wafer form for the Communion), but ordinary leavened bread, blessed by the priest after mass, cut up into small pieces and given to the people.

Holy-bread-skep, O. E. A vessel for containing the holy bread.

Holy Water Pot, Chr. A metal vessel frequently found at the doors of Roman Catholic churches, to contain the consecrated water, which was dispensed with the *aspergillum*.

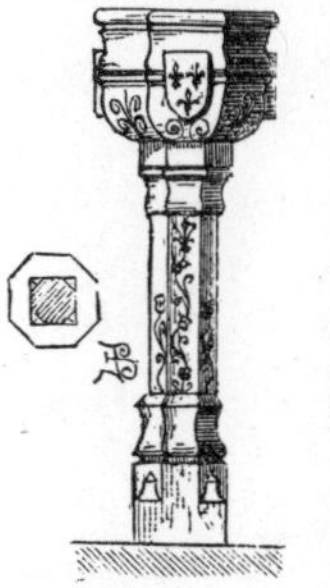

Holy Water Sprinkler or **Morning Star,** O. E. A military club or flail set with spikes, which *sprinkled* the blood about as the *aspergillum* sprinkles the holy water.

Holy Water Stone or **Stoup,** Chr. A stone receptacle placed at the entrance of a church for holding the holy water.

Fig. 387. Holy Water Stone (Renaissance).

Honeysuckle Pattern. A common Greek ornament, fully described by its name. (See FLEURON.)

Honiton Guipure. Lace was made in Devonshire, as well as in other parts of England, of silk and coarse thread until 1567, when the fine thread now used was introduced, it is said, by Flemings, who had escaped from the persecutions of the Duke of Alva. (See OLD DEVONSHIRE.) Honiton lace owes its great reputation to the sprigs made separately on a pillow, and afterwards either worked in with the beautiful pillow net or sewn on it. This net was made of the finest thread from Antwerp, the price of which in 1790 was 70*l.* per pound. (See MECHLIN LACE, 18th century.) Heathcoat's invention, however, dealt a fatal blow to the trade of the net-makers, and since then

Fig. 388. Honiton Guipure.

Honiton lace is usually made by uniting the sprigs on a pillow, or joining them with a needle by various stitches, as shown in the engraving.

Honour, Legion of. Instituted 3rd June, 1802, by Napoleon I. as first consul.

Hoodman-blind. Old English for BLINDMAN'S BUFF (q.v.).

Hoods (A.S. *Hod*) were probably introduced by the Normans. They are constantly represented, with great variation of fashion, in illustrations of the 11th to 18th century, as a part of the costume of both sexes. They were finally displaced by caps and bonnets in the reign of George II. (See CHAPERON, COWL.)

Hoops, in ladies' dress, were introduced in the reign of Queen Elizabeth, displacing the

FARTHINGALE ; and were finally abandoned in that of George III.

Hop-harlot, O. E.   A very coarse coverlet for beds.

Horatia Pila, R.   A pillar erected at the west extremity of the Roman forum to receive the trophy of the spoils of the three Curiatii brought back by Horatius.

Horns. A portion of a lady's head-dress, mentioned in the 13th century. They appear to have been formed by the foldings of the *gorget* or *wimple,* and a disposition of the hair on each side of the head into the form of rams' horns. For the horned head-dress of the 15th century, see the illustration to CORONET.

Horologium.   (1) *Sun-dials* preceded all other instruments for the measurement of time. The *gnomon* or *stocheion* of the GREEKS was a perpendicular staff or pillar, the shadow of which fell upon a properly marked ground ; the *polos* or *heliotropion* consisted of a perpendicular staff, in a basin in which the twelve parts of the day were marked by lines. (2) The *clepsydra* was a hollow globe, with a short neck, and holes in the bottom ; it measured time by the escape of water, and was at first used like an hour-glass to regulate the length of speeches in the Athenian courts. The escape of water was stopped by inserting a stopper in the mouth, when the speaker was interrupted. Smaller *clepsydrata* made of glass and marked with the hours were used in families. A precisely similar history applies to the *horologia* of ROME.

Horreum (dimin. *horreolum*), R.   (1) Literally, a place in which ripe fruits were kept ; a granary, or storehouse for grain ; *horreum publicum* was the public granary. (2) Any storehouse or depôt ; *horrea subterranea,* cellars. (3) It was applied to places in which *works of art* were kept, and Seneca calls his library a *horreum.*

Horse. In Christian art, the emblem of courage and generosity ; attribute of St. Martin, St. Maurice, St. George, and others. The Chinese have a *sacred horse,* which is affirmed to have appeared from a river to the philosopher Fou-hi, bearing instruction in eight diagrams of the characters proper to express certain abstract ideas.

Horse-shoe, Arch.   A form of the stilted arch elevated beyond half the diameter of the curve on which it is described. (See ARCH.)

Hortus (dimin. *hortulus*), R.   A pleasure-garden, park, and thence a kitchen garden ; *horti pensiles* were hanging gardens. The most striking features of a Roman garden were lines of large trees planted in regular order ; alleys or walks (*ambulationes*) formed by closely clipped hedges of box, yew, cypress, and other ever greens ; beds of acanthus, rows of fruit-trees especially of vines, with statues, pyramids, fountains, and summer-houses (*diætæ*). The

Romans were fond of the art of cutting and twisting trees, especially box, into figures of animals, ships, &c. (*ars topiaria*). The principal garden-flowers seem to have been violets and roses, and they had also the crocus, narcissus, lily, gladiolus, iris, poppy, amaranth, and others. Conservatories and hot-houses are frequently mentioned by Martial. An ornamental garden was also called *viridarium,* and the gardener *topiarius* or *viridarius.* The common name for a gardener is *villicus* or *cultor hortorum.* (Consult *Smith's Dict. of Ant.*)

Hospitium, R. (*hospes,* a guest).   A general term to denote any place in which a traveller finds shelter, board, and lodging. [The word had a very wide meaning of *hospitality,* regulated in all its details by the religious and social and politic sentiments of the nations.]

Hostia, R. (*hostio,* to strike).   A victim offered in sacrifice.

Hot Cockles, O. E.   A game common in the Middle Ages.

Hot-houses, O. E.   The name for Turkish baths ; 16th century.

Houppeland, O. E.   A very full loose upper garment with large hanging sleeves ; 14th century. It was probably introduced from Spain, and was something like a cassock.

House. (See DOMUS.)

Houseling Bread, O. E., Chr. (See SINGING BREAD, HOWSLING BELL.)

Housia or **Housse,** O. E.   An outer garment, combining cloak and tunic ; a tabard.

Howsling Bell, O. E.   The bell which was rung before the Holy Eucharist, when taken to the sick.

Howve (Saxon, from the old German *hoofd*). A hood. A common phrase quoted by Chaucer, "to set a man's *howve,*" is the same as to "set his cap," *cap* him or cheat him.

Huacos. (See GUACAS.)

Huircas or **Pinchas,** Peruv.   Subterranean aqueducts of the ancient Peruvians, distinct from the *barecac* or open conduits.

Hullings or **Hullyng.**   Old English name for hangings for a hall, &c.

Humatio, R. (*humo,* to bury).   The act of burying, and thence any mode of interment whatever.

Hume's Permanent White.   SULPHATE OF BARYTES (q.v.).

Humerale.   (See ANABOLOGIUM, AMICE.)

Humettée, Her.   Cut short at the extremities.

Hunting Flask. M. Jacquemart thinks that that represented in Fig. 389 may be reasonably attributed to Palissy. It is glazed in green, and diapered with little flames of a deeper shade. Upon the body, in relief, is the escutcheon of the celebrated Anne de Montmorency, round it the collar of St. Michael, and on each side the Constable's sword sup-

Fig. 389. Hunting Flask of Jaspered Ware,
1554—1556. Louvre Museum.

ported by a mailed arm and the motto of his house, "A Planos" (unwavering). A mask of Italian style and rayonnated suns complete the decoration of this curious sealed earthen-ware.

Hurst, Her. A clump of trees.

Hurte, Her. A blue roundle.

Hutch, O. E. (Fr. *huche*). A locker, which generally stood at the foot of the bed, to con-tain clothes and objects of value. It was com-monly used for a seat.

Huvette, Fr. A close steel skull-cap.

Hyacinth. (1) A precious stone of a violet colour. (2) The colour formed of red with blue, blue predominating. (3) The flower hyacinth among the ancient Greeks was the emblem of death.

Hyacinthia, Gr. A national festival, cele-brated annually at Amyclæ by the Amyclæans and Spartans, in honour of the hero Hyacinthus, who was accidentally killed by Apollo with a quoit.

Hyalotype (ὕαλος, glass, and τυπεῖν, to print). An invention for printing photographs from the negative on to glass, instead of paper.

Hycsos, Egyp. (lit. impure). A people of unknown origin, nomad tribes, but not savages, as has hitherto been believed, who came from Sinai, Arabia, and Syria. They are known as *Poimenes* (the Shepherds), *Mentiou Sati, Asian Shepherds,* and even *Scourges,* from their invasion of some part of Eastern Egypt.

Hydra, Gr. (a water-serpent). A hundred-headed monster of Greek mythology, sprung, like the Chimæra, from Typhon and Echidna ; he was killed by Hercules. In Heraldry the hydra is represented with only nine heads. The illustration (Fig. 390) is of the device adopted by Curtio Gonzaga, an Italian poet, to symbolize the constancy of his love, with the motto, " If I kill it, more strong it revives."

Fig. 390. Hydra with seven heads.

Hydraletês, Gr. (1) A mill for grinding corn, driven by water. (2) A waterfall or cur-rent of water.

Hydraulis, Gr. (ὕδρ-αυλις). A water-organ. The hydraulic organ, invented about B.C. 200, was really a pneumatic organ ; the water was only used to force the air through the pipes. It is represented on a coin of Nero in the British Museum. Only ten pipes are given to it, and there is no indication of any key-board. It had eight stops, and consequently eight rows of pipes ; these were partly of bronze, and partly of reed. It continued in use so late as the 9th century of our era.

Hydria, Gr. A large, heavy vessel, used principally for holding a store of water. It is represented urn-shaped, with a broad base and a narrow mouth, sometimes with one and some-times with two handles at the top, and smaller ones on the belly. The name is applied to other pails of bronze or silver, &c. (Fig. 391.)

Hydriaphoria, Gr. (water-bearing). (1) Fune-real ceremonies performed at Athens in memory of those who had perished in the deluges of Ogyges, Deucalion, &c. (2) A service exacted from married alien women in Athens by the female citizens, when they walked in the great procession at the Panathenaic feasts, and the former carried vessels of water for them.

Hydroceramic (vessels), Gr. Vessels made of a porous clay, in which liquids were put for the purpose of cooling them ; they were a kind of *alcarazas*.

Fig. 391. Hydria, or Water-jug, in black glaze.

Hydroscope. Another name for the clepsydra. (See HOROLOGIUM.)

Hypæthral, Gr. and R. (lit. under the sky, or in the open air). The term was applied to

Fig. 392. Hypæthrum.

any building, especially a temple, the *cella* of which had no roof. On the roofs of Egyptian temples, hypæthral temples are arranged with regard to astronomical observations, by which the calendar was regulated.

Fig. 393. Hypocausis of a Roman villa at Tusculum.

Hypæthrum, Gr. and R. A grating or *claustra* placed over the principal door of a temple for the purpose of admitting light into a part of the *cella*. Fig. 392 shows one of the bronze doors of the Pantheon at Rome, with its *hypæthrum*.

Hyperthyrum, Gr. and R. (over the door). A frieze and cornice arranged and decorated in various ways for the decoration of the lintel of a door.

Hypocastanum. Greek for CHESNUT BROWN (q. v.).

Fig. 394. Hypocausis discovered at Paris.

Hypocaust, Gr. and R. (ὑπό-καυσις and ὑπό-καυστον). A furnace with flues running underneath the floor of an apartment or bath, for heating the air. Fig. 393 represents the sectional elevation of a bath-room discovered in a Roman villa at Tusculum. Fig. 394 represents a *hypocausis* discovered at Paris in the old Rue de Constantine, near Notre Dame.

Hypogeum, Arch. A building under-ground ; a sepulchral vault. They form a principal part of Egyptian architecture of every period. The

Greek term is a synonym of the Latin CONDI-TORIUM (q.v.)

Hyporchema, Gr. A lively dance, accompanied by a mimic performance, at the festivals of Apollo among the Dorians. A chorus of singers danced round the altars, and others acted comic or playful scenes.

Hypotrachelium or **Cincture,** Arch. The part of the Doric capital included between the astragal and the lower annulets or fillets.

Hysteria, Gr. (from ῦs, a pig). Greek festivals, in which swine were sacrificed in honour of Venus.

I.

Ich Dien. I serve. The popular belief that Edward the Black Prince adopted this motto and the "Prince of Wales's feathers," at the battle of Cressy, from the blind King of Bohemia, is not sustained by investigation. It was at the battle of Poitiers that he first adopted this crest, joining to the family badge the old English word *Ic den* (Theyn), "I serve," in accordance with the words of the Apostle, "The heir, while he is a child, differeth nothing from a servant." (*Mrs. Palliser; Historic Devices.*)

Ichnography. The art of making maps or plans.

Iconic (sc. *statues*), Gr. and R. (εἰκονικὰ, i.e.) Portrait-statues; especially statues raised in honour of athletes who had been victorious in the contests.

Iconoclasts, Chr. Image-breakers. The name originated in the 8th or 9th century in the Eastern Empire, from which finally Theophilus banished all the painters and statuaries in 832. It has been since generally applied to those who, at various outbreaks of fanaticism, have destroyed ecclesiastical objects of art, and is especially applicable to the disciples of Savonarola in 1497, and to the Puritans of Scotland and England during the civil wars.

Iconography (i. e. image-description). The science that deals with statues and images, bas-reliefs, busts, medals, &c. Thus we have an Egyptian, Greek, Roman, mediæval iconography, &c. The best work on this science is "Christian Iconography; or the History of Christian Art in the Middle Ages," by M. Didron. The second volume contains a manual on the subject by a painter of the 12th century.

Iconostasis, Chr. The screen of the chancel in ancient churches, so called because it was there that images (εἰκόνες) were displayed for the adoration of the faithful.

Ideal and **Real.** "Any work of art which represents, not a material object, but the mental conception of a material object, is in the primary sense of the word *ideal;* that is to say, it represents an *idea,* not a *thing.* Any work of art which represents or realizes a material object is, in the primary sense of the term, *un-ideal.*" (*Modern Painters,* vol. ii. chap. 13.) In a practical sense an *ideal* picture or statue (e. g. the Medici Venus) is not the portrait of an individual model, but the putting together of selected parts from several models. Raphael said, "To paint a beautiful woman I must see several, and I have also recourse to a certain *ideal* in my mind;" and Guido said, "The beautiful and pure *idea* must be in the mind, and then it is no matter what the model is."

Ides, Idus, R. One of the monthly divisions in the Roman year; it fell on the 15th in months of thirty-one days, excepting January, August, and December; in months with only twenty-nine or thirty days, the *ides* fell on the 13th. The *kalends* are the first of every month; the *nones* are the 7th of March, May, July, and October, and the 5th of all the other months; and the ides always fall eight days later than the nones; and the days are reckoned backwards: thus the 13th of January is the ides of January, and the 14th of January the 19th day *ante diem* (or before) the February kalends. The morrow of the ides was looked upon as an unlucky day (*nefas*).

Illapa, Peruv. One of the divisions of the temple of the Sun (*Inti*) among the ancient Peruvians, so called because it was dedicated to the thunder (*Illapa*). (See INTI.)

Illumination. This art originated simply in the application of *minium* (or red lead) as a colour or ink, to decorate a portion of a piece of writing, the general text of which was in black ink. The term was retained long after the original red lead was superseded by the more brilliant *cinnabar,* or vermilion. Ornaments of all kinds were gradually added, and the term includes the practice of every kind of ornamental or ornamented writing. From the 3rd century Greek and Roman specimens exist of golden lettering upon purple or rose-coloured vellum, and the art prevailed wherever monasteries were founded. Anglo-Saxon and Irish MSS. of the 6th and 7th centuries exhibit a marvellous perfection, characterized by wonderfully minute interlacements of the patterns. Nearly all the best specimens of illumination were destroyed on the dissolution of monasteries. (Consult "*The Art of Illuminating*," *by W. R. Timms.*)

Imagines a vestir, It. Wooden images set up in Italian churches, with the heads and extremities finished, and the bodies covered with real drapery.

Imagines Majorum, R. Portraits of ancestors, or family portraits; they usually consisted of waxen masks, which were kept in the cases of an *armarium* or in an *ædicula;* or small statues which were carried before the corpse in a funeral procession.

Imbrex, R. A ridge-tile of semi-cylindrical form, and thus distinct from the *tegula*, which was a flat tile. It was called *imbrex* from its collecting the rain (*imber*). *Imbrex supinus* was the name given to a channel or gutter formed of ridge-tiles laid on their backs.

Imbrications. Architectural ornaments which take the form of fishes' scales, or of segmental ridge-tiles (*imbrices*) which overlap; whence the name given to them.

Imbricatus, R. Covered with flat and ridgetiles (*tegulæ* and *imbrices*).

Imbrothered, O. E. Embroidered.

Imbrued, Her. Stained with blood.

Immissarium, R. (*immitto*, to send into). A stone basin or trough; any receptacle built upon the ground for the purpose of containing water supplied from the *castellum*.

Impale, Her. To conjoin two separate coats of arms on one shield (as a husband's and wife's, &c.). The device of Queen Mary (Fig. 395) is the *impalement* of the double Tudor rose with the arms of Catherine of Aragon.

Impannata, It. Oiled paper.

Impasto, It. The thickness of the body of pigment laid on to a painting. Rembrandt, Salvator Rosa, and others used a thick *impasto;* Raphael, Guido, and others, one extremely thin.

Imperial. Anything adapted by its excellence for royal uses, or distinguished in size, is generally so called. (1) O. E. A sort of precious silk, wrought partly with gold, used by royalty and for ecclesiastical purposes, brought to England from Greece in the 12th century. (2) The largest kind of slate for roofing. (3) Paper 27 inches by 23. (4) Sp. The roof of a coach; hence, in English, a trunk made to fit the top of a carriage. (5) Russian. A gold coin of 10 silver roubles.

Impluviata, R. A cloak of square shape and brown in colour, worn as a protection against rain.

Impluvium, R. (1) A cistern on the floor of the atrium in a Roman house, into which the

rain was conducted. (2) The aperture in the roof of the atrium. (See DOMUS.)

Impost, Arch. The horizontal mouldings on a pillar, from which an arch is projected.

In antis, Arch. A name given to those temples, the pronaos or entrance porch of which was formed by two antæ or pilasters, and two columns. (See ANTÆ.)

Fig. 395. Device of Philip and Mary. Arms of Tudor and Aragon Impaled (*Rayonnant*).

Inauguratio, R. Generally the term applies to the ceremony by which the sanction of the gods was invoked upon any decree of man, such as the admission of a new member into a corporation or college, or the choice of the site of a theatre, city, or temple, &c.

Inaures, R. (*auris*, the ear; Gr. *enotion*). Earrings. Among the Greeks and Romans they were worn only by women. (See EARRINGS.)

Incensed, Inflamed, Her. On fire. (See FOCULUS.)

Incisura, R. (*incido*, to cut). Hatchings made by means of a brush.

Incitega, R. A kind of tripod or stand for vessels rounded or pointed at the bottom.

Incle, Inkle. A sort of tape used as a trimming to a dress.

Incrustation. The word has a general signification, "a coat of one material applied to another." Technically it should be applied to marble alone ; thus a thin slab of marble is *incrusted* upon a body of slate or stone, metals are DAMASCENED, fused pigments are ENAMEL, and woods are VENEERED.

Incubones, R. Genii who were supposed to guard treasure hidden under the earth.

Incunabula. (1) Swaddling-clothes for infants. (2) Ancient specimens of printing are so called.

Incus, R. (*incudo*, to beat on). An anvil.

Fig. 396. Indented.

Indented, Her. One of the dividing and border lines. It resembles the teeth of a saw.

Indian Art. The study of the forms and principles of Indian Art is indispensable to an appreciation of the true principles of ornamental design in general. The excellence of Indian manufactures is due to the system of Guilds rigidly adhered to for ages, which has resulted in the production of a race of hereditary craftsmen unequalled for their skill and taste in execution and design. Their pottery is distinguished above all others for purity and simplicity of form, obvious fitness to purpose, and individual freedom of design. Its origin

Fig. 397. Printed Calico (Indian) illustrating the treatment of flowers.

antedates the Institutes of Manu, and is lost in antiquity. Indian gold and metal work is supposed by Dr. Birdwood to owe its origin to Greek influence, but has acquired in its development a purely Oriental character. The Hindoos exhibit the greatest skill in the Oriental arts of damascening and enamelling, as well as in lacquer work and wood and ivory carving. All their designs are deeply symbolical, and closely interwoven with the primitive religious impulses of humanity. India was probably the first country in which the art of weaving was brought to perfection, and the fame of its cloudy gauzes and its gold and silver brocades is more ancient than the Code of Manu. The art is repeatedly mentioned in the Vedas. The purity of Indian Art is endangered in modern days by the introduction of machine-made goods and European design. (Consult *Dr. Birdwood's Handbook of Indian Art.*)

Indian Ink or **Chinese Ink.** A black pigment for water-colour painting, made from oil and lamp-black, thickened with some vegetable gum, and scented with musk or camphor. Many cheap and poor imitations of it are made.

Indian Ochre. A red pigment. (See RED OCHRES.)

Indian Paper. A delicate yellowish paper used for proof impressions in engraving. A Japanese paper of a similar quality is now frequently used.

Indian Red or **Persian Red.** A purple earth commonly sold under this name is the peroxide of iron. It is of a deep hue, opaque and permanent, and useful both in oil and water-colour painting ; mixed with white it forms valuable flesh-tints. (*Fairholt.*) (See OCHRE, AMATITA.)

Indian Rubber, Caoutchouc. An elastic gum ; the sap of the *Siphonia elastica*, and several of the fig tribe in India and South America. It was brought into use early in the 18th century. In its natural state it is of a pale yellow brown.

Indian Yellow. A golden yellow pigment and dye, said to be procured from the urine of the cow, or else from camel's dung. It is used in water-colour painting, but is not usually permanent. In some parts of the East it is called PURREE.

Indigetes (sc. *Di*), R. Indigenous gods. Heroes who were deified and worshipped as protectors of a place. The term is derived from *inde* and *genitus*, meaning born in that place. Æneas, Faunus, Romulus, &c., were indigenous gods.

Indigo. A deep blue pigment prepared from the leaves and branches of a small shrub ; it is transparent, tolerably permanent, and mixes well with other pigments, forming excellent greens and purples. A deep brown, known as *indigo brown*, and a deep red resin, known as *indigo red*, may be extracted by purifying the blue colour obtained from this dye. The old blue dye of the aboriginal Britons was produced from *woad* (isatis tinctoria). (*Fairholt.*) (See INTENSE BLUE.)

Inescutcheon, Her. An heraldic shield borne as a charge.

Inferiæ, R. Sacrifices or offerings made at the tombs of the dead.

Infiammati. A literary society of Padua in Italy. Device : Hercules upon the funeral pile on Mount Œta. Motto : "*Arso il mortal al ciel n' andrà l' eterno.*"

Infocati. One of the Italian literary societies. Device : a bar of hot iron on an anvil, beaten by two hammers. Motto: "*In quascunque formas.*"

In Foliage, Her. Bearing leaves.

Infrenatus (sc. *eques*), R. A horseman who rides without a bridle (*frenum*), controlling his horse solely by the voice or the pressure of the knees upon its side. (Fig. 282.)

Infula, R. A flock of red and white wool worn by priestesses and vestals and other Romans on festive or solemn occasions. In sacrificing also an infula was tied with a white band (*vitta*) upon the victim. Hence—

Infulæ, Chr. Ribands hanging from a bishop's mitre.

In Glory, In Splendour, Her. The sun irradiated.

Inlaying. Inserting ornaments in wood-work for decorative furniture. (See BOULE, MARQUETRY.)

In Lure, Her. Wings conjoined, with their tips drooping.

Inoa. Greek festivals in honour of Ino, esp. on the Corinthian Isthmus ; they consisted of contests and sacrifices. (See MATRALIA.)

In Pretence, Her. Placed upon, and in front of.

In Pride, Her. Having the tail displayed, as a peacock's. The illustration is the device of

Fig. 398. Peacock in pride.

Joan of Castile : "A peacock, in his pride, upon the terrestrial globe." (Fig. 398.)

Insensati of Perugia. One of the Italian literary academies. Their device was a flock of cranes, arranged in order, flying across the sea, each with a stone in its foot and sand in its mouth. Mottoes, "*Vel cum pondere*" (even with this weight), or "*Iter tutissimum,*" in allusion to Pliny's statement that the cranes used stones and sand for *ballast*, "wherewith they fly more steadily and endure the wind."

Insignia, R. (*in*, and *signum*, a mark). Generally, any object which serves as a mark or ornament for distinguished persons ; a ceremonial badge, a badge of office, &c. (See ENSIGNS.)

Insubulum, R. A weaver's beam or roller, round which he rolled the cloth as it was made.

Insula, R. A house, or block of houses, having a free space all round them. [Under the emperors the word *domus* meant any house, detached or otherwise, where a family lived ; and *insula* meant a hired lodging.]

Intaglio, It. A stone in which the engraved subject is sunk beneath the surface, and thus distinguished from a cameo, which is engraved in relief.

Intaglio-relievato (It.), or *cavo-relievo*. Sunk-relief, in which the work is recessed within an outline, but still raised in flat relief, not projecting above the surface of the slab ; as seen in the ancient Egyptian carvings.

Intense Blue. A preparation of indigo, very durable and transparent.

Intense Madder Purple. (See MADDER.)

Intercolumniation, Arch. The space between two columns. This space varies according to the orders of architecture and the taste of the architect. According as the space is greater or less between the columns of a temple, the latter is called *aerostyle, eustyle, systyle*, and *pycnostyle*. Generally speaking, in the monuments of antiquity, whatever be the intercolumniation adopted, the space comprised between the two columns which face the door of the building is wider than the intercolumniation at the sides.

Intermetium, R. The long barrier running down the arena of a circus between the two goals (*metæ*). (See META.)

Intermodillions, Arch. The space included between two modillions (projecting brackets in the Corinthian order). This space is regular, and often decorated with various ornaments. In the Romano-Byzantine and Renaissance styles, modillions are often united by arcades.

Intertignium, R. The space between the tie-beams (*tigna*) in the wood-work of a roof.

Interula, R. (*interior*, inner). An under-tunic ; a kind of flannel chemise worn by both men and women.

Intestinum (opus), R. (*intus*, within). The inner fittings or work of any kind in the inside of a house, and thence wood-work, JOINERY.

Fig. 399. Part of the Façade of the Peruvian temple Inti-huasi.

Inti or **Punchau,** Peruv. The Sun or supreme god, inferior deities being called *conopa* and *canopa*. The temple of the Sun was called *Inti-huasi* (house of the Sun) ; it comprised seven principal divisions ; the *inti* or sanctuary, situated in the centre of the temple ; the second division was called *mama-quilla*, from the fact of its being dedicated to the moon, which was thus named ; the third was dedicated to the stars, called *cayllur;* the fourth to the thunder, and called *illapa;* the fifth to the rainbow, and called *ckuichi;* the sixth division was occupied by the chief priest (*huilacuma*) ; the seventh and last division formed the dwelling of the priests.

Intronati of Siena. One of the Italian literary academies. Their device was a gourd for containing salt, with the motto, " *Meliora latent*" (the better part is hidden).

Iodine Scarlet (*pure scarlet*). A pigment more brilliant than vermilion, very susceptible to metallic agency.

Iodine Yellow. A very bright yellow pigment, very liable to change.

Fig. 400. Ionic capital.
From the Erechtheium, Athens.

Ionic, Arch. One of the orders of Grecian architecture, distinguished principally by the ornaments of its CAPITAL, which are spiral and are called VOLUTES, four in number. The Ionic SHAFT is about nine diameters high, including the BASE (which is half a diameter) and the CAPITAL, to the bottom of the volute. The PEDESTAL is a little taller and more ornamented than the Doric. The BASES used are very various. The Attic base is very often used, and, with an *astragal* added above the upper *torus*, makes a beautiful and appropriate base for the Ionic. The CORNICES are (1) plain Grecian, or (2) the *dentil* cornice, or (3) the *modillon* cornice. The Ionic shaft may be fluted in twenty-four semicircular flutes with fillets between them. The best Ionic example was the temple on the Ilissus at Athens. The temple of Fortuna Virilis at Rome is an inferior specimen. (See also Figs. 69, 184.)

Irish Cloth, white and red, in the reign of King John was much used in England.

Iron. *Indian red, Venetian red, Mars red, Mars orange, Mars yellow* are all coloured by iron (see MARS), and are valuable for their great durability. (See METALLURGY.)

Irradiated, Her. Surrounded by rays of light.

Iseia, Gr. and R. ('Ισεια). Festivals in honour of Isis. Among the Romans they degenerated into mere licentiousness, and were abolished by the senate.

Iselastici Ludi, Gr. and R. Athletic contests which gave the victor the right of returning to his native city in a chariot (εἰσελαύνειν) ; whence the name *iselastici*. These contests formed part of the four great games of Greece, viz. the Olympic, Pythian, Isthmian, and Nemean games.

Isodomos or **Isodomum,** Gr. and R. (ἰσόδομος, i. e. equal course). A structure built in equal courses, that is, in such a way that the surface

Fig. 401. Ivory carving. Sword-hilt of the 16th century.

each stone is of one uniform size, and that the joints of one layer are adjusted with those of another so as to correspond symmetrically.

Fig. 400 a. Isodomum opus.

Isokephaleia (Gr. ἴσος, equal ; κεφαλή, head). A rule in Greek sculpture by which the heads of all the figures on a bas-relief were of the same height from the ground.

Isometrical Perspective, used for representing a bird's-eye view of a place, combines the advantages of a ground-plan and elevation ; only the lines of the base are made to converge, leaving the whole figure cubical, and without the expression of *distance* from the point of sight.

Ispahan Tiles, of the period of Shah-Abbas—16th century—are remarkable for exquisite design.

Italian Earth. Burnt *Roman ochre*; resembles Venetian red in colour ; and, mixed with white, yields valuable flesh-tints. (*Fairholt.*)

Italian Pink, or *yellow lake*. A transparent bright-coloured pigment, liable to change. (See YELLOW LAKE, PINKS.)

Italian Varnish. A mixture of white wax and linseed oil, used as a vehicle in painting. It has good consistency, flows freely from the pencil, and is useful for glazing.

Ivory Black. A pigment prepared by heating ivory shavings in an iron cylinder ; when from bone, it is called *bone black* (q.v.). The real ivory black is a fine, transparent, deep-toned pigment, extremely valuable in oil and water-colour painting. The *bone black* (commonly sold as *ivory black*) is much browner.

Ivory Carving. This art, in considerable perfection, was known to prehistoric man at the period of the so-called stone age. Egyptian and Assyrian specimens of the art are of a date at least as early as that of Moses. From the year 1000 B.C. down to the Christian era, there was a constant succession of artists in ivory in the western Asiatic countries, in Egypt, in Greece, and in Italy. From the time of Augustus, ivory carving shared in the general decline of art. Increasing in number as they come nearer to the Middle Ages, we can refer to carved ivories of every century, preserved in museums in England and abroad. The most important ivories up to the 7th century are the consular *diptychs*, originally a favourite form of presents from newly-appointed consuls to eminent persons ; subsequently adapted to

Fig. 402. Ivory carving. Spoon of the 16th century.

Christian uses, or as wedding presents, &c. In the Middle Ages, from the 8th to the 16th cen-

Fig. 403. Ivory carving, 15th century.

tury, the use of ivory was adopted for general

purposes. The favourite subjects of the carvings are those drawn from the romances of the Middle Ages—especially the romance of the Rose—and in the 15th century, scenes of domestic life, illustrating the dress, armour, and manners and customs of the day. Combs of every date, from the Roman and Anglo-Saxon period, and earlier, are found in British graves. In short, from the time when the first prehistoric carvings of antediluvian animals were made to the present, every age of human civilization appears to be more or less fully illustrated in carvings upon ivory and bone. (See also CHESSMEN.) The earliest material was found in the tusks of the mammoth : from Iceland we have beautiful carvings of the 7th century in the teeth of the walrus. Fossil tusks of the mammoth are found in great quantities in Siberia, and are almost the only material of the ivory-turner's work in Russia. African and Asiatic elephant ivory are the best, and differ, the former, when newly cut, being of a mellow, warm, transparent tint. Asiatic ivory tends to become yellow by exposure. A fine specimen of carving in ivory is given in Fig. 403 from a MIRROR-CASE of the 15th century. (See also Fig. 185, and illustrations to PYX, TRIPTYCH, &c.)

Ivy, Chr. The symbol of eternal life.

Iwbwb, Celt. The ancient military cry, which has given name to many places ; as Cwm Iwbwb, in Wales, the Jujupania of Ptolemy. (*Meyrick*.)

Izeds, Persian. Beneficent genii of the mythology of Zoroaster. Ormuzd, the supreme god, created twenty-eight of them to be the attendants of the *amchaspands*.

J.

Jacinth. A precious stone. (See HYACINTH.)

Jack-boots (O. E.) were introduced in the 17th century.

Jackes, O. E. (1) Towels. (2) The roller for a well-rope.

Jacket or **Jack**, **Jerkin**, &c., O. E. ; worn over the doublet ; but the names are applied indiscriminately to a great variety of such garments.

Jacob's Staff, O. E. A pilgrim's staff.

Jacobus. An English coin of James I., value

25s., weighing 6 dwt. 10 grains. The *Carolus*, a similar coin, value 23s., weighed 5 dwt. 20 grains.

Jaculatores, R. Soldiers armed with a javelin (*jaculum*), who formed part of the light troops of the Roman army.

Jade. Spanish *piedra de la yjada*. A green stone, closely resembling jasper, much used by prehistoric man, and to which supernatural virtues have in all ages been attributed, especially by the ancient Mexicans. Fine specimens of jades are carved in China, where they are of a whitish colour, and are called *Yu*. The clear white and green specimens are the most prized by collectors. (See NEPHRITE, SAUSSURITE.)

Jagerant. (See JAZERINE.)

Jamb, Arch. The side of any opening in a wall.

Jambe, Gambe, Her. The leg of a lion or other beast of prey.

Jambes. Armour for the legs ; 14th century.

Janua, R. (*Janus*). The front door of a house opening on the street. The inner doors were called *ostia*, in the singular *ostium*, while the city gates were called *portæ*.

Januales, Janualia, R. Festivals held at Rome, in honour of Janus, on the first or kalends of January in each year ; the offerings consisted of incense, fruits, and a cake called *janual*.

Japanese Paper of a creamy tint is frequently used for proof impressions of etchings, &c.

Japanning. A species of lac-varnishing, in imitation of the lacquered ware of Japan. (See LAC, LACQUER.)

Jasper. A kind of agate, the best known description of which is of a green colour. Many colours and varieties are used for gem-engraving, such as agate-jasper, striped jasper, Egyptian red and brown, and porcelain jasper. In the Christian religion the jasper symbolizes faith ; its hardness expresses the firmness of faith ; its opaqueness the impenetrability of the mysterious.

Jasponyx. An onyx mixed with jasper.

Javelin. A light hand-spear. (See HASTA.)

Jayada. (See VIMANA.)

Jazel. A precious stone of an azure blue colour.

Jazerine (It. *ghiazerino*). A jacket strengthened with overlapping plates of steel, covered with velvet or cloth, and sometimes ornamented with brass ; 13th century.

Jennet. A Spanish or Barbary horse.

Jerkin, O. E. The jerkin was generally worn over the doublet ; but occasionally the doublet was worn alone, and in many instances is confounded with the jerkin. Either had sleeves or not, as the wearer pleased.

"My jerkin is a doublet." (*Shakspeare*.)

Jessant, Her. Shooting forth, as plants growing out of the earth.

    Jessant-de-lys, Her. A combination of a lion's face and a fleur-de-lys.

    Jesse, O. E. A large branched chandelier.

    Jesse, Tree of, Chr. An ornamental design common in early Christian art, representing the genealogy of our Lord in the persons of his ancestors in the flesh.

Fig. 404. Jessant-de-lys.

Jesseraunt. (See JAZERINE.)

Jesses. Straps for hawk's bells. (See Fig. 405.)

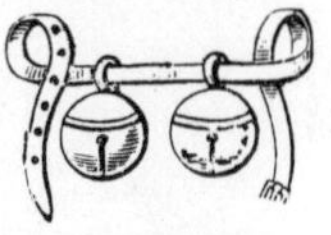

Fig. 405. Hawk's bells and Jesses.

Jet. A variety of soft bituminous coal, admitting of a fine polish, which is used for ornaments. It is, in its natural state, soft and brittle, of a velvet-black colour, and lustrous. Ornaments of jet are found in ancient *tumuli*.

Jet d'Eau, Fr. A fountain. That at Chatsworth springs 267 feet in the air, and is the highest in existence.

Jew's Harp or **Jew's Trump** (from the French *jeu* and *trompe*). A small musical instrument, known for centuries all over Europe, consisting of a metal frame with two branches, and a vibrating tongue of steel in the middle. It has suggested a number of modern instruments, including the HARMONIUM.

Jew's Pitch. A kind of *asphaltum* used as a brown pigment. It attracts dust, and never dries perfectly.

Jewes Light, O. E. (See JUDAS LIGHT.)

Jogues or **Yugs.** In Hindoo chronology, eras or periods of years. (1) The *Suttee Yug*, or age of purity, lasted 3,200,000 years ; the life of man being then 100,000 years, and his stature 21 cubits. (2) The *Tirtar Yug*, in which one-third of man was corrupted, lasted 2,400,000 years ; the life of man being then 10,000 years. (3) The *Dwapaar Yug*, in which half the human race became depraved, lasted 1,600,000 years ; the life of man being 1000 years. (4) The *Collee Yug*, in which all mankind are corrupt, is the present era, ordained to subsist 400,000 years (of which about 5000 have elapsed) ; the life of man being limited to 100 years. There are, however, conflicting accounts of the duration of the different *Jogues*. (See *Halhed's Preface to the Gentoo Laws*.)

Joinery (in Latin, *intestinum opus*) has to deal with the addition in a building of all the fixed wood-work necessary for convenience or ornament. The most celebrated work on the subject is *Nicholson's Carpenter's Guide, and Carpenter's and Joiner's Assistant*, published in 1792. The *modern art* of joinery properly dates from the introduction of the geometrical staircase, or stair supported by the wall only, the first English example of which is said to have been erected by Sir Christopher Wren in St. Paul's. [See JOINERY in *Ency. Brit.* 8th ed.]

Joseph, O. E. A lady's riding-habit, buttoned down the front.

Jousting-helmets were made wide and large, resting on the shoulders, and decorated with a crest. It was common to make them of comical, fantastic designs ; such as weathercocks with the points of the compass, immense figures of birds and beasts, &c.

Jousts or **Justs.** Duels in the tilting-ground; generally with blunted spears, for a friendly trial of skill.

Jousts à Outrance. Jousts in which the combatants fought till death ensued.

Jousts of Peace (*hastiludia pacifica*; Fr. *joutes à plaisance*). These differed from real jousts or tournaments in the strength of the armour worn, and the weapons used. The lance was topped with a *coronel* instead of a steel point; the sword was pointless and blunted, being often of whalebone covered with leather silvered over.

Fig. 406. Chinese vase decorated with signs of longevity.

Jouy (wishes of good fortune). Chinese porcelain vases so called, used for birthday and other presents. In the vase represented on Fig. 406, the handles form the word expressive of the greeting above mentioned.

Jowlopped, Her. Having wattles and a comb, as a cock.

Joys of the Virgin, Chr. The seven joys and seven sorrows are frequently painted together in churches. The joys are, (1) The Annunciation. (2) The Visitation. (3) The Nativity. (4) The Adoration of the Three Kings. (5) The Presentation in the Temple. (6) The finding of Christ, by his mother, in the Temple. (7) The Assumption and Coronation of the Virgin. The seven sorrows are, (1) The prophecy of Simeon. (2) The Flight into Egypt. (3) The loss of the child in the Temple. (4) The Betrayal. (5) The Crucifixion. (6) The Deposition from the Cross. (7) The Ascension.

Jubé (Arch. Mod.). A structure of carved stone-work, separating the chancel from the choir in a church. From this position the daily lessons were chanted, preceded by the words " *Jube*, Domine, benedicere ;" hence its name. In English it is called indifferently, the rood-loft, holy-loft, rood-screen, or jubé.

Jubilee. (1) Heb. (from *jobel*, a ram's horn (trumpet) ; or from *jabal*, to recall). A Jewish festival celebrated every fifty years, when slaves were restored to liberty, and exiles recalled. (2) Chr. A commemoration ceremony at Rome, during which the Pope grants plenary indulgences ; held at irregular intervals.

Judas Light, Judas Candlestick, Jewes Light, O. E. The wooden imitation of a candlestick which held the Paschal candle.

Jugalis (sc. *equus*). A horse harnessed to a yoke (*jugum*), instead of traces (*funalis*).

Jugerum. A Roman superficial measure, 240 feet by 120 feet. In the original assignment of landed property, two *jugera* were allotted to each citizen, as heritable property.

Jugum (Gr. ζυγόν). (1) A yoke for draught cattle. (2) Metaphorically, subjugation —" *sub jugum mittere*" = to pass under the yoke, as nations conquered by the Romans were made to. This ceremonial yoke was constructed of a horizontal supported by two upright spears, at such a height that those passing under it had to stoop the head and shoulders. (3) In a general sense the word signifies that which joins two things together, a cross-beam, &c.

Jugumentum. Door-head, transverse beam on the uprights (*limen superius*).

Jumps, O. E. (1) A loose bodice for ladies.

" Now a shape in neat stays, now a slattern in jumps :
Now high on French heels, now low in your pumps ;
Like the cock on the tower that shews you the weather,
You are hardly the same for two days together."
(*Universal Magazine*, 1780.)

(2) A jacket or loose coat reaching to the thighs, buttoned down before, with sleeves to the wrist. A precisely similar lounging-coat, still in vogue at Cape Colony, is called a *jumper*.

Junones. Tutelary genii of women, as the *genii* were of men. They are represented as females, clothed in drapery, having bats' wings.

Jupon, Fr. Another name for a *pourpoint*, or close tunic, worn over the armour by knights in the Middle Ages. (See Fig. 463.)

Juruparis (Amer. Indian). A mysterious trumpet of the Indians, an object of great veneration. Women are never permitted to see it; if any does so, she is put to death by poison.

No youths are allowed to see it until they have passed through an ordeal of initiatory fastings and scourgings. It is usually kept hidden in the bed of a stream, deep in the forest ; and no one dares to drink of the water of that stream. It is brought out and blown at feasts. The inside of the instrument is a tube made of slips of the Paxiaba palm, wrapped round with long strips of bark. A specimen is preserved in the museum at Kew Gardens.

Juvenalia, R. Scenic games instituted by Nero in commemoration of his shaving his beard for the first time. They consisted of theatrical performances in a private theatre erected in a pleasure-ground (*nemus*). The name was afterwards given to the JANUALIA.

K.

For Greek words not found under this initial, see C.

Kalathos, Gr. (κάλαθος). Literally, made of wicker-work. A drinking-cup, so called because it resembled the wicker-work basket of the Greek women. It was usually furnished with a ring, through which a finger might be put in order to lift it. The word is also written *calathos.*

Kaleidoscope (καλὸs, beautiful ; εἶδos, a form ; σκοπέω, to see). An optical instrument invented in 1814 by Sir David Brewster, which by means of mirrors inserted in it exhibits repetitions of objects placed within it, in certain symmetrical combinations. There are several different kinds, called *polycentral, tetrascopes, hexascopes, polyangular,* &c., according to their construction.

Kang, Hind. A bracelet or ring ; *kang-doy,* a bracelet for the wrist or arm ; *kang-cheung,* a bracelet or ring worn by the Khmers above the ankle.

Kaolin. The name first applied by the Chinese to the fine white porcelain earth derived from the decomposition of the feldspathic granites ; used for fine pottery.

Kayles (Fr. *quilles*). Modern ninepins, represented in MSS. of the 14th century.

Keep of a castle. The DONJON (q. v.).

Keeping in a picture. Harmony and the proper subordination of parts.

Kendal. A kind of green woollen cloth or baize, first made at the town of Kendal, in Westmoreland ; 16th century.

> " Misbegotten knaves in *Kendal green.*"
> (*Shakspeare.*)

Kerchief of Pleasaunce. An embroidered cloth worn by a knight for the sake of a lady, in his helmet, or, in later times, round his arm ; which is the origin of crape being so worn for mourning.

> " Moreore there is ykome into Enlond a knyght out of Spayne wyth a kercheff of plesunse i-wrapped about hys arme, the gwych knyght wyl renne a course wyth a sharpe spere for his sov'eyn lady sake." (*Paston Letters,* vol. p. 6.)

Kerchiefs or **Coverchiefs** (*chief* = the head), O. E. Head-cloths of fine linen worn by ladies.

Kermes (Arabic = little worm). An insect produced on the *Quercus coccifera.* The dead bodies of the female insect produce a fine scarlet dye stuff.

Kern. The Irish infantry were formerly so called.

Kersey. A coarse narrow woollen cloth ; hence "Kersey-mere," so called from the *mere* (or miry brook) which runs through the village of Kersey in Suffolk, where this cloth was first made.

Kettle-drum. A drum with a body of brass.

Kettle-hat, O. E. The iron hat of a knight of the Middle Ages ; also the leather *burgonet* of the 15th century.

Fig. 407. Kettle-hat.

Kettle-pins, O. E. (See KAYLES.)

Key-note. In Music, the foundation or lowest note of the scale. Whatever note this is, the *intervals* between the third and fourth notes, and between the *seventh* and *eighth* above it, must be *semi-tones.*

Key-stone, Arch. The central stone of an arch.

Keys. In Christian art, the attribute of St. Peter, signifying his control over the entrances of Heaven and Hell ; hence the insignia of the Papacy. They also denote, *in heraldry,* office in the State, such as that of chamberlain of the court.

Khan, Orient. The name used by Eastern nations to denote a caravanserai.

Kher, Egyp. The quarter of tombs ; the whole number of burial-places or *hypogæa* collected together at one spot.

Fig. 408. Khmer Architecture. Base of a pillar in a Temple of Cambodia, showing the god Brahma with four faces.

Khmers, Hind. The ancient inhabitants of Cambodia, a territory in South-East Asia, who had attained a high stage of civilization, to judge by the artistic remains of the Khmer nation which survive.

Khopesh, Egyp. The dagger of the Egyptian kings ; its curved blade bore some resemblance to the thigh of an ox, which was called in Egyptian *khopesh* or *khopesk.*

Kin-chung, Chinese. A golden bell.

King-fisher. (See HALCYON.)

King-post. The central upright post supporting the gable of a roof.

King's Yellow. (See ORPIMENT.)

Kings of Arms. Officers of Heralds' College. There are three—*Garter, Clarenceux,* and *Norroy.*

Kinnor, Heb. A stringed instrument of the Hebrews ; it had eight, ten, or twenty-four strings, which were played either with the fingers or a plectrum.

Kinschall. A small curved Turkish dagger.

Kiosk, Kiosque. A Turkish pleasure-house.

Kircher, Kirchowe, O. E. A kerchief.

Kirtel, O. E. A loose gown, a tunic or waistcoat ; also a monk's gown.

Kiste, O. E. A chest.

Kistvaen, Celt. A Celtic monument more commonly known as a DOLMEN (q.v.).

Kit-cat. Canvas for portraits—28 or 29 inches by 36—of the size adopted . by Sir Godfrey Kneller, in painting the portraits of the Kit-cat Club. The club had taken its name from Christopher Cat, a pastrycook, who supplied them at their meetings with mutton-pies. Addison, Steele, Walpole, Marlborough, and other staunch Whigs were the principal members. It dissolved about 1720.

Klaft, Egyp. A royal head-dress of striped cloth forming a kind of hood, and terminating in two flaps which fall over the breast. A great many Egyptian statues are represented with the *klaft.* It is suggested by M. Soldi that the invention of this ornament was for the purpose of strengthening the figure, by avoiding the thinness of the shape of the neck.

Knapsack. A case for a foot-soldier's stores, carried at the back. *Knap* means a protuberance.

Knife, Chr. (See FLAYING-KNIFE.) This is also the attribute of Sts. Agatha, Albert, and Christina ; and a sacrificing-knife of St. Zadkiel the Angel.

Knighthood. The principal English orders are of the GARTER, established 1343, and the *Bath* shortly afterwards ; of ST. PATRICK for Ireland, established in 1783 ; and the *Order of the Thistle,* at least as ancient as Robert II. of Scotland. There is a French order of the *Thistle,* founded in 1463 ; but the most ancient French order is the *Gennet,* in 706. In France are also the orders of *St. Michel* and of *St. Louis ;* but these French orders are now all superseded by the Legion of Honour. [See *An Accurate Historical Account of all the Orders of Knighthood.*]

Knight-service, O. E. A tenure of lands formerly held by knights, on condition of performing military service.

Fig. 409. Architectural *Knop* or *Boss.*

Knol, Hind. A road or high road which frequently passes over very low bridges.

Knop, O. E. A button.

Knop, Knob, Arch. A boss.

Knop and Flower Pattern. An ornament of remote antiquity, original basis of a great branch of decorative art in all nations, common on early Indian monuments, and with different variations in the art of Assyria, Egypt, Greece, and Rome. The variations are regulated according to the flora of the various countries, the *knop* (or bud) and *flower* being always the radical idea.

Knot, Her. An intertwined cord, borne as a badge. Cords intertwined about other figures and devices form so-called compound badges, which significantly declared the union of two houses ; thus the Dacre knot is entwined about the Dacre escallop and the famous "ragged staff" of Beauchamp and Neville. An ORDER OF THE KNOT was established at Naples in 1252. The badge of silk, gold, and pearls was tied in a knot upon the arm, and those who were invested with it made a vow to untie it at Jerusalem. (Fig. 410 and 410 a.)

Fig. 410.
Bourchier Knot.

Knuckle-bones. (See TALUS.)

Koope, O. E. A cope.

Koukim, Heb. Kilns for the cremation of the dead, such as are occasionally found in

Fig. 410 a. Dacre Knot and Badge.

the ancient tombs of the Valley of Hinnom (Gehenna).

Kourganes, Or. Grassy mounds, such as are frequently met with in Russia in Europe, and which bear a strong resemblance to *tumuli* and *barrows*. (See TUMULUS.)

Krems White or **Vienna White.** A pigment manufactured at Krems in Austria. It is the finest white lead used in oils.

Krouts, Hind. An ornament resembling embroidery. The monuments of Khmer art are adorned with krouts of a rich ornamentation, somewhat similar to certain ornaments of the French Renaissance. (See Fig. 408.)

Krumhorn. An old musical instrument of the cornet kind.

Kufic. (See CUFIC.)

Kussier. A Turkish musical instrument, consisting of five strings, stretched over a skin that covers a kind of basin.

Kymbium. (See CYMBIUM.)

Kyphi, Egyp. A perfume which was burnt before the statues of the gods ; it was composed of sixteen different ingredients.

L.

Labarum, Chrism, R. The standard of the Roman emperors from the time of Constantine ; in form it resembled the *vexillum* of the cavalry. The Labarum is the banner of the Chrism, or sign that appeared to Constantine, viz. the Greek letters XP in a monogram (the two first letters of the Name XPIΣTOΣ) ; sometimes followed by the Roman letters IHSV, or the motto in full, "*in hoc signo vinces*." It is, under several variations, a common ecclesiastical emblem.

Labellum. Dimin. of LABRUM (q.v.).

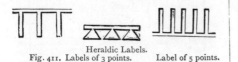

Heraldic Labels.
Fig. 411. Labels of 3 points.   Label of 5 points.

Labels, in heraldry, are marks of *cadency*. (1) A band crossing the shield, with three points de-

pending, marks the coat of an eldest son. (2 Broad ribands hanging from a knight's helmet. (3) In mediæval architecture and church decoration, images of saints and angels bear *labels* inscribed with texts and mottoes.

Labis. (See SPOON.)

Labrum, R. (lit. a lip). A general term to denote any kind of vessel the brim of which turned over on the outside like the lip of the human mouth ; a wide flat basin which stood in the thermal chamber or CALDARIUM (q.v.) of the Roman baths.

Labyrinth, Gen. (λαβύρινθος). A building of considerable size, usually underground, containing streets and cross-roads, like the

Fig. 412. Labyrinth.

catacombs, &c. The term is also applied to intricate designs executed on the grass-plots of gardens, and on the mosaic or glazed tiles n pavements. (Fig. 412.) (See MINOTAUR.)

Lac or **Gum Lac** (Arabic, *lakah*). A resin produced on an East-Indian tree by the punctures of the *Coccus lacca* insect. It forms a brittle substance of a dark red colour, and when in grains is called *seed lac*, and in thin flat plates *shell lac*. (See LACQUER.) The chief use of

Fig. 413. Point de France (pillow-made), 17th century.

Fig. 414. Old Brussels or Point d'Angleterre.

lac in Europe is for making sealing-wax, and as a basis for *spirit varnishes* and *French polish.*

Lace was originally of a heavy texture, more like embroidery. It was of two kinds, *lacis*, or "darned netting," and "*cutwork.*" *Lacis*, often worked in coloured silks and gold thread, was also called "opus araneum" or "spiderwork." In "*cutwork,*" a net of threads was laid on to cloth, and the cloth sewn to it in parts, and the other parts cut away; or, by another method, the threads were arranged on a frame, all radiating from a common centre, and then worked into patterns. This was the old convent lace of Italy, called "*Greek lace.*" *Point laces* are lace made with a needle on a parchment pattern. The principal are the ancient laces of Italy, Spain, and Portugal; and the modern *point d'Alençon* of France. *Pillow laces* are made by the weaving, twisting, and plaiting of the threads with bobbins on a *cushion;* such are Mechlin, Lille, Valenciennes, Honiton, Buckingham, and many manufactories in France. *Brussels lace* is both *point* and *pillow*. The thread is scarcely visible for fineness, and costs 240*l*. per pound. This lace is called in France *point d'Angleterre*, or *English point*. (Fig. 414.)

Lace Glass. (See GLASS.)

Lacerna, R. An open cloak worn by the Romans over the *toga*, and fastened on the right shoulder with a brooch or fibula. It frequently had a cowl attached. (See ABOLLA, PÆNULA, PALLIUM.)

Lachrymatory. A tear-bottle; so called from the use attributed to it of holding tears consecrated to the dead. These phials are made of glass or earthenware, with a long neck, and the mouth formed to receive the eye-ball. The figure of one or two eyes has sometimes been found impressed upon them.

Lacinia, R. The two excrescences, like a divided dewlap on the throat of a goat, which were represented on the necks of fauns and satyrs.

Laciniæ, Gr. and R. The hanging corners of the *toga* and *chlamys*, and the metal knobs attached to make them hang straight.

Lacis. A kind of embroidery, of subjects in squares, with counted stitches (called also "point conté," darned netting, &c.). (See LACE.)

Laconicum, R. A semicircular termination to a room in a set of baths (*caldarium*), so called because of Spartan origin. Under the word BALNEÆ will be found the *laconicum* of Pompeii, restored. (Fig. 56.)

Lacquer (Fr. *laque*) is made of a solution of shell lac and alcohol, coloured with saffron or other colouring matters. Specimens of ancient Chinese red lacquer deeply carved with figures of birds, flowers, &c., and generally made in the form of trays, boxes, and sometimes vases, are met with in the more northern Chinese towns, and are much prized. What is called the *old gold Japan lacquer* is also esteemed by Chinese connoisseurs, and the specimens of this are comparatively rare at the present day. (*Fortune.*)

Lacs d'amour, Fr. True-lovers' knots.

Lacuna, R. (*lacus,* a hollow). An ash-pit placed beneath a lime-kiln to receive the ashes from the kiln.

Lacunar, Arch. A flat roof or ceiling, in contradistinction to a *camera,* vaulted roof.

Lacunaria, Arch. Panels in a flat ceiling (*lacunar*), formed by the rafters crossing one another at right angles. The edges of these panels are often decorated with carved and gilt ornaments, and the centres filled in with paintings.

Lacus, R. (λάκκος). A lake, and thence a large, shallow, open basin, or artificial reservoir; also, a pit made below the level of a wine-cellar (*cella vinaria*), or of an oil-cellar (*cella olearis*), to receive the wine or oil as it comes from the presses.

Lady. A word of Saxon origin, generally supposed to signify "loaf-giver," from *klaf,* a loaf. As a title it belongs to the daughters of all peers above the rank of a viscount, but is extended by courtesy to the wives of knights.

Lady Day, Chr. The 25th of March. Festival of the Annunciation.

Læna, R. (1) A cloth with a long nap. (2) A thick woollen cloak worn over the toga for the sake of warmth. In later times the læna was often worn as a substitute for the toga.

Lagena, Gr. and R. An earthenware vessel with a swelling body, used for holding wine or vegetables and dried fruits.

Laid Papers. Papers with a ribbed surface; as cream-laid, blue-laid, &c.

Lake, Cloth of, O. E. Linen for under-garments.

Lakes. (See CARMINE.) Pigments of a fine crimson red colour, of which there are several kinds; they are prepared from cochineal, kermes, lac, and the best from madder-root. Common lake is obtained from Brazil wood, which affords a very fugitive colour. (See YELLOW LAKE, PURPLE LAKES, GREEN LAKES, CARMINATED LAKES, DROP LAKE, RED LAKE, MINERAL LAKE, MADDER, &c.)

Lakes of *Florence, Paris, Vienna,* &c. (See CARMINATED LAKES.)

Lamb. The peculiar symbol of the Redeemer, generally the emblem of innocence, meekness, modesty. It is properly called the Paschal Lamb, and with a flag, or between two stars and a crescent, was the badge of the Knights Templars. (See AGNUS DEI.)

Lamboys (Fr. *lambeau*). A kind of skirt over the thighs, worn over the armour. (See Fig. 463.)

Lambrequin. A covering for the helmet. (See MANTLING.)

Lamb's-wool, O. E. A drink of ale with the pulp of roasted apples in it.

Lames, Fr. Flexible plates or *blades* of steel, worn over the hips.

Lametta. Brass, silver, or gold foil or wire.

Lamiæ, Gr. and R. Vampires who fed at night on the flesh of human beings. The Lamiæ of Pliny are animals with the face and head of a woman, and the tail of a serpent, inhabiting the deserts of Africa.

Laminated. Disposed in layers or plates.

Lammas, O. E. The 1st of August.

Fig. 415. Roman Lamp.

Lamp, Lantern, or **Taper,** in Christian art, was an emblem of piety; an attribute of St. Lucia. (See LUCERNA, LYCHNUS, LANTERN.)

Lampadephoria, Gr. (torch-bearing). A game common throughout Greece, in which the competitors raced, either on foot or horseback, six stadia (about three-quarters of a mile), carrying lamps prepared for the purpose. (See LAMPAS.)

Lampas, Gr. and R. A general term denoting anything which shines or affords light; a torch, a lamp, and especially a link. The word was frequently used for *lampadephoria,* the *torch-race.*

Lamp-black. A soot used as a pigment. It is very opaque, and dries slowly in oil. It is also the basis of all printing and lithographic inks.

Lance. In Christian art, the attribute of St. Matthias, in allusion to the method of his martyrdom. (See AMENTUM, LANCEA, HASTA.) A shivered lance with the motto "Lacrymæ hinc, hinc dolor," was a device adopted by Catherine de' Medicis after the fatal accident to her husband, Henry II., in a tournament. (Fig. 416.)

Fig. 416. Device of Catherine de' Medicis.

Lance-rest. A projecting iron fixed to a breastplate to support the end of the lance in a joust or tournament.

Lancea, R. A long, light spear, serving both as a pike and a missile.

Lanceola. Dimin. of LANCEA (q.v.).

Lanceolated, Arch. Having the form of a spear-head. The term is applied to lancet windows, arches, and members of architecture forming a rose.

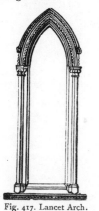

Fig. 417. Lancet Arch. 13th century.

Lancet Arch. A pointed arch, obtuse at the point, resembling a surgeon's lancet, from which a style of architecture, common in England in the 13th century, is named. (Fig. 417.) (See EARLY ENGLISH ARCHITECTURE.)

Lancula, R. (dimin. of LANX). The scale which was placed, when necessary, at one of the ends of a Roman steelyard(*statera*). (Fig. 418.)

Landgrave (Germ. *Land*, *Graf*). A title given to those Counts of Germany who take their rank from a large tract of land. The first *Landgraves* were those of Thuringia, Hesse, Alsace, and Leuchtenberg.

Langue-de-bœuf, Fr. A blade fixed to a pikestaff; named after its shape.

Langued, Her. To denote the tincture of an animal's tongue.

Laniarium, Laniena, R. (*lanius,* a butcher). A slaughter-house or butcher's shop.

Laniers, O. E. Leather straps for various uses; as armlets to a shield, or as garters or bands, &c.

Lanipendia, R. (*lana,* wool, and *pendere,* to weigh). A woman whose duty it was to weigh the wool for spinning, and distribute it among the slaves for their daily tasks.

Lanista, R. A man who trained gladiators for the Roman circus. They were frequently his own property, and he let them out for hire; or he received them from their owners into his *school* (ludus) for training.

Fig. 418. Lancula.

Fig. 419. Old English Horn Lantern.

Lansquenet, Fr. A game at cards.

Lantern. In Christian art, the attribute of St. Gudula, in allusion to the legend of her miraculous lantern, which her prayers rekindled as often as Satan extinguished it. In Architecture, a small turret above the roof of a building, having windows all round it.

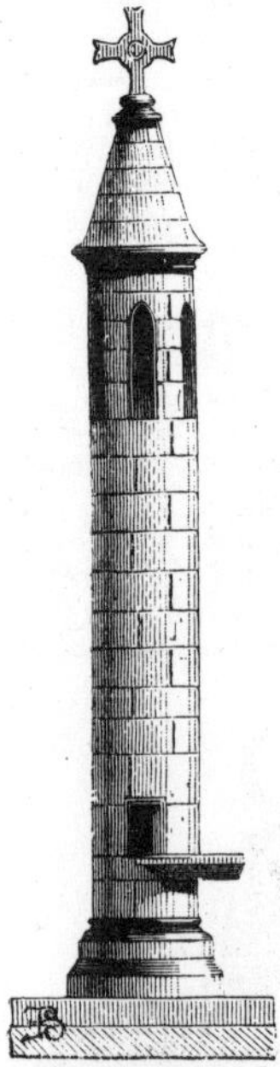

Lanterne des Morts or **Churchyard Beacon,** Arch. A small tower raised upon a base, and generally round, but sometimes square or polygonal; with windows at the top to emit the shining rays from the lamp inside. Fig. 420 represents a "lanterne des morts" at Ciron, France.

Lanx, R. This term denotes (1) a circular dish of silver or other metal, often embossed, used especially at banquets. (2) The scale of a balance (*libra*). (3) A salver for handing fruits or other dainties at dessert.

Laocoon. A magnificent sculpture, found in 1506 among the ruins of the palace of Titus, now in the Vatican. It represents Laocoon and his two sons struggling in the folds of two monster serpents. According to Pliny it is the work of three Rhodian sculptors, Agesander, Polydorus, and Athenodorus, and stood in the palace of Titus. He said that it was made of one stone, but the joining of five pieces has been detected. [See *Lessing's* "*Laokoon.*"]

Fig. 420. Lanterne des Morts.

Laphria, Gr. An annual festival, celebrated at Patræ in Achaia, in honour of Artemis, surnamed Laphria.

Lapidary. An artist who cuts, grinds, and polishes gems and stones. In the lapidary's *scale of hardness* of minerals there are 10 standard degrees, represented as follows:—No. 1, *talc,* which is very easily cut; No. 2, *compact gypsum;* No. 3, *calc-spar;* No. 4, *fluor-spar;* No. 5, *apatite;* No. 6, *felspar;* No. 7, *quartz;* No. 8, *topaz;* No. 9, *sapphire;* No. 10, *diamond.* Diamonds are for the most part cut at Amsterdam.

Lapis Lazuli. A beautiful blue mineral stone of various shades of colour. (See ULTRAMARINE.)

Laquear, Laqueare. Synonym of LACUNAR (q.v.).

Laqueatores, R. An order of gladiators who used a noose to catch their adversaries.

Laqueatus, R. A ceiling decorated with panels (*lacunar*).

Lararium, R. A small shrine consecrated to the gods called Lares ; a room in which the images of the Lares or tutelary genii of the house were placed. It is said to have been customary for religious Romans, immediately after they rose in the morning, to pray in the Lararium.

Larentalia, Larentinalia, or **Laurentalia,** R. A Roman festival in honour of Acca Larentia, the nurse of Romulus and Remus ; or, according to another tradition, a festival instituted by Ancus in honour of a wealthy courtezan named Larentia, who had bequeathed all her property to the Roman people. It was celebrated on the 10th of December.

Lares, R. The Lares Privati, Domestici, or Familiares, were the guardian deities of the house. The spot peculiarly sacred to them was the *focus,* or hearth, in the Atrium, where the altar for domestic sacrifice stood, and near it was a niche, containing little images of these gods, to whom offerings of flowers, frankincense, and wine were made from time to time, and regularly on the kalends of each month. There were many classes of Lares Publici : (1) The Lares rurales, who presided over the flocks, herds, &c. (2) The Lares compitales, worshipped where two cross-roads met, &c. [Cf. Ovid, Fasti, v. 129.]

Larghetto, It. In Music, less slow than *largo.*

Largo, It. In Music, a slow movement, one degree quicker than *adagio.*

Latch, O. E. A cross-bow.

Lateen Sail. A triangular mainsail on a tall sloping yard, which reaches down to the deck.

Later, R. A brick ; the πλίνθος of the Greeks. Among the Romans bricks were of various forms ; the largest was called *pentadorum ;* the next size, *tetradorum. Later coctus, coctilis* was the term applied to a baked brick ; *later crudus* was an unbaked brick, i. e. one dried in the sun. Pliny calls the brick-field LATERARIA.

Latericium (opus), R. A structure built of bricks.

Laterna, Lanterna. A LANTERN (q.v.).

Laton or **Latten,** O. E. An alloy of brass, of which candlesticks, sepulchral monuments, crosses, &c., were made in the Middle Ages. White Laton was a mixture of brass and tin.

Latrunculi, R. (Gr. πεσσοί). The ancient game of draughts. It is mentioned by Homer. The Romans often had twelve lines of squares (*mandræ*) on the draught-board. The number of pieces varied from five to twelve, and in later times the game was played with the *tesseræ* or dice.

Lattice, Arch. A trellis or cross-barred work ; a network window.

Laura, Chr. The origin of the name is obscure. It signifies a collection of separate cells in a wilderness, where a community of monks lived each in his own cell, meeting together only during two days of the week. The most celebrated *lauras* were in Palestine.

Laurel, Gen. The emblem of glory and victory. Sacred also to Apollo. In modern times an emblem of peace.

Lautumiæ, R. (λα-τομία). A stone-quarry, and thence a prison hewn out of a quarry, more particularly the public prison of Syracuse, hewn into the solid cliff, but roofless. The Tullianum at Rome was called Lautumiæ also.

Lava. The scoria from an active volcano, which is well adapted to ornamental carving.

Lavabo. (See LAVATORIUM.)

Lavacrum, R. (*lavo*, to wash). A bath of hot or cold water, in contradistinction to a vapour-bath (*caldarium*).

Lavatorium, R. (*lavo*, to wash). A small building in a monastery, in which the monks washed their hands before and after a repast. The

R. Dudley del.

Fig. 421. Stamped gilt and painted leather hangings illustrating a pictorial arrangement of pattern.

lavatorium was usually placed near the refectory.

Lawn. This fine linen fabric was introduced in the reign of Queen Elizabeth.

Lay Figure. A large wooden jointed doll, used by artists to display drapery.

Lead-glazed Wares. (See POTTERY.)

Leather was used instead of tapestry for the hangings of rooms in the 16th century, and was beautifully gilded and chased. (Consult "L'Art de travailler les Cuirs dorés ou argentés," by M. Fougeroux de Bondary, in "Description des Arts et Métiers," 1762.) (Fig. 421.)

Leaves, Her. Their peculiarities are blazoned as laurel leaf, oak leaf, &c.

Leaves, Leafage. (See FOLIAGE.)

Lebes, Gr. (λέβης; λείβω, to pour out). A brass saucepan or caldron (*pelvis*, *ahenum*); it was a deep vessel with swelling sides. It was sometimes made with a pointed bottom to fit into a stand, which was called INCITEGA.

Lebiton, Lebitonarium. (See COLOBIUM.)

Lecanê, Gr. A drinking-bowl used by the Etrurians (basin-shaped, with a lid).

Lectern. A reading-desk in a Christian church; most frequently of brass in the form of an eagle, but often decorated with more elaborate emblems.

Lectica, R. (*lectus*, a couch). A couch or litter carried by bearers, used both by men and women; it was introduced from the East, and was quickly adopted in Greece and Rome. The Greek litter had a roof made of the skin of an ox, and the sides covered with curtains. Among the Romans it was seldom used excepting for travelling, until the luxurious days of the empire, when the lectica became a very splendid affair. It was sometimes constructed with gold and ivory, and instead of curtains it was closed at the sides, with windows of transparent stone (*lapis specularis*). When standing, it rested on four feet. It was borne upon poles (*asseres*) by two or more slaves, and was called hexophron, octophron, &c., according to the number of *lecticarii* employed to carry it.

Lecticula. Dimin. of *lectica*; it denoted a litter for the conveyance of the sick, or a bier on which a dead body was carried out.

Lectisternium, R. (*lectus*, and *sterno*, to spread out). A religious ceremony consisting of a banquet offered to the gods, at which the statues of the latter were present stretched out on couches, with tables and viands before them as if they were partaking of the feast.

Lectorium, Chr. (*lector*, a reader). An old term afterwards replaced by that of AMBO (q.v.).

Lectrin, Chr. An old term now replaced by *jubé* or rood-loft and desk.

Lectrum, Chr. An old term denoting a praying-desk.

Lectus, R. (*lego*, to put together). A bed or couch complete ; *lectus cubicularis*, a sleeping-couch ; *lectus genialis*, a nuptial bed ; *lectus adversus*, a symbolical marriage-bed ; *lectus triclinaris*, a dining-couch, a couch for three persons, placed in the *triclinium* or dining-room ; *lectus funebris*, a funeral bier. The diminutive of this term is *lectulus*. The *lectus cubicularis* resembled an old-fashioned sofa with a high back ; being of considerable height, it was reached by means of a footstool (*scamnum*), or a set of steps (*gradus*). The *lectus genialis* (Gr. εὐνή) or marriage-bed was still higher, larger, and handsomely decorated ; it is represented with a flight of steps at the foot. The *lectus adversus* was a symbolical marriage-bed, and stood in the atrium, opposite to the entrance of the house, and was, as it were, the throne or seat of office, from which the housewife superintended the spinning, weaving, and similar duties of the servants. The *lectus triclinaris* used at meals is described under the article. *Lectus funebris* is the name of the bier upon which the dead were borne to burial or the pyre.

Fig. 422. Lecythus.

Lecythus, Gr. A cylindrical vase made to contain oil or perfumes. It often figures in the hands of goddesses, or of females at the toilet; and is mostly ornamented with delicate paintings and choice subjects. (Fig. 422.)

Ledger, Arch. A stone slab.

Ledger Lines. In Music, extra lines above or below the five ruled lines.

Ledgment, Arch. A horizontal course of stone or mouldings, particularly the base moulding.

Leet, O. E. An ancient Anglo-Saxon court of justice; a manor court.

Legato, It. Literally, "bound ;" in Music signifies "in a smooth and gliding manner."

Legend. In Numismatics, the words round the *edge* of a medal or coin.

Leghorn. A kind of straw plait, first invented at Leghorn.

Legio, R. (*lego*, to collect). A Roman legion ; a division of the army consisting of from three to six thousand heavy-armed soldiers, who were called *legionarii*. Twelve thousand legionaries were required to make up a consular army. The legion contained troops of all arms ; infantry, cavalry, and the ancient substitutes for artillery ; and was an army complete in itself. The numbers varied, as well as the organization, at different periods. Livy speaks of legions of 5000 infantry and 300 horse. The subject is one demanding voluminous description. The legion was subdivided into Cohortes, Manipuli, Centuriæ, Signa, Ordines, Contubernia.

Leice, Celt. Also called *meanal leice*. The stone of destiny ; a large crystal kept by the Druids for soothsaying.

Leister or **Lister**, Scotch. A trident or many-pronged spear for striking fish.

Leming Star, O. E. (from A.S. *leme*, brightness). A comet.

Lemman (A.S. *leof*=loved, and *man*). A sweetheart, &c.

Lemnian Reddle. An *ochre* of a deep red colour and firm consistence, used as a pigment.

Lemniscus, R. (λημνίσκος ; λῆνος, wool). A fillet or ribbon awarded, as a mark of honour, to a person who had distinguished himself in any way. The person who wore it was called *lemniscatus*. It hung down from crowns or diadems at the back of the head. *Lemnisci* were also worn, without *coronæ*, by ladies for ornament. Hence, in Geometry, a curve of the form of the figure 8 is called *lemniscata*.

Lemon Yellow. A bright pigment, brighter and clearer than Naples yellow or masticot, and not liable to change.

Lemures or **Manes**, R. The souls of the dead, who, according to the religious belief of the Romans, were transformed into beneficent or evil genii, according as the individual had been during his life good or bad, virtuous or worthless. "*Lares* si meriti boni sint; *Lemures* sive *Larvas* si mali ; *Manes* autem cum incertum est," says St. Augustine.

Lemuria. Festivals in honour of the Lemures celebrated at Rome, at night and in silence, on the 9th, 11th, and 13th of May. During them the temples of the gods were closed, and marriage was considered unlucky ; hence the proverb, *Mense Maio male nubent.* Those who celebrated the Lemuria walked bare-footed, washed their hands three times, and threw black beans nine times behind their backs. On the second of the three days there were games in the circus in honour of Mars, and on the third day the images of the thirty Argei, made of rushes, were thrown from the Pons Sublicius into the Tiber by the Vestal virgins. On the same day there was a festival of merchants.

Lenn or **Linn**, Celt. A woollen wrap with a

long nap, or simply the skin of some animal, worn in severe weather as a kind of upper garment by the poorer class of Gauls.

Lens (lit. a lentil). A convex or concave glass, which, by changing the direction of rays of light, magnifies or diminishes objects.

Lent (A.S. *lencten*, Spring), Chr. The forty days' fast preparatory to Easter. Pope Gregory the Great speaks of this fast as of thirty-six days' duration; i. e. six weeks, not counting the Sundays, which, it is suggested, amounts to one-tenth, or a *tithe* of the year.

Lent Rose or **Lent Lily**, O. E. The daffodil.

Lentiform. Shaped like a double convex lens.

Lentiner, O. E. A hawk taken in Lent.

L'Envoy. "The conclusion of a ballet, or sonnet, in a short stanzo by itselfe, and serving oftentimes as a dedication of the whole." (*Cotgrave.*)

Leonine Verses. Rhyming Latin compositions, very popular in the Middle Ages. In the 3rd century a piece of 1200 such verses was written by Commodianus. St. Augustine and the venerable Bede also wrote some. The proper *leonine* consists of a couplet rhyming at the end; but the rhymes may be otherwise distributed: e. g.—

"O miseratrix! O dominatrix! præcipe dictu;
Ne devastemur, ne lapidemur, grandinis ictu."

Leontarium, Chr. A fountain of lions spouting water; frequently placed in the courtyard or atrium of basilican churches.

Leopard, Her. A lion in any other attitude than "rampant" was blazoned by the early heralds as a "leopard." Till the 14th century the lions of the Royal Shield of England were designated leopards.

Leou, Chinese. (1) A building of many stories, like a pagoda. (2) An upper floor in a Chinese house.

Lepastê, R. (λεπάς, a limpet; Lat. *patella*). A large vessel, in form like the *cylix*, but resting on a broad stand; employed from the earliest times for holding pure wine.

Leporarium, R. (*lepus*, a hare). A hare

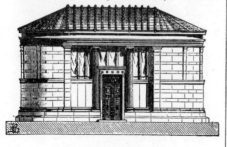

Fig. 423. The Leschê at Delphi.

warren; a walled paddock in which four-footed game were preserved.

Leschê, Gr. (λέσχη, i. e. a place for talking). A public place of assembly and conversation, or a small exchange for transacting business, &c. The leschê of Delphi (Fig. 423) was celebrated for the painting which it contained by Polygnotus (470 B.C.). At Athens there were 360 leschai, small buildings or porticoes furnished with seats and exposed to the sun, where the poor could rest in warmth and shelter.

Lesina, It. An awl. The device of the Lesina Academy, with the motto, "*L'assotigliar la più, meglio anche fora.*"

Lettern, Arch. The *Lectern* of a church is often so called, when made of *Latten* or brass. The word is used instead of *Latten*.

Letters of the Alphabet are sometimes used as charges in heraldry. The practice of weaving letters into the ornamentation of textile fabrics is very ancient in the East. Pliny says, "Parthi *literas* vestibus intexunt." Fanciful designs imitating or copying oriental letters without meaning were worked in church textiles in early Christian times; and the artists of Italy up to the middle of the 16th century represented such devices on the hems of the garments of great personages in their paintings.

Leucite (λευκός, white). *White spar*, or *white garnet*; a white stony substance found among volcanic productions.

Leucomb, O. E. A dormer window.

Leucopyrite. A mineral used in the production of artificial *orpiment*.

Levacion, O. E. The elevation of the host in the mass.

Levant. The Eastern shores of the Mediterranean.

Levecel, O. E. A penthouse or projecting roof over a door or an open shed.

Levesele, O. E. A lattice. The original of the *chequers* on the door-posts of inns.

Levitonarium. (See COLOBIUM.)

Lew, O. E. (modern *lea*). Sheltered from the wind; hence **Lewe Water** (modern *luke*-warm water).

Lewins, O. E. A kind of bands put about a hawk.

Libbard, O. E. A leopard.

Libella, R. (*libra*, a level or balance). (1) A level, or instrument employed by masons, joiners, and carpenters, in the same way as with us, for testing the evenness of the surface of their work. (2) A small Roman silver coin, afterwards substituted by the *As*, which it equalled in value.

Libellus or **Libellulus**, R. A small book, pamphlet, letter, or notice.

Liber (literally, the *rind* of the papyrus; Gr. βιβλίον, from the Egyptian word *byblos*, the papyrus plant). A book.—Parchment (*membrana*) was invented by Eumenes, king of Pergamos;

O

hence its name of *pergamentum*. The paper (*charta*) or parchment was only written upon on one side; the other side was stained yellow. Writings were frequently washed off, and the parchment used again was called *palimpsestus*. The sheets forming a book were joined together and rolled round a staff, and then called a *volume* (*volumen*). The stick was usually ornamented with balls or bosses, ornamented or painted, called *umbilici*. The ends of the roll, carefully cut, polished with pumice-stone, and coloured black, were called *geminæ frontes*. The reader held the staff in his left hand to unroll the sheet (*evolvere librum*), as he proceeded, with his right. The roll, if valuable, was kept in a parchment case, which was stained with a purple colour, or yellow. The title of the book (*titulus* or *index*) was written on a small strip of papyrus or parchment with a light red colour (coccum or minium); and this practice was the origin of the art of illumination.

Liber Pontificalis, *seu de gestis Romanorum pontificum.* A work of the 15th century, of great value to the student of early Christian art work, and in particular of textiles and embroidery.

Libra, R. (1) A balance with two scales (*lanx*), depending by chains from the ends of the beam (*jugum*); in the centre of the latter was a handle (*ansa*). (2) The As or pound; the unit of weight. (See As.)

Libretto, It. The words of an opera, oratorio, &c.

Librile, R. (*libra*). A term denoting the ends of the beam (*jugum*) in a balance, and thence the balance itself; it is thus synonymous with LIBRA (q.v.).

Liburna, Liburnica, R. A vessel of war so called from the fact that it was built on a model invented by the Illyrian pirates, or Liburni.

Lichanos, Gr. (*forefinger string*). The note below the MESE of the seven-stringed lyre. (See MESE.)

Lich-gate. A shed over the gate of a churchyard to rest the corpse under. (See CORPSE-GATE.) (Fig. 197.)

Lich-stone—near a churchyard gate, for resting coffins on—is generally raised about three feet from the ground, shaped like a coffin, and has stone benches round it for the bearers to rest upon.

Liciæ, Med. Lat. (Fr. *lices*), from the Italian *lizza*, palings. The lists; an enclosed space surrounding a camp or castle.

Licium, R. A leash, or thick thread, employed to divide in two a set of threads in a warp, in order to allow the shuttle to pass through them. By analogy, any kind of thread or cord used for fastening.

Lictor, R. (See FASCES.)

Lieberkuhn. A reflecting mirror on a microscope, named after the inventor.

Lierne Rib (in a vault), Arch. (From *lier*, to bind.) "Any rib that does not arise from the impost, and is not a ridge rib, but crosses from one boss or intersection of the principal ribs to another. Vaults in which such *liernes* are employed are termed LIERNE VAULTS." (*Parker's Glossary.*)

Light Red. A pigment of a russet orange tint, produced from burnt ochre.

Lights. The openings between the mullions of a window. (See DAYS.)

Ligula, R. (1) A small tongue-shaped sword.

Fig. 424. Ligula.

(Fig. 424.) The term is derived from *lingua*, a tongue. (2) A liquid measure, a *large* spoonful, distinguished from *cochlear*, which is a *small* spoonful. (3) The leather tongue of a shoe.

Lilies, in Christian art, are the symbols of purity; the special attribute of the Virgin Mary. They are frequent in the catacombs on the tombs of Christian virgins.

Lily or **Iris Green** (It. *verde giglio*). A pigment anciently used in Italy. It was prepared by dipping linen rags into the juice of plants, and then preserving them dry.

Lima, R. (1) A file or rasp, applied to the same purposes as at the present day. (See SCOBINA.) (2) In Med. Lat., a tool or weapon worn by archers in the French service, either as a kind of sword or for sharpening arrows with. (*Meyrick.*)

Limbeck, O. E. An alembeck.

Limbo, O. E. Hell.

"Beholde now what owre Lord Jhesu dide one the Saturday, as sune as he was dede. He went downe to helle to owre holy fadyrs that ware in *lymbo* to tyme of his Resureccione." (*MS. Lincoln.* A. i. 17, f. 186.)

Limbus. An ornamental band or border resembling scroll-work or architectural foliage, employed as an ornament on dress, vases (especially on Etruscan vases), &c.; and thence (1) a ribbon worn as an ornament in the hair; (2) the zodiacal circle described on a globe (see Fig. 48); (3) a stout cord forming the main rope in a fishing-net; (4) in Med. Latin, a military tunic—the German *Wapenrock*; or a wrapper worn by soldiers round the head, *temp.* John, usually termed *cargan*. (*Meyrick.*)

Lime. Slaked lime, alone or mixed with pulverized white marble, was a white pigment used in fresco-painting.

Lime-hound, O. E. A sporting-dog in a *lime* or leash.

Limen, R. The threshold or step laid down before the entrance of a door; the same term is also applied to the lintel. *Limen superius* is the lintel, and *limen inferius* the threshold properly so called.

"Limen superum inferumque, salve!" (*Plautus.*)

Limer, O. E. A bloodhound. "A dogge engendred betweene an hounde and a mastyve, called a *lymmer*, or a mungrell."

Limitour, O. E. A begging friar.

Limning, O. E. Painting, especially portrait painting.

Limoges Enamel. A kind of incrusted enamel on the system called *champlevé*; perfected at Limoges, in France, in the 15th century, and hence called *Opus de Limogia*. (See ENAMEL.) The enamels and METAL WORK of LIMOGES, in furniture, decoration of armour, and church utensils, are very important. The monument of Aylmer de Valence in Westminster Abbey is Limoges workmanship.

Limus, R. A kind of apron bordered with a purple hem, worn by the *popa* or attendant who killed the animal offered at a sacrifice.

Lincei. An academy for natural history, founded in Rome in 1603. They adopted the lynx for their device "because the academicians should have the eyes of a lynx to penetrate the secrets of nature." (*Mrs. Bury-Palliser.*)

Line of Beauty. A curve like an elongated S. (See *Hogarth's Analysis of Beauty.*)

Line of Life. One of the lines in the hand; a term in palmistry.

Linea, R. (*linum*, a flax-thread). A line or any kind of string; *linea alba*, a rope whitened with chalk and stretched across the arena in a circus for the purpose of giving a fair start to runners, chariots, or riders.

Lined, Her. (1) Having a cord attached. (2) Having a lining.

Lineleon. Linseed oil. "*Lineleon ex semine lini fiet.*"

Linen. Painting on linen was largely practised in England during the 14th century; and a drawing sent by Albert Durer to Raphael is described by Vasari as having been painted "in water colours on a fine linen cloth, which showed the transparent lights on both sides, without white; water-colours only being added, while the cloth was left for the lights; which thing appeared wonderful to Raphael." (*Vasari, Vita di Raffaello.*)

Linen-scroll. A decorative ornament, common in German wood-carving of the 15th and 16th centuries. It resembles a napkin stood on end, and partly opened into scroll-shaped cylinders.

Linset, O. E. The stool on which women sat while spinning.

Linsey-woolsey (O. E. Lylse-wulse). Coarse woollen stuff first made at Linsey in Suffolk.

Linstock, O. E. (15th century). A pike, with branches on each side to hold a lighted match for firing artillery.

Lintel. The stone or beam placed across a door or window overhead (*limen superius*).

Linteolum, R. and Chr. (*linteum*). Any small piece of linen, such as a napkin or handkerchief.

Linter, R. A flat boat, frequently formed of the trunk of a tree, used in shallow waters for the transport of produce; it was also used in the construction of bridges of boats.

Linum, R. (λίνον). Flax, and thence anything made of that fibre.

Lion, O. E. (from *lie on*). The main beam of a ceiling.

Rampant.   Statant guardant.   Rampant guardant.

Passant guardant.   Statant.   Passant.

Fig. 425. Heraldic Lions.

Lion. In Heraldry, the lion *couchant* represents sovereignty; *rampant*, magnanimity; *passant*, resolution; *guardant*, prudence; *saliant*, valour; *seiant*, counsel; and *regardant*, circumspection. (See LEOPARD, MARZOCCO.)

Lioncel, Her. A lion drawn to a small scale, generally rampant.

Lions, in Christian art, typify the resurrection of the Redeemer; because, according to an oriental fable, the lion's cub was born dead, and in three days its sire licked it into life. The lion also typifies solitude, and is therefore the attribute of hermits; and as the type of fortitude and resolution it was placed at the feet of martyrs.

Lip Moulding, Arch. So called from its resemblance to an overhanging lip. It is common in the Perpendicular period.

Liquid Madder Lake or **Rubiate.** A brilliant rose-coloured pigment, used in oil or water-colour painting.

Liripipes, O. E. The long tails of hoods, which hung down the back. Worn also by the Italians. (Fig. 426.)

List, Arch. A straight upright ring encircling the lower part of a column, just above the torus, and next to the shaft.

List, Listel, Arch. A small square moulding, also called a *fillet*. Fig. 427 represents a base, the ornamentation of which is made up of numerous *listels* or fillets.

Litany Stool. In a church, a small low desk at which the Litany was sung.

"The priest goeth from out of his seat into the body of the church, and (at a low desk before the chancel door, called the *faldstool*) kneels and says or sings the Litany." (*Eliz.* xviii. 1559.)

Q 2

Fig. 426. Liripipes. Italian, 16th century.

Literatus or **Litteratus**, R. (*litera*, a letter). In general, anything that is marked with letters; and thence (1) a slave who has been branded on the forehead with a hot iron, also called *inscriptus, notatus, stigmatus*. (2) A grammarian, learned man, or commentator.

Fig. 427. Listels.

Litharge. An ingredient of *drying-oil* (q.v.).
Lithochrome. Another name for CHROMO-LITHOGRAPHY, or colour-printing.
Lithography, or drawing on stone, was invented by Aloys Senefelder of Munich in 1796. Drawings are made on a polished surface of calcareous stone, with ink and chalk of a soapy nature. The *lithographic ink* is made of tallow-soap, pure white wax, lamp-black, and a small quantity of tallow, all boiled together, and, when cool, dissolved in

distilled water; the ingredients for the *lithographic chalk* are the same, with a small quantity of potash added during the boiling. After the drawing on the stone is perfectly dry, a very weak solution of sulphuric acid is poured over it, which takes up the alkali from the ink or chalk, and leaves an insoluble substance behind it, while it lowers in a slight degree the surface of the stone not drawn upon, and prepares it for the free absorption of water. Weak gum-water is next applied to close the pores of the stone, and to keep it moist. The stone is then washed with water, and the printing-ink applied in the ordinary way. It then passes through the press, the washing with water and daubing with ink being repeated after every impression. As many as 70,000 copies have in this way been taken from one stone, the last being nearly as good as the first. Copper-plate and steel engravings can be transferred to stone. (See the article "Lithography" in the *Encyclopædia Britannica*, 8th ed.)

Lithostrotum, R. (λιθό-στρωτον). The pavement of a Roman road, and thence any ornamental pavement, mosaic, incrusted marble, coloured inlaid-work, &c.

Litmus or **Lacmus.** The red, violet, and blue colours known as *archil, cudbear*, and *litmus*, are derived from certain lichens; *litmus* from the *roccella tinctoria*.

Liturgy (λειτουργός). The printed formulary according to which the public services in a church are performed.

Lituus, R. (an Etruscan word, signifying *crooked*). (1) A brass trumpet formed of a long, straight tube, but curved and opening out wide at the end like a tobacco-pipe. The *tuba* was straight, the *cornu* spiral. (2) An augur's staff curved into the form of a crook, with which they divided the expanse of the sky into regions in their divinations.

Livery (Fr. *livrée*). Literally, the *distribution*; that is to say, of clothes to be worn by the servants of palaces, &c. (See BADGES.)

Livery Colours. In the Middle Ages all great houses had their own livery colours. Thus those of the House of York were blue and crimson, those of the House of Lancaster white and blue, of the House of Tudor white and green, of the House of Stuart scarlet and gold.

Loaves, in Christian art, are the emblems of charity to the poor; the attribute of St. Philip the Apostle and other saints.

Lobe (of an arch), Fr.; Anglicé *foil;* e. g. a trefoil arch is *arc trilobé.*

Local Colour is the real fundamental colour of an object, considered apart from all accidental variations of light and reflexion.

Locellus, R. A box or casket; this term is a diminutive of LOCULUS.

Lochaber Axe. A short pole with a sharp

axe at one end, an ancient weapon of the Highlanders of Scotland.

Locker, Chr. Arch. A cupboard for sacred vessels generally left in the thickness of the wall on the north side of the altar of a church. (See SECRETARIUM.)

Locking up. Any process by which a colour, liable to be affected by damp, can be rendered durable.

Loculamentum, R. (*loculus,* a little place). Any box, chest, or case, the interior of which is divided into compartments.

Loculus, R. (dimin. of *locus,* a place). (1) A coffin, generally of stone. (See SARCOPHAGUS.) (2) A compartment in the manger of a stable. (3) A small chest fitted with compartments.

Locutorium, Chr. Of a convent, &c., the *parlour.*

Figs. 428, 429. Badge of Richard II. in Westminster Hall.

Lodged, Her. Said of animals of the chase *in repose.* The illustration shows the favourite badge of Richard II.: a white hart chained, and in an attitude of rest. " This device is repeated in *Westminster Hall* 83 times; and all are equally consistent with heraldic truth and accuracy, without any of them being an exact counterpart of any other." (*Boutell, English Heraldry.*) (Fig. 428.)

Loegria, O. E. England. (*Geoffry of Monmouth.*)

Logan Stones (properly *logging stones,* from O. E. *log,* to oscillate). ROCKING STONES (q.v.).

Logeum, Gr. (λογεῖον). A Greek term synonymous with PULPITUM (q.v.).

Loggia, It. The gallery, or corridor, of a palace.

Lombard Architecture. " A style invented by the Lombards (Longobardi) in the 7th century in imitation of the Roman. It continued in use till the 10th century, and gave place to the Norman style. It is rude, heavy, and massive, with small narrow windows." (*Parker.*) The above is only one application of the term, which is applied by different writers to a great number of different styles. The *Lombardesque* style (It. *lo stile Lombardesco*) applies to the architectural works of the family of Pietro Lom-

bardo (15th century). The *Lombard Gothic* is still another style (of the 12th century).

Loops, Loups, Arch. Another name for CRENELS (q.v.), or embrasures.

Lord. The word is Saxon ; from *hlaf* or *klaf,* a loaf of bread ; and *ford,* to give ; hence it means originally *bread-giver.*

Fig. 430. Gallic cuirass in the Louvre.

Lorica, Gr. and R. (*lorum,* a thong). A cuirass; it was made either —for officers, of two γύαλα, the breast and back-pieces; or, for the soldiers, of a number of small metal scales or bands, fastened together with rivets or rings, and flexible. Among the Asiatics the cuirass was frequently made of cotton ; and among the Sarmatians, and other nations, of horn.

Fig. 431. Fragment of a Gallic cuirass.

Lorimers, O. E. Bit-makers.

Lorraine Cross. A cross with two projecting arms on each side.

Lorraine Glass for painted windows ; obtained from the Vosges as early as the 13th century, and then called Burgundy glass. "When any one means to paint, let him choose the Lorraine glass, which inclines to the white yellow because that bears the fire best, and receives the colour better than any other." (*Félibien,* 1619.)

Lota. A sacred utensil in India, used in ceremonial and other ablutions. It is a globular bowl with a low narrow neck, sometimes chased or engraved and incrusted.

Lotus (λωτός). The lotus is a frequently recurring *cyma* in Hindoo architecture. In Egyptian archæology, the lotus, of which two partially opened buds may be seen in Fig. 432, was the symbol of the rising of the sun, of fertilization, life, and resurrection. The lotus appears in the ornamentation of the largest as well as of the smallest monuments of Egyptian art; and is the motive of many of the columns and capitals of the temples and palaces of a certain period, as well as of the decoration of vases and other small objects. Three lotus-stems issuing from a basin symbolized Upper Egypt.

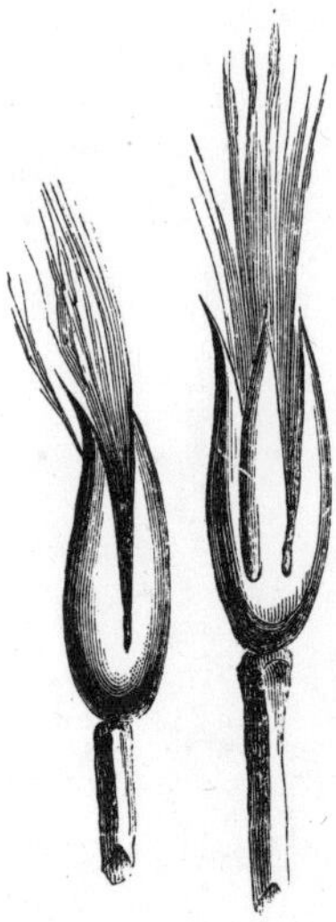

Louis d'Or, Fr. A gold coin, value about 20s., first struck in 1640.

Louis Treize Style (Arch.), a French version of Italian art, prevailed from 1625 to 1650, and produced *Jean le Pautre*, the ornamentist, and the following styles :—

Fig. 432. Lotus-flowers.

Louis Quatorze, Arch. A style of ornament developed towards the close of the 17th century (1643—1715). It is described as "essentially an *ornamental* style, its chief aim being effect by a brilliant play of light and shade ; colour, or mere beauty of form in detail, having no part in it. This style arose in Italy, and the Chiesa del Gesù at Rome is mentioned as its type or model. The great medium of the Louis Quatorze was gilt stucco-work, which, for a while, seems to have almost wholly superseded decorative painting ; and this absence of colour in the principal decorations of the period seems to have led to its more striking characteristic,— infinite play of light and shade." (*Wornum, Analysis of Ornament.*) In this style symmetry was first systematically avoided. In the *Furniture* of the period the characteristic details are the scroll and shell. The classical ornaments and all the elements of the *Cinque-cento*, from which the Louis Quatorze proceeded, are admitted under peculiar treatment, as accessories ; the panels are formed by chains of scrolls, or a combination of the scroll and shell. Versailles is the great repertory of the Louis Quatorze (Fig. 433), and the designs of Watteau ts finest exemplification.

Louis Quinze, Arch. This style (1715—74) is the exaggeration of the Louis Quatorze, rejecting all symmetry, and introducing elongation of the foliations of the scroll, mixed up with a species of crimped conventional *coquillage* or shell-work. The style found its

culmination in the bizarre absurdities of the Rococo.

Louvre, Arch. The open turret in the roofs of ancient halls, through which the smoke escaped before the introduction of modern chimneys.

Louvre-boarding or **Luffer-boarding, Arch.** A series of overlapping boards sloping from the top downwards, and from within outwards, and fixed in a framework of timber. They are placed in the apertures of towers and belfries for the sake of ventilating the timbers, and are sloped to prevent rain and snow from penetrating within, and to direct the sound of the bells downwards. Sometimes the wooden boardings are covered with lead, slate, or zinc, in order to preserve them.

Louvre-window, Belfry-arch, Arch. The large lights fitted with louvre-boarding in belfries.

Love-apple. The tomato is so called.

Love-feast. An annual feast celebrated in some parishes in England on the Thursday before Easter. (See *Edwards's Old English Customs.*)

Love-in-Idleness, O. E. The heart's-ease.

Love-knot. A complicated figure by which an interchange of affection is supposed to be figured.

Love-lies-bleeding, O. E. A flower; a kind of amaranth.

Love-lock. A long ringlet of hair worn on the left side of the head, and allowed to stream down the shoulder sometimes as far as the elbow. The love-lock is mentioned in Queen Elizabeth's reign. "Will you be Frenchified, with a love-lock down to your shoulders, wherein you may weave your mistress's favour?" (*Quip for an Upstart Courtier.*)

"Why should thy sweete love-locke hang dangling downe,
Kissing thy girdle-stud with falling pride ?
Although thy skin be white, thy haire is browne ;
Oh, let not then thy haire thy beautie hide."
(*The Affectionate Shepheard.*)

Lovel, O. E. A dog.

"The Ratte, the Catte, and Lovell our dogge,
Rule all England under the hogge." (1484.)

Low Side-window, Arch. A peculiar small window found in many churches near the west end of the chancel, and very near the ground. It was never glazed, but closed with wooden or iron gratings. Its object has never been ascertained. Most of the examples are of the 13th or 14th century. (See *Archæological Journal*, vol. iv. p. 314.)

Low Sunday, Chr. The Sunday next after Easter.

Lozenge. In Heraldry, the diamond-shaped figure used for a shield to display the arms of spinsters and widows. The *lozenge* is always

Fig. 433. Heraldic Decoration at Versailles—Louis Quatorze.

Lucerna, R. (*luceo*, to shine). An oil-lamp of terra-cotta or bronze. (Fig. 435.) On one side they had a handle, and on the other one or more places for wicks (*myxæ*). The oil was poured in through an opening in the centre. *Lucerna bilychnis, trilychnis, polylychnis,* and *lucerna bimyxos, trimyxos,* or *polymyxos,* were respectively lamps with two, three, or several nozzles, or with two, three, or several wicks; *lucerna pensilis* was a hanging lamp. (See Fig. 435.)

Lucidæ, Med. Lat. Lustrous varnishes.

Lucifer (*lux*, light; *fero*, to bring). The morning or evening star.

Lucta, Luctamen, Luctatio (Gr. πάλη, πάλαισμα, παλαισμοσύνη, or καταβλητική). Wrestling. In the Homeric age the wrestlers contended naked, excepting the *perizoma* round the loins; about B.C. 720 (the 15th Olympiad) this was discarded. The Cretans and Lacedæmonians, and afterwards the Greeks, anointed the body with oil, and then strewed it over with sand or dust. The Lucta or Palé differed from the *Pancratium.* In the latter,

placed upright on the shield, and its true proportions are as 5 to 4. (See MASCLE.)

Lozenge Moulding or **Lozenge Fret.** An ornament used in Norman architecture, presenting the appearance of diagonal ribs, enclosing diamond-shaped panels.

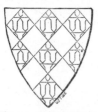

Fig. 434. Shield of Hubert de Burgh, Earl of Kent.

Lozenges. A term in wood-engraving for a class of fine gravers used for outlines and very fine shading.

Lozengy, Her. A field divided lozengewise. (Fig. 434.)

Lucariæ, R. Festivals instituted at Rome to commemorate the refuge which the Roman army had once found in a wood (*lucus*) between the Via Salaria and the left bank of the Tiber. At the time of the invasion of the Gauls in the year 365 B.C., the Roman army would have been entirely cut to pieces but for this refuge.

Lucarne, Fr. Arch. A dormer or garret window.

Luce, Her. The fish now called a pike. (Fig. 380.)

Fig. 435. Bronze Lucerna. Roman.

boxing and wrestling were combined, and the contest continued until one party was killed, or unable to continue. In wrestling, on the other hand, the victory was awarded to the man who first threw the other three times. The most famous wrestler of antiquity was Milo of Crotona, who flourished B.C. 509, and was seven times crowned at the Pythian games, and six times at Olympia.

Lucullite. A variety of black marble, first brought to Rome from an island at Assouan on the Nile by Lucullus.

Ludi. Games at festivals, or a general name for such festivals as consisted entirely of games and contests. *Ludi circenses* were games held in the circus, gladiatorial and other. (See CIRCUS.) *Ludi scenici* were theatrical representations. *Ludi stati*, like the *Feriæ statæ*, were those held regularly on certain days marked in the calendar. *Ludi imperativi*, on the other hand, were held by special appointment, and *votivi* in fulfilment of vows. The games were superintended by the ÆDILES. The principal games will be found described under the headings Apollinares, Augustales, Capitolini, Circenses, Compitalia, Floralia, Funebres, Liberales or Dionysia, Megalesia, Plebeii, Sæculares, &c.

Ludus, R. A game or pastime; *ludus litterarius*, or *ludus* simply, was a school for the instruction of youth; *ludus duodecim scriptorum*, a kind of backgammon played by the ancients; *ludus fidicium*, a music school; *ludus gladiatorius*, a school for gladiators directed by a *lanista*.

Lumachel (It. *lumachella*, a little snail). A marble full of fossil shells, and of beautiful iridescent colours, sometimes a deep red or orange; called also *fire marble*.

Luna, R. (lit. moon). An ivory or silver shoe-buckle worn by Roman senators. (Compare LUNULA.)

Lunated. Crescent-shaped.

Lunette. (1) In Fortification, a work with two *faces* and two flanks, i. e. a REDAN to which flanks or lateral wings have been added; in form, therefore, it resembles a BASTION. (2) In Architecture, a crescent or semicircular window, or space above a square window beneath a rounded roof. Hence the *paintings* on such a space are called *lunettes*; e. g. those of Raffaelle in the Vatican.

Lunula, R. (dimin. of *luna*). (1) An ornament in the form of a crescent worn by women round the neck. (2) The white moon-shaped marks at the roots of the finger-nails. (Cf. MENIS.)

Lupatum, R. A jagged bit with teeth like a saw (*lupus*); whence its name.

Lupercalia, R. Festivals held at Rome on the fifteenth of the calends of March (15th of February), in the *Lupercal*, a sacred

enclosure or cave on the Palatine, regarded as the den of the she-wolf who nursed Romulus and Remus. The *luperci* assembled together and sacrificed goats and young dogs, with the skins of which they ran through the streets half naked. [Lupercus, or Februus, was the god of fertility. The festival was originally a shepherd festival; the ceremony was symbolical of a purification of shepherds, and commemorated the time when Rome was a nation of shepherds.]

Lupus, R. (lit. wolf). (1) A hand-saw. (2) *Lupus ferreus*, a huge iron hook, lowered from the walls of a besieged place to catch the point of the battering-ram. (See HARPAGA.)

Lura, R. Literally, the mouth of a large leathern sack for wine and oil, and thence the sack itself.

Lure. A falconer's decoy, made of feathers on a cord, to attract a hawk back to the wrist. The illustration is a heraldic *lure.* (See Fig. 91. See also IN LURE.)

Fig. 435 a. Hawk's Lure.

Lusiad. The great epic of the Portuguese poet Camoens.

Lustratio (Gr. κάθαρσις). A purification, originally by water, afterwards by solemn ceremonies of sprinkling, or the smoke of sacrifice; made privately after deaths or accidental pollutions, and publicly on the occasion of public disasters, prodigies, or the like; and at certain fixed periods, especially at the close of every *lustrum*.

Lustricus (sc. *dies*), R. (*lustrum*, a lustration). The day of purification for a new-born infant, when it received its name.

Lustrum, R. (*luo*, to wash). A solemn purification performed by the censors on laying down their office, that is to say, every *five years*; whence the term was used to denote that space of time.

Lute (Arabic, *el oud*). A stringed instrument of great antiquity, first mentioned in Persia in 682 A.D. Before the 10th century the lute had only four strings, or four pairs producing four tones, each tone having two strings tuned in unison. About the 10th century a string for a fifth tone was added. The strings were made of silk neatly twisted. The neck of the instrument was provided with frets of string, regulated according to the system of seventeen intervals to an octave. The Chinese god of music is represented playing on a lute with four strings. The lute was very popular in England in Elizabeth's time. Originally it had eight catgut strings, arranged in four pairs, each pair being in unison. The number of strings varied from time to time, and in the 17th century they were twenty-four. The size of the lute also varied; the treble lute was the smallest, and the bass lute the largest. There were also the ARCHLUTE, the CHITARRONE, THEORBO, &c. (Consult Thomas Mace's *Musick's Monument*, 1676.)

Lycæa. A festival of the Arcadians in honour of Zeus Λυκαῖος.

Lyceium. A sacred enclosure at Athens, dedicated to Apollo Lycius, where the *polemarch* originally held his court. It was decorated with fountains, plantations, and ornamental edifices by Peisistratus, Pericles, and Lycurgus. Here Aristotle delivered his lectures, as he *walked about* with his followers, hence called "*Peripatetics.*"

Fig. 436. Lychnus.

Lychnus, Lychnuchus, R. (λύχνος, λυχνοῦχος). The former of these terms is of by far the most frequent occurrence. It denotes a kind of lantern or candlestick made to support oil lamps (*lucernæ*). Fig. 436 represents a lychnus supporting three *lucernæ*.

Lydian. *Of music*, soft and slow; *generally* effeminate.

Lydian Stone (*Lydius lapis* or *Heraclius lapis*) was a kind of flinty slate used by the ancients as a touchstone for the trial of gold and silver.

Lymphad, Her. An ancient galley, the feudal ensign of the house of Lorn, and as such quartered by the Dukes of Argyle. It is borne also by the Prince of Wales as "Lord of the Isles." (Fig. 437.)

Lynx Sapphire. A lapidary's term for dark-grey or greenish-blue varieties of the sapphire.

Lyon King at Arms. The Scotch Herald, Lord Lyon. The regalia of

Fig. 437. Lymphad.

this officer are, a crown of gold, with a crimson velvet cap, &c.; a velvet robe reaching to his feet, with the arms of the kingdom embroidered thereon, both before and behind, in the proper tinctures; a triple row of gold chains round his neck, with an oval gold medal pendent thereto, on one side of which is the royal bearing, and on the other St. Andrew with his cross enamelled in proper colours, and a baton of gold enamelled green, powd ed with the badges of the kingdom.

Lyra, Gr. and R. (λύρα). A lyre; a stringed instrument which assumed var.ous forms. On Assyrian monuments the lyre occurs in three different forms, and is held horizontally in playing. Its front bar was generally either oblique or slightly curved. It was played with a *plectrum* or with the fingers. The HEBREW lyre is represented on coins of Judas Maccabæus. Some have three strings, others five, and others six. The two sides of the frames appear to have been made of horns of animals. The Hebrew square-shaped lyre is probably the PSALTERION; the KINNOR, a lyre of triangular shape, the instrument of King David, is named in the Bible as the oldest stringed instrument, the invention of Jubal. The Rabbis record that King David used to suspend his over his pillow at night. On Egyptian monuments, at Beni Hassan, a Hebrew lyre is represented, probably of the date of Joseph, 1700 B.C. The GREEKS had lyres of many kinds, distinguished by different names; LYRA, a generic term, and also the lyre oval at the base, to be held in the lap; KITHARA, with a square base, to be held against the breast; CHELYS, a small lyre with body made of tortoise-shell; PHORMIX, a large lyre, &c. Some lyres have a bridge, others have none; the largest were probably held on or between the knees, or were tied by a band to the left arm. The strings of catgut or sinew were twanged with a *plektron* or short stem of ivory or metal, pointed at both ends. The lyre was the most favourite instrument of the ROMANS, under various names. The CORNU had a frame ending at the top in two long horns; the BARBITOS was a lyre with a large body; the PSALTERIUM was of an oblong square shape, &c. The lyre is represented in early CHRISTIAN monuments of the 4th century. In one of them the Saviour is represented as Apollo touching the lyre. ANGLO-SAXON MSS. of the 9th century also represent the lyre. A GERMAN fiddle of the 9th century, with only one string, is called *lyra* in the MS. In Christian symbolism the lyre represented "the attractive power of the Lord." (See MESE.)

Lysis, Arch. A plinth, or step above the cornice of the *podium* which surrounds the PEDESTAL.

M.

M-roof, Arch. A roof formed by the junction of two common roofs, with a valley between them.

Macabre. (See DANCE OF DEATH.)

Macaronic Verses. A burlesque of Latin, chequered with Italian, Tuscan, and plebeian words, described by the author :—

"Ars ista poetica nuncupatur Ars Macaronica, a Macaronibus derivata ; qui Macarones sunt quoddam pulmentum, farina, caseo, butyro compaginatum, grossum, rude et rusticanum. Ideo Macaronica nil nisi grossedinem, ruditatem, et *Vocabulazzos* debet in se continere."

Macchia, It. (lit. a spot or stain). "The blocking out of the masses of light and shade." (See *Eastlake's Materials*, &c., ii. 355.)

Mace (Fr. *masse* or *massue*). A military club or staff, generally of iron with a wooden handle, useful for breaking defensive armour. The mace was generally worn at the saddle-bow ; and was subsequently perforated to form a pistol, and finally superseded by the pistol. In the Middle Ages the mace became an emblem of office ; and is so still—usually surmounted by a crown. (See CLAVA, CLUB.)

Macellarius, R. (*macellum*, a market). A keeper of a shop for the sale of fruit and cooked provisions. His shop was called *taverna macellaria*.

Macellum, Gr. and R. (μάκελλον). A covered market in which were sold all kinds of provisions, such as fish, poultry, and game ; it was distinct from the open market called FORUM (q.v.).

Maceria, R. (1) A rough wall formed of materials of every description, and having no *facing*. (2) An enclosed place unroofed. (Fig. 438.)

Fig. 438. Maceria.

Machæra, Gr. and R. (μάχαιρα). A sword with only one edge, made rather for cutting than thrusting.

Machærium, Gr. and R. (μαχαίριον). Dimin. of *machæra*, a knife employed chiefly by fishermen.

Machærophorus, Gr. and R. (μαχαιρο-φόρος). Literally, *armed with the hunting-knife*, the *machærium ;* an epithet of the so-called *barbarous* nations, such as the Egyptians, Persians, Medes, Thracians, and Gauls.

Machicolated, Arch. Furnished with machicolations.

Machicolations (Fr. *machicoulis*), Arch. Openings or grooves made under the parapet of a fortified place, through which stones, pitch, boiling water, or hot sand were thrown down.

Macrochera, Gr. (μακρό-χειρ, long-armed). A tunic with long sleeves, called by the Romans CHIRIDOTA.

Macrocolum, **Macrocollum**, R. Paper of the largest size, that is to say, in sheets formed of a number of pieces of parchment or papyrus glued together.

Macula, R. The mesh of a net ; in the plural *maculæ*.

Madder. The root of "rubia tinctoria" (Fr. *garance*), from which a number of valuable pigments are made, which are transparent and permanent, working equally well in oil and in water colours. They vary from the lightest and most delicate rose to the deepest purple, and are known as *rose madder, pink madder, madder-carmine, purple madder, brown madder, intense madder-purple,* and *orange madder-lake.*

Madonna, It. The Virgin Mary. (See JOYS.)

Mæander, Gr. (Μαίανδρος). An ornamental design so called from the numerous windings it described, like the river *Mæander*. Its proper name is the GREEK FRET. (Figs. 334 to 336.)

Mælium. (See MELIUM.)

Mæmacteria, Gr. (μαιμακτήρια). Festivals held at Athens in honour of the boisterous or stormy Zeus (Μαιμάκτης), with the object of obtaining a mild winter.

Mænad, Gr. (μαινάς). Literally, a frenzied woman, and thence a bacchante. (See BACCHA.)

Mænhir. (See MENHIR.)

Mænia Columna, R. A column situated in the Roman forum, near which certain magistrates (*triumviri criminales*) judged criminals, slaves, and vagrants.

Mæniana, Mænianæ Scholæ, R. Celebrated schools of Gaul founded by Augustus at Autun (*Augustodunum* or *Bibracte*), so called because the buildings were furnished with balconies (*mæniana*). (See MÆNIANUM.)

Mænianum, R. A structure supported on corbels ; a balcony projecting from the wall of a house ; in a theatre or amphitheatre, one range of seats comprised between two landing-places (*præcinctiones*). Originally a balcony erected round the Roman forum, B.C. 318, to give accommodation to the spectators of gladiatorial contests. Afterwards balconies in general were so called.

Maes, Celt. A Welsh word for a field of battle, common in topographical nomenclature.

Mafil. (See MAHFIL.)

Mafors or **Mavors** (Gr. μαφώριον) was a short veil covering the head and neck and flowing down on the shoulders, such as nuns wear in imitation of the Virgin Mary.

Magadis, Gr. (μάγαδις). A musical instrument invented by the Lydians ; it was a kind of harp, which changed its form and was afterwards called SAMBUCA (q.v.). (See LYRA.)

Maghreb Pottery. (See GARGOULETTE.)

Magi. The adoration of the Magi (commemorated on Christmas Day) is the subject of some of the earliest specimens of Christian art. A fresco in the catacomb of St. Agnes, representing the Magi before Herod, is attributed to the 2nd century, and the mosaics of St. Maria Maggiore at Rome, in which the same subject occurs, are of the 5th century.

Magnase Black. A colour which dries rapidly when mixed with oil, and is of intense body.

Mahfil, Arab. A raised seat in a mosque, for the *imaum mocri* who reads the Koran, and for the *imaum khatib*, who recites prayer, preaches, and acts as the minister of the services generally.

Mahl-stick. A stick with a pad at the end, upon which the painter rests the wrist of his right arm while working.

Mahogany. Wood of the *Swietenia mahogoni* of Jamaica and Honduras. Satin-wood, or green mahogany, is the *Chloroxyllon ;* mottled, or African mahogany, is the *Khaya ;* Indian mahogany is the *Cedrela toona.*

Mahoitres, O. E. The name of a singular fashion of the 15th century—"of prankyd gownes, and *shoulders up set*, moss and flocks sewed within"—of padding up the shoulder to give a broad appearance to the chest. (See Figs. 51, 355, and 469.)

Mail (from the Fr. *maille*, the meshes of a net). Applied to chain or ringed armour. "Rich *mayles* that ronke (*strong*) were and round."

Mainefaire, O. E. The covering for a horse's mane. It was made of overlapping plates, like a lobster's tail ; and was fastened to the *testière* by buttons, and round the animal's neck by straps. (*Meyrick.*)

Maintenance, Cap of, Her. (See CHAPEAU.)

Maiolica or **Majolica.** The Italian name for the glazed earthenware introduced by Moorish potters from the island of Majorca. Originally these terms were only applied to "*lustre wares*," but from the 16th century they were generally applied to the *glazed earthenware* of Italy. A coarser lead-glazed lustred ware was known as mezza-majolica. The distinguishing characteristics of the Majolica ware are "coarseness of ware, intricacy of pattern, and occasionally prismatic glaze." It is also named FAIENCE, from the *botega* at FAENZA, and, when decorated with subjects after designs of Raphael, "Raffaelle ware." FAYENCE, *terraglia*, as distinct from PORCELAIN, is formed of potter's clay (hence its English name Pottery) mixed with marl and

Fig. 439. Majolica Plate (Urbino Ware).

sand, and is *soft* or *hard* according to the nature of the composition, and the degree of heat under which it is fired in the kiln. English *earthenware* is soft, while *stone-ware, Queen's-ware*, &c., are hard. Soft wares are either unglazed, or *lustrous*, or *glazed*, or enamelled. The Italian lustrous ware is properly, and the glazed ware improperly, but generally called MAJOLICA.

Majesty (It. *Maesta*), Chr. A conventional representation of the Saviour in glory, on a throne, encompassed by a *nimbus*, and surrounded by cherubim, and the four evangelistic symbols, and the letters A and Ω. "The only existing document relating to Cimabue shows that he was employed in 1301 on a mosaic 'Majesty' in the tribune of the Duomo at Pisa." (*Eastlake.*)

Mala Pioba. Irish (*mala*, a bag). The bag-pipe.

Malachite. A native carbonate of copper, forming a beautiful and permanent green pigment, used for oils and water-colours. *Incrusted* upon other materials it is used for articles of ornament. *Blue* malachite is pure carbonate of copper ; *green* malachite is green carbonate of copper ; *emerald* or *royal* malachite is dioptase of copper, a still rarer green and the best of all, which is a mixture of copper and silica ; *false* or *pseudo*-malachite is phosphate of copper, soft and silky, and of a rich velvet green marred by black spots or lines, and not so rich as the three kinds of true malachite.

Malchus, R. An old term for a confessional having only one stool for penitents ; it signified that which has only one ear, from the fact that Malchus, Caïaphas' servant, was deprived of his right ear by Peter.

Malleability. The property of extension under the hammer (*malleus*). *Gold* is the most malleable of metals. The art of rendering *glass* malleable was discovered by an architect in the reign of Tiberius. Buried treasures of glass vessels have been found to be malleable when first disinterred, but to harden quickly on exposure to the air.

Malleus, R. (1) A hammer. (2) Med. The MAULE (Gothic *Miölner*), Thor's hammer ; a military weapon.

Malluvia, Malluvium, R. A wash-hand basin.

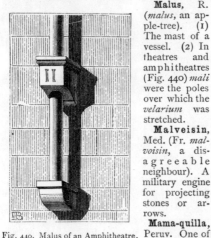

Malus, R. (*malus*, an apple-tree). (1) The mast of a vessel. (2) In theatres and amphitheatres (Fig. 440) *mali* were the poles over which the *velarium* was stretched.

Malveisin, Med. (Fr. *malvoisin*, a disagreeable neighbour). A military engine for projecting stones or arrows.

Mama-quilla, Peruv. One of the divisions of

Fig. 440. Malus of an Amphitheatre.

the temple of the Sun, INTI (q.v.) ; so called because it was dedicated to the moon, *Mamaquilla*.

Mamillare, R. (*mamilla*, the breast). (1) A broad band made of soft leather, a kind of small stays, used by the Roman ladies to support the breasts. (2) In Mediæval Latin, circular plates on the surcoat with rings from which two chains depended, one of which was attached to the sword and the other to the sheath. The fashion was introduced under Edward I., and continued until Henry V.

Mancop Oly, Dutch. Poppy oil, "a very white oil used by the painters in the Netherlands, who execute delicate works requiring lively colours, such as the vases of flowers of De Ghein, &c." (*Eastlake*.)

Mandorla, Chr. (lit. an almond). (See AUREOLE and VESICA PISCIS.)

Mandra, Chr. (lit. *a fold*). A favourite appellation for monastic establishments in the East.

Manducus, R. (*mando*, to chew). A comic masked character, distinguished by his ugliness and *voracity* (whence his name). (See PERSONA.)

Mandyas, Chr. In the Greek Church, an outer garment worn by monks. It is a long cloak, reaching almost to the feet, and fastened at the throat. It is originally a Persian dress, and is frequently mentioned as worn by emperors and kings.

Manefaire, O. E. A covering of armour for a horse's *mane*.

Manes, R. The shades of the dead. (See LEMURES.)

Manganese Brown. A rich semi-opaque brown pigment, permanent and drying well. (See CAPPAGH.)

Manger, Chr. The boards of the manger in which the Infant Saviour was laid, are said to be preserved in the crypt of the church of St. Maria Maggiore at Rome. They are called the *culla*, and are the object of a solemn procession on Christmas Eve.

Mangonell, Med. A military machine for hurling stones ; the spelling is frequently varied : —

"Vous peussez bugles, mangoniaux
Veoir pardessus les carniaux."
(*Roman de la Rose.*)

Manica, R. (*manus*, a hand). (1) An armlet, or piece of armour which protected the arm of the gladiator. (2) A leather glove worn by barbarous nations. In the plural, *manicæ* denotes (1) manacles ; (2) a grappling-iron called HARPAGA (q.v.).

Manicora, Manicore, Chr. In Christian iconography, the manicora is a hybrid animal with a human head, and a globular body ending in a serpent. It is a symbol of the World, the Flesh, and the Devil. (Fig. 441.)

Maniple, Chr. A short stole held in the left hand, originally used as a napkin by the officiating priest. Afterwards it was worn pendent from the wrist, and richly decorated. (See FANON.) The word is derived from—

Manipulus, R. (lit. a handful). (1) A maniple, the earliest ensign of the Roman legion ; it consisted of a handful of hay attached to the end of a pole. (2) A body of infantry in a legion, consisting of about 180 to 200 men.

Mansard Roof, Arch. (so called from *Mansard*, the French architect, who introduced it),

Fig. 441. Manicore.

or **Curb Roof** (from the French *courber*, to bend). A roof with two sets of rafters, of which the upper part is, as it were, broken off, and not so steep as the lower. According to *Mesanges*, Mansard took the idea of his roof from a frame composed by Segallo, and Michael Angelo employed it in the construction of the dome of St. Peter's. The houses in Lower Brittany were covered with these roofs in the end of the 15th century.

Manse, O. E. The parsonage-house.

Mansio, R. (*maneo*, to remain). Stations placed at intervals along the high roads, to serve as halting-places for the troops on a march. (See MUTATIO.)

Mantapa, Hind. A *porch* to a temple.

Mantel-piece, Arch. (formerly *mantil*). A cloak or covering; hence the slab which covers a part of the fireplace; the canopy over a shrine (Latin *mandualis*).

Mantelet or **Mantlet.** A shed used for protecting soldiers from missile weapons. (See PLUTEUS.)

Mantica, R. (*manus*, the hand). A double wallet serving as a portmanteau for riders or pedestrians.

Mantle. A flowing robe worn over the armour, as shown in the costume of the knights in the ivory mirror-case. (Fig. 463.)

Mantling or **Lambrequin.** A small mantle, of some rich materials, attached to the helmet, and worn hanging down, and ending in tassels.

(See Fig. 177.) It is usually represented, in Heraldry, with jagged ends, to represent the cuts it would be exposed to in actual battle.

Manuale, R. (*manus*, the hand). A wooden case for a book.

Manuballista, R. A hand-ballista. (See ARCUBALLISTA.)

Manubrium, R. (i. e. what is borne in the hand). A general term for a handle of any kind. (See Fig. 377.)

Manus Ferrea, R. Literally, a *hand of iron*; an iron hook which served as a grappling-iron, differing from the *harpaga*, as it was launched at the end of a chain, while the *harpaga* was fixed on a long beam (*asser*).

Marble. The finest for statuary, from *Carrara*, is of a pure white; that from *Paros* is of a waxy cream colour; others coloured with metallic oxides are available for ornamental purposes. Many cements have been produced as " artificial marble." (See SCAGLIOLA.)

Marble Silk had a weft of several colours so woven as to make the whole web look like *marble* stained with a variety of tints. On the 6th of November, 1551, "the old qwyne of Schottes rod thrught London; then cam the lord tresorer with a C. great horsse and ther cotes of *marbull.*" Its use prevailed for three centuries.

Marbling " is an art which consists in the production of certain patterns and effects by means of colours so prepared as to float on a mucilaginous liquid. While so floating they form into patterns, which are taken off on to a sheet of paper (for book-covers), or to the smoothly cut edges of a book, by dipping." (*Woolnough, The Whole Art of Marbling*, 1881.)

Marcus, R. A blacksmith's hammer; a sledge-hammer. (See MALLEUS.)

Mardelles, Margelles, or **Marges,** Celt. Excavations met with in several parts of Europe, supposed to be Celtic.

Mark, O. E. An ancient coin, value 13*s.* 4*d.*; formerly the equivalent of 30 silver pennies.

Marmouset, Arch. Fr. (monkey). A grotesque figure introduced into architectural decoration in the 13th century.

Marouflage, Fr. (*maroufler*, to line). A method of house-painting in France, upon a lining of prepared canvas fixed upon the surface to be decorated.

Marquess, Marquis, Her. The second order of the British peerage, in rank next to that of duke, was introduced into England in 1387 by Richard II. The coronet, apparently contemporary in

Fig. 442. Marquess's coronet.

its present form with that of the dukes, has its golden circlet heightened with four strawberry-leaves and as many pearls arranged alternately.

Marquetry. Inlaid-work of ornamental woods and stones of various colours put together and mixed with metals. The art has existed from the earliest ages; but no nation has brought it to a higher degree of perfection than the Italians of the 15th century. The Florentines especially have produced work of this kind which is unapproached; the Medici chapel at Florence may be particularly instanced. Figs. 443 and 444 represent specimens of antique work. The Venetian marquetry, derived from Persia and India, is a fine inlay of ivory, metal, and woods, stained to vary the colour. This work is in geometric patterns only. In France, in the early marquetry designs, picturesque landscapes, broken architecture, and figures are

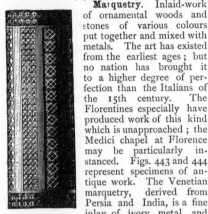

Fig. 443. Shaft ornamented with Marquetry.

Fig. 444. Marquetry.

represented. Colours are occasionally stained on the wood. Ivory and ebony are the favourite materials. In England, it is an art imported from Holland in the reign of William and Mary. The older designs on Dutch marquetry represent tulips and other flowers, foliage, birds, &c., all in gay colours, generally the self colours of the wood used. Sometimes the eyes and other salient points are in ivory and mother-of-pearl. (Compare BOULE. CERTOSINA WORK, EMBLEMATA, MUSIVUM OPUS, REISHER-WORK, &c.)

Marra, R. A kind of hoe with indented teeth, used for tearing up weeds. (Fig. 445.)

Mars Brown. A brown pigment.

Mars (Reds, &c.). Calcined earths of which the brightness of the redness is regulated by the duration of the roasting.

Fig. 445. Marra.

Marseilles Faience. This ancient city has at all times been celebrated in the ceramic arts. Fig. 446 gives a representative specimen of modern polychrome work, decorated with flowers easily recognized by the disposition of their long stalks. These flowers are, in

Fig. 446. Teapot of Marseilles faience.

other specimens, accompanied by marine landscapes. Other polychrome services are called from their designs "services aux insectes."

Marsupium, R. (μαρσύπιον). A purse for containing money; it was made of leather and shaped like a pear, being confined at the top with a string. (Hence the adjective *marsupial* applied to the kangaroo, &c.)

Martel de Fer, Med. A weapon which had at one end a pick, and at the other a hammer, axe-blade, half-moon, mace-head, or other fanciful termination. (*Meyrick.*)

Martlet, Her. Bird, usually represented without feet. (Figs. 447, 448.)

Fig. 447. Early Heraldic   Fig. 448. Heraldic
Martlet.   Martlet.

Martyrium, Chr. An altar erected over the tomb of a martyr.

Marzocco, It. The Lion of Florence. The heraldic emblem of the city. (Fig. 449.)

Fig. 449. Il Marzocco, the bronze Lion now in the Bargello at Florence. By Donatello (about A.D. 1420).

Mascaron, Arch. Fr. A mask ; the face of a man or animal employed as an ornamentation for decorating the key-stones of arches or vaults, or the stones of an arch, &c. (Fig. 450.)

Fig. 450. Etruscan Mask in terra-cotta.

Mascle, Her. The central *lozenge* of a diapered surface ; it is drawn with right angles.

Maser or **Mazer,** O. E. A bowl of maple-wood. The name is applied to similar bowls or goblets of other woods.

"The mazers four,
My noble fathers loved of yore,"

are mentioned by Scott in "The Lord of the Isles." They were richly ornamented, frequently with legends on the rim, such as

"In the name of the Trinitie
Fille the kup and drinke to me,"

and the rim was often covered with silver or gold.

Massicot. The name of an ancient pigment of a dull orange colour.

Mastaba, Mastabê, Egyp. An outer chapel attached to Egyptian burial-places ; it was generally a small quadrangular building, the door of which faced the East.

Master Arch, O. E. The central or widest arch of a bridge.

Mastic. A resin used for varnish. (Dissolve one part of mastic resin in two of oil of turpentine.) (See VARNISH.) In France, the term is applied to a cement used to fill up joints in masonry ; in *joinery*, to a composition of wax, resin, and pounded brick, applied to fill up knots and chinks in the wood. Putty is also so called.

Mastigophorus, Gr. and R. (μαστιγο-φόρος). A slave-driver, and thence an officer who fulfilled the same functions as our policemen. The mastigophori were so named because they carried a whip (μάστιγα φέρειν), in order to put down any crowding or tumult ; it was also part of their duty to repress any infringement of the regulations at the public games.

Match-lock. A gun which was exploded by means of a match, before the introduction of the flint and steel. (See FIRE-LOCK.)

Materiatio, R. (*materia*, materials). The timber-work of a roof, consisting of two principal rafters (*canterii*), a tie-beam (*tignum*), a ridge-piece (*calcimen*), beams (*trabes*), struts (*capreoli*), purlines (*templa*), and common rafters (*asseres*).

Materis, R. A Celtic javelin with a broad head.

Matralia, R. (i. e. pertaining to a mother). The festival of *Matuta* (the Ino of the Greeks), which was held at Rome every year on the third of the ides of June (11th of June). Prayers were offered by the Roman matrons on behalf of their nephews, they being afraid to pray for their own children, since those of Matuta had turned out so unfortunately.

Matronalia, R. A festival of the Roman matrons held on the calends of March, at which matrons offered sacrifices to Mars and Juno Lucina.

Mattucashlash. An ancient Scotch weapon, sometimes called the *armpit dagger*, being worn on the arm ready to be used on coming to close quarters.

Maule. (See MALLEUS.)

Maunde, O. E. A basket.

Mausoleum, R. The tomb of Mausolus, king of Caria, at Halicarnassus, ranked among the seven wonders of the world. The name was afterwards applied to tombs of an imposing size and splendour, such as the tomb of Augustus in the Field of Mars, and that of Hadrian, on the banks of the Tiber, now known as Fort St. Angelo. A representation of it, in its original state, is shown in Fig. 451.

Mauve is the colour of a peach blossom ; obtained as a dye from *aniline* found in gas tar.

Maze, Chr. Labyrinthine figures in the pavements of churches and on the turf of greens.

Fig. 451. Mausoleum of Hadrian at Rome. In its original state.

To trace the former kneeling was a species of penance.

Mazmorra, Sp. A tank lined with cement, sunk in the ground and used for storing grain. (See *Murray's Handbook, Spain,* p. 361, *Granada,* &c.)

Mazonum, Gr. (μαζο-νομεῖον ; μᾶζα, barley-bread). A wooden platter for domestic use, and thence a salver of bronze or gold on which perfumes were burnt in the religious processions of Bacchus.

Mechlin Lace is fine, transparent, and effective. It is made in one piece on the pillow ; its distinguishing feature is the flat thread which forms the flowers, and gives to the lace the character of embroidery. In 1699—when Charles II.'s prohibition to the introduction of Flanders lace was removed—Mechlin lace became the fashion in England, and continued so during the succeeding century. In the 17th century the Beguinage nuns were celebrated for their lace-making, and they supported their house by their work. Previous to 1665 the name of Mechlin was given to all pillow lace,

and much of it was made like our modern insertion. The engraving shows a specimen

Fig. 452. Old Mechlin Lace, 17th century.

Fig. 453. Mechlin Lace, 18th century.

of old Mechlin lace formerly in great favour as head-dresses and other trimmings.

Medallion. (1) A medal of a larger size than the ordinary coinage. (2) In Architecture, a circular or oval tablet on the face of a building.

Mediæval. (See MIDDLE AGES.)

Medimnus, Gr. (μέδιμνος). The principal Greek measure of capacity, holding as much as six Roman *modii.* It was especially used for measuring corn.

Meditrinalia, R. (*medeor*, to remedy). Roman festivals in honour of Meditrina, the goddess of healing, celebrated on the 11th of October, at which new wine was tasted, it being looked upon by the Romans as a preservative of health.

Medium. The liquid in which pigments are ground. The best are linseed oil and nut oil.

Fig. 454. Medusa Head on a shield.

Medusa Head was frequently used as an ornament for the centre of a shield. (Cf. GORGONEIA.)

Megalartia, Gr. (μεγαλάρτια). Festivals held at Delos in honour of Ceres, who was called *Megalartos* (Μεγάλαρτος) from her having bestowed bread on mankind.

Megalesian (games), R. (*Ludi megalenses*). Festivals celebrated annually on the 4th of April in honour of Cybelê, who was called the Great (Μεγαλεῖα), in which the people went in procession to the Field of Mars to witness scenic spectacles. The magistrates attended these spectacles in a purple toga, or "toga prætexta ;" hence the expression " Purpura Megalensis."

Megylp. A vehicle used by some oil-painters, condemned as tending to destroy the permanency of the picture.

Melides, Gr. Nymphs of fruit-trees. (Cf. HAMADRYADES.)

Melina, R. A pouch made out of the skin of a marten (or a badger, *meles*).

Melium, R. A collar for sporting-dogs, studded with nails and iron spikes (*clavulis, capitatis*).

Mell. (See MALLEUS.)

Melotte, O. E. A garment worn by monks during laborious occupation. (*Halliwell.*)

Membrana, R. (*membrum*, skin). Parchment for writing on was introduced as a substitute for the Egyptian papyrus by Eumenes II., king of Pergamus. It was usually written over on one side, and the back was stained with saffron. The writings were frequently erased, and the paper or parchment used again. It was then called a *palimpsest*. All the sheets used for one work were joined together into a long scroll, which was folded round a staff, and then called *volumen ;* usually there were ornamental balls or bosses, projecting from the ends of the staff, called *umbilici* or *cornua*. The ends of the roli were carefully cut and blackened ; they were called *geminæ frontes*. The roll itself was kept in a parchment case, which was stained purple or yellow. (See also LIBER.)

Membranula, R. (dimin. of *membrana*). A small strip of parchment on which the title or contents of a volume were inscribed in minium.

Menat, Egyp. An Egyptian amulet worn on a necklace. The menat evidently formed some symbol, the meaning of which has hitherto not been discovered.

Menehis or **Minihis,** Fr. This term, derived from the Celtic *menech-ti* (house of a monk), or *manach-li* (free spot of earth), was formerly used in Brittany to denote a place of asylum which had been consecrated in any way.

Menhir, Celt. A Celtic monument consisting of a huge stone fixed upright in the ground. Menhirs are found associated with *dolmens, tumuli,* and circles of stones. (Consult Bertrand, *Archéologie Celtique et Gauloise*, p. 84.)

Menis, Meniscus, Gr. and R. (μηνίσκος ; μήνη, the moon). A crescent-shaped piece of metal which was placed on statues of the gods to hinder birds from settling on them. The same term was used to denote an ornament, likewise in the shape of a crescent, placed by the Romans at the beginning of their books ; hence the expression *a menide*, from the beginning. (Cf. LUNA.)

Mensa, R. (Gr. τράπεζα). A board, tablet, or table ; *mensa escaria*, or *mensa* simply, a dining-table ; *mensa prima, secunda*, the first, second course of a meal ; *mensa tripes*, a table with three feet, in contradistinction to *monopodium*, a table with a single leg ; *mensa vinaria*, a drinking-table (see DELPHICA) ; *mensa sacra*, an altar-table ; *mensa vasaria*, a table for holding vessels ; *mensa publica*, a public bank ; hence *mensarii*, bankers.

Mensao, Celt. A Celtic monument more usually called MENHIR (q. v.).

Mensole, Arch. A term denoting the keystone of an arch.

Menzil, Orient. Houses in the East for the reception of travellers, in places where there are neither caravanserais nor *khans*.

Mereack, Hind. A sort of thick black varnish employed by the Khmers to coat over statues made of any soft stone, which are exposed to the changes of the weather. This varnish was, in many instances, itself covered with gold-leaf.

Merkins, O. E. A name given to ringlets of false hair, much worn by ladies *temp.* Charles I.

P

Merlons, Arch. The COPS or raised parts of a battlement. Figures of warriors or animals are sometimes carved on the tops. (See BATTLE-MENT.)

Fig. 455. Mermaid and Pillars of Hercules. Arms of the Colonna family.

Mermaid. An ancient device of the Colonna family was the mermaid between the pillars of Hercules, with the motto *Contemnit tuta procellas.*

Mesaulæ (μέσ-αυλα). (1) The narrow passage or corridor which, in a Greek house, connected the *andron* with the *gynæceum.* (2) The door in this passage.

Mese (the middle, sc. χορδή). The central note of the seven-stringed lyre. The Greeks had no names to distinguish musical notes. They were expressed by the names of the strings of the lyre. Thus, NETE, *d*; PARANETE, *c*; PARAMESE, *b* flat; and MESE, *a*, in the treble or upper tetrachord; and LICHANOS, *g*; PARHYPATE, *f*; and HYPATE, *e*, in the base or lower tetrachord.

Mesjid, Arab. A small mosque. These exist in great numbers. The Sultan Mohamet II. alone consecrated 170 *mesjids* in Constantinople.

Messe, A.S. The Mass.

Messle-house or **Meselle-house,** O. E. (from the obsolete word *measle,* a leper). A hospital or lazar-house.

Meta, R. (*metior,* to measure). Any object with a circular base and of conical shape; in a circus the term *meta,* or rather *metæ* (for there were two sets of goals), was applied to a set of three cones placed together upon a pedestal, as shown in Fig. 456, to mark the turning-points of the race-course. In a mill for grinding corn

Fig. 456. Meta of a Roman race-course.

the name of *meta* was applied to the lower part of the mill, which was hewn into the form of a cone. (See CIRCUS, OVUM, SPINA, &c.)

Metal, Tech. (1) A mass of glass in the state of paste, adherent to the pipe and already blown; it may be regarded as the first stage in the production of a piece. (2) Broken glass. (3) Broken stones for repairing roads.

Metal, Her. The tinctures *or* and *argent.*

Metallic Canvas. A combination of metal and canvas; waterproof for various uses.

Metallic Lava. A composition of gravel, pounded chalk, tar, and wax, forming an artificial stone to be cast into ornamental shapes in moulds. The vestibule of the Euston Station is paved with this preparation. (*Builder,* vi. 502.)

Metallurgy. It was at a comparatively late period of human civilization that the art of working in iron was brought to perfection. The ancient Egyptians, probably aware of its resources, had a superstitious objection to its use; but they hardened bronze to a degree unknown to later ages, and their bronze statuary of the most ancient period is worthy of any age. The bronze-work of Britain and Ireland is as ancient as any; and, in beauty of form and perfection of casting, rivals the best modern work. Of the work in Greece we are told that Athens alone contained 3000 bronze statues in the year 130 B.C., and vast treasures of metallurgy have been discovered in Herculaneum and Pompeii. In mediæval times Ireland was famous for metallurgy, and of its admirable copper-works of the 11th century many splendid relics remain, especially the so-called Bell of St. Patrick. Oriental bronzes, of characteristic design, are plentiful from all ages; especially beautiful and perfect in execution are those of China and Japan. The best period of workmanship in *Iron* is the Middle Ages; gates and hinges, keys, and especially weapons and defensive armour being the chief objects produced. (Consult *Pugin, Digby Wyatt.*) (See also BRONZE, COPPER, DAMASCENING, GOLD, &c.)

Fig. 457. One of the carved Metopes of the Parthenon, representing the War of the Centaurs and the Lapithæ.

Metope, Arch. ($\mu\epsilon\tau$-ό$\pi\eta$, i. e. the space between the ό$\pi\alpha l$). A kind of panel between the triglyphs in the Doric frieze (Fig. 458);

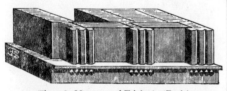

Fig. 458. Metopes and Triglyphs (Doric).

in some Greek examples quite plain, in others ornamented with sculpture. The metopes of the Parthenon in the British Museum are carved with representations of the war of the Centaurs and Lapithæ. (Fig. 457.) (See ELGIN MARBLES.) In Roman buildings the metopes are usually carved, and are exact squares ; but in the Greek Doric this was not necessary.

Metreta, Gr. ($\mu\epsilon\tau\rho\eta\tau\grave{\eta}s$, i. e. measurer). The unit in the Greek measures of capacity ; it held two *cotylæ*, or about eight gallons.

Meurtrière, O. E. "A black knot, that unties and ties the curles of the hair." (*Ladies' Dict.*, 1694.)

Mews, O. E. Originally a courtyard for "mewing" (i. e. moulting) hawks.

Mexican Architecture. The principal monu-

ments of the valley of Mexico are situated in a small tract in the centre of the table-land of Anahuac. These consist of pyramidal temples (*teocallis*) formed in terraces, with flat tops, and always surmounted by a chamber or cell, which is the temple itself. In *Yucatan* there are more architectural remains than anywhere in the world, with palaces of all dates, generally pyramidal, and often rich with elaborate carvings. (See *Stephens's Incidents of Travel in Yucatan.*) (Fig. 458 a.)

Mezza-majolica was the coarser majolica ware formed of potter's earth, covered with a white "slip," upon which the subject was painted, then glazed with the common lead glaze, over which the lustre pigments were applied ; the *majolica*, on the other hand, being the tin-enamelled ware similarly lustred. (See MAJOLICA.)

Mezzanine, Entresole, Half-story, Arch. A small story intermediate between two others of larger size. A mezzanine or Flemish window was a window either square or broader than it was long, made in an attic,

Fig. 458 a. Mexican temple—*Teocalli.*

or in a lower story lying between two higher stories.

Mezzo-relievo, It. Sculpture in relief, in

Fig. 459. Jardinière—Milan Faience.

which one half of the figure projects ; sometimes called DEMI-RELIEVO.

Mias, Hind. A commemorative monument.

Mica, Micatio, R. (*mico*, to move quickly).
A game called by the Italians of the present day

Fig. 460. Milan Reticella Lace.

mora ; two players simultaneously
stretching out one or more fingers, and
each guessing the number held up by
his adversary.

Middle Ages. The mediæval period
—of transition between ancient and
modern times—between the 10th and
the 15th centuries is one of the grandest
periods in art. It begins with the
decay of Rome, and merges into the
Renaissance.

Middle Distance, in a landscape :—
between the foreground and the background. Great skill is displayed in
the expression of distance by the
effects of intervening atmospheres, and
by the design of intermediate *plans*
carrying the eye onward and suggest-
ing space.

Middle Ground in a landscape. (See MID-
DLE DISTANCE.)

Middle Pointed Period of Architecture is a
name given to that period of Gothic architecture
in England, which is generally described as "*the
Decorated Period."*

Middle Post. The KING POST in the truss of
a roof.

Milan Faience. Fig. 459 is an illustration of
the Oriental imitations for which Milan was
famous. "It is," says M. Jacquemart, "of
such beautiful enamel that it might be taken for
porcelain. The upper and lower edges are
decorated with shells, scrolls, and rocailles in
relief, heightened with gold ; the whole surface
has a decoration of peonies ,and sprigs in blue,
red, and gold, which rival in beauty the richest
specimens of old Delft."

Milan Lace. The engraving shows a specimen of Old Milan Point or Reticella from the
convent of Santa Maria delle Grazie in that
city. (See RETICELLA.) (Fig. 460.)

Miliarium, R. (1) A tall narrow copper
vessel employed in baths for heating the
water. (2) The column of an olive-press (*trapetum*), which rose from the centre of the mortar
(*mortarium*).

Military Architecture. The science of building fortresses and fortifying town walls, &c.
[See *Viollet le Duc,* " *Essai sur l'Architecture
militaire au Moyen Age."*]

Milled Money, with grooved edges, was first
coined in this country in 1561.

Millefiori. Mosaic glass. (See GLASS.)

Milliarium, R. (*mille,* a thousand, sc. paces).
A column placed at intervals of a mile (1618
English yards) along a Roman road to indicate
the distance. (Fig. 461.) It was also called *lapis.
Milliarium aureum* was the name given to the
golden mile-stone erected by Augustus in the
Forum, where the principal roads of the Empire
terminated. A stone, called the "London

Stone," in Cannon Street, E.C., is supposed to have marked the centre of the Roman roads in Britain.

Fig. 461. Roman Mile-stone at Nic-sur-Aisne in France.

Mill-rind, Fer-de-Moline, Her. The iron fixed to the centre of a millstone.

Millstone-grit. The name of a good building stone, plentiful in the north of England. It is supposed to be formed by a re-aggregation of the disintegrated materials of granite. (See the *Builder*, vol. ix. 639.)

Millus, R. (See MELIUM.)

Mimbar, Arabic. A pulpit in a mosque. A finely-carved mimbar is in the South Kensington Museum.

Minah, Minar, Hind. A tower or pillar. The *Surkh Minar* and *Minar Chakri,* among the topes at Cabul, are almost the only *pillars* existing in India. They are generally ascribed to Alexander the Great, but are probably Buddhist monuments of the 3rd or 4th century of our era.

Minaret (Arabic *menarah,* a lantern). A feature peculiar to Mohammedan architecture. A tall, slender shaft or turret, rising high above all surrounding buildings of the *mosque* to which it is attached ; in several stories, with or without external galleries, but usually having three. From these galleries the *muezzin* summon the faithful to prayer. Blind men are generally selected for this duty, because the minaret commands a view of the house-tops used as sleeping-chambers in the East.

Mineral Black. A native oxide of carbon.

Mineral Blue. A native carbonate of copper which is liable to change its tint to green, if mixed with oil. (*Fairholt.*)

Mineral Brown. (See CAPPAGH.)

Mineral Green. MALACHITE (q.v.). (See CARBONATES OF COPPER.)

Mineral Lake is a French pigment, a kind of orange chrome.

Mineral Yellow. A pigment of chloride of lead, which becomes paler by time. The name has also been applied to YELLOW OCHRE and YELLOW ARSENIC (q.v.).

Minerval, R. A present or fee which Roman scholars took to their masters every year, on the fourteenth of the calends of April (19th of March), that is, on occasion of the festivals of Minerva.

Minever, O. E. (1) Either the pure white fur with which the robes of peers and judges are trimmed—"*minever pure;*" or (2) the ermine with minute spots of black in it—*minutus varius*—in lieu of the complete tails ; or (3) the fur of the ermine mixed with that of the small weasel. (Consult *Planché's Cyclopædia;* see also VAIR.)

Miniature. Literally, a painting executed in *minium* (vermilion). Now used for any small picture, and especially for a small portrait.

Ministerium, Chr. All the sacred ornaments and utensils of a church taken collectively.

Minium. A kind of *red lead* obtained by exposing lead or its protoxide to heat, till it is converted into a red oxide. It is a fine orange pigment, but fugitive and liable to decomposition when mixed with other pigments. The ancient *minium* was *cinnabar,* or vermilion. (See ILLUMINATING.)

Minnim, Heb. Stringed musical instruments of the lute or guitar kind.

Fig. 462. Minotaur. Device of Gonzalvo Perez.

Fig. 463. Mirror-case of carved ivory—14th cent.

Minotaur, R. A monster, half man, half bull, confined in the labyrinth constructed by Dædalus in Crete. It was assumed as a device by Gonzalvo Perez, with the motto from Isaiah xxx. 15. (Fig. 462.)

Minster, Abbey-church, O. E. (Germ. *Münster*). A church to which a monastery was attached; a cathedral. The name survives in "West-*minster*."

Minstrel Gallery, O. E. The LOFT in a church was so called.

Minuscule. (See SEMI-UNCIALS.)

Minute, It. A subdivision of the *module* in the measurement of architectural proportion. It is the twelfth, the eighteenth, or the thirtieth part of the MODULE.

Mirador, Sp. A belvedere, or overhanging bow-window.

Mirror. In the Middle Ages mirrors were often enclosed in cases of metal or carved ivory. The example (Fig. 463) gives a representation of the Siege of the Castle of Love from one of the romances of the period. (See GLASS.)

Mirror, Arch. A small oval ornament cut into the deep mouldings, and separated by wreaths of flowers.

Miserere. A projecting bracket, on the *sellette* of a church stall, on which, when the seat was turned up, there was a leaning-space,

available to the infirm during the parts of the service required to be performed standing. (See SELLETTE.)

Misericorde. The narrow-bladed dagger used to put the victory with sword or lance to the test, by obliging a fallen antagonist to cry for *mercy*, or by despatching him.

Mis'rha, Hind. Hindoo temples built with two kinds of materials; whence their name of mixed (*mis'rha*). (See SUD'HA, VIMANA, and SANCIRA.)

Missilia, R. (i. e. things thrown). Presents of cheques or tickets thrown by the emperor and wealthy persons among the people. The cheques were payable to the bearer at the magazine of the donor. (See CONGIARIUM.)

Mistarius, Mixtarius, R. Any vessel of large size used for mixing water with wine.

Mitella, Gr. (dimin. of *mitra*). (1) A head-band or coif of peaked form worn by Greek women. (2) A scarf used as a bandage or support for a broken arm.

Mithriatic (Festivals), Pers. and R. Festivals held in honour of Mithras, the Persian sun-god.

Mitis Green. (See EMERALD GREEN.)

Mitra, Gr. and R. (μίτρα). (1) A mitre or head-dress of the Galli or priests of Cybelê; it was a Phrygian cap of felt, which was tied under the chin by lappets; it was also called a *Phrygian tiara*. (2) A cable fastened round the hull of a vessel to strengthen the timbers.

Mitre, Chr. Her. The ensign of archiepiscopal and episcopal rank, placed above the arms of prelates of the Church of England, sometimes borne as a charge, and adopted by the Berkeleys as their crest. The contour of the mitre has varied considerably at various times, growing continually higher and more pointed. It was first worn by bishops about the close of the 10th century. Bishops had three kinds of mitres: the *simplex*, of plain white linen; the *auri-frigata*, ornamented with gold orphreys; and the *pretiosa*, enriched with gold and jewels, for use at high festivals. (Fig. 464.) In Architecture, the corner line formed by the meeting of mouldings intercepting each other at an angle.

Mitten, Mitaine, Anglo-Norman. A glove; not restricted to gloves without fingers. "Gloves made of linnen or woollen, whether knit or stytched : sometimes also they call so gloves made of leather without fingers." (*Ray.*) (See MUFFETEE.)

Fig. 464. Mitre. Arms of St. Alban's Abbey.

Moat, Mote. (1) Originally a heap or hillock ; the *dune* on which a tower was built, forming the original castle. The Saxons assembled on such *moats* or mounds to make laws and administer justice ; hence their word *witten-mote* for parliament. (2) Mod. Usually applied to the fosse of a rampart, the side next the fortress being the *scarp*, and the opposite the *counterscarp.*

Mobcap, O. E. A cap tying under a woman's chin by an excessively broad band, generally made of the same material as the cap itself. (*H.*)

Moccinigo. A small Venetian coin, worth about 9*d.* (*H.*)

Mochado, Mokkado, O. E. (1) A silk stuff, commonly called "mock velvet," much used in the 16th and 17th centuries. (*Fairholt.*) (2) A woollen stuff of the same kind. (*Halliwell.*) It was probably a mixture of silk and wool. (*Planché.*)

Modena Pottery. The antique pottery of Modena is referred to by Pliny and Livy, but there is no exact record or marked example of wares produced there during the Renaissance. The manufacture flourishes now at *Sassuolo*, a town ten miles south of Modena.

Modesty Bit or **Piece,** O. E. " A narrow lace which runs along the upper part of the stays, before, being a part of the tucker, is called the modesty piece." (*Guardian.*) "Modesty bits—out of fashion" is an announcement in the *London Chronicle*, vol. xi. 1762.

Modillions, Arch. Small brackets under the coronæ of cornices ; when *square* they are called MUTULES. In the Corinthian order

they have carved leaves spread under them. Fig. 465 is taken from the temple of Mars the Avenger, at Rome.

Fig. 465. Modillion.

Modius, R. (*modus*, a measure or standard). The largest Roman measure of capacity.

Module, Arch. A measure adopted by architects to determine by the column the proportions of the different parts of a work of architecture. It is usually the diameter or the semidiameter of the shaft of the column.

Mœnia, R. A term synonymous with MURUS (q.v.) ; but more comprehensive, in that it implies not merely the idea of walls, but also of the buildings attached to them.

" *Mœnia* lata videt, triplici circumdata *muro.*" (*Virgil.*)

Mogul Architecture is that of the buildings erected in the reigns of the Mogul emperors, kings of Delhi, from A.D. 1531 to the present century.

Moilon (Fr. *moellon*), Arch. Rubblemasonry.

Mokador, Mocket, O. E. A napkin, handkerchief, or bib.

" Goo hom, lytyl babe, and sytt on thi moderes lap,
   And put a *mokador* aforn thi brest,
And pray thi modyr to fede the with the pappe."
                (*Twentieth Coventry Mystery.*)

Fig. 466. Mola versatilis.

Mola, R. (*molo,* to grind). A mill ; *mola manuaria,* a hand-mill ; *mola buxea,* a box-wood mill, or mill for grinding pepper ; *mola aquaria,* a water-mill ; *mola asinaria,* a mill worked by a beast of burden ; *mola versatilis,* a grindstone (Fig. 466 represents Love sharpening his arrows, from an engraved gem) ; *mola olearia,* a mill for crushing olives.

Mold, O. E. (for *mould*). Earth ; ground. The word is constantly applied to the *ground* in works of art. (See *Degrevant,* 1039 ; *Halliwell.*)

Moline, Her. A cross terminating like the MILL-RIND. In modern cadency it is the difference of the eighth son.

Mollicina, Molochina (sc. *vestis*), R. (μολό-χινα, i. e. mallow-coloured). A garment made from the fibres of a mallow (*hibiscus*).

Mona Marble. A beautiful marble of a greenish colour, obtained in the Isle of Anglesea.

Monastic Orders consisted of Benedictine or black monks, and Cistercian or white monks. There were the *Regular Orders,* the *Military Orders,* the *Conventual Orders, Colleges,* &c.

Monaulos, Gr. and R. (μόν-αυλος, single-flute). A Greek pipe made of a reed, of Egyptian origin, blown at the end without a reed mouthpiece, and remarkable for the sweetness of its tone.

Monelle, Monial, Moynel, Arch. (See MULLIONS.)

Moneris, Gr. (μον-ήρης, single). A galley or ship with a single bench of rowers.

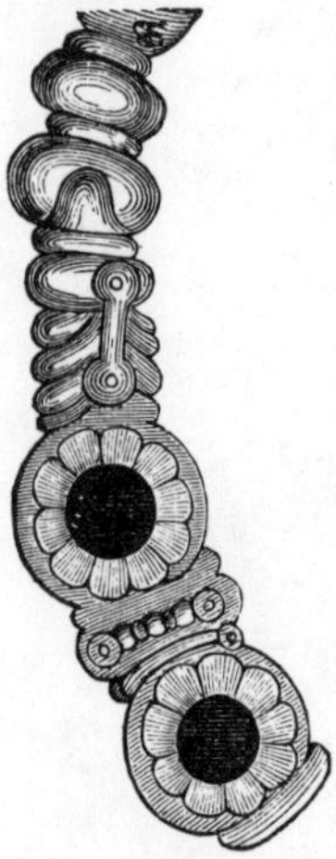

Monile, Gr. and R. A necklace or collar. Fig. 468 represents a bronze necklace belonging to the Gaulish period, and Fig. 467 a part of the same necklace on a larger scale. By analogy the term was applied to the ornaments worn by horses about the neck. (See NECKLACES.)

Monks, Chr. In the religious iconography of the Gothic period, especially the 14th and 15th centuries, there frequently occur grotesque representations of monks. (See Fig. 351.)

Monmouth Cap, O. E. A cap worn by soldiers and sailors.

Fig. 467. Monile. Details of ornament.

Monochord. A one-stringed musical instrument, much used for measuring the proportions of length which yield the various sounds within an octave.

Fig. 468. Monile. A Gaulish collar.

Monochrome Painting. (1) Painting in a single colour, as, for instance, red upon a black ground, or white upon a red ground. The most numerous class of specimens of this kind of painting are upon terra-cotta, as the Etruscan vases. (2) The term is applied to paintings in tints of one colour, in imitation of bas-reliefs.

Monogram. A combination of two or more letters into one design, illustrated especially in ecclesiastical decoration of the 14th and 15th centuries, &c. The abbreviation IHS is said to have been invented by St. Bernardino of Siena about 1437. For *Artists' monograms,* see *Stellway, Heller, Brulliot* (*Dictionaries of Monograms*).

Monolith (μονό-λιθος). An object formed of a single block of stone.

Monolium, Monolinum, R. A necklace formed with a single string of pearls. (See MONILE.)

Monoloris, R. (Gr. μόνος, one, and Lat. *lorum,* a thong. A hybrid word). Decorated with a single band of purple and gold, like the PARAGAUDA (q.v.).

Monopodium (sc. *mensa*), R. (μονο-πόδιον). A table with a single foot.

Monopteral, Arch. (μονό-πτερος). With a single wing ; a circular temple or shrine, consisting of a roof supported on columns, without any *cella.*

Monostyle, Arch. (1) Piers of a single shaft are sometimes distinguished by this name from *compound piers,* then called for distinction *poly-style.* (2) A building which is of one *style* of architecture throughout ; or (3) surrounded by a single row of pillars.

Monota, Gr. A vase with one *ear* (or handle).

Monotriglyph, Arch. The intercolumniation in the Doric order, which embraces one triglyph and two metopes in the entablature. (*Parker's Glossary of Architecture.*)

Monoxylos, Monoxylus, Gr. and R. (*μονό-ξυλος*). Literally, hewn or made out of a single piece of wood.

Monsters, in Architecture. (See CENTAUR, GRIFFIN, GROTESQUES, SPHINX, &c.) ,

Monstrance, Expositorium, Chr. (*monstrare*, to show). An ornamental vessel of gold, silver, silver-gilt, or gilded or silvered copper, representing usually a sun with rays, in the centre of which is a *lunule* or glass box in which the consecrated wafer is carried and exposed on the altars of churches. The earliest monstrances, which are now called *expositories*, do not date beyond the 12th century. Very ancient specimens exist at Rheims, Namur, &c.

Montem. An annual custom at Eton ; a procession of boats *ad montem*. (See *Brand*, i. 237.)

Montero. "A close hood wherewith travellers preserve their faces and heads from frost-biting and weather-beating in winter." (*Cotgrave.*)

Monteth, O. E. A vessel used for cooling wine-glasses in. (*Halliwell.*)

Mont-la-haut. "A certain wier (wire) that raises the head-dress by degrees or stories." (*Ladies' Dict.*, 1694.)

Montmorency Escutcheon. (See the illustration to HUNTING-FLASK.)

Monumentum, R. (*moneo*, to remind). In general, any token, statue, or monument intended to perpetuate the memory of anything. *Monumentum sepulchri* is the name given to a tomb. The Monument of the Great Fire of London, erected by Sir Christopher Wren, is of the Italo-Vitruvian-Doric order, of Portland stone, and consists of a *pedestal* about 21 feet square, with a *plinth* 27 feet, and a fluted shaft 15 feet at the base ; on the *abacus* is a balcony encompassing a moulded cylinder, which supports a flaming vase of gilt bronze, indicative of its commemoration of the Great Fire. Defoe describes it as " built in the form of a *candle* with a handsome gilt frame." Its entire height is 202 feet, and it is the loftiest isolated column in the world. Its interior contains a spiral stair-case of 345 black marble steps. (See COCHLIS.)

Monyal, O. E. for MULLION (q. v.).

Moorish Architecture, or Arabian or Mohammedan architecture, arose at the beginning of the 7th century in the East, and in Spain, Sicily, and Byzantium in Europe. The style originated in a free adaptation of different features of Christian architecture, and their earliest mosques were built by Christian architects. The horse-shoe arch is a very early characteristic of their style, and the pointed arch appears at Cairo and elsewhere three centuries earlier than in Europe. The most perfect specimen of the luxury of decoration of which this style is capable is found in the Alhambra. (See ALHAMBRAIC ARCHITECTURE ; consult the *Essai sur l'Architecture des Arabes et des Mores*, by *Girault de Prangy*, 1841.)

Moor-stone. A very coarse granite found in Cornwall and some other parts of England, and of great value for the coarser parts of building ; it is also found in immense strata in Ireland. Its colours are chiefly black and white.

Moot-hall, O. E. A public assembly-house ; a town-hall, &c. (See MOAT.)

Mora, R. (*mora*, an obstacle). A projection or cross-bar on a spear to prevent its penetrating too far.

Mordaunt, Fr. The catch for the tongue of the buckle of a belt.

Moresco-Spanish, or Saracenic **Textiles** wrought in Spain, are remarkable for an ingenious imitation of gold, produced by shreds of gilded parchment cut up into narrow flat strips and woven with the silk.

Moresque or **Moresco-Spanish Architecture** is the work of Moorish workmen, executed for their Christian masters in Spain. The most remarkable examples are in the city of Toledo (described by *Street*, *Gothic Architecture in Spain*).

Morion. A head-piece of the 16th century, introduced by the Spaniards, who had copied it from the Moors, to the rest of Europe about 1550. It was worn as late as the reign of Charles I. There were peaked morions, coming to a point at the top ; and high combed morions, surmounted by a kind of crest or ridge.

Moriones, R. (1) Idiots, dwarfs, or deformed persons, used as slaves, to afford amusement in the houses of the great. (2) A dark-brown gem ; perhaps the smoky topaz.

Morisco, O. E. (See MORRIS DANCE.)

Moristan, Arab. A hospital.

Morne, Mornette. The head of a blunted tilting-lance, the point being turned back.

Morning Star, O. E. A club called also a HOLY WATER SPRINKLER (q.v.).

Morris Dance, O. E. (or Moorish). A very ancient dance, of masked and costumed performers, with bells, &c.

Morris Pike, O. E. (for Moorish). Long pikes copied from those of the Moors, the staves of which were covered with little nails.

Morse, Chr. (Fr. *mordre*, to bite). The clasp or brooch which fastened the cope on the breast. (See the illustration to POPE.)

Mort, O. E. (death). The notes blown on the horn at the death of a deer.

Mortuary Palls, in the Middle Ages, for the covering of the biers of dead people were richly decorated. One at Amiens is decorated, upon white stripes on a black ground, with skulls and bones and the words " memento mori " interspersed.

Mosaic, or more correctly **Mosaic Work.**
OPUS MUSIVUM, glass mosaic; OPUS TESSE-
LATUM, clay mosaic; OPUS LITHOSTROTUM,
stone mosaic.

Mosaic Glass, Millefiori. (See GLASS.)

Mose. (1) Probably a dish ("Dyschmete"
made of apples was called "Appulmoce").
(2) For MORSE (q.v.).

Moton, O. E. A piece of armour intended to
protect the right arm-pit, used in the reigns of
Henry VI., Edward IV., and Richard III.

Mottoes, in Heraldry, are words, or very short
sentences, sometimes placed above the crest,
but generally below the shield. Mottoes are
sometimes emblematical or allusive, and frequently punning, as the "Set on" of the Setons,
the "Tight on" of the Tittons, and the "Est
hic" of the Eastwicks. (See LABELS [2].)

Mould. (See MOLD.)

Mouldings. A general term for the varieties
of outline given to subordinate parts of architecture, such as *cornices, capitals, bases,* &c. These
(described in their places) are principally: the
FILLET or LIST, the ASTRAGAL or BEAD, the
CYMA REVERSA or OGEE, the CYMA RECTA
or CYMA, the CAVETTO or *hollow moulding,*
the OVOLO or *quarter round,* the SCOTIA or
TROCHILUS. These are frequently enriched by
foliage, egg-and-tongue and other ornaments, &c.
(See the article in *Parker's Glossary of Architecture* for a history of the diversities of the
mouldings in the different styles.)

Moulinet. A machine for winding up a cross-
bow.

Mound, Her. A globe encircled and arched
over with rich bands, and surmounted by a cross-
patée; an ensign of the royal estate. (See
CROWN, ORB, RE-
GALIA.)

Mountain or **Mi-
neral Blue (Green).**
(See CARBONATES
OF COPPER.)

Moustiers Faience.
Moustiers in Pro-
vence is one of the
most important of
the French ceramic
centres. The mug
represented in Fig.
469 is coloured with
varied enamels, and ornamented with medallion
and wreaths.

Fig. 469. Mug of Moustiers
make.

Muckinder, Muckinger, O. E. A pocket-
handkerchief (sc. dirty).

Mueta, Med. Lat. (Old Fr. *muette*). A
watch-tower.

Muffler. A handkerchief covering the chin
and throat, and sometimes used to cover the face
(*muffle* or *muzzle*).

"I spy a great peard under her *muffler.*" (*Shakspeare.*)

Muffs were introduced into England from
France in the reign of Charles II. They were
previously known in England, but were subsequently more common, and used by both
sexes. Very little variation has occurred in
their manufacture.

Muglias, Arab. A kind of pastilles; a substance employed in the Middle Ages for making
odoriferous beads; they were burnt for fumiga-
tions.

Mulctra, Mulctrale, Mulctrum, R. and Chr.
(*mulgeo,* to milk). A milk-pail for milking
cows. In Christian archæology it is a pastoral
vessel which is a eucharistic symbol.

Mullets, Her. Stars generally of five, but sometimes of
six or more rays. Fig. 470 is
of the date 1295, and Fig. 471
its development in 1431.

Fig. 470.

Mulleus, Mule, R. (*mullus,*
a red mullet). A red half-boot,
which only certain magistrates
had the right of wearing, viz.
the ancient dictators, consuls,
prætors, censors, and ædiles.

Fig. 471.

Mullions or **Munnions,**
Arch. The slender piers which
separate a window into several compartments.

Multifoiled, Arch. Having
many FOILS (q.v.). This term is
synonymous with POLYFOILED.

Mummy. This pigment *should* be made of
the pure Egyptian asphaltum, ground up with
drying oil or with amber varnish.

Mummy-cloths (Egyptian) were of fine unmixed flaxen linen, beautifully woven, of yarns
of nearly 100 hanks in the pound, with 140
threads in an inch in the warp, and about 64 in
the woof.

Muniment-rooms, to be strong and fire-proof,
were erected over porches, gateways, &c. They
contained charters, archives, &c. (See CHAR-
TER-HOUSE.)

Munnions, Arch., for MULLIONS (q.v.).

Mural. Generally, on a wall; as—

Mural Arch. An arch against a wall, frequent
in the aisles of mediæval buildings.

Mural Crown (Her.)
represents masonry, and
is embattled. (See
CORONA.)

Mural Monument. A
tablet fixed to a wall,
&c.

Fig. 472. Mural
crown.

Mural Painting. (See
FRESCO, TEMPERA, &c.)

Murex, R. (1) A Triton's horn or conch;
(2) *murex ferreus,* a caltrap, thrown down
to hinder the advance of cavalry, its long
spikes being so arranged as to pierce into the

horses' feet, and so disable them. (See CAL-TRAPS.)

Murrey, O. E. A reddish purple or mulberry colour. The livery of the House of York.

Murrhina, Murrhea, and **Myrrhina,** R. Murrhine vases; they are spoken of by Pliny, and have given rise to interminable treatises and discussions, with the sole result that no light whatever has been thrown on the nature of these vases.

Murrhine Glass. (See GLASS.)

Fig. 473. Walls of Megalopolis.

Murus, R. Walls as defences and fortifications, in contradistinction to *paries*, the wall of a building. Fig. 473 represents a portion of the walls of Megalopolis. (See MŒNIA.)

Muscarium, R. (*musca*, a fly). (1) A flyflap. Hence (2) The tail of a horse. (3) A case in which papers were shut up in order to preserve them from fly-stains.

Muses, the personifications of the liberal arts, are represented conventionally as follows :—

Calliope. The Muse of epic poetry ; a tablet and stylus, sometimes a roll.

Cleio. The Muse of history; seated in an arm-chair with an open roll of paper, sometimes with a sun-dial.

Euterpe. The Muse of lyric poetry; with a double flute.

Melpomene. The Muse of tragedy ; with a tragic mask, the club of Hercules, and sword ; crowned with the vine-leaves of Bacchus, and shod in the *cothurnus;* often heroically posed with one foot on a fragment of rock.

Terpsichore. The Muse of choral dance and religious song ; with lyra and *plectrum.* As the Muse of religious poetry, her expression is dignified and earnest.

Erato. The Muse of erotic poetry and soft Lydian music ; sometimes has the lyre, sometimes is represented dancing, always gentle and *feminine* in expression.

Polyhymnia. The Muse of the sublime hymn and divine tradition ; usually appears without any attribute, in an attitude of meditation ; sometimes the inscription ΜΥΘΟΥΣ (*of the myth*).

Urania. The Muse of astronomy; points

with a staff to a celestial globe. (Lachesis, one of the Parcæ, has the same attributes.)

Thaleia. The Muse of pastoral life, of comedy, and of idyllic poetry ; appears with the comic mask, a shepherd's staff, and a wreath of ivy, or basket ; sometimes dressed in a sheepskin.

The Muses are sometimes represented with feathers on their heads, alluding to their contest with the Sirens, whom they stripped of their wing feathers, which they wore as ornaments. (*Hirt. Mythologisches Bilderbuch,* p. 203.)

Museum, Gr. and R. (Μουσεῖον). Literally, a temple of the Muses. The term was afterwards applied to an establishment founded by Ptolemy I., called Soter, at Alexandria in Egypt, in which scholars and literary men were maintained at the public expense. In a villa, it was a grotto or retreat to which people retired for meditation.

Fig. 474. Opus musivum.

Musivum (opus), R. (μουσεῖον). This term was used by the Romans to denote a mosaic of small cubes of coloured glass or enamel, in contradistinction to LITHOSTROTUM (q.v.), which was a pavement made of real stones and marbles of different colours ; but in a more extended sense, the term Musivum denotes any kind of mosaic. Figs. 474 and 475 show examples of various kinds. Fig. 476 is a mosaic forming a border.

Muslin, originally esteemed for the beauty with which gold was woven in its warp, took its name from the city of Mousull in Turkey in Asia.

Fig. 475. Opus musivum.

Musquet. A long heavy match-lock gun, introduced from Spain in the Dutch wars of the 16th century, which eventually displaced the harquebus. (See SNAPHAUNCE and WHEEL-LOCK.)

Fig. 476. Opus musivum—bordering.

Musquet-rest. A staff with a forked head required to support the musquet. It was trailed by a string from the wrist.

Mustarde Villars, O. E. Either (1) a kind of cloth, probably so named from Moustier de Villiers, near Harfleur; or else (2) (as Stowe says) "a colour, now out of use." *Mustard* was a favourite colour for liveries and official dresses in the 15th century.

Mutatio, R. Literally, *change.* The Romans gave the name of *mutationes* to the post-houses for relays of horses established along the high roads for the service of the state.

Mutch, O. E. An old woman's close cap. (*Fairholt.*)

Mute, Fr. This term, derived from the Latin *muta,* is employed by ancient authors as a synonym for *belfry, turret,* or *bell-tower.*

Mutule, Arch. In a general sense, any stone or wooden projection which stands out beyond the surface of a wall, such as a rafter, for instance. In a more restricted sense, it denotes an architectural ornament characteristic of the Doric order, consisting of a square block placed at equal intervals above the triglyphs and metopes in a Doric cornice. In the Corinthian order *mutules* are replaced by modillions.

Mynchery, A.S. A nunnery. The word survives in local dialects, and is applied to the ruins; e. g. of the ancient *mynchery* at Little-more, near Oxford.

Myrtle Crown for bloodless victors. The *myrtle* was sacred to Venus. It flourished on the sea-coast of Italy and Greece. The wood is very hard, and is used for furniture, marquetry, and turning. Another myrtle wood from Van Diemen's Land is beautifully veined for cabinet work.

Myth, Gen. (μῦθος, lit. that which is spoken). The name given to obscure traditions handed down from remote antiquity, antecedent to written or precise history; opposed to *legendary* record (which can be *read*).

N.

Nablia, Nablum. A stringed musical instrument; a kind of *cithara* in the shape of a semi-circle.

Nacre, Fr. Mother-of-pearl, the iridescent inner lining of the pearl mussel or oyster.

Nacreous Shells. Iridescent shells. Several kinds are used for manufactures, as some species of *Meleagrina, Turbo, Nautili,* &c.

Nadir (Arab. *nadhir,* opposite). The part of the heavens directly under our feet; opposite to the ZENITH.

Nænia. (See NENIA.)

Naga, Malay. Jars with the figure of a dragon traced on them.

Naga Architecture (Hind. *naga,* a poisonous snake). Temples dedicated to the worship of the seven-headed snakes are found in Cashmere, remarkable for their identity of style with the Grecian Doric, unlike anything found in any other part of India. [Consult *Fergusson, History of Architecture,* ii. 703—732.]

Nagara. A Hindoo name for a music-gallery in front of the Jain temples.

Nahinna. A Persian manufacture of majolica. The Comte de Rochechouart says that the ancient faience of Persia is as admirable as the modern is detestable, though it retains a degree of oriental elegance.

Naiad. A water-nymph.

Nail. In cloth measure, 2¼ inches.

Nail-head Moulding, Arch. An ornament formed by a series of projections resembling round or angular *nail-heads.*

Nainsook, Hind. A thick sort of jaconet muslin.

Naipes, Sp. Playing-cards. The word is supposed to be derived from the initials of Nicolao Pepin, the inventor. (*Diccionario de la Lengua Castellana.*) Hence the Italian *naibi.*

Naked Flooring, Arch. The timber-work which supports a floor.

Namby-pamby. Affectedly pretty. The

term originated in criticism of an English poet of the 17th century—Ambrose Phillips.

Nancy Biscuit. A peculiar porcelain made at Nancy. The faïencerie was established in 1774 by Nicolas Lelong.

Nankeen. A buff-coloured cotton cloth, introduced from the province of Nankin, in China.

Nân-mo, Chinese. A beautiful wood, resembling cedar, used for temples, palaces, and houses of state.

Nantes. Manufactories of white faience were established here in 1588 and 1625 ; and that of Le Roy de Montilliée and others in the 18th century.

Naology. The science of temples. (See *Dudley's Naology, or a Treatise on the Origin, Progress, and Symbolical Import of the Sacred Structures of the World.*)

Fig. 477. Narghilly—Persian.

Naos, Gr. The interior apartment of a Greek temple ; the *cella* of the Roman temple.

Napery. A general term for made-up linen cloth.

Naphthar, Heb. (lit. *thick water*). The name given by Nehemiah to the substance that they found in the pit where the sacred fire of the temple had been hidden during the Captivity. This "thick water," which" (the legend says) " being poured over the sacrifice and the wood, was kindled by the great heat of the sun and then burnt with an exceedingly bright and clear flame," was the naphtha of modern commerce.

Napiform (Lat. *napus*, a turnip). Turnip-shaped.

Napkin (little *nape*). A pocket-handkerchief.

"Your napkin is too little." (*Othello.*)

Napkin Pattern. A decorative ornament very common in German wood-carving of the 15th and 16th centuries. (See LINEN SCROLL.)

Naples Majolicas were already celebrated early in the 16th century. M. Jacquemart describes some vases of colossal size, evidently constructed for "la grande décoration," being painted on only one face ; handles in the form of caryatids add to the majestic appearance of these vases ; the subjects are scriptural, executed in blue camayeu picked out in black ; the design is free, elegant though rather straggling, and the touch is bold and spirited.

Naples Yellow (It. *giallolino*). A compound of the oxides of lead and antimony, having a rich, opaque, golden hue. As a pigment for oil-painting and for porcelain and enamel, it is now superseded by chromate of lead. As a water-colour pigment it is liable to blacken upon exposure to damp or bad air.

Napron. An apron used by mediæval masons. *Limas* was another kind of apron worn by them.

Nard (Lat. *nardus*). Ointment prepared from the spikenard shrub.

Nares, Lat. (the nostrils). (1) The perforations in the register-table of an organ, which admit air to the openings of the pipes. (2) The issue of a conduit.

Nargilé or **Narghilly,** Persian. A tobacco-pipe with an arrangement for passing the smoke through water. The illustration is the bowl of a Persian pipe of this description, in Chinese porcelain. (Fig. 477.)

Nariform (Lat. *naris*, the nostril). Nose-shaped.

Narthex, Chr. The vestibule of a church ; sometimes within the church, sometimes without, but always further from the altar than the part where the "faithful" were assembled. Hence it was a place for the catechumens. The narthex communicated with the *nave* by the " beautiful gates," and with the outside by the "great gates." In monastic churches the narthex was the place for the general public.

Nasal, O. E. The bar of a helmet which protected the nose.

Nask, Hind. A *quoin*, or coin-stone.

Natalitii Ludi, R. Games in the circus in honour of an emperor's birthday.

Natatorium. A cold swimming-pool in the baths. That at Pompeii is of white marble twelve feet ten inches in diameter, and about three feet deep, with three marble steps, and a seat round it raised about ten inches from the bottom. There is a platform or *ambulatory* round the bath, also of marble. (See SIGMA.) The ceiling is vaulted, with a window in the centre. (See BAPTISTERIUM.)

Natatorium, Chr. A baptismal font ; Gr. κολυμβήθρα (*piscina probata*).

Natinz. A Persian manufacture of majolica. (See NAHINNA.)

Nativity. While the Adoration of the Magi is one of the commonest subjects of early Christian art, the Nativity is one of the rarest. It is not found in any catacomb frescoes, or the mosaics of any basilicas or churches. The only examples are sculptural, and this on ivories, gems, &c. On these generally the Child is seen wrapped in swaddling clothes as the central object, the star appears above, the Virgin on a rude couch, and sometimes St. Joseph rapt in thought, his head resting on his hand ; the ox and the ass appear behind, and shepherds with curved staves stand by adoring.

Natural. In Music, a character marked ♮ used to correct the power of a previous *sharp* or *flat*. A *natural scale* is a scale written without sharps or flats.

Naturalisti, It. Artists who work on the principle of a close adherence to the forms and colours actually combined in natural objects. The epithet was particularly applied as a term of reproach to the founders of the modern Dutch school of painting. (See IDEAL.)

Fig. 478. Naumachia, from a coin of Domitian.

Naumachia (ναῦς, a ship, and μάχη, a battle). (1) A spectacle representing a sea-fight, a subject frequently represented on coins and sculptures. (2) A building erected for such shows. Napoleon I. had a theatre at Milan filled with water for a sea-fight.

Nautilus. A shell-fish that sails on the surface of the sea in its shell. Its spiral univalve shell is a common motive in ornamental design.

" Learn of the little nautilus to sail,
  Spread the thin oar, and catch the driving gale."
                                        (*Pope.*)

Fig. 479. Nautilus. Device of the Affidati Academy.

The illustration is the device of the Affidati, an Italian literary Academy, with the motto " Safe above and below."

Fig. 480. Naval crown.

Navalis Corona. (See CORONA NAVALIS.) (Fig. 480.)

Nave, Arch. (so called from its vaulted roof resembling in shape an inverted ship (*navis*); or from *nave*, the centre of anything). The middle part or body of a church between the aisles, extending from the *choir* to the principal entrance. The Germans call this part of a church " Schiff."

Navette, Navicula, Chr. The vessel, in the shape of a boat, in which incense is placed for the supply of the thurible.

Navicella, Chr. A celebrated mosaic, at Rome, of a ship tossed by storms and assailed by demons ; emblematic of the Church.

Neanderthal. A valley near Dusseldorf, in which bones and skulls were found of men asserted to have been *præadamite.*

Neat-house, O. E. A cattle-shed.

Nebris, Gr. (from νεβρὸς, a fawn). A fawn's skin, worn originally by hunters ; an attribute of Dionysus, and assumed by his votaries. It is represented in ancient art as worn not only by male and female *bacchanals*, but also by Pans and Satyrs. It was commonly put on in the same manner as the *ægis*, or goat's skin, by tying the two fore-legs over the right shoulder, so as to allow the body of the skin to cover the left side of the wearer.

Nebular (Lat. *nebula*, a mist). Belonging to the nebulæ, or clusters of stars only visible as a light, gauzy appearance or mist in the skies.

Nebule Moulding. A decorated moulding of Norman architecture, so called from the edge

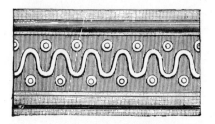

Fig. 481. Nebule Moulding.

forming an undulating or waving line. (See Fig. 481.)

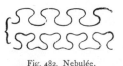

Fig. 482. Nebulée.

Nebulée, Her. A dividing and border line, as represented in Fig. 482.
Nebulous. Cloudy or hazy.
Nebuly, Her. Ornamented with light wavy lines.

Neck, Arch. The plain part at the bottom of a Roman Doric or other capital, between the mouldings and the top of the shaft. (See HYPOTRACHELIUM.)

Necklaces. An ornament common to all ages and nations. The ancient EGYPTIANS of both sexes wore them of gold or beads, generally with a large drop or figure in the centre, and strung of the various religious emblems; amethysts, pearls, gold or cornelian bottles, imitations of fish, shell, and leaves ; finally, an infinite variety of devices. (See *Wilkinson's Ancient Egyptians,* ii. 343.) An illustration of a common form of GREEK necklaces is given under *Crotalium.* The BRITISH women of the earliest ages wore necklaces of jet, ivory, and amber, beads, shells, &c., besides gold links hooked together. (See also MONILE, TORQUE.) The Anglo-Norman ladies do not appear to have worn necklaces, and no mediæval examples are found earlier than the 15th century. (See Figs. 303, 304, 483.)

Neck-mouldings, Arch. The mouldings at the bottom of the capital, in Gothic architecture.

Necrodeipnon, Gr. A feast after a funeral ; a common subject on tombs. A horse's head is usually placed in one corner of the representation, as an emblem of death as a journey.

Necrologium, Chr. A book kept in religious houses for the names of the founders and benefactors to be mentioned in the prayers.

Necromancy (Gr. νεκρὸς, the dead, and μαντεία, prophecy). Calling up the spirits of the dead for divination ; hence generally applied to con-

juring. Necromancy was practised in two ways : by inspection of the entrails, and by invoking the dead.

Fig. 483. Necklace. Costume of a Roman lady of the 16th century.

Necropolis, Gr. A city of the dead ; a cemetery.

Nectar, Gr. The drink of the gods.

Necysia, Gr. Offerings of garlands of flowers and other objects made at the tombs of deceased relatives on the anniversary of the day of death, or, as some suppose, on their birthdays. (See GENESIA.)

Needfire, or Fire of St. John Baptist (Old Germ. *Nodfyr, Niedfyr*). A superstitious practice of the ancients, derived from a pagan source, of celebrating the birthday of St. John Baptist at the midsummer solstice (St. John's Eve) by lighting fires, carrying about firebrands, or rolling a burning wheel. The practice is one of many examples of the caution with which the evangelizing ecclesiastics of the Middle Ages refrained from abruptly disturbing the deeply-rooted superstitions of the ancient Germans. [Consult *Grimm's German Mythology; Brand, Popular Antiquities.*]

Needle, Arch. An *obelisk* (q.v.).

Fig. 484. Needle Point Lace.

Needle Point in relief. To Venice belongs the invention of the two most perfect productions of the needle—"Point coupé," and Venetian point in relief. Various other wonderful products of the needle are included under the general name of Venetian point, all of exquisite workmanship. The needle point in relief is made by means of cotton placed as thick as may be required to raise the pattern; an infinity of beautiful stitches are introduced into the flowers, which are surrounded by a pearl of geometric regularity. The engraving is an exquisite specimen of the fine raised needle point.

Nef or **Ship**. A costly and curious piece of plate for the table, used as an épergne in the Middle Ages. In the 16th century they were perfect models of actual ships, with masts, yards, shrouds, and sailors climbing in the rigging. They were filled with sweetmeats, and were sometimes put on wheels; and there is one at Emden in Hanover from the hull of which wine was drunk.

Negative. In Photography, a picture on glass having the lights and shadows reversed, from which *positives* may be printed.

Neginoth, Heb. A general term for stringed musical instruments.

Nehiloth, Heb. (root *chalal*, to perforate). A general term for perforated wind instruments of music.

Nelumbo, Chinese. A fruit-tree closely connected with the Buddhist legends, and from its symbolical significance and adaptability to ornamentation, commonly represented on porcelain. (See *Jacquemart, Hist. de la Céramique.*)

Nenia, R. The funeral song which the hired mourners sang at a Roman funeral, in praise of the deceased. *Lessus* was their wailing or cry of lamentation.

Nenuphar (It. *nenufar*). The great white water-lily of Europe.

Neocori, Gr. and R. (1) Originally sweepers of the temple. (2) In early times applied to the priests in charge of temples. (3) Under the Roman emperors, to all Asiatic cities which had temples dedicated to an emperor; it occurs in this sense (Νεωκόρος) on the coins of Ephesus, Smyrna, and other cities.

Neoteric, Gr. Of recent origin; modern.

Nepaul Paper. A strong unsized paper, made in Nepaul from the pulverized bark of the *Daphne papyracea.* Sheets of this paper are sometimes made many yards square.

Nephrite. A mineral. (See JADE.)

Neptunalia. Festivals celebrated at Rome on the 23rd of July, in honour of Neptune. The people built huts of branches and foliage about the streets.

Nereids, Gr. Nymphs of the sea, who were the constant attendants of Neptune.

Nero Antico, It. Antique marble of Egyptian and other ancient statuary, of an intense black, probably the result of ages of exposure, as no marble of the same intensity of blackness is found in any quarries. Marble, called also *nero antico*, of two degrees of beauty, is quarried at Aubert (Girons) in France; and the mausoleum of Napoleon I. is constructed of this stone.

Nerved, Her. Having fibres, as leaves.

Nerves, Arch. The name is sometimes applied to the ribs and mouldings on the side surface of a vault.

Nessotrophium, Gr. A place in a Roman villa for breeding domestic ducks. It was surrounded by a high wall, on which was a high ledge with nests for the birds. A pond was dug in the middle of the enclosure, which was planted with shrubs.

Net Tracery, Arch. A simple and beautiful form of tracery of the *Decorated* period, consisting of a series of loops resembling the meshes of a net, each loop being quatrefoiled. An example occurs in the east cloister of Westminster Abbey.

Nete, Gr. The shortest string, or highest note, of the seven-stringed lyre. (See MESE.)

Netherstocks, O. E. The name given to *stockings* in the 16th century, as continuations of the trunk-hose or *upper stocks*.

Nethinim, Heb. (from *nathan*, to give). The servants of the priests and Levites about the Temple.

Nettle-cloth. A material made in Germany of very thick cotton, used as a substitute for japanned leather, on the peaks of caps, &c.

Network (*filatorium opus*). An ancient method of embroidery in England, used for church use or household furniture, by darning or working the subject upon linen netting. This method chiefly prevailed in the 14th century.

Neuma or **Pneuma** (lit. a breath). A musical passage consisting of a number of notes sung to one syllable, or simply to a sound, as " āh " prolonged. " In hujus fine *neumatizamus,* id est jubilamus, dum finem protrahimus, et ei velut caudam accingimus."

Neutral Colour is that resulting from a combination of blue, red, and yellow, resulting in grey.

Neutral Tint. An artificial pigment used in water-colours, composed of sepia, and indigo and other blues, with madder and other lakes; producing a scale of *neutral colours*.

Neuvaines, Fr. Chr. Set prayers repeated for *nine* consecutive days.

Nevers Faience. (See NIVERNAIS.)

Newcastle Glass. A *crown* glass, held the best for windows from 1728 to 1830, when it was superseded by the improved make of *sheet* glass. It was of an ash colour, subject to specks, streaks, and other blemishes, and frequently warped.

Newel, Arch. The upright central pillar supporting a geometrical staircase.

Newel Stairs, Arch. Where the steps are *pinned* into the

Fig. 485. *Niche* in the *Sigma* of the *Caldarium*.

wall, and there is no central pillar, the staircase is said to have an open or hollow newel. (See JOINERY.)

Niche, Arch. (It. *nicchia*, a sea-shell). A recess in a wall for a statue or bust. (Fig. 485.)

Niche-vaulting, Arch. (Germ. *Muschelgewölbe*). A form of roofing in a semi-cupola design, common in the choirs of churches.

Nick, Old Nick, O. E. (Icelandic *nikr;* A.S. *nicor,* a water-god). The devil.

Nickel (contraction of *Kupfernickel,* or Nick's copper, a term of derision given to it by the German miners). A white or reddish-white metal, from which nickel-silver is made. It is used to a large extent in the arts, being remarkable for the peculiar whiteness and silver-like lustre which it communicates to other metals when alloyed with them.

Nickel-silver. German silver, or white metal, a compound of tin and nickel.

Niello. The art of chasing out lines or forms, and inlaying a black composition called *nigellum* or niello, was probably well known to the Greeks. The Byzantines compounded for this purpose silver, lead, sulphur, and copper, and laid it on the silver in a powder; being then passed through the furnace, it melted and incorporated with the solid metal. A process producing a similar result of black tracery is practised in porcelain painting, and called NIELLO-ENAMEL.

Nigged Ashlar, O. E. Stone hewn with a pick or a pointed hammer, presenting a gnawed or nibbled surface : from the Swedish *nagga,* to gnaw.

Nilometer. A building erected, A.D. 847, in the island of Rhoda, opposite to Cairo, for recording the annual rise of the Nile (i. e. 16 cubits). It is a slender octagonal shaft about 20 feet in height, with a Corinthian capital. (See the *Builder,* xvii. 255.)

Nimbed, Her. Having the head encircled with a *nimbus ;* usually represented by a circular line.

Nimbus (Lat. *nimbus,* a bright or black cloud). In Christian art, a disc or plate, commonly golden, sometimes red, blue, or green, or banded like a rainbow, placed vertically behind the heads of persons of special dignity or sanctity as a symbol of honour. After the 8th century living persons were, in Italy, distinguished by a square nimbus, which sometimes assumed the form of a scroll partly unrolled. The nimbus is of heathen origin. Virgil describes Juno as " nimbo succincta." The heads of the statues of the gods, and the Roman emperors, after they began to claim divine honours, were decorated with a crown of rays. On medals of the Christian emperors also the nimbus is found, e.g. Constantine. In illuminated MSS. it is found on Pharaoh, Ahab, and other kings. It

Q

is a familiar symbol of dignity or power in the East, but does not appear as a Christian emblem before the 6th century. [See the article NIMBUS in the *Dict. of Christian Antiquities.*] (See AUREOLE, GLORY, VESICA PISCIS, &c.)

Nincompoop, O. E. A corruption of the Latin *non compos;* a fool.

Ninth. In Music, an interval consisting of an octave and a tone, or semi-tone.

Nisan, Heb. The month in the Jewish calendar answering to our April.

Nitrate of Silver, used in photography, is silver dissolved in nitric acid.

Nivarius (saccus), R. A bag of snow used as a wine-cooler. (See COLLUM VINARIUM.)

Nivernais Faience. An important branch of the ceramic art, established in 1608 at Nevers in France by the brothers Conrade. (Fig. 486.)

Nobbled Stone, Arch. Stone roughly rounded at the quarry to diminish its bulk for transport.

Noble. A gold coin worth 6s. 8d. (Fig. 487.)

Fig. 486. Jar. Nivernais Faience.

Nodes. In Astronomy, the two points where the orbit of a heavenly body intersects the ecliptic.

Nodus, Arch. The Latin name for a key-stone, or a *boss* in vaulting.

Nog, O. E. Timbers built into walls to strengthen the structure. They show on the plastering of houses in ornamental patterns. In Kent these houses are called "wood noggen" houses.

Noggin, O. E. "A mug or pot of earth with a large belly and narrower mouth."

Nogging, Arch. Brickwork in panels carried between quarters.

Nome, Egyp. (νομός). A division or district of Egypt; there were forty-four in all. Each nome was placed under the protection of a special divinity, and ruled by a resident military governor.

Nonagon. A nine-sided polygon.

Nones. (1) R. One of the three divisions of the Roman month; the ninth days before the IDES of each month. (2) Chr. One of the HOURS OF PRAYER (q.v.).

Nonunia, O. E. A quick time in music, containing nine crotchets between the bars. (*Halliwell.*)

Norman Architecture. It was introduced into England at the Conquest, A.D. 1066, and was superseded in the 12th century by the Early English style. Solid massive masonry, round-headed doors and windows, and low square central tower are (broadly) its characteristics. Among details the zigzag and the billet mouldings are the most noticeable. (Fig. 488.)

Norman Pottery, Mediæval. The illustration is from a pavement of a church of the 12th century. "Nothing," says Jacquemart, "is more curious than the study of these tiles, in which, with rudimentary means, art already begins to manifest its power. There, in a graceful chequer-work, the fleur-de-lis of France heightens at intervals a semé of trefoils and rosettes; scrolls of notched leaves combine in graceful borders; circles divided crossways receive in their sections stars and heraldic suns; here are armour-clad warriors, mounted upon horses richly caparisoned, &c.— all that picturesque fancy assisted by the resources of heraldry could invent to animate the cold compartments of the pavement, and give a meaning to the vast naves trodden every day by the Christian multitude." (*Histoire de l'Art Céramique.*) (Fig. 489.)

Norns, Nornas, Icelandic. The three Fates, whose names signify the Past, the Present, and the Future.

Norroy King at Arms. The third of the kings at arms, whose jurisdiction lies to the north of the Trent.

North Side of a church "was regarded as the source of the cold wind, and the haunt of Satan. In some Cornish churches there is an entrance called the devil's door, adjoining the font, which was only opened at the time of the renunciation made in baptism, for the escape of the fiend. In consequence of these superstitions, and its sunless aspect, the northern parts of churchyards are

Fig. 487. Noble of Henry V.

Fig. 488. Norman Architecture. The Round Church, Cambridge.

usually devoid of graves." (*Wallcott, Sacred Archæology*.)

Norwegian Architecture. The timber-built churches are of great interest, and exhibit the wonderful durability of the Norwegian pine. They are generally in the form of a cross, with a tower in the centre ending in a cupola or spire, and with high pitched roofs. The ornamental details are elaborate and richly carved. The whole is often painted of a rich brown

Fig. 489. Incrusted Tile. Norman. Middle Ages.

colour; sometimes of a bright red. Some o these churches date from the 11th or 12th century, and are an imitation in wood of the masonic style of the period.

Nosocomium, R. (νοσο-κομεῖον). A hospital.

Notatus, R. (*noto*, to mark). A slave branded with a hot iron.

Note of a Room. The vibrations of the air in a chamber or vaulted space produce a musical *note* proper to the dimensions and other conditions of the place, which a good musical ear can recognize and identify. [See *T. R. Smith's Acoustics*, pp. 83—87.]

Nottingham White. White lead. (See CARBONATE OF LEAD.)

November (Lat. *novem*, nine). The *ninth* month of the Roman year, which began with March. It consisted originally of thirty days, but Julius Cæsar added one to it. Augustus, however, reduced it to its original number.

Nowed, Her. Coiled in a knot, as a snake. The illustration (Fig. 490) is the ordinary device of the house of Savoy—the "true lovers' knot ;" with the Latin motto, " It binds but constrains not."

Nowel, O. E. (Fr. *noel*, from *natalis*). A cry of joy ; properly that at Christmas, of joy for the birth of the Saviour. It originally signified the feast of Christmas.

Nubilarium, R. A shed used as a barn ; it was situated close to the threshing-floor.

Numella, Numellus, R. A kind of pillory

for keeping men and animals in a fixed position. It was made use of in surgical operations, and as an instrument of torture.

Fig. 490. Nowed. Device of the House of Savoy.

Numismatics (*numisma*, coined money). The science of coins and medals. The earliest known coins were issued by the Greeks, probably in the 8th century B.C. (See the Article in the *Encyclopædia Britan.*, 8th edition, from which reference can be taken to exhaustive treatises on the various ramifications of this science.)

Nummud, Persian. A carpet of felt much used in Persia.

Nun's Thread. A kind of thread formerly made to a large extent in Paisley.

Fig. 491. Nuremberg Vase, enamelled in relief.

Nun's Work (Fr. *œuvre de nonnain*). As early as the 14th century needlework was generally so described. Ancient lace is still so called in many parts of the country.

Nundinæ (*novemdinæ*; from *novem*, nine, and *dies*, days). Roman weeks; the nomenclature including the day before and that after the seven days. The name was given to the weekly *market*-days at Rome.

Nupta, R. (*nubo*, to wed). A married woman.

Nuremberg Vase. Fig. 491 is one of the gems, of the Renaissance period, issued from Nuremberg; a vase with portraits heightened with enamels and gold. (*Jacquemart.*)

Nurhag (Sardinian *Noraga*). Primitive buildings in the island of Sardinia, of remote antiquity, having turrets as high as 30 to 60 feet, and containing stones of 100 cubic feet each in their structure. [See *Waring, Stone Monuments.*]

Nurspell. An old English game like trap, bat, and ball. It is played with a *kibble*, a *nur*, and a *spell*. When the end of the *spell* is struck with the *kibble*, the *nur* rises into the air, &c.

Nut. In Christian symbolism, an emblem of

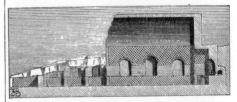

Fig. 492. Nymphæum of Egeria, near Rome.

the Divinity of Christ hidden in His manhood. St. Augustine has a long treatise on the symbolism of the husk, shell, and kernel of the nut. (*Serm. de temp. Dominic. ante Nativ.*)

Fig. 493. Nymphæum at Nismes (restored).

Nut Oil. This medium for colour-grinding is derived from the walnut ; as a vehicle it is preferred to linseed oil, and is the quickest dryer. (See MEDIUMS, OILS.)

Nutmeg Ornament, Arch. A common feature in Early English work in the *north* of England, but not in the south. It resembles half a nutmeg, and is carved at certain distances apart in the hollow of a dripstone at St. Mary's Church, Nunmonkton, Yorkshire.

Nuttoo, Hind. A nose-stud or ornament worn by Indian women, often set with brilliants, rubies, emeralds, and pearls.

Nymphæum, Nympheum (νύμφαιον and νυμφεῖον). Literally, *a building consecrated to the nymphs.* It was a large and richly-decorated chamber, with columns, niches, and statues, and a fountain in the centre. Nymphæa were often erected near the head of a spring, and formed cool and agreeable retreats. Fig. 492 represents a portion of the ruins of the nymphæum of Egeria, near Rome ; and Fig. 493 the interior of the nymphæum at Nismes, restored. In Christian times the fountains or cisterns common at the doors of churches were called *nymphæa.*

Nymphs. Inferior goddesses of the mountains, forests, waters, or meadows. Those presiding over rivers, &c., were OCEANIDES, NAIADS, NEREIDS ; those over mountains, OREIADS ; those over woods and trees, DRYADS and HAMADRYADS ; those over valleys, NAPÆÆ, &c. They were represented in art as beautiful young women. The waters of Hades had their presiding nymphs, the AVERNALES.

O.

O was used as a numeral by the ancients to represent 11, and with a dash over it (Ō) to denote 11,000.

O, O. E. Anything circular. Shakspeare calls the stars "those fiery O's."

Oak-apple Day, O. E. The 29th of May, in commemoration of the escape of King Charles in the oak-tree.

Oak-tree, the emblem of virtue, force, and strength, is frequently introduced in ancient sculpture. In Christian art an attribute of St. Boniface, in allusion to his cutting down a Druidical oak.

Oasis (from the Coptic *ouah,* a resting-place). One of the verdant spots that occur at intervals in the deserts of Africa ; hence any fertile spot in a desert, with the obvious symbolical application.

Oast-house, O. E. A kiln for drying hops.

Oban. The principal gold coin of Japan, worth about 4*l.* 2*s.*

Obba, Gr. and R. (ἄμβιξ). A drinking-vessel of earthenware or wood, probably funnel-shaped ; hence—

Obbatus, Gr. and R. Made in the shape of an *obba,* that is, terminating in a point. The term is often applied to the cap of the Dioscuri.

Obelisk (ὀβελίσκος, lit. a small spit). Also called a needle. A tall, rectangular, monolithic column, of slightly pyramidal shape, invented by the Egyptians ; in nearly every case they are covered from the base to the top, and on all four sides, with hieroglyphic symbols. (Fig. 494.)

Oberon. The king of the fairies.

Obex, R. (*objicio,* to obstruct). Any contrivance to keep a door closed, such as a bolt, lock, latch, iron bar, &c.

Oblata, Chr. The sacred bread. This word was more commonly applied to the *unconsecrated* loaf, and HOSTIA to the *consecrated.* (For particulars respecting the preparation and the form of *oblates,* see the article ELEMENTS in *Smith and Cheetham, Dict. of Christian Antiquities.*) In the same manner OBLATI were lay-brothers in a monastery who had not taken the vows.

Oblate. Flattened or shortened like the earth at the poles. The earth is an *oblate* spheroid.

Oblationarium, Chr. A small table placed near the high altar, or at the end of one of the side aisles, on which the people laid their offerings. It was also used, when in the choir, to hold the sacred utensils in place of the *credence-table.* In the Greek Church the *oblationarium* is still used for the bread, wine, and sacred vessels required in the mass.

Oble, Oblete (Lat. *oblata*), O. E. The consecrated wafer distributed to communicants at mass.

> "Ne Jhesu was nat the *oble*
> That reysed was at the sacre."
> (*Harl. MS.*)

Hence, a wafer-cake, sweetened with honey, and made of the finest wheaten bread.

Oboe or **Hautboy** (from Fr. *haut,* high, and *bois,* wood). A wind instrument like a flute, sounded through a reed.

Obolo, Mod. A copper coin, worth about a halfpenny, circulated in the Ionian Islands.

Obolos, Gr.(derived from ὀβολὸs, a brooch, originally). A small copper coin worth the sixth part

Fig. 494. Egyptian Obelisk.

of a drachm. The obolos in later times was of bronze ; but in the best times of Athens it was of silver. Its value in the Æginetan standard was 1·166 of a penny.

Obscœna, Chr. Obscene representations frequently met with in Christian iconography, which, according to De Canmont, are "to warn the faithful that they ought to enter the temple with pure hearts, leaving outside all the passions that soil the soul."

Obsidian. A volcanic glass found near volcanoes, used in antiquity for the manufacture of mirrors, axes, knives, &c. (See GLASS.)

Obstragulum, R. A long leather strap (*amentum*) worn as a fastening to the *crepida*.

Obstrigillum, R. A shoe, the sides of which were lengthened into a lappet over the instep.

Obturaculum, Obturamentum, R. (*obturo*, to stop up). A stopper for the neck of a bottle or the mouth of a vessel.

Obverse. Of a coin, the face, or side which bears the principal symbol. The other side is the REVERSE.

Ocal, Span. Coarse silk.

Occabus, R. (ὄκκαβοs). A kind of spoon.

Occidental Diamond. A precious stone of inferior hardness and beauty.

Occultation. The disappearance or eclipse of one heavenly body behind another.

Ocellata, R. (lit. marked with *ocelli* or spots). Marbles used as playthings by children.

Ocellated. Full of eyes ; said of a peacock's tail. (See Fig. 398.)

Ochre. Argillaceous earth of different colours which, when finely ground, is used as a pigment. *Red ochre* is a form of specular iron ore ; *brown ochre* is a variety of hæmatite. The *yellow ochres* become red when calcined, but the finest reds are made from those which are brown in the bed. Native red ochre is called *red chalk* or *reddle* in England. *Spanish Brown, Indian Red, Venetian Red,* and the yellow ochres have nearly the same composition. The other ochres are known as *Oxford, Roman,* and *stone ochres,* and as *terra di Sienna* and *umber.* They are all valuable and durable pigments for oil, water, or enamel painting. (See AMATITA.)

Ocrea, R. A greave ; a piece of armour which covered the shin-bone from below the knee to the ankle. It was generally richly ornamented by designs embossed or chased upon it. (Modern JAMBES.)

Octagon. A figure of eight equal sides, considered as an emblem of regeneration ; consequently the proper form for baptisteries and fonts. (*Fairholt.*)

Octahedron. A solid contained by eight equal sides, which are equilateral triangles.

Octastyle, R. (ὀκτά-στυλος). An *octastyle* portico is a portico having eight columns in front ; *octastyle* pediment, a pediment supported by eight columns. The pediment of the Parthenon at Athens, from which the Elgin Marbles come, is an *octastyle*.

Octave. (1) In Music, the longest interval in the diatonic scale ; as from *do* to *do*, or C to c. (2) Chr. Eight days, or the eighth day after a Church festival (the festival being included) kept as a repetition or prolongation of the festival. It is a Western custom unknown to the Eastern Church.

October. The eighth month of the old Roman year, but the tenth in the calendar of Numa, Julius Cæsar, &c. It was sacred to Mars, and a horse called the *October equus* was annually sacrificed to Mars.

Octofoil, Her. A double *quatrefoil;* the *difference* of a ninth son.

Octophoron or **Octaphoron**, Gr. and R.

(ὀκτώφορον). A litter (*lectica*) borne by eight slaves.

Ocularium, Med. Lat.

The narrow slit or opening for the sight in a helmet. (See Fig. 495.)

Oculus, Chr. A round window of frequent occurrence in the tympanum of the pediment in Latin basilicas, and occasionally in certain churches of the 11th century.

Ode (ᾠδή, a song). A short lyrical poem, intended to be sung to the accompaniment of an instrument, especially the *lyre*; hence the expression *lyric* poetry.

Odeon (ᾠδεῖον; ᾠδή, a song). A small theatre at Athens, built by Pericles for musical performances. By analogy, the name was applied to any theatre built on a circular plan and covered with a roof, like that of Athens, shown in Fig. 496.

Fig. 495. Ocularium in a helmet.

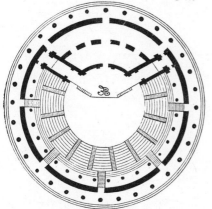

Fig. 496. Ground-plan of the Odeon at Athens.

Œcos, Œcus, Gr. (οἶκος). A Greek house; the term, however, denoted rather a large apartment resembling the atrium, but entirely shut in, that is to say, without impluvium. In Fig. 497, A is the œcus; B, C, two rooms forming offices; D, a tablinum; E, a portico; G, the entrance to the house; H, work-rooms; J, the triclinium. *Œcus tetrastylos* was a house in which four columns supported the roof; *œcus Corinthius*, having one order of columns supporting an archi-

trave, cornice, and an arched roof; *œcus Egyptius*, in which the pillars supported

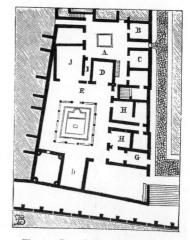

Fig. 497. Ground-plan of a Greek house.

gallery with a paved floor, forming a walk round the apartment; above these pillars others were placed, one-fourth less in height; and between the upper columns were placed windows; and the *œcus Cyzicenus*, which looked to the north, and, if possible, faced gardens, to which it opened by folding-doors, was a summer-house. (See DOMUS.)

Œil-de-bœuf, Arch. A small round or oval window in a roof.

Œillets. (See OILLETS.)

Œnochoê (Gr. οἶνος, wine, and χέω, to pour). An earthen vase used to take the wine out of the crater and distribute it into cups. It is the vase carried by the goddesses, and used for libations. (Figs. 498, 498 a.)

Œnophorum, Gr. and R. (οἰνοφόρον). A light case or basket for carrying wine.

Œnopolium, Gr. and R. (οἰνοπώλιον). The shop of a dealer who sold wine to be

Fig. 498. Œnochoê, decorated with *zoophori*, or bands of animals.

carried away; distinct from the *taberna meritoria*
or *deversoria*, which was a public tavern.

Offendix, R. A string by which the *apex*,
or cap worn by the flamens, Salians, or other
members of priestly colleges, was fastened under
the chin.

Offertoria, Chr. (1) The anthems sung in a
Christian church while the oblations were received; mentioned by Isidorus, A.D. 595:
"Offertoria quæ
in sacrificiorum
honore canuntur."
(2) Large plates,
which, in the
C h r i s t i a n
churches of Gaul,
served to collect
the bread which
the Christians had
just laid on the
altar. A beau-
tiful specimen of
such dishes, found
in Siberia in 1867,
and described by
Rossi, is 6 inches
in diameter, and
weighs 1½ lbs. It
has a relief in
repoussé w o r k,
consisting of a
cross planted on a
small globe stud-
ded with stars,
beneath which
issue the four rivers of Paradise; and on either
side stand two nimbed angels, holding a rod in
the left hand, and raising their right hand
towards the cross in token of adoration. De
Rossi regards this dish as the work of Byzantine
goldsmiths of the 6th century. (3) At Rome,
acolytes went in and out among the people, and
collected the offerings in napkins of fine linen or
richer material called also *offertoria*.

Fig. 498 a. Œnochoê, or Wine-jug,
in black glazed earthenware.

Offertories, in Egyptian archæology, are offerings made to the gods, of various shapes; such
as outstretched hands supporting a cup, or
spoons of ivory, wood, or bronze, the handle of
which is formed by a human figure.

Officina, R. A workshop, in contradistinction to *taberna*, a store, and *apotheca*, a shop;
thus, *officina ærariorum* was a goldsmith's
workshop; *officina fullonum*, a fuller's establishment.

Offuscati. One of the Italian literary academies. They bore for their device a bear,
roused from his natural heaviness by the stings
of bees, with the motto, "Stings (or points) will
sharpen steel." (Fig. 499.)

Ogam, Celtic. The sacred writing of the
Druids. (Cf. OGHAM.)

Ogee Arch or **Contrasted Arch** or **Moulding**, Arch. An arch or moulding described

Fig. 499. Device of the Offuscati Academy.

by means of four centres, so as to be alternately concave and convex. It was frequently employed in fifteenth-century monuments, and its constant recurrence in the *later
Gothic* or *flamboyant* architecture has given
rise to its French name of *ogival*.

Ogham. A kind of short-hand writing or
cipher in use among the ancient Irish. (*S.*)

Ogivale, Fr. A French architectural term
of constant occurrence, applied to the architecture of the mediæval period in France, during
which the *pointed arch* was used.

Ogive, Fr. Arch. A *pointed* arch; *not* the
OGEE.

Ogivette, Arch. A small ogee.

Ogress, Her. A pellet or black roundle.

Oil Painting was introduced in Flanders by
the brothers Van Eyck in 1410, and in Italy by
Antonello da Messina in or about 1455.

Oillets or **Oylets.** Loopholes.

Oils. The fixed oils used in painting are
linseed, *walnut*, and *poppy*, purified and rendered
drying by the addition of *litharge*. They
should be pale in colour, limpid, and transparent, and should dry quickly: *nut oil* in a
few hours, *linseed* in a day, and *poppy oil* in
thirty-six to forty hours. The essential oils used
in painting are *turpentine*, for diluting the pigments ground in oil, and *spike*, or *lavender*, for
wax and enamel painting.

Oinerusis, Gr. (οἰν-ήρυσις). (See ARYSTI-
CHOS.)

Ointment-box, in Christian art, is the attribute of St. Mary Magdalene, St. Joseph of
Arimathæa, and other saints.

Oiron, a small town in France (so named from the flocks of geese which circle round it

Fig. 500. Covered Tazza ; Faience of Oiron. In the Louvre.

Oi-rond in winter), is the place where the fine faiences, usually called Henri II. ware, were made. "Here is France," says M. Jacquemart, "in the 16th century in possession of a pottery, the discovery of which is attributed 200 years later to England." There are only about fifty pieces known, five of which may be seen in the South Kensington Museum.

Okel, Egyp. A caravanserai. A large covered court surrounded by two stories of galleries, of which the lower is used as shops, &c., and the upper one as lodging-rooms.

Oldham. A coarse kind of cloth originated at Oldham in Norfolk, *temp.* Richard II.

Olibanum. A gum-resin used for incense.

Oliphant, A.S. An elephant ; hence a hunting-horn of ivory.

Olive. A blue-grey colour ; violet mixed with green.

Olive(-tree). (1) In Christian art, the emblem of peace and concord, and frequent on early Christian tombs in the catacombs, with or without the dove. (2) Arch. Its leaf was introduced into sculpture by the ancients, in wreaths or garlands. The Corinthian order is enriched with *olive*-leaves, as are almost all the antiques at Rome of this order. (3) R. The *corona oleagina*, an honorary wreath made of olive-leaves, was conferred by the Romans on soldiers and commanders through whose instrumentality a triumph

had been obtained when they were not personally present in the action. (4) Gr. It was the *olive*-tree that Minerva caused to spring from the ground in the citadel at Athens. (5) The colour and grain of the wood, and of the root portion especially, are very beautiful, and valuable for decorative and cabinet work.

Olivette. A Flemish name for *poppy oil.*

Olivine. A variety of *chrysolite* of a dark green, commonly called bottle-green colour.

Olla, R. An earthenware vessel of very common make. It resembled our flower-pots, but had swelling sides, and was covered with a lid. It was used for cooking meat and vegetables and for preserving grapes (*uva ollaria*), and as a cinerary urn (*olla ossuaria* or *cineraria*). Hence—

Olla-podrida, Sp. A stew of meat and vegetables mixed, common in Spain. The word is used to describe any other incongruous mixture.

Ollarium, R. A niche in a sepulchral chamber, in which the *olla ossuaria* was placed. (See CINERARIUM, Fig. 160.)

Olpê, Gr. (ὄλπη). A kind of *aryballos* with a curved handle, but no spout (originally a leather oil-flask).

Olympiad, Gr. ('Ολυμπίας). The period of four years between two consecutive celebrations of the Olympic games. The first Olympiad began B.C. 776.

Olympic Games, Gr. Games instituted by Hercules in honour of Jupiter Olympius ; they were the most ancient and celebrated in all Greece. They derived their name from Olympia, in Greece, where they were celebrated. They were finally suppressed by Theodosius, A.D. 394.

Ombre. A kind of damask.

Ombros. The name for a particular quality of *madder.*

Omophagi, Gr. (ὠμο-φάγοι, sc. δαῖτες, i. e. flesh-eating banquets). Festivals held at Chio and Tenedos in honour of Bacchus.

Omophorion. (1) An article of female dress, worn on the *shoulders.* (2) A vestment of the Greek Church, consisting of a long woollen band with embroidered crosses. It is typical of the lost sheep borne home on the shoulders of the Shepherd.

Onager, Onagrus, R. An engine for hurling stones of great size.

Onicolo or **Nicolo.** A variety of the onyx, with a deep-brown ground, on which is a band of bluish white, used for making cameos.

Onocentaurs. Fabulous animals, half man, half ass.

Onychomancy (*onyx,* a nail). Divination by means of the marks on the nails of the hands.

Onyx (ὄνυξ, a finger-nail). (1) A general name for the varieties of the agate which consist of alternate layers of white, brown, or black, greatly valued by the ancients for cameos.

In the Christian symbolism the onyx typifies innocence and candour. (See ONICOLO.) (2) The name has also been applied by the ancients to Oriental alabaster. (3) Onyx marble was a name given to Algerian marble from Oran, of which "pure white, brilliant red, golden yellow, and hues of green, with every variety of striation and flocculence, exist." [See the *Building News*, xiv. 489.]

Opa, Opê, Gr. Arch. (ὀπή). A cavity in which a tie-beam (*tignum*) rests ; whence the space included between two ὀπαί or *tigna* was called *metopa* or *intertignum*.

Opacity. Want of transparency.

Opaion, Gr. Arch. The panels on a ceiling formed by the intersection of its beams.

Opal. A semi-transparent stone, remarkable for the play of colours that it exhibits. Three varieties are, the *oriental opal*, called also the *noble* opal and the *harlequin* opal, remarkable for its flashes of brilliant colours having a triangular disposition. The affection that the ancients entertained for this beautiful gem was unbounded. The Roman senator Nonnius preferred exile to parting with a brilliant opal the size of a filbert which Marc Antony coveted. The *fire opal* is furnished principally by Mexico. Its colour, more pronounced than that of the *oriental* opal, and the carmine or vinous red tint of its fires, permit it to be easily recognized. The *common opal* displays very little fire ; its colour is milk-white, which, joined to a texture extremely homogeneous, renders it semi-transparent. [*L. Dieulafait.*]

Opal Glass, called also Milk-white Glass ; prepared for globes to lamps, &c.

Opales, Opalia, R. Festivals of Ops, the wife of Saturn, which were held every year on the fourteenth of the calends of January (19th of December).

Opalescent. Having a play of colours like the *opal*.

Open-tide, O. E. The season between Epiphany and Ash-Wednesday, when marriages were publicly solemnized.

Opera. A lyrical drama set to music ; originated at Florence in the 16th century. [Consult *Doni* (passim), *Arteaga Manfredini, Signorelli*, &c. ; also *Dr. Burney's Tours and Correspondence*, and *Grimm's Correspondence*.]

Operculum, R. A cover for any kind of earthenware vessel.

Ophicleide (ὄφις, a serpent, and κλείς, a key). A wind instrument of brass or copper made in the form of a serpent. Generally, the bass of a military band.

Ophiomancy, Gr. Divination by snakes.

Ophiomorphous. Snake-shaped.

Ophite or **Ophiolite**. Green porphyry or SERPENTINE.

Ophites, Chr. A sect which arose in the 2nd century in the Christian Church. They believed that the Serpent who tempted Eve was Christ himself. They are also called SERPENTINIANS. (*S.*)

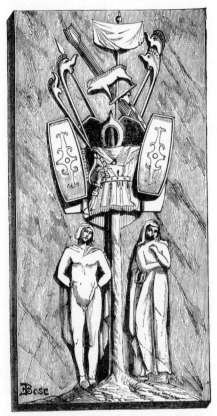

Fig. 501. Opima Spolia. Trophy of Gallic Ensigns.

Opima Spolia, R. The "spoils of honour," consisting of armour set up as a trophy and dedicated in the temple of Jupiter Feretrius at Rome. These were spoils taken from the chief of a hostile army, who had been killed by the hand of a Roman general. Plutarch asserts that the *spolia opima* were actually taken only three times.

Opinicus, Her. A fabulous heraldic monster; a dragon before and a lion behind, with a camel's tail.

Opisthodomos, Gr. (ὀπισθό-δομος). Latin, **Posticum**. A small chamber placed at the back of a temple, to which the priests alone had access.

Oporotheca, Gr. (ὀπωρο-θήκη). A store-house for fruits.

Oppidan. At Eton College, a boy who is not a king's scholar, and boards in the town.

Fig. 502. Oppidum and carceres of the circus of Caracalla.

Oppidum, R. A fortified town, and thence the mass of buildings occupying the extremity of a circus, in which were the stalls for the chariots and horses (*carceres*). Fig. 502 gives a representation of the *oppidum* in the circus of Caracalla.

Optical Correction is a name given to the task of adapting art objects, or architectural proportions and ornaments, to the circumstances of distance or comparison in which they are to be exhibited. Belzoni observes that the heads of colossal Egyptian statues are proportionally larger than the lower members. (For numerous examples of this contrivance, see the article in the *Architectural Publication Society's Dictionary.*)

Optics (Gr. ὄπτομαι, to see). The science of the nature and properties of light ; of its changes as it penetrates or is reflected or absorbed by bodies ; of the structure of the eye, and the laws of vision ; and of instruments in connexion with sight. It is thus closely connected with the science of colour, and the arts in general. The earliest treatise extant on this science is Euclid's *Optica et Catoptrica*. (Cf. *Dr. Smith's Optics*, &c.)

Optigraph. A telescope for copying landscapes. (See CLAUDE GLASS.)

Optostratum, R. (ὀπτὸς, brick, and στρωτὸν, strewn). A brick pavement, often arranged in a herring-boned pattern, as in the OPUS SPICATUM. (Fig. 509.)

Opus Albarium. (See STUCCO.)

Opus Alexandrinum. A mosaic flooring

Fig. 503. Alexandrinum opus.

much used by the Romans, consisting of geometric figures, and generally of only two kinds of tessera, red and black on a white ground. (See MUSIVUM OPUS.)

Opus Araneum (spider-work). A kind of embroidery, 13th century ; modern "guipure d'art."

Opus Consutum. Appliqué work in embroidery. (See APPLIQUÉ.)

Opus Filatorium. A kind of embroidery, 14th century ; modern "filet brodé."

Opus Græcum, R. Inlaid pavement. (See MUSIVUM OPUS.)

Opus Incertum, R. A Roman method of building ; the construction of walls of very small rough stones, not laid in courses, but held together by the mortar.

Fig. 504. Pseudisodomum opus, with a course of opus insertum.

Opus Insertum, R. A Roman method of building, of courses of flat tiles, the most durable of all. Such courses were also introduced in the other kinds of stone and brick walls, in which they served as bond-courses, and also kept the damp from rising from the ground.

Fig. 505. Musivum opus.¶

Opus Musivum. Mosaic. (See MUSIVUM.)

Opus Pectineum (comb-wrought). Woven work imitating embroidery.

Opus Phrygianum, R. Fine embroidery. (See ORPHREY.)

Opus Plumarium (feather-stitch). Embroidery

of which the stitches overlap one another like the feathers of a bird.

Fig. 506. Pseudisodomum opus.

Opus Pseud-iso-domum, Gr. (lit. *quasi-equal* structure). A Greek method of building in which the courses are (1) parallel and unequal,

Fig. 507. Gate of Lions at Mycenæ.
Pseudisodomum opus.

but regular among themselves, as in Fig. 506 ; or (2) irregular altogether, as in the Gate of Lions at Mycenæ, Fig. 507 (or in Fig. 504).

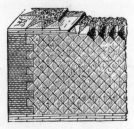

Fig. 508. Structura reticulata.

Opus Pulvinarium (cushion-style). Embroidery like modern Berlin work, generally used for cushions.

Opus Reticulatum, R. A Roman method of construction, with an ornamental surface resembling the meshes of a *net*.

Opus Spicatum, R. Herring-bone masonry.

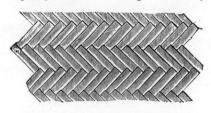

Fig. 509. Spicatum opus.

Or, Her. The metal gold, expressed in engraving by small dots, as on Fig. 375.

Or basané, Fr. Leather stamped in gold, used as hangings in the 16th and 17th centuries.

Ora, R. The cable which fastened the stern of a ship to the shore, while the ANCORALE kept her head out to sea.

Ora. An old Saxon coin of 16 or 20 pence in value.

Orange. The colour formed by the mixture of 5 parts of red and 3 parts of yellow. It is the complementary of blue. The nearest pigment is *cadmium yellow*.

Orange Chrome. A sub-chromate of lead, which yields a beautiful orange pigment.

Orange Madder-lake. (See MADDER.)

Orange Minium. (See MINIUM.)

Orange Vermilion. A durable pigment for oil and water colours, in colour resembling *red lead*.

Orange Yellow. A yellow inclining to red, represented by molybdate of lead. (*Ansted, Elementary Course.*)

Orange-tree. In Christian art, symbol of the " Heavenly Bride."

Oranti, It. The name given to certain male and female figures found in the catacomb frescoes at Rome, represented with the hands spread in the Eastern attitude of prayer.

Orarium, R. A scarf or handkerchief thrown to the crowd in a circus, to wave to the chariot-drivers. In Christian archæology, (1) A scarf affixed to the pastoral staff; as early as the 13th century. (2) The stole. (3) The border of an ecclesiastical vestment. (*Planché.*) (See STOLE, SUDARIUM.)

Orb. One of the emblems of sovereignty with which kings are solemnly invested at their coronation. It is a globe surmounted by a cross, and is held in the palm of the left hand. In Art it is a common attribute of the Infant Saviour.

Orca, Gr. and R. (ὅρκη or ὕρχα). An earthenware vessel of large size, but smaller than the amphora; it was used for holding salted fish. The diminutive is *orcula*; the modern Italian *orcio*.

Orchestra, Gr. and R. (ὀρχήστρα, i.e. dancing-place). The lowest part of the Greek and Roman theatres; usually occupied by the chorus. It contained an altar, on which sacrifices to Bacchus were sometimes made.

Orchestrino. A modern musical instrument invented by Poulleau. It was shaped like a pianoforte with similar finger-keys, and the sounds were produced by the friction of a bow upon strings.

Orchestrion. A modern portable organ, invented by the Abbé Vogler about 1789. A similarly-named instrument invented in 1796 by Kunz, a Bohemian, consisted of a pianoforte combined with some organ-stops.

Orcula. Diminutive of *orca*.

Order. In classical architecture, a column entire; i.e. base, shaft, capital, and entablature. There are usually said to be five *orders*: the Tuscan, Doric, Ionic, Corinthian, and Composite.

Orders of Knighthood. (See KNIGHTHOOD.)

Ordinary, Her. An early principal charge of a simple character.

Oread. A mountain-nymph.

Oreæ, R. (*ora*, the mouth). A snaffle-bit for horses.

Oreiller, Her. A cushion or pillow.

Oreillettes, Fr. Ear-pieces on helmets; 15th and 16th centuries.

Orfrays. The gold, silver, or silk embroidery on rich garments, chiefly sacerdotal ornaments. The term has two derivations;

Fig. 510. Regals or Portable Organ.

some derive it from *aurum Phrygium*, because the Phrygians, who were excellent embroiderers, were considered to have invented the style; others take it to be from *aurum fractum* (broken). In mediæval Latin the term for orfrays was *aurifrigia, aurifrisa, aurifrisus*, and *aurifrixus*.

Organ. Organs are said to have been first introduced into France, A.D. 289, from Greece. A large organ existed in Westminster Abbey in the 10th century. Portable organs called also RE-GALS were also common. The antique organs had no key-boards, which were introduced in the 11th century, simultaneously with the invention of the musical *stave*. (Cf. HYDRAULA.) The REGALS or portable organ is an attribute of St. Cecilia. (Fig. 510.)

Organdi. A kind of muslin.

Organistrum, O. E. A musical instrument, resembling the modern hurdy-gurdy, played by two persons, of whom one turned the handle, while the other played the keys.

Organolyricon. A musical instrument invented in Paris in 1810 by M. de St. Pern. It consists of a pianoforte with two rows of keys, and contains twelve different wind instruments, viz. three flutes, an oboe, a clarionet, a bassoon, horns, trumpet, and fife.

Organzine. Thrown silk of a very fine texture. (*S.*)

Orgies, Gr. (ὄργια). Festivals of Bacchus at which all who were present were carried away by frenzy. The same term was also used to denote the festivals of Ceres and those of the CABIRI.

Orgues, Fr. Med. (1) Pieces of timber, pointed and shod with iron, hung like a portcullis over a gateway, to be let down in case of attack. (2) An arrangement of gun-barrels, the precursor of the mitrailleuse. (*S.*)

Orgyia (from ὀρέγω, to extend). A Greek measure of length, representing the distance from end to end of the *outstretched* arms, or the height of the human figure. It was equal to four cubits or six feet, and was one-hundredth of a stadium.

Orichalcum (from ὄρος and χαλκὸς, i.e. *mountain bronze*). A metallic compound, akin to copper and bronze, which was highly prized by the ancients. It was probably *brass*.

Oriel or **Oriole,** Chr. (*oriolum*, a little entrance). A projecting angular window, generally triangular or pentagonal in shape. A large bay or recessed window in a church or in an apartment. The word has been used in many senses, with the general meaning of a recess within or a projection from a building. A small oratory.

Orientation, Chr. The arrangement of a church by which a worshipper faces the *east* at prayers.

Oriflamme. The ancient royal banner of France, coloured purple-azure and gold. It was split into five points, and sometimes bore upon it a *saltire* wavy, from the centre of which golden rays diverged.

Orillon, Fr. A mass of earth lined with a wall on the shoulder of a bastion, for the protection of a gun.

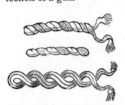

Fig. 511. Orle or crest-wreath.

Orle. (1) Arch. A fillet or listel placed beneath the ovolo of a capital. (2) In Heraldry, a subordinary formed of a border of a shield which is charged upon another and a larger shield. (3) The wreath or torse which encircled the crest, composed ordinarily of silk of two colours twisted together, and representing the principal metal and tincture in the wearer's armorial bearings. (*Planché.*)

Orleans. A cloth made of worsted and cotton.

Orlo. A Spanish musical instrument.

Orlop-deck of a ship. That over the hold, on which the cables are stowed.

Ormolu, Fr. (*or*, gold, and *moulu*, ground). 72·43 copper, 25·2 zinc, and 2·65 tin ; used for cheap jewellery, &c. *Mosaic gold*, another name for such a metal, is composed of 65 copper and 35 zinc.

Ormolu Varnish. A copper, bronze, or imitation-gold varnish.

Ornithon, R. (ὀρνιθών). A poultry-yard or aviary.

Orpharion, O. E. A kind of lute. (*Halliwell.*)

Orpheon. A musical instrument.

Orphrey. An old English word for gold embroidery, from the Latin *auriphrygium*. (See ORFRAYS.)

Orpiment (Lat. *auripigmentum ;* Ang. *king's yellow*). A yellow pigment of arsenic with sulphur, or, when the arsenic predominates, an orange colour. The finest native orpiment comes from Persia, and is called *golden orpiment*.

Orpin, O. E., contraction of **Orpiment.** Yellow arsenic.

Orrery. A machine for representing in a model the motions and relative positions of the heavenly bodies.

Orrice or **Orris.** A peculiar pattern in which gold or silver lace is worked. The edges are ornamented with conical figures, placed at equal distances, with spots between them.

Orthostata, Gr. (ὀρθόστατα, i. e. standing upright). (1) The facings of a wall, consisting of

different materials from the internal part of it. (Fig. 512.) (2) An anta or pilaster.

Orthron. (See HOURS OF PRAYER.)

Oscen, *plur.* **Oscines,** R. (*os*, mouth, and *cano*, to predict). A bird or birds from whose singing it was possible to draw auguries.

Fig. 512. Orthostata. Facing of a Greek wall.

Oschophoria, Gr. (ὀσχο-φόρια, i. e. vine-branch-bearing). Athenian vintage festivals, instituted in honour of Bacchus and Ariadne by Theseus, or according to other authorities, in honour of Dionysus and Athena, in which those who took part carried vine-boughs loaded with grapes. The festival was concluded by a race on the seashore from the temple of Bacchus to that of Minerva. The victor's prize was a cup called PENTAPLOA, because it contained *five* ingredients: wine, honey, cheese, meal, and oil.

Oscillatio, R. A swing. The Roman swings are represented having legs like a chair.

Oscilla, R. (dimin. of *os*, mouth or face). Small images or masks, generally of Bacchus, hung up in vineyards to ensure a good crop, and practically useful to scare off birds from the grapes.

Osculare, Osculatorium, Chr. (See PAX.)

Ossarium and **Ossuarium,** R. (*os*, a bone). A sarcophagus of earthenware, stone, or marble, in which the vessel containing the cremated ashes of the dead was placed.

Ossature, Arch. (from the Italian *ossatura*, skeieton). The skeleton or framework of a Gothic roof or a window. In the roof, the ossature comprises the nerves, the transverse or longitudinal arches, the diagonal rib, &c. ; in a window, the iron framing.

Osteau, Arch. An old term used to denote the rose placed in the upper part of a mullioned window; it was also applied to a rosace and a medallion.

Ostinati. An Italian literary academy, whose device was a pyramid blown from all quarters by the winds, with the *obstinate* motto, "*Frustra*" (in vain).

Ostium, R. A lobby inside the entrance door of a Roman house, deep enough to contain a small porter's lodge on one side, and leading to an inner door which opened on the ATRIUM. The street door was called JANUA. (See DOMUS.)

Ostrich Eggs, Chr. The practice of suspending eggs of ostriches in churches was probably introduced from the East by Crusaders.

"In some churches two eggs of ostriches, and other things which cause admiration, and which are rarely seen, are accustomed to be suspended: that by their means the people may be drawn to church, and have their minds the more affected." (*Durandus on Symbolism.*)

Ostrum, R. A purple colour used by the ancients, produced from the juice of the *murex* fish.

Othone, Chr. (See STOLE.)

Ottone, It. Brass.

Oubliettes, Fr. Subterranean dungeons, into which prisoners were thrown to be *oubliés* (forgotten). The side walls were in some cases armed with strong sharp blades, which cut the victims to pieces as they fell. It should be mentioned that in many cases cesspools have been mistaken for oubliettes.

Ouch or **Nouche**, O. E. An ornament of the brooch kind; a jewel. (Mod.) The setting of a precious stone.

Oudenardes. Tapestry landscapes first made at that place; called also "*tapisseries de verdure.*"

Ourania, Gr. (οὐρανια, i. e. in the air). A game at catch-ball.

Outline, which has no real existence in nature, is defined by Aristotle as πέρας στερεοῦ, "the boundary of solid form." The only light and shade used in outlines is the greater lightness or darkness of the lines.

Outré, Fr. Exaggerated, fantastic, absurd.

Oval (Lat. *ovum*, an egg). The oval, formed of a continuous curve, differs from the ELLIPSE, which is equally broad at both ends, in having one end narrower than the other, and is sometimes called a false ellipse. *Ovals* in windows, arches, and other parts of architecture exist, but are rare.

Ovatio. A lesser triumph distinguished from TRIUMPHUS. The general entered the city *on foot*, and dressed in the toga prætexta of a magistrate, attended only by musicians, and knights and plebeians; and the sacrifice by which the ceremony concluded was a *sheep* (ovis) instead of a bull; hence the word *ovation.*

Overstory, Arch. The CLERESTORY.

Overture (Fr. *ouverture*, an opening; It. *sinfonia*). Instrumental music preceding an opera, &c.

Ovile, R. Literally, a *sheep-fold*, and thence an enclosure in the Campus Martius in which

each century assembled before proceeding to place its votes (*tabellæ*) in the urn (*cista*). It was divided into compartments approached through narrow passages called *pontes* or *ponticuli*. On entering, the citizens received their voting-tablets (*tabellæ*), and when they had consulted within the enclosure, they passed out by another *pons*, at which they threw votes into the chest (*cista*).

Fig. 513. Ovolo or Quarter-round.

Ovolo, Arch. (from the Latin *ovum*). (1) A convex moulding showing the quarter of a circle,

Fig. 514. Egg and dart moulding.

and thence called quarter-round. (2) The echinus of the Doric capital. (3) An ornament composed of eggs, separated either by tongues (Fig. 277) or by darts (Fig. 514). (See ECHINUS.)

Ovum, **Egg**, R. Conical egg-shaped balls which were placed upon the *spina* of a circus, on a stone table supported by four columns. (Fig. 515.) There was a second table at the other end of the *spina*, on which were placed small marble dolphins. *Ovum Orphicum*, or Orphic egg, was the mysterious symbol employed by Orpheus to denote the procreative principle with which the whole earth is pervaded. *Ovum anguinum* was an oval ball of glass worn by the Druids round their neck; so named because, as was asserted, it was produced from the mingled saliva of two serpents (*angues*).

Fig. 515. Ovum. Egg-shaped balls.

Owl. With the Athenians the owl was the

emblem of prudence and wisdom ; the bird of Athenê. In Christian art it symbolizes darkness and solitude, and hence unbelief.

Ox. In Christian art the attribute of St. Luke ; the emblem of the priesthood and of sacrifice. In representations of the Nativity an ox and an ass are commonly introduced.

Ox-gall. The bile or bitter fluid secreted by the liver of the ox ; when refined it is used in oil and water-colour painting to fix and thicken the colours. (See GALL.)

Oxford Ochre. An oxide of iron used as a pigment of a brownish yellow in oil and water colours. (See OCHRE.)

Oxide of Zinc. A *white* pigment which is more permanent in resisting gases than the white lead.

Oxides of Copper. The pigments derived from these were well known to the ancients. Modern pigments are *Blue Verditer, Brunswick Green, Verdigris,* and *Emerald* or *Scheele's Green* (q.v.).

Oxybaphoi, Gr. Small cymbals in the shape of vinegar-saucers.

Oxybaphon (ὀξυβάφον). A Greek term applied to a bell-shaped vase with a plain foot and a moulded rim, synonymous with the Latin ACE-TABULUM (q.v.).

Oyelet, Oylet. (See OILLETS.)

Oyer and **Terminer.** Ancient law-French. The words mean *to hear and to determine,* and express the authority or commission given to an appointed court of justice.

P.

Packfong or **Pakfong.** A Chinese name for Argentine, or German silver.

Pæan (Gr. παιάν). A hymn to Apollo, of gratitude or propitiation. It was also used as a battle-song before and after an engagement.

Pænula, R. A thick cloak with a hole to put the head through ; it was furnished with a hood, and was worn in travelling, or as a protection against cold and rain.

Pagai, Hind. A kind of short double oar, with broad ends resembling small scoops.

Paganalia, Paganales, R. A rustic festival which took place yearly towards the end of January or the beginning of February, seven days after the *Sementivæ.* It was the festival of villages (*pagi*) and of villagers (*pagani*), whence its name. Sacrifices were offered in honour of Proserpine, goddess of vegetation. As the old religion continued to prevail in the villages long after that of Christ was established in the towns, the words *pagan* and unbeliever gradually became synonymous.

Paganica (sc. *pila*), R. A ball covered with leather and stuffed with feathers or down ; it took its name from the peasants or country people (*pagani*), who used it for playing a game the nature of which is not known.

Pagina, R. (lit. a thing fastened). This term, when synonymous with *scheda,* signifies a page of paper, the page of a volume ; or else it serves to denote one of the columns of writing which cover a sheet of paper.

Pagoda, Hind. (1) A religious building of the Hindoos. The great ancient pagodas of India are monolithic temples hewn out of rocky mountains ; but the term is also applied to temples built in the open air. (2) Gold coins formerly current in India were called pagodas.

Pagoda-stone. A limestone containing tapering fossil shells shaped like a Chinese pagoda at the top.

Pagodite. A stone much used by the Chinese for carving into pagodas and other ornaments.

Pagus, R. Any lofty site in the country capable of being easily turned into a fortified post by means of a few siege works. The name was extended to the country surrounding a fortified village ; and each of the country tribes was divided by Numa into a certain number of pagi.

Paile. An old term used to denote a striped cloth of floss silk manufactured at Alexandria in Egypt, and thence a mantle, canopy, or pavilion.

Pala, It. An altar front. The *Pala d'oro* of St. Mark's, Venice, is a celebrated specimen of Byzantine art. It is of silver-gilt ornamented with gems and enamels, with Greek and Latin inscriptions in niello, and representations from sacred and profane history. It was originally made at Constantinople in 976, but has been repaired in 1105, in 1209, and in 1345, by which it has lost much of its original character.

Pala, R. A spade, or scoop in the form of a spade, and thence the bezil of a ring.

Palæstra (παλαίστρα). A place for wrestling, formerly part of the gymnasium. (See GYMNA-SIUM.)

Palanga. (See PHALANGÆ.) Hence :—

Palanquin. A covered conveyance for one person, carried on the shoulders of men in India and China. They are often very splendidly carved, and decorated with tapestry, ornamental woods, and inlaid-work.

Palaria, R. An exercise practised by young Roman recruits, which consisted of hurling javelins (*pila*) against a stake (*palus*) fixed in the ground. (See PEL.)

Palê, Gr. (πάλη). A Greek term having the same meaning as LUCTA, LUCTAMEN, LUCTA-MENTUM (q.v.).

Pale, Her. One of the ordinaries. **Pale-wise** or **In Pale,** arranged vertically one above the other, as the lions of England. (See PER.)

Paleste, Gr. (παλαιστή, i. e. palm of the hand). A lineal measure used by the Greeks equal to the quarter of a foot, or a little more than three inches. (See PALMUS.)

Palette. " Setting the palette " is arranging the colours for use. This is always done in a certain order regulated by the key in which the picture is to be painted. The order generally recommended is to begin with white, and then proceed through the yellows, reds, and blues to black. The Egyptians used palettes of a long rectangular form ; one side higher than the other, had two or three saucers sunk in it to hold cakes of colour or ink ; the other side was notched to receive the *calami* or cut reeds used as writing-pens.

Palettes or **Rouudels,** in Armour, are round plates or shields hung on the armour to defend the joints of the arm, necessarily left free for action.

Palilia, R. A festival in honour of Pales, the goddess of shepherds and flocks ; it was held on the 21st of April.

Palimpsest (παλίμ-ψηστος, lit. scraped again). A parchment the writing on which had been erased, so that it might be used again. Monumental brasses are found to have been reversed and used a second time. In both cases the most ancient writing or inscription is generally the most valuable and interesting.

Palindrome (πάλιν, again, and δρόμος, a course). A sentence which reads the same when read backwards or forwards. Such is the Greek inscription on the ancient font in the chapel of Dulwich College : " νίψον ανομημαμημονανοψιν." "Purify the heart and not the countenance alone."

Palissy Ware. The pieces to which Palissy owes his reputation, in the first place, are the so-called " rustic pottery " (*rustiques figulines*), " dishes or vases where upon a rough ground strewn with fossil shells, lizards and salamanders are running, frogs jumping, snakes crawling or sleeping, or more still, in a streamlet of water wriggling eels, pointed-nosed pikes, trout with spotted scales, and a thousand others of

our fresh-water fishes are swimming." When afterwards he worked in the capital, he did not give up his rustic compositions, but mixed them with the human figure. " There is an identity of

Fig. 516. Palissy Jug.

style in all his figures and compositions ; such as the Diana, Plenty, &c., framed round with delicate and ingenious ornaments drawn in the taste of the period." (*Jacquemart.*)

Paliurus. A thorn-bush with long sharp spikes, common on the coasts of the Mediterranean, where it is called *Christ's thorn,* because it is said to have furnished material of which the Crown of thorns was woven.

Palla, Gr. and R. A robe of state worn by patrician ladies, and frequently represented on statues of goddesses. *Palla cithærædica* was the name given to a long robe which musicians wore upon the stage ; Apollo is often represented with this garment, especially when he is surnamed *Citharædus* and *Musagetes*. *Palla Gallica* was a short garment like a TABARD, open in front and behind ; it was worn by the Gauls and adopted by the Romans, who called it CARACALLA (q.v.).

Palla Corporalis, Chr. The veil for the Pyx. (See CORPORAL.)

Palladium. (1) An image of Pallas Athenê, kept carefully hidden, and revered as the safeguard of the place where it lay. The most celebrated was the *Palladium* of Troy, said to have been

R

thrown from Olympus by the hand of Zeus. It was about three cubits high, and represented the goddess sitting with a spear in her right hand, and in her left a distaff and spindle. (2) The term has been applied to a metal discovered by Dr. Wollaston in 1803, obtained from platinum, which it resembles in colour and lustre.

Pallium (Gr. ἱμάτιον). A large square woollen sheet or blanket worn by the Greeks over the shoulders, and fastened like the ABOLLA round the neck with a brooch (*fibula*); it formed the principal article of the *amictus* or Greek dress. (Hence the expression to *palliate*, or cloak over, an offence.) (2) Chr. A vestment bestowed by the Pope on all patriarchs and archbishops on their accession to office as the symbol of their ecclesiastical power. The material is obtained from the wool of two lambs slain on the Eve of St. Agnes. The modern pallium of the Church is a short white cloak ornamented with a red cross, which encircles the neck and shoulders, and falls down the back. The pall or pallium is a charge in the arms of the Sees of Canterbury, Armagh, and Dublin.

Pall-mall. The ancient form of the game of croquet, "wherein a round box bowle is with a mallet strucke through a high arch of yron standing at either end of an ally." (*Cotgrave.*) "This game is used at the long alley near St. James's, and vulgarly called Pell-Mell." (*Blount's Glossary,* 1681.)

Palm. The ancient classical emblem of victory and triumph was early assumed by the Christians as the universal symbol of martyrdom. In England we understand by palm, not the leaves of a palm-tree, but "the yelowe that groweth on wyllowes."

Fig. 516 a. Palm-leaf Ornament.

Palm-leaf, Arch. An architectural ornament bearing more or less resemblance to a palm-leaf, employed for mouldings, and for the decoration of the corners of the ceilings in Doric cornices; and in antefixæ, as crownings for the pediment and as acroteria. Figs. 516a and 516b represent palm-leaves of terra-cotta.

Palmus, Gr. and R. A measure of length. Of the Greek *palmus* the greater (σπιθαμή) contained nine finger-breadths, and the less (παλαιστή) four. The greater Roman *palmus* contained twelve finger-breadths or about nine inches, and the less four finger-breadths. The greater *palmus* was taken from the length of the hand or span, the less from the breadth of it.

Palstave, Celt. A wedge-shaped axe used by the Celtic nations in war for battering the armour of the enemy. (See Fig. 255.)

Fig. 516 b. Architectural Palm-leaf Ornament.

Paltock (modern *paletôt*). "A short cloake with sleeves," i. e. a great-coat.

Paludamentum, R. A military cloak worn over their armour by the generals and superior officers of the Roman army; an officer thus dressed was said to be *paludatus.* (See Fig. 44.)

Palus, R. (*pango,* to fix). A stake planted in the earth, against which recruits hurled their javelins (*pila*). The mediaeval PEL (q. v.).

Pam, O. E. The knave of clubs. (*Halliwell.*)

Pammachium (παμμάχιον). A synonym for PANCRATIUM (q.v.).

Panache, Her. A plume of feathers set upright and borne as a crest. Fig. 517 is from the seal of Edward Courtenay, A.D. 1400.

Fig. 517. Panache.

Panarium, R. (*panis,* bread). A bread-basket; a pantry in which bread was kept.

Panathenæa, Gr. (Παναθήναια). Festivals of Minerva Athenê among the Athenians, so called because they formed the festival of all the peoples placed under the protection of Minerva (πᾶν, all, and Ἀθήνη). There were the Greater and Lesser Panathenæa; the former being held every five years, the latter every three years. The procession at the Greater festival is the subject of the friezes from the Parthenon now in the British Museum. (See ELGIN MARBLES.) They represent the solemn transportation of the *peplus* of Athenê to her temple, in which nearly the whole of the population took part, on foot, on horseback, or in chariots. Old men carried olive-branches, young men attended in armour, and maidens carried baskets of flowers.

Panaulon. An enlarged German flute with sixteen finger-keys; invented recently by Trexler of Vienna. It is available as a bass to other flutes.

Pancratium, R. (from πάν every : and κράτος force). A wrestling and boxing match, in which the combatants employed every means to disable each other; and the contest was continued until one of the combatants owned himself disabled by holding up a finger, or was killed.

Paned, O. E. Striped.

Paned Hose. Breeches formed of stripes, with small panes or squares of silk or velvet. (*Halliwell.*)

Panegyris, Egyp. (πανήγυρις). A popular festival of Egypt, to which the whole country was summoned in order to celebrate the thirtieth anniversary of the reigning monarch.

Panels, Arch. The sunken compartments in wood and stone-work; very abundant in Gothic architecture as ornaments on walls, ceilings, &c. After the expiration of Gothic architecture, panelling in great measure ceased to be used in stone-work.

Panel Picture. A painting on a board or panel.

Panisci, R. (Πανίσκοι, dimin. from Πάν). Literally, *small Pans*, small rustic gods no bigger than pigmies.

Pannetier Green. A handsome and durable emerald green, prepared by a secret process by its inventor, M. Pannetier. It is sold at a high price.

Panoply (πανοπλία). A complete suit of armour. (See ARMOUR.)

Pantables (for PANTOFLES). Slippers.

"Hee standeth upon his *pantables*, and regardeth greatly his reputacion." (*Saker's Narbonus*, 1580.)

Pantaloon. From the Italian *pianta leone* (plant the lion); the Venetian standard-bearers (of the *lion* of St. Mark) being so called, who wore tight hose, the name came to be given to tight hose in general. In ancient pantomimes, Pantaloon was always a Venetian. (See HARLEQUIN.)

Pantaloons, O. E. "Garments made for merry-andrews, that have the breeches and stockings of the same stuff, and joined together as one garment." (*Halliwell.*)

Panthea, Gen. (πάν-θεια). Statues or figures which combine the symbols of several divinities.

Pantheon (πᾶν, every, and θεὸs, god). A temple dedicated to all the divinities collectively. That at Rome is now a Christian church. It is circular, 150 feet in height and in diameter, with a domed roof.

Pantherinæ, R. Panther-tables; of wood striped like the skin of a panther. (See TIGRINÆ.)

Pantobles, Pantoffles, O. E. Slippers.

Pantofles, O. E. Slippers or wooden pattens.

Pantograph. An instrument for enlarging or reducing plans and designs, largely used in the arts, e. g. in machine embroidery.

Pantomime (παντὸs, of everything; μῖμος,

mimic). Gesture and action applied, without speech, to represent emotion; hence applied to the form of theatrical performance which consists entirely or principally of gesture and action.

Paper. (See CHARTA.)

Papier-maché, Fr. Paper-pulp; made by compressing the pulp, or by pasting together different thicknesses of paper, to the hardness and consistency of wood. It is an invention of the 18th century, and originated in snuff-boxes called after their manufacturer "Martins." The process has since been developed to great perfection by the invention of new varnishes and methods of ornament, the principal of which are gilding and bronzing, pearl and gem inlaying, &c. (See a paper by *R. Hunt* in the *Art Journal*, 1851.)

Papilio, R. (lit. a butterfly). A military tent, so called because the curtains opened and shut like the wings of a butterfly.

Papyrus. The paper made of the papyrus plant, used by the Egyptians and other nations of antiquity. The *Papyrus rolls* on which important relics of Egyptian literature and art have come down to us, were formed of a sheet of papyrus rolled on a slender wooden cylinder. They have mostly been discovered in mummy cases, and contain illustrations of funeral ceremonies and religious emblems relating to the future of the soul. Others are historical or literary, and some have been discovered containing caricatures and comic illustrations. (Cf. LIBER.)

Parada, Celt. A tent or awning stretched over the deck of a vessel, and thence a cabin hung with tapestry.

Paradise or **Parvise**, Chr. (1) A vestibule or courtyard in front of a church. The term must thus, at a certain period, have been synonymous with *narthex* or porch. At the present day the term is applied to the open space to be found in front of cathedrals or public buildings. (2) The word is sometimes applied to the room that is often found above church porches. (See CLOISTER GARTH.)

Paradisus (παράδεισος). A Persian park or pleasure-garden, enclosed within a wall, elaborately planted and irrigated, and stocked with animals for the chase. Hence the Garden of Eden was so called.

Paragauda, Paragaudis, R. An embroidered band of silk or gold thread sewn on to a tunic.

Paraison, Fr. A term in glass, equivalent to the English METAL (q.v.).

Paralus (πάραλος). The name of an Athenian state vessel, kept, like that of the Doge of Venice in modern times, for state and religious ceremonies. A sister vessel was named the SALAMINIA; they were both fast-sailing triremes.

Paramese, Gr. (next to middle), or TRITE (third). The third treble note, immediately above the mese, of the seven-stringed lyre. (See MESE.)

Paranete, Gr. (beside the shortest). The second treble note of the seven-stringed lyre. (See MESE.)

Parapet, It. (*parare petto*, to defend the breast). A wall breast-high on a fortification, roof, or other gallery. (See CRENELS.)

Paraphernalia (from the Greek παράφερνα). That which a wife brings besides her dower ; i.e. her personal attire and ornament.

Parasang. A Persian measure of distance, about 30 Greek stadia or 3¾ English miles.

Paratorium. (See OBLATIONARIUM.)

Parazonium, R. (παραζώνιον). A short sword or kind of dagger worn by the tribunes and superior officers of the Roman army attached to their belt on the right side. This sword was shorter than the *gladius* worn by the common soldier on the right side.

Parchment. The finer kind of parchment known as *vellum* is from the skins of calves, kids, and dead-born lambs. The stout parchment of drum-heads is from the skin of the wolf, although that of the ass or calf is sometimes used. The parchment of battledores is from the skin of the ass, and that used for sieves from the skin of the he-goat. The green parchment used in book-binding is coloured by means of Verdigris. (See LIBER.) The name comes from the Latin Pergamentum. Eumenes, King of Pergamus, has the honour of the invention.

Parentales, Parentalia, R. Festivals, also called *Februales*, which were held by the Romans in honour of deceased ancestors.

Pargetting, Parge-work, O. E. In Architecture, an old term for the ornamental plaster-work common on the outside walls of timber-built houses of Queen Elizabeth's and earlier periods.

Parhypate, Gr. (beside the longest). The second bass note of the seven-stringed lyre (See MESE.)

Parian Chronicle. A slab of Parian marble, among the so-called ARUNDEL MARBLES in the University of Oxford, containing a chronological record of Greek history from B.C. 1582 to B.C. 264.

Parian Marble from the island of Paros was of extremely fine grain, easy to work, and of a creamy white. The marble *now* called Parian has a coarse sparkling grain, which, however, takes a high finish. (*Redford, Ancient Sculpture.*)

Paries, R. The wall of a house or any building, in contradistinction to *murus, muri*, which denoted the walls of a city.

Paris Black. A name for IVORY BLACK (q.v.).

Paris Blue. A very handsome dark violet-blue pigment. "Its great qualities of body and intensity of coloration will always ensure it a large sale ; moreover, its mixture with chrome yellow produces a fine *green-cinnabar* or *leaf-green.*" (*Habich.*)

Paris Lake. (See CARMINATED LAKES.)

Parlour (Lat. *parlatorium*). (1) The old "speke-house" in a convent for inmates to speak with their friends. (2) Any private room.

Parma, R. (πάρμη). A shield, usually of circular form, carried in the Roman army by the light-armed troops or light infantry (*velites*) and the cavalry (*equites*). The *parma thracidica* used by the class of gladiators called *Thraces* was not round, but in the form of a small SCUTUM (q.v.).

Parquet. French flooring of inlaid wood-work.

Parsley, Arch. In every period, but especially in Romano-Byzantine and Gothic art, parsley-leaves have been abundantly made use of in architectural decoration.

Parthenon. The famous temple of Minerva in the Acropolis at Athens. The finest example of the GRECIAN-DORIC style of architecture ; built by Pheidias, 454—438 B.C. Fergusson says, "For beauty of detail, and for the exquisite perception of the highest and most recondite principles of art ever applied to architecture, it stands utterly and entirely alone and unrivalled—the glory of Greece." (*Hist. of Architecture.*) The celebrated frieze, 525 feet in length, ran all round the outer wall of the *cella* close up to the ceiling. The best work on the Parthenon sculptures is by Michaelis (*Der Parthenon*, Leipzig, 1871). (See ELGIN MARBLES.)

Partisan, O. E. A kind of short pike, introduced *temp.* Edward III.

Partlet, O. E. A ruff. "A maydens necker-chefe or lynnen parlette."

Party, Parted, Her. Divided. (See PER.)

Parvise. (See PARADISE.)

Paschal Taper, Chr. A large wax-candle which was consecrated during the service on Easter Eve, and lighted on Sundays from Easter to Whitsuntide, with five grains of incense attached to it to indicate the five movable feasts of the year.

Pasquinade, It. A lampoon ; so called from *Pasquino*, an Italian barber at Rome, whose door was opposite to the statue of a gladiator on which such satirical writings were posted.

Passamen, O. E. A kind of lace. (*Hall.*)

Passant, Her. Walking and looking forward. *Passant guardant*, walking and looking out from the shield ; *passant reguardant*, walking and looking back ; *passant repassant*, walking in opposite directions. (Fig. 518, 519.)

Passe-partout, Fr. A light picture-frame of cardboard, having the inner edges generally gilt.

Passementerie, Fr. Trimming, lace, or tape of gold, silver, lace, or thread.

Fig. 518. Passant.

Fig. 519. Passant guardant.

Passion, Instruments of the—a frequent subject in ecclesiastical decoration of the Middle Ages—are, the PITCHER from which Jesus poured water; the TOWEL—represented as hanging on a ring—wherewith He wiped the Apostles' feet; the TWO SWORDS which they showed Him, when He said, " It is enough ;" the EAR of Malchus; ST. PETER'S SWORD, represented as a small *falchion*; the POST to which the Saviour was bound; the SCOURGE; the CROWN OF THORNS; the REED wherewith He was smitten on the head; the CROSS; the LADDER; the NAILS; the SPEAR of Longinus, crossed by the REED with the SPONGE; the FIRE at which St. Peter warmed himself; the COCK; the PINCERS, and a HEART pierced with five wounds.

Passus, R. A pace, from the point where the heel leaves the ground, to where the same heel is set down; five Roman feet. *Mille passuum*, or a thousand such paces, formed the Roman mile.

Pasta Verde, It. Sap-green; a vegetable green pigment prepared from the berries of the buckthorn.

Pastel. The French name for coloured crayons. Pastel-painting was much used for portraits in the beginning of the 19th century.

Pasticcio, It. An imitation of the style of another painter in an independent design.

Pastophori, Gr. and Egyp. (πασ το-φόροι). Priests who, at certain ceremonies, carried small shrines (ναὸs) containing the image of a deity, which were hidden from the eyes of the crowd by a veil of different colours called πασος, παστὸν φέρειν (to carry the *pastos*), the term applied to the priests who performed this duty. The keepers of the temple were also so called.

Pastophoria, Chr. Small apses flanking the principal apse in a basilica, in which the consecrated bread was kept.

Fig. 520. Bishop's Pastoral Staff.

Pastoral Staff, Chr. The *pedum* of antiquity and emblem of a bishop's pastoral responsibility is distinct from the CROZIER (q.v.) of an archbishop, and has a crook head.

Pastouraux, Cubical stones, usually of two colours, applied in the ornamentation of Romano-Byzantine architecture.

Patagium, R. A band of purple, or with gold ornaments or embroidery, which was placed round the neck and down the front of a woman's tunic (*tunica muliebris*).

Patee or **Pattee**, Her. A small cross with the arms widening towards the ends.

Patella. Diminutive of PATERA (q.v.).

Patena, R. and Chr. A manger of wood, stone, or marble for holding food for horses; when it was divided into several compartments, these were called *loculi*. (See LOCULUS.) In Christian archæology, *patena* was the term applied to a small plate of gold or silver, used in the celebration of mass to cover over the chalice, and to hold the pieces of the host after it has been broken by the priest.

Patent Yellow. (See TURNER'S YELLOW.)

Patera, dimin. **Patella** (φιάλη). Flat plates or dishes for holding fluids for domestic use, and wine for libations in the sacrifices. The common kinds were of red earthenware, ornamented with designs in black. Others were of bronze or silver, often richly decorated with chasing, &c. (Compare PATINA.) In Architecture, a great variety of flat ornaments used in all styles of architecture are improperly called *pateræ*, the word applying properly to circular ornaments resembling the classical dish often found on friezes of classical architecture. (Fig. 521, 522.)

Fig. 521. Patera.

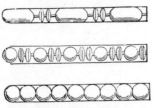

Fig. 522. Side view, showing the depth of the patera.

Paternosters or **Bead-ornament.** (1) A rosary. (2) Architectural ornaments in the form of

Fig. 523. Paternosters.

berries or beads (Fig. 523), which decorate bands or other mouldings, and which often occur above ovolos.

Patibulum, R. An instrument of punishment in the form of a fork (*furca*), between the prongs of which the criminal's neck was placed. His hands were fastened to the prongs of the fork, and in this condition (*patibulatus*) he was flogged through the city. The name of *patibulum*, or *crux patibularia*, was also given to a cross to which criminals were nailed.

Patina. The rust of antiquity found on bronzes and coins; it cannot be removed by rubbing or wetting it. It varies with the nature of the soil, and in some cases the surface acquires the smoothness and colour of malachite.

Patina, R. An earthenware vessel, used generally for cookery. It was deeper than the *patera*, but less deep than the *olla*.

Patonce, Her. A variety of the heraldic cross.

Patriarchal, Her. A variety of the heraldic cross, with a short cross-bar on the upper limb.

Patrick, Order of St., indicated by the letters K.P., was instituted by George III. in 1783. The badge or jewel is of gold enamelled and oval in form, and is worn suspended from a collar formed of alternate roses and harps, or from a broad sky-blue ribbon.

Fig. 524. Badge of St. Patrick.

Patten, Fr. (1) A woman's clog. (2) The base of a column.

Patulous. Spreading.

Paul Veronese Green. An *arsenite* or *arseniate of copper*. A fine and durable colour, used either for oil or water-colour painting. (See EMERALD GREEN.)

Pavilion, Arch. A projecting apartment, usually with a dome or turret.

Fig. 525. Pavimentum (sectile).

Fig. 526. Pavimentum (sectile).

Pavimentum, R. A pavement formed by means of pieces of tile, crushed stones, flints, and other materials set in a bed of ashes or cement, and consolidated by beating down with the rammer (*pavicula*), whence its name of *pavimentum*. There were various kinds of *pavimenta*: the *sectile* (Figs. 525, 526), the *tessellatum* or *tesseris structum*, the *vermiculatum*, the *sculpturatum*, and the *testaceum*, &c.

Pavo. (See PEACOCK.)

Pavonaceum (sc. *opus*), R. An arrangement of materials placed so as to overlap one another, and bearing more or less resemblance to the feathers in a peacock's tail.

Pavonine. Coloured like a peacock's tail.

Pax, Paxboard, Chr. A representation of the Crucifixion upon a piece of wood or metal, with a handle at the back. It was kissed by the priest in the mass at the words "*Pax Domini sit semper vobiscum,*" and afterwards passed round to be kissed by the congregation. It was also spelt *Paxbrede.* Also called OSCULA-TORIUM.

Peach-stone Black, prepared from calcined stones of fruits, is a handsome colour, but has a reddish tinge. Ground with oil and white lead, the colour called *old gray* is obtained.

Peacock, R. and Chr. In antiquity the peacock was sacred to Juno, and is called *Junonia avis.* It is represented on Roman imperial coins bearing the empresses up to heaven, as the eagle does the emperors; and hence in Christian archæology is the symbol of the resurrection. (Her., see Fig. 398, IN PRIDE.)

Pea-green. (See CHRYSOCOLLA.)

Pean, Her. One of the furs; represented in gold spots on a black ground.

Pean or **Pæan.** A song or shout of triumph.

Pearl. A secretion of the mollusc; in its normal development a thickening of the shell, which supplies *mother-of-pearl*; abnormally, forming globules for the purpose of encysting foreign substances intruded within the shell, which are the precious pearls used in jewellery.

Pearl, in Chinese the emblem of *talent*, is put by the Chinese on porcelains destined for rewards of poets and other *laureati* in China.

Pebble. A name given by lapidaries to many different stones.

Pechblende or **Pech-urane,** Germ. An ore of uranium and iron, used in porcelain painting and glass, producing a handsome greenish-yellow pigment.

Pecten, Egyp. and R. (*pecto*, to comb). (1) A comb for the hair; among the Egyptians and Romans they were made of boxwood or ivory. (See COMB.) (2) A weaver's comb for pressing the threads of the web firmly together. (3) A comb for carding flax or wool. (4) A reaper's "comb," used in several countries, especially Gaul, instead of a sickle, for plucking the ears of wheat from the stalk. (5) A haymaker's rake, &c.

Pectinated. Having teeth like a comb.

Pectoral, Gen. (*pectus*, the breast). A plate forming the front of a cuirass, and thus covering the chest.

Peculium, R. Property or earnings which a slave or a *filius familias* was permitted to acquire and consider as his own, although in strict law it belonged to the master or father. The slave was sometimes allowed by agreement to use this peculium for the purpose of purchasing his liberty.

Pecunia, R. Money; so called from *pecus*, a herd of cattle, Man's primitive medium of exchange.

Pedal. In Music, a passage where the harmony moves upon a sustained sound, which is either the dominant or the tonic of the key.

Pede-cloth, Chr. A carpet laid on the space between the altar and the rails.

Pedestal, Gen. The base of a structure; the base supporting a statue, group, or monumental column. A pedestal has three parts : the *base* or *foot* next the ground, the *dado* or *die* forming the centre, and the *cornice* or *surbase* mouldings at the top. Fig. 527 represents a half-section of the base of Trajan's column at Rome ; Fig. 528 a half-section of the base of the column dedicated to Antoninus Pius, and preserved in the Pio Clementino Museum at Rome ; lastly, Fig. 529 gives a part of the pedestal or base of the Pandrosium at Athens ; when, however, pedestals support caryatides or columns, they are more commonly called STYLOBATES (q.v.).

Fig. 527. Pedestal of Trajan's Column.

Fig. 528. Pedestal. of Column of Antoninus Pius.

Pedica, R. (1) A snare by which an animal is caught by the foot (*pes*). (2) Fetters or irons worn on the feet by slaves.

Pediculated, Arch. Sustained or supported by a PEDICULE (q.v.).

Pedicule, Arch. A small pillar which serves as a support to anything ; whence the expressions *monopediculated* (with a single pedicule) (Fig. 387), and *polypediculated* (with several pedicules).

Fig. 529. Pedestal of the Androsium at Athens.

Pediluvium. (See ABLUTIONS.)

Pediment, Arch. The triangular crowning of a portico, usually supported by a row of columns. (Fig. 26.) The temples of antiquity generally had two pediments, one on each face. The inner part of the pediment is called the TYMPANUM (q.v.).

Pedum, Gen. (*pes,* a foot). A shepherd's crook,or curved stick for catching goats or sheep by the leg. Fauns and satyrs are often represented carrying the pastoral crook, and it is the attribute of Thalia, as the muse of pastoral poetry. (See under PEPLUM.) In Egyptian archæology it is a symbol of authority, and is frequently to be seen in the hands of Osiris and the Pharaohs ; the Egyptian term for it is *hyq.* (Cf. HYCSOS.) In early Christian art it is an attribute of Our Lord as the *Good Shepherd.* Representations of the pedum are of frequent occurrence in the catacomb paintings. (See PASTORAL STAFF.)

the Museum at South Kensington, shows his device given above. (Fig. 530.)

Pegma, R. (πῆγμα, i.e. a thing fastened). (1) This term denotes generally anything made of a number of boards joined together. (2) In a more restricted sense it means a theatrical machine of several stages (*tabulata*), one above the other, which could be raised or lowered by balance weights. On such stages gladiators called *pegmares* fought in the amphitheatres, and battles and other scenes were represented. When they were used in sacrifices, the victim was slaughtered in an upper stage and the priest stood in one under the ground, and was afterwards brought up to be shown to the people with the blood of the victim upon him. In theatres similar *pegmata* were employed for the purpose of changing the scenery. (3) Lastly the term was used to denote any kind of wooden furniture or joinery in a house, such as shelves, sideboards, bookcases, &c.

Pegola, It. Greek pitch; boiled resin for varnishes.

Pel, O. E. (Lat. *palus*). A post, six feet in height, set firmly in the ground, to be hewn at with sword or mace for exercise. The weapons were double the ordinary weight, and the swordsman had to cover himself from imaginary blows in return with a shield, called a *fan,* also of double weight. (See QUINTAIN.) (Consult *Meyrick,* vol. i. 145.) The pel was in the same way set up as a mark to throw spears at, and for archery practice.

Pelecinon, Gr. A sun-dial so called because it ended in a "dove-tail " (πελεκῖνος).

Pelican tearing open her breast to feed her young with her own blood was an early symbol of the Redemption and of the virtue of Charity. As a device it was borne by William of Orange, with the appropriate motto " *Pro lege, grege et*

Fig. 531. A Pelican in its piety.

Fig. 530. Pegasus. Device of Cardinal Bembo.

Pegasus. A horse with wings ; emblem of fame, eloquence, poetic study, and contemplation. A bronze medal of Cardinal Bembo, the great Italian author of the 16th century, in

rege" (for the law, the people, and the king); a slight modification of that of Alphonso the

Wise. (Fig. 531.) It is described in Heraldry as "*a pelican in its piety.*"

Pelisse (from *pellis*, a skin). A robe made of fur.

Pellet, Her. A black ROUNDLE.

Pellicatus, R. (*pellis*, a skin). Literally, covered with *skin*. The term was specially applied to earthenware vessels which were covered over with skin in order to keep the provisions they held fresh.

Pellitus, R. (*pellis*, skin). Clothed by means of skins; dressed in furs.

Pelluvia, Pelluvium, R. (*pes*, a foot, and *luo*, to wash). A basin in which the feet were washed, in contradistinction to the vessel called *malluvium*.

Pelta, Gr. (πέλτη). A small shield made of some light material, such as wood or wicker-work, and covered with leather. In shape it was sometimes elliptical, but more often cut away at the top, so that at that part it resembled a crescent. (Compare CLIPEUS.)

Pelvis, R. A general term used in ancient times to denote any kind of circular-shaped vessel. The term corresponded to the Greek πελίκα.

Penates (*penus*, food). Household gods who were believed by the ancients to be the bestowers of all the worldly blessings enjoyed by a family.

Pencil. A collection of rays of light converging to a point is so called.

Pendant. In Heraldry, drooping.

Pendant Key-stone. A synonym of PENDENTIVE. (See this word and FURCA.)

Pendants, Arch. Ornaments hanging down from the ceilings and roofs of Gothic architecture. Generally, a pair of pictures or statues appropriate to each other are called *pendant* each of the other.

Pendentives, Arch. In a spherical roof intersected with groined compartments, the term *pendentives* was applied to the surfaces included between such compartments. The same term is applied to the surfaces included in the angles formed by a groined vaulting at its spring.

Penetrale, R. An inner apartment. (Cf. ADYTUM.)

Penicillum, Penicillus, R. (*penis*, a tail). (Gr. ὑπογραφίς.) A painter's pencil or brush. The brushes of the ancients were made either with hair or a kind of seaweed or sponge.

Peniculus. Synonym of PENICILLUM.

Penna, R. A quill, a large and strong feather, in contradistinction to *pluma*, which denotes the small feathers spread over a bird's body; and thence a writing-pen, which was used instead of the *arundo* or *calamus*.

Penna, Med. During the Middle Ages this term was used to denote the battlements of a castle wall, and thence the castle itself.

Pennon, Her. An armorial lance-flag, pointed or swallow-tailed at the fly, borne by knights.

Fig. 532. Pennon.

Pentachord. Any musical instrument having five strings; a system of five sounds.

Pentacle (It. *pentacolo*). A talisman; a figure formed of two triangles, intersecting so as to form a six-pointed star. A frequent object in early ornamental art.

Pentagon. A figure of five sides and five angles.

Pentagraph. A mechanism contrived to facilitate the copying of drawings on a different scale, invented by Christopher Scheiner, a Suabian Jesuit, in the 16th century.

Pentahedron. A solid figure having five equal sides.

Pentalpha. The pentacle was so called. "A star of five points, composed of five A's interlaced, was formerly made by physicians the symbol of health, under the name of Pentalpha." (*Menestrier.*)

Pentaptych. An altar painting of five or more leaves. (See DIPTYCH.)

Pentaspastos, Gr. (παντά-σπαστος). A kind of pulley, the *block* of which contains a system of five pulleys (*orbiculi*). This engine was employed to lift great weights.

Pentastyle, Arch. A portico of five columns.

Pentathlon, Gr. Greek games similar to the QUINQUERTIUM (q.v.) of the Romans, frequently represented on ancient vases.

Pentelic Marble from a mountain of that name near Athens, of which the Parthenon and other temples are built, has a beautiful *warm* yellowish tone, comparable to ivory. All the Athenian statues are of this marble.

Penteloris. (See PARAGAUDA.)

Pent-roof, Arch. A roof sloping only from one side; hence a *pent-house* for a house or shed covered by such a roof.

Penula. (See PÆNULA.)

Penumbra (Lat. *pene*, almost, and *umbra*, shade). The part of a picture where the light and shade blend together.

Peperino, It. (*pepe*, pepper). A pepper-coloured building-stone much used in the construction of ancient Rome, formerly called *Lapis Albanus*.

Peplum and **Peplus,** Gr. (πέπλον and πέπλος). The robe peculiarly proper to Minerva. (See PANATHENÆA.) A large full robe or shawl worn by women, corresponding to the *himation* or *pallium* of the men. On occasions of funerals or weddings this shawl was thrown over the head as a veil.

The choicest productions of the loom in antiquity were *pepli*; and the most splendid dyes, and curious workmanship, and skilful designs were lavished upon their manufacture. They were a common form of offering to the treasures of the temples. A fine statue in the British Museum represents the Muse Thalia wearing the *peplos* and *chiton*, and holding the pastoral *pedum* in her hand. (Fig. 533.)

Fig. 533. Thalia, the Muse of Comedy.
Wearing the chiton and peplos.

Per, Her. In blazoning the divisions of a shield the term "*per*," signifying " by " or " by means of," is employed sometimes alone, and sometimes (having the same signification) with the word " party " or " parted." The following are the primary divisions of a shield :—Fig. *a*,

Per Pale, or *Parted per Pale*, or *Party per Pale* ; Fig. *b*, *Per Fesse* or *Parted per Fesse*; Fig. *c*, *Per Cross* or *Quarterly* (*Per Pale* and *Per Fesse* together); Fig. *d*, *Per Bend* ; Fig. *e*, *Per Bend Sinister* ; Fig. *f*, *Per Saltire* (*Per Bend* and *Per Bend Sinister*) ; Fig. *g*, *Per Chevron* ; Fig. *h*, *Per Tierce* or *Tiercé* (divided into three equal divisions by two vertical lines). (*Boutell*.)

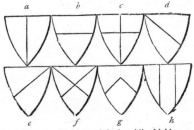

Fig. 534. Divisions of the heraldic shield.

Pera, R. (πήρα). A wallet or haversack of leather or hide, which was carried, slung over the shoulder, by travellers, peasants, and beggars. The Cynic philosophers, anticipating the fraternity of the GUEUX, adopted the wallet as a distinctive part of their costume.

Pergula, R. (*pergere*, to continue on). Generally, any construction added to another beyond the original plan, generally in the way of a lean-to ; e. g. a balcony built over the colonnades of a forum, or a gallery placed on a house-top ; a room in which paintings were exhibited ; a lecture-room, &c.

Periactos, R. (περί-ακτος, i.e. that turns round). A theatrical machine used by the ancients ; it was of very simple construction, being formed of three frames arranged so as to form a triangular prism, on each face of which a different scene was painted. At each side of the stage there was a *periactos* which turned on pivots as required, so as to admit of a rapid change of scene.

Periapts, O. E. Charms worn about the neck. (*Shakspeare*.)

Peribolê, Gr. and R. (περιβολή, an enclosing). The sacred enclosure of a temple, which was in some instances of sufficient size to contain not only altars and statues of the god, but shrines and a sacred wood. In Christian architecture the word was used for the wall of enclosure of the choir, &c.

Peridot, Fr. A yellow gem supposed to be the *topaz* of the ancients.

Peridromê, Gr. and R. (περι-δρομή, a running-round). A gallery or covered promenade which ran round a temple or other building.

Perigee. Near the earth ; *figuratively* "at its lowest."

Perihelion. Near the sun ; *figuratively* "at its highest."

Perimeter. The outline of a rectilinear figure.

Peripatetics. Disciples of Aristotle, who *walked about* during his lectures in the Lyceum at Athens.

Peripetasma (περι-πέτασμα). A general term including anything that is flat and hung up or spread out, such as a covering, tapestry, hangings, curtains, &c.

Periphery, Gr. and R. (περι-φέρεια). (1) The circumference of a curvilinear figure. (2) Ornaments in relief executed on the sides of vases, *running round* them. (See CRUSTÆ.)

Fig. 535. Ground-plan of a *pseudo-peripteral* temple.

Periptery, Arch. (περί-πτερος, lit. with wings around). A building surrounded by columns at equal distances one from the other ; the distance between the wall of enclosure and the colonnade being equal to that between the columns. *Peripteral temples* are distinguished as *monopteral*, or those with a single row of columns ; *dipteral*, those with two rows ; *pseudo-dipteral*, or buildings with one row of columns standing apart and one embedded ; lastly, *pseudo-peripteral* (Fig. 535), or buildings whose columns are embedded in the wall.

Periscelis, Gr. (περι-σκελίς). (1) An anklet worn by Oriental and Greek women, and less frequently by Roman ladies also. (2) The word is sometimes used for *feminalia* (q.v.).

Peristerium, Chr. A kind of canopy surrounding the sacred vessels containing the host. The eucharistic doves are called *peristera*.

Peristroma, R. (περί-στρωμα). In general, anything used as a covering, in especial that which is spread over a bed, and thence curtains, carpets, or hangings.

Peristyle, Arch. (περί-στυλον). A building the *interior* of which is surrounded with columns, the opposite of PERIPTEROS ; a building may, however, be peripteral and yet possess a peristyle. The term is also a Greek name for the ATRIUM.

Perivalium, Med. A Latin word used in the Middle Ages to denote the choir of a church, or the stalls of the choir.

Permanent White. (See CONSTANT WHITE.)

Pero, R. A tall boot reaching to the calf, made of untanned leather with the fur on, worn by shepherds and agricultural labourers, and still common in Italian villages.

Perogue. (See PIROGUE.)

Perpend-stone, Arch. A large stone reaching through the wall, visible on both sides.

Perpendicular Style of Architecture. The third and last of the pointed or Gothic styles of architecture used in England. It was developed from the Decorated during the latter part of the 14th century, and continued in use till the middle of the 16th, when it gave way to the style called ELIZABETHAN. It is peculiar to England. Its chief characteristics are a general prevalence of perpendicular lines, panelling of flat surfaces, and the multiplicity of small shafts with which the piers, &c., are overlaid.

Perron, Arch. A staircase, or flight of steps, outside a building.

Perse, Fr. Chintz.

Fig. 536. Persian Bowl.

Fig. 537. Flask. Persian.

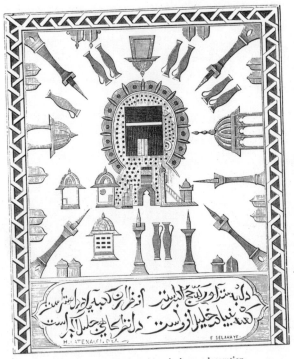

Fig. 538. Persian Plaque, with polychrome decoration.

Persian. A thin inferior *silk* used for lining garments.

Persian Blinds (Fr. *Persiennes*). Venetian blinds.

Persian Pottery. The illustrations (from Jacquemart's *History of the Ceramic Art*) are (Fig. 536) a bowl of soft porcelain, blue externally and decorated with abundant vegetation and fantastic birds with peacocks' tails; (Fig. 537) a flask, also of soft porcelain, characterized by a blackish-blue scroll encircling the principal subject; and (Fig. 538) a faience tile which M. Jacquemart considers pure Mohammedan art, is very interesting for the subject that it represents—the caaba or sacred mosque of Mecca, the object of the Mohammedan pilgrimage. (Consult *Souvenir d'un voyage en Perse, Comte de Rochchouart.*)

Persian Red. (See INDIAN RED.)

Persiana, It. (1) A silk with a pattern of large flowers. (2) Venetian blinds; Persiennes.

Persians, Gr. and R.(περσικά). Columns the shafts of which consist of figures of Persian slaves; they are also known as *Persian columns.*

Persona, Gr. and R. A mask worn by actors upon the stage; there were *personæ tragicæ, comicæ* (Fig. 539), *mutæ,* &c., that is, masks for tragic, comic, or mute persons, &c. The custom is attributed to that of smearing the face with certain juices and colours, and appearing in disguise at the festivals of Dionysus; and is probably as old as the drama itself.

Perspective. The art of representing on a flat surface the appearance of objects from one given point of view. *Linear perspective* is the science by which the principles of geometry are applied in this art. (See AERIAL and ISOMETRICAL PERSPECTIVE.)

Pertica, R. A rod, pole, or stick; a foot, or measure of length divided into twelve inches (*unciæ*) and sixteen fingers (*digiti*).

Perticæ, Chr. In mediæval architecture, beams behind the altar in a church, from which relics were suspended on days of festival.

Peruque. (See WIGS.)

Peruvian Architecture. The Peruvian temples and palaces were generally low and spacious, constructed of great blocks of stone often 38 feet by 18 and 6 feet in thickness. The interiors were richly ornamented, the sides of the apartments being thickly studded with gold and silver. Niches in the walls were filled with images of plants and animals, also of the precious metals. The Western wall of the temple was placed to receive the first rays of the rising sun upon a statue of the god engraved on a plate of gold and thickly studded with emeralds and precious stones.

Pes, R. A foot; the standard measure of length, composed of 12 *unciæ* or

Fig. 539. Persona comica.

inches, or 16 *digiti, finger-breadths.* It equalled 11·6496 inches English.

Pesante, It. A weight = half a drachm.

Fig. 540. Vase of Pesaro Ware.

Pesaro Ware. The particular characteristic of the mother-of-pearl majolica of Pesaro is a pale, limpid yellow, associated with a pure blue; under the effect of luminous rays these colours become animated and shoot out in pencils of red, golden yellow, green, and blue of remarkable intensity. (*Jacquemart.*) (Fig. 540.)

Peseta, Sp. A silver coin, about the fourth of a Mexican dollar; about 10½*d.*

Pesillo, It. Small scales used for weighing gold and silver, and gems.

Pessi (Gr. πεσσοί). Draughts. (See LATRUN-CULI.)

Pessulus, R. A bolt for a door.

Petasus, Gr. and R. (πέτασος, i. e. that which spreads out). (1) A soft felt hat with broad brim. (2) The winged cap of Mercury. Most of the horsemen in the Panathenaic procession (see ELGIN MARBLES) wear the petasus. In Greek art it is a conventional sign of a traveller. (Compare PILEUS.)

Petaurum, R. (πέταυρον, lit. a perch for fowls). A machine employed in the Roman games; probably a fixed " see-saw."

Peter-boat, O. E. A river *fisherman's* wherry.

Petit Canon, Fr. A kind of printing-type; *two-line* in English.

Petit Gris, Fr. Minever fur. (See VAIR.)

Petit Texte, Fr. A kind of printing-type; *brevier.*

Petoritum, R. An open four-wheeled carriage, a kind of cart used for conveying slaves. Its Gallic origin is indicated by the etymology of the word, viz. *petoer,* four, and *rit,* a wheel.

Petronel (Fr. *poictrinal*). A piece of artillery or fire-arm, used in the 16th century, which was afterwards converted into a clumsy gun called a *blunderbuss.* It was the medium between the arquebus and the pistol.

Petunse, Chinese. A fine clay used for porcelain ; a kind of kaolin.

Peulvan, Celt. (See MENHIR.)

Pewter. An alloy of 100 parts of tin to 17 of antimony ; or 89 tin, 7 antimony, and 2 copper. Tin and zinc, and lead and tin, are sometimes used to make pewter. The ancient guild of the Pewterers' Company have their hall in Lime Street.

Phæcasia, Gr. and R. (φαικάσιον). White shoes worn by different classes among the Greeks and Romans, but more especially by the priests and gymnasiarchs.

Phalæ or **Falæ,** R. Wooden towers which were erected temporarily in a circus for the display of sham fights and captures of cities. (Compare PEGMA.)

Phalangæ, Palangæ, R. (φάλαγξ). A pole employed for carrying purposes. Two men took the ends of this pole upon the shoulders, the burden being suspended from it in the middle. The same term was also applied to the rollers placed beneath objects whose weight rendered them difficult to move. The persons who made use of *phalangæ* for carrying anything were called *phalangarii.*

Phalanx, Gr. A close compact mass of infantry soldiers drawn up in files, usually eight deep. The Theban phalanx was twenty-five in depth.

Phalarica. (See FALARICA.)

Fig. 541. Gallic Phalera.

Phaleræ, R. (φάλαρα). Medals of gold, silver, or bronze (Fig. 541), worn upon the breast as a military decoration, and frequently displayed on the harness of the horses.

Phannel, O. E. (See FANON.)

Phantasmagoria. Literally, a procession of images. A name applied especially to dissolving views shown by the alternate use of each of two magic lanterns.

Pharetra, Gr. and R. (φαρέτρα). A quiver. This was made of hide or leather, often richly ornamented with gold, painting, or braiding. It had a lid, and hung, from a belt over the right shoulder, on the left hip. (See CORYTUS, QUIVERS.)

Pharos, Pharus, Gr. and R. (φάρος). A lighthouse ; the name was derived from that which Ptolemy Philadelphus erected in the island of Pharos, at the entrance to the harbour of Alexandria, in Egypt.

Phaselus, Egyp. (φάσηλος). A light Egyptian boat, long and narrow in shape, and made

Fig. 544. Part of the Frieze of the temple of Apollo Epicurius near Phigalia.

of very slight materials, such as osier, papyrus, and terra-cotta ; it derived its name from the resemblance it bore to the pod of a bean (φάσηλος).

Phaskon, Gr. A vessel of a flattened ovoid form, with a long spout, and a handle at the top, like the askos.

Fig. 542. Phaskon.

Phenakistoscope (φενακιστικὸs, deceptive, and σκοπέω, to view), or **Spectroscope.** A toy for illustrating the duration of impressions on the retina of the eye. (See SPECTRA.)

Phenicine. An indigo purple pigment.

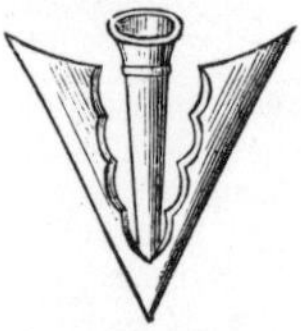

Pheon, Her. A pointed spear-head borne with the point in base. (*Boutell.*) "The *peon*, or *pheon*, was a barbed javelin ; the heads of these are still heraldic bearings, and from their figure, we find the barbs *escalloped*, or *invecked* as the heralds term it, aside." (*Meyrick.*)

Fig. 543. Pheon.

Pheretrum. (See FERETRUM.)

Phiala, Phialê, Gr. (φιάλη). The Greek term synonymous with the Latin PATERA. But *Jacquemart* says, "Quant à la phiale, sorte de *petite bouteille* qui nous a donné le mot *fiole;* elle figure assez souvent dans les mains des divinités."

Phigalian Marbles. Friezes in the Hellenic room of the British Museum, from a temple to Apollo Epicurius, near the ancient Phigalia in Arcadia. There are twenty-three slabs in high relief, eleven representing the battle between the Centaurs and the Lapithæ, and the rest the contest of the Greeks and Amazons. They are attributed to the same period as the Parthenon, but are considered inferior in style and workmanship. (Fig. 544.)

Philactery. (See PHYLACTERY.)

Philomel. Poetical for the nightingale.

Philyra and **Philura,** Gr. (φιλύρα). Strips of papyrus used for making a sheet of writing-paper ; ten or twelve strips of papyrus were first glued together lengthwise, and at the back of these a sufficient number of strips were fastened crosswise to double the thickness of the surface so obtained.

Phimus, Gr. (φιμόs). A Greek term synonymous with FRITILLUS (q.v.).

Phiolæ Rubricatæ. (See SANGUINOLENTA.)

Fig. 545. Phœnix. Device of Cardinal Trent.

Phœnix, Chr. In Christian archæology the

phœnix, which is consumed by concentrating the sun's rays in its body, and immediately rises again from its ashes, represents the mystery of the resurrection after death. In this sense it was adopted frequently as a device by ecclesiastics. (See BENNOU.) In blazon it is always represented as issuant from flames. (Fig. 545.)

Phorminx, Gr. (φόρμιγξ). Homer's epithet for the ancient *lyre*. It was a large lyre, and resembled the *cithara* of later times, or the modern guitar. It was used at an early period singly, or for accompanying recitations.

Photogalvanography. An art invented by Mr. Paul Pretsch, of Vienna, for printing from photographs by the medium of gutta percha. For a description of the process, see the *Manual of Photography*, 5th edition, pp. 269, 270.

Photoglyphic Engraving. An invention of Mr. Fox Talbot (1858) for engraving on metal plates by the action of light. (See *Photographic Journal*, vol. v. p. 58.)

Photography. A great many processes of producing pictures by the action of the sun's rays upon a sensitive surface are included under this general term, such as the Daguerreotype, the Talbotype, &c. [Consult in the first instance *R. Hunt's Manual of Photography*, from which reference can be taken to other authorities.]

Photolithography. The art of preparing lithographic stones for printing from, by the medium of photography.

Photometallography. A process of etching on metal plates, by the action of light, invented by Mr. C. J. Burnett (1858). (See *Photographic Journal*, vol. v. p. 97.)

Photometer. An instrument for measuring the *intensity* of light.

Phototype. A plate, like an engraved plate, produced from a photograph, for printing from.

Photozincography. The art of preparing zinc plates for printing from, by the medium of photography.

Phrase. In Music, a passage of melody or harmony containing a musical idea, more or less complete in respect of cadence.

Phrygian. Applied to music of a lively kind. (Cf. LYDIAN.)

Phrygian Work, O. E. Embroidery. (See ORFRAYS.)

Phrygianum (opus). A name given to all fine embroidery by the Romans, at a period when the work of the Phrygian women was most perfect.

Phrygio, R. A Phrygian, or embroiderer, because the inhabitants of Phrygia had the reputation of being excellent embroiderers.

Phylactery, Gen. (φυλακτήριον, a preservative). (1) A general term which included any kind of amulet worn about the person as a protection against dangers of all kinds. (2 Strips of parchment or vellum, upon which the Jews transcribed passages from the sacred books, and which they either wore upon the arm or the forehead, in a small leather box. (3) In the Middle Ages the term was applied to the scrolls held in the hands of angels or other persons represented in painting or sculpture. These scrolls bore inscriptions. (See LABELS.)

Phylaka, Gr. (φυλακή). A prison; a Greek term corresponding to the Latin words CARCER and ERGASTULUM (q.v.).

Phytography. A process of nature-printing from plants, by passing them between soft metal plates through a rolling press.

Piazza, It. A square or open place surrounded by buildings, generally supported by pillars, and forming a vaulted promenade; hence the term is sometimes applied to the archways of a colonnade.

Pibroch, Scotch. Bagpipe music.

Pica (*pic*). Printing type of the size formerly used in printing the *pic*, or service-book.

Piccadilly, Old Fr. A high, broad, peaked collar or ruff, *temp.* James I. The tailor who made these ruffs is said to have built the street called by this name.

Piccagium, Med. Lat. (English use). Money paid in fairs for breaking ground.

Piccolo, It. A small flute. Small pianofortes are so called also.

Pictura, R. (*pingo*, to paint). The art of painting; *pictura in tabula*, a painting on wood; *pictura in linteo* or *in sipario*, a painting on canvas; *pictura inusta*, a painting in encaustic or wax; *pictura udo tectorio*, a fresco-painting. Embroidery was called *pictura textilis*.

Picturatus, R. Painted; *tabella picturata*, a painted panel; *linteum picturatum*, embroidered linen.

Pièce de Maitrise, Fr. A test-work produced by an apprentice to prove his competence to become a *master* of his art or craft.

Piedouche, Fr. A bracket-pedestal.

Pieds de Hérisson, Fr. Fabulous animals so called represented on Persian pottery, mentioned by Jacquemart (p. 152); having the legs of a stag, the tail of a tiger, and the head of a woman. The legend is that Mohamet and Ali will mount such beasts on the Day of Judgment.

Piers, in Architecture, are the perpendicular supports from which *arches* spring.

Pietà, It. A picture or statue of the Body of Christ, attended by the Virgin Mary, or by holy women and angels.

Pietra Dura. Mosaic panelling of hard pebbles of variegated colours, representing fruit, birds, &c. in relief, and used as a decoration for coffers and cabinets in the 15th century.

Pietré Commesse, It. Costly inlaid-work representing flowers, fruit, &c., in precious stones —such as agates, jaspers, lapis lazuli, &c.—introduced in Florence in the 17th century, and still maintained in the royal manufactory of that city.

The finest examples are in the chapel of the Medici attached to the cathedral church of St. Lorenzo.

Pig. A black pig was represented at St. Anthony's feet, representing his victory over sensuality and gluttony. The monks of the order of St. Anthony used to keep herds of consecrated pigs.

Pigments. The colours used in painting. A large number are described in their order. Standard works on ancient and modern pigments are *Eastlake's Materials for a History of Painting*; *Merrifield's Ancient Art of Painting*; *Hundertpfund's Art of Painting restored to its Simplest and Surest Principles.* An exhaustive catalogue of other works on the subject has been issued by the Librarian of the South Kensington Museum.

Pike. A celebrated infantry weapon now replaced by the bayonet, consisting of a strong spear or lance with a spike at the butt for fixing in the ground. The shape of the head has varied at different periods.

Pila, R. This word has different meanings, according as the first syllable is long or short. In the first case it denotes (1) a mortar ; (2) a pillar or conical pier for supporting the superstructure of a bridge ; (3) a breakwater. When the first syllable is short, the word denotes (1) a playing-ball. The game of ball, from the earliest times to the fall of the Roman Empire, was one of the favourite exercises of the Greeks and Romans. In the baths and the gymnasiums a room (*sphæristerium*) was set apart for the purpose. *Pila* was a small ball ; *follis*, a large one filled with air : other balls were the *paganica* and the *harpastum*. (2) *Pila vitrea*, a glass globe. (3) A dummy made to roughly imitate the human form.

Pilaster, It. A square pillar on a wall, partly embedded in it, one-fourth or one-fifth of its thickness projecting.

Pile. (1) Her. One of the ordinaries, in form like a wedge. (2) An arrow used in hunting, with a round knob below the head, to prevent it penetrating too far. (3) The nap or surface on velvet.

Pileatus, R. One who wears the *pileus*, or skull-cap of felt ; it was specially worn by the seafaring classes, and also by the Dioscuri (Castor and Pollux).

Pilentum, R. A state carriage in which the Roman ladies rode when attending any ceremony, whereas for purposes of recreation or for visiting they made use of the *carpentum* or the *harmamaxa*.

Pileolus, R. Diminutive of PILEUS ; it was a small felt skull-cap which hardly covered the top of the head.

Pileus, Pileum, R. (πῖλος, felt). A kind of close-fitting felt cap worn more particularly by the seafaring classes. The *pileus* varied in form amongst the different nations by whom it was adopted ; it was worn exclusively by men. The most familiar form of the pileus, in art, is the Phrygian bonnet, or cap of liberty. (Cf. PETASUS.)

Pillar Dollars are Spanish silver coins, stamped on the obverse with the royal arms of Spain supported by two columns.

Pillion, O. E. A soft pad-saddle with a foot-rest, for a woman or child to ride on behind a man.

Pillow or **Head-stool,** Egyp. A kind of rest for the head, made sometimes of stone (onyx, alabaster, or sandstone), but more generally of wood, and used by the Egyptians to support and raise the head during sleep. In form it was a half-cylinder, and the base was more or less raised above the ground. This kind of pillow is still in use at the present day among various peoples, particularly the Nubians, the Japanese, and the Ashantees of Western Africa.

Pillow-beres, O. E. Pillow-cases. They were at all times an object of rich ornamentation.

Pillow Lace. Lace worked by hand, by throwing *bobbins* upon a cushion or pillow. (See LACE.)

Pilum, R. A javelin ; the missile weapon of the Roman infantry, but used likewise as a pike for charging the enemy. It was a thick strong weapon, 6 feet 3 inches in length, half of wood and half of iron, with a barbed head of 9 inches of solid iron. The term also denotes a heavy pestle for bruising things in a mortar.

Pilus, Med. Lat. (Fr. *pieu*). A pointed club or javelin.

Pina, Sp. An amalgam of silver.

Pinacotheca, Gr. and R. (πινακο-θήκη). A picture-gallery, one of the ordinary adjuncts to Greek or Roman houses of wealthy private persons.

Pinaculum, Gr. and R. (a ridge or crest). A roof terminating in a ridge, the ordinary covering for a temple, whereas private houses had a flat roof.

Pinchbeck. An alloy of 85 per cent. copper or brass, and 15 per cent. zinc ; named after its inventor. It is sometimes called *tomback*.

Pindaric. Of verses, irregular in metre ; like the verses of the lyric poet Pindar.

Pingle Pan, Scotch. A small tin ladle used for mixing children's food.

Pink Madder. (See MADDER.)

Pinking. Stamping out borders and edges upon textile fabrics with a cutting instrument.

Pinks (Fr. *stil de grain*). These are water-colour pigments of a yellow or greenish-yellow colour produced from the precipitation of vegetable juices, such as saffron, aloes, buckthorn-berries, broom-flowers, &c., upon chalk or whiting. They are *Italian pink*, sometimes called *yellow lake*; *brown pink*, *rose pink*, and *Dutch pink*.

Pinna, R. (lit. a wing). (1) The top of an embattled wall, the *battlements*. (2) The blade of a rudder.

Pinnacle, Arch. A small spire, generally with four sides and ornamented; it is usually placed on the tops of buttresses, both external and internal.

Pins. Metal pins were introduced into this country from France in 1543, previous to which ladies were accustomed to fasten their dresses with skewers of box-wood, ivory, or bone.

Pipe. A musical wind-instrument, represented in the 14th century, in *Strutt's Sports and Pastimes*, as used with the TABOR to accompany mountebanks, &c. (See also AULOS, PITO, &c.)

Pipe-clay. An oily clay found in large quantities in Devonshire; used for moulding earthenware, but chiefly for tobacco-pipes.

Piriform, Arch. Pear-shaped. The term is applied to roofs domed in the form of a pear; the Baptistery of Parma may be cited as an example.

Pirogue. An Indian canoe, hollowed out of a solid tree.

Piscina, R. (*piscis*, a fish). (1) A fish-pond, an indispensable appendage to the villa of a wealthy Roman. (2) A large uncovered tank in the open air used as a swimming-bath, and distinct from the *baptisterium*, which was under cover. (3) *Piscina limaria* was the reservoir of an aqueduct. In mediæval archæology the name was given (1) to credence-tables; (2) to baptisteries. (See BAPTISTERIUM, NATATORIUM.)

Pisé-work. A method of constructing very durable walls of blocks of *kneaded earth*. It was probably suggested by the building processes of the ants, and Pliny calls such walls *formaciæ*.

Pistillum, Pistillus, R. A pestle for a mortar.

Pistol. Invented at Pistoia in Tuscany. (See *Pallas Armata, Sir James Turner*, 1670; *Meyrick*, iii. 76.)

Pistole. A Spanish gold coin, worth about 16s.; the fourth of a *doubloon*.

Pistolese, It. A long dagger or stabbing-knife of Pistoia.

Pistrina, Pistrinum, R. (*pistor*, a miller). Originally this term denoted a mill for grinding grain; later on it was used exclusively to denote a house of correction for slaves who had to turn the mill. The work was of a most laborious kind.

Pistris, Pistrix, R. (πίστρις). (1) A marine monster, representations of which are to be seen on the walls of several houses at Pompeii (in the legend of Theseus and Andromeda). It is always represented with the head of a dragon, and the fins and tail of a fish; and was adopted in early Christian art for the fish that swallowed Jonah. (2) A military engine.

Pitch-blende. An ore used in porcelain painting. It produces a fine orange colour; also a black.

Pitch-pipe. A sort of whistle for ascertaining the *pitch* of a musical instrument, or for setting the key-note.

Pithos, R. (πίθος). A large earthenware jar with a narrow neck, used in ancient and modern times for storing wine and oil. It appears upon a bas-relief in the Villa Albani as the tub of Diogenes.

Pito, Sp. A Mexican name for the *pipe* of the Aztecs, which resembled a *flageolet*. It was made of red clay, and had four finger-holes. The young man selected as a victim at the sacrifice to Tezcatlepoca was carefully instructed before his death in the art of playing this instrument, and as he ascended the temple or TEOCALLI to the sacrifice, he broke a flute upon each of the steps of the temple.

Piu, It. Rather; used in Music, as *piu forte*, *rather* loud.

Pix or **Pyx**, Chr. (πυξίς). (1) A box to keep the unconsecrated altar-breads in. It was generally circular, with a pointed cover, and richly enamelled. (2) The vessel in which the holy eucharist was suspended over the altar. (3) The box kept at the British Mint to contain the coins selected to be tried in assay, to ascertain whether the coinage is of the standard purity. (See CIBORIUM [3], MONSTRANCE, &c.)

Pizzicato (It.). An expression in music; playing on the violin like a harp.

Placage, Fr. Veneering or inlaying.

Plack, Scotch. A small copper coin formerly current in Scotland; equal to the third of an English penny.

Placket, O. E. A petticoat. (*Shakspeare.*)

Plafond, Plafonner, Fr. Arch. (*plat-fond*). The French term for a ceiling, often the subject of elaborate architectural, carved, or painted decoration. The peculiar foreshortened perspective characteristic of figure-pictures on a ceiling is hence described as "plafonné;" and it is generally said of a painter distinguished for bold foreshortenings, "Il excelle à *plafonner*." *Plafonds* of different periods are found of wood, lath and plaster, or stone.

Plaga, R. A hunting-net, the diminutive of which is *plagula* (small net); the latter term also denotes the curtains hung round a couch or litter, a width of cloth, a strip of paper, &c.

Plagula. (See PLAGA.)

Planchet. A name for the smooth coin prepared for stamping before it has passed under the die.

Planeta. A robe worn by *priests*, resembling the DALMATIC (see Fig. 236) worn by *deacons*. (See CHASUBLE.)

Planetary Machine. (See ORRERY.)

s

Planisphere. A projection of the sphere and its various circles on a plane surface.

Planta Genista, Her. The broom-plant badge of the Plantagenets.

Plaque, Fr. A flat plate of metal or painted china. Limoges enamels of the 15th century are described as *plaques*.

Plasm. A mould or matrix.

Fig. 546. Planta Genista.

Plasma. A green transparent chalcedony found in India and China.

Plaster of Paris. The cement or plaster obtained from gypsum, originally prepared near Paris. It is usually sold in the form of white powder, and is largely used in the arts. Verrocchio (1435—1488) is said to have been the first sculptor to cast moulds in plaster of Paris. (See GYPSUM.)

Plastic Art. Sculpture ; opposed to *Graphic Art*, or painting, &c.

Plastron, Fr. A fencing-pad to cover the body. *Plastron-de-fer* was an iron breastplate worn under the hauberk, especially when the latter was of ringed mail.

Plat-band. (See TÆNIA.)

Plata, Sp. Silver (hence our *plate*).

Plate, Her. A silver roundle.

Plate-armour, consisting entirely of metal *plates*, became general during the 15th century.

Plate-glass. A superior kind of thick glass, used chiefly for mirrors and for large windows.

Plate-jack, O. E. Coat armour.

Plate-marks. (See HALL-MARKS.)

Plate-paper is a thick soft paper expressly prepared for printing engravings upon.

Platea, Gr. and R. (πλατεῖα, i.e. broad). A wide fine street in a city, in contradistinction to a small street called *angiportus*, which means literally a narrow street.

Platen. Of a printing-press, the flat part by which the impression is made.

Plateresca, Sp. A name given to goldsmiths' work of the 14th and 15th centuries, which reflected the complicated and delicate forms of ornament applied in the pointed architecture of the period.

Plates are properly illustrations taken from copper or steel engravings ; *cuts* are impressions from wood-blocks.

Platina. Twisted silver-wire.

Platina Yellow. Two pigments, one of a pale yellow colour, the other resembling *cadmium yellow*, are sold under this name.

Plating is the art of covering metals with a thin surface of silver or gold for ornament.

Platinum (Sp. *plata*, silver). A white metal exceedingly ductile, malleable, and difficult of fusion. It is found in the Ural Mountains and in South America, and is much used in goldsmiths' work in Russia.

Plaustrum, R. (*plaudo*, to rumble). A two-wheeled cart drawn by two oxen, and used for conveying agricultural produce'; *plaustrum majus* was a much larger cart mounted on four wheels. It had a long pole projecting behind, on which blocks of stone or other cargo could be balanced on planks attached. The wheels (*tympana*) were of solid wood nearly a foot in thickness, and their creaking was heard to a great distance (hence the name).

Plectrum or **Plektron,** Gr. and R. (from πλήσσειν, to strike). A short stem of ivory or metal pointed at both ends, used to strike the chords of the lyre, the *barbiton*, the *cithara*, and some other stringed instruments.

Plemochoê, Gr. and R. (πλημο-χοή, i. e. that pours a flood). A vessel in the shape of a top ; it resembled the *cotylê*.

Plenitude, Her. Said of the moon when in full.

Plenshing-nail. A large nail for fastening the planks of floors to the joists.

Plethron, Gr. The basis of land measurement, being 100 feet square, or 10,000 square feet. As a lineal measure, 100 feet, or about 101 of English measurement.

Plinth, Arch. (πλίνθος). Lit. a *tile* or *brick*, and thence the lower projecting base of a column, pedestal, or wall, which resembles a strong square tile placed beneath the last torus at the base of a column. (See ABACUS.)

Plinthium, R. (πλινθίον). A sun-dial, so called because its divisions were marked on a flat surface (πλίνθος).

Plocage, Fr. Carding-wool.

Plombage. Lead work.

Plombagine. Plumbago.

Plostellum. Diminutive of PLAUSTRUM.

Ploughs are mentioned in Deuteronomy (1451 B.C.), and represented on Egyptian sculptures of still earlier date. The Roman plough of the date of our era is described by Virgil.

Plough Monday was the name given by our ancestors to the first Monday after the Epiphany, the return to labour after the Christmas holiday.

Plumæ, R. (lit. feathers). The scales of armour, arranged to imitate feathers. (See PENNA.)

Plumarium Opus. (See OPUS P.)

Plumbago. A carburet of iron commonly known as black lead, also called GRAPHITE, used for making crucibles and black-lead pencils.

Plumbeous Wares. Lead-glazed, by the addition of an oxide of lead in the preparation of the glaze. (See POTTERY.)

Plumbum, R. (lit. lead). A general term denoting anything that is made of lead, such as a lead pipe, a slinger's bullet, &c.

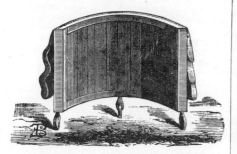

Fig. 547. Pluteus.

Pluteus, R. A general term including anything made of boards adapted to afford a support, cover, passage, &c.; and thus sometimes used as a synonym for *musculus* or protective shed. Fig. 547, a *pluteus* upon three wheels, was used for protecting soldiers conducting an approach at the foot of a rampart. These *plutei* were covered with the skins of animals, which were wetted to protect the machines from fire; and helped to deaden the shock of missiles.

Plynteria, Gr. (πλυντήρια, washing). Festivals held at Athens in honour of Athena Aglauros, in which the statue of the goddess was stripped of its garments and ornaments and washed. It was carefully concealed in the mean time, and the city being thus in a manner deprived of its protecting divinity, the day was considered an ill-omened one.

Pnigeus, R. (πνιγεὺς, lit. a choker). A kind of funnel employed to stop or repress the air in a hydraulic organ.

Pnyx, Gr. The site in Athens where the ECCLESIÆ were held. It was a semicircular rising ground, with an area of 12,000 square yards, levelled with a pavement of large stones, and surrounded by a wall, behind which was the BEMA or platform from which speakers addressed the people.

Pocillum or Poculum, R. Any cup or glass for drinking, distinct from the CRATER for mixing, and the CYATHUS for ladling the wine. (Cf. POKAL.)

Poddisoy, Padusoy, O. E. (Fr. *pou de soie*). A rich plain silk.

Podera, Gr. (ποδήρης, i.e. reaching to the feet). A rich linen dress worn by Greek women, the edges of which were indented.

Podium, Arch. (πόδιον, lit. a small foot). A low wall or basement, generally with a *plinth* and *cornice,* running round a room or in front of a building, forming a sort of shelf or seat. Fig. 548 shows the *podium* of a sepulchral chamber. In an amphitheatre, *podium*

Fig. 548. Podium running round a sepulchral chamber.

was the name for a raised basement which ran like a high enclosure round the whole circumference of the arena. Lastly, the term is sometimes used as a synonym for a socle, and a console or bracket.

Fig. 549. Point Lace à bride picotée.

Poêle, Fr. (lit. a frying-pan). A square shield with a raised edge and a grating on it, which resembled the German baking-dish. In a tournament, the joust "*à la poêle*" was the most dangerous of all, as the champions fought bare-headed and without armour. Their horses were blindfolded, and a coffin was brought into the course before the combat commenced. (*Meyrick.*)

Point Lace à *bride picotée* ground. This lace is made with the needle (see NEEDLE POINT), some parts of the pattern only slightly raised in relief being united by stitches called *bride picotée*. (Fig. 549.)

Point of Sight. The principal vanishing point, in perspective, to which the horizontal lines converge.

Pointed or **Christian Architecture** is generally called GOTHIC ; and is a general term, descriptive of all the styles that have prevailed subsequent to the introduction of the *pointed arch*, commencing with the 11th century.

Pointel. The mediæval *stylus* or *graphium* (q.v.).

Points. In the 15th and 16th centuries, before the introduction of buttons, the different parts of dress were fastened with ribands, having ornamental *points* or metal tags at the end. (See Fig. 559.)

Poitrine, Fr. A breastplate for man or horse.

Pokal, Germ. (Lat. *poculum*). A drinking-cup. (Fig. 550.)

Poke, O. E. A bag ; modern pocket.

Poker Pictures. Drawings burned upon wood with hot irons ; much patronized in the 18th century.

Fig. 550. Pokal, or German Tankard.

Pol, Edepol, R. A familiar oath or adjuration especially employed by the Roman women ; it was an abbreviation of *By Pollux !*

Polariscope. An instrument for exhibiting the polarization of light.

Pole-axe. A weapon of the 15th century, combining a hatchet, a pike, and a serrated hammer. Used principally by cavalry.

Poleyns, Fr. (See GENOUILLIÈRES.)

Pollubrum and **Polubrum,** R. An old term for which there was substituted later on *malluvium, aquimanale, aquiminarium, trulleum ;* it was a kind of basin for washing the hands, the χέρνιψ, χερόνιπτρον of the Greeks.

Polos, Gr. A kind of sun-dial. (See HOROLOGIUM.)

Polyandrion, Chr. (Gr. πολυ-άνδριον). A common sepulchre in which more than four bodies were buried. (See LOCULUS.)

Polychord. An instrument for application to the pianoforte for coupling together the strings of two octave notes.

Polychromy. Colouring statuary, bas-reliefs, and architecture ; to be distinguished from forming them of variously-coloured materials. This was not done by painting with an opaque colour, but a sort of staining of the surface by thin, transparent colouring matter. M. de Quincy states that the fine preservation of the surface of some antique statues, such as the Apollo Belvedere, Hercules of Glycon, and Venus de Medici, is attributable to the use of wax colouring. Stones of various colours were used to represent different parts of the figure, and in busts of the Roman emperors the dress is frequently of coloured marble, while the flesh is of white. [Consult *Redford's Ancient Sculpture.*]

Polyhedron. A solid with many faces or planes.

Polyptyca, Gr. (πολύ-πτυχα). (1) Tablets, a sufficient number of which are put together to

Fig. 551. A Silver Engraved Pomander, or Scent-box, shown open and closed.

form what we now call a note-book. (2) A polyptych; a picture with several compartments. (Cf. DIPTYCH.)

Polystyle, Arch. Surrounded by several rows of columns, as in Moorish architecture. The porticoes of a Greek temple had never more than ten columns in front (decastyle).

Pomander, O. E. (from *pomme d'ambre,* perfume apple). A scent-box worn at the end of the hanging girdles of the 16th century. (See POUNCET-BOX.) (Fig. 551.) Consult an interesting monograph by *R. H. Soden Smith,* "*Notes on Pomanders.*"

Pomme, Her. A green roundle.

Pomœrium, R. (*post* and *mœrium* (*murus*) behind the walls). A line enclosing a town, marked out at intervals by stone pillars. When the limits of the town were extended, the *pomœrium* could not be changed without augury by the *jus pomœrii,* and, in any case, only by a town whose inhabitants had contributed to the extension of the limits of the empire.

Pompa, R. and Gr. (πομπή). A solemn procession, especially that with which the games of the circus were preceded.

Pondus, Weight, R. (*pendo,* to suspend). An object used for weighing, either with the balance (*libra*), or the steel-yard (*statera*). The same term was also applied to a weaver's weights; these were of stone, terra-cotta, or lead.

Fig. 552. Pons.

Pons, R. (Gr. γέφυρα). (1) A bridge; the causeway (*agger*) which traversed the Roman bridge was paved with large polygonal stones; on either side of it was a pathway (*crepido*). Fig. 552 shows the Roman bridge at St. Chamas, at the ends of which were erected triumphal arches (*fornices*). (See FORNIX.) *Pons sublicius* was a wooden bridge built upon piles; *pons suffragiorum,* the voting-bridge over which the electors passed as they came out of the *septum* to cast their vote (*tabella*) into the urn (*cista*). It is pro-

bable that the Greek bridges were of wood. (2) A wharf or landing-stage by the water-side.

Poongi, Hindoo. A curious musical instrument made of a gourd, or sort of cocoa-nut, into which two pipes are inserted. It is the instrument played by the Sampuris, or snake-charmers, to the performing cobras.

Pope. The illustration represents the Pope of Rome in full pontificals, viz. the *tiara,* consisting of three crowns of gold decorated

Fig. 553. Pope in full pontificals.

with precious stones and surmounted by a cross, and over a *rochet* (surplice) of silk a mantle of gold work plentifully ornamented with pearls. The under vestment, which is long, is of hyacinth colour. The slippers are of velvet with a cross of gold, which all who wish to speak to the Pope reverently kiss. Late mediæval artists attributed this costume to the First Person of the Trinity. It is given also to St. Clement, St. Cornelius, St. Fabian, St. Gregory, St. Peter, and St. Sylvanus.

Popina, R. A tavern or refreshment-place where food was sold, in contradistinction to *caupona,* which was a shop for selling wine.

Popinjay, O. E. A parrot.

Poplin. A textile of modern introduction, woven of threads of silk and worsted.

Poppy, Chr. This plant, the seed of which affords a soporific oil, symbolizes, in Christian iconography, death.

Poppy Oil. A bland drying oil, obtained from poppy-seed, and used in painting. (See OILS.)

Poppy-head. A term in decorative art for the carved ornaments with which the tops of the uprights of wood-work, such as the ends of benches, backs of chairs, bedposts, &c., were crowned.

Popularia, R. The second *mænianum* or tier of seats in an amphitheatre.

Porcelain (Ancient Chinese) (from the Portuguese *porcellana,* little pigs ; a name given to cowrie-shells by the early traders, and applied to porcelain, which they thought was made of them, or because it resembled the interior of a shell). A fine species of transparent earthenware, the chief component part of which is silex. (*Fairholt.*) The most ancient examples of porcelain in China are circular dishes with upright sides, very thick, strong, and heavy, and which invariably have the marks of one, two, or three on the bottom thus: I. II. III. The colours of these rare specimens vary. The kinds most highly prized have a brownish-yellow ground, over which is thrown a light shot sky-blue, with here and there a dash of blood-red. The Chinese say there are

but a few of these specimens in the country, and that they are more than a thousand years old. (*Fortune.*) The first imitations of Chinese porcelain in Europe date from the 16th century, under the Medici family, and include specimens supposed to have been designed by the immediate pupils of Raffaelle. (See RAFFAELLE-WARE.) Among the next earliest produced is that of Fulham, by Dr. Dwight, in 1671, and of St. Cloud in France about 1695.

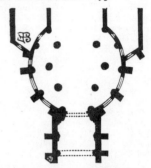

Fig. 555. Ground-plan of a Cupola Porch.

Porch, Arch. A structure placed in front of the door of a church or other building, and very variable in form. In the ancient basilicas the vestibule is more commonly called NARTHEX (q.v.). Fig. 554 shows a wooden porch also called a *pent-house porch,* and Fig. 555 a plan of what is called a *cupola* porch, from the fact that, its ground being circular, it is surmounted by a dome.

Porcupine (Fr. *porc epic*). Hereditary device

Fig. 554. Pent-house Porch.

Fig. 556. Porcupine. Device of Louis XII.

of the Valois family. The "Order of the Por-cupine" was instituted in 1397 by Louis, Duke of Orleans, and abolished by Louis XII., who retained the badge (Fig. 556), and had his cannon marked with a porcupine. In numismatics his golden "écus au porc epic" are rare and highly valued.

Porcupine-wood. The ornamental wood of a palm, the markings of which in the horizontal section resemble porcupine quills.

Porphyry. A hard stone much used in Egyptian sculpture, and for sarcophagi. It was of a fine red colour, passing into purple and green, and susceptible of a fine polish. (See also ROSSO ANTICO.)

Porporino, It. A yellow powder substituted for gold by mediæval artists. It was compounded of quicksilver, sulphur, and tin.

Fig. 557. Porta (Gate of Perusium).

Porta, R. This term denotes the gate of a city, a large gate in any enclosure, in contra-distinction to JANUA and OSTIUM (q.v.), which denote the doors of a building. Fig. 557 shows the ancient gate of Perugia.

Portcullis. A kind of iron grating, form-ing an outer door, which slided up and down perpendicularly in the grooves of a bay. It was suspended by a chain, which could instantly be lowered, as occasion required, in order to pre-vent ingress and cut off all communication. By the Greeks and Romans they were called *portæ cataractæ*, and in the Middle Ages they were known as Saracenic gates.

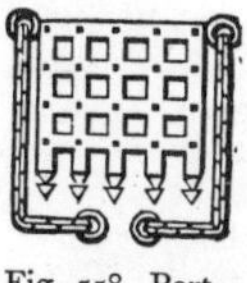

Portcullis, Her. A defence for a gateway, borne as a badge by the Houses of Beaufort and Tudor. Motto, "*Altera securitas.*" (Fig. 558.)

Fig. 558. Port-cullis.

Porticus, Portico, R. (*porta*). A long colonnade serving as a covered promenade. In an amphitheatre, the covered gallery at the top which was appropriated to women or slaves. A wooden gallery covered over with a roof, but in some cases entirely open on the side of the country. (See TEMPLUM.)

Portisculus, R. A director's staff wielded on board ship by the officer who gave the time to the rowers to make them row in unison.

Portrait Painting. The earliest portrait on record is that of Polygnotus, painted by himself, B.C. 400. Giotto is said to have been the earliest successful portrait painter of modern times. The different sizes of portraits are the following :—

	ft.	in.		ft.	in.
Bishop's whole length	8	10	by	5	10.
Whole length	7	10	,,	4	10.
Bishop's half-length	4	8	,,	3	8.
Half-length	4	2	,,	3	4.
Small half-length	3	8	,,	2	10.
Kit-cat	3	0	,,	2	4.
Three-quarter size	2	6	,,	2	1.
Head size	2	0	,,	1	8.

Portula. A wicket made in a large gate in order to give admittance into a city without opening the *porta* or large gate.

Posnett, O. E. A little pot.

Postergale, Chr. A DORSAL (q.v.).

Postern (*posterna*, a back-door). A private gate in a rampart, either upon the platform or at the angle of a curtain, and opening into the ditches, whence it was possible to pass by the *pas-de-souris*, without being seen by the besiegers, into the covered way and the glacis.

Posticum, R. (Gr. παραθύρα). (1) A back door to a Roman house. (2) In Architecture, the part of a building opposite to the façade ; the posterior façade.

Postis, R. The jamb of a door, supporting the lintel or *limen superius.*

Postscenium, R. The part of a Roman theatre behind the stage, in which the actors dressed, and the appointments and machines were kept.

Potichomanie. A process of ornamenting glass with coloured designs on paper, in imita-tion of painted porcelain.

Potter's Clay, found in Dorsetshire and Devonshire, is used for modelling and for pottery ; mixed with linseed oil, it is used as a *ground* in painting.

Pottery (Fayence, Terraglia), as distinct from porcelain, is formed of potter's clay mixed with marl of argillaceous and calcareous nature, and sand, variously proportioned, and may be classed under two divisions : *Soft* (Fayence à pâte tendre), and *Hard* (Fayence à pâte dure), according to the nature of the composition or the degree of heat under which it has been fired in the kiln. What is known generally in England as *earthenware* is soft, while *stone-ware, Queen's-ware*, &c., are hard. The characteristics of the soft wares are a paste or body which may be scratched with a knife or file, and fusibility generally at the heat of a porcelain furnace. These soft wares may be again divided into four subdivisions : *unglazed, lustrous, glazed*, or *enamelled*. Among the three first of these sub-divisions may be arranged almost all the ancient pottery of Egypt, Greece, Etruria, and Rome ; as also the larger portion of that in general use among all nations during mediæval and modern times. The *glazed wares* may be again divided into *silicious* or *glass-glazed wares*, and *plumbeous* or *lead-glazed*. In these subdivisions the foundation is in all cases the same. The mixed clay or "paste" or "body" is formed by the hand or on the wheel, or impressed into moulds ; then slowly dried and baked in a furnace or stove, after which, on cooling, it is in a state to receive the glaze. This is prepared by fusing sand or other silicious material with potash or soda to form a translucent glass, the composition of the glaze upon vitreous or *glass-glazed* wares. The addition of oxide of lead constitutes the glaze of *plumbeous* wares ; and the further addition of the oxide of tin produces an enamel of an opaque white of great purity, which is the characteristic glazing of *stanniferous* or *tin-glazed wares*. Most of the principal seats of the manufacture of pottery, and a description of the objects manufactured, and methods used in the manufacture, will be found mentioned under their respective headings.

Poulaines, Fr. Long-toed boots and shoes, introduced in 1384. (See CRACOWES.)

Pounce-paper. A kind of transparent tracing-paper, free from grease, &c.; made in Carlsruhe.

Pounced. In Engraving, *dotted* all over.

Pouncet-box, O. E. A perfume-box, carved with open work. (See POMANDER.)

Pouranamas, Hind. Very ancient books of India, which give a part of Hindoo history from the beginning of the Hindoo monarchy, or the time of the king Ellou or Ella.

Pourpoint, Fr. A quilted doublet, worn in the 14th and 15th centuries. The illustration

represents a Venetian gallant of the 16th century. (See GAMBESON.)

Fig. 559. Pourpoint. Worn by a Venetian youth of the 16th century.

Powder-blue is pulverized pipe-clay, a good "pounce" for transferring designs upon linen for embroidery.

Powdered, Her. (See SÉMÉ.)

Powers, Chr. Guardian angels, usually represented bearing a staff. (See ANGELS.)

Præcinctio, R. (*præcingo*, to gird). A lobby running quite round the circle formed by the *caveæ* in the interior of a theatre or amphitheatre ; the same term is also used to denote the passages between the tiers of seats comprised within each *mænianum*. According to their importance, theatres and amphitheatres were divided into two, three, and sometimes four præcinctiones.

Præfericulum, R. A metal basin without handles, used for holding sacred utensils.

Præficæ, R. Women hired as mourners at the funerals of wealthy persons.

Præfurnium, R. The mouth of a furnace placed beneath a *hypocausis* or heating-stove in a set of baths. Fig. 560 shows the *præfurnium* of a hypocausis which was drawn upon the walls of a *laconicum* situated near the church of St. Cecilia at Rome. (See HYPOCAUSIS.)

Fig. 560. Præfurnium hypocaust.

Prætexta, R. A TOGA with a broad purple border. It was introduced by the Etruscans, and was the costume assigned to priests and magistrates, to boys before they came of age, and to women before their marriage. (See TOGA.) (Fig. 561.)

Prætorium, R. The tent of the commander-in-chief of the army ; it was so called because in the earliest times of Rome the consul who commanded the army bore the title of *prætor*. The residence of a governor of a province was also called *prætorium*, and finally the name was given to any large house or palace.

Prandium, R. (*prandeo*, to breakfast). The midday meal, which came between breakfast (*jentaculum*) and dinner (*cœna*).

Prastura. (See UPAPITHA.)

Préa-koul, Hind. An upright stone or sacred boundary among the Khmers.

Préasat, Hind. The tower of the Khmers ; *préasat-stupaï* means little tower ; *préasat-phra-damrey*, the elephant tower of the king.

Precarium, Chr. A temporary benefice granted to a layman by the Church ; the holder of the benefice was, however, bound to pay the Church certain dues.

Predella, It. A ledge behind the altar of a church on which the altar-piece was placed, containing small pictures, of similar subjects to the altar-piece.

Prefericulum, R. A shallow metal bowl used in sacrifices for carrying the sacred vessels. Its shape resembled the *patera*.

Premier Coup. (See PRIMA PAINTING.)

Pre-Raphaelites. A modern school of painters, who, throwing aside all conventional laws and traditions in art, direct their study to the forms and colours of Nature.

Presentoir, Fr. An épergne or table-stand for flowers ; made very shallow, on a tall and richly-decorated stem. A favourite subject of the goldsmith's art in the 16th century.

Fig. 561. Roman maiden wearing the *toga prætexta*.

Pressed Glass. Glass pressed into a mould by a machine ; differing from *blown glass*.

Presto, It. In Music, quickly.

Priapeia, R. (πριάπεια). Festivals in honour of Priapus ; they were held chiefly at Lampsacus.

Pricket. A young stag of two years, when his horns begin to sprout.

Prie-Dieu. A kneeling-desk for prayers.

Prima Painting (in French, *peinture au premier coup*) is a modern style directed to the avoidance of extreme finish, described in a work by *Hundertpfund*, "*The Art of Painting restored to its Simplest and Surest Principles.*"

Primary Colours. Blue, yellow, and red, from which all colours are derived.

Primero, O. E. A game at cards mentioned by Shakspeare.

Primicerii, Chr. This term had several meanings, but it was usually employed to denote the first person inscribed on a list, because the tablet on which the names were written was covered with wax; whence *primi-cerius* (from *cera*, wax), the first upon the wax. In cathedral churches the primicerius presided over the choir, and regulated the order and method of the ceremonies.

Priming. (See GROUNDS.)

Prince's Metal or **Prince Rupert's Metal.** An alloy of 72 parts of copper and 28 parts of zinc, which has a resemblance to gold.

Princedoms or **Principalities**, Chr. An order of THRONES of angels; usually represented in complete armour, carrying pennons. (See Fig. 24.)

Principes, R. A body of heavy-armed foot-soldiers; thus named, because, in the order of battle, they were placed first.

Principia, R. (*princeps*, chief, foremost). The headquarters in a Roman camp, comprising not only the tents of the general and the superior officers, but also an open space in which justice was administered and sacrifices offered to the gods; it was in the same open space that all the standards of the legion were set up.

Priory, Chr. A monastery attached, as a rule, to an abbey; there were also, however, priories which formed the *head of an order*. In the order of Malta each *tongue* comprehended several great priories.

Fig. 562. Prismatic mouldings.

Prismatic (mouldings). A kind of moulding resembling the facets of a prism (Fig. 562), which is sometimes met with in archivolts of the Romano-Byzantine period. The same term is likewise applied to mouldings characteristic of the flamboyant style, which assume, especially in their base, the form of prisms.

Proaron, Gr. and R. (πρόαρον; ἀρύω, to draw water). A vessel of a flattened spheroid form, with two handles.

Proaulium, R. (*pro*, in front of). The vestibule of any building.

Prochous, Gr. (πρόχοος, i. e. thing for pouring out). A small jug for pouring liquid into a cask; it had a narrow neck, a very large handle, and a pointed mouth.

Procœton, Gr. and R. (προ-κοιτών). An antechamber or room preceding other rooms or chambers.

Prodd, O. E. A light cross-bow, used by ladies, *temp.* Elizabeth.

Prodomos, Arch. (πρό-δομος). The façade of a temple or building, and sometimes the porch of a church.

Profile. The side view of the human face. It is observed by Fairholt that "a face which, seen directly in front, is attractive by its rounded outline, blooming colour, and lovely smile, is often divested of its charms when seen in profile, and strikes only as far as it has an *intellectual* expression. Only where great symmetry exists, connected with a preponderance of the intellectual over the sensual, will a profile appear finer than the front face."

Projectura, R. The beaver of a helmet.

Proletarii, R. The proletariate, or Roman citizens of the lowest class of the people, so called because they contributed nothing to the resources of the republic except by their offspring (*proles*); being, as they were, too poor to pay taxes.

Prom, Hind. An ornamented carpet in Khmer art.

Prometheia. An Athenian festival in honour of Prometheus, with a torch-race (*lampadephoria*).

Promulsis. The first course at a Roman dinner, arranged to stimulate the appetite; eggs were a principal ingredient, whence the proverb *ab ovo usque ad mala* (from first to last).

Pronaos, R. (πρό-ναος). A portico situated in front of a temple; it was open on all sides, and surrounded only by columns, which, in front, supported not only the entablature, but the pediment (*fastigium*).

Proper, Her. Said of a thing exhibited in its natural, or proper, colour.

Proplasma, Gr. and R. (πρό-πλασμα). A rough model or embodiment of the sculptor's first idea, executed by him in clay.

Propnigeum, Gr. and R. The mouth of the furnace of the HYPOCAUSIS (q.v.).

Propylæa, Gr. The open court at the entrance to a sacred enclosure; e. g. an Egyptian temple, or especially the Acropolis at Athens.

Prora, R. (πρῷρα). The prow or fore-part of a ship, whence *proreta*, a man who stood at the ship's head; *proreus* was a term also used. (See ACROSTOLIUM.)

Proscenium, R. (πρό-σκήνιον). The stage in a Greek or Roman theatre; it included the whole platform comprised between the *orchestra* and the wall of the stage ; the term was also used sometimes to denote the wall of the stage itself.

Proscenium, Mod. The ornamental frame on which the curtain hangs.

Prostylos, R. (πρό-στυλος). A building or temple which has a porch supported by a row of columns.

Proteleia, Gr. (προ-τέλεια). Sacrifices which were offered to Diana, Juno, the Graces, and Venus prior to the celebration of a marriage.

Prothyrum, Gr. (πρό-θυρον). With the Greeks, the vestibule in front of the door of a house, where there was generally an altar of Apollo, or a statue or laurel-tree; with the Romans, the prothyrum was the corridor or passage leading from the street to the atrium (Fig. 563).

Fig. 563. Entrance (Prothyrum) of a Roman house.

Prototype (πρῶτον, first ; τύπον, mould). The model of a plastic design; hence figuratively, a *type* or forerunner.

Protractor. An instrument for laying down and measuring angles upon paper.

Protypum, Gr. and R. (πρό-τυπον). A model,

first model or mould for making any object in clay, such as antefixæ.

Prussian Blue. A valuable pigment of a greenish-blue colour, of great body, transparency, and permanency ; a mixture of prussiate of potash and rust, or oxide of iron. (See CYANOGEN.)

Prussian Brown. A deep-brown pigment, more permanent than madder.

Psaltery. A stringed instrument or kind of lyre of an oblong square shape, played with a rather large plectrum.

Pschent, Egyp. The head-dress of the ancient kings of Egypt, which should properly be called *skhent*, since the *p* only represents the article *the*. This head-dress is the emblem of supreme power, the symbol of dominion over the south and north. It is a diadem composed of the united crowns of the Upper and Lower Egypts.

Psephus, Gr. (ψῆφος). A round stone used by the Athenian voters to record their votes.

Pseudisodomum (*opus*). (See OPUS PSEUDISODOMUM.)

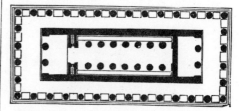

Fig. 564. Ground plan of a Pseudodipteral Temple.

Pseudodipteros, Gr. and R. (ψευδο-δίπτερος). A building or temple which presents the appearance of being surrounded by a double colonnade, though it possesses only a single one, which is separated from the walls of the cella, as in the dipteral arrangement. (Fig. 564.)

Pseudoperipteros, Gr. and R. (ψευδο-περίπτερος). A building or temple which presents the appearance of being surrounded by a colonnade, although in reality it does not possess one, the columns being embedded in the walls of the cella. (See PERIPTEROS, under which an example of this kind of temple is given.)

Pseudothyrum, Gr. and R. (ψευδό-θυρον). Literally, a false door, and thence a secret door, or door hidden by some means or other.

Pseudourbana (sc. *ædificia*), R. The dwelling-house of the owner of a farm, which was distinct from the buildings set apart for the farm people and the slaves, the *familia rustica*.

Psili, Gr. (ψιλοί). Light-armed troops, who wore skins or leather instead of metal armour, and fought generally with bows and arrows or slings.

Psychè, Fr. A cheval-glass or mirror.

Psycter, Gr. (ψυκτήρ). A metal wine-cooler, often of silver, consisting of an outer vessel to contain ice, and an inner vessel for the wine.

Pterotus, R. (πτερωτός). That which has wings or ears ; an epithet applied to the drink-ing-cup called *calix*.

Puggaree, Hind. A piece of muslin worn as a turban.

Pugillares, R. Writing-tablets small enough to be held in the hand (*pugillus*), whence their name.

Pugio, R. (Gr. μάχαιρα). A short dagger, without a sheath, worn by officers of high rank.

Pulpitum, R. The tribune of an orator, or the chair of a professor. In a theatre the term was used to denote the part of the stage next to the *orchestra*. (See PROSCENIUM.)

Pulvinar, R. (*pulvinus*, a cushion). A cushion or bolster, and thence a state couch or a marriage-bed.

Pulvinarium, R. (1) A room in a temple, in which was set out the *pulvinar* or couch for the gods at the feast of the LECTISTERNIUM. (2) See OPUS PULVINARIUM.

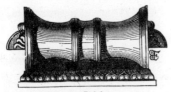

Fig. 565. Pulvinatus.

Pulvinatus, R. Having a contour similar to that of a cushion or bolster, and thence the cylinder formed by the swelling of the volute at the side of the Ionic capital. (Fig. 565.)

Pumice-stone. A kind of lava of less specific gravity than water. The dome of the mosque of St. Sophia at Constantinople is built of pumice-stone.

Punchau. (See INTI.)

Punctum, R. A vote or suffrage, because in early times each citizen, instead of laying down a *tessera* or tablet with his vote, passed in front of the *rogator*, or voting officer who had the list of candidates before him, and pricked a hole (*punctum*) in the tablet against the name of the candidate for whom the vote was given.

Punkahs. Swinging fans suspended from the ceilings of houses in India, often richly embroidered and decorated with feathers, brilliant insects, gold and silver, &c.

Puntilla, Sp. A narrow point-lace edging.

Pupa, R. A doll ; a child's plaything. Dolls of terra-cotta have been found in various countries. In Egypt dolls have been found, made out of wood, painted, and in perfect proportion, with glass beads on the head in imitation of hair. As a rule, the ancient dolls are made with movable joints.

Puppis, R. The poop or after-part of a vessel as opposed to the *prora* or prow. (See PRORA.)

Purbeck-stone. A rough grey sandstone from Dorsetshire, largely used for building purposes in London.

Purim (Festivals of), Heb. Jewish festivals called *Festivals of the Lots*, instituted in memory of Esther, who had averted the peril with which Haman threatened the Jews ; they were so called because the favourite of Ahasuerus was to have decimated the Jews by casting lots to see who should be put to death.

Purple, Gen. An insignia of authority pertaining to certain magistrates who wore purple robes or bands of purple on their attire. There were two kinds of purple, the amethyst and the Tyrian ; the former was a deep violet, and obtained from a shell-fish (*murex trunculus*) ; the Tyrian was more brilliant and had a redder tinge ; it was obtained from the *murex brandaris*.

Purple is red graduated with blue, the red predominating ; red with black makes purple-black. Purple pigments are *madder purple*, *violet mars*, *burnt carmine* (for water-colours).

Purple Lakes and *Green Lakes* are made by mixing *yellow* lakes with blue pigments. (See YELLOW LAKE.)

Purple Madder. (See MADDER.)

Purple-wood. A beautiful deep-coloured Brazilian wood, used for marquetry and inlaid-work, but principally for the ramrods of guns.

Fig. 566. Puteus. Manhole of an Aqueduct.

Purpure, Her. Purple.

Purree, Hind. A bright golden-yellow pigment prepared from camel's dung. (See INDIAN YELLOW.)

Pursuivants. The lowest order of officers in Herald's College ; of whom there are four, called respectively Rouge Croix, Rouge Dragon, Blue Mantle, and Portcullis. In the Middle

Ages these officers were attached to the households of the nobility, and bore titles generally taken from the armorial insignia of their lords.

Puteal, R. A place struck by lightning, and thus rendered sacred; in order to keep it from the tread of profane feet, it was surrounded by a low wall similar to that which protected a well (*puteus*); whence the name of *puteal.*

Puteus, R. (1) A well fed by a spring or an underground stream of water; (2) an opening or manhole of an aqueduct (Fig. 566); (3) a pit for preserving grain.

Puticuli, Puticulæ, R. Common pits in which the bodies of those slaves and paupers were buried, who had not the means to pay for a funeral pyre or a private tomb.

Puttock, O. E. A base kind of hawk. (*Shakspeare.*)

Pyanepsia, Gr. (πυανέψια). Ancient "Beanfeasts." Athenian festivals in honour of Apollo, instituted by Theseus after his victory over the Minotaur; they were so called because beans were cooked for the banquet in honour of the god (πύανος, a bean, and ἕψειν, to cook).

Pyat, O. E. A magpie.

Pykers, O. E. A kind of fishing-boats.

Pylon, Egyp. (πυλών). A monumental gate composed of two lofty and massive pyramidal towers, forming the entrance to the enclosure of the great Egyptian temples. The interior of a pylon contained staircases and chambers. A splendid example in full preservation is that of the temple at Esneh on the Nile.

Pyra, Gr. and R. (πυρὰ, lit. the burning-place). A funeral pile before it was set on fire, in contradistinction to *rogus*, a funeral pile which has been lighted. It was built in the form of an altar with four equal sides, which were frequently covered with foliage of dark leaves; and cypress-trees were placed in front of the pile. The corpse was placed on the top, in the bier (*lectica*) on which it had been borne to the place. (See FUNERAL CEREMONIES.)

Pyræum, Pers. (πυρεῖον). A place in which the Persians kept the sacred fire (*puros*, fire). At Bactria there were seven pyræa, in honour of the seven planets.

Pyramid (Egyptian, *Pi-rama*, a mountain). In the hieroglyphics called *Abumer*, "a great tomb," which it essentially is, or rather a great cairn over the cave tomb excavated in the live rock immediately under its apex. This sepulchral chamber having been connected with the upper world by a passage sloping downwards from the north, the graduated structure was regularly built over it, the proportions of the base to the sides being constantly preserved, and the whole forming always a perfect pyramid; so that the building could be continued during the whole lifetime of its destined tenant, and covered and closed in

immediately upon his death. It is on record that from Seneferoo, the first king whose name has been found upon monuments, to the last of the Sixth Dynasty, i. e. during the whole period of the Ancient Empire, every king of Egypt built a pyramid. (Consult *Vyse, Pyramids of Gezeh.*)

Pyrotechny (πῦρ, fire, and τέχνη, art). The art of making fireworks. The Chinese had great skill in this art long before its introduction into Europe, and are at this day unrivalled in it. The best English work on the subject is perhaps that by *G. W. Mortimer* (London, 1853).

Pyrrhica, Gr. (πυρρίχη). A war-dance in great favour with the early Greeks, and frequently represented in sculptures, in which warriors brandished their weapons and went through a mock combat.

Pythia, Gr. (πύθια). (1) A priestess of Apollo at Delphi, represented seated on the sacred *tripod.* (See CORTINA.) (2) Games instituted at Delphi in honour of Apollo, and of his killing the Pytho, the monstrous serpent born from the waters in Deucalion's flood.

Pythoness. Synonym of PYTHIA (q.v.). The term was also used to denote certain sorceresses, such as the pythoness of Endor.

Pyx, or **Pix, Cloths.** (See CORPORALS.)

Fig. 567. Small Ivory Pyx. Ninth Century (?).

Pyx. The word in its earliest meaning included any small box or case, and often in the Middle Ages it contained relics. Thus in the Durham treasury there was "a tooth of St. Gengulphus, good for the falling sickness, in a small ivory pyx." The pyx used for the sacrament was usually ornamented with religious subjects, other than the incidents of the lives of saints. (Fig. 567.)

Pyxis, Gr. and R. (πυξίς, lit. a box-wood box). A casket, trinket-box, or jewel-case.

Q.

Many Old English words are indifferently spelt with qu, ch, *and* c ; *such as* quire, choir ;
quoif, coif, &c.

Quadra, R. Generally, any square or rectangular object; such as a table, plinth, or abacus.

Quadragesima, Chr. Lent is so called, because it has *forty* days.

Quadrans, R. (a fourth part). A small bronze coin worth the quarter of an *as,* or about a farthing.

Quadrant. An instrument for measuring celestial altitudes; superseded by the CIRCLE. (See SEXTANT.) (Consult *Lalande, Astronomie,* § 2311, &c., 3me edition).

Quadrantal, R. A square vessel used as a measure, the solid contents of which were exactly equal to an amphora. A standard model was kept in the temple of Jupiter Capitolinus.

Quadrelle, O. E. A mace, with four lateral projections, somewhat like the leaves of a flower. (See *Planché, Cycl. of Costume,* Plate xii. 16.)

Quadrellus, Med. Lat. A quarrel for a cross-bow.

Quadriforis, R. A door folding into four leaves.

Quadriga, R. Generally **Quadrigæ** (Greek τετραορία or τέθριππος). A chariot in which four horses were yoked abreast. The two strongest horses were harnessed under the yoke in the centre ; the others were fastened on each side by means of ropes. (See CURRUS.)

Quadrigatus, R. A silver denarius, so called from its having a quadriga on the reverse.

Quadrilateral. Four-sided.

Quadriliteral. Consisting of four letters.

Quadrille, Med. (It. *squadriglia,* dimin. of *squadra*—our "squadron"—a small party of troops drawn up in a square). Small parties of richly-caparisoned horsemen, who rode at tournaments and public festivals. The modern dance so called was introduced in 1808.

Quadriremis, R. A galley with four banks of rowers.

Quadrisomus, Chr. A sarcophagus with compartments for four bodies. One discovered in the Vatican cemetery at Rome contained the bodies of the first four popes called Leo. (Cf. BISOMUS.)

Quadrivalves, Arch. (See QUADRIFORIS.)

Quadrivium (lit. of four ways). The four minor arts of arithmetic, music, geometry, and astronomy. (See TRIVIUM.)

Quadrivium, R. A place where four roads meet.

Quadrumane. Having four prehensile hands or feet, like monkeys.

Quadruplatores, R. Public informers, who were rewarded with a *fourth part* of the criminal's property on obtaining a conviction.

Quæstiones Perpetuæ, R. Permanent tribunals established at Rome to take cognizance of criminal cases.

Quæstorium, R. In a Roman camp, the *quæstor's* tent ; this was in some cases near the porta decumana, or the rear of the camp ; in others, on one side of the PRÆTORIUM (q.v.).

Quaich, Queish, or **Quegh,** Scotch. An old-fashioned drinking-cup or bowl, with two handles. (English MASER [?].)

Quality-binding, Scotch. A kind of worsted tape used in the borders of carpets.

Qualus, R. (Gr. KALATHOS, q.v.). A wicker-work basket.

Quandary, O. E. (from Fr. *qu'en dirai-je?*) Doubt and perplexity.

Quannet. A tool for working in horn and tortoise-shell.

Quarnellus, Med., in fortification. (See CRENEL.)

Quarrel (Fr. *carreau*), Arch. A lozenge-shaped brick, stone, or pane of glass ; a glazier's diamond.

Quarrel, O. E. An arrow for the cross-bow with a four-square head.

Quarter-deck, on a ship of war. The deck abaft the mainmast, appropriated to the commissioned officers. These were originally of great height, corresponding with the lofty forecastle for soldiers, and helped to make the ships top-heavy and unmanageable. A commission on ship-building in 1618 says,—

"They must bee somewhat snugg built, without double gallarys, and too lofty upper workes, which overcharge many shipps, and make them coeme faire, but not worke well at sea."

Quarter-gallery of a ship. A balcony round the stern.

Quarter-round, Arch. The ovolo moulding (q.v.).

Quarter-tones (Gr. *diesis*), in Music, were the subject of much discussion among the ancient Greeks, but they were used on the lyre for an occasional "grace-note." Aristoxenos says "no voice could sing three of them in succession, neither can the singer sing *less* than the quarter-tone correctly, nor the hearer judge of it." (Consult *Chappell's Hist. of Music.*)

Quartering, Her. Marshalling two or more coats of arms in the different quarters of the same shield. (Fig. 568.)

Fig. 568. Royal Arms of England, *temp.* Edward III., quartered with the fleur-de-lys of France.

Quartet, Quartetto, It. A piece of music for four performers, each of whose parts is *obligato*, i. e. essential to the music.

Quartile. In Astronomy, distant from each other 90 degrees, or a *quarter* of a circle.

Quasillum (dimin. of QUALUS, q.v.) was a small basket in which the quantity of wool was measured, which was assigned to a slave to spin in a day's work.

Fig. 569. Quatrefoil.

Quatrefoil. An ornament in pointed architecture consisting of four foils. The term is likewise applied to a rosace formed of four divisions, which figures frequently in the upper part of pointed windows.

Quatrefoil or **Primrose**, Her. A flower or figure having four foils or conjoined leaves.

Quattrocento, It. (lit. *four hundred*). A term applied to the characteristic style of the artists who practised in the 15th century ; it was hard, and peculiar in colour as well as in form and pose. It was the intermediate of that progressive period of art, which, commencing with Fra Angelico, Masaccio, Mantegna, Botticelli, and other celebrated painters, between A.D. 1400 and 1500, reached excellence in the 16th century (the *cinque cento*) with Leonardo da Vinci and Raphael.

Fig. 570. Crown of Her Majesty the Queen.

Quaver. A musical note of very short time = half a crotchet.

Queen. Crown of Her Majesty. (See Fig. 570.)

Queen-post (anciently *prick-post*

or (*side-post*), Arch. An upright post similar in use and position to the KING-POST, but rising, not in the centre to the point of the gable, but midway between the wall and the centre.

Queen's Boots. The interesting fact in English archæology is not generally known, that Her Majesty's *boots* are provided for by an annual tax of two shillings (on the whole) upon the village of Ketton in Rutlandshire "*pro ocreis reginæ.*"

Queen's Ware. A cream-coloured glazed earthenware of the Wedgwood manufacture at Burslem, 1759-70.

Queen's Yellow. A colour formed from the subsulphate of mercury.

Queintise, O. E. A dress curiously cut or ornamented. (See COINTOISE.)

Querpo (for **Cuerpo**). Partly undressed.

Querpo-hood. A hood worn by the Puritans. (*P.*)

"No face of mine shall by my friends be viewed In Quaker's pinner, or in *querpo*-hood. (*Archæologia*, vol. xxvii.)

Queshews, O. E. *Cuisses;* armour for the thighs.

Queue, Fr. A support for a lance. It was a large piece of iron screwed to the back of the breastplate, curved downward to hold down the end of the lance.

Queue Fourchée, Her. Having a double tail, or two tails.

Quichuas. Remarkable specimens of pottery, from this Peruvian coast province, doubtless of remote antiquity, resemble in their freedom from conventionality and successful imitation of natural forms all primitive Egyptian and other sculpture. Jacquemart describes the vase of the illustration (on page 214) as the *chef-d'œuvre* of American ceramics ; and, from the close resemblance of the features of the figure represented to certain groups of prisoners on the Egyptian bas-reliefs, as well as to the ethnic type of the ancient Japanese kings, makes important deductions with reference to the dispersion of mankind, and the commerce of the old and new worlds in prehistoric times.

Quicksilver, alloyed with tin-foil, forms the reflecting surface of looking-glasses, and is largely used in the operations of gilding and silvering metals.

Quilled, Her. A term used to blazon the quills of *feathers;* thus a blue feather having its quill golden is blazoned—a feather *az., quilled or.* (*Boutell.*)

Quilts for bed-coverings, in England, were formerly made of embroidered linen with emblems of the evangelists in the four corners. At Durham, in 1446, in the dormitory of the priory was a quilt "cum iiijᵒʳ evangelistis in corneriis." The Very Rev. Daniel Rock (*Tex-*

tile Fabrics) suggests that this gave rise to the old nursery rhyme :—

"Matthew, Mark, Luke, and John,
Bless the bed that I lie on."

Quinarius. A Roman coin = half a *denarius*, or five *asses*.

Quincaillerie, Fr. A general term for all kinds of metallurgical work in copper, brass, iron, &c.

Fig. 571. Quince. Device of the Sforzas.

Quince, Her. The "*Pomo cotogno*," the emblem of the town of Cotignola, adopted by the founder of the Sforza family who was born there. The Emperor Robert of Bavaria added a lion in 1401 as a reward of an act of bravery, to "support the *quince* with his left hand and defend it with his right," adding " guai a chi lo tocchi ! " (Fig. 571.)

Quincunx, R. (i. e. five-twelfths of anything). (1) A Roman bronze coin, equivalent to five-twelfths of an *as,* and weighing five ounces (*unciæ*). (2) An arrangement of five objects in a square ; one at each corner, and one in the middle. (3) In *gardening,* said of trees planted in oblique rows of three and two, or in a *quincunx* (No. 2).

Quincupedal, R. A rod five feet in length, for taking measurements in masonry.

Quindecagon. A plane figure having fifteen sides and fifteen angles.

Quinite. A Spanish textile of hair with silk or other thread.

Quinquagesima, Chr. The *fiftieth* day before Easter ; Shrove Sunday. (*S.*)

Quinquatrus (or —ia), R. Festivals of Minerva, celebrated on the 19th of March. They lasted five days ; on the first no blood was shed, but on the last four were contests of gladiators. Another festival called *Quinquatrus minores,* also in honour of Minerva, was celebrated on the ides of June.

Quinquennalia, R. Games celebrated every

four years at Rome ; instituted by Nero, A.D. 60. They consisted of music, gymnastical contests, and horse-races.

Quinqueremis, R. A galley with five banks of oars.

Quinquertium, R. (Gr. *Pentathlon*). A gymnastic contest of Greek origin, so called because it consisted of five exercises, viz. *leaping, running, wrestling, throwing the discus,* and *throwing the spear.* Introduced in the Olympic games in Ol. 18.

Quintain, O. E. A post set up to be tilted at by mounted soldiers ; sometimes a man turning on a pivot ; sometimes a flat board, on a pivot, with a heavy bag of sand at the other end, which knocked the tilter on the back if he charged unskilfully. (See *Strutt, Sports and Pastimes,* p. 89, Plates ix. and x.)

Quintana, R. A causeway fifty feet wide in a Roman camp.

Quintetto, It. A piece of music for five performers, *obligati.* (Cf. QUARTET.)

Quintile. In Astronomy, distant from each other 72 degrees, or a *fifth* of a circle.

Quippa, Peruv. (lit. a knot). A fringe of knotted and particoloured threads, used to record events in ancient Mexico.

Quippos or **Quippus,** Peruv. A plaited cord of strings of different colours and lengths, used as a substitute for writing among the ancient Peruvians.

Quire. O. E. for CHOIR.

Quirinalia, R. A festival sacred to Romulus —Quirinus—held on the 17th of February, as the anniversary of the day on which he was supposed to have been carried up to heaven. The festival was also called *Stultorum feriæ.* (See FORNACALIA.)

Quirk, Arch. An acute channel by which the convex parts of Greek mouldings (the ogees and ovolos) are separated from the fillet or soffit that covers them. In Gothic architecture quirks are abundantly used between mouldings.

Quishwine, Qusson, and **Qwissinge.** Old ways of spelling the word " cushion."

Quivers. The ancient Greeks and Etruscans, the Normans and Saxons wore quivers (*pharetra*) on a belt slung over the shoulder. Archers of the 12th to 14th century carried their arrows stuck in their belts.

"A shefe of peacock arwes bryght and kene
Under his belt he bare ful thriftely."
(*Chaucer.*)

Quivers were probably introduced into England in the 15th century.

Quoif or **Coif,** O. E. A close-fitting cap worn by both sexes, and by lawyers, *temp.* Elizabeth.

Quoin or **Coin.** (1) Arch. The external angle of a building. (2) O. E. A wedge.

Quoits. A very ancient game derived from the Roman DISCUS (q.v.).

R.

Ra. The sun-god with hawk head is a common object of Egyptian pottery and architectural ornament, subsequent to the Asiatic invasions. It typifies the union of the yellow Asiatic and the native Egyptian races.

Rabato, Sp. A neck-band or ruff. (See REBATO.)

Rabbet (from *rebated*). In Joinery a groove in the edge of a board.

Rabyte, O. E. (for Arabyte). An Arab horse.

Racana, Chr. A blanket of hair-cloth prescribed for the couches of monks, &c., in summer.

"Pro anis *rachinis* propter æstus utantur."

Rack, O. E. The last fleeting vestige of the highest clouds.

Racon, O. E. The pot-hook by which vessels are suspended over a fire. (See GALOWS.)

Radiant, Rayonée. Encircled with rays. (Fig. 395.)

Radius, R. A pointed rod employed by certain professors of astronomy and mathematics for tracing figures on the sand. Also the spoke of a wheel, a ray of light, and lastly, a stake used in constructing intrenchments (*valla*).

Radula, R. A scraper, an iron tool used for paring or scratching off.

Raffaelle-ware. A fine kind of Urbino majolica, the designs for which were probably furnished by pupils of the great master.

Rag. In Masonry, stone that breaks in jagged pieces.

Ragged Staff, Her. (See RAGULÉE.)

Ragman's or **Rageman's Roll,** O. E. (1) In History, a roll of the nobles of Scotland, who swore fealty to Edward I. at Berwick, in 1296; hence (2) a game of chance, in which a number of versified descriptions of character were drawn from a roll by the members of a company; 13th to 15th century. The game survives among children of the present age in the custom of drawing *Twelfth-Night* characters.

Ragstone. A rough kind of sandstone found in Kent.

Ragulée, Raguly, Her. Serrated. A "ragged staff," or "staff *ragulée*," is a part of a stem from

Fig. 572. Ragulée.

which the branches have been cut off roughly. The illustration is the well-known device of the Earls of Warwick, originating with Arthgal, one of the Knights of the Round Table; because, says Leland, "this Arthgal took a bere in his arms, for that, in Britisch, soundeth a bere in Englisch." (Fig. 573.)

Fig. 573. Bear and Ragged Staff.

Rahal, Arabic. A load for a camel; about 5 cwt.

Rains, or **Raynes, Cloths** (A.D. 1327 —1434, &c.). Fine linen woven at *Rennes* in Brittany.

Rajeta, Sp. A coarse cloth of mixed colours.

Rallum, R. A piece of iron on the end of a stick, used to scrape off earth from the plough-share.

Fig. 574. Assyrian Battering-ram.

Ram, in Christian iconography, is a symbol not fully explained. It was probably connected with the idea of a manful *fight* with the powers of evil. Two rams face to face with a cross between them are a frequent symbol. (Consult

T

Martigny, Dict. des Antiq. Chrét. s. v. Belier.)

Ram, O. E. for rain. (*Shakspeare.*)

Ram or **Battering-ram.** (See ARIES.) The illustration (Fig. 574) is from the Assyrian sculptures, showing the invention of the *testudo* to be of great antiquity.

Ramadhan. The ninth month of the Arabian calendar, and the Mohammedan month of fasting ; it is followed by the festival of the *Little Bairam.*

Ramalia, R. (*ramus*, a ram). Roman festivals instituted in honour of Ariadne and Bacchus.

Ramillete, Sp. A nosegay ; a pyramid of sweetmeats and fruits.

Rampant, Her. Erect, one hind paw on the ground, the other three paws elevated; the animal looking forward, and having his tail elevated.

Rampant guardant, Her. The same as rampant, but looking out of the shield.

Rampant reguardant, Her. The same as rampant, but looking backwards.

Ranseur, Fr. A sort of partisan in use in the time of Edward IV., having a broad long blade in the centre, and projecting shorter blades on each side.

Fig. 575. Lion Rampant.

Fig. 576. Demi-lion Rampant.

Rantle-tree, Scotch. (1) The beam in the chimney from which the crook is suspended, when there is no grate (Angl. GALOWS. See also REEKING-HOOK). (2) A tree chosen with two branches, which are cut short, and left in the shape of a Y, built into the gable of a cottage to support one end of the roof-tree.

Rapier, introduced from Spain in the 16th century, remained the favourite weapon of gentlemen. It is a light sword with a narrow blade adapted only for thrusting. It used to be called a *tuck.*

Rapier-dance. A theatrical dance still practised in Yorkshire, consisting of evolutions of the dancers with naked rapiers round a performer who kneels in the centre and finally simulates death. (Compare SWORD-DANCE.)

Raploch, Scotch. Coarse undyed woollen cloth.

Rareca. Peruvian aqueducts ; distinct from the subterranean aqueducts called HUIRCAS or *Pinchas* (q. v.).

Rash. " A species of inferior silk, or silk and stuff manufacture." (*Nares.*)

Raster, Rastrum, R. (*rado*, to scrape). A rake.

Rat. In Chinese symbolism, the month of November. (See TCHY PERIODS.)

Rath, Celtic. An ancient fortress or castle of the Irish chiefs, consisting of a circular intrenched enclosure, with buildings in the centre.

Rational, Heb. A square piece of richly-embroidered cloth worn by the Jewish high priest upon the breast, above the ephod.

Ratis, R. A raft of strong beams or planks ; and thence a flat boat, a bridge of boats, &c.

Raunle-tree. Scotch ; for RANTLE-TREE (q. v.).

Raven, the ensign of the ancient Danes, was the bird of Odin. In Christian art, the emblem of Divine Providence (in allusion to the history of Elisha) ; attribute of certain saints, especially of ascetics. (See CROW.)

Ray, Chr. The fish (*rina diaudan*) which was burned by Tobias (vii. 2, 3), and the eggs of which are still burnt for intermittent fevers among the Greeks. (*Harris*, 408.)

Ray, O. E. (i. e. *rayed*). Striped cloth much worn in the 13th and 14th centuries.

Raynes, O. E. (from Rennes in Brittany). Fine linen.

" Cloth of raynes to sleep on soft." (*Chaucer.*)

Rayonnée, Her. (See RADIANT.)

Real (Eng. ROYAL). A Spanish coin. There are two kinds : a *real of plate*, worth 4¾d., and a *real of vellon*, worth 2½d. (Cf. RIAL.)

Realgar. A red pigment, formed of arsenic in combination with sulphur. A fugitive and *corrosive* pigment. (See *Merimée, De la Peinture à l'huile,* p. 124.)

Realism, Realistic, in Art. (See IDEAL and REAL.)

Rebated. Turned back, as the head of a MORNE or jousting-lance.

Rebato, Sp. The turn-down collar of the 15th and 16th centuries.

Rebec, Sp. A musical instrument of three strings, tuned in fifths, and played with a bow like a fiddle. It was originally introduced into Spain by the Moors.

Rebiting. A process of renewing the lines of a worn-out plate, by etching them over again ; a difficult and delicate operation, which is rarely performed with entire success.

Rebus, Her. An allusive charge or device. A *ton* or *tun* pierced by a bird-bolt is in the church of Great St. Bartholomew, of which Prior Bolton was the last prior.

"Prior Bolton
With his bolt and tun."
(Ben Jonson.)

Fig. 577. Rebus (Prior Bolton).
The Bolt and Tun.

Fig. 578. Cross
Recercelée.

R e c a m o, Sp. Embroidery of raised work.

Recel, Sp. A kind of striped tapestry.

Receptorium, R. *(recepto,* to receive). A kind of parlour, also called *salutatorium,* which generally adjoined the ancient basilicas.

R e c e r c e l é e, Her. A variety of the heraldic cross.

Recheat, O. E. A sound on the horn to call dogs away from the chase.

Recinctus. Equivalent in meaning to DISCINCTUS (q.v.).

Recorders. A musical instrument mentioned by Shakspeare. It resembled a very large clarionet. Milton also speaks of

'the Dorian mood
Of flutes and *soft recorders.*"
(Paradise Lost, i. 550.)

Recta, R. A straight tunic, made out of a single piece, which took the form of the body ; it hung from the neck, and fell down as far as the feet.

Rectilinear figures are those composed entirely of straight or *right* lines.

Red. One of the three primary colours, producing with YELLOW, *orange,* and with BLUE, *violet.* The principal red pigments are *carmine, vermilion, chrome red, scarlet lake, madder lake, light red, burnt sienna,* for *yellow* reds ; and *Venetian red, Indian red, crimson lake,* for *blue* reds. Red, in Christian art, represented by the ruby, signified fire, divine love, the Holy Spirit, heat or the creative power, and royalty. In a bad sense, red signified blood, war, hatred, and punishment. Red and black combined were the colours of purgatory and the devil. (See REALGAR, INDIGO.)

Red Chalk or **Reddle** is a mixture of clay and red iron OCHRE, used as a crayon in drawing. (See OCHRE.)

Red Lake. (See CARMINE.)

Red Lead. A pigment which mixes badly with other pigments. (See MINIUM.)

Red Ochre includes *Indian red, scarlet ochre, Indian ochre, reddle,* &c.

Red Orpiment. (See REALGAR.)

Redan, the simplest kind of work in field fortification, generally consists of a parapet of earth, divided on the plan into two faces, which make with one another a salient angle, or one whose vertex is towards the enemy.

Reddle. (See RED CHALK.)

Redimiculum, R. *(redimio,* to bind round). A long string or ribbon attached to any kind of head-dress.

Redoubt is a general name for nearly every kind of work in the class of field fortifications.

Redshank, Scotch. A Highlander wearing buskins of red-deer skin, with the hair outwards.

Reduction. In Art, a copy on a smaller scale. The work is done mechanically by a process of subdivision of the original into segments or squares.

Reekie, Scotch. Smoky ; hence *Auld Reekie,* the city of Edinburgh.

Reeking-hook, O. E. A pot-hook hung in the chimney, to suspend vessels over an open fire. (See GALOWS.)

Re-entering, in Engraving, is the sharpening or deepening with a graver the lines insufficiently *bitten in* by the acid.

Refectory, Mod. *(reficio,* to refresh). A hall in which the monks of a monastery assembled to take their meals ; one of the most important rooms of the establishment ; it was often divided into two naves by a row of columns called the spine *(spina),* which received the spring of the vaultings forming the roof of the refectory.

Fig. 579. Regals or Portable Organ.

Reflected Lights thrown by an illuminated surface into the shadows opposed to it, modify the LOCAL COLOUR of every object that we observe in nature, and should accordingly be made to do so in painting.

Reflexed, Reflected, Her. Curved and carried backwards.

Refraction is the diversion of a ray of light which occurs when it falls obliquely on the surface of a medium differing in density from that through which it had previously moved. The differently-coloured rays have different degrees of refrangibility. Refraction is the cause of the phenomena of the *mirage, Fata Morgana,* &c., and presents to us the light of the sun before his actual emergence above the horizon.

Regal or **Regals,** O. E. (1) A small portable organ, with single or double sets of pipes (the attribute of St. Cecilia, and of saints and angels of the heavenly choir). The illustration (Fig. 579) of an angel playing the regals, is taken from an ancient MS. (2) A kind of harmonica, with sonorous slabs of wood.

Regalia. The ensigns of royalty. The regalia of England are the crown, sceptre, verge or rod with the dove, St. Edward's staff, the orb or mound, the sword of mercy called Curtana, the two swords of spiritual and temporal justice, the ring of alliance with the kingdom, the armillæ or bracelets, the spurs of chivalry, and some royal vestments ; and are kept in the Jewel Office in the Tower of London. The Scottish insignia, a crown, a sceptre, and a sword of state, are kept in the Crownroom at Edinburgh. The illustration shows the regalia and state vestments of the Grand Duke of Tuscany, in the 16th century. (Fig. 580.)

Regifugium, R. (lit. flight of the king). An annual festival held on the sixth day of the calends of March (24th of February), in commemoration of the flight of Tarquin and the establishment of the Roman republic.

Regioles, Fr. Chr. Small doors in the *confessio* or *martyrium* of an altar, containing relics of a saint or martyr. The faithful used to introduce handkerchiefs by these doors, that they might consecrate them by contact with the relics.

Regrating or **Skinning,** in Masonry, is the process of scraping or hammering off the outer surface of old stones to make them look white and new ; it has been greatly abused in the restoration of ancient buildings.

Reguardant, Her. Turning the head and looking back ; emblematic of circumspection and prudence.

Regula, R. A straight rule used by artisans.

Regulares, Chr. Horizontal *rods* of wood or metal in churches for the suspension of veils or curtains. These were often made of gold or silver, with a row of images on the upper part.

Fig. 580. Regalia. Grand Duke of Tuscany in state costume, with crown and sceptre, &c.

Regulus (in Greek βασιλίσκος) is the name given by ancient astronomers to a line drawn from the polar star, between the pointers, &c., to the bright star called α Leonis or Cor Leonis (the lion's heart).

Reindeer, Her. A hart with double antlers, one pair erect, the other drooping.

Reisner-work. A corrupt spelling of the name of Riesener, a celebrated worker in marquetry in France in the 18th century.

"Riesener used tulip, rosewood, holly, maple, laburnum, purple-wood, &c. Wreaths and bunches of flowers, exquisitely worked and boldly designed, form centres of his marquetry panels, which are often plain surfaces of one wood. On the sides, in borders and compartments, we find diaper patterns in three or four quiet colours." (See *Pollen, Ancient and Modern Furniture,* &c.)

Relief (It. *rilievo*). Sculpture projecting— ALTO-RELIEVO, more than half ; MEZZO-RE- LIEVO, exactly half; BASSO-RELIEVO, less than half. (See also RONDO BOSSO, INTAGLIO RELIEVATO, STACCIATO.)

Reliquary, Chr. A portable shrine or casket made to contain relics. A reliquary made to be worn round the neck was called *encolpium* (*ἐν κόλπῳ*, in the bosom), *phylacterium*, &c.; one to be carried processionally, *feretrum*. (See FERE- TORY, Fig. 307.)

Remarque, Fr. A slight sketch on the mar- gin beneath an etching or engraving, to denote the earliest proof impressions.

Removed, Her. Out of its proper position.

Remuria, R. A Roman festival in honour of Remus, held on the third of the ides of May (13th of May) on the Palatine mount, on the spot where Remus had taken the auspices, and where he was buried.

Renaissance (lit. new-birth or revival). The term is popularly applied to the gradual return to classical principles in Art in the 13th and 14th centuries. The Italian renaissance, begun by NICCOLA PISANO in architecture and sculpture, and by GIOTTO in painting, was fostered by the Medici family, and culminated in Leonardo, Michelangelo, and Raphael. Teutonic art (Flemish, German, and Dutch) had also their periods of revival. It is, however, impossible to indicate their representatives without entering upon debateable questions. Goldsmith's work, pottery, and other useful arts passed through parallel periods of revival concurrent, or nearly so, with those in painting.

Rengue, Sp. A kind of gauze worn on official robes in Spain.

Reno and **Rheno,** R. A very short cloak, often made of skins, peculiar to the Gauls and Germans, and adopted by the Roman soldiery.

Repagula, R. (lit. fastening back). A double fastening to a door ; of two bolts (*pessuli*), one of which was shot towards the right, and the other to the left.

Replica. A duplicate of a picture, done by the same painter.

Repose. (See RIPOSO.)

Repositorium, R. (*repono*, to lay down). A sideboard for plates and dishes in a dining-room; it was divided into several stories, and formed a kind of dinner-wagon ; and many examples were richly ornamented, and inlaid with varie- gated woods, or tortoise-shell and silver, &c.

Repoussé, Fr. Metal-work hammered out from behind into ornaments in *relief.*

Requiem, Chr. The Roman *Missa pro De- functis,* or service for the dead, beginning with the anthem "*Requiem æternam dona eis, Domine.*"

Rerebrace, O. E. (for the French *arrière bras*). Armour for the upper part of the arm.

Rerebrake, O. E. A pommel at the back of a saddle to support the horseman under the shock of a tilting-bout. (See *Meyrick*, vol. ii. p. 137.)

Reredos, Chr. (1) The wall or screen at the back of an altar. In the primitive churches, in which the bishop's seat was at the back of the altar, there was no *reredos.* Its introduction dates from the period (about the 12th century) when the episcopal seats and the choirs were established in front of the altars. (2) The ROOD-SCREEN was sometimes so called. (3) The open hearth was so called. Hollinshed relates that, before the invention of chimneys, "each man made his fire against a *reredosse* in the hall, where he dined and dressed his meat."

Rere-supper (Fr. *arrière souper*). The last meal taken in the day ; 15th century.

Resins. (See AMBER, COPAL, DAMARA, MASTIC, &c.)

Ressaunt, O. E. Arch. An obsolete term applied to members of architecture inflected or curved like an OGEE moulding.

Rest. In Music, a character denoting silence for a length denoted by the character used to express the rest, i.e. *semi-breve, minim, crotchet, quaver,* &c.

Restoration. In Architecture, a drawing of an ancient building in its original design.

Retable (Fr.), Chr. (See REREDOS.)

Rete and **Retis,** R. A net.

Retiarius. A gladiator whose only arms were a trident and net ; with the latter he tried to embarrass the adversary by casting it over his head, and, having done so, to wound him with the trident ; failing in their throw, their only resource was to run round the arena preparing the net for a second attempt. They fought generally with the Mirmillones, and had no helmet nor other protective armour excepting for the left arm. (See GLADIATORS.)

Reticella (Lat. *reticulus*, a little net). This was the first known needle-made lace, produced in all lace-making countries under different names. (See GREEK LACE.) It was made in several ways: the first consisted in arranging a network of threads on a small frame, crossing and interlacing them in various complicated patterns. Beneath this network was gummed a piece of fine cloth, open like canvas, called quin- tain (from the town in Brittany where it was made). Then with a needle the network was sewn to the quintain by edging round those parts of the pattern which were to remain thick, then cutting away the superfluous cloth : hence the name of cutwork in England. A more simple mode was to make the pattern de- tached without any linen ; the threads radiating at equal distances from one common centre served as a frame-work to others, which were united to them in geometric forms worked over

Fig. 581. Venetian Reticella Lace.

with button-hole stitch (or *point noué*). The engraving shows a fine specimen of reticella

Fig. 582. Reticulated Vase. Japanese.

from Venice, 1493. (See also MILAN RETI-CELLA.)

Reticulated. Latticed like the meshes of a net (*rete*).

Reticulated Glass. (See GLASS.)

Reticulated Porcelain is an Oriental product, of which the outer side is entirely cut out in geometric patterns, honeycomb, circles intercrossed and superposed to a second vase of similar, or of simply cylindrical form. Fig. 582 is a specimen of this style.

Reticulated Work, Arch. (Lat. *reticulata structura*, literally, made like a net). Masonry constructed with diamond-shaped stones, or QUARRELS, shown in Figs. 493 and 583. The

Fig. 583. Reticulatum opus.

latter shows one of the mouths of the *cloaca* opening on the Tiber. *Reticulata fenestra* was a window grated over with bars of wood or metal crossing in the form of network.

Reticulum, R. Diminutive of *rete*, a net.

Retinaculum, R. (*retineo*, to hold back). A rope used to moor a vessel to the shore.

Retorted, Her. Intertwined.

Retro-choir, Chr. Arch. Chapels behind or about the choir.

Reverse. The back of a medal. In very ancient coins this had no mark except that of the instrument by which it was fixed to receive the stamp of the *obverse*. By degrees this grew into a figure of a dolphin or some other animal. Some ancient Greek reverses are *intaglios* of the stamp in relief of the *obverse*. Complete reverses appear on Greek coins about 500 B.C., and are of exquisite execution. (Cf. OBVERSE.)

Revinctum (opus), R. (*revincio*, to bind fast). Dove-tailed masonry. (See Fig. 269.)

Rhabdion (lit. a small rod). An instrument used in *encaustic painting*, with which the wax

Fig. 584. Rhyton. Greek Drinking-cup.

tints were blended. It was probably flat at one end, and kept heated in a small furnace close at hand. (See *Eastlake, Materials*, &c., i. 154.)

Rheda, R. A roomy four-wheeled carriage, of Gallic origin, with several seats. The driver was called RHEDARIUS.

Rheno, Gr. (ῥῆν, a sheep). A sheepskin cloak, covering the shoulders and as far as to the waist, worn by the ancient Germans as a protection against rain.

Rhingrave. The petticoat breeches worn in the reign of Charles II. (*Planché.*)

Rhomboid. "An equilateral oblique parallelogram."

Rhomphæa, Romphæa, Rumpia, R. A sword with a long blade, used by the Thracians.

Rhyton, Gr. and R. (ῥυτόν, lit. flowing). A drinking-vessel of earthenware in the form of a horn or trumpet; in many instances with a handle.

Rial or **Royal** (Sp. *real*). A Spanish coin introduced into England in 16th cent. (See REAL.)

Fig. 585. Rial. Queen Elizabeth.

Riband or **Ribbon** (Welsh *rhibin*; Irish *ruibin*, &c.). A long narrow web of silk worn for ornament or use; especially for a *badge* of devotion in love or war.

"See in the lists they wait the trumpet's
    sound:
Some love-device is wrought on every
    sword,
And every ribbon bears some mystic
    word."

(*Granville.*)

The Ribbons of the various orders of Knighthood are:—of the GARTER, a broad dark blue ribbon passing over the left shoulder; of the THISTLE, a broad dark green ribbon; of St. PATRICK, a light blue; of the BATH, red; of the STAR OF INDIA, pale blue with white borders.

Ribbon, Riband, Her. A diminutive of a BEND.

Ribibe. A kind of fiddle; 15th century.

Ribs, Arch. Projecting bands on ceilings, &c.

Rica, R. A square piece of cloth with a fringe, worn by priests and women on the head, and especially by the former when they were offering a sacrifice; *ricula* was a smaller veil worn in the same fashion. (Cf. FLAMMEUM.)

Rice-paper. A delicate vegetable film brought from China, and used as a substitute for drawing-paper in the representation of richly-coloured insects or flowers, &c.

Ridels. French word for bed-curtains; 15th century.

Rimenato, It. (See CRUSCA.)

Ring Mail. Flexible armour of iron rings interwoven; introduced from the East by the Crusaders.

Rings. The symbolic use of signet-rings is mentioned in many passages of the Holy Scriptures, especially as a transfer of authority; as Pharaoh to Joseph (Gen. xli. 42), Ahasuerus to Haman, &c. A large collection of Egyptian signet-rings is in the British Museum, many being much too large to be worn on the hand. EGYPTIAN rings were of ivory, porcelain, or stone, but generally of gold. The ETRUSCANS and SABINES wore rings at the foundation of Rome, 753 B.C., those of the former being remarkable for beauty and intrinsic value. The LACEDÆMONIANS wore iron rings. The ROMANS also under the Republic were proud of wearing an iron ring; under the Empire the privilege of wearing a ring raised the wearer to the equestrian order. GREEK and ROMAN rings were, generally speaking, massive and simple, and

Fig. 586. Ring of chiselled iron. French. 16th century.

Fig. 587. Venetian Ring. 16th century.

of obvious value in metal and stone, until in the degenerate times of the Empire luxury spread, and the lower classes began to disfigure themselves with cheap jewellery. Solid rings were carved out of rock-crystal in Christian times; and others were made of stone, chiefly of calcedony. Rings of amber, glass, earthenware, and other materials were exhumed at Pompeii. The

BRITONS and SAXONS had beautiful jewellery. The former wore the ring on the middle finger; the Anglo-Saxons on the third finger of the right hand, which was thence poetically called the "golden finger." A beautiful specimen of enamelled art is the gold ring of Ethelwulf, king of Wessex (the father of Alfred the Great), now in the medal room of the British Museum. Among the niello rings of the Saxon period is one in the British Museum inscribed "Ahlreds owns me, Eanred engraved me." Plain wire rings, or plain bands of metal merely twisted round the finger, are common objects in Saxon tombs; but the most beautiful specimens of this, as of other branches of the goldsmith's art in antiquity, are from IRELAND. In SCANDINAVIA the earliest forms are spiral, and of simple workmanship. RINGS were a part of the official jewellery of kings, bishops, and cardinals; and the fisherman's ring, with a representation of St. Peter in a boat fishing, was the papal ring of investiture. A copious literature on this special subject deals with the superstitions, ceremonies, customs, and anecdotes connected with finger-rings, as well as with their exemplification of the history of the development or decadence of art. A collector divides his rings into Antique, Mediæval, and Modern; the former period ending A.D. 800, and classified by nationalities. The later collections are classified as Official: ecclesiastical, civil, and military; or Personal, viz. signet-rings, love and marriage, mourning, &c.; historical, religious (i.e. devotional, &c.), magic, and simply ornamental.

(The substance of the above is drawn from Finger-ring Lore, &c., by W. Jones, Chatto, 1877; and Antique Gems, by the Rev. C. W. King. For the significance of rings in connexion with the history of Christianity, see Smith and Cheetham, Dict. of Christ. Ant. s. v.)

Rinman's Green. (See COBALT.)

Rip-rap, Arch. A builder's term for a foundation of loose stones.

Riposo, It. The rest of the Holy Family during the Flight into Egypt is often shortly designated the Riposo; it is treated by different masters in a great variety of styles.

Riscus, R. (ρίσκος). A wardrobe or chest for clothes.

Rising, Roussant, Her. Said of birds about to take wing.

Rivers, Chr. The four rivers of Paradise are variously represented in primitive Christian art; e. g. the LAMB standing on a mountain, from which they flow; or they are personified, and symbolize the four Evangelists: the Gihon is St. Matthew; Pison, St. John; Tigris, St. Mark; and Euphrates, St. Luke. The following lines in one instance accompany such a representation on an engraved copper plate :—

" Fons paradisiacus per flumina quatuor exit ;
Hec quadriga levis te Χρε per omnia vexit."

In CLASSIC art generally, rivers are personified as half-prostrate figures reclining upon an urn, and marked by certain attributes; e. g. of the Nile, a hippopotamus; of the Tiber, a wolf suckling Romulus and Remus; other rivers by the flora or by certain cities of their banks, &c. (Consult Didron, Iconographie Chrét.; Martigny, &c.)

Roan. (1) A kind of leather much used for bookbinding; it is of sheepskins tanned with

Fig. 588. Robur. Prison at Rome.

sumach. (2) Said of a *bay* or *sorel* horse marked with grey.

Robigalia, R. Roman festivals held every year on the sixth of the calends of May (25th of April), in honour of the god Robigus, to preserve the wheat from mildew.

Roborarium (*robur*, strength). An enclosure within a wooden palisade.

Robur, R. The subterranean dungeon of a prison (*carcer*), in which criminals were executed. In Fig. 588 the character of the *robur* is clearly seen ; it is that of the prison of Ancus Martius and Servius Tullius at Rome, of which some ruins still remain.

Rochet, Chr. (Lat. *rochetum ;* Anglo-Saxon *roc,* a loose upper garment). A short surplice without sleeves, open at the sides ; imitated from a linen outer garment of the same name, much worn by women in the 14th century. Chaucer says,—

"There is no clothe sytteth bette
On damoselle than doth rokette."

Rock-crystal. A material much used for carving in China. *Fortune* says, "Fine specimens of rock-crystal, carved into figures, cups, and vases, are met with in the curiosity shops of Foo-chow-foo. Some of these specimens are white, others golden yellow, and others again blue and black. One kind looks as if human hair was thrown in and crystallized. *Imitations* of this stone are common in Canton, made into snuff-bottles, such as are commonly used by the Chinese." The GREEK name (κρύσταλλος, ice) refers to the belief that it was frozen water ; the INDIANS believe it to be the husk of which the *diamond* is the kernel, and call it the *unripe diamond ;* in JAPAN it is cut into round balls used for cooling the hands; in CHINA also it is extensively carved ; in the MIDDLE AGES it was highly valued throughout EUROPE as a detector of poison. Still more recently crystal balls have been supposed to have magical influence, and used for divination and conjuring.

Rockets, O. E. Slabs of wood used on lances, during exercise, for the same purpose as the buttons of foils.

Rococo, It. The style of decoration into which that of the Louis Quinze period culminated, distinguished for a superfluity of confused and discordant detail. (See LOUIS XV.)

Rod. In measurement, 16½ feet linear, or 272½ square feet.

Rodomel, O. E. The juice of roses, mixed with honey.

Rogus, R. A funeral pile when in process of burning, in contradistinction to PYRA (q.v.).

Rokelay, O. E. A short cloak.

Roll-moulding (Arch.), profusely used in the Early English and Decorated styles, is a round moulding, divided longitudinally along the middle, the upper half of which projects over the lower. *Roll and fillet moulding* is a roll-moulding with a square *fillet* on the face of it.

Rolls of Arms. Heraldic records of ancient armorial insignia, preserved on strips of parchment. The earliest known are of the 13th century. (Consult *Boutell.*)

Romal, Hind. A silk fabric, of which cotton imitations are made in England.

Fig. 589. Temple of Vesta at Tivoli, with Roman-Corinthian columns.

Roman Architecture is a combination of the *Etruscan* and the *Greek*, principally distinguished from the latter by the circular arch, and the *monopteral* or circular temple unknown to the Greeks, but a favourite form with the tomb-building ancestors of the Etruscans. The *orders* of Roman architecture were the Doric and Ionic, detrimentally modified ; the Corinthian, which they greatly enriched ; and the Composite, of which the upper part of the capital was Ionic, and the remainder Corinthian. The distinguishing feature of the Roman architecture is, however, less in the modifications of the orders, than in their application in *composite arcades*, or plain arches of Etruscan design, faced by and supporting a purely ornamental arrangement of a long horizontal entablature on two columns. (Consult *Fergusson, Hist. of Arch.*, vol. i.)

Roman-Doric Order of Architecture. A deteriorated imitation of the Grecian-Doric, adopted, with considerable modifications, by modern Italian architects.

Roman Ochre or **Italian Earth.** A pigment of a rich orange-yellow, used both raw and burnt in oil and water-colours. (See OCHRE.)

Roman Sepia is *sepia* (q. v.) mixed with red.

Romanesque. A degenerated and hybrid style of architecture and ornament, transitional from the classical Roman to the introduction of the Gothic. In the architecture there is an incongruous combination of the horizontal and arched methods of construction; and in the ornament a similar dissonance of natural and conventional or fanciful objects. *Fairholt* calls it the *classic rococo. Fergusson* (*Hist. of Arch.*, vol. i. p. 352) defines the *Romanesque* as "that modification of the classical Roman form, which was introduced between the reigns of Constantine and Justinian, and was avowedly an attempt to adapt classical forms to Christian purposes." He says, "If *Romanesque* is to be applied to our Norman architecture, the Parthenon ought to be called *Egyptianesque*, and the Temple at Ephesus *Assyrianesque*." There seems to be no universally-received definition of this term.

Rondache, Fr. A round shield for foot-soldiers. It had a slit near the top to look through, and another at the side for the sword.

Ronde Bosse (It. *rondo bosso*). Sculpture in relief with a complete rounded outline, detached from the ground.

Rood, Chr. (1) A cross or crucifix. (2) A space of 1210 square yards; the fourth of an acre. (3) In building, 36 square yards of work. (4) As a linear measure variable, from 21 feet to 36 yards.

Rood-beam, Chr. The beam across the church by which the *rood* was supported when there was no *rood-loft.*

Rood-cloth, Chr. The veil by which the large crucifix or *rood* was hidden during Lent.

Rood - loft, Rood - screen, Chr. A gallery, generally placed over the chancel screen in parish churches, in which the cross or *rood* was set to view.

Rood-tower, Rood-steeple, Chr. Arch. A tower or steeple of a cruciform church, built above the intersection, i. e. immediately over the *rood.*

Roquelaure. "A short abridgment or compendium of a cloak, which is dedicated to the Duke of Roquelaure."

Rorarii, R. (*ros*, the dew). A body of light skirmishers in the Roman army, who were ranged in the second rank of the *triarii*, with the *accensi* behind them in the third line. They took their name from the light missiles which they scattered upon the enemy, which were like the drops of rain before a thunder shower. It was their business to begin the attack, and retire behind the *triarii* when pressed. Their skirmishing was a prelude to the charge of the heavy-armed spears (*hastati*).

Rosary, Chr. A string or chaplet of beads for numbering prayers, an Oriental and ante-Christian custom of great antiquity. They are called *tasbih* by the Indian Mohammedans; in Sanscrit *Japanata*, "the muttering chaplet," &c.

Rose, Her. Represented in blazon without leaves. The rose of England is generally drawn like the natural flower, or with natural stem, branches, leaves, and buds, but with heraldic

Fig. 591. Rose-window in the Church of St. Croix, Orleans.

rose-flowers. (See Fig. 395.) In Classic art, a rose upon a tomb is an emblem of a short life. The an-

Fig. 590. Heraldic Roses.

cient Romans were passionately fond of roses, and cultivated them assiduously in their gardens, and introduced them plentifully in their feasts and symposia. In *mediæval* England roses were the favourite presents on birthdays ; and Whitsuntide was called, from the plenty of them, Rose Easter. Sticking a rose in the ear was the boast of an accepted lover.

"That in mine ear I durst not stick a rose,
  Lest men should say, Look where three farthings goes."
(*Shakspeare*.)

The allusion refers to a thin silver coin of the reign of Elizabeth, called the three-farthing rose. (*Planché*.)

Rose-engine Pattern (Fr. *guillochis*). (1) An architectural moulding, also called Greek fret, meanders, and quirked torus. (2) In goldsmiths' work it is an ornament of network made by means of a machine called a rose-engine. (*Bosc*.)

Rose Lake, Rose Madder. A rich tint prepared from lac and madder. (See MADDER.)

Rose Pink. A coarse kind of lake ; a delicate and fugitive colour. (See PINKS.)

Rose-quartz. A massive quartz of a rose-red colour, common in Ceylon.

Rose-window (sometimes called a Catherine wheel), Arch. A large circular window divided into compartments by curved mullions. The most beautiful examples are met with in churches of the Florid Gothic period. (Fig. 591.)

Rose-wood, Rhodes-wood, largely used in furniture as a favourite veneer, is a name applied to a large variety of trees, mostly imported from Brazil.

Rosemary, in Old England, was closely connected with wedding-feasts and with funerals.

" There's rosemary ; that's for remembrance ; pray you.
love, remember : and there is pansies ; that's for thoughts."
(*Hamlet*.)

" There's Rosemarie ; the Arabians justifie,
  It comforteth the braine and memorie."
(*A Dialogue between Nature and the Phœnix,
  by R. Chester*, 1601.)

Rosetta-wood. A beautifully-veined East Indian wood, of a bright-red orange colour.

Rosettes. (See RIBANDS.)

Rosins. (See RESINS.)

Rosso Antico, It. Ancient marble of a deep red tint, probably deepened in colour by antiquity, like the NERO ANTICO (q.v.). It is the

material of many ancient Egyptian and early Greek sculptures, unequalled in tone by the products of any modern quarries. It contains white spots and veins.

Rostrum, R. (Gr. *Embolos*). The prow of a ship. The plural *rostra* was used to denote a tribune in the Roman forum, from which orators addressed the people ; it was so called because it was decorated with the figure-heads of the ships taken from the Volscians in the Latin War.

Rota, R. (1) A wheel composed of a nave (*modius*), spokes (*radii*), felloes (*absides*), and iron tires (*orbes* or *canthi ferrarii*). (2) It was also an instrument of punishment. *Rota aquaria* was a hydraulic wheel ; *rota figularis*, a potter's wheel.

Rotta (Germ. *rotte*; Eng. *rote*), a stringed instrument of the early Middle Ages, sounded either as a harp or a fiddle.

Rotunda. A dome-shaped or *monopteral* (q.v.) structure. The largest *rotunda* ever made was that of the Vienna Exhibition in 1873.

Rouelle, Fr. (lit. a small wheel). A French term which has been applied by antiquaries to numerous objects more or less resembling a wheel, such as brooches and coins. The Gallic coin (Fig. 592) is from the bas-reliefs on a Roman arch at Orange.

Fig. 592. Gallic coin.

Rouennais Faience. This style, of strongly Oriental character, and mostly applied to the decoration of what are called "lambrequins" (or mantlings) and "dentelles"

Fig. 593. Rouen Plate. Decorated à la Corne.

(lace), has been the object of universal imitation in France and other countries. Figs. 593 and

Fig. 594. Slipper in Rouen Faience.

594 are representative specimens remarkable for great originality.

Rouge Croix, Rouge Dragon. Two of the four *Pursuivants* (heralds of the lowest type) of Herald's College.

Rouge Royal, Arch. A kind of red marble.

Round Towers. There are upwards of a hundred in Ireland, of which about twenty are perfect. Generally the tower is a hollow circular column from 50 to 150 feet high, capped by a short pointed roof of stone. The base, frequently of cyclopean masonry, measures from 40 to 60 feet in circumference, and the form of the whole tower is tapering towards the summit. The single entrance door is always from 8 to 15 feet above the ground ; the windows, scattered, light the internal stories or rooms. Innumerable and wild conjectures of the origin and purpose of these towers have been made. The most sober appears to be that they were the earliest form of buildings of a monastic order, adapted to the exigencies of a Christian settlement in the midst of pagans and pirates. (See *Petrie, The Round Towers of Ireland.*)

Roundels. (1) Wooden platters decorated with painting and gilding ; 16th century. (2) Small round shields borne by soldiers in the 14th and 15th centuries. (3) Arch. The bead or astragal moulding.

Fig 595.
Bezant.

Roundle, Her. A circular figure in Heraldry, of which there are many kinds : as the BEZANT, PLATE, TORTEAU, &c. (q.v.). In modern Heraldry a roundle *gules* is called TORTEAU; *azure*, HURT; *sable*, PELLET or OGRESS ; *vert*, POMME ; *purpure*, GOLPE. (See also FOUNTAIN, ANNULET.)

Roussant, Her. About to fly.

Rowan-tree, Scotch. The mountain ash.

Rowel. The wheel of a spur.

Rowel Lights, Chr. Lights in a church, let up and down by a pulley, especially a star-like light made to move at the Epiphany, when the coming of the wise men was acted as a religious play. Any small hoop or ring movable on the place that holds it is a "*rowel.*"

Rowell or **Ricel,** O. E. A vessel mentioned, but not described, in Church records (of *Walberswick,* Suffolk), to be used twice in the year ; " whereby, and the great quantity of Wax and Frankincense, a ceremonial Imitation of the Birth and Burial of our *Saviour* seems to have been celebrated." (*Gardner, T., Historical Account.*)

Royal. (1) *Paper*: 21 inches by 19. (2) *Artillery*. A very small mortar. (3) *Sailing*. The upper sail above the top-gallant. (4) O. E. A RIAL (q.v.), a coin of the value of ten shillings.

Royal Blue (Fr. *bleu du roi*). A vitreous pigment used in porcelain painting, resulting in a rich, deep blue colour. It is prepared from *smalt.*

Rubelite. A precious stone not much used for jewellery. It is a species of *tourmaline,* red and pink in colour.

Rubens Brown. A rich brown pigment.

Rubiate. A name for *Liquid Madder Lake* (q.v.).

Rubicelle. An orange-coloured stone, a variety of the *spinel ruby.*

Rubrica, R. Red ochre ; and thence *rubric,* an edict or ordinance of the Civil Law written in red ochre, while the ordinances and rules of the prætors were written in black on a white ground on the ALBUM (q.v.).

Ruby, in Christian art. (See RED.)

Ruby or **Red Sapphire.** A *corundum,* the most valuable of all gems ; when perfect and large, exceeding even the diamond in value. The colour varies from the lightest rose tint to the deepest carmine. The most valuable kind is called " pigeon's blood," a pure deep rich red, without any admixture of blue or yellow. Brahmin traditions speak of the abode of the gods lighted by enormous rubies ; and one name of the Kings of Pegu was " Lord of Rubies." In mediæval times the ruby was regarded as an amulet against poison, plague, sadness, evil thoughts, wicked spirits, &c. It also kept the wearer in health, and cheered his mind, and blackened when he incurred danger. (Consult *Emanuel, Diamonds and Precious Stones,* &c.)

Rudder. On ancient coins, &c., with the orb and fasces, emblem of the supreme power.

Rudens, R. The smaller ropes in a ship.

Rudiarii. Veteran gladiators discharged from the service by the presentation of a wooden sword (*rudis*).

Rudis, R. (1) A spoon or similar instrument. (2) A wooden sword. (See RUDIARII.) When a gladiator received his discharge, a *rudis* was given him, together with a freedman's cap, by way of declaration that he had been granted his liberty, a fact expressed by the phrase *rude donari.*

Rue, Her. A *chaplet of rue* is blazoned *bend-wise* (see PER BEND) across the shield of Saxony. (See CRANCELIN.)

Ruffles. Lace frills worn over the wrists, introduced *temp.* Henry VIII.

Ruff and Honours. An ancient game of cards from which Whist is derived.

Fig. 596. Silesian Maiden with Ruff.

Ruffs. Large collars of lace or muslin. A fashion of the 16th century ; it commenced at the end of the reign of Henry VIII. Cambrics and lawn for making ruffs were first imported under Elizabeth. For illustrations of various modifications of this fashion, see Figs. 267, 283, 304, 559, 561, 580, &c. (Consult *Planché, Cycl. of Costume.*)

Rugæ, Chr. The metal *cancelli* or screens of the more sacred parts of a church. The presbytery of St. Peter's was fenced in with silver "rugæ," and the confessional with rugæ of gold. (See *Smith and Cheetham.*)

Rullions, Scotch. Shoes made of untanned leather.

Rum-swizzle. "The name given in Dublin to a fabric made from undyed foreign wool, which, while preserving its natural property of resisting wet, possesses the qualities of common cloth." (*Simmonds' Commercial Dict.*)

Rumex, R. A weapon of similar character to the SPARUM, the head of which was formed like a spear with a hook on the blade.

Runcina, R. A carpenter's tool of the nature of a plane.

Runco, R. A hoe.

Runes, Scand. Magical inscriptions in a character believed by the northern nations to have been invented by Woden. "The Runic alphabet," says *Mr. Wheaton,* "consists properly of sixteen letters, which are Phœnician in their origin. . . . They are only Roman, with the curves changed into straight lines for the convenience of engraving on hard substances." (*Hist. of the Northmen,* p. 61.)

Ruskie, Scotch. A coarse straw hat ; a basket or beehive of plaited osiers or straw.

Russells, O. E. A kind of satin.

Russet. A *red* grey colour ; violet mixed with orange. Its complementary is *green* grey.

Rust (oxide) of iron. "The best *rust*" is mentioned in a list of colours of the 17th century. (*Brown, Ars Pictoria, Appendix,* p. 5.)

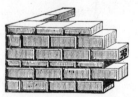

Fig. 597. Rustic Work. Bossage.

Rustic Work (Fr. *bossage*). Ashlar masonry, the joints of which are worked with grooves or channels to render them conspicuous ; sometimes the whole of the joints are worked in this way, and sometimes only the horizontal ones. (See Fig. 597.)

Rustre, Her. A LOZENGE pierced with a circular opening.

Rustred Armour seems to have grown out of the *ring armour.* It consisted of one row of flat rings about double the usual size, laid half over the other, so that two in the outer partly covered one.

S.

S, as a *numeral*, was used to represent **7** ; as an *abbreviation* it generally means *socius* or Fellow (of a society) ; S. P. Q. R., on Roman monuments, stands for *senatus*, populusque Romanus.

Sabanum, R. (σάβανον). A kind of cloth, towel, or napkin.

Sabaoth, Heb. Armies; hosts of angels. It is also written *Zabaoth*.

Sabatines, O. E. (1) Steel armour for the feet ; 16th century. (2) Slippers, or clogs.

Sabianism. The worship of the heavenly bodies.

Sable. (1) The best and most costly brushes for painting are made from this fur. (2) In Heraldry, the colour black, represented in engraving by crossed lines. (See Fig. 375.)

Sabre, Fr. A curved sword with a broad and heavy blade.

Sabretasche, Fr. A pocket worn, suspended from the sword-belt, by a cavalry officer.

Sac-friars. (See SACCUS.)

Sacciperium, R. A large sackcloth bag. A pocket.

Saccus, R. (σάκκος). A large sack of coarse cloth for wheat, flour, &c. (2) A beggar's wallet. (3) Chr. (Angl. *sack*). A coarse upper garment of sack or hair-cloth, worn by monks ; hence called SAC-FRIARS. (Cf. SACQUE.)

Sacellum, R. (dimin. of *sacrum*). A small precinct enclosing an altar, and consecrated to a divinity. In Christian architecture, small monumental chapels within churches.

Sachem. The chief of a tribe of North American Indians.

Sackbut, O. E. (9th century). A wind instrument resembling the *trombone*.

Sacque. Part of a lady's dress in the reign of Louis XIV. It was a silk cloak, and hung from the shoulders, spreading over the dress to the ground. In England it was worn in part of the reign of George III. (Fig. 598.)

Sacrarium (*sacrum*, holy). A place in which sacred things are kept ; the sacristy in a temple. In a private house a place used as a chapel or oratory.

Sacring Bell, Chr. A hand-bell rung at the elevation of the Host.

" Her eye was as bright as the merry sunlight,
    When it shines on the dewy grass ;
    And her voice was as clear as a *sacring bell*,
    That is rung at the holy mass."

(See also SANCTUS BELL.)

Sacristy, of a church, the apartment where the vestments and vessels are kept.

Sacro Catino, It. An extraordinary hexa-

gonal glass dish preserved in the cathedral at Genoa, which was for a long time supposed to have been formed of a single emerald ; and to have been either "a gift from the Queen of Sheba to Solomon, or the dish which held the Paschal Lamb at the Last Supper," &c. It was obtained in the Crusades in 1101, and was for many generations an object of superstitious reverence. Its principal interest now is in the evidence it bears to the early perfection of the art of making and colouring glass.

Sadda, Pers. (lit. a hundred gates). An abridgment of the Zend-Avesta or sacred books of the ancient Persians.

Saddle-bars. Said of small iron bars, in glazing casements, to which the lead panels are fastened.

Fig. 598. Sacque of the time of Louis XIV.

Saddle-roof, Arch. A roof of two gables. (French, *en batière.*)

Safety-arch, Arch. An arch in a wall over a door or window, to keep the weight of the wall above off the lintel.

Safflower. A delicate red colour obtained from the flower of that name.

Saffron (It. *zafferano*). Produced from the flowers of the crocus ; a yellow pigment principally used as a glazing.

Saga, R. A woman skilled in religious mysteries ; and thence a witch or sorceress.

Sagaris, Orient. (σάγαρις). A two-edged axe, also called *bipennis* ; it was used by the Amazons, Massagetæ, and Persians. (See BI-PENNIS.)

Sagena, Gr. and R. (σαγήνη). A large fishing-net ; modern *seine*. It was fitted with leaden weights at the bottom and corks at the top.

Sagitta, R. (1) An arrow; primitively with heads of flint, afterwards of bronze and iron. The heads of the arrows of the Greeks and Romans were oval ; among other nations they were triangular and barbed, like those carried by the SAGITTARIUS in Fig. 599. This kind of arrow was called *sagitta hasta* or *adunca.* (2) A lancet for bleeding animals.

Fig. 599. Sagittarius.

Sagittarius, R. An archer ; a sign of the zodiac, represented as a centaur. (Fig. 599.) In Christian art, a symbol of Divine vengeance.

Sagma, R. (σάγμα). A wooden pack-saddle. **Sagmarius,** R. A beast of burden carrying the *sagma.*

Sagochlamys, R. A military cloak which combined the Roman *sagus* and the Greek *chlamys.*

Sagus or **Sagum,** Celt. A woollen cloak with a long nap, worn folded and fastened round the neck by a clasp, especially by soldiers on a campaign (Fig. 44) ; hence *saga* is a sign of war, as *toga* is of peace. At a later period the same name was given to a kind of blouse, striped or checked in staring colours, and adorned with flowers and other ornaments, and bordered with bands of purple and gold and silver embroidery, worn by the Gauls in Artois and Flanders.

Saic, Turk. A sailing-vessel common in the Levant.

Saie, O. E. A delicate serge or woollen cloth.

Saints-bell, O. E. for SACRING-BELL.

Salade, Sallet. A light helmet resembling the KETTLE-HAT (Fig. 407), introduced from Germany in the 15th century.

Salam-stone. A name given to the blue or oriental sapphire from Ceylon.

Fig. 600. Salamander. Device of Francis I., the "Father of Letters."

Salamander, Chr. In Christian art, a symbol of fire, and supposed to live in fire ; or, according to Pliny, "to quench it as if ice were put into it." In Heraldry it is either represented as a lizard, or as a kind of dog breathing flames. Fig. 600 is the device of Francis I. of France, with a motto implying that a good prince nourishes that which is good, and expels the bad. At the meeting of the Field of the Cloth of Gold, the king's guard at the tournament was clothed in blue and yellow, with the salamander embroidered thereon.

Salamander's Hair. The variety of asbestos called *amianthus.*

Salet, O. E. A light helmet. (See SALADE.)

Salic Dances. (See SALII.)

Salient, Her. In the act of leaping or

bounding, the hind-paws on the ground, both the fore-paws elevated.

Salinum, R. (*sal*, salt). A salt-cellar.

Saltatio, R. (*salto*, to dance). Dancing; applied to religious dances, gymnastic or war dances, CORYBANTIC, SALIC, MIMETIC or theatrical dances, &c.

Saltire or **Saltier**, Her. An ordinary in the form of St. Andrew's Cross. The illustration (Fig. 601) is "*argent a* SALTIRE *gules.*"

Salutatorium. (See RECEPTORIUM.

Salute at Sea. The English claim the right, formerly claimed by the Venetians, of being saluted *first* in all places, as sovereigns of the seas. The naval salute to the British flag began in the reign of King Alfred.

Fig. 601. Argent a *saltire* gules.

Sambuca, R. (σαμβύκη). (1) A stringed musical instrument, which varied in form, but resembled a harp. (2) Military. A scaling-ladder.

Sam-cloth, O. E. (needlework). A sampler. "A *sam-cloth*, vulgarly a sampler."

Samit, for **Exsamit** (ἑξ, six ; μίτοι, threads). A splendid tissue, having six threads of silk in the warp, and the weft of flat gold shreds.

Sammaron-cloth, O. E. A woven mixture of linen and hemp.

Samnites. Gladiators armed like the Samnite soldiers, with a close helmet, shield, and greaves.

Sampan. A Chinese canoe or small boat.

Sampler (Lat. *exemplar*). A piece of ornamental needlework, done for a sample or specimen.

Sanctus Bell, Chr. A fixed bell rung at the elevation of the Host, at the words "*sanctus, sanctus, sanctus, Deus Sabaoth.*" It was fixed outside the church, generally on the eastern gable of the nave. (See SACRING BELL.) (2) In the absence of a fixed bell, small bells carried by acolytes, often the subject of rich ornamentation, sometimes consisting of a carillon of three small bells hidden within one large one, thus blending their sounds.

Sandal. (See CENDAL.)

Sandal-wood. Ornamental wood highly valued for cabinet-work ; when old it becomes yellow and highly odoriferous.

Sandalium, Gr. and R. (σανδάλιον). A richly-ornamented sandal worn exclusively by women.

Sandapila, R. A rough kind of bier for the poor. (See LECTICA.)

Sandarac. A resin used for spirit varnishes.

Sandyx, Gr. (σάνδυξ). A Lydian tunic, of a fine and transparent texture, dyed with the juice

of the sandyx, which gave it a flesh-coloured tint.

Sang-réal (Saint Graal). The Holy Grail said to have been brought to England by Joseph of Arimathea. The legend is that it is an emerald cup, or the cup used at the Last Supper, containing the real (or it may mean "royal") Blood (*sang-réel* or *réal*).

"The cup, the cup itself, from which our Lord
Drank at the last sad supper with his own."
(*Tennyson.*)

Sanglier, Her. A wild boar.

Sanguine. A deep blood colour, prepared from oxide of iron.

Sanguinolentæ (sc. ampullæ). Glass vessels found in the catacombs at Rome, containing a red sediment, ascertained by analysis to be *blood*; and canonically pronounced by the Roman Church to be that of the early Christian martyrs in whose tombs it has been found. (The subject is discussed at length by *V. Schultze: die Katakomben*, Leipzig, 1882.)

Sanhedrim, Heb. The supreme council of the Jews, which sat at Jerusalem in a circular hall, one half of which was within the temple, and the other outside. (*Bosc.*)

Sap-green. The only green vegetable pigment ; used in water-colour painting. Obtained by evaporating the juice of the berries of the buckthorn, mixed with lime.

Sap-wood. The soft white wood immediately under the bark of a tree.

Sapphire (Syriac *saphilah*). The *oriental sapphire* from Arabia, which has been known from the earliest antiquity, was one of the stones on the breastplate of Aaron, and was dedicated to Apollo by the Greeks, by whom it was regarded as the gem of gems—the sacred stone *par excellence*. The sapphires from Brazil are also called oriental sapphires. The sapphires of Puy, found in a mountain in Central France, vary from the deepest to the palest blue, passing sometimes to a reddish blue or even to a yellowish green. The sapphire, although extremely hard, has been engraved by the ancients. There is a beautiful sapphire among the crown jewels of Russia, representing a draped female figure : the stone is of two tints, and the artist has skilfully used the dark tint for the woman and the light for the drapery. (*L. Dieulafait.*)

Sapphire, in Christian art. (See BLUE.)

Saraballa, Sarabara, Gr. and R. (σαράβαλλα). Loose trousers, which reached from the waist to the instep, worn by the Parthians, Medes, and Persians.

Saraband, Sp. A slow dance derived from the Saracens ; the music for *sarabands*, by Corelli and other old masters, is interesting. (See *Chappell's History of Music*, &c.)

Saracenic Architecture. (See ALHAMBRAIC, MOORISH, MORESCO-SPANISH.)

Sarapis, Pers. (σάραπις). The tunic of the kings of Persia ; it was made of a fine purple-coloured cloth, with a white band in front embroidered with gold.

Sarcenet. A fine thin woven silk. An improved *cendal*, introduced in the 15th century by the Saracens of the south of Spain ; hence its name. (See CENDAL.)

Sarcilis, Chr. A woollen garment—not described.

Sarcoline (Gr. σὰρξ, flesh). Flesh-coloured.

Sarcolite. A stone of a rose-flesh colour.

Sarcophagus, Gen. (σαρκοφάγος ; σὰρξ, flesh, and φαγεῖν, to eat). A coffin of a limestone called Lapis Assius, in which the corpse was rapidly consumed. The great sarcophagus called "of Alexander the Great," in the British Museum, is a celebrated specimen. (See BISOMUS, QUADRISOMUS, and TRISOMUS.)

Sard or **Carnelian.** A brownish-red variety of chalcedony.

Sard-achates. A name given by the ancients to varieties of *agate*, which contained layers of *Sard* or carnelian.

Sardonic Laughter. A distortion of the features of the dying, the closing symptom of several fatal diseases; named from the poisonous herb Sardonia.

Sard-onyx. A precious stone composed of alternate layers of carnelian and *chalcedony ;* extensively used for gem-engraving.

Sardel, Sardine, Sardius. A precious stone mentioned in Scripture in the description of Aaron's breastplate.

Sarissa, Gr. (σάρισσα). The longest and heaviest spear of the Greeks peculiar to the Macedonian phalanx.

Sarrazinois Carpets. Embroidered stuffs resembling tapestry, made in the 10th and 11th centuries, doubtless imitated from work by the Saracens.

Sarsen-stones. Boulders of sandstone found on the Chalk downs in Wiltshire.

Sarsnet. (See SARCENET.)

Sartago, R. A frying-pan ; in the patois of Languedoc, *sartan.*

Satin. This fine silk, originally imported from China, was first known in England in the 14th century. It is thicker than ordinary silk, and remarkable for its smooth glossy surface, not exhibiting the marks of the reticulations of the threads.

Satin-spar. An ornamental stone, having a soft *satiny* surface when polished.

Satin-wood. An ornamental yellow wood much used in cabinet-making.

Satinet. A thin kind of satin.

Saturn, Her. The black colour in the arms of sovereign princes.

Saturnalia, R. Festivals of Saturn, held on the seventh of the calends of January (14th of December), instituted by Numa. During the four or five days that this festival lasted, both public and private business was interrupted ; and banquets and festivities were held, in which masters and slaves met on a temporary footing of equality. In the feasts at rustic places, the hollow statue of Saturn was filled with oil ; he held a pruning knife in his hand, and his feet were surrounded with a band of wool.

Satyrs. Greek deities of the wooded plains, as the Roman *fauns* were of the fields. They are usually represented as the attendants of Bacchus, or the lovers of the Nymphs, with goat's legs and horns, and human bodies covered with short hair ; often with LACINIA on the neck.

Saunders' Blue (Green) (from the French *cendres' bleu*). The blue ashes of calcined *lapis lazuli*. (See CARBONATES OF COPPER.)

Saurians. Animals of the lizard tribe, crocodiles, &c., antediluvian and other.

Fig. 602. Device of Charles d'Amboise, Sieur de Chaumont.

Savage-man or **Wood-man**, Her. A wild man, naked, or clothed in skins or leaves, and carrying a club. The illustration is the device of De Chaumont, Marshal of France (+ 1510), with the motto, "*Mitem animum agresti sub tegmine scabro,*" which he bore embroidered on the pennon of his company.

Savonnerie. (See TURKEY-STITCH.)

Saxon Blue. Sulphate of indigo used as a dye-stuff.

Saxon Gold-work of elegant design and skilful workmanship, may be attributed to the 5th and 6th centuries. The art was doubtless imported by Roman colonists. Specimens may be studied in the South Kensington Museum. (See METALLURGY.)

Scabellum, R. (dimin. from SCAMNUM, q.v.) (1) A stool or step to get into bed with. (2) A shoe with a castanet in the sole, with which the wearer beat time, as an accompaniment to music.

Scagliola (It. *scaglia*, a chip of marble). Artificial marble made of gypsum, glue, &c., of variegated colours, in imitation of marble, applied in ornamental work like *stucco*, but admitting a fine polish.

Scalæ, R. (*scando*, to climb). A ladder or staircase.

Scald, Scand. A poet or bard.

Scaldino, It. A copper.

Scale, in Music (It. *scala*, a ladder). (See TONES.)

Scalmus, R. (σκαλμός). The thole, or strong peg with a thong, with which an oar was attached to the side of a ship.

Scalper, Scalprum, R. (*scalpo*, to cut). A general term for all kinds of cutting tools, such as chisels, knives, &c.

Scalptura. Engraving in precious stones. (See INTAGLIO, CAMEO.)

Scamnum, R. (*scando*, to climb). A stool for a bed or arm-chair, or a stone bench with a step.

Scandula, R. A wooden shingle used for tiles (*tegulæ*).

Scansoria Machina or Scansorium, R. (*scando*, to mount). A scaffolding, such as a tower, which enables work to be carried on at various heights from the ground.

Scantling. In *Masonry*, the size of a stone, in length, breadth, and thickness. In *Carpentry*, the dimensions of a timber in breadth and thickness only. Any piece of timber less than five inches square is called *scantling*.

Scapha, R. (σκάφη, i.e. dug out). A long-boat or cutter attached to a larger vessel; obviously, from the etymology, a sort of canoe in its origin; our "skiff."

Scaphium, R. (σκάφιον). A vessel of Greek origin and of small size, and in the form of a boat (*scapha*), which, though used as a drinking-cup, is especially to be classed among sacrificial utensils.

Scapple. In Masonry, to reduce a stone to a straight surface, without making it smooth.

Scapulary, Chr. A part of the monastic dress, worn by both sexes over the shoulders (*scapula*). It is generally a narrow strip of cloth contrasting with the colour of the dress, reaching almost to the feet.

Scapus, Gr. and R. (σκᾶπος). A shaft or stem. This term is applied to several distinct things, which all, however, imply an idea of use in support of some other thing; as, for instance, the shaft of a column, which supports a capital, and occasionally an entablature; the central shaft or newel which supports the stair-

Fig. 603. Scarabæus, sacred.

case of a column; the stem of a candelabrum or lamp-rest, and so on.

Scarabæus (Egyp.), or sacred ateuchus, is an attribute of Phtha, and the symbol of creation. Under the name of *Kheper* (creator), the scarabæus was given to the soldiers in exchange for their oath of fidelity, and worn by them as a finger ring. With wings extended (as in Fig. 603) it is a funereal ornament.

Scarlet. (See IODINE SCARLET.)

Scarlet Ochre. (See VENETIAN RED.)

Scarpe, Escarpe, Her. A diminutive of a bend sinister.

Scauper. A tool used by engravers; a kind of gouge. (Angl. *scooper*.)

Scena, Gr. and R. (σκηνή). (1) The stage of a theatre, including not only the part so called at the present day, but the wall at the back, which was provided with three doors, one in the centre (*valvæ regiæ*), and two lateral ones (*valvæ hospitales*). (2) A double-edged axe, used in the sacrifices; one of the iron sides of this axe had the broad blade of the *securis*, and the other that of the *dolabra*. In the sense of "an axe," *scena* is the contracted form of an old Latin word *sacena*.

Scene-painting was invented by Inigo Jones, about 1610.

Scenographia, R. (σκηνο-γραφία). The drawing of a building in *perspective*. A *geometrical* plan is called *orthographia*.

Sceptre, Gr. and R. (σκῆπτρον). Originally, in early antiquity, a long staff similar to the shaft of a spear, which was carried by great persons to lean on when walking. Afterwards it became the *truncheon*, and a weapon of offence and defence. Later on, an ornament was added to the upper end of this staff, and it became the insignia of power and authority. The ivory sceptre of the kings and consuls of Rome was surmounted by an eagle. The sceptre was an attribute of Jupiter and Juno, as sovereigns of the gods.

Schafte, O. E. (See SHAFT.)

Scheele's Green. A green pigment; an arsenite

of copper ; arsenite of potash mixed with sulphate of copper ; used in oil and water-colours.

Scherzo, It. (*playful*). A lively style in music; faster than the minuet (such as in *Beethoven's* Second Symphony, op. 36, in D major).

Schleswig Lace. North Schleswig (or South Jutland) is the only province of Denmark in which there was a regular manufacture of lace. The art itself is supposed to have been introduced, in 1515, by Queen Elizabeth (sister of the Emperor Charles V., and wife of Christian II. of Denmark). About 1712 lace-making was much improved by Brabant women. The earlier specimens are all of Flemish character, made on the pillow in the same way, occasionally imitating the Mechlin ground with the pattern apparently run in with the needle. All Schleswig laces are remarkable for their fine quality and

Fig. 604. Schleswig Lace.

excellent workmanship. The engraving shows part of a shirt-collar of Christian IV., of a Brabant pattern to be seen in his portrait in Hampton Court Palace.

Schmeltz, Germ. Glass ornament ; produced by fusing lumps of coloured glass together to imitate marble, cornelian, and other stones. (See GLASS.)

Schweinfurth's Green. A brilliant sea-green pigment.

Scimitar. (See SCYMETAR.)

Scimpodium, Gr. and R. (σκιμπόδιον, lit. footprop). A couch or long chair for an invalid.

Scintillant, Her. Emitting sparks. (See Fig. 342.)

Sciolist (from σκιὸs, a shadow). A man of superficial acquirements, who sees only the *shadows* of things.

Scioptics (σκιὰ, a shadow). The branch of the science of optics applied in the construction of the *camera obscura.*

Sciothericon (σκιοθηρικόν). A sun-dial.

Scipio. An official staff. (See SCEPTRE.)

Scirophoria. Athenian festivals held in the month Scirophorion or June.

Scirpea, R. A waggon formed of basketwork of plaited rushes (*scirpus*), and used principally for agricultural operations.

Scobina, R. (*scabo,* to scrape). A rasp for wood ; distinct from *lima,* a file for metals.

Scobs. Shreds of ivory, metals, &c., turned off the lathe or rasp, &c.

Sconces. Brackets projecting from the wall, supporting candlesticks : originated in the 15th century, and from that date form an important branch of metallurgical art-work.

Scopæ, R. A broom made of small twigs of wood. This term survives in the Languedoc *escoube.* **Scopulæ,** R. A little broom.

Scorpers. In wood engraving, tools used for cutting away large spaces after outlining or engraving, so as to leave only the drawing in relief.

Scorpio, Gr. and R. (lit. a scorpion). (1) A kind of cross-bow. (2) A pyramid of stones raised for a landmark in country places.

Fig. 605. Scotia or Trochilus.

Scotia or **Trochilus,** Arch. (σκοτία, τροχίλος). A concave moulding employed especially in the decoration of the bases of columns or pilasters, between the fillets of the tori. In plain bases the *scotiæ* are smooth, and in decorated bases they are ornamented with sculptures, as shown in Fig. 605.

Scourge. (See FLAGELLUM and FLAGRUM.)

Scraper. An engraver's tool for removing BURRS (q.v.).

Screen, Chr. An open barrier of woodwork or stone enclosing the choir or chancel of a church, chapel, or tomb ; generally highly enriched by carving and gilding, and the lower panels decorated with painting. (See ROODLOFT.)

Scrinium, Scrinia, Chr. and R. (1) Chr. A chest which held chiefly liturgical writings; according to the writings they contained, these cases were variously distinguished as *scrinia epistolarum, scrinia dispositionum, scrinia libellorum, scrinia memoriæ, scrinia sacra,* &c. *Scrinia* were generally kept in the *diaconicum* or *scevophylacium.* (2) Cylindrical boxes or cases used for carrying volumes (i.e. rolls) and papers (cf.

HANAPER).   (3) *Scrinia unguentaria* were used
to contain phials of oils and perfumes, &c.,
for the toilette.

Scriptorium, Chr.   An apartment in large
monasteries where manuscripts were transcribed.

Scripulum. (See SCRUPULUM.)

Scrupulum, R. (*scrupus*, lit. a small stone).
A scruple, the smallest Roman gold coin; it
weighed a third of the *denarius aureus.* (See
DENARIUS.)

Scrutoire, Fr.   An old way of spelling
escritoire.

Scudo, It.   A silver coin worth about 4*s.*
In Rome the gold scudo is worth 65*s.*

Sculponeæ, R.   A common kind of boot,
with a wooden sole; it was worn by the
familia rustica, or slaves who worked in the
country.

Sculpture (from *sculpo,* to carve) includes all
carved work, in wood, ivory, stone, marble,
metal, or other material; and also those works
formed in a softer material not requiring carving, such as wax or clay. It includes STA-
TUARY, carved ornament, and GLYPTICS or
incised gems and cameos. From the practice of
preparing the model in clay, sculpture is also
called *the plastic art.* A most remarkable incident in the history of sculpture, is the fact that
the most ancient specimens are carved of the
hardest stones, such as basalt, granite, and porphyry; and that this work was done at a period
antecedent to the introduction of steel tools.
(Consult *Redford's Ancient Sculpture.*)

Scumbling. The process of going over a
painting with a nearly dry brush, to soften and
blend the tints.

Scutage, O. E. (from *scutum,* a shield).
A tax upon lands held by *knight-service.*

Scutale, R. (from *scutum,* i. e. shield-
shaped). The hollow in the thongs of a sling
in which the missile is laid.

Scutarius, Med.   An esquire or shield-
bearer.

Scutcheon, for ESCUTCHEON (q.v.).

Scutella. Diminutive of SCUTRA (q.v.).

Scutica, Gr. and R. A whip made with a
leather thong (σκυτικός).

Scutiform. Shaped like a shield.

Scutra, R. (from *scutum,* i. e. shield-shaped).
Diminutive *scutella.* A square wooden tray for
plates, dishes, and cups.

Scutum, R. and Egyp. The large oblong
shield of the Roman infantry, in contradistinction to *clipeus,* a round shield. (See SHIELDS.)

Scymetar. A sword of oriental origin, with
a curved blade, very sharp.

Scyphus, Gr. and R. (σκύφος). A drinking-
cup of wood or silver, of smaller capacity than
the BROMIAS (q.v.). It was sacred to Hercules.

Seals. Ancient porcelain seals, to which the

Chinese attribute an antiquity of from 1000 to
2000 years, are met with in collections; and
precisely identical specimens have been found in
the bogs of *Ireland.* They are of a peculiar
white or cream-coloured porcelain, such as has
not been made in China for several hundred
years. It is believed that the Irish specimens
must have lain buried there from a period
anterior to history. (*Fortune.*) (See SIGILLUM,
RINGS.)

Seax. A Saxon sword.

Secco, It.   Fresco-painting *in secco* is that
kind which absorbs the colours into the plaster,
and gives them a dry sunken appearance. (*Fairholt.*)

Second Distance. In a picture, the part of
the *middle distance* next the foreground.

Secondary Colours. The three *primary colours*
(containing nothing of any other colour)—blue,
red, and yellow—when mixed in *equal* proportions produce three *secondary* colours:—blue and
yellow produce *green;* blue and red, *violet;* and
yellow and red, *orange.* Mixed in *unequal*
proportions they produce what are called
TONES (q.v.).

Secos, Egyp. (σηκός). The name for the
NAOS in an Egyptian temple.

Secretarium, Chr. (*secretum,* secret). A
sacristy (not a *tabernacle,* as maintained by some
authors) in the apse, at the side of the altar. In
the ancient basilicas there were two such re-
cesses, one on each side of the altar.

Sectilis. (See PAVIMENTUM.)

Securicula (diminutive of *securis*). In Architecture, a dove-tail mortise.

Securis, R. (*seco,* to cut). An axe or hatchet
of any kind; but esp. that borne by the lictors
in the FASCES. (See DOLABRA, BIPENNIS, FAS-
CIS, &c.)

Securis Dannica, Med. (See BIPENNIS.)

Secutores, R.   Gladiators appointed to fight
with the *Retiarii* (whom they were constantly
pursuing round the circus); or those who replaced others killed were so called.

Sedes, Sedile (dimin. *sedicula*). Any kind of
seat.

Sedilia. (1) R. The rows of seats in the
amphitheatre. (2) Chr. In a Catholic church,
the stone seats on the south side of the altar, for
the use of the clergy in the intervals of the services.

Segestrium, R. (lit. of straw). A coarse
wrapper made of skins or straw-matting.

Segmenta, R. (*seco,* to cut off). Strips of
rich cloth or tissues of gold or silver worn as a
border to the dresses of wealthy Roman ladies.

Segno. In Music, a direction to repeat :—
al segno, as far as the sign; *dal segno,* from the
sign.

Segreant, Her. A griffin or wyvern rampant. (See Fig. 369.)

Fig. 606. Sejant.

Fig 607.
Sejant Rampant.

Sejant, Her. Sitting:— of a lion, at rest with his fore-legs stretched on the ground, but awake, and his head and tail elevated.

Sejant Rampant. Seated like a cat, with his fore-legs erect.

Sejugis, R. (*sex*, six, and *jungo*, to join). A chariot drawn by six horses abreast.

Seliquastrum, Chr. A seat of highly archaic character met with on certain monuments of Christian art.

Sella, R. (*sedeo*, to sit). A low seat without back, a stool; *sella curulis*, a curule chair; its feet were of ivory, and took the form of an X, and it folded like a camp-stool; *sella castrensis*, a real camp-stool; *sella balnearis*, a bath-seat, we possess a specimen in ancient red marble of the greatest beauty, another name for it was *sella pertusa; sella tonsoria*, a barber's chair. Again, the term *sella* was applied to a sedan-chair (*sella portatoria, gestatoria, fertoria*), and a pack-saddle for beasts of burden (*sella bajulatoria*), and to a riding-saddle (*sella eques-tris*).

Sellaria, R. A large reception-room, so called because it was furnished with a number of *sellæ*.

Sellaris (sc. *equus*), R. A saddle-horse.

Sellula, R. (dimin. of SELLA). A small sedan-chair.

Sembella, R. A nominal subdivision of the *denarius*, of which it was worth a twentieth part, or about fivepence.

Fig. 608. *Fleur-de-lis* (*semée*). Ancient France.

Semée or Aspers-ed, Her. Sown broadcast, or scattered, without any fixed number, over the field. (Fig. 608.)

Sementivæ, R. (*sementis*, a sowing). A festival which took place at seed-time in honour of Ceres and Tellus.

Semi- (ἡμι-), as an adjunct, is the Greek form of *demi* = half.

Semibreve. In Music, half a breve; the longest note in modern music, marked ⊂.

Semicinctium, R. (*semi*, half, and *cingo*, to gird). A short kilt worn by men when going through violent exercises or severe bodily labour; it reached from the waist to the knees.

Semidiapason. In Music, an octave lessened by a semitone.

Semiquaver. A sixteenth of a semibreve—♪.

Semis, Semissis. The half of an As, or six ounces; hence *Semisses* = six per cent. interest.

Semita, R. (*se* and *meo*, i. e. going aside). A pathway in a field; a narrow lane in a town.

Semitarge, Med. Fr. A scimitar. (See TARGE.)

Semitone. In Music; the smallest interval in modern music; the ancients had *quarter-tones* (q.v.).

Semi-uncials. During the 6th and 7th centuries, a transition style of illuminating prevailed, the letters of which have been termed *semi-uncials*. This, in a further transition, became more like the old Roman cursive, which was called then *minuscule*; it began to prevail over *uncials* about the 8th century, and in the 10th its use was established. (See UNCIAL LETTERS.)

Semuncia. Half an ounce.

Senaculum, R. A place in which the senate used to meet. There were at Rome three *senacula*; one between the Capitol and the Forum, a second near the Porta Capena, and a third near the temple of Bellona.

Senio, R. The number *six* inscribed on the face of dice, and thence the throw when all the sixes turned up.

Sentina, R. The well or hold of a ship.

Sentinaculum, R. A ship's pump.

Sepia. A warm, brown, water-colour pigment obtained from the ink-bag of the cuttle-fish. (See ROMAN SEPIA.)

Sept-foil, Chr. A figure of *seven* foils, typical of the seven sacraments of the Church, and other mysteries of religion linked to the number seven.

Septilateral. Having seven sides.

Septimontium, R. A festival of the seven hills, celebrated at Rome in December.

Septizonium, Septemzonium, R. A building of great magnificence, which had seven stories of columns one above the other; each set supported an entablature and cornice running right round the building (*zona*), whence the name Septizonium.

Septum, R. and Chr. (*sepio*, to fence in). In general, any enclosure shut in by walls, palisades, barriers, hedges, &c. In Christian archæology, *septum* was the name given to a barrier, which, in the ancient Roman basilicas, separated the nave from the absides.

Septunx, R. (*septem* and *uncia*). Seven-twelfths of any quantity, whatever its nature.

Sepulchre, Chr. The Holy Sepulchre is a favourite subject of architectural sculpture, in cathedrals and continental churches. It is generally found on the north side of the chancel near the altar.

Sepulcrum, R. (*sepelio*, to bury). A sepulchre, the general term for any kind of tomb in which the dead were buried, or in which their ashes were deposited in urns. *Sepulcrum familiare*, a sepulchre erected for a single person, or for the members of a family. The *sepulcrum commune* was a tomb held in common by a number of persons belonging either to a single family, or several families, or a group of individuals, such as that given in Fig. 182, which represents the tomb of the freedmen of Octavia.

Sequin (It. *zecchino*). A gold coin in Italy, worth about 9*s.* 6*d.*; and in Turkey worth about 7*s.* 6*d.*

Sera, R. (*sero,* to fasten). A padlock or movable lock to a door.

Serapeum, Egyp. (σαραπεῖον).. A general term for sepulchral monuments in Egypt, but more especially that of Memphis. (*Bosc.*)

Seraph; pl. **Seraphim,** Heb. (See ANGELS, CHERUBIM.) "They are usually represented with wings and a flaming heart, to typify spiritual emotion and divine affection; or covered all over with eyes, to denote their knowledge of all human events as counsellors of the Most High. The Seraph's head in Heraldry, is usually delineated with six wings, two above and two below, which cross each other, and one on each side of the head." (*Fairholt.*)

Serges, Chr. Fr. The large wax candles used in churches. They are often covered with texts and devices.

Seria, R. An earthenware vessel used chiefly for holding wine and oil; it was larger than the amphora, and smaller than the *dolium.*

Serpent. A musical wind-instrument, of a powerful bass; invented by a French priest at Auxerre in 1590.

Serpent. (1) In Christian archæology an emblem of the principle of evil; the Virgin Mary is frequently represented trampling on the head of the serpent. It is especially a symbol of cunning, lying, and envy. (2) Generally. The serpent with its tail in its mouth describes a circle which is the symbol of eternity. In Classic Art it is an attribute of Æsculapius, and of Apollo; and a symbol of the *Genius Loci* (esp. of temples, &c.).

Serpentine Verses begin and end with the same word:

"Ambo florentes ætatibus, Arcades ambo."

Serrated. Having an edge like the teeth of a saw (*serra*).

Set-offs, Arch. The mouldings and slopes on *buttresses,* dividing them into stages.

Setting drawings in pencil or crayon is done by simply passing them through a dish of milk, or by washing the surface with a weak solution of isinglass.

Severey, Arch. A bay, or compartment in a vaulted ceiling.

Sèvres Porcelain. The celebrated manufactory at Sèvres was established in 1756. Soon afterwards it became the property of the king, Louis XV., and was much patronized both by

him and Madame de Pompadour. Some of the first artists of France were employed to decorate the plaques and vases, and the productions of this

Fig. 609. Sèvres Vase, with jewelled ornament.

factory are more highly prized than any others in the world. In 1870 three *jardinières* were sold by auction in London for over 10,000*l.*

The finest colours of this porcelain were the *bleu du roi* and the *rose de Pompadour*.

Sewer. (See CLOACA.)

Sextans, R. (*sextus*, sixth). A copper coin worth the tenth of an as, in weight about two ounces (*unciæ*).

Sextant. The sixth part of a circle ; an arc of 60 degrees.

Sextarius, R. (*sextus*). A measure of capacity used for liquids, grain, &c. ; it held the tenth of a CONGIUS (q.v.).

Sextertius, R. A coin originally of silver, and afterwards of fine copper (*aurichalcum*) ; it was worth two ases and a half.

Sextula, R. The sixth part of the ounce (*uncia*) ; the smallest denomination of Roman money.

Sforzato (It.). In Music ; with force, louder than the rest.

Sfregazzi or **Sfregature,** It. By this term is meant a peculiar thin kind of glazing, which is executed by dipping the finger into the colour, and drawing it once lightly and evenly along the part of the picture on which it is to be applied —such as the shade on the cheek, the limbs, &c., or wherever it is wished to lay a soft thin shadow. (Consult *Mrs. Merrifield, Ancient Practice of Painting*, vol. ii. p. 879.)

Sgraffito, It. (lit. scratched). A method of painting on stucco, in which a ground of dark stucco is covered with a coat of white, and the design is formed by scraping this away for the shadows. (Consult an article by *Mr. Alan Cole* in the *House Furnisher and Decorator*, May 10, 1873.)

Fig. 610.
Shackle.

Shackle and **Padlock,** Her. A badge of the Yorkist party during the wars of the Roses ; called also a FETTER-LOCK.

Shades. (See UMBRÆ.)

Shaft, Arch. The part of the column comprised between the base and the capital.

Shaft, O. E. The May-pole. May-poles seem to have existed in most villages until the Civil War. They were abolished by an ordinance of the Long Parliament, April 6, 1644, as heathenish vanities "generally abused to superstition and wickednesse."

Shaftman, O. E. A measure roughly six inches ; "the measure of the fist with the thumb set up." (*Ray*, 1674.)

Shagreen. A grained leather prepared from the skin of a species of shark, and stained green. A close imitation is made from horses' or asses' skins, in Russia, and dyed red, blue, or black.

Shalm or **Shawm.** A musical instrument, a pipe with a reed in the mouth-hole.

Shamrock, Her. A trefoil plant or leaf, the badge of Ireland.

Shard, O. E. A piece of broken pottery. (It has other meanings. Consult *Halliwell*.)

Shay-le, Chin. A relic of Buddha.

Sheaf. (1) A bundle of ripe corn bound up in the field ; the device assumed by Alfonso d'Avalos, when he was made captain-general of

Fig. 611. Sheaf. Device of Alphonso d'Avalos.

the army of Charles V., with the motto implying incessant devotion to his work,—that, as soon as one harvest is reaped, its successor must be sown. (2) A bunch of twenty-four arrows, enough to fill a quiver.

Sheep. In Christian art, the twelve apostles occur in early mosaics as twelve sheep, and our Lord in the midst as their Shepherd.

Shekel. A Jewish coin, value about 2s. 6d.

Shell, Chr. In Gallic as in Christian tombs shells are of frequent occurrence ; there is no doubt that they symbolize the resurrection, the body of man being looked upon as a shell which he leaves behind him at death. Different kinds of shell are met with, but that of most frequent occurrence is the common snail-shell (*helix pomatia*). (See ESCALLOP.)

Shell-cameos. Cameos carved on shells. These are certain conch shells or strombs, the substance of which consists of two distinct layers of different colours. The black conch offers the most decided contrast in the colours.

Shell-lac. Crude lac-resin melted into plates or *shales*. (See LAC.)

Shenti, Egyp. A short pair of drawers, fastened round the hips by a belt, worn by the ancient Egyptians.

Shepherd's Crook. (See PEDUM.)

Shepherds. (See HYCSOS.)

Shingles. Wooden tiles ; frequently used for church spires.

Ship. A symbol of the Church. (See NAVETTE.)

Fig. 612. Shrine of the Three Kings in Cologne Cathedral. 13th century.

Shoes. The shoes worn by the Greeks generally reached to the middle of the leg; the ROMANS had the *calceus* and the *solea* or sandal; the former was worn with the toga on ordinary occasions; the sandal on a journey or at a feast; but it was considered effeminate to appear in public with them. Black shoes were worn by the citizens of ordinary rank (see ATRAMENTUM, CHALCANTHUM), and white ones (sometimes red) by the women; on ceremonial occasions the magistrates wore red shoes. Patricians and their children wore a crescent shoe-buckle (see LUNA). Slaves went barefooted. The Jews had shoes of leather, wood, &c., tied with thongs passed under the soles of the feet; to "untie the latchets" of a man's shoes was a sign of deep subservience. In ancient as in modern times the Oriental peoples put off their shoes as we uncover the head. (Consult *Herbert Spencer on Ceremonies*.)

Shop. (See TABERNA.)

Shrine. A repository for relics; either fixed, as a tomb; or movable, as a *feretory.* (See Fig. 307.) The Shrine of the Three Kings in Cologne Cathedral is one of the most celebrated and costly in the world. (Fig. 612.)

Sibina, Sibyna, Gr. and R. (σιβύνη). A kind of boar-spear employed in hunting.

Sibylline (Books), R. The Sibylline books were a series of oracles of the destiny of the Roman Empire; they were three in number, and were placed by Tarquin in a vault of the temple of Jupiter Capitolinus, and were consulted in cases of difficulty by an order of the senate. They perished in 670 A.U.C., when the Capitol was burnt. A set of Sibylline oracles in existence, which predict very clearly the establishment of the Christian religion, have been ascertained to be a forgery of the 2nd century of the Christian era.

Sibyls, Gr. and R. (Σίβυλλα). Prophetesses of antiquity recognized by the ancient Christian Church, and a common object of symbolical ecclesiastical sculpture, with reference to their foreknowledge of the fulfilment of inspired prophecy; they are twelve in number, having each a proper emblem. (Cf. *Smith and Cheetham.*)

Sica, R. (dimin. *sicilla*). A curved dagger or scimitar; distinct from PUGIO, a straight dagger. It was the weapon preferred by thieves and assassins on account of the convenience of its

Fig. 614. Silver gilt dish and ewer ; the property of St. John's College, Cambridge. (Work of the late 17th century.)

shape for concealment. (From this word our English *sickle* is derived.)

Siccative. A synonym for DRYING (q.v.).

Sicilis, R. A sickle.

Sienite. A statuary marble from Syene (Assouan) on the Nile.

Sienna, Terra di Sienna. A brown pigment. (See OCHRES.)

Sigilla, R. (dimin. of *signum*, an image). (1) A seal or signet. (2) Small sculptured or moulded bosses, used to decorate vases or architecture. (3) Small statuettes, called also SIGILLARIA.

Sigillaria, R. (1) The last days of the festival of the Saturnalia, when *sigilla*, or statuettes of gold and silver or terra-cotta, were offered to Saturn, and amongst the people, as presents to each other.

Sigillatus, R. Ornamented or decorated with *sigilla*. (See SIGILLUM.)

Sigla, It. (contraction of *sigilla*). A conventional sign used instead of a word or phrase ; such as = for *equal to*, and + for *plus ;* A.U.C. for *ab urbe conditâ*, &c.

Sigma, R. A semicircular couch, so called because it assumed the form of the Greek Σ, which was originally written like our C. Hence, the seat which ran round the walls of the PIS-CINA in a bath. (See STIBADIUM.)

Signa Militaria. (See ENSIGNS.)

Signature, in printing, is a letter put at the bottom of the first page in every sheet, as a direction to the binder in collating them.

Signets. (See RINGS.)

Signinum (opus), R. A kind of concrete for floorings, invented at *Signia*, and formed of broken tiles consolidated with mortar, and levelled with a pavior's beetle.

Signum, R. A general term for any kind of sign or mark by which anything can be recognized ; such as an image or figure, the intaglio on a ring, the sign of a shop, or a military standard or ensign (*signa militaria*), as represented in Fig. 665.

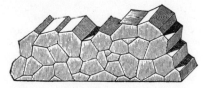

Fig. 613. Wall of Silex.

Silex, R. In general a flint or flint-stone, and thence, by extension, any kind of hard stone hewn into polygonal blocks, as shown in Fig. 613.

Silhouette, Fr. A profile portrait, or representation of the shape contained in the outline of an object, with no attempt to fill in the parts.

Silicernium, Gr. and R.   A funeral feast in honour of the dead.

Silicious Wares.   (See POTTERY.)

Sill or **Cill** of a window or door.   The LIMEN INFERIUS (q.v.).

Fig. 615. Silver tankard of the 16th century.
(Belonging to the Norwich Corporation.)

Silver. The history of working in silver is identical with that of Goldsmiths' work in general. (See GOLD.) *Pollen* remarks that though Phidias and his contemporaries made great statues of gold, many artists who devoted themselves mainly and altogether to working in the precious metals executed their best work in silver. Silver was also largely used for the surfaces of mirrors, which were hung on the walls of temples. The best collection of antique silver plate was found at Hildesheim, in Germany, in 1869, and is now in the Berlin Museum. The silver stoup (Fig. 615) belonging to the Corporation of Norwich, is of the time of Elizabeth. The illustration (Fig. 614) of the silver dish and ewer at St. John's College (1670), is representative of the change that the goldsmiths' style

underwent about the middle of the 17th century, after which time the light and graceful leaf work gave way to heavier designs. (Consult *Pollen, Gold and Silversmiths' Work.*)

Silver. In Christian art, an emblem of purity. (See WHITE.) As one of the two *metals* among the *tinctures* of Heraldry, represented by a white space. (See ARGENT.)

Silver, Cloth of. Josephus tells us that the royal robe of Herod Agrippa was a tunic made of silver. In the Middle Ages it was woven, like gold, in long narrow shreds unmixed with anything else, into a web for garments.

Sima, Arch.   (See CYMA.)

Simikion, Gr. (σιμίκιον). A musical instrument of the Greeks ; it had thirty-five strings.

Simpulum or **Simpuvium,** R.   A small cup used for libations. It was in the form of a ladle with a long handle.

Sinciput. The front part of the head. The back part is the *occiput.*

Sindon (σινδών).   (See CORPORAL.)

Singing-bread, Chr. The larger altar breads used in the mass were called *singing-bread ;* the smaller ones consecrated for the people were known as *houseling-bread.* (See also HOLY BREAD.)

Sinister, Her. The left side of a shield (considered from the back, or wearer's point of view). The *bendlet* or *baton sinister* is generally (not rigorously) regarded in modern Heraldry as the most appropriate *difference* of illegitimacy. (Consult *Boutell's English Heraldry,* p. 194.)

Sinopia. A fine red pigment found upon ancient mural paintings.

Sinum or **Sinus,** R. A vessel of small dimensions, but tolerably wide and deep, which was used for holding wine or milk.

Siparium, R. The curtain of a theatre. It was divided in the middle and withdrawn to the sides to disclose the stage.

Sipho, Gr. (σίφων, a hollow body). A siphon for exhausting liquids from a vessel by the pressure of the atmosphere. A painting at Thebes shows that the principle of the siphon was known to the Egyptians as early as the eighteenth dynasty. The same name was applied to a suction and forcing pump, which was generally employed as a fire-engine.

Sirens (Gr. Σειρῆνες [probably from σειρά, a *chain,* to signify their attractive power]). These mythical representatives of the evil side of the seductive power of music, are represented in art as lovely women to the waist, and fishes or birds below. Sometimes they have wings, which the Muses are said to have plucked (see MUSES) of their feathers ; as Orpheus, by opening their minds to the unattainable higher music, drove them to suicide in the end. In Christian symbolism the sirens typify the three carnal lusts. (See Fig. 455.)

Sirpea. (See SCIRPEA.)

Sispa-sastra, Hind. A Hindoo work, the title of which means literally the science of manual art. It was a kind of encyclopædia, and comprised about thirty treatises on the manual arts, and included a treatise on architecture written by a Hindoo whose name has not come down to us; but a sage or mage called Dupayana compiled, abridged, and edited, about 1500 B.C., the lost treatise of the Hindoo architect. (*Bosc.*)

Sistrum, Egyp. (σεῖστρον; σείω, to shake). A kind of rattle formed by a certain number of metallic rods which passed through a framework also of metal; this was attached to a short handle ending in a head of Athor. By shaking the instrument by the handle the metallic rods and the movable rings suspended from them were made to give out a sharp rattling sound. The Egyptians made use of the sistrum in the ceremonial worship of Isis and at funerals. Roman coins of Hadrian present a personification of Egypt as a female figure seated with the sacred ibis at her feet, and a *sistrum* in her hand. The instrument is still in use on the Nile.

Sitella. Diminutive of SITULA (q.v.).

Situla, R. A bucket for drawing water from a well.

Situlus. Synonym of SITULA (q.v.).

Sixfoil, Her. A flower of six leaves.

Fig. 616.
Sixfoil.

Size is used to prepare paper for printing upon, and as a *vehicle* in oil painting. (See DISTEMPER.)

Skeens, Celtic. Long sharp knives; "*skeen dubh,*" black knife, the Highlander's *dernier ressort.*

Skinning, in Masonry. (See REGRATING.)

Skirophorion. (See SCIROPHORIUM.)

Sling. (See BALEA, FUNDA.)

Slipped, Her. Pulled or torn off.

Smalt. A vitreous substance coloured by cobalt, used for painting on china, not being affected by fire. It makes also a bad pigment in water-colour painting, and is largely used for giving a blue tinge to writing-paper, linen, &c. (See COBALT.)

Smalti, It. Cubes of coloured glass applied in the modern MOSAICS.

Snail, Chr. In Christian iconography the snail is an emblem of sloth and of the resurrection.

Snood (A.S. *snód*). A head-band for ladies, of the Anglo-Saxon period, similar to that now used by young unmarried women in Scotland.

Soapstone. (See STEATITE.)

Socculus. Diminutive of *soccus.*

Soccus, Gr. and R. A slipper worn in Greece both by men and women, but at Rome by women only. It was worn by actors upon the stage.

Socle, Arch. A plain block or plinth forming a low pedestal to a column; or a plinth round the bottom of a wall.

Soffit, Arch. The flat surface on the lower side of an arch or cornice.

Solarium, R. (*sol,* the sun). (1) A sun-dial; (2) a water-clock or clepsydra (*solarium ex aquâ*); (3) a terrace constructed on the top of a house or portico.

Soldurii, Gaul. A body of Gallic warriors forming a CLAN under one chief.

Solea, R. and Chr. (*solum,* sole of the foot). A sandal of the simplest kind, consisting of a sole fastened with straps over the instep. *Solea ferrea,* a horse-shoe, or *soccus* of iron; *solea sparta,* a sock of Spanish broom for the feet of beasts of burden or of cattle; *solea lignea,* wooden clogs fastened to the feet of criminals. Lastly the term denoted a machine for crushing olives, the nature and shape of which are entirely unknown. In Christian archæology, the term *solea* was used to denote, in the early basilicas, a space in front of the choir.

Soler (Lat. *solarium;* A.S. *up-flor*). The upper floor of a house, approached by a *staeger* (Ang. stair) outside.

Soles of the Feet, Egyp. and Chr. On a great number of Christian tombs there occur representations of the soles of the feet. This symbol has been variously explained. In our opinion, one which has never been broached before, it denoted that the dead were in the power of God; for among the Egyptians, whenever a god or powerful king was spoken of, it was said of him that he put his enemies under the sole of his foot. Ezekiel uses the same terms in speaking of Jehovah. Whenever an Egyptian went on a pilgrimage to a distant place, he never left the country without engraving on some stone the impression of his feet, to which he added his name and titles. (*Bosc.*)

Soliferreum or **Solliferreum,** R. A javelin made entirely of massive iron.

Solium, R. This term denotes (1) a chair or arm-chair with a high back; (2) a bier of wood or terra-cotta for a dead body; (3) the granite or marble seat in an ancient bath.

Solstice. The time when the sun appears to *stand still,* at one of the solstitial points, i.e. at his greatest distance from the equator; the summer solstice is the longest day, June 22nd; the winter solstice December 22nd, in the North Hemisphere; reversed in the South.

Sonata, Ital. A piece of music with various movements, composed for a single instrument with or without accompaniment. *Sonate di camera,* sonatas adapted for chamber music; *sonate de chiesa,* for churches.

Sonnachiosi of Bologna. One of the Italian Academies, having for their device a bear, which sleeps through the winter ; and the motto *spero avanzar con la vigilia il sonno.* (I hope by vigils to make up for sleep.)

Sorrows of the Virgin. (See JOYS OF THE VIRGIN.)

Sortes, R. Lots ; small tablets or counters thrown into a SITELLA or urn full of water, and withdrawn for soothsaying.

Soteria, Gr. and R. (σατήρια, i.e. of saving). Sacrifices in honour of the gods offered by way of thanksgiving for escape from any danger.

Sounding-board, Chr. A sort of dome or canopy, placed above pulpits to convey the voice of the preacher to his auditory. In the centre of the lower part of the canopy there is often a carved dove, symbolizing the Holy Ghost. Sounding-boards must be placed five feet above the speaker's head, and their diameter should exceed that of the pulpit by six to eight inches on either side.

Soutane, Fr. A white woollen cassock, worn by priests under the *rochet.*

Sow, Chr. In Christian iconography, the sow is a symbol of evil, impurity, gluttony, and fecundity. It is borne in the crest of Hamilton, Duke of Hamilton, with the motto, " Through."

Span. Of an arch, the breadth between the imposts.

Spandril, Arch. The triangular space between the upper arch of a door and the square mouldings which form a frame to it.

Spangles, of gold and silver, were, in the Middle Ages, artistically shaped concave, and sewed on like tiles, one overlapping the other, producing a rich and pleasing effect. Our present flat spangles are quite modern.

Spanish Black. A pigment of burnt cork.

Spanish Brown. (See OCHRE.)

Spanish Ferreto. A rich reddish-brown pigment.

Spanish Red. An ochreous red pigment, yellower than the *Venetian red.*

Spanish Stitch. A kind of embroidery introduced into England by Katharine of Aragon in 1501.

Span-roof, Arch. Having *two* inclined sides ; not a *pent-roof.*

Spartea. (See SOLEA.)

Sparum, R. A weapon specially employed by the agricultural population, whence its name of *sparum agreste, telum rusticum.* It was a kind of halberd. A form *sparus* was also in use.

Spatha, Gr. and R. (σπάθη). (1) A *batten* or wooden blade used by weavers for beating the threads of the woof. (2) The spatula of a druggist or chemist. (3) A long, broad, two-edged sword, with a sharp point.

Spathalium, Gr. and R. (σπαθάλιο:). A kind of bracelet with bells attached, so that it bore some resemblance to the flower-sheath of the palm-tree (*spatha*), whence its name.

Speak-house, O. E. A parlour.

Spean, Hind. A monumental bridge, of no great height, among the Khmers or ancient inhabitants of Cambodgia. The balustrade of this bridge was formed by means of NAGAGAS (q.v.).

Spear, Her., is seldom seen in blazon, though it appears as a "punning device" in the arms granted to Shakspeare's father. (See LANCE, CUSPIS, &c.)

Specillum, R. A surgeon's probe, of iron, bronze, or silver.

Spectra. Impressions which remain for a time on the retina of the eye, after looking at certain bright and coloured objects. They are either similar in colour and form to the objects which excited them, or vary according to the laws of the spectrum ; e.g. if the eye is fixed on a *red* wafer, lying on a sheet of *white* paper, it will appear fringed with a faint *green;* then if, after a time, the eye is turned to another part of the paper, where there is no wafer, a *green* wafer will appear.

Spectrum. The series of colours that a beam of white light slips into under refraction : — red, orange, yellow, green, blue, indigo, and violet.

Specula, R. A watch-tower.

Specularia, Gr. and R. Window-panes made with a kind of transparent stone (*lapis specularis*).

Speculum, R. (*specio,* to behold). A mirror ; they were made in ancient times of a white composition of copper and tin, and afterwards of silver. The back of the mirror was decorated with beautiful engraved or enchased designs. There were also glass mirrors backed with a thin leaf of metal. Mirrors were not contrived to be hung against a wall, or to stand on a table, but were generally held by female slaves in front of their mistresses. (See MIRRORS.)

Specus, R. Originally a dark grotto or cave ; later the covered canal of an aqueduct.

Spence, O. E. The buttery attached to the hall ; 13th, 14th century.

Speos, Egyp. (σπέος). HYPOGEA or subterranean Egyptian temples. *Hemispeos* was the name given to temples built partly above and partly under the ground.

Sperlings, O. E. Sprats.

Sperthe, O. E. A battle-axe.

Spetum, Med. A kind of PARTISAN, but narrower and lighter.

Sphæristerium, Gr. and R. (σφαιριστήριον, lit. place for ball). An apartment attached to a gymnasium or set of baths for playing with balls.

Sphæromachia, Gr. and R. (σφαιρο-μαχία). A game of ball.

Sphendone, Gr. A band or fillet with which Greek ladies confined their hair. (See DIADEMA, HAIR, &c.)

Fig. 617. Andro-Sphinx.

Sphinx, Egyp.(Σφίγξ). An emblem peculiarly Egyptian, signifying the religious mystery; in this sense it was adopted by the Romans and placed in the pronaos of their temples. The ANDRO-SPHINX (Fig. 617), a human head upon a lion's body, typified generally the union of in-

Fig 618. Crio-Sphinx.

tellectual and physical power; the CRIO-SPHINX (Fig. 618) had the head of a ram; and the

Fig. 619. Hieraco-Sphinx.

HIERACO-SPHINX (Fig. 619) that of a hawk. The two latter are complex emblems; the hawk being the sun-god's and the king's special figure, and the ram that of the god Neph. The sym-

bolical importance of these figures was completely disregarded in the course of their application to the purposes of Greek art.

Sphyrelata, Gr. Hammered metal-work; the earliest form of art manufacture in metal. Archaic statues, antecedent to the invention of the art of casting, were formed of hammered plates fastened together with rivets. (See METALLURGY.)

Spicæ Testaceæ, R. (*spica*, ear of corn). Oblong bricks for pavements; applied in the Spicatum Opus.

Spicatum (opus), R. A term answering to our HERRING-BONE work; it was a kind of

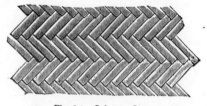

Fig. 620. Spicatum Opus.

construction in which the stones were arranged so as to resemble the setting of the grains in an ear of corn. (Fig. 620.)

Fig. 621. Spiculum.

Spiculum, R. (dimin. of *spicum*, a point). The barbed iron head of an arrow or lance. The custom of barbing weapons dates from a very early period, since it is met with in prehistoric times. Fig. 621 shows a barbed bone arrow.

Spider-work (*opus araneum*). A kind of embroidery; specimens of the 13th and 14th centuries are in South Kensington Museum.

Spike. *Oil of spike* used in wax painting is prepared from the wild lavender.

Spina, R. (lit. a spine). A long, low wall along the middle of a circus, marking off the course in a race. At each end were the goals, (*metæ*). (See CIRCUS, META.)

Spinet (Ital. *spinetta*). An old-fashioned musical instrument on the principle of the *harpsichord* and pianoforte. Brass and steel wires were struck by quills fixed to the tongues of jacks which were moved by the keys of a finger-board. (Fig. 622.)

Spinther, R. (σφιγκτήρ). A bracelet; it was worn upon the left arm, and retained in its place merely by the elasticity of the material.

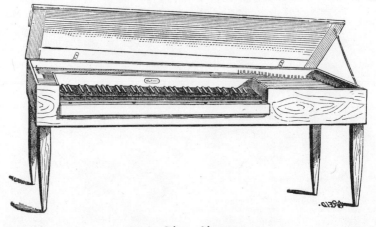

Fig. 622. Spinet. 18th century.

The term is really a corruption of *sphincter*, the muscle which remains naturally contracted. (See ARMILLA.)

Fig. 623. Carved ivory Spoon with figure of "January."

Spira, R. (σπεῖρα). Anything spiral or coiled; such as (1) a coil of rope; (2) an ornament worn by women on the head; (3) the string by which the cap of the Salian priests was fastened under the chin; (4) the base of a column.

Spire, Arch. An acutely-pointed termination crowning a steeple. (See CHAMFER.)

Spirit Fresco. A new method of painting in *fresco*, introduced by Mr. Gambier Parry, 1880.

Spirits of Wine are used to dissolve resins in the preparation of varnishes.

Spirula. Diminutive of *spira*.

Spittle or **Spittle-house**, O. E. A hospital.

Spolarium, R. (*spolio*, to strip off). A cloak-room in the baths, where the bathers left their clothes; in an amphitheatre or circus the term was applied to a cella in which gladiators who had been killed in the arena were stripped of their clothes and weapons.

Spolia, R. Booty taken in war. PRÆDA means plunder generally; MANUBIUM, the share of the commander or the state; EXUVIÆ, the personal spoils of an enemy; and SPOLIA, properly speaking, arms or implements of war. (See OPIMA SPOLIA.)

Fig. 624. Folding Spoon of carved box-wood.

Spoon, Chr. In early times, especially among the Greeks, Syrians, and Copts, the sacrament in one kind only was administered with a small gold or silver spoon, into which a few drops of the consecrated wine were poured. In the Middle Ages spoons were frequently ornamented with figures, some carved in ivory or wood, and others of metal. APOSTLE SPOONS had figures of the Apostles on the handles. (See LABIS and COCHLEAR.)

Sporta, R. A broad plaited basket made of wood and usually furnished with two handles. Diminutives of this term are *sportella* and *sportula*.

Springers, Arch. The lowest stones of an arch resting on a column, pilaster, or cluster of small colums.

Spurs with rowels appear first in the 13th century; in early times and in antiquity they were merely sharp goads fixed to the heel. In the middle of the 15th century spurs were of extravagant length. In Heraldry, the *knightly spur* had a single point, up to about 1320, and was known as the "pryck-spur;" the later form is called the "rouelle-spur."

Spurn, O. E. A piece of stone or wood protecting a corner house or gate-post from wheels. One end is fixed in the ground, and the other attached at an angle to the post or wall.

Squinch, Arch. Small arches built across angles of towers to support projecting masonry above.

Stadium, Gr. (στάδιον). The course for the foot-race at Olympia, which measured exactly one stadium (606¾ feet). The stadium was the principal Greek measure for distance, and equalled the eighth of a Roman mile.

Stag (*cervus*). Representations of the stag occur in many Christian bas-reliefs and paintings. It is the emblem of many dissimilar moral ideas, but more especially of a longing desire for baptism, from an application of the text in the 42nd Psalm, "Like as the hart," &c. (See HART.)

Stalactite (Gr. στάλαγμα, an icicle). Spar, in the form of icicles hanging from the roof of a cavern. **Stalagmites** are heaped up from their droppings on the floor, forming when they unite with the Stalactites the so-called Organ-pipes.

Stalagmium, Gr. and R. (σταλάγμιον). An ear-ring decorated with pearls, or small gold or silver drops, which bore more or less resemblance to the shape of a drop of water (στάλαγμα), whence its name.

Stall-plate, Her. The plate bearing the arms of a knight, and placed in his stall in the chapel of his order.

Stalls, Chr. Seats in a chapel ; made to be used in two ways : either with the flap of the seat let down called "sellette," which formed the regular seat, or with the flap raised, affording only a small resting-place called *miserere*. The elbows are often called "museaux" from their being in many cases ornamented with the head of some animal. (See MISERERE.)

Stamen, R. The spun thread as it comes off the spindle.

Stamnos, Gr. and R. A vessel in the shape

of a Panathenæan water-jar or amphora, but with a wider neck, and with two ears and no handle.

Stanchion, Arch. The upright iron bar between the mullions of a window.

Standard or **Banner,** Chr. The symbol of victory over sin, death, and idolatry. (See ENSIGNS, LABARUM, SIGNA, &c.) In heraldry, a long narrow flag introduced in the 14th century. The ROYAL STANDARD bears the blazonry of the Queen's arms. The UNION JACK was produced in the reign of James I., in 1606, as the national flag of united England and Scotland, combining the banners of St. George and St. Andrew. The latest UNION JACK shows, over the saltire of St. Andrew, the *gules* of St. Patrick, and was introduced upon the occasion of the *union* with Ireland. The word "Jack" is a corruption of the French "Jacques," for James.

Standing Stones. Celtic monuments, also called *megalithic*, consisting of a row of stones standing in a line. (See DOLMEN, MENHIR, MEGALITHIC, &c.)

Standish, O. E. A case for pens and ink; an inkstand.

Stanniferous Wares. (See POTTERY.)

Stapes, Stapia, Med. Lat. A stirrup.

Fig. 625. Badge of the Star of India.

Star of India. An order of knighthood instituted by Queen Victoria in 1861. The INSIGNIA are the *Badge* (Fig. 171); *collar* of heraldic roses and lotus - flowers alternating with palm-branches, a crown being in the centre ; *ribbon* of pale blue with white borders, crossing the left shoulder; and *star* of diamonds, having a mullet upon an irradiated field in its centre, with the motto "Heaven's Light our Guide."

Stars, Her. (See ESTOILE, MULLET.)

Stars, Chr. Emblematic of the canopy of Heaven, are generally represented on the domed ceilings of churches. These were usually forged in metal and fixed on to an azure ground. They are attributes of the Virgin Mary as queen of heaven, and of St. Dominic and other saints.

Stars, Star-moulding, Arch. An ornament of the Romano-Byzantine period, in the shape of a star with four rays only. (Fig. 627.) It is met with as a decoration in various mouldings.

Mullet.   Estoile.
Fig. 626. Heraldic Stars.

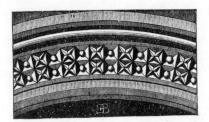

Fig. 627.   Star-moulding.

Fig. 628. Statera.

Statera, R. A steelyard or Roman balance, of much later invention than the scales called *libra*. It consisted (Fig. 628) of a rod or yard (*scapa*), divided by equidistant points (*puncta*), and was suspended by means of a handle (*ansa*) consisting of a hook or chain. The weight (*æquipondium*) forms a counterpoise to any object suspended from one of the hooks or the scale (*lancula*). (Fig. 418.) The term is sometimes looked upon as a synonym of LIBRA (q.v.). It denotes besides (1) a wooden bar or yoke placed across the withers of a pair of horses harnessed to a BIJUGUS (q.v.); (2) a plate or dish, probably of circular form.

Statuettes. Small statues in bronze or porcelain for the decoration of rooms. For **Porcelain Statuary,** consult Jacquemart's *History of the Ceramic Art.*

Stauracin (Gr. σταυρὸς, a cross) was a silken stuff figured with small plain *crosses;* hence *polystauron,* having many crosses.

Steatite or **Soapstone.** A soft, unctuous, magnesian mineral, used by the Chinese for statuary and decorative purposes.

Steel, Engraving in, was invented during the present century. The process is nearly the same as engraving in copper. (See CHALCOGRAPHY.)

Stega, Gr. and R. (στέγη, i.e. a covering). The deck of a ship; a synonym for CONSTRATUM (q.v.).

Steganography, Gr. (στεγανὸς, secret). Cypher, or secret writing, by substitution of signs for letters.

Steinkerque was a twisted necktie, and owed its origin to the battle of that name fought in 1692 by Marshal Luxembourg against William of Orange. When the French princes were suddenly ordered into action, hastily tying their cravats—in peaceful times an elaborate proceeding—they rushed to the charge and gained the day.

Fig. 629. Steinkerque.

In honour of this event ladies also wore their lace neckerchiefs twisted in this careless fashion. Steinkerques became the rage, and were worn in England and France by men and women for many years afterwards. The engraving represents the Grand Dauphin of France wearing a Steinkerque.

Stela, Stelè, Gr. A pillar, or stone of a cylindrical or quadrangular shape, often surmounted by an ornament in the form of a palm. These *stelæ* served to mark out burial-places. Fig. 631 represents a Roman, and Fig. 630 a Greek stelê.

Fig. 630. Greek Stelè.

Stemma, Gr. and R. (στέμμα, i. e. that which crowns). Among the Greeks this term served to denote a wreath bound round with woollen fillets; among the Romans the same term denoted a long roll of parchment ornamented with garlands. This roll contained the genealogy of the family. *Stemmata* were hung upon the busts of ancestors, and in front of the *imagines majorum.*

Fig. 631. Roman Stela.

Stencil. A plate of any material in which patterns have been cut out. The use of stencil plates is of great antiquity. They were used in the schools of ancient Rome to teach writing, and by the emperors for affixing their sign manual to documents.

Stereobate. The base of a plain wall, (See STYLOBATES.

Stereochromy. A new method of wall-painting, with water colours sprinkled over with fluoric acid, adapted permanently to resist all the influences of climate.

Stereo-graphy (στερεὸs, solid). Geometrical drawing of solids on a plane surface.

Stereoscope. A binocular glass, arranged in conformity with the natural convergence of the sight of each eye to a focal centre. An object is photographed twice, as it would appear to each eye if the other were closed ; and when the two pictures are looked at together in the stereoscope, an effect of rounded solidity

(*stereon*) is produced. The effect is particularly beautiful in photographs of statues.

Stereotype. Solid type, obtained from a cast of the forme of movable type, for permanent use in printing works of which many editions are required.

Steyre, O. E. A stair.

Stiacciato, Ital. Sculpture in very low relief, less than *basso-relievo.*

Stibadium, Gr. and R. (στιβάδιον). A circular dining-couch generally made of wicker-work. Another name for it was SIGMA.

Sticharium, Chr. (στιχάριον). A white tunic worn by the Greek bishops and deacons in certain ceremonies.

Stigma, R. (στίγμα, lit. a mark by pricking). A mark, impression, or brand. Thieves were branded with the letter F, which stood for *fur*, thief. A *stigma* tattooed on the arm was the mark by which conscripts were declared capable of military service, &c., hence

Stigmata, Chr. The marks of the five sacred wounds on the hands, feet, and side of Our Lord ; said to have been miraculously printed on the persons of saints.

Stil-de-grain. (See PINKS.)

Still Life. Inanimate objects.

Stilted Arch. One having the capital or impost mouldings of the jambs below the level of the springing of the curve, the moulding of the arch being continued vertically down to the impost mouldings.

Stilus, Stylus, R. A style, or instrument of bone, ivory, iron, bronze, or silver, about five inches long, having one end pointed, and the other flattened like a spatula ; the latter served either to spread the wax on the writing-tablet, or to erase by smoothing down what had been written upon it ; the other and pointed end served for writing upon the wax-covered tablet. The term also denoted (1) the needle or index of a sun-dial ; (2) a bronze needle ; (3) a probe employed for garden purposes. (4) A sharp stake in a pitfall. It was also called *graphium.*

Stimulus, R. (στίζω, to prick). A goad for driving cattle.

Stipple. Etched imitations of chalk drawings of the human figure, called *engravings in stipple*, have a very soft effect, but are inferior to engraving. In this variety the whole subject is executed in dots without strokes on the etching-ground, and these dots are bitten in with aqua-fortis. The dots may be harmonized with a little hammer, in which case the work is called *opus mallei.* In the method known as *mezzo-tinto*, a dark *barb* or ground is raised uniformly by means of a toothed tool ; and the design being traced, the light parts are scraped off from the plate by fitting instruments, according to the effect required. (See ENGRAVING.)

Stips, R. A small bronze coin, equal to the

X

twelfth part of an *as*, or about a quarter of a farthing ; it bore on the reverse the prow of a vessel.

Fig. 632. Stola. Costume of a Roman Matron.

Stocheion, Gr. A form of sun-dial. (See HOROLOGIUM.)

Stockings were introduced into England with knitting in 1501, when Queen Elizabeth was presented with a pair of black knit silk stockings by her tirewoman, and immediately discontinued the cloth hose she had previously worn. The Scotch claim the invention of knitting, and a French company of stocking-knitters established at Paris in 1527 took for their patron St. Fiacre, who is said to have been the son of a King of Scotland. (See NETHERSTOCKS.)

Stola, R. (στολή, lit. an equipment). The robe worn by Roman matrons; it consisted of a wide tunic with long sleeves. It came down to the ankles or feet, and was confined at the waist by a girdle, leaving broad loose folds over the breast. The pallium was worn over the *stola*. It was the distinguishing dress of the Roman matron, and the *meretrices* or divorced women were forbidden to wear it. The *stola* was also worn by a certain class of priests. (See PALLIUM, TOGA.)   (See Fig. 632.)

Stole, Chr. This term, a synonym of *orarium*, denoted, with the early Christians, according to Fleury, a piece of fine linen which was worn round the neck. It was used as a kind of pocket-handkerchief, long before the introduction of Christianity, by the Romans, who named it indifferently *linteolum*, *strophium*, and *sudarium*. In the Christian Church it is represented by a narrow band of embroidered stuff, and worn over the left shoulder by deacons ; and across both shoulders by bishops and priests. It is sacred to the memory of the cloth with which the Saviour is alleged to have wiped away the sweat from His face as He passed to the Crucifixion. (See SUDARIUM, ORARIUM.)

Fig. 633. Stole.

Stone Ochre. A pigment. An earthy oxide of iron. (See OCHRES.)

Stone-ware. (See POTTERY.)

Stopping-out. In etching, arresting the action of the acid on the fainter lines of a plate, by covering them over with a preparation called *stopping ground*, while the deeper and broader parts corrode. (See ETCHING.)

Stoup, Chr. A small niche with a basin, at the entrance of a church, placed there for the holy water. O.E. A kind of tankard. (See Fig. 615.)

Stragulatæ. Striped or barred silks ; 13th century.

Stragulum, R. (*sterno*, to throw over). A general term to denote any kind of covering used for bed-clothing, or a covering for men, horses, or beasts of burden, and thence a caparison.

Fig. 634. Strasburg Porcelain.   Open-work Basket.

Strap-work, Arch.   A form of architectural ornament, by the tracery of a narrow band or fillet in convolutions similar to those that a leather strap thrown down at hazard would form. It is characteristic of the Renaissance period.

Strasburg Porcelain.   The manufacture of this ware, which was begun by Charles Hannong about 1721, became very celebrated for about sixty years.   (Consult Jacquemart's *History of the Ceramic Art.*)   (Fig. 634.)

Strasburg Turpentine.   A varnish made of the resin from the silver fir (*pinus picea*), diluted with naphtha, drying linseed, or nut oil.

Strena, R.   A new year's gift or present made on the calends of January.

Stria, R.   The fluting of a column.

Striated.   Fluted like a column.

Strigilis, R. (*stringo*, to scrape).   A bronze scraper for the skin, curved and hollowed like a spoon, used in the bath.   The same term is used in architecture for a fluting which resembles the bath-strigil in form.

String-course, Arch.   A narrow moulding projecting from the wall of a building in a horizontal line.

Stroma, Gr. (στρῶμα).   A Greek term synonymous with the Latin STRAGULUM.

Strontian Yellow.   A pale canary-coloured pigment.

Strophe (στρέφω, to turn).   In Greek poetry, the first division of a choral ode, of which the other parts were the *antistrophe* and the *epode*.

Strophium, R. (στρόφιον, lit. a thing twisted). (1) A long scarf which the Roman women rolled into a band, and fastened round the body and breast.   (2) A girdle for the same purpose, generally of leather.   (3) The term likewise denoted the cable of an anchor.   (See ORARIUM.)

Structura, R. (*struo*, to build up).   A

general term for any kind of masonry.   (See OPUS.)

Struppus or **Strupus,** R.   A rope or other fastening by which the oar is attached to the thole (*scalmus*).

Stucco, It.   A fine plaster, for covering walls, prepared by various methods, as a mixture of *gypsum* and glue; or white marble, pulverized with plaster of lime and mixed with water; the *opus albarium* of the ancients.

Stump, for drawing in pencil or crayon.   It is a thick roll of strong paper made into a kind of pencil, and used for rubbing over lines to soften them down for ground tints, gradation of shading, &c.

Stylites, Chr. (στυλίτης). "Pillar saints." Anchorites of the early Church who passed their lives on the top of a column, in order to give themselves up to meditation.   There were some of them in Syria down to the 12th century.   They derived their name from στῦλος, a column.

Fig 635. Stylobates.   Fig. 636. Stylobates.

Stylobate, Arch.   A pedestal supporting a row of columns; Figs. 635 to 637 represent three richly-decorated stylobates found in the baths and other Roman ruins at Nismes. (See PEDESTAL, STEREOBATE.)

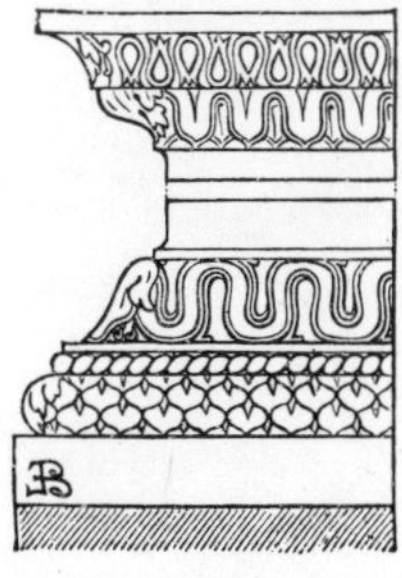

Fig. 637. Stylobates.

Stylus, R. (Gr. στῦλος). A pointed instrument with which the Romans wrote on their waxed tablets. (See STILUS.)

Subarmale, Subermale, R.   A garment worn by soldiers underneath their ar-

X 2

mour ; it formed the tunic of the legionaries, and representations of it are very frequently met with on the bas-reliefs of monumental columns and triumphal arches.

Subjugium, R. Curved pieces of wood placed at each end of a yoke, *underneath* it ; whence their name.

Sublicius, R. (*sublica*, a pile). Any wooden structure supported on piles. (See Pons.)

Subligaculum, **Subligar**, R. (*subligo*, to tie below). A cloth worn by acrobats, drawn between the legs and made fast to the girdle.

Subsecus, R. A tenon, in carpentry ; that is, the tongue or wedge which fits into a mortise.

Subsellium, R. (i. e. lower than a *sella*). A movable bench without a back, which was used in large assemblies. In a theatre or circus the same term was applied to the circular rows of seats in the *cavea*.

Subsericum. Partly, not all, silk ; opposed to *holosericum*.

Substructio, R. (*substruo*, to build underneath). Any work of solid masonry, such as a foundation wall, abutment walls, &c. (See Suspensura.)

Subtrefoiled, Arch. Decorated with foils placed underneath ; a term applied to what are called *trefoil-headed* arches.

Subucula, R. (*sub*, and *duo*, to put on). Under-garments of wool which the Romans wore next the skin, underneath the tunic.

Suburbanum, R. A villa in the suburbs of Rome.

Succinctus, R. (*succingo*, to gird beneath). Wearing a girdle round the waist above the tunic ; applied to a person prepared for active exertion.

Sucula, R. A capstan.

Sudarium, Chr. A name of the miraculous portrait of our Lord, impressed on the cloth presented to Him by St. Veronica on the way to the Crucifixion. (See Stole, Vera Icon.) A representation of this legendary portrait is given in Albert Dürer's "Little Passion."

Sudatorium, R. (*sudor*, sweat). The hot room in a Roman bath. (See Caldarium.)

Sud'ha, Hind. A temple of the Khmers or ancient inhabitants of Cambodgia, built of one unmixed material, and thence called *pure* (*sud'ha*).

Suffibulum, R. A large square piece of white cloth worn by vestals and priests during the discharge of their functions.

Suggestus, R. (*sub* and *gero*, to heap up). (1) A stage or platform from which an orator addressed a crowd. The Rostra at Rome was a celebrated *suggestus*. (2) In a camp the *suggestus* was formed of stones and clods of turf, or constructed of woodwork, from which the general harangued the troops. (3) The raised seat from which the Emperor saw the games.

Suile, R. A stable for pigs ; among the Romans a building of considerable size, containing a number of separate sties (*haræ*).

Fig. 638. Suggestus.

Sulphate of Barytes. (See Barytes.)

Sulphate of Zinc, or white vitrol, is used as a *dryer*.

Sulphurs. Impressions taken by the goldsmiths of the 16th century from the engravings executed on plates, paxes, &c. ; and which they obtained by spreading a layer of melted sulphur on the face of the plate, producing a cast in *relief* of the lines engraved. Some few of these proofs exist in the British and continental museums, and are known as "sulphurs." They are amongst the rarest specimens connected with the art of engraving. (*Fairholt*.)

Fig. 639. Device of Louis XIV.

Sun, Her. When represented shining and surrounded by rays, he has a representation of a human face on his disc, and is blazoned "In splendour," or "In glory ;" when "eclipsed" the representation is the same, but tinctured sable.

Sundials. The sundial of Ahaz is mentioned by Isaiah, 713 B.C. Sundials with appropriate mottoes have been at all times fashionable. Mrs. Palliser gives a long selection of such mottoes : e.g. :—

Nulla hora sine linea, "No hour without a line." (Nec momentum sine linea, was Cardinal Richelieu's motto.) Pereunt et imputantur—"They pass and are imputed "— (*Martial*). *Of the passing hour*, Dubia omnibus, ultima multis—("Uncertain to all, the last to many "); or, suprema hæc multis forsitan tibi—(' The last to many, perhaps to thee "). The old sundial at the Palais de Justice in Paris is inscribed, in letters of gold, Sacra Themis mores, ut pendula dirigit horas—(" Holy Justice guides manners, as this dial does the hours). The largest number are *allusions to Death*, as :

Io vado e vengo ogni giorno. Ma tu andrai senza ritorno—("I go and come daily, but thou shalt go and never return.") And on a sundial at Bourges is the following :

"La vie est comme l'hombre,
Insensible en son cours.
On la croit immobile :
Elle s'avance toujours."

More cheerful mottoes are found from Horace, as : Carpe diem. Horas non numero nisi serenas (at Venice), &c.

(Consult *Mrs. Alfred Gatty, "Book of Sundials."*)

Super-altar, Chr. A small portable altar.
Superaria. (See EPENDYTES.)
Supercilium, R. (lit. eye-brow). (See LIMEN SUPERIUS.)
Superindum. (See EPENDYTES.)
Superpellicum, Chr. A surplice.
Suppedaneum. A synonym for SCABELLUM and SCAMNUM (q.v.).
Supplicatio, R. (*supplico*, to kneel down).

The act of praying when kneeling ; opposed to *precatio*, a prayer uttered standing. Solemn thanksgivings offered to the gods in their temples.

Supporter, Her. A figure that stands by a shield of arms, as if supporting or guarding it. Supporters came into use during the 14th century. (See Fig. 24.)

Surahé, Pers. A Persian wine-bottle. The illustration represents a beautiful specimen of hard porcelain decorated in patterns, of Chinese character, executed under the glaze with cobalt. A legend on the medallions contains the words *Deh surahé,* "Give me the bottle." (Fig. 640.)

Surbase, Arch. The shaft of a PEDESTAL.

Surcoat. Any garment worn over armour ; more especially the long flowing garment worn by knights until 1325. (See Fig. 463.)

Surface-rib, Arch. The rib of a groined vaulting.

Surinda, Hind. A stringed instrument played with a bow.

Surod, Hind. A kind of guitar, sounded with a plectrum.

Surplice. Chr. The Protestant *alb.* See *Stevens,* in a note to *All's Well that Ends Well,* Act i., scene 3, for notices of the Puritan aversion to this article of clerical costume.

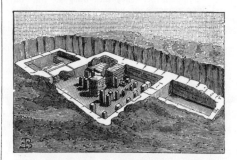

Fig. 641. Suspensura, showing the pillars supporting the floor of a bath-room.

Suspensura, R. In a general sense this term denotes anything that is supported, *suspended* above arcades, columns, or pillars, and more especially the flooring of a bath-room, when it is supported by small low pillars. Fig. 391 shows the flooring of a bath-room, and Fig. 641 the pillars supporting the suspensura. See HYPOCAUST.)

Svastika, Hind. A kind of Greek cross, each branch of which ends in a hook. This cross has a sacred character, and is met with on a great variety of objects. Its origin dates back to the bronze age, and it is represented on the weapons of that period. (See FYLFOT.)

Fig. 640. Surahé or Wine bottle. Persian Porcelain.

Swallow. In Christian symbolism, the emblem of pride and of conversion.

Swallow-tail. (See DOVE-TAIL.)

Swan, Her. When blazoned "proper"— white with red beak and legs—it is the badge of the Bohuns, Staffords, and some other families.

Swathbondes, O. E. Swaddling clothes (mentioned by Shakspeare).

Swine's Feather, O. E. A kind of bayonet about six inches long, affixed to a musket-rest and projected by the action of a spring; 17th century.

Sword. (See GLADIUS.)

Sword, in Christian art, is a symbol of martyrdom; it is also the attribute of martyrs who were soldiers. In Heraldry, when borne as a charge, it is straight in the blade, pointed, and with a cross-guard. The custom of swearing on the sword, the hilt of which took the shape of a cross, or had crosses engraved on it, is mentioned in very ancient history. (Cf. *Hamlet.*)

Sympathetic Inks. Inks of which the marks are invisible until the moisture is absorbed by the application of heat. (See COBALT.)

Symposium, Gr. A drinking-party, distinguished from *deipnon*, a feast. A very common subject of representations on ancient vases.

Syndon or **Sindon.** A better kind of *cendal* (q.v.).

Synoikia, Gr. (1) Athenian festivals held in honour of Athena in the month Hecatombeion (July—August). Their object was to commemorate the union of the government of all the towns of Attica in Athens. (2) A lodging-house adapted to hold several families (Latin, *insula*), for the convenience of foreigners and others who by Athenian law were prohibited from acquiring house property of their own.

Synthesis or **Synthesina,** Gr. and R. (σύν-θεσις). One of the *vestes cœnatoriæ* which the master of the house, the Amphitryon, provided for his guests. The parable of the "Wedding Garment" has reference to this practice. It was a kind of tunic worn over the other garments, and during the Saturnalia by all classes alike. It was usually dyed some colour, and was *not* white like the toga.

Sypirs, O. E. Cloth of Cyprus.

Syrinx (O. E. 9th and 10th cent.). An instrument resembling Pandean pipes.

Syrinx, Gr. and R. (σῦριγξ). The pastoral pipe invented by Pan; it was called by the poets *arundo* and *fistula*. It was formed of seven hollow reeds of regulated lengths adjusted to form an octave.

Syrma, Gr. (σύρω, to sweep). A robe with a train worn on the stage by those actors who had to represent the parts of gods or heroes. Hence the word is poetically used for tragedy.

Systyle, Gr. and R. (σύστυλος). An arrangement in architecture, the intercolumniation of which is of the width of two diameters of the shaft, measured at its lower part, just above the *apophyge;* the distance between the *plinths* being exactly equal to the diameter of the plinths, as in the Parthenon at Athens.

T.

Fig. 642. Tabard.

Tabard, O. E. (Lat. *colobium*). A tunic with sleeves, worn over the armour by knights of the Tudor period, and blazoned on the sleeves, front, and back; it is the official costume of a herald; Chaucer's ploughman wears a *tabard*, like the modern smock - frock. (See COAT-ARMOUR.) Fig. 642.

Tabaret. A stout, satin-striped silk.

Tabbinet, O. E. Another name for POPLIN.

Tabby, O. E. A silk *watered* or figured.

Tabella, Gen. (dimin. of *tabula*). A small board, or tablet, of any kind, esp. (1) a wax-tablet; (2) a voting-tablet (*tessera*); (3) a letter sent by a messenger (*tabellarius*); (4) *tabella absolutoria*, a receipt for a debt; (5) *tabella damnatoria*, a judicial record of a verdict and sentence; (6) *tabella liminis*, the leaf of a door, &c.

Taberna, R. (1) A retail shop; Fig. 643 shows a shop at Pompeii, restored. (2) *Taberna deversoria, taberna meritoria*, or simply *taberna*, a wine-shop or *tavern*. (Fig. 643.)

Tabernacle Work, Arch. The ornamented open work over the *stalls* (of a cathedral church, &c.), and, in general, any minute ornamental open-work is called *tabernacle work*.

Tabernaculum, Tabernacle, R. and Chr.

Fig. 643. Taberna.

(Lit. a tent). (1) A booth of planks, or a wooden hut covered with hides. (2) In Christian archæology, the *tabernacle* is a small shrine placed on the altar for the consecrated wafer. It succeeded the *pyx*, which was anciently deposited in one of two chambers arranged on each side of the altar. Originally of goldsmith's work, in the 15th and 16th centuries they became stone shrines decorated with sculpture, approached by steps, rising into lanterns and pinnacles to the roof of the church. A cast of a beautiful tabernacle of late 15th century, marble with a gilt metal door, is in the South Kensington Museum. Tabernacles of ivory were common in the 16th century. (3) Ornamental niches in a hall. (4) Accurately applied the term signifies a *canopy*, (of stone, wood, or other material) such as was placed over a NICHE, a stall, &c.

Tabernula. Dimin. of TABERNA (q.v.).

Tabinet. (See TABBINET.)

Tabl shamee, Egyp. The Syrian drum, used by the modern Egyptians; a kind of kettledrum of tinned copper, with a parchment face.

Tablature, Fr. One part of a painted wall or ceiling, forming a single piece or design.

Table, O. E. The ancient meaning of this word was "any level expanded surface," such as a flat piece of board. A picture was called a table (Latin *tabula*) as late as the 17th century. (See TABULA.)

Table-base, Arch. A BASE-MOULDING, near the ground, immediately over the plinth.

Table Diamond. A gem cut with a flat surface.

Tablementum, Arch. Synonym of TABULA.

Tables, O. E. (1) Backgammon. (2) Ivory writing-tablets, so called, were used in the middle ages in England by people of all ranks :—

"His felaw had a staff tipped with horn,
A pair of *tables* all of ivory,
And a pointed ypolished fetishly,
And wrote alway the names, as he stood
Of alle folk that gaue hem any good."
    (*Chaucer.*)

Tablet. (Fr. *tablette.*) Any flat surface for inscriptions; leaves for memoranda.

Tablets. In architecture a general term for small projecting mouldings or strings, mostly horizontal. The tablet at the top, under the battlement, is called a *cornice*, and that at the bottom a *basement*, under which is generally a thicker wall. The tablet running round doors and windows is called a *dripstone*, and if ornamented a *canopy*. (*Rickman*, p. 42.)

Tabletterie, Fr. Turned work in ivory or shells, &c.

Tablinum, R. One of the apartments in a Roman house; it was a recess in the ATRIUM, and contained the wax or ivory portraits and statues in bronze and marble of ancestors, and carved representations of their honourable achievements in the state, and the family archives. (See DOMUS.)

Tabor, Tabour, O. E. A very loud drum "which is bad for people's heads, for, if stretched tight and struck hard, it may be heard at half a league's distance."

Tabouret. An embroidery frame.

Tabret, Heb. A small *tabor*.

Tabula, R. and Chr. (1) Literally, a *plank*, and thence used to denote a variety of objects made of wood or planks, as for instance a bench; a dice-table; a waxed writing-tablet (*tabula cerata*); a panel-painting; a votive-tablet; a voting-ticket. (2) Arch. Properly any solid construction adapted for superficial decoration, as the *frontal* of an altar. "The most remarkable example of the *tabula* destined for the front of the Altar, is preserved in Westminster Abbey; it is formed of wood, elaborately carved, painted and enriched with a kind of mosaic work of coloured glass, superficially inlaid, a species of decoration of Italian origin." (Consult *Parker's Glossary* s.v.) (3) In Christian archæology, *tabulæ nuptiales* or *dotales* was the name given to the parchment scrolls in the hands of persons who figure in the marriage scenes represented on tombs.

Tabularium, R. A place set apart in the temples at Rome where the public records were kept.

Tace, Chr. The cross or crutch of St. Anthony.

Taces. (See TASSETS.) The *skirts* or *coverings* to the pockets. (*Meyrick*.)

Taces. Overlapping plates of armour to envelope the abdomen (see TACHES), introduced in the 14th century, under Richard II.

Tack or **Dag, O. E.** A kind of pistol : something like a *petronel*.

Tæda or **Teda, R.** A resinous torch made with pieces and slips of the pine called *teda*.

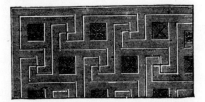

Fig. 644. Tænia.

Tænia, Gr. and R. (1) The ribbon with which a wreath or fillet round the head was attached. (2) In architecture, the band which separates the Doric frieze from the architrave ; it is, in many cases, ornamented with painting similar to that shown in Fig. 644.

Taffeta (Pers. *taftah*, from *taftan*, to twist). A thin, glossy silken fabric, having a wavy lustre ; a less costly silk than CENDAL (q.v.), 16th century. *Stow* records that it was first made in England by John Tyce, of Shoreditch, London, 41 Elizabeth, 1598.

Taille de bois, Fr. Wood engraving.

Taille douce, Fr. Copper-plate engraving.

Taille dure, Fr. Steel engraving.

Tail-piece. An ornamental design placed at the end of a page or chapter of a book. In French *cul-de-lampe*.

Takel, O. E. An arrow,—

"Wel could he dress his *takel* yeomanly." (*Chaucer*.)

Talaria, R. (*talus*, the ankle). Wings fixed to the ankles ; the attribute of Mercury, Perseus, and sometimes Minerva. They are represented either attached to sandals, or growing from the limb.

Talbot, Her. A badge of the Earl of Shrewsbury of that name (the "Scourge of France"). A silver running hound or *talbot*.

Talbotype. The photographic process of multiplying impressions from a *negative*, invented by Mr. Fox Talbot. (See CALOTYPE.)

Talc (from Germ. Talg, tallow). A translucent mineral, resembling *mica* but much softer. "Being calcined and variously prepared, it maketh a curious whitewash, which some justify lawful, because clearing not changing the complexion." (*Fuller.*) The Chinese make lanterns, shades, and ornaments of talc.

Talent, Gr. and R. (τάλαντον, lit. a balance). A weight of silver with the Greeks, and of copper with the Romans ; applied as a unit of value. The GREEK talent of silver is estimated at rather less than 250*l*. sterling—it contained 60 *minæ*, or 6000 *drachmæ*. The ATTIC talent was of much smaller value, of less than an ounce of gold, and is that generally intended by the word. The silver talent was called *talentum magnum*. The JEWISH talent of silver=about 396*l*., and of gold = about 5475*l*. From its application as an expression of a man's available wealth, metaphorically applied *in Scripture* to resources of any kind, as of intellect, position, &c., for the due unselfish administration of which he is responsible.

Talero, It. A Venetian silver coin = about five francs.

Talevas, Talvas. (See TAVOLACE.)

Tali, R. (Gr. ἀστράγαλος). Knuckle-bones of sheep or goats, used from the earliest times, exactly as they are by children now, to play with. When they were marked with black dots on each face they were used as dice. The numbers were 1, 3, 4 and 6 ; 1 being opposite to 6, and 3 opposite to 4 ; and each number, and each cast, had its appropriate name : 1 was called in Greek μονάς, εἷς, κύων, Χῖος ; Ionic οἴνη ; Latin, *unio, vulturius, canis* ; 3 was τριάς, and *ternio ;* 4, τετράς, and *quaternio* ; 6, ἑξάς, ἑξίτης, Κῷος, and *senio*. The best throw was that called *Venus* or *jactus Venereus*, in which the four *tali* showed different numbers. By this cast the player became king of the feast or symposium ; in the *canis* (dog-throw), on the other hand, all four dice turned up the same number.

Talisman (Arab. tilsam, a magical image). A charm worn about the person as a protection from dangers, especially from the effects of magic and the "evil eye." The *bullæ* worn by children, and the rings of the ladies among the Greeks and Romans frequently contained such charms. The practice has survived in all ages and nations, and is not at all unfrequent in the 19th century, and even among the educated classes.

Tall-boys, O. E. High cups or glasses.

Tall-men, O. E. Loaded dice.

Tall-wood, O. E. "Pacte wodde to make byllettes of, *taillee*." (*Palsgrave*.)

Talleh, Arab. Myrrh from Abyssinia.

Tallow-cut (Fr. *en cabuchon*). This is a term applied by lapidaries to precious stones not cut into regular *facets*, but ground down and polished.

Tally, O. E. (Fr. *tailler*, to cut.) An ancient method of keeping record of monies advanced to the Royal Exchequer. A *tally* was a piece of wood inscribed with a receipt, which was split by an officer, and one part delivered to the lender, and the other, called the *Stock*, preserved in the Tally-office in the Exchequer. Hence the name Stocks for the Government securities. After the disuse of the tallies in 1782 the old ones were used for firing in the Houses of Parliament, and caused their destruction in 1834.

Talmud (Chaldean, lit. instruction,) consists of two parts, the MISHNA and GEMARA ; and contains the whole body of Hebrew law and traditions.

Talus. (1) R. The game of knuckle-bones. (See ASTRAGALUS.) (2) Arch. The sloping part of a work, a term in fortification.

Talvace, O. E. A shield or buckler, circular and projecting.

Talvas, O. E. An oblong *wooden shield*, 14th century.

Tambour, Fr. A small drum. Rich embroidery work done on a drum-shaped frame.

Tamboura. An ancient musical instrument of the lute or guitar kind. The Hindoos represent Ganesa, the god of wisdom, as a man with the head of an elephant, holding a tamboura in his hands.

Tambourine. A small drum with only one skin, played on by the hand.

Fig. 645. Flemish Tankard, silver-gilt 17th century.

·Tamine, Taminy, Tammy (Fr. *tamis*, a sieve). A thin woollen textile, highly glazed.

Tampion. (See TOMPION.)

Tang-fish. Seals are so called in the Shetlands.

Tankard. (Norman Fr. Tankar.) A drinking-jug with a cover. The name is said to be compounded of *étain*, tin, and *quarte*, a quart measure. The Flemish had tankards of wood, with pegs down the sides, to measure the quantity drunk. (See Figs. 615 and 645.) (See POKAL.)

Tapestry. The introduction of *tapestry* properly so called dates from the 12th century, when it began to rival the more ancient embroidered stuffs called *Sarrazinois carpets*. Tapestry is woven on looms, i. e. on a *warp* rolled round two cylinders, and stretched out between them either vertically or horizontally, for the insertion of the *woof* between and among the threads. When woven on a vertical warp, it is called high-warp (*haute-lisse*) ; when horizontal, low-warp (*basse-lisse*). The former produces, for many reasons, incomparably the finest work, and is the method adopted for the Gobelins and Savonnerie tapestries. The progress of the art has followed, especially in Flanders, that of painting, from which its models are derived. It has become less popular than it was during the present century, from the general disuse of hangings in the decoration of houses. Perhaps the best condensed account of this extensive subject is the work of M. Alfred de Champeaux, translated for the South Kensington Museum. (See BAYEUX TAPESTRY.)

Tapul, O. E. The perpendicular ridge down the centre of a breastplate.

Tar-black. A kind of *lamp black* prepared by the combustion of coal tar, or of the heavy oils of tar and schist.

Targe, Fr. Med. A dagger or small sword : "Les autres gens avoient *targes* et *semitarges*, qui sont espées de Turquie." (See SEMITARGE.)

Targe or **Target,** O. E. A round shield.

Targe (or **Pavoise**) **Futée,** Fr. A shield composed of several pieces, which loosened on being struck, and fell asunder. The Swabian jousters at Maximilian's triumph are described (*Meyrick*, vol. ii.) as bearing these shields.

Targe, Target. (Welsh *targa*, wicker-work.)

Targum, Chaldee (lit. interpretation). A paraphrase, or lesson from the Old Testament in the Chaldee language.

Tarn. A mountain lake.

Tarots. Emblematical cards still used in Switzerland and parts of Germany. "They are unknown, except as curiosities, to the Parisians and to ourselves ; but they are, nevertheless, the sole representatives of the original cards which the Gipsies brought with them into Europe." (*Rev. E. S. Taylor.*)

Tarpaulin. A tarred *palling* or covering. ·

Tars, Cloth of. A web of silk and the downy wool of goats of Tibet, the forerunner of *cashmere*.

Tarsia or **Intarsia.** A kind of mosaic in woods ; representing views of buildings and ornament of various kinds, by inlaying pieces of wood, of various colours and shades, into panels of walnut wood.

Tarsus. In *Anatomy*, the instep and socket of the ankle-bone.

Tartan, Fr. (*not* Gaelic). The Highland plaid, the dress of the Scottish Highlanders, said to be derived from the Celta ; the *Galli non braccati.*

Tartarium. Cloth of Tars was a costly cloth of royal purple, probably a mixture of silk and goat's-hair from Thibet. It is mentioned by Chaucer :—

"His coat armure was of cloth of Tars,
Couched with perles."

Tas or **Tats,** Egyp. Amulets of gilded sycamore wood, cornelian, jasper, glass, &c., found suspended from the necks of mummies.

Tassel-gentle, O. E. (for tercel-gentle). A species of hawk. (*Shakspeare.*)

Tasses. Flaps of armour attached to the bottom of the breast-plate for the protection of the thighs.

Tat or **Dad,** Egyp. A sculptor's stool ; a religious emblem worn by gods and sacred animals round the neck. The term was also probably a name of Mendés.

Tau, Taucross. (1) Her. A cross formed like the letter T, so-called in Greek. This charge is also called the Cross of St. Anthony. (2) Chr. As a motive for ornamental design the *tau* is the ancient form of the episcopal staff as represented in the catacombs. Originally curved like the pagan *lituus*, it became in the 8th century straight. The Taus were often hollowed to contain relics, &c. (Consult *Ivories*, by *W. Maskell*, pp. 84, 85.)

Tauntons. A kind of broad cloth made at Taunton in Somersetshire.

Tavolace or **Talevas** (It. *tavolaccio*). A large thick wooden shield ; like a *table* (*tavola*) of wood (hence its name), 15th century.

Tawdry. Showy. The word is *said* to be derived from *Ethelreda torquem*, St. Ethelred's necklace, which was composed of rows of twisted lace, an ornament much used by Anglo-Saxon ladies. (*Stormont.*)

Tawdry Lace. A kind of fine lace alluded to by Shakspeare, Spenser, &c. (*Halliwell.*)

"Fimbriæ nundinis sanctæ Ethelredæ emptæ." (*Coles.*)

Tawney, O. E. A deep orange colour, used in the Middle Ages as a *livery* colour.

Tawney Coat, O. E. The dress of a summoner or apparitor. (*Shakspeare.*)

Taxidermy. The art of preserving the skins of animals.

Tazza, It. An ornamental cup or vase, with a flat shallow bowl, standing on a foot, and with handles.

Tchy, Chinese. Twelve recurrent periods of the cycle of sixty years, represented by animals assigned to the twelve months, i.e. the signs of the Chinese Zodiac. They are: November, the *rat ;* December, the *ox ;* January, the *tiger ;* February, the *rabbit ;* March, the *dragon ;* April, the *serpent ;* May, the *horse ;* June, the *hare ;* July, the *ape ;* August, the *hen ;* September, the *dog ;* October, the *boar*. The above are accordingly frequent accessories of designs on porcelain.

Te Deum, Chr. The first words and title of a hymn composed by St. Augustin and St. Ambrose about 390.

Tegillum, R. (dimin. of *tegulum*, a roof). A short mantle with a hood, made of a coarse material ; worn by country people and fishermen.

Tegula, R. (Gr. κέραμος ; Lat. *tego*, to cover). A roofing tile ; originally of baked clay or wooden shingles. At an early date (620 B.C.) tiles of marble were introduced, and were followed by tiles of gilded bronze ; *per tegulas exire* means to go out by the opening in the roof of the atrium, the compluvium.

Teheran Ware. An inferior Persian majolica.

Tela, R. A loom, an essential adjunct to every large establishment in ancient Rome ; *tela jugalis* was the simplest description of weaving-loom. The *warp* was called *stamen* from its upright position ; the *woof* subtegmen or trama. In Greek στήμων and κρόκη.

Telamones, R. Figures of men, which were employed in lieu of columns to support an entablature. (See ATLANTES.) (Fig. 646.)

Temo, R. The pole of a carriage, waggon, plough, &c.

Tempera Painting. Painting with pigments mixed with chalk or clay, and diluted with weak glue or size ; chiefly used in scene-painting and decoration. (See DISTEMPER.)

Templars. An order

Fig. 646. Telamon.

of knighthood introduced about A.D. 1118, and suppressed A.D. 1309. They wore a red Maltese cross on a white field, and bore a *banner* showing that cross on a white field ; and a second banner of black and white called Beau Séant, this word Beau Séant being their battle-cry. Their *badges* were the AGNUS DEI, or Lamb and Flag ; and a device representing two knights on one horse, indicating the original poverty of the order. This is blazoned in modern times as a *pegasus*, the two knights being mistaken for wings on a *flying horse*.

Template. (1) A model in thin board of an ornament to be produced in sculpture. (2) A short timber under a girder.

Temple. (See TEMPLUM.)

Temple Church, London—a round church—is a representative specimen of the transition period of architecture in England from the NORMAN to the EARLY ENGLISH. "The Eastern part is a most excellent specimen of plain light Early English, and its growing and slender piers are perhaps unequalled." (*Rickman, Architecture in England,* &c.)

Templet. (See TEMPLATE.)

Templum, Temple, R. (τέμνω, to cut off). A Greek temple was not originally intended for worshippers, but as a shrine for the gods. In the earliest times the Greek temples were made of wood, and the primitive origin of them was probably a hollow tree in which the image was placed as in a niche. The early Greek temples were dark and gloomy, having no windows, but lighted through the door, or by lamps. At a very early stage in history, temples of great grandeur and beauty are mentioned. All temples were built in an oblong or round form, and were mostly adorned with columns ; they were classified accordingly as *astyle*, without any columns ; *in antis*, with

Fig. 647. Templum in antis.

two columns in front, between the *antæ ; prostyle*, with four columns in front ; or *amphiprostyle*, with four columns at each end ; *peripteral*, with columns at each end and along the sides ; or *dipteral*, with two ranges of columns all round, one within the other, &c. They were also described according to the number of columns in the porticoes, as *tetrastyle, hexastyle, decastyle,* &c.,—this number was never uneven ; or according to the intercolumniation, as *pycnostyle, systyle, eustyle, diastyle,* or *aræostyle*. Many of the great temples consisted of three parts : the *pronaos* or vestibule ; the *cella*, properly the *naos ;* and the *opisthodomos.*

Tendrils of a vine or other creeping plant, with which it clasps the objects that support it, furnish abundant suggestions for ornamental designs in scroll-work.

Tenebrosi. A school of Italian artists who devoted their attention to striking *Rembrandt* effects of light and shade ; represented by Caravaggio.

Tenent, Tenant. A term in French heraldry applied to human figures as SUPPORTERS.

Tennée or **Tawney,** Her. A deep orange colour, indicated by vertical lines crossing PURPURE.

Tenon. The end of a piece of wood, shaped to fit into another piece.

Tenor. In Music, a high male voice.

Tensa or **Thensa,** R. A triumphal car, probably in the form of a platform on wheels, and richly decorated, upon which the images of certain gods were paraded during the Circensian games. The ceremony was regarded as one of the highest solemnity, and the car was escorted by the senators in robes of state, who helped to drag the carriage or to lead the horses, with thongs attached for the purpose.

Tenture, Fr. Paper or tapestry hangings.

Tepidarium, R. (*tepidus,* lukewarm). (1) A warm room in a bath ; used as a preparation for the SUDATORIUM. (2) The vessel in which the water was heated.

Tercel, O. E. The male hawk. (*Shakspeare.*)

Terce major. A sequence of three best cards.

Terebenthina. Turpentine.

Terebra, R. (*tero,* to rub or wear away). (1) Any tool used for boring, such as a drill, a gimlet, an auger, &c. (2) A mechanical ram contrived to pierce the walls of a fortification.

Terginum, R. (*tergum,* the back). A leathern lash used for flogging slaves.

Terminal Figures. Statues of the god Terminus. (See TERMINI, HERMÆ.)

Terminalia, R. Festivals in honour of Terminus the god of boundaries ; they took place yearly on the eighth day of the calends of March

(23rd of February), which was the last day of the old Roman year.

Termini, Terms, R. The statues of the god TERMINUS, which consisted merely of posts or pillars for landmarks, were crowned with garlands by the proprietors of co-terminous lands.

" When Tarquin the Proud desired to build a temple to Jupiter upon the Tarpeian rock, he begged all the inferior divinities to give up the altars they had upon the rock in favour of the master of them all. All the gods cheerfully consented except Terminus. This Terminus, therefore, who refused to yield to Jupiter, was chosen by Erasmus for his haughty device, with the motto *Cedo nulli*. (*Mr. Palliser, Historic Devices, &c.*) (See Fig. 648.)

Fig. 648. Terminus.

Terra-cotta, It. Baked clay; largely used in architectural ornament.

Terra da Boccali, It. (See TERRA DI LAVA.)

Terra di Lava, It. A clay which was anciently used in combination with charcoal to form a white ground for the reception of oil colours.

Terra di Siena. An ochreous earth producing a yellow and a deep orange pigment; useful for oil and water-colour painting. (See SIENA.)

Terra Nera. Black earth; an ancient pigment.

Terra Verde. (See GREEN EARTH.)

Terraglia. (See POTTERY.)

Terretta, It. (See TERRA DI LAVA.)

Terry Velvet. A kind of silk plush or ribbed velvet.

Tertiary Colours, produced by the mixture of two secondary colours, are *greys*, inclining to the primary or secondary colour which is in excess in their composition. (Consult *Chevreuil on Colours.*)

Teruncius, R. A silver coin equal in value to one-fourth of an as.

Tessela, R. (diminutive of *tessera*). A small cube of stone or marble used for making mosaic pavements (*tesselatum opus* or *tesselata structura*).

Tesselated pavement. Inlaid or mosaic work composed of *tesselæ*. *Tesselatum flagrum.* (See FLAGRUM.) Cf. MUSIVUM OPUS. (Consult

Buckman and Newmarch, Remains of Roman Art in Cirencester.)

Tessera, R. (Gr. κύβος). A cube, a die; *tesseræ, tesseræ lusoriæ,* dice of ivory, bone, or wood; the dice-box is *fritillus.* (Compare TALUS.) *Tessera hospitalis* was an oblong token of wood or earthenware, exchanged among families agreed to mutual hospitality. Many of these tokens have the bust of Jupiter Hospitalis impressed; *tessera theatralis,* a pass to the theatre; *tessera militaris* (Gr. σύνθημα), a tablet on which the watch-word or war-cry of the day was written; it was passed about the ranks before joining battle. *Tesseræ frumentariæ* or *nummariæ,* vouchers for bread or money distributed by the magistrats among the poor. (Cf. TESSELA, TALUS, TABULÆ.)

Testa, R. A sherd of tiles or pottery, and thence an earthenware vase.

Testaceum, R. (*testa*). Made of tiles; the term was used to denote a roofing or pavement made with the fragments of broken tiles.

Tester. (1) Any flat *canopy.* The framework over a four-post bedstead. (2) A silver coin so called from the head (*teste*) of the king upon it. In the reign of Henry VIII. it was worth 12*d.* and afterwards 6*d.* French testers were struck by Louis XII. in 1513, and Scotch under Queen Mary in 1559.

Testière, Med. Fr. Originally, mailed armour for a horse's head, subsequently a plate between the ears on which a crest was fixed. (See CHANFRON.)

Testif, Fr. Camel's hair.

Testudinatus, R. Made in the form of a TESTUDO (q.v.); the term was applied either to a roof or to a ceiling.

Testudineus, R. Made with tortoise-shells.

Fig. 649. Testudo.

Testudo, R. (*testa,* a shell). (1) A tortoise, and thence a lyre of which the sounding bottom was made out of a tortoise-shell. (2) In Architecture, an arched ceiling, the four sides of which converge to a centre. (3) *Testudo arietaria* was a movable wooden shed covered with skins and containing a battering-ram (Fig. 574). (4) Lastly the term denoted a kind of defensive roof formed by the shields of soldiers when advancing to the foot of a rampart (Fig. 649).

Tetra-chordon, Gr. and R. (τετρά-χορδον). Literally, having four strings; *hydraulos tetrachordon* was a hydraulic organ with four pipes.

Tetra-comus, Gr. A banqueting-song sung at the festival of Bacchus during the fourth course (κῶμος).

Tetra-doros (sc. *later*), Gr. A peculiar kind of brick described by Vitruvius; it was called from its measuring four hand-breadths.

Tetra-drachmum, Gr. (τετρά-δραχμον). An Attic silver coin of the value of four *drachmæ*, or about 3s. 3d.

Tetra-foliated, Arch. Said of any architectural decoration showing four foils.

Tetragon. A plane figure having four angles; a four-sided figure.

Tetra-morph, Chr. (Gr. τέσσαρα, four; μορφή, shape). The union of the four attributes of the Evangelists (the angel, eagle, lion, and ox), in one figure, e. g. as a woman crowned and seated on an animal which, with the body of a horse, has the four heads of the mystic creatures; and of the four feet one is human, one hoofed for the ox, one clawed like an eagle's, and one like a lion's; underneath is inscribed *Animal Ecclesiæ.*

Tetra-style, Gr. and R. (τετράστυλος). Having four columns. (See TEMPLUM.)

Tetra-vela, Lat. "The veils or curtains placed between the pillars which supported the canopy of the altar, at the sides and in front, and which were drawn round it when the priest was not officiating." (*Fairholt.*)

Teutonic Order. A military order of knights, established in the Holy Land about 1191. They first subdued and Christianized Prussia.

Tewel, Arch. (From the French *tuyau*.) A pipe or flue to convey smoke: it is mentioned by Chaucer:

" . . . Soche a smoke gan out wende
Blacke, blue and greenish, swartishe, rede,
As doith where that men melte lede,
Lo! all on hie from the *tewell.*"
(*House of Fame.*)

Textile, R. (*texo*, to weave). Woven. Anything capable of being woven.

Texture. In Art, the *surface* appearance of a representation not of textiles only, but of the other parts of a picture—wood, marble, skin, hair, &c. Gerard Dow excels in *texture.*

Thalamifera, Gr. A term applied, in describing ancient sculpture, to kneeling figures supporting tablets, on which figures of the gods or inscriptions are carved.

Thalamus, Gr. and R. (θάλαμος). The nuptial chamber in a Roman house; the others were called DORMITORIA.

Thalysia, Gr. (θαλύ-σια). Greek festivals of the harvest and vintage.

Thargelia, Gr. (θαργήλια). Very ancient festivals held at Athens on the occasion of a plague or other public disaster in honour of Apollo and Artemis; in which two persons, generally criminals, were put to death for the *purification* of the city.

Thaumaturgi, Chr. (θαυματο-εργός). Workers of miracles.

Theatrum, Theatre, Gr. and R. (θέατρον, lit. a place for seeing). The construction of the ancient GREEK theatre was similar to that of modern theatres. The seats rose one behind and above the other in concentric half-circles, and the whole space enclosed was called *cavea*, the pit, being in most cases a real excavation from the rock. The central level space within and below the circles for spectators was covered with boards, upon which the *chorus* danced and performed their part. This was the ORCHESTRA, the central point of which and of the plan of the whole building was the THYMELE, or altar of Dionysus. This altar became a *property* of the piece, doing duty as a funeral monument, an altar, or a pulpit for the leader of the chorus or flute-player, according to the nature of the performance going on, in which it must be remembered that the part assigned to the *chorus* in the orchestra below was quite as important as any other, and in its original intention was in fact the centre of interest, to which the performance on the stage was *accessory.* The whole theatre and orchestra were open to the sky. The cavea of the former accommodated about 50,000 spectators. The arrangements of the stage were elaborate and ingenious, and the art of *scene-painting* developed at a very early period. The ROMAN theatre differed from the Greek principally in the absence of an *orchestra*, that space (the modern *pit*) being used for the seats of senators, foreign ambassadors, &c. Remains of ancient theatres still exist in Greece, Italy, and France. The most perfect of these are the Colosseum at Rome, and the amphitheatre at Nismes.

Theca Calamaria, Gr. and R. (θήκη; τίθημι, to put into). A portable inkstand.

Thenard's Blue. (See COBALT.)

Thensa. (See TENSA.)

Theo-gamia, Gr. (θεο-γάμια). Greek festivals held in honour of Proserpine and commemorating her marriage with Pluto.

Theorbo. A stringed musical instrument; a kind of lute, having supplementary strings by the side of the finger-board.

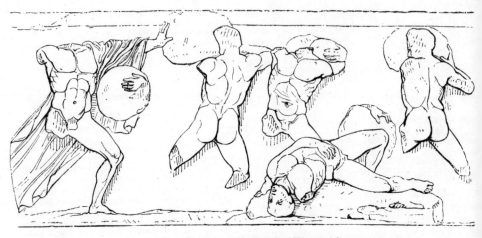

Fig. 650. Part of the Frieze of the Temple of Theseus, Athens.

Thermæ, Gr. and R. (θέρμαι, lit. hot-springs). Distinguished from *balneæ.* The luxurious establishments for bathing, gymnastics, and conversation which grew up under the Roman Empire, on which all the resources of architecture and decorative art were lavished. The ruins of the *thermæ* of Titus, Caracalla, and Diocletian are still visible. They contained, besides the baths properly so called, "*exedræ* for philosophers and rhetoricians to lecture in, *porticoes* for the idle, and libraries for the learned, and were adorned with marbles and fountains, and shaded with walks and plantations."

Thermography. A chemical process for copying prints and drawings upon paper or metal by the agency of *heat* without light.

Thermopolium, R. (θερμο-πώλιον). A refreshment-room, in which warm drinks were sold, such as mulled wine, mead, &c.

Thermulæ (dimin. of *thermæ*). Baths on a small scale.

Thesaurus, Gr. A treasure-house. In the monuments of the heroic period many subterranean buildings of great extent and peculiar construction have been attributed to this purpose; but they may more probably have been sepulchral. In historical times the public treasures were in the *agoræ* or the temples. (See ÆRARIUM.)

Theseum. An Athenian temple built in the 5th century B.C., to receive the bones of Theseus. It was richly ornamented with statuary and sculpture. The former has been destroyed; but some metopes and sculptured friezes in high relief remain, of which castings exist in the British Museum. Our illustration represents an incident of the "Battle of the gods and the giants," and is remarkable for anatomical precision. In these sculptures Greek art has entirely emerged from the *archaic* stage, and they were doubtless the inspiring models for Pheidias and his contemporaries, and the forerunners of the Parthenon sculptures. (See ELGIN MARBLES.)

Thesmo-phoria. Greek festivals of women and maidens in honour of Demeter, in commemoration of the traditions of civilized life. The solemnities opened with processions of women bearing on their heads the books of the sacred laws (ascribed to Demeter). On the second day, of fasting and mourning, the women remained all day grouped round the statue of Demeter in the temple, taking no other food than cakes of sesame and honey, and in the afternoon walked barefoot in procession behind a waggon on which baskets with mystical symbols were borne to the *thesmophorion.* On the third day they commemorated the smiles of Demeter, under the epithet of καλλιγένεια.

Thibet Cloth. A fabric of goat's hair; called also *camlet.*

Thick-pleached, O. E. Thickly interwoven. (*Shakspeare.*)

Thieves' Vinegar. A kind of aromatic vinegar for a sick-room, consisting of the dried tops of rosemary, sage-leaves, lavender-flowers, and bruised cloves, steeped in acetic acid and boiling water. It derives its name and popularity from a story that thieves who plundered the dead bodies during the plague with perfect security, attributed their impunity to the use of this disinfectant. (*Simmonds' Commercial Dictionary.*)

Thimbles are said to have been found at Herculaneum. The manufacture was introduced into England, from Holland, about 1695.

Thistle, Her. The national badge of Scotland represented after its natural aspect and tinctured proper. The Order of the Thistle of Scotland was instituted a long time before the union of the two kingdoms (commemorated in the badge selected by James I. of the rose and thistle combined). (Fig. 293.) The badge or jewel is of gold ena-melled, having a figure of St. Andrew holding his silver saltire and surrounded by rays, and an oval border with the motto. It is borne from the collar of the order formed

Fig. 651. Badge of the Thistle.

of thistles alternating with bunches of rue sprigs, or on a dark-green ribbon across the shoulder. The order of the *Ecu d'Or*, instituted by Louis of Bourbon (1410), had also a *thistle* in the jewel and girdle.

Tholus, Gr. and R. (θόλος). A dome and cupola of a circular building.

Thorax, Gr. (θώραξ). (1) A breastplate; Latin LORICA (q.v.). (2) A bust of wax, marble, or bronze.

Three-pile, O. E. Rich velvet.

Three-quarter. A size of portrait; 30 inches by 25. (See PORTRAIT PAINTING.)

Thrones, Chr. An order of angels, usually represented with double wings, supporting the Throne of the Almighty in ethereal space.

Through-stone or **Throwstone,** O. E. (vari-ously spelt, derived from Anglo-Saxon, *thruh,* a coffin.) A flat grave-stone. Parker gives in his "Glossary" the following quotation :—

"Over the midst of the said vault did lie a fair *throw-stone,* and at each either side of the stone it was open, through which were cast the bones of the monks whose graves were opened for other monks to lie in; which vault was made to be a charnel-house to put dead men's bones in."

(*Ancient Rites of Durham.*)

Thurible, Chr. An incense-burner. Gene-rally of bronze. The practice of burning incense in religious functions is very ancient, and origi-nated in the East. The illustration (Fig. 652) is a beautiful specimen of Arabian work devoted to this object.

Thurles, O.E. (holes through the wall). The small windows of a house; 12th century.

Thyas or **Thias,** Gr. A Bacchante, the Greek equivalent for the Latin BACCHA.

Thymela, Thymelê, Gr. (θυμέλη). (Lite-rally, a place for sacrifice.) An altar placed in the orchestra of a Greek theatre and dedicated to Bacchus.

Thyroma, Gr. (θύρωμα). A synonym for the Latin JANUA (q.v.).

Thyrsus, R. (θύρσος). A long staff, sur-mounted with a fir-cone, or a bunch of vine-leaves or ivy, with grapes or berries, carried by Bacchus, and the satyrs, mænads, and others, during the celebration of religious rites. Be-neath the garland or fir-cone the thyrsus ends in the sharp point of a spear, a puncture from which induces madness.

Tiara, Gr. (τιάρα). A hat with a tall high crown; the characteristic head-dress of the north-western Asiatics; especially the Armenians, Parthians, Medes, and Persians. *Tiara recta* or cidaris was an upright tiara, the regal head-dress of Persia. *Tiara Phrygia* was a synonym for MITRA. Fig. 183 represents the head-dress and costume of a Persian soldier.

Tiara, Chr. The Pope's triple crown, em-blematic of his authority in the three kingdoms of heaven, earth, and the lower world. (See Fig. 653.)

Tibia, R. (Greek, *aulos*). A pipe or flute of reed, bone, ivory, horn, or metal, perforated with holes for the notes like a flute; the prin-

Fig. 652. Thurible. An Arabic incense-burner in brass, inlaid with silver.

cipal varieties were:— the *monaulos* or single pipe, including the bagpipe (*utricolarius*);

Fig. 653. Persian soldier wearing the *tiara*.

the *diaulos*, or double pipe, bound round the cheeks with a bandage called by the Romans *capistrum*, and in Greek *phorbeia*; and the *syrinx* or Pandæan pipe, of three to nine tubes.

Tibia Curva, R. A kind of flute curved at its broadest end.

Tibia Dextra, R. The right-hand pipe of the *diaulos*, usually constructed of the upper and thinner part of a reed.

Tibia Gingrina, R. A flute made of a long thin tube of reed with a mouth-hole at the side of one end.

Tibia Ligula, R. A flute resembling the modern flageolet.

Tibia Longa, R. A flute used especially in religious worship.

Tibia Obliqua, R. A flute having the mouth-piece at right angles to the tube.

Tibia Sinistra, R. The left-hand pipe of the *diaulos*, usually constructed of the lower and broader part of a reed.

Tibia Utricolarius, R. The ancient bag-pipe

Tibia Vasca, R. A flute having the mouth-piece at a right angle.

Tibiæ Pares, R. A name for the double

flute when the tubes were exactly alike, *impares* when they differed.

Tie-beam, Arch. The strong horizontal on which the king-post and other uprights rest, which support the beams of a roof.

Tierce, Per Tierce, Her. Divided into three equal parts.

Tig, O. E. A shallow drinking-bowl with four handles, made to pass round the table from hand to hand as a *loving cup*.

Tiger-wood, obtained from Guiana, is a valuable ornamental wood for cabinet-work.

Tignum, R. In a general sense wood used in carpentry, a beam or joist; in a more restricted sense, a tie-beam, rafters, brackets, &c.

Tigrinæ. Tiger-tables Great importance was attached in Roman decorative art to the grain of the wood. Tables having " veins arranged in wavy lines," were called Tigrinæ, from the resemblance of their pattern to that of a tiger's skin. Those having " veins which formed spirals, or little whirlpools," were called *pantherinæ*, or panther-tables.

Tiles for roofs are of two kinds :—plain tiles and pan tiles ; they are mentioned in an ancient statute of King Edward IV. (1477), regulating the

" Fesure, whitying, et anelyng de tewle, appelez pleintile, autrement nosmez thaktile, roftile, ou crestile, cornertile et guttertile fait et affaire deinz cest Roialme."

Glazed or *encaustic tiles* were anciently much used for paving sacred edifices. English designs are generally heraldic in character. In Spanish architecture tiles were used for the decoration of walls instead of hangings ; and richly decorated pavements are found in Asia Minor and the East Indies. (Consult *Parker's Glossary, J. G. Nichols, Examples of Tiles,* &c.)

Tilt, O.E. The word is properly applied to the exercises in training for the joust, against the QUINTAIN, the PEL, the ring, and other objects.

Timbre, Her. (1) Anciently, the *crest ;* (2) Modern French, the *helm,* in a coat of arms.

Timbrel. An ancient *tambourine,* with a double row of gingles.

Tin-glazed Wares. (See POTTERY.)

Tina, R. A large vessel used for holding wine ; its shape is unknown.

Tinctures, Her. The two metals and the five colours of heraldry.

Tint of colour = degree of intensity. In painting in oils this is lowered by the addition of a white pigment, in water colours by dilution. " *Tint* is any unbroken state of any colour, varying between the intensity of its parent colour and the purity of white." (*J. B. Pyne, in the Art Union of* 1844.) (See TONES.)

Tint-tools. In copper and wood engraving, gravers used for skies, still waters, architecture, &c. The word " tint " in engraving means colour, and skies are *tints* cut horizontally.

Tintinnabulatus, R. Carrying a bell (*tintin-nabulum*); a term applied especially to animals which carried a bell hung round their neck.

Fig. 654. Tintinnabulum. Front view.

Tintinnabulum, R. (Gr. κώδων). A bell used as a hand-bell; they took very various forms in antiquity, hemispherical, pear-shaped, or cylindrical, and some were square. The Romans also made use of a kind of swinging gong similar to that shown in Figs. 654 and 655, of a specimen discovered at Pompeii, and now in the Naples museum.

Tintinnabulum, O. E. A musical instrument made of a set of bells, arranged in order within a frame.

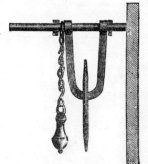

Fig. 655. Tintinnabulum. Side view.

Tints. (See TONE.)

Tiraz, Arab. The ancient name of the apartment in an Arab palace set apart for weaving; also of the rich silken stuffs woven there.

Tire Valiant or **Volant,** O. E. A kind of head-dress. (*Shakspeare.*)

Titulus, R. (1) The title or INDEX of a book. (2) A notice in front of a house to be let or sold. (3) An epitaph or other inscription on monuments. (4) A large board mounted on a spear and inscribed with the numbers of the prisoners, cities, and standards that had been captured from the enemy; carried in a TRIUMPH or OVATION.

Tobine. A stout twilled silk.

Toga, R. (*tego*, to cover). The principal outer garment of a Roman, as the PALLIUM (q.v.) was the national dress of the Greek. Among the different kinds of toga were the *toga restricta, toga fusa, toga prætexta, toga pura* or *virilis, toga palmata, toga picturata,* &c.

The colour of the toga was ordinarily white. *Candidates* (from *candidus,* white) were so called from their whitening their togas with chalk; the *toga pulla,* of the natural colour of black wool, was worn in mourning; the *toga picta,* or embroidered toga, was for generals on their triumphs. (See also PRÆTEXTA, TRABEA, &c.) The illustration (Fig. 656) represents the statue of a Roman senator of the Augustan age.

Togatus, R. Wearing the *toga;* essentially the Roman costume, opposed to *palliatus,* a man in the Greek dress.

Togula, R. (dimin. of *toga*). (1) A toga of a fine texture; or (2) the short and thread-

Fig. 656. Roman Senator wearing the toga.

Y

bare toga of coarse texture, worn by a poor man, who then went by the name of *togatulus*.

Toilinet. A textile of silk or cotton warp, with woollen weft.

Toise. In French lineal measurement = 76 inches.

Toison d'Or, Her. The Golden Fleece. A French order of knighthood, instituted by Philip the Good in 1429. The order has a king-at-arms called Toison d'Or. The collar is composed of flint-stones, alternately with double *fusils* placed two and two together, forming double B's. From this suspends a Golden Fleece. The motto is, " Pretium non vile laborum." (See FUSIL.)

Tokens. Small coins issued by tradesmen for current money. (Consult *W. Boyne's Tokens,* &c.)

Tolleno, R. (*tollo,* to lift). (1) A contrivance for drawing water from a well, made of a strong cross-bar poised from the top of an upright beam, with a weight at one end and a rope and bucket at the other. (2) A similar apparatus was used in siege operations to lift soldiers up to a wall.

Tom-tom. Oriental small drum, of a barrel form, covered at each end with skin, carried obliquely, and beaten with one hand at each end.

Fig. 657. Lycian Tomb of great antiquity.

Tomb. From the earliest ages tombs similar in general design to those of modern times have been used to mark the resting-places of the dead. Fig. 657 represents an ancient monument in Lycia. (See STELA, SHRINE.)

Tombac. Red brass ; the white tombac is an alloy of copper and zinc, containing not more than 20 per cent. of zinc.

Tompion. The plug to the mouth of a cannon.

Tondi, It. A name given to a series of twelve circular medallions, painted by Luca della Robbia, with impersonations of the twelve months.

Tondino, It. A name given to small plates or dishes, which it was a mediæval fashion for the gallants to present, filled with confectioneries, to ladies. They are described as small, with a wide flat brim and sunk centre ; in this, the central medallion generally occupied by a figure of Cupid, hearts tied by ribbons or pierced with arrows, or by joined hands, and similar amatory devices, or with a shield of arms and initial letters, &c.

Tones are the modifications which a colour, in its greatest intensity, is capable of receiving from *white*, which *lowers* its tone, or *black* which *heightens* it. A *scale* is an assemblage of tones of the same colour, thus modified. The pure colour is the *normal tone* of the scale. *Hues* are the modifications which a colour receives from the addition of a small quantity of another colour. (*Chevreuil on Colour,* pp. 34, 35.)

Tonometer. A delicate instrument for tuning musical instruments, by marking the number of vibrations.

Tonstrina, R. A barber's shop ; frequented only by the middle classes ; the rich were shaved at their houses ; and the poor allowed their beards and hair to grow.

Tonsure, Chr. The clerical crown, adopted, it is said, in imitation of St. Peter, or of the Crown of Thorns, was disapproved of in the 4th century as pertaining only to penitents ; and not made essential till the end of the 5th or beginning of the 6th centuries.

Tontisse, Fr. Flock-paper ; paper-hangings ornamented with flock-wool.

Tooth Ornament, Arch. A name of the NAIL-HEAD moulding. It is the peculiar distinction of the Early English style, to which it is nearly, if not exclusively, confined. It is the regular progression from the Norman *zigzag* to the delicate *quatrefoil* of the DECORATED ENGLISH. It resembles a succession of low, square, pierced pyramids set on the edges of a hollow moulding.

Toothing, Arch. Projecting bricks left at the end of a wall, to form a *union* with any further buildings.

Topaz. There are two varieties of this gem ; the Brazilian yellow, which is the best known, and the Oriental.

Topaz, Her. In blazoning arms of nobles, the names of *gems* were sometimes substituted for *tinctures ;* the topaz for gold (OR).

Topes, Hind. Bhuddist sepulchral monuments, cone-shaped, and round at the tops, like the *dagobs* of Ava and Ceylon.

Topiaria (Ars), R. Artificial training of shrubs and trees into fantastic shapes. Painted representations of landscapes on the walls of houses were called TOPIA. (See HORTUS.)

Topiarius, R. A gardener skilled in the ARS TOPIARIA (q.v.).

Torale. R. (*torus,* a couch). The hanging valance of a couch.

Torch, R. The emblem of marriage, from the custom of forming wedding processions in the evening by torch-light. Upright, the torch was the emblem of rejoicing ; reversed, of death or sleep ; hence its application upon funereal monuments.

Torcular, Torculum, R. A wine or oil press. Hence—

Torcularium, R. The press-room.

Toreador, Sp. A bull-fighter.

Toreuma, Gr. and R. (τόρευμα). *Carving upon ivory* executed on the lathe.

Toreutic Art (from τορεύω, to bore through ; or from τορός, clear, distinct). Sculpture ; especially of metals, ivories, metallic castings in relief, &c. A long essay on the meaning of this word occurs in the works of De Quincy.

Tormentum, R. (1) (*Torqueo,* to twist.) A general term for such instruments as the *balista, catapulta, onager, scorpio,* &c., from the twisting of the strands of the ropes that were used as the string to the bow. (2) Torture. By the Greek law the evidence of slaves was *always* extracted by torture. In Rome free persons *in humble circumstances* were also subjected to it in cases of treason.

Tornus, Gr. and R. A lathe or potter's wheel.

Torquatus, R. Wearing the Gallic TORQUE. *Torquatus miles,* a soldier who received such a collar as a reward, and wore it, not round the neck, but on the breast, like a decoration.

Torques, Gen. (*torqueo,* to twist). A necklace, or armlet, or collar of gold or other wire spirally twisted. (See ARMILLA, MONILE, &c.)

Torse, Her. A crest wreath. (See ORLE.)

Torso, It. In Sculpture, the trunk regarded apart from the head and limbs. The celebrated Torso of Hercules, in the Vatican, by Apollonios, about 336 B.C., is said to have been the favourite inspiration of Michael Angelo. Another fine torso is that known as the Farnese, in the Naples Museum, representing probably a seated figure of Bacchus.

Torteau, Her. A red ROUNDLE (q.v.).

Tortoise. Among the Egyptians the tortoise was an emblem of darkness and of death. Fig. 129 is the remarkable device of Cosmo, Grand Duke of Tuscany, with the motto, " Hasten slowly," i. e. have caution with energy.

Fig. 658. Tortoise. Device of the Duke of Tuscany.

Tortoise-shell is largely used for making combs, and for veneering on cabinet-work. When it is softened with hot water, it receives impressions which become permanent if it is suddenly cooled. The plates used are those found on the back of the sea-turtle (*chelone imbricata*). Five large plates are obtained from the middle of the carapace or upper buckler, and four large ones from the sides, called " blades," and twenty-five smaller plates from the edges, called "feet or noses." The belly shells are of a yellow colour, and are used for the purposes of horn.

Torus, R. Anything swelling like the strand of a rope. A bed covered with sheets or blankets (*toralia*).

Fig. 659. Torus moulding.

Torus, Arch. A convex moulding used in architectural decoration (Fig. 659) at all periods and by all nations.

Touchstone is a kind of black jasper, known as *Lydian stone,* used for testing gold. This is done with *touching*-needles tipped with metal in various states of alloy, and the streaks that they make on the touchstone determine the fineness of the gold. In Architecture, certain black marbles were anciently so called, from their supposed identity with the *lapis Lydius.*

Tough, Turkish. A Turkish standard ; a *horse-tail* attached to the upper part of a pike which ends in a crescent and ball.

Tourelle, Fr. A small tower on a castle, with a winding staircase.

Towers. (See ROUND TOWERS.)

Trabea, R. (lit. shaped like a *trabs* or beam). A rich toga, either made entirely of purple cloth or decorated with horizontal stripes of that colour. The purple toga was an attribute of the *gods*, and afterwards of the *emperors*; purple and white, or purple and saffron, of augurs; purple and white, of *royalty* (kings).

Trabs, R. A beam; especially a long beam supporting the joists of a ceiling.

Tracery. In architecture or decorative work, geometrical ornament, such as is inserted on the upper parts of Gothic windows, in Alhambraic architecture, &c.

Tracing-paper is made of tissue-paper soaked in oil or thin varnish.

Trajan Column, in Rome, the work of Apollodorus, A.D. 114, is 10½ feet in diameter, and 127 feet high, made of 34 blocks of white marble—23 in the shaft, 9 in the base, which is finely sculptured, and 2 in the capital and torus. The sculptures show about 2500 figures besides the horses, and represent the battles and sieges of the Dacian War. The column is a perfect *handbook* of the military costume of Rome and other countries of its period. (Consult the work of *Alfonso G. Hispano*, published at Rome, 1586, which contains 130 plates representing all the sculptures; or the more modern work of *Pietro Santo Bartoli*, which contains beautiful engravings of all the reliefs.) A plaster cast of the column in two pieces is in the South Kensington Museum, with a handbook by J. H. Pollen on a desk near its base, with the aid of which it can be perfectly studied at leisure.

Trama, Sp. The weft or woof; a kind of silk thread so called.

Transenna, R. and Chr. A snare for birds. It consisted of a net stretched over a circular framework. In Christian archæology, the name was given to a marble lattice placed in the catacomb chapels to protect the relics.

Transept, Arch. A transverse nave, passing in front of the choir, and crossing the longitudinal or central nave of a church. It is sometimes called the *cross*, and each of its parts to the right and left of the nave are called *cross-aisles*.

Transfluent, Her. Flowing through.

Transition Periods of Architecture. Generally speaking, all periods deserve this title, as the progressive change of the styles is continuous. Those with more precision so described are, in English Architecture, three:—from the NORMAN to the EARLY ENGLISH; and then to the DECORATED; and thirdly to the PERPENDICULAR styles.

Transmuted, Her. Counter-changed.

Transom, Arch. The horizontal cross-bar in a window.

Transposed, Her. Reversed.

Transtrum, R. (*trans*, across). In a general sense a horizontal beam. In the plural, *transtra*, the cross-benches of a ship occupied by the rowers.

Trapeso, It. A weight for gold and silver; the twentieth part of an ounce.

Trapetum, R. A mill for crushing olives.

Trapezophorum, R. (τραπεζο-φόρον). A richly-carved leg for sideboards or small tables; sometimes called DELPHICA (q.v.).

Trasformati of Milan. One of the Italian Academies who bore as a device a plane-tree, and the verse from Virgil, "*et steriles platani malos gessere valentes*, "the barren planes have borne good fruit" (cut out of a wild olive-tree and grafted in).

Travagliati. One of the Italian literary academies, whose device was a sieve (*vaglio*) with the motto "*donec purum*" (until clean).

Traversed, Her. Facing to the *sinister*.

Travertine, Travertino, It. A compact kind of TUFA stone, used in architecture; part of St. Peter's and the Colosseum of Rome are built of this stone. (See TUFA.) It is a stone of a white or yellowish tint, and was used by the ancient painters to give *body* to lakes.

Trebuchet, Fr. Med. A mechanical contrivance for projecting stones and darts; a kind of enormous cross-bow or sling.

Tredyl, O. E. (See GRYSE.)

Treflée, Her. (See BOTONNÉE.)

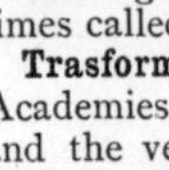

Fig. 660.
Trefoil slipped.

Trefoil, Arch. An ornament of three foils peculiar to the Romano-Byzantine and pointed styles. This ornament occurs in bands or string-courses, and also forms *entablatured* foliage. A synonym for it is *tiercefoil*. In Heraldry, a leaf of three conjoined foils generally borne *slipped*. (Fig. 660.)

Trellis. Open lattice-work.

Trenchers (Fr. *tranchoirs*). Originally thick *slices* of bread on which the meat was served, instead of plates; 13th century.

Trental, O. E. Chr. for Trigintale. Thirty masses for the dead.

Tresson, Fr. A net for the hair, worn by ladies in the Middle Ages. (See CALANTICA.)

Tressure, Her. A variety of the ORLE, generally set round with *fleurs-de-lys*. A striking example is to be seen in the Royal Shield of Scotland, now displayed in the second quarter of the Royal Arms, blazoned as—*Or, within a double Tressure flory; counterflory, a lion rampant guardant.*

Trevat. A weaver's cutting instrument for severing the pile-threads of velvet.

Triangle, Chr. An equilateral triangle is a symbol of the Holy Trinity, and therefore the motive, only second in frequency and importance to the CROSS, of the construction and decoration of Christian churches.

Triangle. A musical instrument of early occurrence, producing sound by the striking of a metal triangle with a metal rod.

Triblet. A goldsmith's tool used in making rings.

Tribometer. An instrument for estimating the friction of different metals.

Tribon, Gr. and R. (τρίβων). Literally, worn threadbare ; and thence a coarse and common sort of mantle worn by the Spartans or by Romans who affected Spartan manners.

Tribula or **Tribulum,** R. (*tero,* to rub). An apparatus for threshing corn ; consisting of a heavy platform armed with iron teeth or sharp flints.

Tribulus, R. (τρί-βολος, three-pointed). A CALTRAP (q.v.).

Tribunal, R. A raised platform for the curule chairs of the magistrates in the Basilica.

Tribune, R. and Chr. The semicircular recess in a Latin basilica in which the chief magistrate had his raised seat and administered justice. In Christian archæology, a gallery in a church ; the *triforium* and the organ-loft are tribunes. In Italian, *tribuna,* a picture-gallery.

Tricerion, Chr. (τρὶς, thrice ; κέρας, a horn). A candlestick with three branches, symbolizing the Holy Trinity. (See DICERION.)

Tricked, Her. Sketched with pen and ink in outline.

Triclinium, Gr. R. and Chr. (τρι-κλίνιον). A set of three dining-couches arranged round a table, and thence the dining-room itself, especially the summer dining-room. In Christian archæology the *triclinium* was an apartment attached to a Christian basilica, in which pilgrims were entertained.

Tricolor. The French national standard—red, white, and blue—introduced at the period of the revolution of 1789.

Tricomos, Gr. and R. A song for the third course of a banquet (κῶμος) at the festivals of Bacchus. The *comus* was peculiar to the first, and the *tetracomos* to the fourth course.

Tricot, Fr. (1) Silk net. (2) A knitted cotton fabric.

Fig. 661. Trident.

Trident, R. A three-pronged fork, the attribute of Neptune, used (1) for spearing fish ; (2) by the class of gladiators called RETIARII ; (3) as a goad for horses and cattle.

Triens, R. A small copper coin current among the Romans ; it was worth the third of an as, or about one farthing. It bore on the obverse a ship's prow or a horse's head, and four balls indicating four ounces (*unciæ*).

Trieterides, Gr. (τρι-ετηρίδες). Festivals of Bacchus, held in Bœotia every third year.

Triforium, Chr. A gallery over the side aisles of a church, open to the nave in arcades of three arches (*tres fores*).

Triga, R. A car drawn by three horses yoked either abreast or with one in front.

Trigarium, R. A field for the exercise of *trigæ* and other chariots.

Triglyph, Arch. (τρίγλυφος). An ornament consisting of three flutings or upright groovings separating the metopes in a Doric frieze. (Fig. 458.)

Trigonalis, R. Three-cornered " catch-ball ;" a subject on frescoes.

Fig. 662. Trigonum opus.

Trigonum, Gr. and R. (τρίγωνον). (1) A mosaic of triangular pieces of marble, glass, terracotta, or other material (*sectilia*). Fig. 662 is from a pavement at the entrance of a house at Pompeii. (2) A musical stringed instrument ; a triangular lyre, probably derived from Egypt.

Trilith, Celt. (τρί-λιθος). A Celtic monument of three stones forming a kind of door.

Trilix, R. In weaving, triple thread. (Compare BILIX.)

Trilobate, Arch. Presenting three foils.

Trimodia, R. A basket or vessel made to contain three modii (*tres modii*).

Trinity, Chr. For a detailed account of the progressive series of representations in Art of the Holy Trinity, consult *Fairholt's Dictionary, Didron's Iconographie Chrétienne,* &c.

Triobolum, Gr. A Greek silver coin of the value of three oboli. It was the established fee payable to an Athenian *dikast* for the hearing of a cause.

Tripetia. A Gallic term signifying a three-legged stool.

Tripod (Gr. τρί-πους). A vessel or table on three feet ; esp. the slab at Delphi upon which the priestess of Apollo sat. (See DELPHICA, CORTINA.)

Fig. 663. Tripod.

Tripping, Her. In easy motion, as a stag.

Triptych (τρί-πτυχος, three-fold). A form of picture, generally for ecclesiastical purposes, in three panels ; a centre, and two hanging doors worked on both sides. (Fig. 664.)

Tripudium, R. The noise made by the grain

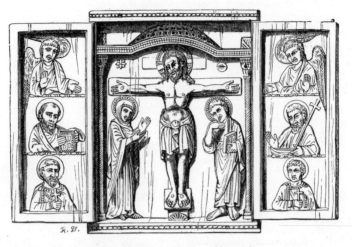

Fig. 664. Triptych carved in ivory with open doors.

as it fell from the beaks of the sacred chickens on to the ground; it was looked upon by the priest as a favourable omen; another name for it was *terripavium* (striking the earth). (See AUSPICIUM.)

Triquetra, Arch. A symmetrical interlaced ornament of early northern monuments. An endless line forming three arcs symmetrically interlaced will describe the figure.

Trireme, R. (*tres,* and *remus,* oar). A galley with three banks of rowers.

Trisomus, Chr. (τρί-σωμος). A triple sarcophagus. (Cf. BISOMUS.)

Trispastus, R. (τρί-σπαστος, drawn threefold). A block for raising weights; of three pullies (*orbiculi*), set in a single block (*trochlea*).

Triton. A sea-monster; generally represented as blowing a shell (*murex*), and with a body above the waist like that of a man, and below like a dolphin.

Triumphal Arch. A monumental structure, usually a portico with one or more arches, erected across a public road for a triumphal procession to pass under.

Triumphalia, R. Insignia conferred upon a general on the occasion of a triumph; consisting of a richly embroidered toga and tunic, a sceptre, a chaplet of laurel leaves with a crown of gold, and a chariot.

Triumphalis (Via), R. The road traversed by a triumph.

Triumphus, Triumph, R. The pageant of the entry of a victorious general into Rome.

Trivet, Her. A circular or triangular iron frame with three feet, borne by the family of Tryvett.

Trivium, R. (*tres,* and *via,* a way). A place where three roads meet.

Trochilus, Arch. A concave moulding in classic architecture. (See SCOTIA.)

Trochlea, R. (τροχιλέα). A machine for raising weights, very similar to the TRISPASTOS.

Trochus (τροχὸς, a wheel). A hoop represented on ancient gems as driven by naked boys with a crooked stick, precisely in the existing school fashion. It was of bronze, often with rings attached.

Trombone. A large trumpet with an arrange-

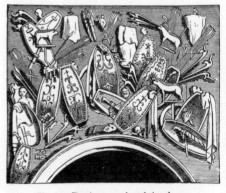

Fig. 665. Trophy on a triumphal arch.

ment of sliding tubes for modulating the tones by which every gradation of sound within its compass can be exactly produced.

Trophy, Gr. (τρόπαιον). A monument of victory (τροπή). Fig. 665 represents a trophy of Gallic spoils, from a bas-relief on the triumphal arch at Orange.

Trotcosie, Scotch. A warm covering for the head, neck, and breast, worn by travellers.

Fig. 666. Trulla.

Trua, dim. **Trulla,** R. (1) A large flat ladle or spoon perforated with holes and used for skimming liquids when boiling. (2) A kind of drinking-cup. (3) A portable brazier or earthenware vessel perforated with holes (Fig. 666) for carrying hot coals about. (4) A mason's trowel.

Trullissatio, R. A coating of plaster or cement laid on by the trowel (*trulla*).

Trumeau, Fr. A pier looking-glass.

Trumpet, Her. The Roman *tuba*; a long straight tube expanded at its extremity.

Truncated. With the top cut off parallel to the base.

Trunnions. The side supports on which a cannon rests on its carriage.

Truss, Arch. The system of timbers mutually supporting each other and the roof.

Trussed, Her. Said of birds, with closed wings.

Fig. 667. **Trussing,** Her. Said of birds of Trumpet. prey, devouring.

Tuba, R. A straight bronze trumpet with a small mouthpiece at one end, the other being wide and bell-shaped. (Cf. CORNU.)

Tubilustrum, Quinquatrus, R. Festivals held at Rome twice a year, for the purification of trumpets (*tubæ*).

Tubla. Assyrian drums, with skin at the top only.

Tuck, O. E. A short sword or dagger, worn in the 16th and 17th centuries by all classes.

Tucket, O. E. (It. *toccata*). A flourish on a trumpet.

Tudesco, Sp. A wide cloak.

Tudor Arch, Arch. An arch of four centres, flat for its span; having two of its centres in or near the spring, and the other two far below it. (*Rickman.*)

Tudor Flower, Arch. An ornament common to Elizabethan buildings. A flat flower, or leaf, as a crest or finish on cornices, &c.

Tudor Rose, formed by the union of the white and red roses of York and Lancaster; is described in heraldry as a white rose charged upon a red one. (See Fig. 395.)

Tudor Style, Arch. The style which prevailed under the Tudor dynasty. The term is loosely applied to various periods. (See PERPENDICULAR.)

Tufa. A porous variety of limestone deposited by calcareous water. It hardens on exposure to the air; and was much used by the Romans for facing buildings, and generally, on account of its lightness, for vaulting. (See TRAVERTINE.)

Tugurium, R. (*tego*, to cover). A thatched roof, and thence, a peasant's hut.

Tulip-tree. The wood of this tree is smooth and fine-grained, very easily wrought, and not liable to split. It is largely used in carving and ornamental work, and for panels in coach building.

Tulle. A plain silk lace, blonde or net.

Tumblers. The drinking-glasses so called take their name from their original shape, rounded at the bottom, so that they *tumbled* over unless they were very carefully set down. Similar goblets are still made of wood in Germany; often with the inscription—

"Trink' mich aus, und leg' mich nieder:
Steh' ich auf, so füll' mich wieder."

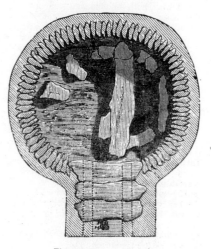

Fig. 668. Plan of a Tumulus.

Tumulus (*tumeo*, to swell). Sepulchral mounds of ancient and prehistoric construction. The illustrations, figs. 668 and 669, show the plan and section of a Gallic tumulus opened at Fontenay le Marmion.

Tumulus Honorarius. (See CENOTAPHIUM.)

Tunbridge Ware. Inlaid work of variously-coloured woods made at Tunbridge Wells in Kent.

Fig. 669. Section of a Tumulus.

Tunica, Gr. and R. A tunic; the principal garment worn both by men and women among the Greeks and Romans. It was a kind of woollen shirt confined round the neck and the waist; it came down as far as the knee; it had short sleeves which only covered the upper part of the arm. Tunics were classed as follows: the *exomis*, the *epomis*, the *chiton*, the *manicata* or *manuleata*, the *talaris*, the *muliebris*, the *interior* or *intima*, the *recta*, the *angusticlavia*, the *laticlavia*, the *patagiata*, the *palmata*, the *asema*, and the *picta*. (*Bosc.*) (Fig. 670.)

Tunicatus, Gr. and R. Wearing a tunic.

Tunicle, Chr. (Lat. *subtile*). The vestment of the sub-deacon; it resembled the dalmatic, but had tight sleeves.

Turbo, R. (Gr. βέμβιξ). A child's whipping-top; the whorl of a spindle.

Turibulum. (See THURIBLE.)

Turicremus. (See THURICREMUS.)

Turkey Carpets are made entirely of wool, the loops being larger than those of Brussels carpeting, and always cut; the cutting of the yarn gives the surface the appearance of velvet.

Turkey-stitch (*point de Turquie*). A kind of carpet made at the Savonnerie, established 1627.

Turma, R. A squadron of legionary cavalry; it consisted of thirty-two men commanded by a decurion, and led under a *vexillum.*

Turnbull's Blue. A light and delicate variety of *Prussian blue.*

Turner's Yellow. An oxychloride of lead, known also as *patent yellow*, and *Cassell yellow*.

Turquoise. A valuable blue gem for ornamental purposes. (*S.*) Fossil ivory impregnated with copper. (*F.*)

Turrets, Arch. (Fr. *tourette*, a small tower). Towers of great height in proportion to their diameter, and large pinnacles, are called turrets; these often contain staircases, and are sometimes crowned with small spires. Large towers often have turrets at their corners.

Turricula, R. (dimin. of *turris*). A small tower; also, a dice-box in the form of a tower,

Fig. 670. Tunica muliebris, *talaris.*

to which the Greeks applied the term of *pyrgus* (πύργος). *Turricula* has a synonym FRITILLUS (q.v.).

Turriger, R. Bearing a tower ; the term applies both to an elephant and a ship of war when thus armed.

Turris, Tower. In a general sense, any building or collection of buildings either lofty in themselves or built upon an elevation, and thence, fortifications, such as a tower of defence, the tower of a city gate or a castle, a DONJON (q.v.).

Tus or **Thus**, R. Frankincense, imported from Arabia and used in great quantities by the ancients either for religious ceremonies or to perfume their apartments.

Tuscan Order of Architecture. The simplest of the five ORDERS of classical architecture, having no ornament whatever ; unknown to the Greeks ; a variety of ROMAN-DORIC (q.v.). The *column* is about seven diameters high, including the base and capital. The *base* is half a diameter in height ; the *capital* is of equal height, having a square *abacus*, with a small projecting fillet on the upper edge—under the abacus is an ovolo and a fillet with neck below ; the *shaft* is never fluted ; the *entablature* is quite plain, having neither *mutules* nor *modillions* ; the *frieze* also is quite plain.

Tusses or **Toothing-stones**, in building, are projecting stones for joining other buildings upon.

Tutulatus, R.. Having the hair arranged in the form of a cone, or wearing the sacerdotal cap called *tutulus*, and thence a priest who usually wore the TUTULUS (q.v.).

Tutulus or **Apex**, R. (1) A flamen's cap ; it was conical and almost pointed. (2) A mode of arranging the hair on the crown of the head in the shape of a pyramid or cone. An example is seen in the Medicean Venus.

Twill. A kind of ribbed cloth.

Tympanium, R. (τυμπάνιον). A pearl shaped like a kettle-drum, namely, with one surface flat and the other round.

Tympanum, R. (τύμπανον). (1) A tambourine, like that of modern times : a piece of stiff parchment stretched over a hoop with bells. (2) A drum-shaped wheel ; *tympanum dentatum*, a cogged wheel. (3) In architecture, the flat

Fig. 671. Tympanum. Romano-Byzantine.

surface, whether triangular or round, marked out by the mouldings of a pediment. Fig. 671 shows a tympanum of the Romano-Byzantine period. (For TRIANGULAR PEDIMENT, see Fig. 26.)

Tynes, Scotch. (1) Branches of a stag's antlers. (2) Teeth of a harrow.

Tyrian Purple. An ancient dye of a brilliant colour, obtained from shells of the *murex* and *purpura*.

U.

U. The letter repeated so as to mark the feathering upon tails of birds, is a peculiarity of Sicilian silks.

Udo, R. A sock made of goat-skin, or felt.

Ulna, R. A measure of length, subdivision of the foot measure.

Ultramarine or **Lapis Lazuli** (*azurrum transmarinum*). A beautiful blue pigment obtained from lazulite, highly esteemed by early painters. In consequence of the costliness of this pigment its use in a picture was regulated by special contract, and it was either supplied or paid for by the person who ordered the picture. Lely has recorded that he paid for his as much as 4*l*. 10*s*. the ounce. The pigment is now artificially compounded. (Cf. GUIMET'S U.)

Umbella, Umbraculum, R. (*umbra*, shade). An umbrella, made to open and shut like those of modern times. It is represented on vases held by a female slave over the head of her mistress. (See also UMBRELLAS.)

Umber. A massive mineral pigment used by painters as a brown colour, and to make varnish dry quickly. *Raw umber* is of an olive brown, which becomes much redder when *burnt*. (See OCHRES.)

Umbilici, R. (lit. *navels*), were the ornamental bosses which projected from each end of the staff round which a volume of papyrus or parchment (*liber*) was rolled. They were also called *cornua*, and *geminæ frontes*. (See LIBER.)

Umbo (Gr. ὀμφαλός). (1) The boss of a shield, often sharp and projecting so as to form an offensive weapon in itself. (2) A bunch formed by the folds of the toga tacked in to the belt across the chest.

Umbræ, R. The shades of the departed; represented in the forms in which they abandoned life. Those killed in battle, *mutilated*, &c.

Umbrellas. ANGLO-SAXON manuscripts sometimes represent a servant holding an umbrella over the head of his master. In the sculptures of ancient EGYPT and ASSYRIA they are represented borne by the attendants on a king. The GREEK and ROMAN ladies used parasols in all respects resembling those of modern times. In the PANATHENAIC procession the daughters of foreign settlers in Athens had to carry parasols over the heads of the Athenian maidens taking part in the procession. They were substituted later on by broad hats, the Roman PETASUS and the Greek THOLIA. In the SIAMESE empire an umbrella is the emblem of the royal dignity.

Umbrere, Umbril. In mediæval armour, a projection on a helmet acting as a guard to the eyes. **Umbril.** (See UMBRERE.)

Fig. 672. Umbril.

Uncia (Gr. οὐγκία, *Angl.* ounce). The *unit* of measurement. The twelfth part of anything. In currency, a copper coin; the twelfth part of an As. Its value was expressed on the obverse and reverse by *one* ball; in lineal measurement, the twelfth of a foot, whence our *inch;* in square measure, the twelfth of a *jugerum;* of liquids, the twelfth of a *sextarius;* in weight, the twelfth of a pound (*libra*).

Uncial Letters. When writing on papyrus or vellum became common, many of the straight lines of the capitals, in that kind of writing, gradually acquired a *curved* form. From the 6th to the 8th, or even 10th century, these *uncials*, or partly rounded capitals, prevail in illuminated MSS. (See also MINUSCULE, SEMI-UNCIALS.)

Uncus, R. (ὄγκος). A hook such as (1) that with which the corpses of gladiators were dragged out of the arena ; or those of criminals from the carnificina where they were executed. (2) The fluke of an anchor, &c.

Under-croft, Arch. A subterranean chamber.

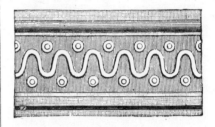

Fig. 673. Undulated moulding.

Undulated, Arch. (*unda,* a wave). Moulded or sculptured in the form of a *wave;* as for instance the *undulated torus.* (See NEBULE.) (Fig. 673.)

Undy, Undée, Her. Wavy.

Unguentaria, R. Flasks or boxes of costly workmanship for holding perfumes, essences, oils, and salves, for use in the baths, &c. (See NARTHECIA.)

Unicorn. In Christian art a symbol of purity, especially of female chastity. Attribute of St. Justina of Antioch. In Heraldry it is famous as the sinister supporter of the Royal Shield of England. The legend was that its body took the form of a horse and antelope, and

Fig. 674. Unicorn. Device of the Orsini family.

it had one horn on its head. It was believed to live solitary in the woods, and could only be caught by a maiden. The property of detecting poison was attributed to its horn, and Hentzner, who visited England in 1598, says :—

"We were shown at Windsor the horn of an Unicorn, of about eight spans and a half in length, valued at above 100l."

It is frequently mentioned in ancient inventories :—

"1391. Une manche d'or d'un essay de lincourne pour attoucher aux viandes de Monseigneur le Dauphin." *Comptes Royaux*, quoted by Mrs. Bury Palliser."

In allusion to this property, Alviano, the champion of the Orsini family, adopted as his device a unicorn at a fountain surrounded by snakes, toads, and other reptiles, and stirring up the water with its horn before he drinks, with the motto, " I expel poisons."

Union Cloths. Fabrics of wool with wefts of cotton.

Union Jack. The National Ensign of the United Kingdom of Great Britain —exhibiting the Union of the crosses of St. George and St. Andrew combined —first displayed in the reign of James I., 1606. The flag as it is now used, dates from the beginning of this century. It is borne on a shield, charged in pretence upon the escutcheon of the Duke of Wellington.

Fig. 675. Present Union Jack.

Upapitha, Hind. The pedestal of the Hindoo orders, which included, besides the pedestal properly so called, the base (*athisthama*), the pillar or shaft (*stambu*) which was either square or polygonal and only rounded at the upper part near the capital or *cushion* which took its place, and lastly the entablature (*prastura*).

Uræus, Egyp. A transcription of the Egyptian word *ârâ* or the asp *hajé*, a kind of serpent called by the Greeks *basilicon* (βασιλικόν). The *uræus* as an emblem of the sovereign power forms the distinctive ornament in the head-dress of the Egyptian kings.

Urbino Ware, made at Urbino, under the patronage of its Duke. " A city," says Jacquemart, " which has supplied potters and painters to the greater part of the workshops of Italy ; which has sent ceramic colonies to Flanders and

Corfu, and yet we are scarcely acquainted with its works, except those of its decline." (Fig. 676.) (See MAJOLICA.)

Fig. 676. Plate of Urbino Ware, Louvre Museum.

Urceolated (Basket), Arch. The corbel of the capital which narrows a little underneath its upper part.

Urceolus. Diminutive of URCEUS (q.v.).

Urceus, R. An earthenware pitcher used in religious ceremonies ; represented on coins in the form of a modern ewer.

Uriant, Her. Said of a fish when it swims in a vertical position ; head downwards. (Cf. HAURIANT.)

Urn. The common urn, the κάλπις of the Greeks, had a narrow neck and swelling body ; it was used for conveying water from the fountain. The funereal cinerary urn was in general quadrangular, but there were a large number which resembled the *kalpis*, with the exception that they had a wider neck and were furnished in every case with a lid.

Fig. 677. Funereal urn, Indian.

Fig. 677 represents a funeral urn of Indian pottery, of very ancient date. The electoral urn, from which lots were drawn at the comitia to decide the order of voting, was of an oval form and had a narrow neck to prevent the possibility of more than one number being drawn out at a time. An urn is always introduced as an appropriate emblem of the river-gods. The *urna* was a measure of capacity containing eight *congii* or half an AMPHORA.

Urnarium, R. A square table or hollow slab on which *urnæ* or earthenware vessels were placed.

Ustrina, Ustrinum, R. (*uro,* to burn). A public place for burning the bodies of the dead, in contradistinction to BUSTUM, a private place of cremation, situated within the sepulchral enclosure. It was in the public ustrina that the bodies of people of moderate means as well as the poor were burned.

Uter, R. A wine-skin or large leathern bag made of goat-skin, pig-skin, or ox-hide, and used for holding wine or other liquids. *Uter unctus* was a goat-skin inflated with air and thoroughly greased on the outside. The peasants of Greece were fond of dancing and leaping upon these wine-skins, which it was extremely difficult to do without frequent falls. This was a very popular rustic game, and formed a principal feature of the second day of the festival of Bacchus, called by the Greeks *Ascolia* (Ἀσκώλια), ἀσκὸς being the Greek equivalent of *uter.*

Uti Rogas, R. A voting formula affirmative of the proposition in debate, written on the ticket in the abbreviated form V. R. for *uti rogas* (as you propose).

Utricularius, R. (from *uter*). A performer on the bag-pipe.

Utriculus. Diminutive of UTER (q.v.).

V.

In mediæval words the initials V and B occasionally interchange:—as Vanneria for Banneria, a banner, &c.

Vacerra, R. (*vacca,* a cow). An enclosure in which cattle were kept.

Vacons, Hind. Hindoo genii which figure in the celestial hierarchy immediately after Brahma. They are eight in number, and each of them protects one of the eight regions of the world: Paoulestia is the guardian of the North or mineral wealth; Ima, god of the dead and the infernal regions, is the guardian of the South; Indra, god of the ether and the day, the guardian of the East; Pratcheta, god of waters and the ocean, the guardian of the West; Içania, who is looked upon as an incarnation of Siva, is the guardian of the North-East; Pavana, king of the winds, the guardian of the North-West; Agni or Pacava, the god of fire, is the guardian of the South-East; and Nirouti, the prince of the evil genii, is the guardian of the South-West. (*Bosc.*)

Vagina, R. The scabbard of a sword, made of wood or leather, and generally ornamented with plates and bosses of metal. (See Fig. 44.)

Vails (from *Vale,* farewell!). Fees to servants from parting guests.

Vair. The fur of the squirrel, much worn in state costumes of the 14th century. In Heraldry —one of the furs—represented as a series of small shields placed close together, alternately blue and white.

Valance. Drapery hangings for furniture, cornices, &c.; hence—

Valenced. Fringed with a beard. (*Shakespeare.*)

Fig. 678. Gilded Vase of Valentia, with votive inscription.

Valencia Pottery. M. Jacquemart considers this the most ancient and the true centre of the ceramic fabrication in Spain, carried back by tradition to the Roman domination. On the conquest of Spain from the Moors the Saracen potters of Valencia were protected by special charter. Fig. 678 is an illustration of the gilded ware for which Valencia is famous.

Fig. 679. Valenciennes.

Valenciennes. The date of the introduction of the manufacture of this lace is unknown, although it existed before the time of Louis XIV., under whose reign it flourished and reached its climax between 1725 and 1780. Valenciennes lace is made entirely on the pillow, of simple combinations, with one kind of thread for the pattern and for the ground. (See engraving.) No lace is so expensive to make from the number of bobbins required. The flax used is of the finest quality, so fine that the lace-makers worked in underground cellars to keep their work from the air, and scarcely completed an inch and half of lace in a day.

Valendar Clay. A kind of potter's clay from Nassau. (*Simmonds.*)

Valet, O. E. (Med. Lat. *valeti*). Sons of the nobility and of knights bore this title, until they acquired the military belt. (*Meyrick.*)

Valle Cypre. A silk mourning crape, called also Bologna crape.

Vallum, Gr. and R. (*vallus*, a stake). A palisade made with strong branches of trees, which was placed on the top of the embankment (*agger*) surrounding a camp.

Valvæ, R. (Gr. σανίς). Folding doors or shutters; synonym of FORES.

Vambrace (Fr. *avant bras*). The ancient BRACHIALE, the covering of the lower arm, from the elbow to the wrist. Originally it covered only the outside of the arm, but afterwards was made like a sleeve of iron. (C f. RERE-BRACE.)

Fig. 680. Vambrace.

Vamp. Upper leathers for shoes. In Russia and the East they are richly embroidered.

Vampire. A monster of mediæval iconography. A well-known example is the one which decorates the angle of one of the towers in Paris Cathedral.

Vamplate (Fr. *avant plaque*). A guard of metal over the handle of a tilting-lance.

Van (from Fr. *avant*). Of an army, the front.

Vandyke-brown. A pigment of a fine, deep, semi-transparent brown colour obtained from peat.

Vane, or **Fane,** O. E. (from the German *Fahne*, a banner). (1) A broad flag to be carried by a knight in a tournament. (*Meyrick*, i. 155.) Hence (2) a weathercock, in Mediæval buildings generally in the form of a heraldic banner supported by a figure. (See FANE.)

Vanishing Point. In perspective. (See POINT OF SIGHT.)

Vannerie, Fr. Basket-work.

Vannus, R. A winnowing-van; i.e. a broad flat basket used for winnowing the chaff from the corn. It was among the agricultural symbols borne in the processions of Ceres. A sculpture in the British Museum represents the infant Bacchus riding in such a basket in the hands of a pair of dancing bacchantes.

Vantbrace. (See VAMBRACE.)

Vaquero, Sp. A jacket worn by women and children.

Vardingale, O. E. The *farthingale* or hooped petticoat of Elizabeth's reign, fig. 681.

"Supporters, postures, *farthingales*,
Above the loins to wear,
That, be she ne'er so slender, yet
She cross-like seems four square."
(*Warner, in Albion's England.*)

Varnishes are made by dissolving *resins* or gum-resins in alcohol, ether, &c., so that as the spirit evaporates the varnish dries down into a

Fig. 681. Farthingale, temp. Elizabeth.

transparent film; varnishes are coloured with aloes, annotto, cochineal, dragon's blood, gamboge, indigo, red saunders, saffron, or turmeric. *Amber varnish* is hardest and most durable in colour, but dries very slowly. *Animé varnish* dries quickly, but is liable to crack, and deepens in colour with exposure to the air. *Copal* ranks next to amber in durability, and the varnish becomes lighter by exposure; the best copal varnishes are slow in drying unless mixed with animé. *Mastic* is a favourite spirit varnish used as a picture varnish and for delicate works of a pale colour. *Damar* mixed with mastic makes an appropriate varnish for maps and similar work. The qualities to be sought in varnishes for a painting are that they should resist damp, exclude air, and not injure the colour. (See also ITALIAN VARNISH, STRASBURG TURPENTINE, &c.)

Vas, R. A vase. Any kind of vessel, e.g. *Vasa Corinthia, Vasa Deliaca, Vasa Samia, Murrhina*, &c. The manufacture and ornamentation of vases was one of the most important branches of Classical Art. Illustrations of vases are found in this work under:

	Fig.		Fig.
Acratophorum	7	Egyptian	279
Amphora	20	Funeral Urn	340
Arezzo Vase	37	Hydria	391
Aryballos	46	Chinese Vase	406
Bifrons	85	Lecythus	422
Cantharus	132	Nuremberg	491
Cylix	232	Oinochoe	498
Ecuelle	278	Valentia	678

Vatillum. (See BATILLUM.)

Vaunt-brace, O. E., or **Warn-brace.** Armour for the body.

Vectis, R. (*veho*, to carry). A bar of wood or iron used as a lever, crow-bar, capstan bar, or pole for carrying burdens on the back; the workman who made use of a *vectis* was called *vectiarius*.

Vedas (from Sanskrit *vid*, to know), Hind. Four collections of sacred books said to have been collated about 3000 B.C. from earlier documents. They are the RIGVEDA, a collection of hymns and prayers; the YAJURVEDA, liturgical and ceremonial ordinances; SAMAVEDA, lyrical pieces; and ATHARVAVEDA, chiefly incantations. Besides the above, each Veda contains fragmentary writings called *Samhuta*, and dogmatic treatises called *Brahmana*; and certain Commentaries, called *Upavedas, Vedangas*, and *Upangas* are regarded as forming a fifth Veda. The above form the sacred books of the Hindoo religion.

Vegetable Blue Black. (See BLUE BLACK.)

Vegetable Ivory. Nuts of a South American palm (*Phytelephas macrocarpa*) resembling ivory, and much used for ornamental carving.

Vehicles or **Mediums.** The liquid in which pigments are applied. In *fresco* and water-colour painting gum-water is used; in *distemper painting*, size; in *oil painting*, the fixed oils of linseed, nut, and poppy. In *encaustic* wax is used. (See also MEDIUM, COPAL, ITALIAN VARNISH, MEGYLP, &c.)

Velamen and **Velamentum**, R. (*velum*, a veil). A veil worn by women, concealing the whole person. (See FLAMMEUM.)

Velarium, R. (*velum*, a covering). An awning stretched over a theatre; usually of woollen cloth, but sometimes of more costly materials.

Velatura, It. A mode of glazing, adopted by the early Italian painters, by which the colour was rubbed on by all the fingers or the flat of the hand, so as to fill the interstices left by the brush, and cover the entire surface of the picture thinly and evenly. (*Fairholt.*)

Velatus, R. (*velo*, to cover). Veiled or wearing flowing garments; having the forehead encircled with a garland. *Milites velati* were supernumerary soldiers who filled the places of those who were killed or disabled.

Velites, R. A body of light-armed infantry not forming part of the legion, who skirmished in small companies.

Vellum. Fine parchment from the skins of calves; any parchment binding is by librarians technically described as vellum. It is a beautifnl substitute for paper, for luxurious printing of books for presentation, &c., and was much used by mediæval artists for painting and illuminating.

Velours (Fr. Velvet). A kind of velvet or plush for furniture, carpets, &c., manufactured in Prussia, partly of linen, and partly of double cotton warps with mohair yarn weft. (*Simmonds' Commercial Dict.*)

Velours d'Utrecht. A woollen velvet, for tapestry, &c., made in the Netherlands.

Veloute, Fr. Velvet lace.

Velum, R. (1) A general term for any kind of sail, esp. the square *main-sail* of a ship in contradistinction to the other sails. (2) The curtain or drop-scene of a theatre. (3) The curtain or hanging put up as a covering in front of a door. (4) A synonym for VELARIUM.

Fig. 682. Venetian point in relief, English made.

Velufe (Fr. *velours*). Velvet. (*Shakespeare.*)

Velvet (Ital. *velluto*; hairy or shaggy, like an animal's skin) was introduced into England in the 13th century. *Velvet upon velvet* is that where the pattern shows itself in a *double pile*, one pile higher than the other. "*Purshed*" velvet was velvet raised in a network pattern.

Velvet Painting. The art of painting on fine velvet.

Velveteen. A kind of FUSTIAN.

Venabulum, R. (*venor*, to hunt). A hunting-spear, a strong staff with a broad lozenge-shaped iron head.

Venationes. Hunting scenes and sports in the arena in which wild beasts were introduced fighting with each other and with men, a common subject of representation on bas-reliefs on ancient tombs.

Veneering is the art of covering wooden objects with a thin slice of ornamental wood, so as to give the whole the false appearance of being made of the superior wood. It is distinct from MARQUETRY or INLAID-WORK (q.v.).

Veneficium, R. The crime of poisoning; an accusation abused by the ancient Romans almost as that of witchcraft was in the middle ages.

Venetian Blinds are those made of laths strung together.

Venetian Chalk. A white talc used for marking cloth, &c.

Venetian Door. A door lighted by panes of glass on each side.

Venetian Point. The engraving represents an exquisite specimen of Venetian point lace in relief, shown at the International Exhibition, 1874, among other wonderful reproductions of ancient needle-made lace. (For method of working, see NEEDLE POINT.)

Venetian Porcelain. (See ECUELLE.)

Venetian Red or **Scarlet Ochre.** A burnt ochre, used as a pigment in oil and water colours. Its colour is red, alloyed with blue and yellow.

Venetian Window. A window with three separate lights.

Venew (Fr. *venu*). A bout at a fencing-school.

Venice, Doge of. The illustration represents the state costume of the Doge of Venice, wearing the traditional cap of liberty, the ermine, and richly-embroidered robes of his office.

Venice Turpentine. A product of the larch, used for varnishing pictures. It is liable to crack.

Venice White. (See CARBONATE OF LEAD, BARYTES.)

Ventaile or **Aventail.** A movable front to a helmet, through which the wearer breathed:—
"quâ ventus hauritur."

"L'escu au col, la ventaille fermée."
(*Roman de Roncevaux.*)

Ventrale, R. (*venter*, the belly). A girdle of peculiar shape, fastened round the loins over the abdomen.

Vents, Scotch. Chimneys.

Venturina, Sp. A precious stone, of a yellowish-brown colour. Hence :—

Venturine. A powder of gold used to sprinkle over japanned surfaces.

Ver Sacrum, R. (lit. a holy (or dedicated) Spring). The dedication to sacrifice of all that is born in a certain year, in the months of March and April, was a common practice of the early Italian nations, especially of the Sabines. In the most ancient times actual infanticide was a

Fig. 683. Venice, Doge of, in state costume, 16th century.

part of this offering; but in later years the practice was modified as regarded children. They were brought up, under a vow of dedication, to the age of twenty-one, and then with veiled faces expelled across the frontiers. Many colonies resulted from this practice.

Vera Icon, Chr. The *true image* impressed upon the SUDARIUM (q.v.) of St. Veronica. In St. Peter's at Rome, in a chapel dedicated to that saint, a painting on linen is shown as the veritable napkin of St. Veronica ; and a fine mosaic over the altar, after a design by Andrea Sacchi, represents the incident. (See STOLE.)

Verandah. An open portico to a house. In the tropical countries the open verandah is the principal apartment of a house, and Society appear to the passers-by, in their illuminated verandahs, like the actors on the stage of a theatre.

Verbena, R. Sacred herbs torn up by the roots from the enclosure of the Capitoline hill ; which the Roman *fetiales* or ambassadors always carried in their hands on foreign embassies. (Compare VINDICIÆ.)

" When an injury had been received from a foreign state four fetiales were deputed to seek redress, who again elected one of their number to act as representative. He was styled *pater patratus populi Romani.* A fillet of white wool was bound round his head, together with a *wreath of sacred herbs* gathered within the enclosure of the Capitoline hill (*verbenæ*, Sagmina), whence he was called Verbenarius." (*Dr. Smith.*)

Verber, R. In a general sense, any kind of leather thong ; as, for instance, the thong of a sling, the thong of a whip for driving horses or scourging slaves, &c.

Verde Antico. A green mottled serpentine marble, used by ancient sculptors, found at Taygetos. It is much valued for its beautiful markings.

Verde Azurro, It. (1) A native carbonate of copper, of a greenish-blue colour; the *Armenian stone* of Pliny. (2) A blue-green pigment.

Verde Eterno. A dark green pigment, anciently used by the Venetian painters.

Verdigris. A bright acetate of copper, used as a green pigment.

Verditer (Blue and **Green).** A hydrated percarbonate of copper. It is generally prepared by decomposing the solution of nitrate of copper, by the addition of chalk. The refined blue and green verditers, see CARBONATES of COPPER (*Mountain blue*). The verditer known as *Bremen Green* is produced by subjecting copper to the action of sea salt and vitriol for three months. (Cf. CHRYSOCOLLA.)

Veretonus, Med. Lat. The VIRETON (q.v.).

Verge, O. E. A rod. In Mediæval Architecture the shaft of a column.

Verge Board, Arch. The external gable-board of a house, which is often elaborately ornamented with carvings. (See BARGE BOARD.)

Vergers (Fr. *verge*, a staff). Officers who carry a rod or staff of office. In the law courts a white wand, before the judges; in cathedrals, &c., a rod tipped with silver.

Verguilla, Sp. Gold or silver wire, without silk.

Vermeil, Fr. Silver gilt, or gilt bronze.

Vermiculatum. A kind of pavement disposed in wreathed lines like the undulations of worms (*vermes*). (See PAVIMENTUM.)

Vermilion. The *minium* of the ancients. A bright and beautiful red colour.

Vermilion. The bisulphuret of mercury in powder, a delicate bright red pigment which is *pale* or *deep*; supposed to be the pigment known to the Romans as *minium*. (Cf. CINNABAR, RED LEAD.)

Vernacle, Chr. A term for the VERA ICON.

Vernation. See ESTIVATION.

Vernis-Martin Work. A Japanese style of painting and enamelling on furniture, carriages, and small objects, named after the introducer, who was born about 1706.

Vernon Gallery, founded in 1847 by the gift of Mr. Robert Vernon of 157 pictures of the British school, is now in the South Kensington Museum.

Verona Green. A variety of GREEN EARTH (q.v.). (See APPIANUM.)

Verona Serge. A thin textile fabric, made of worsted, or mohair, and of cotton.

Veronese Green. (See CARBONATE OF COPPER.)

Veronica. (See VERA ICON.)

Vert, Her. Green, represented in engraving by lines sloping downwards from left to right.

Vert bleu, Fr. (See VERDE AZURRO.)

Verticillus, R. (*verto*, to turn). The whorl of a spindle, a small disk of wood, stone, or metal, by means of which a rotary movement is given to the spindle. (Cf. TURBO.)

Veru, R. Literally, a roasting-spit made of wood and with an iron point. The term was also applied to a weapon of Samnite origin used by the Roman infantry, and bearing much resemblance to a spit. (2) An arrow or dart. (Fr. *vire*.)

Veruculum, R. (dimin. of *veru*). A small javelin used by the Roman infantry.

Vervels, Varvals, Her. Small rings.

Vesara, Hind. A Hindoo temple built on a circular plan.

Vesica Piscis (in Italian, *mandorla*, almond). The oblong glory surrounding the whole person of Our Lord, or the Virgin, or saints ascending into heaven. The *seals* of abbeys, colleges, and other religious establishments were all of this form. (See Fig. 684.)

It is in form symbolical of the monogram Ἰχθὺς. (See ACROSTIC.)

Fig. 684. Vesica Piscis.

Vespæ, Vespillones, R. The bearers of a bier in a funeral were so called by the common people, because they came to fetch the bodies in the evening (*vespertino tempore*).

Vespers, Chr. In the Roman Church, the afternoon service; in the English Church, Evening Prayer.

Vessets. A kind of cloth.

Vest, O. E. "A wide garment reaching to the knees, open before, and turned up with a facing or lining, the sleeves turned up at the elbows." (*Randle Holme*, 1683.)

Vestalia, Gr. and R. Festivals in honour of Vesta. Asses were driven through Rome, carrying wreaths of flowers and rolls.

Vestals, R. The priestesses of the goddess Vesta, to whom the charge was committed of the sacred fire. They were originally four, subsequently six in number. Their distinctive dress was the *infula* fitting close to the head, with *vittæ* depending, a long tunic of white linen, and the purple TOGA, or mantle, with a long train to it.

Vested, Her. Clothed.

Vestibule, Arch. An entrance-court or vacant space before the entrance to a house, temple, or other building. (See DOMUS.)

Vestment, Chr. The hangings of an altar, and the robes of the clergy; the term often comprises also the sacred vessels.

Vestry, Chr. The modern *vestiarium* in a church; called also the SACRISTY.

Vethym, or **Vathym**, O.E. A fathom—six feet.

Vettura, It. (Fr. *voiture*). A travelling carriage.

Vexillatio, R. Troops under one *vexillum*; and thence the troops of the allies.

Vexillum, R. A cavalry standard consisting of a square piece of woollen cloth spread upon a cross. (See SIGNA MILITARIA.)

Vexillum Regale, Med. Lat. The Royal Standard.

Via, R. The high road. These were so constructed by the Romans that following gene-

Z

rations used them without repair for more than a thousand years. The earliest was the *Appian* or the *Great South Road* from Rome to Brindisi, made B.C. 312 ; the *Great North Road* continued through Gaul was the *Flaminian Road*. The construction of a Roman road was the following :—between trenches thirteen to fifteen feet apart, the *gremium* or foundation was made firm, if necessary, in a marsh, with piles ; this was covered with large stones of a regulated size, such as London streets were formerly paved with (*statumen*), and this with macadamized stones cemented with lime (*rudus*), rammed down hard, and nine inches thick ; then came small shards of pottery, six inches thick, also cemented with lime (*nucleus*), and over this the pavement of large blocks of the hardest stone (see SILEX), irregular, but fitted and joined with the greatest nicety, and perfectly smoothed with a slope for drainage.

Viaticum, R. A provision for a journey. Adopted by the Christian Church in reference to the last offices of religion to the dying, with the obvious symbolical significance.

Vibia, R. A cross-bar and uprights forming a trestle.

Vibrella, Med. Lat. A cannon.

Vices. The seven VICES commonly met with in Christian allegory are : Anger, Avarice, Envy, Lust, Pride, Revenge, and Sloth.

Vicessis, R. Twenty pounds weight = 14·987 lbs. avoirdupois.

Victima, R. The animals used for sacrifices were mostly domestic; as bulls, sheep, goats, pigs, dogs, or horses ; each god had his favourite animals. The head of the victim was generally strewed with roasted barley meal, mixed with salt, and adorned with garlands, and sometimes its horns were gilt. A bunch of hair was cut from its forehead and thrown into the fire as *primatiæ*. It was killed by a person called the *popa*, not by the priests ; and part of the intestines were burned, or to river-gods, thrown into the river, &c.

Fig. 685. Victoria Cross.

Victoria Cross is of bronze, and was instituted by the Queen in 1856 to render honour to "conspicuous bravery" in actual conflict by sea or land. It is worn on the left breast attached to a blue ribbon for the Navy, and a red for the Army.

Victoriatus R. A silver coin stamped with a figure of Victory, while its ob-

verse represented a bearded Jupiter. (Fig. 686.)

Fig. 686.

Victory is represented by the ancients winged, and bearing a *palm* branch and a *laurel* crown. Fig. 687 is the beautiful device adopted by Martin, King of Aragon, in 1396, with the motto, "Not in the Darkness."

Fig. 687. Victory. Device of Martin, King of Aragon.

Vicuna. A kind of alpaca wool.

Vicus, R. (Gr. κώμη). A quarter in a city.

Vidrecome, Fr. A large drinking-glass.

Vielle, Fr. The "hurdy-gurdy," an ancient stringed instrument played with finger-keys, and producing sound by the friction of a wheel instead of a fiddle-bow.

Vienna Lake. (See CARMINATED LAKES.)

Vienna White. (See CARBONATE OF LEAD.)

Vigessis, R. (See VICESSIS.)

Vignette (Fr. *a little vine*). A small woodcut or illustration on a page. In Architecture, a running ornament of leaves and tendrils, common in the hollow mouldings of Gothic Architecture ; especially in the Decorated and Perpendicular styles. (*Parker*.)

Vihuela. A musical instrument, represented in the celebrated Portico della Gloria of Santiago da Compostella, in Spain. It closely resembles the REBEC (q.v.).

Villa, R. A Roman farmstead or country house. It was divided into three distinct parts : the *urbana*, or house of the owner; the *rustica*, or farm building in which the slaves and animals lived; and the *fructuaria* or magazine for storing the produce.

Villicus, R. A gardener. (See HORTUS).

Vimana, Hind. A Hindoo temple consisting merely of a building in the form of a pyramid, allowing of several stories which recede one above the other. Vimanas are divided into five groups: the medium vimana, called *santiaca;* the victorious (*pantica*), the enormous (*jayada*), the admirable (*atb' huta*), and the amiable (*sarvacama*).

Vina, Hind. A kind of Hindoo lyre furnished with a small number of strings.

Vinalia. Roman festivals of two kinds—*urban* and *rustic*. The former were kept on 23rd April, when the wine of the previous year was first broached; the *rustic* on 19th August, when the vintage opened by the priest solemnly plucking the first bunch of grapes, after a sacrifice of lambs to Jupiter.

Vinatico. A coarse mahogany wood, obtained in Madeira, from *Persea Indica.*

Vinculum, R. (*vincio*, to bind). A general term to denote anything that binds, fastens, or clasps; such as a string, lace, ribbon, chaplet, or garland, strap, dog or slave-collar, manacles, fetters. (See AMENTUM, COLLARE, COMPES, CORONA, &c.)

Vindiciæ (*vindico*, to claim). A fragment of any property under dispute which, under the old Roman jurisprudence, the plaintiff was compelled to bring before the court and to place beneath his foot while stating his case; if the property in question were a flock, the *vindiciæ* consisted of a tuft of wool; if an estate or field, of a clod or turf taken from the said estate or field.

Vindicta, R. (*vindico*, to deliver). The rod with which the prætor or his lictor struck a slave on the head in the ceremony of *manumissio*, by way of declaration that he was free. (See FESTUCA.)

Vine. (See VITIS.)

Vine Black. Ink used in copper-plate printing; prepared from the charred husks of grapes and the residue of the vine press.

Vinea, R. (lit. a bower of vine-branches). The *vineæ*, also called under the emperors *causiæ*, were a kind of mantelets or sheds employed in siege operations, made of light timbers covered with planks and the skins of animals.

Vinum Saccatum. (See COLLUM VINARIUM.)

Viol. (See FIDDLE.)

Viola or **Alto-viola.** A *tenor* violin; tuned an octave above the *violoncello.* It is larger than the ordinary violin and has four gut strings, of which the third and fourth are covered with silver-plated copper wire. Its name in the ancient "set of viols" was *viola di braccio.*

Viola da Gamba. An instrument closely resembling the modern violoncello. (See Fig. 689.)

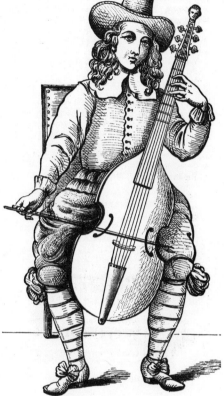

Fig. 689. Viola da Gamba.

Viola d'Amore, It. An obsolete species of violin producing a very sweet and peculiar tone by an arrangement of metal wires vibrating in unison with the gut-strings.

Violet is a combination of equal red and blue. It is complementary to yellow. In Christian art, the colour violet or the amethyst, signified love and truth, or passion and suffering.

Violet Wood. A turnery wood of Guiana, the produce of *Andira violacea.*

Violin. This instrument has three gut strings, and a fourth of silver wire. The *back, neck, sides,* and *circles* are generally made of sycamore; the *belly, bass-bar, sound-post,* and six *blocks,* of deal; the *finger-board* and *tail-piece* of ebony. The

Hindus claim the invention of the *bow*, for a period about 3000 years B.C. (See FIDDLE.)

Violoncello. A large and deep-toned instrument of the *viol* kind, the two lowest strings being covered with silver wire.

Violone, It. Contre-basso or double bass ; the largest instrument of the violin kind.

Virago Sleeves. A fashion of ladies' dress in the reign of Charles I., perpetuated in the bishop's sleeves.

Vire, Fr. A barbed arrow, used with the early cross-bow.

Vireton, It. A peculiar form of arrow, the feathers in which are spirally arranged to produce a spinning movement in its flight.

Virga, R. A general term for any kind of rod or wand ; as, for instance, a riding-whip ; a switch for chastising children or slaves ; a very slight stick carried by a lictor to aid him in opening a way through the crowd for the magistrate before whom he walked.

Virgatus, R. Striped ; a term applied to

Fig. 690. Virginal. 16th century.

cloth or drapery ornamented with bands (*virgæ*), or to anything plaited with twigs of osier, such as a basket.

Virginal. A musical instrument which originated in the middle ages. A specimen of the time of Elizabeth, in the form of a miniature *pianoforte*, is in the South Kensington Museum. (Fig. 690.) It was followed by the SPINET (q.v.).

Virgins are usually represented soberly robed with long hair streaming down their backs. The parable of the wise and foolish virgins is a very common subject of mediæval sculpture and church decoration.

Viria, R. A very ancient term replaced by ARMILLA (q v.).

Viridarium, R. An ornamental garden. (See HORTUS.)

Virtu, Fr. The quality of rareness, or art ex-

cellence sought in the selection of specimens of art-work by a *Virtuoso*.

Virtues. A degree of the second order of ANGELS. They are usually represented in complete armour bearing pennons and battle-axes. The *Cardinal* virtues are : Power, Prudence, Temperance, and Justice ; and the *Theological* virtues are : Faith, Hope, and Charity. There are innumerable other virtues variously represented in Christian allegory, opposed to corresponding VICES.

Virtuoso, It. A man skilled in the selection of specimens of art-work.

Fig. 691. Viscount's Coronet.

Viscount (vice-comes). The fourth degree of rank and dignity in the British peerage. Originally an earl's deputy in his county, made an arbitrary title of honour, next in rank to an earl, by Henry VI. in 1440. A viscount's mantle is two doublings and a half of plain fur. His coronet, granted by James I., has only a row of sixteen pearls set close to the circlet.

Vise, Arch. A spiral staircase. (See NEWEL.)

"Vyce, a tourning stayre, *vis*." (*Palsgrave*.)

Visitation, Chr. (It. *La visitazione;* German, *die Heimsuchung Mariä*). A frequent theme of Christian art, representing the meeting of the Virgin Mary and Elizabeth, the mother of St. John the Baptist. (Consult *Mrs. Jameson's Legends of the Madonna*.)

Visor. The part of a helmet made to cover the face. (See UMBRIL.)

Vitis, Vine, R. and Chr. A vine or vine-branch with which a centurion punished any soldier who had neglected his duty. In Christian symbolism, the vine-stock with clusters of grapes is an emblem of the Church. Representations of it are frequently met with on monuments of Christian art.

Vitreous Wares. Wares having a glassy surface. (See POTTERY.)

Vitro di Trino (Ital.). An ornamental glass-work invented by the Venetians in the 15th century, consisting of a sort of lace-work of white enamel or transparent glass, forming a series of diamond-shaped sections ; in the centre of each an air-bubble was allowed to remain as a decoration. (*Fairholt*.)

Vitrum, R. GLASS (q.v.).

Vitruvian Scroll, Arch. A name given to a peculiar pattern of scroll-work, consisting of convolved undulations, used in classical architecture. (*Parker*.)

Vitta, R. A ribbon or band worn round the head by Roman women of free birth to confine their hair. *Vitta sacra* was a long ribbon confining the flocks of wool which formed an *infula*, and worn by the priests or the victim destined for sacrifice. The term was further applied to the ribbon which passed round garlands or festoons of leaves and fruits, and thence to any ribbon employed in the decoration of an architectural motive, such as tori for instance, as shown in Fig. 693.

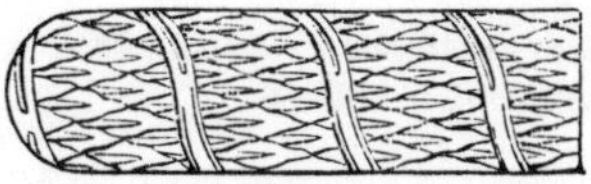

Fig. 693. Vitta.

Vittatus, R. Adorned with the *vitta*; a term applied to women, victims, and certain architectural ornaments.

Vivarium, R. (*vivum*, a living thing). A general term for any kind of place in which live animals are kept; such as aviaries, warrens, fish-ponds, game preserves, &c.

Vivianite. A blue phosphate of iron, occasionally used as a pigment.

Vizard. A mask for the face.

"On with this robe of mine,
This *vizard* and this cap!"
(*Old Play.*)

Vizor. (See VISOR.)

Voided, Her. Having the central area removed.

Volant, Her. Flying.

Volante Piece. A piece of jousting-armour fastened to the GRAND-GARDE above it, protecting the neck and breast.

Volets, Fr. (1) The side *wings* of a TRIPTYCH. (2) A gauze veil worn at the back of the head, by ladies, in the Middle Ages. (See Fig. 704.)

Volumen, R. (*volvo*, to roll). A very long, narrow sheet made of strips of papyrus glued together. This sheet was gradually rolled round a wooden cylinder as the reader perused what was written on it, an operation expressed by the term *evolvere volumen*. When a work was of considerable length, each book or chapter was rolled round a separate stick or wooden cylinder, so that a single volume (*volumen*) consisted of a large number of rolls.

Volupere, O. E. A woman's cap or nightcap.

"The tapes of her white *volupere*."
(*Chaucer, The Miller's Tale.*)

Volute, Arch. (*volvo*, to roll). (1) The spiral scroll peculiarly distinguishing the capital in the Ionic order. (Fig. 694.) (2) The small volutes of the Corinthian capital which are placed at the four angles of the *abacus*; they are called *helices majores*, while the volutes beneath the

cinque-foils are called *helices minores*. (See HELIX.)

Vomer, Vomis, R. A plough-share; it resembled almost exactly our modern ones.

Fig. 694. Ionic Volute.

Vomitoria, R. (*vomo*, to discharge). Doors in a theatre or amphitheatre opening on the corridors of the building, or on to the *scalæ*

Fig. 695. Vomitorium.

leading into the *cavea*. Fig. 695 represents a *vomitorium* (restored) in the Coliseum or Flavian amphitheatre, at Rome.

Votive Tablets. Sculptured representations of parts of the body affected with disease, offered to the gods, either in gratitude or propitiation. The superstition introduced by the ancient Egyptians has survived all religious revolutions, and survives in Roman Catholic countries at the present day. Wilkinson says:—

"After the cure of a disease was effected they (the ancient Egyptians) frequently suspended a model of the restored part in the temple of the god whose interposition they had invoked, precisely in the same manner as in the sheikh's tombs in modern Egypt, and in the Roman Catholic chapels of Italy and other countries, consecrated to the Virgin or a saint; and eyes, distorted arms and other members were dedicated as memorials of their gratitude and superstition." (*Ancient Egyptians.*)

Voulge. (See LANGUE DE BŒUF.)

Voussoir, Arch. A French term for the

wedge-shaped stones (ring-stones) of which an arch is composed.

Vulcanalia. Roman festivals to Vulcan, celebrated with games in the Flaminian circus on the 23rd August. The sacrifices were of *fishes*, which the people threw into the fire ; and it was the custom to commence the work of the day by candle-light, in honour of the god ot fire.

Vulned, Her. Wounded or bleeding. The pelican in its piety (Fig. 531) s described as *vulning herself*.

Vulture, Egyp. Among the Egyptians, the vulture is the symbol of maternity, and accordingly a representation of it served to write the word *mother*, and the name of the goddess MAUT.

Vulture Feathers. Largely used for making artificial flowers ; the feathers of species of *accipitres* imported from Bombay.

Vulturius, Vulture, R. A throw at dice. It is not known how many points made up a vulture, but it is clear from certain authors that it was a bad throw, although not so bad as the *canis* or dog.

Vuyders or **Guiders.** Straps to draw together the parts of armour.

W.

This initial interchanges frequently with gu :— *as ward*, guard ; *wicket*, guichet, &c.

Wafters, O. E. Blunted swords for exercise.

Wain, O. E. A wagon.

Wainscot, Arch. (from the German *Wand-Schotten*, wall-covering), wooden panelling used to line the inner walls.

Waist. The central part of the upper deck of a ship, between the fore and main masts.

Wait. An old English wind instrument resembling the SHAWM (q.v.). It was used by the watchmen or *waights*, to proclaim the time of night.

Waka-tana. The war canoe of New Zealand ; some of these are fifty feet long, by four feet beam, with a high stern-post. This and the carved prow are both richly decorated with a profusion of feathers. (*Simmonds.*)

Wakes (A.S. *wæcan*). Originally vigils or eves of Saints' days. The *late-wake* of the Highlanders ; the *lyke-wake* of the early English, and the *wake* of the Irish are the remains of the ancient northern custom of watching the body of a deceased friend before burial. (Consult *Brand's Popular Antiquities*.)

Wales. The strong side-planks of the body of a ship, running fore and aft.

Walking-sticks. (See BOURDON.) (See also Fig. 91.) Fairholt (*Costume in England*) gives the following quotation from an inventory of Greenwich Palace, *temp*. Henry VIII.

"A cane, garnished with sylver and gilte, with astronomie upon it. A cane, garnished with golde, having a perfume in the toppe, under that a diall, with a pair of twitchers, and a pair of compasses of golde, and a foot rule of golde, a knife and a file the haft of golde, with a whetstone tipped with golde."

Under Charles II. bunches of ribands on the tops of canes were fashionable.

Wall Painting. The GREEK temples were brilliantly decorated with painting and gilding internally. The method has been investigated and is described to be the colouring of the body of the wall of a pale yellow or golden colour, the triglyphs and mutules blue, the metopes and the tympanum red, and some other portions of the building green, and varying these tints or using them of greater or less intensity as the judgment of the artist dictated." (*Hittorf, Essay on the Polychromy of Greek Architecture.*) The colouring of the EGYPTIAN bas-reliefs is familiar. The buildings of HERCULANEUM and POMPEII were decorated with *frescoes* and *mosaics*, in the Augustan age of Roman art. In the Middle Ages the custom was continued of decorating with colour the architecture of sacred edifices ; and many old palaces and mansions in England show relics of the practice of decorating the walls with tempera, especially under Henry III. (See FRESCOES, STEREOCHROMY, WATERWORK, &c.)

Wallet. The badge of the Gueux ; two hands clasped through the handles of a beggar's wallet. (See GUEUX.)

Wall-plates, in building. Horizontal timbers, called *plates*, *properly* those at the top of a building under the roof.

Walled, Muraillée, Her. Made to represent brick or stonework.

Walling Wax. The composition with which etchers make a *wall* round the plate upon which they are proceeding to pour the acid. (See ENGRAVING.)

Walnut, Chr. In Christian iconography the walnut is the symbol of perfection. (See NUT.)

Walnut Oil. (See NUT OIL.)

Wambais (Saxon *wambe*, the belly). A stuffing of wool in the quilted tunic or GAMBESON.

The best illustration is the conventional figure of Punch.

Fig 696. Wallet—Badge of the Gueux.

Wampum, North American Indian. Strings of shells worn as belts and used for money.

Wang, Chinese. Yellow. The sacred colour.

Wapentake, O. E. A hundred, or district. The term is derived from *weapon-taking* (or counting).

Wapinshaw, O. E. A review of weapons.

"Et fiat visus armorum, quod dicitur Wapinschaw."
(*Scotch Statute.*)

Wappenrock, Germ. A military cloak, with armorial charges. (See TABARD.)

Ward, of a castle. The BAILEY or court-yard. (See BALLIUM.)

Warnbrace. (See VAUNTBRACE.)

Wassail or **Wassel**, O. E. (Saxon *waes hael*, "to your health."). (1) A drinking-bout generally. (2) A drink made of roasted apples.

Watchet, O. E. Pale blue.

"The saphyre stone is of a *watchet* blue."
(*Barnfield's Affectionate Shepherd*, 1594.)

Water, of a diamond ; its lustre.

Water-colour Painting was gradually raised from the hard dry style of the last century to its present brilliancy, by the efforts of Nicholson, Copley Fielding, Sandby, Varley, the great Turner, Pyne, Cattermole, Prout, &c., within the present century. The Water Colour Society's Exhibition was begun in 1805. (*Haydn's Dict. of Dates.*)

Water Colours. The principal are *lemon yellow, gamboge, Indian yellow, yellow ochre, chrome, vermilion, light red, Indian red, rose madder, carmine, purple madder, Vandyke brown, sepia, brown pink, sap green, emerald green, indigo, ultramarine, smalt,* and *cobalt.*

Water-gilding. Gilding with a thin coat of amalgam.

Water-mark, on paper. A device resembling a transparency in the texture, which is printed during the process of manufacture, by means of wire or brass plates on the mould of the paper machine.

Water-scape. A fanciful term sometimes used to distinguish a sea view from a *landscape.*

Water-table, Arch. A horizontal set-off in a wall, sloped to throw off the wet.

Water-work, O. E. Wall painting in distemper.

"A pretty slight drollery, or the German hunting in *waterwork*, is worth a thousand of these bed-hangings, and these fly-bitten tapestries." (*Shakespeare.*)

Watered (silk) having a shaded or diversified surface ; produced by placing two pieces of silk lengthways between metallic rollers, where they are subjected to different degrees of pressure.

Watteau Pictures. Idyllic scenes of imaginary Arcadian enjoyment, and a certain fanciful style of costume characteristic of Watteau's pictures, called in French "scènes de la vie galante."

Wattle. An Australian name for various woods of the Acacia species.

Wattled, Her. Having a comb and gills, as a cock.

Wayn-cloutt, O. E. A waggon-cloth.

Wax. Bleached bees'-wax is the vehicle in *encaustic* painting.

Wax-painting. (See ENCAUSTIC PAINTING.)

Weathercock. (See FANE.)

Weathering, Arch. The slope of flat surfaces, for drainage.

Webbing Tape. A kind of broad tape.

Wedgwood Ware. The manufacture of Josiah Wedgwood begun in 1759, at Etruria, in Staffordshire. A fine white, cream-coloured ware, having a clear and hard body, with more compact glaze and more perfect substance than the majolica. Many of the groups on Wedgwood vases and plaques were designed by Flaxman. (Fig. 697.)

Weepers, O. E. Statues in niches round tombs, representing the mourners.

Welding. The union of two pieces of metal together, by heat and pressure.

Welkin. The sky ; hence *welkin eyes*, blue eyes. (*Shakspeare.*)

Well-staircase. A spiral staircase. (See NEWEL.)

Welsh Hook. A mediæval weapon, a kind of bill with a *hook* at the back, used to drag a horse-soldier from his saddle.

Welt. A joint or fold in a texture. The term is variously explained as synonymous with *guard*, a facing to a gown; or *purfles*, i.e. fringes. (Consult *Fairholt*, s.v.)

Welted Brocades and **Quilts.** Articles with folds in the texture ; lined and ribbed.

Weued, A. S. The altar.

"In chyrche to vore the *heye weued* Constantyn hym sleu."

(*Robert of Gloucester.*)

Whalebone is the commercial name for the *baleen* plates found in the mouth of the whale, of which there are about 300 in each animal.

Fig. 697. Wedgwood Vase.

What-not. A modern piece of furniture, a light sideboard or stand.

Wheel. In Christian art, the attribute of St. Catherine, in allusion to the manner of her martyrdom.

Wheel, Catherine Wheel. Represented in heraldry with curved spikes projecting from its rim.

Wheel Engraving upon Glass. (See GLASS.)

Wheel-lock. A crude invention in gunnery, of the 16th century, for winding up the trigger of a gun with a hand-winch.

Whinyard, O. E. A sword.

Whipping-tops are represented in Anglo-

Saxon manuscripts; the thongs of the whips are *knotted,* which would add to the difficulty of the game.

Whisk, O. E.
A *ruff* or *band.*

"A woman's *nec whisk* is used both plain and laced, and is called of most a gorget or *falling whisk,* because it falleth about the shoulders." (*Randle Holme.*)

Whisket, O. E. A basket. S.

Whistle. Prehistoric specimens of whistles made of bones have been disinterred among relics of the Stone Age. The Mexicans in antiquity made curiously grotesque whistles of baked clay representing caricatures of the human face and figure, birds, beasts, and flowers. (Consult *Musical Instruments by Carl Engel.*)

Fig. 698. Falling "Whisk."

White, in Christian art represented by the diamond or silver, was the emblem of light, religious purity, innocence, virginity, faith, joy, and life. (*J.*)

White is in theory the result of the union of the three primary colours. The principal white pigments are *white lead, Lake white, Krems white, zinc white, constant white* (q.v.). (See CARBONATE OF LEAD, OXIDE OF ZINC, &c.)

White Copper. German silver.

White Lead is the white pigment universally used for oil-painting; it is considered a good dryer, and is used to render oil more drying. (Consult *Merrifield's Treatise,* &c., vol. i. cl.) (See CARBONATE OF LEAD.)

White Vitriol. SULPHATE OF ZINC (q.v.).

Whiting, as used for wall-painting, &c., is pure chalk, cleansed and ground with water.

Whittle, O. E. A pocket clasp knife. (*Shakspeare.*)

Whole and Halves. Proportional compasses used for the enlargement or reduction of drawings.

Whorler. The wheel of a potter's lathe.

Wicker-work. Texture of osiers, or small twigs; basket-work.

Wicket (Fr. *Guichet*). A small door perforated in a larger one.

Wigs (contraction of Periwigs, from Fr. *perruque*) were brought in from France in the 16th century. They took their greatest proportions in the time of Louis XIV. In the early 18th century also they are described as of immense size, "large enough to have loaded a camel." And of this date is the celebrated wig-maker's sign, in which Absalom was represented hanging by the hair in a tree, and King David weeping beneath, exclaiming,—

> "O Absalom! O Absalom!
> O Absalom, my son!
> If thou hadst worn a *periwig*
> Thou hadst not been undone."

Smaller varieties were called *perukes* or travelling-wigs; and the *campaign wig*, which "hath knots or *bobs*, a *dildo* on each side with a curled forehead." These *dildos* or *pole-locks* were the origin of the pigtail. (See HAIR.)

Wilton Carpets are a kind of Brussels carpeting, with the yarns cut.

Wimple, O. E. A nun's hood, covering the neck and shoulders, adopted by ladies in general, *temp.* Henry VII.

Winchester Bushel. An ancient standard measure of capacity preserved in the Town Hall at Winchester. It dates from the reign of King Edgar. It is 18½ inches wide, and 8 inches deep.

Windows. The earliest of stained glass in Italy were painted by order of Pope Leo III., at Rome, in 795. The windows of some churches were closed with valves or shutters of stone, like those of the Duomo of Torcello, erected in 1008. Others were filled with slabs of transparent talc or alabaster. The earliest painted glass in York Cathedral is of A.D. 1200. The use of glass windows in private houses was not general until the 14th century. During the Middle Ages glass windows were in movable wooden frames, and were taken away by families when they travelled. (Consult *Hallam's Middle Ages*, vol. iii.) Substitutes for glass were thin parchment or linen, painted and varnished, or even paper. (*Le Vieil, de la Peinture sur Verre.*) These paper windows may still be seen in villages in the north of Italy.

Winds (Latin, *Venti*). The impersonations of the *winds* were held in high veneration, especially by the Athenians. The four principal were Eurus or Vulturnus, the east or south-east wind; Auster, the south wind, the Notus of the Greeks, pernicious to plants and men; Zephyrus, the son of Aurora and father of Carpus (fruit), a genial, health-bearing breeze, called also ζωηφόρος, life-bearing; and Boreas, the strong north wind, usually represented with the feet of a serpent, his wings dripping with golden dewdrops, and the train of his garment sweeping along the ground. Inferior *winds* were Solanus, in Greek Apeliotes, answering to the east, and represented as a young man holding fruit in his lap; Africus, south-west, represented with black wings and melancholy countenance; Corus, north-west, drives clouds of snow before him; Aquilo, north-east by north, equally dreadful in appearance, from *aquila*, an eagle, type of swiftness and impetuosity.

Windsor Chairs. A plain kind of strong wooden chairs, so-called.

Wings, from time immemorial, have been the Oriental and Egyptian symbol of power as well as of swiftness; of the spiritual and aerial, in contradistinction to the human and the earthly; also in Chaldaic and Babylonian remains, in the Lycian and Nineveh marbles, and on the gems and other relics of the Gnostics In Etruscan art all their divinities are winged.

Wings, in theatres. The shifting side-scenes on the stage. In costume, the projections on the shoulders of a *doublet*. (See Fig. 91.)

Wise Men, Chr. The MAGI. (See EPIPHANY.)

Wisp, O. E. A broom.

Woad. A dye plant—*Isatis tinctoria.*

Wolf. In Egypt was worshipped at Lycopolis; it figures frequently among hieroglyphic signs. The Greeks had consecrated the wolf to Apollo, the Romans to Mars. In Christian (especially Spanish) art, an attribute of St. Vincent, in allusion to the legend that wild beasts were driven away from his body after his martyrdom, by a raven.

Wood-carving. One of the most ancient manifestations of the art instinct of humanity is found in the very earliest relics of every nation. Especially in Egypt specimens remarkable for fidelity of representation have been recently disinterred, and stand in the Boulac Museum. Among Christian countries Germany is the most distinguished in this branch of art, but Holland and Belgium closely rival it in excellence and abundance of early specimens. Illustrious English carvers in wood were mostly of Dutch or German extraction. The most famous of them is Grinling Gibbons, employed by Sir Christopher Wren in the decoration of St. Paul's Cathedral. He excelled in carving flowers and foliage.

Wood-engraving or **Xylography.** Box-wood is the only kind that can be used. The blocks when smoothed and polished are prepared for drawing on, by rubbing the polished surface with *bath brick* in very fine powder mixed with water. When this thin coating is dry, it is removed by rubbing the block on the palm of the hand; its only use is to make the surface less slippery. There are four descriptions of cutting tools used in wood-engraving. The *graver* is not very different from that used for copper-plate, but has the point ground to a peculiar form by rubbing on a *Turkey stone.* Eight or nine *gravers,* of different sizes, are generally re-

Fig. 699. Carved-wood mirror frame, belonging to Lord Stafford at Costessy.

quired, commencing with a very fine one, which is called the *outline tool,* and increasing in size or breadth. *Tinting* is cutting series of parallel lines, which, when engraved, form an even and uniform tint. For this process there is a dis-tinct set of tools called *tinting tools. Gouges* of different sizes are used for scooping out the wood towards the centre of the block, and flat tools or *chisels* for cutting it away towards the edges. The earliest known wood-engraving, "The Virgin surrounded by four Saints," is dated 1418. A print of it is in the Brussels Museum.

Wood-skin. An American name for a large canoe made of bark.

Woof. The *weft,* or cross-texture of fabrics.

Woolsack. The seat of the Lord Chancellor, in the House of Lords.

Working Drawings (Arch.) are enlarged portions of plans with details of a building, for the practical artificers to work from.

Worsted (properly Worstead, spelt also "*worsett*" and "*woryst*") was the name given to the cloth woven of the hard thread produced by the peculiar carding process that was invented at *Worstead* in Norfolk; 14th century.

Wou or **Wouwou,** Egyp. The Egyptian name for the dog; it is evidently an onomatopœia, like the name for a cat, which is written MAAOU. (See CANIS.)

Wreath. Wreaths have at all times been prominent among symbolical personal ornaments; always with an honourable or pleasant signification; wreaths of ivy distinguished the votaries of Bacchus; appropriate wreaths were invented for sacrifices at the altar for heroic or priestly or literary distinction. (See ORLE, CREST, WREATH, &c.)

Wrest. O. E. An instrument for drawing up the strings of a harp. (*Shakespeare.*)

Wyn, O. E. A narrow flag.

Wyvern, Wivern, Her. A fabulous creature, a species of dragon with two legs, and re-presented having its tail nowed. (Fig. 700.)

Fig. 700.
Wyvern.

X.

(The syllable ξυν- in Greek is generally rendered Syn, q.v.)

X. The Roman numeral for ten.

Xanthian Marbles. Sculptures found in 1838 at Xanthus, in ancient Lycia, now in the British Museum. The figures are Assyrian in character, and of a date not later than 500 B.C. Besides the so-called Harpy tomb (see HARPIES), there are sieges, processions, and many figures, in the energetic action so remarkable in the Nineveh sculptures. Most of the figures are in profile; but the eyes, like those of Egyptian sculptures, are shown in full.

Xebec. A small lateen-rigged three-masted vessel, common in the Mediterranean.

Xenagia, Gr. (ξεναγία). A subdivision of the Greek army consisting of 256 men, and sub-divided into four tetrarchies, commanded by the *Xenagos,* an officer appointed by the Spartans, who had the control of the armies of the Greek states.

Xenia, Gr. (ξένια, lit. friendly gifts). (1) Delicacies, dainties, or pastry which were sent to one another by the Greeks and Romans as a pledge of friendship, chiefly during the Saturnalia. (2) Decorations to the walls of *guest*-chambers consisting of paintings of *still life* representing game, fruits, fish, and flowers.

Xenodochium, R. (ξενο-δοχεῖον). A low-Latin term for a hospice intended for the reception of pilgrims and sick persons. Childebert founded a *xenodochium* at Lyons in the 6th century.

Xerophagia, Chr. (ξηρο-φαγία). A six days' fast throughout Holy Week, during which the Christians of the primitive Church eat only bread with a little salt, and drank nothing but water.

Xestes, Gr. (Lat. Sextarius). A Greek measure of capacity ; very nearly a *pint ;* equivalent to the Latin SEXTARIUS.

Xoïtes, Egyp. A nome or division of Lower Egypt, the capital of which was *Khsonou ;* Ammon-Ra was the principal deity there worshipped.

Xylography. Wood-engraving (q. v.).

Xylon, Gr. (lit. wood). A Greek measure of length, equal to 4 feet and 6·6 inches.

Xylopyrography. Poker-painting ; the art of burning pictures on to wood.

Xyneciæ, Gr. (συν-οίκια). Festivals held at Athens in honour of Minerva, to commemorate the union of the inhabitants of Attica into a single city. These festivals were instituted by Theseus, and held every year in the month of July. Another name for them was *Metœciæ* (μετοίκιαι).

Xystus, Gr. (ξυστός). A covered place situated near a portico, within which, in a palæstra or stadium, athletes went through their exercises. Pausanias tells us that this part of the stadium received its name from the fact that Hercules used every day to clear out the palæstra at Elis in order to inure himself to toil, and that he tore up many weeds by scraping (ξύω, to scrap· ξυστός). The baths and thermæ at Rome were furnished with large xysti, in which young men went through a number of exercises. The term *xystus* was also generally applied by the Romans to the beds of rare flowers and shrubs in the centre of the peristyle ; it also denoted a garden walk perfectly straight, and planted in a regular style ; and lastly, an open walk or terrace in a garden attached to any building.

Y.

The letter **Y** is called the letter of Pythagoras because that philosopher made it the symbol of life. The foot of the letter, he said, represented infancy, and as man gradually rises to the age of reason, he finds two paths set before him, the one leading to good, the other to evil, portrayed by two forks of the letter. The illustration is the device of Jean de Morvilliers (+ 1577), Chancellor of France ; the harrow tied to the Pythagorean **Υ**, a *rebus* on his name *Mort-vie-liers—*" Death and life united." The harrow is the symbol of Death, which makes all things equal. (Fig. 701.)

Yacca. An ornamental Jamaica wood used for cabinet-making.

Yard (from the Saxon *geard* or *gyrd*, from *gyrdan*, to enclose). Originally estimated to measure the *girth* of a man's body ; until Henry I. decreed that it should be the length of his arm.

Yataghan. A Turkish dagger or scimitar.

Yawl. A man-of-war's boat, rowed with six oars.

Ychma, Peruv. The name for wild cinnabar among the ancient Peruvians; it was employed by them for painting the body and drawing figures on the face and arms.

Yellow. One of the three primary colours ; producing with *green*, blue ; and with *red*, orange. The principal yellow pigments are *gamboge* (bluish), *gold ochre* (reddish), *yellow*

Fig. 701. Device of Morvilliers. (The Pythagorean Y.)

ochre, Naples yellow, chrome yellow, lemon yellow, Indian yellow, gall-stone, Roman ochre, Mars yellow, terra di Siena, Italian pink, cadmium yellow, &c.

Yellow, in Christian art, or gold, was the symbol of the sun ; of the goodness of God, initiation or marriage, faith or fruitfulness. In a bad sense yellow signifies inconstancy, jealousy, deceit ; in this sense it is given to the traitor Judas, who is generally habited in dirty yellow.

Yellow Arsenic. (See YELLOW ORPIMENT.)

Yellow Flag. Denoting sickness on board of a ship or quarantine.

Yellow Lake. A bright pigment, very susceptible to the action of light or metal. (See PINKS.)

Yellow Metal. A composition, two-thirds copper and one-third zinc.

Yellow Ochre. An argillaceous earth, coloured by admixture of iron. (See OCHRE.)

Yellow Orpiment (*auripigmentum*). A bright and pure yellow pigment, but not durable, and dries very slowly ; called also *Yellow Arsenic.*

Yeoman of the Guard. A beef-eater ; one of the British sovereign's state body-guard ; below the *gentleman-at-arms.* Instituted at the coronation of Henry VII. in 1485.

Yew. *Taxus baccata.* The word is largely used in cabinet-making. The excellence of the wood for making bows led to the trees being planted in churchyards, to preserve them.

Ymaigier. (See IMAGIER.)

Ymaigerie, Imagery, Med. (1) Illuminated borders on missals and manuscripts executed by the miniaturists of the Middle Ages. (2) Bas-reliefs and sculptures on wood and stone.

Yoke. A symbolical device assumed by Pope Leo X. in allusion to the text " My yoke is easy," expressed in the one word of the motto " *Suave.*" (See JUGUM.) Fig. 702.

York Collar. Her. Was formed of alternate *Suns* and *Roses.*

York Herald. One of the six Heralds of the College of Arms. (See HERALDS.)

York Rose. Her. The *white* rose of the family of York. (See Fig. 589.)

Yorkshire Grit. A stone used for polishing marble and engravers' copper plates.

Fig. 702. Yoke. Device of Pope Leo X.

Ypres Lace is the finest and most costly kind of VALENCIENNES.

Yu, Chinese. (1) A hard and heavy stone, supposed to be a kind of agate which was used for the ancient musical instrument KING, which was a kind of harmonicon made of slabs of sonorous stone of different sizes. (2) An ancient name for a curious wind instrument of high antiquity, which is still in use and is now called *cheng.* It consists of a number of tubes placed in a *calabash,* or bowl, and blown into through a long curved tube.

Yucatan. A province of Mexico remarkable for its architectural monuments of a forgotten civilization, described by *Stephens, Incidents of Travel in Yucatan.* (See MEXICAN ARCHITECTURE.)

Yufts. A kind of Russia leather, red and soft, with a pleasant smell.

Yule, O. E. Christmas time.

Z.

The initials Z and S and Z and C frequently interchange, especially in old words derived from the German, as zither, *cither ;* zentner, centner, *&c. The German Z is pronounced ts.*

Zaba, Zava. An Arabic cuirass. (*Meyrick.*)

Zabaoth. (See SABAOTH.)

Zafferano, It. Saffron. A vegetable yellow pigment.

Zaffre (It. *zaffiro*). An ancient blue pigment,

prepared from *cobalt,* of a *sapphire* blue, resembling *smalt.*

Zamarilla, Sp. A loose jacket of sheepskins.

Zarf. An oriental saucer for coffee-cups.

Zauca, Zaucha, or **Zauga,** Gr. and R. A

soft and flexible leather boot peculiar to Eastern nations; it was worn under the trousers.

Zazahan, Sp. A kind of flowered silk.

Zebec. A common form of sailing vessel in the Mediterranean, rigged with a lateen sail.

Zebra Wood. The *Hyawaballi* of Guiana, a beautiful wood for furniture.

Zebu. The humped species to which the sacred Brahmin bull belongs, represented in Hindu art.

Zema, Gr. and R. (ζέμα). A vessel of earthenware or metal, a saucepan.

Zemzemeeyeh, Arabic. A skin for carrying water in the desert.

Zend-Avesta, Pers. "The Word of Life" or "Living Word." The sacred book of the Parsees; it consists of two parts, one of which is written in *Zend*, the other in *Pehloi* and *Parsee*. The first part is called *Vendidad-Salé*, and the second *Boundehech*.

Zenith. The centre of the arch of the sky overhead. (Cf. NADIR.)

Zephyr Yarn is the dyed worsted thread usually known as *Berlin wool*.

Zeuxite. A gem. (See TOURMALINE.)

Zigzag, Arch. One of the mouldings frequently used in Norman architecture, running in zigzag lines. (See Fig. 488.) Fig. 123 is an illustration of a variety of this ornament on a column. *Zigzig* mouldings in connexion with pointed arches are characteristic of the transition period of architecture, from the Norman to the Early English, frequently called *chevron*.

Zimarra. An Oriental robe, called in England also *Samare*. Described as a lady's jacket: "it has a loose body and four side laps or skirts, which extend to the knee; the sleeves short, cut to the elbow, turned up and faced."—*Randle Holme*.

Zincography. Engraving on plates of zinc, introduced in 1817. (See PHOTOZINCOGRAPHY.)

Zinc White. A pigment recently introduced as a substitute for the preparations of white lead. It is little liable to change, either by atmospheric action or mixture with other pigments. It is the white oxide of zinc, and is also called *Chinese White* (q.v.).

Zipo, Med. Lat. A shirt of mail.

Zircon. A peculiar rare grey and brown earth, found in the true rough and opaque varieties of hyacinth stone, which are met with in Ceylon, Norway, Carinthia, and the Ural. The term *hyacinth* is applied to the transparent and bright-coloured varieties of zircon, and *jargoon* to crystals devoid of colour and of a smoky tinge, occasionally sold as inferior diamonds. (*Simmonds' Com. Dict.*)

Zither. A favourite stringed instrument of a soft and sweet effect, much used in the Austrian Tyrol. It is played lying flat on a table, and the strings struck with a *plectrum* worn on the thumb.

Zocle or **Socle,** Arch. The plinth in classical architecture.

Zodiacus, Zodiac, Gen. (ζωδιακὸς, i. e. pertaining to animals). The zone of the celestial

Fig. 704. Duchess of Parma in richly embroidered robes and zimarra.

sphere which extends to eight degrees on either side of the ecliptic. The Egyptians had representations of it in their temples, the most celebrated being that of *Denderah*, a cast of which is at the Louvre. Other zodiacs have also been found in the great temple of Esneh and at Contra-Lato. Many monuments of the Romano-Byzantine and Gothic periods possess representations of zodiacs. They occur on the doorways and other parts of churches from the end of the 10th century. In particular may be noted the one which figures on the bas-reliefs of the frieze in the side apsides of the Romano-Auvergniate church of St. Paul d'Issoire. One of the largest zodiacs, dating from the beginning of the 11th century, is that of the church of St. Vézelay. The series of medallions which surround the great tympanum representing Christ and the apostles, contain, independently of the signs of the zodiac, representations of the agricultural operations belonging to each month of the year.

Zona, Gr. (1) A girdle, used to gird up the skirts of the dress for freedom of action (Fig. 157); on occasions of solemnity, as sacrifices or fune-

Fig. 705. Zona.

rals, the girdle was relaxed, and the folds of the dress allowed to hang to the feet (Fig. 537); as a part of the marriage ceremony it was taken off. Upon the armour of men it supported the kilt, and was worn round the cuirass (Fig. 705; cf. Fig. 44). It was generally used as a purse. The celebrated girdle (*cestus*) of Venus, which conferred beauty and inspired love, is not represented on the statues of that goddess. There is a town on the Ægean Sea called Zona from the belt of trees upon it, still growing in the processional order in which they arrived when they left their native plantations and followed the music of Orpheus. (2) In Architecture, an entablature which encircles any isolated building. Lofty buildings surrounded by seven *zones* were described as *septizonia*. (3) In painted vases, horizontal annular bands often decorated with animals. (See ZOOPHORI.)

Zonula. Diminutive of ZONA.

Zoomara, Arab. A double clarionet.

Zoophori. Bands of ornament on friezes, vases, &c., representing animals. (See Figs. 706, 707.)

Zophorus, Gr. and R. (ζωφόρος). Literally, bearing animals, and thence a *frieze*, decorated with figures of animals, conventional or real.

Zotheca, Gr. and R. (ζω-θήκη). A small chamber adjoining a larger apartment, whither the occupant might retire for the purpose of study. (2) A small niche for the reception of a statue, vase, or any other object. The Romans had a diminutive for *zotheca*, viz. *zothecula*.

Zummârah, Egyp. A musical instrument; a double reed pipe.

Fig. 706. Greek Vase decorated with Zoophori.

Fig. 707. Vase with bands of Zoophori.

THE END.